# THE POLITICAL ECONOMY OF COMPETITION LAW IN CHINA

*The Political Economy of Competition Law in China* provides a unique perspective of China's competition law that is situated within its legal, institutional, economic and political contexts. Adopting a framework that focuses on key stakeholders and the relevant governance and policy environment, and drawing upon stakeholder interviews, case studies and doctrinal analysis, this book examines China's Anti-monopoly Law in the context of the political economy from which it emerged and in which it is now enforced. It explains the legal and economic reasoning used by Chinese competition authorities in interpreting and applying the Anti-monopoly Law, and offers valuable and novel insights into the processes and dynamics of law- and decision-making under that law. This book will interest scholars of competition law and professionals advising clients that operate in China, as well as scholars of Chinese law, Asian law, comparative law and political and social science.

DR WENDY NG is a lecturer at Melbourne Law School, where she is the Associate Director (China) of the Asian Law Centre and the Deputy Director of the Competition Law and Economics Network. Her research concentrates on competition law, focusing on China, law and development and political economy issues. Previously, Wendy worked as a lawyer at leading international commercial law firms in Melbourne and New York.

# THE POLITICAL ECONOMY OF COMPETITION LAW IN CHINA

WENDY NG
*University of Melbourne*

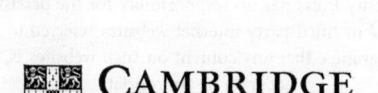

CAMBRIDGE
UNIVERSITY PRESS

# CAMBRIDGE
## UNIVERSITY PRESS

University Printing House, Cambridge CB2 8BS, United Kingdom

One Liberty Plaza, 20th Floor, New York, NY 10006, USA

477 Williamstown Road, Port Melbourne, VIC 3207, Australia

314–321, 3rd Floor, Plot 3, Splendor Forum, Jasola District Centre,
New Delhi – 110025, India

79 Anson Road, #06-04/06, Singapore 079906

Cambridge University Press is part of the University of Cambridge.

It furthers the University's mission by disseminating knowledge in the pursuit of education, learning, and research at the highest international levels of excellence.

www.cambridge.org
Information on this title: www.cambridge.org/9781107154407
DOI: 10.1017/9781316658949

© Cambridge University Press 2018

This publication is in copyright. Subject to statutory exception and to the provisions of relevant collective licensing agreements, no reproduction of any part may take place without the written permission of Cambridge University Press.

First published 2018

Printed in the United Kingdom by Clays, St Ives plc

*A catalogue record for this publication is available from the British Library.*

*Library of Congress Cataloging-in-Publication Data*
Names: Ng, Wendy, 1980–
Title: The political economy of competition law in China /
Wendy Ng, University of Melbourne.
Description: Cambridge [UK] ; New York : Cambridge University Press, 2017. |
Includes bibliographical references and index.
Identifiers: LCCN 2017029301 | ISBN 9781107154407 (Hardback : alk. paper)
Subjects: LCSH: Antitrust law–Political aspects–China. | Antitrust law–Economic aspects–China. | Competition, Unfair–China. | Restraint of trade–China.
Classification: LCC KNQ3220 .N4 2017 | DDC 343.5107/21–dc23
LC record available at https://lccn.loc.gov/2017029301

ISBN 978-1-107-15440-7 Hardback

Cambridge University Press has no responsibility for the persistence or accuracy of URLs for external or third-party internet websites referred to in this publication and does not guarantee that any content on such websites is, or will remain, accurate or appropriate.

For my mother

For my mother

# CONTENTS

*Foreword by Professor Wang Xiaoye* ix
*Acknowledgements* xii
*Table of Legislation, Regulations, Administrative Decisions and Policy Documents* xiv
*List of Abbreviations* xxx

PART I   Introducing the Anti-monopoly Law   1

1 **Competition Law in China and the Importance of Context**   3
  1.1 Introduction   3
  1.2 Evaluations of the Anti-monopoly Law to Date   4
  1.3 Competition Law and the Relevance of Context   16
  1.4 Need for a New Analytical Framework for the Anti-monopoly Law   20
  1.5 A Political Economy Framework for the Anti-monopoly Law   22
  1.6 Methodology and Scope   24
  1.7 Structure of Book   24

2 **Legal Analysis of the Anti-monopoly Law**   27
  2.1 Introduction   27
  2.2 Merger Control   28
  2.3 Non-Merger Conduct   59
  2.4 Conclusion   96

PART II   A Political Economy Framework for the Anti-monopoly Law   99

3 **Demand-Side Analysis of the Anti-monopoly Law**   101
  3.1 Introduction   101
  3.2 Key Stakeholders on the Demand-Side of the Anti-monopoly Law   102
  3.3 Shaping the Demand for Competition Law in China: Economic Reforms and the Governance Gap   120

3.4 Broader Policy Environment Influencing Demand-Side Dynamics  124
3.5 Conclusion  135

## 4 Supply-Side Analysis of the Anti-monopoly Law  136
4.1 Introduction  136
4.2 Key Stakeholders on the Supply-Side of the Anti-monopoly Law  137
4.3 Institutional Design Issues Influencing Supply-Side Dynamics  175
4.4 Broader Governance and Policy Environment Influencing Supply-Side Dynamics  187
4.5 Conclusion  197

### PART III Understanding the Anti-monopoly Law in Its Context  199

## 5 The Making of the Anti-monopoly Law  201
5.1 Introduction  201
5.2 The Anti-monopoly Law Drafting Process  202
5.3 Major Issues Considered in the Drafting of the Anti-monopoly Law  213
5.4 Conclusion  240

## 6 The Public Enforcement of the Anti-monopoly Law  243
6.1 Introduction  243
6.2 Jurisdiction: Enforcement and Scope Issues  244
6.3 Anti-monopoly Law and Other Government Policies  259
6.4 The Relationship between the State and the Market  277
6.5 Conclusion  294

## 7 Conclusion  297
7.1 Introduction  297
7.2 Findings  298
7.3 Implications for Current Evaluations of the Anti-monopoly Law  305
7.4 Final Thoughts  311

### *Appendices*
Appendix A: Research Methods, Materials and Sources  313
Appendix B: Published Anti-monopoly Law Administrative Enforcement Decisions as at 31 December 2016  315
Appendix C: Timeline of the Anti-monopoly Law Drafting Process  332
*Bibliography*  335
*Index*  376

# FOREWORD

Since it came into effect in August 2008, research on China's Anti-monopoly Law, both within and outside China, has grown and spread like bamboo shoots after a spring rain. This research examines the issues of the Anti-monopoly Law itself and the specific decisions made by the competition authorities and courts, and engages in comparative analysis of the Anti-monopoly Law and the competition laws of other jurisdictions, with the aim of improving the Anti-monopoly Law and the effectiveness of its enforcement. I am pleased to recommend Dr Wendy Ng's book on the Anti-monopoly Law, *The Political Economy of Competition Law in China*, to the international community. The author explores the development and implementation of China's Anti-monopoly Law through the study and analysis of China's political, economic and societal contexts.

I believe that this book will justifiably attract a great deal of interest from the international community. Although there is no shortage of foreign academics researching and writing on the Anti-monopoly Law, what distinguishes Dr Ng from many other foreign academics is that she is a 'China hand'. She is fluent in Mandarin Chinese, able to converse and interact face-to-face with Chinese academics and undertakes research using Chinese-language primary and secondary materials. She has the ability, skill and opportunity to deeply understand the background, law-making and enforcement of the Anti-monopoly Law, and China's political, economic and other relevant contexts. As a result of Dr Ng's combined expertise on China and competition law, this book provides many valuable and thoughtful insights into the Anti-monopoly Law that cannot be furnished by other research and published work in English. Further, Dr Ng's Australian background means that she brings a perspective to the Anti-monopoly Law that is different to that taken by Chinese academics, including myself. As a Chinese academic, I am greatly interested in her book.

Another reason for my recommendation of Dr Ng's book is that, in addition to examining the Anti-monopoly Law from a legal perspective, it explores the impact of the political economy on the making and enforcement of the Anti-monopoly Law in considerable depth. In Chapter 3, she adopts a demand-side perspective to explore the stakeholders and wider environment surrounding the Anti-monopoly Law. For example, Dr Ng points out that while China's economic reforms are conducive to developing the Anti-monopoly Law, there is also resistance and opposition to the law on the part of state-owned enterprises and monopoly industries. In Chapter 4, Dr Ng examines the actors and various factors shaping and constraining the Anti-monopoly Law from a supply-side perspective, observing, for example, that it is inevitable that there will be compromise and coordination between competition authorities and industry regulators. The various debates and issues discussed during the drafting and deliberation of the Anti-monopoly Law are analysed in Chapter 5 from a political economy perspective. Such issues include whether the Anti-monopoly Law would prohibit administrative monopoly, protect the state-owned economy, strengthen macroeconomic regulation and control and encourage mergers to expand economies of scale and scope. The clash of these different ideas and views not only demonstrates the difficulties involved in developing the Anti-monopoly Law and the potential problems that may arise in its enforcement, but also reflects China's politics, economy, society and culture. Thus, Dr Ng astutely points out that China's adoption of the Anti-monopoly Law is the product of the coordination and balancing of the different views and ideologies within Chinese society. The impact of China's political economy on the enforcement of the Anti-monopoly Law is studied in Chapter 6. One consequence of the political economy, as the author observes, is that industrial policy and intervention of industry regulators feature in enforcement; her views in this regard are correct.

With this book, Dr Ng commendably provides readers with a clear, sophisticated and critical understanding and analysis of the Anti-monopoly Law, informed by her deep, comprehensive and nuanced understanding of China's political economy. Her critical analysis reveals that the Anti-monopoly Law faces some challenges and problems. Nevertheless, I must also bring attention to the fact that the enactment of the Anti-monopoly Law evidences the market-orientated direction of China's economic reforms; it is therefore a milestone in China's economic reform process. Inevitably, various problems will arise in the enforcement of the Anti-monopoly Law, especially concerning the independence of the competition authorities. However, I believe that the general direction of its enforcement is on the right track. For example, in the case of Qualcomm, where a record-high administrative penalty was imposed, some academics comment that the Anti-monopoly Law could have been enforced more strongly, but virtually no one believed that the Chinese competition authorities were not capable of handling the case simply because Qualcomm was a foreign company.

I met Dr Ng in 2012, when she moved from Melbourne to Beijing to undertake fieldwork and research on the Anti-monopoly Law. During her eight-month stay in Beijing, we met regularly to engage in academic discussions, over the course of which I encountered her rigorous approach to research and solid competition law knowledge. Dr Ng has a strong interest in China, and one that she seeks to share with others. This is demonstrated not only through her research on China's Anti-monopoly Law and in the publication of this book, but also in her tireless efforts as the editor of an online bulletin that provides regular updates to the international community on developments in Chinese competition law. As a Chinese academic, I would like to express my gratitude and respect for her dedication and valuable contribution. On a personal note, I am thankful to Dr Ng for her substantial assistance in helping me to communicate my research to the global competition law community, especially in the publication of my book in 2014 – there are very few native English speakers who speak Chinese proficiently in the global competition law community. Through our common research interests and shared desire to engage with the international community on the Anti-monopoly Law, we have developed a firm friendship. I am delighted to commend her book to readers.

Finally, I would like to express my heartfelt congratulations to Dr Ng on the publication of the first monograph of her academic career! I believe that this valuable book will be welcomed and very well received by the international community. I sincerely hope that Dr Ng continues to work hard and forge ahead in her teaching and research of competition law, and will become a new shining star in the global competition law community.

*Xiaoye Wang*
*Professor of Law, Chinese Academy of Social Sciences*
*Distinguished Professor of Law, Hunan University*
*Member of the Expert Committee of the Anti-monopoly Commission*
*under the State Council of the People's Republic of China*
*Beijing*

# ACKNOWLEDGEMENTS

Many moons ago, as a second-year lawyer working in the competition law group at a law firm in Melbourne, I worked on a global merger that involved coordinating and securing merger approvals from competition authorities in multiple jurisdictions. These jurisdictions were varied: some were rich, developed countries with lengthy experiences of competition law; others were poorer, developing countries with relatively new competition laws and limited enforcement experience. I was intrigued by the fact that these jurisdictions, despite variations in their development levels, economies, cultures and socio-economic situations, all had a competition law. What drives the decision to adopt a competition law and to dedicate resources to enforcing that law, in the face of competing priorities, challenges and considerations, especially for poorer or less developed countries? What are the differences in the ways in which competition laws are understood and enforced in various countries, and why do these differences arise? These questions lingered in my mind long after the merger had closed and I had moved overseas to study and work. Eventually, with the aim of satiating my curiosity, and perhaps with a dash of naiveté, I decided to do a PhD, focusing my research on China's competition law.

This book, which draws substantially from my doctoral research, is the culmination of these efforts. But, much like raising a child, it took a village to develop my initial curiosity into a doctoral dissertation and, eventually, into a book. I am immensely grateful to my village of colleagues, mentors, friends and family.

To my PhD supervisors, Caron Beaton-Wells and Sean Cooney, I will always be grateful for your wise counsel, support and encouragement.

To the participants in my interviews, thank you for giving me your time, sharing your experiences and insights and answering my questions candidly and openly. Your generosity enabled me to engage with my research with more depth and nuance, with an enhanced appreciation and awareness of the very real impact that the law has on its constituents. I hope that the book adequately and appropriately reflects your contributions.

To Wang Xiaoye, Allan Fels, Mark Furse and Mark Williams, who variously read my work, discussed my research at length and provided useful and insightful comments and suggestions; Gabrielle Appleby and John Williams, who offered useful advice at the beginning stages of this book project; and Cate Read and the staff at the Academic Research Service at Melbourne Law School, who provided incredible and unparalleled assistance in the preparation of the manuscript for this book, my sincere thanks for your support, advice and help in this project; I am lucky to have such wonderful mentors and colleagues.

To Kim Hughes, Catherine Smith and Cambridge University Press, thank you for your assistance and considerable patience in preparing and guiding this book to publication.

To my friends, thank you for your understanding, humour, friendship and distraction. To quote The Beatles, who said it best, 'I get by with a little help from my friends'.

And finally, and certainly not least, to my family. Thank you for your unwavering and unconditional support, nourishment and belief, and for instilling in me a love of learning and a curious mind.

# TABLE OF LEGISLATION, REGULATIONS, ADMINISTRATIVE DECISIONS AND POLICY DOCUMENTS

## Legislation

### China

中华人民共和国行政处罚法 [Administrative Penalty Law of the People's Republic of China] (People's Republic of China) National People's Congress, 17 March 1996

中华人民共和国行政诉讼法 [Administrative Procedure Law of the People's Republic of China] (People's Republic of China) National People's Congress, 4 April 1989

中华人民共和国宪法修正案 (1988年) [Amendment to the Constitution of the People's Republic of China (1988)] (People's Republic of China) National People's Congress, 12 April 1988

中华人民共和国反垄断法 [Anti-monopoly Law of the People's Republic of China] (People's Republic of China) Standing Committee of the National People's Congress, 30 August 2007

中华人民共和国反不正当竞争法 [Anti-Unfair Competition Law of the People's Republic of China] (People's Republic of China) Standing Committee of the National People's Congress, 2 September 1993

中华人民共和国宪法 [Constitution of the People's Republic of China]

中华人民共和国法官法 [Law on Judges of the People's Republic of China] (People's Republic of China) National People's Congress, 28 February 1995

中华人民共和国立法法 [Law on Legislation of the People's Republic of China] (People's Republic of China) National People's Congress, 15 March 2000

中华人民共和国全国人民代表大会组织法 [Organic Law of the National People's Congress of the People's Republic of China] (People's Republic of China) National People's Congress, 10 December 1982

中华人民共和国人民法院组织法 [Organic Law of the People's Courts of the People's Republic of China] (People's Republic of China) National People's Congress, 1 July 1979

中华人民共和国价格法 [Price Law of the People's Republic of China] (People's Republic of China) Standing Committee of the National People's Congress, 29 December 1997

中华人民共和国企业国有资产法 [State-owned Assets Law of the People's Republic of China] (People's Republic of China) Standing Committee of the National People's Congress, Order No. 5, 28 October 2008

*Other*

*Verordnung gegen Missbrauch wirtschaftlicher Machtstellungen* [Ordinance against Abuse of Economic Power] (Germany) 2 November 1923, [1923] RGB I, 1067

Treaty Establishing the European Economic Community, Rome, 25 March 1957, in force 1 January 1958, 298 UNTS 11

## Regulations and Similar Instruments

价格违法行为行政处罚规定 [Administrative Regulation on Penalties for Pricing Violations] (People's Republic of China) State Council, 29 November 2010

关于公用企业限制竞争和垄断行为突出问题的公告 [Announcement on Prominent Issues Relating to Anticompetitive and Monopolistic Conduct of Public Enterprises] (People's Republic of China) State Administration for Industry and Commerce, Order No. 54, 7 April 2016

反价格垄断规定 [Anti-Price Monopoly Regulation] (People's Republic of China) National Development and Reform Commission, Order No. 7, 29 December 2010

关于地方各级人民法院不应制定司法解释性文件的批复 [A Reply from the Supreme People's Court that Local People's Courts at Various Levels Shall Not Make Judicial Interpretation Documents] (People's Republic of China) Supreme People's Court, 31 March 1987

关于放开在线数据处理与交易处理业务 (经营类电子商务) 外资股比限制的通告 [Circular on Removing Restrictions on Foreign-owned Equity Interests in Online Data Processing and Transaction Processing Services (Operating E-commerce Business)] (People's Republic of China) Ministry for Industry and Information Technology, Order No. 196, 19 June 2015

全国人大常委会关于完善人民陪审员制度的决定 [Decision of the Standing Committee of the National People's Congress on Perfecting the Layperson Assessors System] (People's Republic of China) Standing Committee of the National People's Congress, 28 August 2004

最高人民法院关于修改《民事案件案由规定》的决定 [Decision of the Supreme People's Court to Amend the Provisions on the Causes of Action for Civil Cases] (People's Republic of China) Supreme People's Court, Order No. 41, 18 February 2011

外商投资产业指导目录 (2011年修订) [Foreign Investment Industry Guidance Catalogue (2011 Revised Edition)] (People's Republic of China) National Reform and Development Commission and the Ministry of Commerce, Order No. 12, 24 December 2011

外商投资产业指导目录 (2015年修订) [Foreign Investment Industry Guidance Catalogue (2015 Revised Edition)] (People's Republic of China) National Reform and Development Commission and the Ministry of Commerce, Order No. 22, 10 March 2015

国务院反垄断委员会关于相关市场界定的指南 [Guideline of the Anti-monopoly Commission of the State Council on Defining the Relevant Market] (People's Republic of China) Anti-monopoly Commission of the State Council, 24 May 2009

关于经营者集中申报的指导意见 [Guiding Opinion on Notification of Concentration of Business Operators] (People's Republic of China) Ministry of Commerce, 6 June 2014

关于经营者集中简易案件申报的指导意见 (试行) [Guiding Opinion on Notification of Simple Cases of Concentrations of Business Operators (Trial)] (People's Republic of China) Ministry of Commerce, 18 April 2014

推进国有资本调整和国有企业重组指导意见的通知 [Guiding Opinion on Promoting the Adjustment of State-owned Assets and Reorganisation of State-owned Enterprises] (People's Republic of China) State Council, Order No. 97, 5 December 2006

未依法申报经营者集中调查处理暂行办法 [Interim Measure for Investigating and Handling Concentrations of Business Operators Not Notified in Accordance with the Law] (People's Republic of China) Ministry of Commerce, Order No. 6, 30 December 2011

制止价格垄断行为暂行决定 [Interim Provision on Preventing Price-Related Monopoly Conduct] (People's Republic of China) National Development Reform Commission, Order No. 3, 18 June 2003

关于评估经营者集中竞争影响的暂行规定 [Interim Provision on the Assessment of the Effect of Concentrations of Business Operators on Competition] (People's Republic of China) Ministry of Commerce, Order No. 55, 29 August 2011

关于经营者集中简易案件适用标准的暂行规定 [Interim Regulation on the Applicable Standards for Simple Cases of Concentrations of Business Operators] (People's Republic of China) Ministry of Commerce, Order No. 12, 11 February 2014

经营者集中审查办法 [Measure on the Review of Concentrations of Business Operators] (People's Republic of China) Ministry of Commerce, Order No. 12, 15 July 2009

国家发展改革委 商务部公告2016年第22号 [NDRC and MOFCOM Order No. 22, 2016] (People's Republic of China) National Development and Reform Commission and Ministry of Commerce, Order No. 22, 8 October 2016

国务院办公厅关于国务院反垄断委员会主要职责和组成人员的通知 [Notice of the General Office of the State Council on the Primary Duties and Composition of the Anti-monopoly Commission of the State Council] (People's Republic of China) State Council, Order No. 104, 28 July 2008

最高人民法院印发《关于推进司法公开三大平台建设的若干意见》的通知 [Notice of the Supreme People's Court on the Issuance of the Several Opinions on the Establishment of Three Major Platforms to Promote Judicial Transparency] (People's Republic of China) Supreme People's Court, 21 November 2013

最高人民法院关于认真学习和贯彻《中华人民共和国反垄断法》的通知 [Notice of the Supreme People's Court on the Study and Implementation of the Anti-monopoly Law] (People's Republic of China) Supreme People's Court, Order No. 23, 28 July 2008

关于在全国开展药品价格专项检查的通知 [Notice on Carrying Out National Drug Price Inspections] (People's Republic of China) National Development and Reform Commission, Order No. 1101, 22 May 2016

关于批评北京奇虎科技有限公司和深圳市腾讯计算机系统有限公司的通报 [Notice on Criticising Beijing Qihoo Technology Co., Ltd. and Shenzhen Tencent Computer System Co., Ltd.] (People's Republic of China) Ministry of Industry and Information Technology, Order No. 536, 20 November 2010

关于加强药品市场价格行为监管的通知 [Notice on Strengthening Supervision of Market Prices of Drugs] (People's Republic of China) National Development and Reform Commission, Order No. 930, 4 May 2015

国家工商总局主要职责内设机构和人员编制规定 [Notice on the Major Duties, Internal Structure, and Staffing Requirements of the State Administration for Industry and Commerce] (People's Republic of China) State Council, Order No. 88, 11 July 2008

国务院反垄断委员会关于印发《关于相关市场界定的指南》的通知 [Notice Regarding the Issue of the 'Guidelines on the Definition of the Relevant Market' by the Anti-monopoly Commission of the State Council] (People's Republic of China) Anti-monopoly Commission, Order No. 3, 6 July 2009

企业国有产权交易操作规则 [Operational Rule on Transactions Involving State-owned Assets] (People's Republic of China) State-owned Assets Supervision and Administration Commission of the State Council, Order No. 120, 15 June 2009

最高人民法院关于全面深化人民法院改革的意见—人民法院第四个五年改革纲要 (2014–2018) [Opinion of the Supreme People's Court on the Comprehensive Reform of People's Courts – Outline of the Fourth Five-Year Reform Plan of the People's Court (2014–2018)] (People's Republic of China) Supreme People's Court, Order No. 3, 4 February 2015

关于在市场体系建设中建立公平竞争审查制度的意见 [Opinion on Establishing a Fair Competition Review System in the Construction of a Market System] (People's Republic of China) State Council, Order No. 34, 1 June 2016

关于建立完善价格监管机制的意见 [Opinion on Establishing and Perfecting the Price Supervision Mechanism] (People's Republic of China) National Development and Reform Commission, Order No. 2099, 22 October 2013

推进药品价格改革意见 [Opinion on Promoting Drug Price Reform] (People's Republic of China) National Development and Reform Commission, National

Health and Family Planning Commission, Ministry of Human Resources and Social Security, Ministry of Industry and Information Technology, Ministry of Finance, Ministry of Commerce, and China Food and Drug Administration, Order No. 904, 4 May 2015

推进医疗服务价格改革的意见 [Opinion on Promoting Medical Service Price Reform] (People's Republic of China) National Development and Reform Commission, National Health and Family Planning Commission, Ministry of Human Resources and Social Security, and Ministry of Finance, Order No. 1431, 1 July 2016

关于做大做强民营经济的意见 [Opinion on the Private Economy Becoming Bigger and Stronger] (People's Republic of China) Suzhou Provincial Government, Order No. 24, 13 February 2004

最高人民法院关于审理因垄断行为引发的民事纠纷案件应用法律若干问题的规定 [Provision of the Supreme People's Court on Several Issues Regarding the Application of Law in the Hearing of Civil Dispute Cases Caused by Monopolistic Conduct] (People's Republic of China) Supreme People's Court, Legal Interpretation No. 5, 30 January 2012

最高人民法院关于巡回法庭审理案件若干问题的规定 [Provision of the Supreme People's Court on Several Issues Regarding the Trial of Cases in Circuit Court Divisions] (People's Republic of China) Supreme People's Court, Legal Interpretation No. 3, 28 January 2015

最高人民法院关于人民法院在互联网公布裁判文书的规定 [Provision of the Supreme People's Court Regarding the Publication of the Judgments and Rulings of the People's Courts on the Internet] (People's Republic of China) Supreme People's Court, Legal Interpretation No. 26, 13 November 2013

外商投资电信企业管理规定 [Provision on the Administration of Foreign-Invested Telecommunications Enterprises] (People's Republic of China) State Council, Order No. 333, 11 December 2001

民事案件案由规定 [Provision on the Causes of Action for Civil Cases] (People's Republic of China) Supreme People's Court, Order No. 11, 29 October 2007

最高人民法院关于北京、上海、广州知识产权法院案件管辖的规定 [Provision on the Jurisdiction of the Intellectual Property Courts in Beijing, Shanghai, and Guangzhou] (People's Republic of China) Supreme People's Court, Order No. 12, 31 October 2014

关于开展和保护社会主义竞争的暂行规定 [Provisional Regulation on the Development and Protection of Socialist Competition] (People's Republic of China) State Council, 17 October 1980

企业国有资产监督管理暂行条例 [Provisional Regulation on the State-owned Assets Supervision and Administration Commission] (People's Republic of China) State Council, Order No. 378, 27 May 2003

最高人民法院发布关于司法解释工作的规定 [Regulation Concerning Judicial Interpretation Work] (People's Republic of China) Supreme People's Court, 23 March 2007

工商行政管理机关查处垄断协议、滥用市场支配地位案件程序规定 [Regulation of the Administration for Industry and Commerce on the Procedures Relating to the Investigation of Monopoly Agreement and Abuse of Dominance Cases] (People's Republic of China) State Administration for Industry and Commerce, Order No. 42, 26 May 2009

工商行政管理机关制止滥用行政权力排除、限制竞争行为程序规定 [Regulation of the Administration for Industry and Commerce on the Procedures Relating to the Prevention of the Abuse of Administrative Power to Eliminate or Restrict Competition] State Administration for Industry and Commerce, Order No. 41, 26 May 2009

工商行政管理机关制止滥用行政权利排除、限制竞争行为的规定 [Regulation of the Administration for Industry and Commerce on the Prohibition of Abuse of Administrative Power to Restrict or Eliminate Competition] (People's Republic of China) State Administration for Industry and Commerce, Order No. 55, 31 December 2010

工商行政管理机关禁止滥用市场支配地位行为的规定 [Regulation of the Administration for Industry and Commerce on the Prohibition of Abuse of Dominance Conduct] (People's Republic of China) State Administration for Industry and Commerce, Order No. 54, 31 December 2010

工商行政管理机关禁止垄断协议行为的规定 [Regulation of the Administration for Industry and Commerce on the Prohibition of Monopoly Agreements] (People's Republic of China) State Administration for Industry and Commerce, Order No. 53, 31 December 2010

国务院关于经营者集中申报标准的规定 [Regulation of the State Council on the Notification Thresholds for Concentrations of Business Operators] (People's Republic of China) State Council, Order No. 529, 3 August 2008

反价格垄断行政执法程序规定 [Regulation on Anti-Price Monopoly Administrative Enforcement Procedures] (People's Republic of China) National Reform and Development Commission, Order No. 8, 29 December 2010

关于外国投资着并购境内企业的规定 [Regulation on Mergers with and Acquisitions of Domestic Enterprises by Foreign Investors] (People's Republic of China) Ministry of Commerce, State Assets Supervision and Administration Commission of the State Council, State Administration of Taxation, State Administration for Industry and Commerce, China Securities Regulatory Commission, and State Administration of Foreign Exchange, Order No. 10, 8 August 2006

关于外国投资者并购境内企业的规定 [Regulation on Mergers with and Acquisitions of Domestic Enterprises by Foreign Investors] (People's Republic of China) Ministry of Commerce, Order No. 6, 22 June 2009

外国律师事务所驻华代表机构管理条例 [Regulation on the Administration of Foreign Law Firms' Representative Offices in China] (People's Republic of China) State Council, Order No. 338, 19 December 2001

关于经营者集中附加限制性条件的规定(试行) [Regulation on the Imposition of Restrictive Conditions on Concentrations of Business Operators (Trial)] (People's Republic of China) Ministry of Commerce, Order No. 6, 4 December 2014

商务部主要职责内设机构和人员编制规定 [Regulation on the Major Duties, Internal Structure, and Staffing Requirements of the Ministry of Commerce] (People's Republic of China) Ministry of Commerce, 24 August 2008

工业和信息化部主要职责内设机构和人员编制规定 [Regulation on the Major Duties, Internal Structure, and Staffing Requirements of the Ministry of Industry and Information Technology] (People's Republic of China) State Council, Order No. 72, 11 July 2008

国家发展和改革委员会主要职责内设机构和人员编制规定 [Regulation on the Major Duties, Internal Structure, and Staffing Requirements of the National Development and Reform Commission] (People's Republic of China) National Development and Reform Commission, 25 August 2008

关于禁止滥用知识产权排除、限制竞争行为的规定 [Regulation on the Prohibition of Abuse of Intellectual Property Rights to Eliminate or Restrict Competition] (People's Republic of China) State Administration for Industry and Commerce, Order No. 74, 7 April 2015

社会团体登记管理条例 [Regulation on the Registration and Management of Social Organisations] (People's Republic of China) State Council, Order No. 250, 25 October 1998

关于加强法律解释工作的决议 [Resolution on Strengthening Legal Interpretation Work] (People's Republic of China) Standing Committee of the National People's Congress, 10 June 1981

规范互联网信息服务市场秩序若干规定 [Several Provisions on Regulating Internet Information Services Market Order] (People's Republic of China) Ministry of Industry and Information Technology, Order No. 20, 29 December 2011

规范价格行政处罚权的若干规定 [Several Provisions on Regulating Price-Related Administrative Penalty Power] (People's Republic of China) National Development and Reform Commission, Order No. 1223, 7 June 2014

国务院关于修改《外商投资电信企业管理规定》的决定 [State Council Decision on Revising the Provisions on the Administration of Foreign-Invested Telecommunications Enterprises] (People's Republic of China) State Council, Order No. 534, 10 September 2008

国务院工作规则 [State Council Work Rules] (People's Republic of China) State Council, Order No. 16, 23 March 2013

中华人民共和国电信条例 [Telecommunications Regulation of the People's Republic of China] (People's Republic of China) State Council, Order No. 291, 25 September 2000

电信业务分类目录(2003版) [Telecommunications Services Classification Catalogue (2003 Version)] (People's Republic of China) Ministry of Industry and Information Technology, 1 April 2003

## Administrative Decisions

*Merger Decisions*

中华人民共和国商务部公告2008年第95号 [Announcement No. 95 of 2008 of the Ministry of Commerce of the People's Republic of China] (People's Republic of China) Ministry of Commerce, Order No. 95, 18 November 2008

关于禁止可口可乐公司收购中国汇源公司审查决定的公告 [Announcement of the Review Decision to Prohibit Coca-Cola's Acquisition of Huiyuan] (People's Republic of China) Ministry of Commerce, Order No. 22, 18 March 2009

中华人民共和国商务部公告 (2009年第28号) [Announcement of the Ministry of Commerce of the People's Republic of China (No. 28 of 2009)] (People's Republic of China) Ministry of Commerce, Order No. 28, 24 April 2009

关于附条件批准美国通用汽车公司收购德尔福公司反垄断审查决定的公告 [Announcement of the Anti-monopoly Review Decision to Conditionally Approve General Motors' Acquisition of Delphi] (People's Republic of China) Ministry of Commerce, Order No. 76, 28 September 2009

关于附条件批准松下公司收购三洋公司反垄断审查决定的公告 [Announcement of the Anti-monopoly Review Decision to Conditionally Approve Panasonic's Acquisition of Sanyo] (People's Republic of China) Ministry of Commerce, Order No. 82, 30 October 2009

公布关于附条件批准诺华股份公司收购爱尔康公司反垄断审查决定的公告 [Announcement of the Anti-monopoly Review Decision to Conditionally Approve Novartis' Acquisition of Alcon] (People's Republic of China) Ministry of Commerce, Order No. 53, 13 August 2010

关于附条件批准乌拉尔开放型股份公司吸收合并谢尔维尼特开放型股份公司反垄断审查决定的公告 [Announcement of the Anti-monopoly Review Decision to Conditionally Approve Uralkali's Merger with Silvinit] (People's Republic of China) Ministry of Commerce, Order No. 33, 2 June 2011

关于附条件批准佩内洛普有限责任公司收购萨维奥纺织机械股份有限公司反垄断审查决定的公告 [Announcement of the Anti-monopoly Review Decision to Conditionally Approve Alpha V's Acquisition of Savio] (People's Republic of China) Ministry of Commerce, Order No. 73, 31 October 2011

关于附条件批准通用电气(中国)有限公司与中国神华煤制油化工有限公司设立合营企业反垄断审查决定的公告 [Announcement of the Anti-monopoly Review Decision to Conditionally Approve the Establishment of a Joint Venture between General Electric (China) and Shenhua] (People's Republic of China) Ministry of Commerce, Order No. 74, 10 November 2011

关于附条件批准希捷科技公司收购三星电子有限公司硬盘驱动器业务反垄断审查决定的公告 [Announcement of the Anti-monopoly Review Decision to Conditionally Approve Seagate Technology's Acquisition of the Hard Disk Drive Business of Samsung Electronics] (People's Republic of China) Ministry of Commerce, Order No. 90, 12 December 2011

关于附加限制性条件批准汉高香港与天德化工组建合营企业经营者集中反垄断审查决定的公告 [Announcement of the Anti-monopoly Review of Concentrations of Business Operators Decision to Impose Restrictive Conditions to the Approval of the Establishment of a Joint Venture between Hong Kong Henkel and Tiande] (People's Republic of China) Ministry of Commerce, Order No. 6, 9 February 2012

关于附加限制性条件批准西部数据收购日立存储经营者集中反垄断审查决定的公告 [Announcement of the Anti-monopoly Review of Concentrations of Business Operators Decision to Impose Restrictive Conditions to the Approval of Western Digital's Acquisition of Hitachi] (People's Republic of China) Ministry of Commerce, Order No. 9, 2 March 2012

关于附加限制性条件批准谷歌收购摩托罗拉移动经营者集中反垄断审查决定的公告 [Announcement of the Anti-monopoly Review of Concentrations of Business Operators Decision to Impose Restrictive Conditions to the Approval of Google's Acquisition of Motorola Mobility] (People's Republic of China) Ministry of Commerce, Order No. 25, 19 May 2012

关于附加限制性条件批准沃尔玛公司收购纽海控股33.6%股权经营者集中反垄断审查决定的公告 [Announcement of the Anti-monopoly Review of Concentrations of Business Operators Decision to Impose Restrictive Conditions to the Approval of Wal-Mart's Acquisition of 33.6 per cent Equity Interest in Newheight (Shanghai)] (People's Republic of China) Ministry of Commerce, Order No. 49, 13 August 2012

关于附加限制性条件批准嘉能可国际公司收购斯特拉塔公司经营者集中反垄断审查决定的公告 [Announcement of the Anti-monopoly Review of Concentrations of Business Operators Decision to Impose Restrictive Conditions to the Approval of Glencore International Acquisition of Xstrata] (People's Republic of China) Ministry of Commerce, Order No. 20, 16 April 2013

关于附加限制性条件批准丸红公司收购高鸿公司100%股权经营者集中反垄断审查决定的公告 [Announcement of the Anti-monopoly Review of Concentrations of Business Operators Decision to Impose Restrictive Conditions to the Approval of Marubeni's Acquisition of 100 per cent Equity Interest of Gavilon Holdings] (People's Republic of China) Ministry of Commerce, Order No. 22, 23 April 2013

关于附加限制性条件批准美国百特国际有限公司收购瑞典金宝公司经营者集中反垄断审查决定的公告 [Announcement of the Anti-monopoly Review of Concentrations of Business Operators Decision to Impose Restrictive Conditions to the Approval of Baxter International's Acquisition of Gambro] (People's Republic of China) Ministry of Commerce, Order No. 58, 13 August 2013

关于附加限制性条件批准联发科技股份有限公司吸收合并开曼晨星半导体公司经营者集中反垄断审查决定的公告 [Announcement of the Anti-monopoly Review of Concentrations of Business Operators Decision to Impose Restrictive Conditions to the Approval of MediaTek's Merger with MStar Semiconductor] (People's Republic of China) Ministry of Commerce, Order No. 61, 26 August 2013

关于附加限制性条件批准赛默飞世尔科技公司收购立菲技术公司案经营者集中反垄断审查决定的公告 [Announcement of the Anti-monopoly Review of Concentrations of Business Operators Decision to Impose Restrictive Conditions to the Approval of Thermo Fisher Scientific's Acquisition of Life Technologies] (People's Republic of China) Ministry of Commerce, Order No. 3, 15 January 2014

关于附加限制性条件批准微软收购诺基亚设备和服务业务案经营者集中反垄断审查决定的公告 [Announcement of the Anti-monopoly Review of Concentrations of Business Operators Decision to Impose Restrictive Conditions to the Approval of Microsoft's Acquisition of Nokia's Device and Service Business] (People's Republic of China) Ministry of Commerce, Order No. 24, 8 April 2014

关于附加限制性条件批准默克公司收购安智电子材料公司案经营者集中反垄断审查决定的公告 [Announcement of the Anti-monopoly Review of Concentrations of Business Operators Decision to Impose Restrictive Conditions to the Approval of Merck's Acquisition of AZ Electronics Materials] (People's Republic of China) Ministry of Commerce, Order No. 30, 30 April 2014

关于禁止马士基、地中海航运、达飞设立网络中心经营者集中反垄断审查决定的公告 [Announcement of the Anti-monopoly Review of Concentrations of Business Operators Decision to Prohibit the Establishment of a Network Centre by AP Møller-Maersk, MSC Mediterranean Shipping Company, and CMA CGM] (People's Republic of China) Ministry of Commerce, Order No. 46, 17 June 2014

商务部关于附加限制性条件批准科力远、丰田中国、PEVE、新中源、丰田通商拟设立合营企业案经营者集中反垄断审查决定的公告 [Announcement of the Anti-monopoly Review of Concentrations of Business Operators Decision to Impose Restrictive Conditions to the Approval of the Establishment of a Joint Venture among Hunan Corun New Energy, Toyota China, PEVE, Changshu Sinogy Venture Capital, and Toyota Tsusho] (People's Republic of China) Ministry of Commerce, Order No. 49, 2 July 2014

商务部行政处罚决定书 [Ministry of Commerce Administrative Penalty Decision] (People's Republic of China) Ministry of Commerce, Order No. 787, 2 December 2014

商务部行政处罚决定书 [Ministry of Commerce Administrative Penalty Decision] (People's Republic of China) Ministry of Commerce, Order No. 788, 2 December 2014

关于解除谷歌收购摩托罗拉案部分义务的公告 [Announcement of the Partial Release of Commitments Relating to Google's Acquisition of Motorola Mobility] (People's Republic of China) Ministry of Commerce, Order No. 2, 6 January 2015

关于附加限制性条件批准诺基亚收购阿尔卡特朗讯股权案经营者集中反垄断审查决定的公告 [Announcement of the Anti-monopoly Review of Concentrations of Business Operators Decision to Impose Restrictive Conditions to the Approval of Nokia's Acquisition of Shares in Alcatel-Lucent] (People's Republic of China) Ministry of Commerce, Order No. 44, 19 October 2015

关于变更希捷科技公司收购三星电子有限公司硬盘驱动器业务经营者集中限制性条件的公告 [Announcement of the Variation to the Restrictive Conditions Imposed on Seagate Technology's Acquisition of the Hard Disk Drive Business of Samsung Electronics] (People's Republic of China) Ministry of Commerce, Order No. 43, 19 October 2015

关于变更西部数据收购日立存储经营者集中限制性条件的公告 [Announcement of the Variation to the Restrictive Conditions Imposed on Western Digital's Acquisition of Hitachi] (People's Republic of China) Ministry of Commerce, Order No. 41, 19 October 2015

关于附加限制性条件批准恩智浦收购飞思卡尔全部股权案经营者集中反垄断审查决定的公告 [Announcement of the Anti-monopoly Review of Concentrations of Business Operators Decision to Impose Restrictive Conditions to the Approval of NXP's Acquisition of Freescale's Entire Share Capital] (People's Republic of China) Ministry of Commerce, Order No. 64, 25 November 2015

关于解除沃尔玛收购纽海控股33.6%股权案经营者集中限制性条件的公告 [Announcement of the Release of Restrictive Conditions Imposed on Wal-Mart's Acquisition of 33.6 per cent Equity Interest in Newheight (Shanghai)] (People's Republic of China) Ministry of Commerce, Order No. 23, 30 May 2016

关于附加限制性条件批准百威英博啤酒集团收购英国南非米勒酿酒公司股权案经营者集中反垄断审查决定的公告 [Announcement of the Anti-monopoly Review of Concentrations of Business Operators Decision to Impose Restrictive Conditions to the Approval of Anheuser-Busch InBev's Acquisition of Shares in SABMiller] (People's Republic of China) Ministry of Commerce, Order No. 38, 29 July 2016

关于附加限制性条件批准雅培公司收购圣犹达医疗公司股权案经营者集中反垄断审查决定的公告 [Announcement of the Anti-monopoly Review of Concentrations of Business Operators Decision to Impose Restrictive Conditions to the Approval of Abbott Laboratories' Acquisition of Shares in St Jude's Medical] (People's Republic of China) Ministry of Commerce, Order No. 88, 30 December 2016

*Non-Merger Decisions*

National Development and Reform Commission, 国家发展改革委对方便面价格串通案调查情况的通报 [National Development and Reform Commission's Report on Its Instant Noodle Price Collusion Investigation] (News Release, 16 August 2007)

National Development and Reform Commission, 湖北省物价局依法查处武昌盐业分公司强制搭售案件 [Hubei Price Bureau Investigates the Wuhan Salt Industry Group Branch Forced Tying Case According to Law] (News Release, 15 November 2010)

江西省泰和县液化石油气经营者从事垄断协议案 [Jiangxi Province Taihe County Liquified Petroleum Gas Monopoly Agreement Case] (People's Republic of China) Jiangxi Province Administration for Industry and Commerce, Order No. 1, 1 April 2011

National Development and Reform Commission, 两医药公司垄断复方利血平原料药收到严厉处罚 [Two Pharmaceutical Companies Strictly Punished for Monopolising Compound Reserpine Raw Materials] (News Release, 15 November 2011)

河南省安阳市旧机动车经营者从事垄断协议案 [Henan Province Anyang City Used Car Operators Monopoly Agreement Case] (People's Republic of China) Henan Province Administration for Industry and Commerce, Order No. 1, 4 January 2012

关于辽阳冀东水泥有限公司协议垄断经营行为的处罚决定 [Administrative Penalty on Liaoning Jidong Cement Monopoly Agreement Conduct] (People's Republic of China) Liaoning Province Administration for Industry and Commerce, Order No. 2, 13 August 2012

National Development and Reform Commission, 广东查处海砂价格垄断案件 确保国家重点工程建设顺利进行 [Guangdong Investigates Sea Sand Price Monopoly Case, Ensures Smooth Progress of Nationally Important Construction Project] (News Release, 26 October 2012)

湖南省永州市保险行业协会组织本行经营者从事垄断协议案 [Hunan Province Yongzhou City Insurance Industry Association Monopoly Agreement Case] (People's Republic of China) Hunan Province Administration for Industry and Commerce, Order No. 1, 30 November 2012

湖南省郴州市保险行业协会组织本行经营者从事垄断协议案 [Hunan Province Chenzhou City Insurance Industry Association Monopoly Agreement Case] (People's Republic of China) Hunan Province Administration for Industry and Commerce, Order No. 3, 3 December 2012

浙江省江山市混凝土经营者从事垄断协议案 [Zhejiang Province Jiangshan City Concrete Businesses Monopoly Agreement Case] (People's Republic of China) Zhejiang Province Administration for Industry and Commerce, Order No. 16, 14 December 2012

National Development and Reform Commission, 六家境外企业实施液晶面板价格垄断被依法查处 [Six Overseas Businesses Investigated and Punished for Implementing LCD Panel Price Monopoly] (News Release, 4 January 2013)

Sichuan Development and Reform Commission, 五粮液公司实施价格垄断被处罚2.02亿元 [Wuliangye Fined RMB 202 Million for Implementing Price Monopoly] (News Release, 22 February 2013)

浙江省慈溪市建设工程检测协会组织本行业经营者从事垄断协议案 [Zhejiang Province Cixi City Construction Quality Assurance Industry Association Monopoly Agreement Case] (People's Republic of China) Zhejiang Province Administration for Industry and Commerce, Order No. 15, 14 March 2013

云南省西双版纳州旅游协会, 西双版纳州旅行社协会组织本行业经营者从事垄断协议案 [Yunnan Province Xishuangbanna Tourism Association, Xishuangbanna Travel Agency Association Organise for Industry Operators to Implement

Monopoly Agreements Case] (People's Republic of China) Yunnan Province Administration for Industry and Commerce, Order No. 1, 7 April 2013

National Development and Reform Commission, 合生元等乳粉生产企业违反《反垄断法》限制竞争行为共被处罚6.6873亿元 [Biostime and Other Infant Formula Producers Restricted Competition and Violated the Anti-monopoly Law, Fined a Total of RMB 668.73m] (News Release, 7 August 2013)

上海黄金饰品行业协会及部分金店实施价格垄断被依法查处 [Price Monopoly Agreement Implemented by the Shanghai Gold Jewellery Industry Association and Some Jewellery Stores Investigated According to Law] (News Release, 13 August 2013)

National Development and Reform Commission, 一批扰乱旅游市场秩序的价格违法案件受到严肃查处 [Some Illegal Price-Related Conduct Cases that Disrupted Market Order in the Tourism Market Severely Punished] (News Release, 29 September 2013)

广东惠州大亚湾溢源净水有限公司滥用市场支配地位案 [Guangdong Huizhou Daya Bay Yiyuan Purified Water Company Abuse of Dominance Case] (People's Republic of China) Guangdong Province Administration for Industry and Commerce, Order No. 2, 16 December 2013

National Development and Reform Commission, 国家发展改革委对美国IDC公司涉嫌价格垄断案中止调查 [NDRC Stops Investigation of InterDigital Suspected Price Monopoly Case] (News Release, 22 May 2014)

关于赤峰中心城区烟花爆竹批发企业以行政机关限定为由实施垄断行为的处罚决定 [Administrative Penalty on Fireworks and Firecracker Wholesale Businesses in Chifeng City Centre for Implementing Monopoly Agreement by Reason of Administrative Restriction] (People's Republic of China) Inner Mongolia Autonomous Region Administration for Industry and Commerce, Order No. 1, 27 May 2014

National Development and Reform Commission, 部分眼镜镜片生产企业维持转售价格行为被依法查处 [Resale Price Maintenance Conduct of Some Glass Lens Manufacturers Handled According to Law] (News Release, 29 May 2014)

内蒙古自治区烟草公司赤峰市公司滥用市场支配地位案 [Inner Mongolia Tobacco Company Chifeng Subsidiary Abuse of Dominance Case] (People's Republic of China) Inner Mongolia Autonomous Region Province Administration for Industry and Commerce, Order No. 2, 4 July 2014

麻阳苗族自治县页岩砖经营者垄断案 [Mayang Miao Autonomous Region Shale Brick Businesses Monopoly Case] (People's Republic of China) Hunan Province Administration for Industry and Commerce, Order No. 1, 5 January 2015

海南省东方市自来水公司垄断案 [Hainan Province Dongfang Water Company Monopoly Case] (People's Republic of China) Hainan Province Administration for Industry and Commerce, Order No. 2, 9 January 2015

行政处罚决定书 [Administrative Penalty Decision] (People's Republic of China) National Development and Reform Commission, Order No. 1, 9 February 2015

国家发展改革委办公厅关于建议纠正山东省交通运输厅滥用行政权力排除限制竞争有关行为的函 [National Development and Reform Commission General Office Letter Recommending That Shandong Province Department of Transportation Correct Its Abuse of Administrative Power Conduct Restricting Competition] (People's Republic of China) National Development and Reform Commission, Order No. 501, 9 March 2015

广州市番禺动漫游艺行业协会垄断协议案 [Guangdong Panyu Animation and Entertainment Industry Association Monopoly Agreement Case] (People's Republic of China) Guangdong Province Administration for Industry and Commerce, Order No. 1, 9 May 2015

辽宁省烟草公司抚顺市公司滥用市场支配地位案 [Liaoning Tobacco Company Fushun Subsidiary Abuse of Dominance Case] (People's Republic of China) Liaoning Province Administration for Industry and Commerce, Order No. 2, 1 June 2015

National Development and Reform Commission, 云南省通信管理局违反《反垄断法》滥用行政权力排除限制竞争被依法纠正 [Yunnan Province Communications Authority's Abuse of Administrative Power to Eliminate or Restrict Competition in Violation of the Anti-monopoly Law Has Been Corrected] (News Release, 2 June 2015)

重庆青阳药业有限公司涉嫌滥用市场支配地位拒绝交易案 [Chongqing Qingyang Pharmaceutical Company Suspected Abuse of Dominance Refusal to Deal Case] (People's Republic of China) Chongqing Administration for Industry and Commerce, Order No. 15, 28 October 2015

National Development and Reform Commission, 四川、浙江省卫生和计划生育委员会及时纠正药品集中采购中违反《反垄断法》、排除限制竞争行为 [Sichuan Province and Zhejiang Province Health and Planning Commissions Promptly Corrects Anti-Competitive Conduct Violating the Anti-monopoly Law in Centralised Drug Procurement] (News Release, 2 November 2015)

甘肃省发改和改革委员会关于建议纠正甘肃省道路运输管理局滥用行政权利排除，限制竞争有关行为的涵 [Gansu Province Development and Reform Commission Letter Recommending that the Gansu Province Road Transport Authority Correct Its Abuse of Administrative Power Conduct Eliminating or Restricting Competition] Gansu Province Development and Reform Commission, Order No. 7, 26 November 2015

内蒙古自治区阿拉善左旗城市给排水公司滥用市场支配地位案 [Inner Mongolia Autonomous Region Alxa Zuoqi Water Supply and Drainage Company Abuse of Dominance Case] (People's Republic of China) Inner Mongolia Autonomous Region Province Administration for Industry and Commerce, Order No. 1, 22 April 2016

湖北省物价局对5家天然气公司价格垄断行为进行处罚 [Hubei Price Bureau Punishes Five Natural Gas Companies' Price Monopoly Conduct] (News Release, 12 July 2016)

安徽信雅达等三家密码器企业垄断协议案 [Three Encryption Device Businesses Monopoly Agreement Case] (People's Republic of China) Anhui Administration for Industry and Commerce, Order No. 9, 4 November 2016

国家工商行政管理总局行政处罚决定书 [State Administration for Industry and Commerce Administrative Penalty Decision] (People's Republic of China) State Administration for Industry and Commerce, Order No. 1, 9 November 2016

北京市住建委纠正混凝土行业管理中滥用行政权力排除限制竞争行为 [Beijing Municipal Commission of Housing and Urban-Rural Development Corrects Conduct that Abuses Administrative Power to Eliminate or Restrict Competition in Its Management of the Concrete Industry] (News Release, 29 December 2016)

## Policy Documents

### China

中国共产党第十一届中央委员会第三次全体会议公报 [Communiqué of the Third Plenum of the Eleventh Central Committee of the Communist Party of China], Communist Party of China, 22 December 1978

中国共产党章程 [Constitution of the Communist Party of China] (People's Republic of China) National Congress of the Communist Party of China, 21 October 2007

中共中央关于全面深化改革若干重大问题的决定 [Decision of the Central Committee of the Communist Party of China on Some Major Issues Concerning Comprehensively Deepening Reform] (People's Republic of China) Third Plenary Session of the 18th Central Committee of the Communist Party of China, 12 November 2013

全国人民代表大会常务委员会关于修改《中华人民共和国外资企业法》等四部法律的决定 [Decision to Revise Four Laws Including the Law of the People's Republic of China on Wholly Foreign-owned Enterprises] (People's Republic of China) Standing Committee of the National People's Congress, 3 September 2016

中华人民共和国国民经济和社会发展第十二个五年规划纲要 [Outline of the 12th Five-Year Plan for National Economic and Social Development] (People's Republic of China) National People's Congress, 14 March 2011

中华人民共和国国民经济和社会发展第十三个五年规划纲要 [Outline of the 13th Five-Year Plan for National Economic and Social Development] (People's Republic of China) National People's Congress, 16 March 2016

国家中长期科学和技术发展规划纲要 (2006–2020) 年 [Outline of the National Medium- and Long-Term Plan for the Development of Science and Technology (2006–2020)] (People's Republic of China) State Council, 9 February 2006

盐业体制改革方案 [Salt Industry System Reform Plan] (People's Republic of China) State Council, Order No. 25, 22 April 2016

关于促进工业企业做大做强若干奖励政策 [Some Incentives on Promoting Industrial Enterprises to Become Bigger and Stronger] (People's Republic of China) Luyang Government, Order No. 12, 23 May 2007

中共中央国务院关于深化体制机制改革加快实施创新驱动发展战略的若干意见 [Some Opinions of the Central Committee of the Communist Party of China and the State Council on Deepening Institutional Reforms and Accelerating the Implementation of the Innovation-Driven Development Strategy] (People's Republic of China) Central Committee of the Communist Party of China and the State Council, 13 March 2015

关于促进市场公平竞争维护市场正常秩序的若干意见 [Some Opinions on Promoting Fair Market Competition and Maintaining Normal Market Order] (People's Republic of China) State Council, Order No. 20, 4 June 2014

国家知识产权战略纲要 [State Intellectual Property Strategic Guideline] (People's Republic of China) State Council, Notice No. 18, 5 June 2008

## Other

Australian Competition and Consumer Commission, 'Merger Guidelines' (November 2008)

Japan Fair Trade Commission, 'Guidelines to Application of the Antimonopoly Act Concerning Review of Business Combination', 14 June 2011

Ministry of Commerce of China and the Directorate-General for Competition of European Commission, Terms of Reference of the EU-China Competition Policy Dialogue, 6 May 2004, available at http://ec.europa.eu/competition/international/bilateral/china_tor_en.pdf

US Department of Justice and Federal Trade Commission, 'Horizontal Merger Guidelines', 19 August 2010

US Department of Justice Antitrust Division, 'Antitrust Division Policy Guide to Merger Remedies' (June 2011)

# LIST OF ABBREVIATIONS

| | |
|---|---|
| AIC | Administration for Industry and Commerce |
| AMC | Anti-monopoly Commission |
| AML | Anti-monopoly Law |
| AUCL | Anti-Unfair Competition Law |
| CAAC | Civil Aviation Administration of China |
| CASS | Chinese Academy of Social Sciences |
| CBRC | China Banking Regulatory Commission |
| CIRC | China Insurance Regulatory Commission |
| CNPC | China National Petroleum Corporation |
| CPC | Communist Party of China |
| CPPCC | Chinese People's Political Consultative Conference |
| CSRC | China Securities Regulatory Commission |
| FCS | Fiscal contracting system |
| FRAND | Fair, reasonable and non-discriminatory |
| HHI | Herfindahl–Hirschman Index |
| IPR | Intellectual property right |
| LAO | State Council Legislative Affairs Office |
| MIIT | Ministry for Industry and Information Technology |
| MOFCOM | Ministry of Commerce |
| NDRC | National Development and Reform Commission |
| NPC | National People's Congress |
| Politburo | Political Bureau of the Central Committee |
| SAIC | State Administration for Industry and Commerce |
| SAPPRFT | State Administration of Press, Publication, Radio, Film and Television |
| SASAC | State-owned Assets Supervision and Administration Commission |
| SCNPC | Standing Committee of the National People's Congress |
| SEP | Standard essential patent |
| SETC | State Economic and Trade Commission |
| Sinopec | China Petrochemical Corporation |
| SOEs | State-owned enterprises |

| | |
|---|---|
| SPC | Supreme People's Court |
| VATS | Value-added telecommunications services |
| VIE | Variable interest entity |
| WTO | World Trade Organization |

# PART I

Introducing the Anti-monopoly Law

# 1

# Competition Law in China and the Importance of Context

## 1.1 Introduction

In December 1978, the Communist Party of China (CPC) made the critical decision to shift its focus from 'class struggle' to 'economic development'.[1] Since then, China has adopted incremental and far-reaching reforms to shift its centrally-planned economy to one that is market-based, open up its economy to foreign investment and participate in global markets. China's entry into the World Trade Organization (WTO) on 11 December 2001 marked its formal integration into the global economic system.

China's economic growth has been hailed as remarkable not only for the high, sustained rate at which it has been achieved, but also because it has been achieved with a relatively weak legal system and underdeveloped financial markets, institutions thought to be critical to economic development.[2] When China first embarked on economic reforms and opening up, its legal system was virtually non-existent, having been effectively abolished during the Cultural Revolution.[3] Since the mid-1990s, China has attached increasing importance to the rule of law and to establishing and improving its laws and legal institutions in order to promote and support economic reforms and the development of a

---

[1] 中国共产党第十一届中央委员会第三次全体会议公报 [Communiqué of the Third Plenum of the Eleventh Central Committee of the Communist Party of China], Communist Party of China, 22 December 1978.

[2] Franklin Allen, Jun Qian and Meijun Qian, 'Law, Finance, and Economic Growth in China' (2005) 77 *Journal of Financial Economics* 57 at 58–9; Yang Yao and Linda Yueh, 'Law, Finance, and Economic Growth in China: An Introduction' (2009) 37 *World Development* 753 at 753; Donald C. Clarke, 'Legislating for a Market Economy in China' (2007) 191 *The China Quarterly* 567.

[3] Stanley Lubman, 'Bird in a Cage: Chinese Law Reform after Twenty Years' (2000) 20 *Northwestern Journal of International Law & Business* 383 at 383–4.

market economy.[4] As part of those law-making efforts, China enacted its first comprehensive competition law in 2007 – the Anti-monopoly Law (AML).[5]

The AML regulates anticompetitive agreements (referred to as 'monopoly agreements'),[6] abuses of dominant market positions,[7] and mergers (referred to as 'concentrations of undertakings'),[8] which are together defined as monopolistic conduct.[9] There are also some provisions in the AML that have been tailored to address China-specific matters such as administrative monopoly, which is the abuse of administrative power to restrict competition and includes exercises of administrative power that impede the free flow of goods within China's internal market or competition in or market entry into particular industries or sectors.[10]

## 1.2 Evaluations of the Anti-monopoly Law to Date

The development, adoption and subsequent implementation and enforcement of the AML has garnered substantial attention and commentary from academics, lawyers, government officials, economists, businesses and media outlets in China and beyond. Drafts produced, investigations launched and decisions made in relation to the AML have been carefully scrutinised and considered.

Generally speaking, the AML is regarded as a modern competition law that is largely consistent in form and substance with prevailing international competition law norms, and in particular the competition laws of the European Union and Germany.[11] Commentators note that many

---

[4] Lubman, 'Bird in a Cage'; Clarke, 'Legislating for a Market Economy in China'; Chen Su, 'The Establishment and Development of the Chinese Economic Legal System in the Past Sixty Years' (2009) 23 *Columbia Journal of Asian Law* 109; Randall Peerenboom, *China's Long March toward Rule of Law* (Cambridge: Cambridge University Press, 2002).
[5] 中华人民共和国反垄断法 [Anti-monopoly Law of the People's Republic of China] (People's Republic of China) Standing Committee of the National People's Congress, 30 August 2007.
[6] Anti-monopoly Law, ch. II.　[7] Anti-monopoly Law, ch. III.
[8] Anti-monopoly Law, ch. IV.　[9] Anti-monopoly Law, art. 3.
[10] Xiaoye Wang, 'Highlights of China's New Anti-monopoly Law' (2008) 75 *Antitrust Law Journal* 133 at 148; Eleanor M. Fox, 'An Anti-monopoly Law for China – Scaling the Walls of Government Restraints' (2008) 75 *Antitrust Law Journal* 173 at 173; Mark Williams, *Competition Policy and Law in China, Hong Kong and Taiwan* (Cambridge: Cambridge University Press, 2005), p. 138.
[11] Wang, 'Highlights of China's New Anti-monopoly Law', 135; Nathan Bush, 'Constraints on Convergence in Chinese Antitrust' (2009) 54 *Antitrust Bulletin* 87 at 92–3; Wentong

substantive provisions in the AML are similar to provisions in European Union competition law, and that a number of legal doctrines from United States antitrust law have also been reflected in the AML.[12] Many commentators observe that decisions made under the AML are increasingly framed in language that is identifiable as and consistent with what they regard as standard antitrust economic theories of harm and legal doctrines and approaches that are adopted in the United States, Europe and other mature competition law jurisdictions.[13] They also note that AML decisions, especially merger decisions, reflect growing analytical depth and sophistication.[14]

Nonetheless, the AML and its enforcement have attracted some criticism. Commentators voice concerns that so-called 'non-competition factors' are influencing the outcomes of investigations and reviews taken by the Chinese competition agencies. They are also worried that the AML is not being applied equally to state-owned enterprises (SOEs) and is being enforced in a manner that discriminates against foreign companies. Another key complaint is the lack of transparency and due process in the

---

Zheng, 'Transplanting Antitrust in China: Economic Transition, Market Structure, and State Control' (2010) 32 *University of Pennsylvania Journal of International Law* 643 at 647–8; Dina Kallay, 'Reflections on China's New Anti-monopoly Law' (Remarks presented at the IBA/SVK 'Europe and the Globalisation of Antitrust' Conference, Berlin, 30 June 2008), pp. 4–5.

[12] Wang, 'Highlights of China's New Anti-monopoly Law', 134–5; Nathan Bush, 'The PRC Antimonopoly Law: Unanswered Questions and Challenges Ahead' [2007] (October) *The Antitrust Source* 1 at 2, available at www.americanbar.org/content/dam/aba/publishing/antitrust_source/Oct07_Bush10_18f.authcheckdam.pdf; H. Stephen Harris Jr et al., *Anti-monopoly Law and Practice in China* (New York: Oxford University Press, 2011), pp. 2–3; Susan Beth Farmer, 'The Evolution of Chinese Merger Notification Guidelines: A Work in Progress Integrating Global Consensus and Domestic Imperatives' (2009) 18 *Tulane Journal of International and Comparative Law* 1 at 6.

[13] See, e.g., Xiaoye Wang and Adrian Emch, 'Five Years of Implementation of China's Anti-monopoly Law – Achievements and Challenges' (2013) 1 *Journal of Antitrust Enforcement* 247 at 251–4; Ping Lin and Jingjing Zhao, 'Merger Control Policy under China's Anti-monopoly Law' (2012) 41 *Review of Industrial Organization* 109 at 123–5; Xinzhu Zhang and Vanessa Yanhua Zhang, 'Chinese Merger Control: Patterns and Implications' (2010) 6 *Journal of Competition Law and Economics* 477 at 492–3; Fei Deng and Cunzhen Huang, 'A Five Year Review of Merger Enforcement in China' [2013] (October) *The Antitrust Source* 1 at 18, available at www.americanbar.org/content/dam/aba/directories/antitrust/oct13_deng_10_29f.authcheckdam.pdf.

[14] Wang and Emch, 'Five Years of Implementation of China's Anti-monopoly Law', 251–4, 259, 265; Deng and Huang, 'A Five Year Review', 18; Yee Wah Chin, 'Mergers & Acquisitions under China's Anti-monopoly Law: Update' (Legal Research Paper No. 23/2012, Victoria University of Wellington, 21 February 2012), p. 19.

investigation process. Critics are also concerned about the effectiveness of the administrative enforcement structure.

### 1.2.1 Consideration of Non-Competition Factors

The inclusion of 'public interest' and 'the healthy development of the socialist market economy' as express objectives of the AML has been viewed as problematic by many commentators.[15] They regard these objectives as being inappropriate for competition law and contrary to international competition law norms.[16] In their view, the objectives of competition law should be limited to enhancing economic efficiency and consumer welfare, and conduct should be assessed by reference to its impact on competition only. Other objectives or considerations such as matters related to industrial policy or foreign investment policy, referred to as 'non-competition' matters, lie outside the realm of competition law and policy and are better addressed in other laws and policies.[17] These objectives are also considered too vague, which critics argue allows the AML to be enforced in a manner such that non-competition objectives such as industrial policy, the interests of SOEs or stability concerns might take precedence over competition concerns such as consumer welfare and efficiency.[18] In addition, other provisions

---

[15] Anti-monopoly Law, art. 1.

[16] See, e.g., Susan Beth Farmer, 'The Impact of China's Antitrust Law and Other Competition Polices on US Companies' (2010) 23 *Loyola Consumer Law Review* 34 at 45–6; Kallay, 'Reflections on China's New Anti-monopoly Law', p. 3; Sections of Antitrust Law and International Law and Practice, American Bar Association, 'Joint Submission to the Ministry of Commerce of the People's Republic of China', 15 July 2003, pp. 2, 7–10.

[17] Bianca Rodriguez Galindo, 'Presentation' (Speech delivered at the International Seminar Review of Anti-monopoly Law, Hangzhou, China, 19–21 May 2006), p. 2–3; Sections of Antitrust Law and International Law and Practice, pp. 9–10; Bruce M. Owen, Su Sun and Wentong Zheng, 'Antitrust in China: The Problem of Incentive Compatibility' (2005) 1 *Journal of Competition Law and Economics* 123 at 142; Huang Yong and Richean Zhiyan Li, 'An Overview of Chinese Competition Policy: Between Fragmentation and Consolidation' in Adrian Emch and David Stallibrass (eds.), *China's Anti-monopoly Law: The First Five Years* (Alphen aan den Rijn, The Netherlands: Kluwer Law International, 2013), pp. 10–11.

[18] Xiaoye Wang, 'The New Chinese Anti-monopoly Law: A Survey of a Work in Progress' (2009) 54 *Antitrust Bulletin* 577 at 584–7; Zhengxin Huo, 'A Tiger without Teeth: The Antitrust Law of the People's Republic of China' (2008) 10 *Asian-Pacific Law & Policy Journal* 32 at 44–5; Deborah Healey, 'An Anti-monopoly Law for China: Weapon or Mirage?' (2008) 16 *Competition & Consumer Law Journal* 220 at 225–7; H. Stephen Harris Jr, 'The Making of an Antitrust Law: The Pending Anti-monopoly Law of the People's Republic of China' (2006) 7 *Chicago Journal of International Law* 169 at 185–6;

of the AML provide for the consideration of industrial policy, economic development and social factors.[19]

A number of commentators believe that non-competition factors have influenced AML enforcement outcomes. For merger enforcement, this issue has generally arisen in situations where a decision reached by China's Ministry of Commerce (MOFCOM) was different to that reached by other competition authorities reviewing the same merger, or where the conditions imposed by the MOFCOM on a merger appeared, in their opinion, not to be directed at addressing the stated competition concerns. Mergers involving products considered important to Chinese economic development or stability, well-known Chinese brands, intellectual property or sensitive or strategic industries also tend to raise such concerns. In such cases, commentators have speculated that non-competition considerations were the reason for the divergent outcomes or perceived disconnect between the stated competition concerns and the conditions imposed.[20] Similarly, concerns that the AML was being enforced to achieve non-competition policy goals have been voiced in non-merger investigations where foreign companies were investigated and/or sanctioned. Some commentators criticised the competition agencies for pursuing industrial policy and/or protectionist goals in these cases, and for setting price controls.[21]

---

R. Hewitt Pate, 'What I Heard in the Great Hall of the People – Realistic Expectations of Chinese Antitrust' (2008) 75 *Antitrust Law Journal* 195 at 200–2.

[19] Anti-monopoly Law, arts. 4, 27, 28.

[20] François Renard and Michael Edwards, 'China Merger Control Practice: A Comparative Analysis' in Adrian Emch and David Stallibrass (eds.), *China's Anti-monopoly Law: The First Five Years* (Alphen aan den Rijn, The Netherlands: Kluwer Law International, 2013), pp. 185–6; Wei Han, 'Merger Remedies in China: Past, Present, and Future' [2013] (2) *CPI Antitrust Chronicle* 1 at 9; Michael Han and Zhaofeng Zhou, 'MOFCOM's Approach to Merger Remedies: Distinctions from Other Competition Authorities' [2012] *Competition Policy International: Asia Antitrust Column* 1 at 4–6, available at www.competitionpolicyinternational.com/assets/Free/cpiasiaantitrusthan.pdf; Deng and Huang, 'A Five Year Review', 15–16; Deborah Healey, 'Mergers with Conditions in China: Caution, Control, or Industrial Policy?' in Lisa Toohey, Colin B. Picker and Jonathan Greenacre (eds.), *China in the International Economic Order: New Directions and Changing Paradigms* (Cambridge: Cambridge University Press, 2015), pp. 266–7; Maureen K. Ohlhausen, 'Antitrust Enforcement in China – What Next?' (Remarks delivered at the Second Annual GCR Live Conference, New York, 16 September 2014), pp. 6–7.

[21] Nate Bush, 'Weathervanes, Lightning Rods, and Pliers: The NDRC's Competition Enforcement Program' [2014] (August) *The Antitrust Source* 1 at 3–5, available at www.americanbar.org/content/dam/aba/publishing/antitrust_source/aug14_bush_7_23f.pdf; US Chamber of Commerce, *Competing Interests in China's Competition Law Enforcement: China's Anti-monopoly Law Application and the Role of Industrial Policy* (2014), pp. 56–67;

### 1.2.2 Protection of State-owned Enterprises

When the AML was first enacted, there were concerns that SOEs would be exempt from or enjoy special treatment under the AML.[22] Commentators were worried that Article 7 of the AML, which recognises and protects the state's controlling position in national economic lifeline, national security and state-granted monopoly industries and confirms that businesses in these industries must not abuse their dominance, would give enforcement authorities too much discretion in the way that the AML is applied (or not) to SOEs.[23] For example, it might justify the exemption of SOEs from the operation of the AML, or the prioritisation of industrial policies or other non-competition considerations over competition concerns where SOEs are involved.[24]

Some of these concerns have been put to rest since the AML came into effect. The AML has been enforced against SOEs, allaying concerns that SOEs were exempt from its operation. However, commentators remain critical of the low level of AML enforcement against SOEs. They believe that the AML has been applied leniently or weakly against SOEs. For example, some authors point out that, although many mergers involving SOEs have been undertaken since the AML came into effect, a number of which would have reached the notification thresholds, only a few of them have been notified to the MOFCOM

---

European Union Chamber of Commerce in China, 'European Chamber Releases Statement on China AML-Related Investigations' (Press Release, 13 August 2014).

[22] Healey, 'An Anti-monopoly Law for China', 228–9; Thomas R. Howell et al., 'China's New Anti-monopoly Law: A Perspective from the United States' (2009) 18(1) *Pacific Rim Law & Policy Journal* 53 at 82–3; Bush, 'Constraints on Convergence in Chinese Antitrust', 113–14; Fox, 'An Anti-monopoly Law for China', 178, 192–3; Harris et al., *Anti-monopoly Law and Practice in China*, pp. 195–7.

[23] Bruce M. Owen, Su Sun and Wentong Zheng, 'China's Competition Policy Reforms: The Anti-monopoly Law and Beyond' (2008) 75 *Antitrust Law Journal* 231 at 246; Howell et al., 'China's New Anti-monopoly Law', 83; Harris et al., *Anti-monopoly Law and Practice in China*, p. 196; Mark Williams, 'Foreign Investment in China: Will the Anti-monopoly Law Be a Barrier or a Facilitator?' (2009) 45 *Texas International Law Journal* 127 at 137; Bush, 'Constraints on Convergence in Chinese Antitrust', 114; US Chamber of Commerce, *Competing Interests in China's Competition Law Enforcement*, pp. 15–16.

[24] Yong Huang, 'Pursuing the Second Best: The History, Momentum, and Remaining Issues of China's Anti-monopoly Law' (2008) 75 *Antitrust Law Journal* 117 at 127–8; Wang, 'Highlights of China's New Anti-monopoly Law', 146–8; Adrian Emch, 'The Antimonopoly Law and Its Structural Shortcomings' [2008] (1) *CPI Antitrust Chronicle* 1 at 9; Howell et al., 'China's New Anti-monopoly Law', 83.

for review, and with no consequences for such non-compliance.[25] There are suggestions that investigations involving SOEs may be insufficiently investigated and that rather than sanctioning SOEs for engaging in anti-competitive conduct, the competition authorities are accepting commitments and terminating investigations instead.[26] There are also concerns that non-competition matters, such as creating and building national champions, broader SOE reforms and industrial policy, have influenced AML outcomes where SOEs are involved.[27]

### 1.2.3 Discrimination against Foreign Companies

Concerns that the AML would be enforced against foreign companies in a discriminatory manner persisted throughout the drafting process and into enforcement. These concerns initially stemmed from what some commentators considered to be the protectionist rhetoric surrounding the drafting of the AML.[28] Further, the insertion of Article 31 into the AML, which provides that acquisitions of Chinese companies by foreign investors are subject to both anti-monopoly review and national security review, also caused alarm among foreign commentators. Many of them believed that the inclusion of Article 31, against a backdrop of growing concerns purportedly held by the public and the Chinese government regarding foreign investment in China,

---

[25] Deng Fei and Gregory K. Leonard, 'The Role of China's Unique Economic Characteristics in Antitrust Enforcement' in Adrian Emch and David Stallibrass (eds.), *China's Antimonopoly Law: The First Five Years* (Alphen aan den Rijn, The Netherlands: Kluwer Law International, 2013), pp. 63–4; Deborah Healey, 'Anti-monopoly Law and Mergers in China: An Early Report Card on Procedural and Substantive Issues' (2010) 3 *Tsinghua China Law Review* 17 at 29–30; Zheng, 'Transplanting Antitrust in China', 710–11; Wang and Emch, 'Five Years of Implementation of China's Anti-monopoly Law', 267.

[26] Wang and Emch, 'Five Years of Implementation of China's Anti-monopoly Law', 267–8; Deng and Leonard, 'The Role of China's Unique Economic Characteristics in Antitrust Enforcement', p. 64.

[27] Zheng, 'Transplanting Antitrust in China', 714–15; Jim O'Connell, 'The Year of the Metal Rabbit: Antitrust Enforcement in China in 2011' (2012) 26(2) *Antitrust* 65; US Chamber of Commerce, *Competing Interests in China's Competition Law Enforcement*, pp. 33–4.

[28] Bush, 'Constraints on Convergence in Chinese Antitrust', 96; Owen, Sun and Zheng, 'China's Competition Policy Reforms', 252–3; H. Stephen Harris Jr and Kathy Lijun Yang, 'China: Latest Developments in Anti-monopoly Law Legislation' (2005) 19(2) *Antitrust* 89 at 90; Rebecca Buckman, 'China Hurries Antitrust Law', The Wall Street Journal, 11 June 2004, available at http://online.wsj.com/news/articles/SB108689271342233967; US Chamber of Commerce, *Competing Interests in China's Competition Law Enforcement*, pp. 19–23; Howell et al., 'China's New Anti-monopoly Law', 62–3.

increased the risk that national security concerns would seep into the anti-monopoly review process.[29] In their view, national security concerns – the definition of which includes national economic interests in China – are political in nature and irrelevant to competition review.[30]

Criticisms that foreign companies are unfairly targeted by the Chinese competition authorities have intensified in enforcement. In relation to merger enforcement, commentators highlight that most conditionally approved or prohibited mergers have involved mergers between foreign companies and that no purely domestic mergers have been subject to conditions or prohibited. They also observe that purely domestic mergers are notified much less frequently than mergers involving foreign companies.[31] The US–China Economic and Security Review Commission argues that this effectively exempts such domestic mergers from the AML, which in turn disadvantages foreign companies because they are exposed to greater scrutiny and uncertainty and incur additional costs associated with anti-monopoly review.[32] Commentators also believe that some merger decisions have been motivated by protectionist, foreign investment or industrial policy concerns, such as promoting national champions.[33] In particular, the decision to prohibit the *Coca-Cola/Huiyuan* merger, whereby Coca-Cola proposed to acquire a well-known

---

[29] Williams, 'Foreign Investment in China', 139; Michael Han and Jessica Su, 'China's Antimonopoly Law: Status Quo and Outlook' [2008] (1) *CPI Antitrust Chronicle* 1 at 6; Howell et al., 'China's New Anti-monopoly Law', 92; Oliver Q. C. Zhong, 'Dawn of a New Constitutional Era or Opportunity Wasted? An Intellectual Reappraisal of China's Anti-monopoly Law' (2010) 24 *Columbia Journal of Asian Law* 87 at 105–6; Bush, 'Constraints on Convergence in Chinese Antitrust', 115–17.

[30] Williams, 'Foreign Investment in China', 139; Howell et al., 'China's New Anti-monopoly Law', 92; Bush, 'Constraints on Convergence in Chinese Antitrust', 116–17.

[31] US Chamber of Commerce, *Competing Interests in China's Competition Law Enforcement*, pp. 27–32; US–China Economic and Security Review Commission, *2015 Report to Congress of the US–China Economic and Security Review Commission* (114th Congress, First Session, November 2015), pp. 90–1; Yuni Yan Sobel, 'Domestic-to-Domestic Transactions – A Gap in China's Merger Control Regime?' [2014] (February) *The Antitrust Source* 1 at 4–5, available at www.americanbar.org/content/dam/aba/publishing/antitrust_source/feb14_sobel_2_20f.pdf.

[32] US–China Economic and Security Review Commission, *2015 Report to Congress*, p. 91.

[33] Ibid., p. 90; US Chamber of Commerce, *Competing Interests in China's Competition Law Enforcement*, pp. 33–7; Chin, 'Mergers & Acquisitions under China's Anti-monopoly Law', 3–4; Markus Masseli, 'The Application of Chinese Competition Law to Foreign Mergers: Lessons from the Draft New Guidelines' (2012) 3 *Journal of European Competition Law & Practice* 102 at 102, 108–9, 104.

Chinese fruit juice brand, attracted substantial criticism for its perceived motivation of economic protectionism.[34]

Commentators are also critical of non-merger enforcement activities and believe that these have disproportionately targeted and impacted on foreign companies.[35] While they acknowledge that domestic companies have been investigated and sanctioned for breaching the AML, they believe that domestic companies face lighter penalties than foreign companies and are not probed for similar violations in industry-specific investigations.[36] There is also a view that foreign companies have been disproportionately targeted in high-profile investigations, with the aim of reducing prices for goods sold to Chinese consumers.[37] Further, US commentators have been especially concerned that the AML is being used to pressure foreign companies to license their intellectual property on terms that are favourable to Chinese licensees and to reduce their

---

[34] US Chamber of Commerce, *Competing Interests in China's Competition Law Enforcement*, pp. 43–4; Chin, 'Mergers & Acquisitions under China's Anti-monopoly Law', 3; Williams, 'Foreign Investment in China', 153–4; Lin and Zhao, 'Merger Control Policy under China's Anti-monopoly Law', 112, 120; Yong Huang, 'Coordination of International Competition Policies: An Anatomy Based on Chinese Reality' in Andrew T. Guzman (ed.), *Cooperation, Comity, and Competition Policy* (New York: Oxford University Press, 2011), p. 240; D. Daniel Sokol, 'Merger Control under China's Anti-monopoly Law' (2013) 10 *New York University Journal of Law & Business* 1 at 24–5. Cf Angela Huyue Zhang, 'Problems in Following EU Competition Law: A Case Study of *Coca-Cola/Huiyuan*' (2012) 3 *Peking University Journal of Legal Studies* 96.

[35] See, e.g., 'Trust-Busting in China: Unequal Before the Law?', *The Economist*, 23 August 2014, available at www.economist.com/news/business/21613348-chinas-antitrust-crackdown-turns-ugly-foreign-carmakers-forefront-unequal; Gordon G. Chang, 'China Mugs Foreign Companies with Price Investigations', *Forbes*, 7 July 2013, available at www.forbes.com/sites/gordonchang/2013/07/07/china-mugs-foreign-companies-with-price-investigations; Nicolas Jenny, 'The Politics of China's Anti-monopoly Investigations', *International Policy Digest*, 17 September 2014, available at www.internationalpolicydigest.org/2014/09/17/politics-china-s-anti-monopoly-investigations; Samson Yuen, 'Taming the "Foreign Tigers": China's Anti-Trust Crusade against Multinational Companies' [2014] (4) *China Perspectives* 53 at 53–5. Cf Michael Han and David Boyle, 'Antitrust Enforcement: China Ups the Ante' [2014] *Competition Policy International: Asia Antitrust Column* 1, available at www.competitionpolicyinternational.com/antitrust-enforcement-china-ups-the-ante.

[36] European Union Chamber of Commerce in China, 'European Chamber Releases Statement on China AML-Related Investigations'; US Chamber of Commerce, *Competing Interests in China's Competition Law Enforcement*, pp. 55–6; Yuen, 'Taming the "Foreign Tigers"', 57.

[37] US Chamber of Commerce, *Competing Interests in China's Competition Law Enforcement*, pp. 53–62.

licensing fees, as well as to give potential Chinese licensees additional leverage in licensing negotiations.[38]

### 1.2.4 Issues Relating to the Administrative Enforcement Structure

The effectiveness of the administrative enforcement structure has also been questioned. Administrative enforcement responsibilities under the AML are divided among three existing ministries: the MOFCOM (responsible for merger enforcement); the National Development and Reform Commission (NDRC, responsible for price-related non-merger conduct); and the State Administration for Industry and Commerce (SAIC, responsible for non-price-related non-merger conduct). The Anti-monopoly Commission was also established to organise, coordinate and guide China's competition policy.

This two-tiered, divided enforcement structure has been criticised by Chinese and foreign commentators. They believe that the distribution of resources and competition law knowledge, which are scarce in China, across three ministries is inefficient and administratively costly.[39] They are also concerned that jurisdictional conflicts and inconsistent decision-making may occur if there is inadequate coordination and cooperation among the enforcement agencies where, for example, conduct falls within the scope of both the NDRC's and the SAIC's authority, or the competition authorities take different approaches to matters such as market definition and competition assessment.[40] In particular, the delineation of enforcement responsibility between the NDRC and the SAIC based on price-related and non-price-related conduct is criticised as being unworkable in practice.[41] In enforcement, commentators point to cases

---

[38] Ibid., pp. 62–7; US–China Economic and Security Review Commission, *2015 Report to Congress*, p. 95.

[39] Wang and Emch, 'Five Years of Implementation of China's Anti-monopoly Law', 268–9; Bush, 'Constraints on Convergence in Chinese Antitrust', 99; Salil K. Mehra and Yanbei Meng, 'Against Antitrust Functionalism: Reconsidering China's Antimonopoly Law' (2008) 49 *Virginia Journal of International Law* 379 at 408; US Chamber of Commerce, *Competing Interests in China's Competition Law Enforcement*, p. 8.

[40] Wang, 'The New Chinese Anti-monopoly Law', 590; Huang, 'Pursuing the Second Best', 126; Bush, 'Constraints on Convergence in Chinese Antitrust', 104–5; Angela Huyue Zhang, 'The Enforcement of the Anti-monopoly Law in China: An Institutional Design Perspective' (2011) 56 *The Antitrust Bulletin* 631 at 639–40; US Chamber of Commerce, *Competing Interests in China's Competition Law Enforcement*, p. 8.

[41] Bush, 'Constraints on Convergence in Chinese Antitrust', 104; Zhang, 'The Enforcement of the Anti-monopoly Law in China', 640.

where the price/non-price distinction has not been followed, resulting in the competition agency investigating and sanctioning conduct outside its authority, or where the distinction was observed but other conduct was left uninvestigated.[42] They also note that there have been situations where local offices of the NDRC and the SAIC in the same province investigated similar conduct in the same industry but did not coordinate their investigations, leading to potentially divergent or conflicting outcomes.[43]

Critics also point to the lack of independence and sufficient authority of the competition agencies as limiting the effectiveness of AML enforcement. Some commentators worry that the non-AML responsibilities and portfolios held by each of the competition agencies will influence their AML enforcement decisions,[44] especially where there is a conflict between the AML outcome and another policy outcome.[45] Others question whether the competition agencies have sufficient administrative and political power to enforce the AML, especially against SOEs or businesses operating in regulated industries.[46]

---

[42] Adrian Emch, 'Chinese Antitrust Institutions – Many Cooks in the Kitchen' (2014) 10 *Competition Policy International* 217 at 227–9; Lei Kuang, 'Celebrating with a Damp Squib: China's Public Competition Enforcement' (2016) 4 *Journal of Antitrust Enforcement* 411 at 426–7; Angela Huyue Zhang, 'The Enforcement of the Anti-monopoly Law in China: An Institutional Design Perspective' (2011) 56(3) *The Antitrust Bulletin* 631 at 640–4.

[43] Emch, 'Chinese Antitrust Institutions', 234–6; Kuang, 'Celebrating with a Damp Squib', 426–8; Zhang, 'The Enforcement of the Anti-monopoly Law in China', 640–4.

[44] The MOFCOM's portfolio includes domestic and foreign trade, international economic cooperation, foreign investment and market regulation; the SAIC is responsible for market regulation and supervision and protecting the rights and interests of businesses and consumers; and the NDRC has a broad mandate which covers industrial policy and pricing.

[45] Wang, 'The New Chinese Anti-monopoly Law', 590; Bush, 'Constraints on Convergence in Chinese Antitrust', 104–5; Hao Qian, 'The Multiple Hands: Institutional Dynamics of China's Competition Regime' in Adrian Emch and David Stallibrass (eds.), *China's Antimonopoly Law: The First Five Years* (Alphen aan den Rijn, The Netherlands: Kluwer Law International, 2013), p. 24; Emch, 'The Antimonopoly Law and Its Structural Shortcomings', 5; US Chamber of Commerce, *Competing Interests in China's Competition Law Enforcement*, p. 8. For a discussion on whether the independence of the Chinese competition agencies has influenced enforcement of the AML, see Wendy Ng, 'The Independence of Chinese Competition Agencies and the Impact on Competition Enforcement in China' (2016) 4 *Journal of Antitrust Enforcement* 188.

[46] Wang and Emch, 'Five Years of Implementation of China's Anti-monopoly Law', 267–8; Owen, Sun and Zheng, 'China's Competition Policy Reforms', 261.

There are also doubts that the AML will be effectively enforced against administrative monopolies. Here, enforcement power lies with the superior authority of the administrative organ in question, and the role of the competition agency is limited to making a recommendation to the superior authority on how to handle the case under the AML. Many commentators are sceptical as to whether a superior authority will have the incentive or sufficient competition law knowledge to properly apply the AML to sanction their lower-level authority or to adequately handle administrative monopoly conduct.[47]

To address these issues, many commentators believe that a unified, independent, ministry-level administrative authority should be established to enforce the AML. In their opinion, the enforcement authority should be a stand-alone ministry that reports directly to the State Council, free from the interference of other government authorities and authorised to administratively enforce all provisions of the AML to the exclusion of other government authorities.[48]

### 1.2.5 Lack of Due Process and Transparency

Last but certainly not least, commentators have been very critical of what they perceive to be a lack of procedural fairness and transparency afforded to parties during merger reviews and non-merger investigations. One of the principal concerns voiced by commentators about merger review is that it is a 'black box'; that is, merging parties are not provided with sufficient information about the substance and process of merger review.[49]

---

[47] Wang, 'Highlights of China's New Anti-monopoly Law', 149; Huo, 'A Tiger without Teeth', 52; Fox, 'An Anti-monopoly Law for China', 177; Williams, 'Foreign Investment in China', 135–6; Changqi Wu and Zhicheng Liu, 'A Tiger without Teeth? Regulation of Administrative Monopoly under China's Anti-monopoly Law' (2012) 41 *Review of Industrial Organisation* 133 at 144, 153.

[48] Huang, 'Pursuing the Second Best', 125; Wang, 'Highlights of China's New Anti-monopoly Law', 145; Owen, Sun, and Zheng, 'China's Competition Policy Reforms', 261; Sections of Antitrust Law and International Law and Practice, pp. 4–5, 26; Rodriguez Galindo, 'Presentation', pp. 3–5.

[49] US–China Business Council, 'Competition Policy and Enforcement in China' (September 2014), pp. 14–15, available at www.uschina.org/reports/competition-policy-and-enforcement-china; US Chamber of Commerce, *Competing Interests in China's Competition Law Enforcement*, pp. 47–9; Maureen K. Ohlhausen, 'Taking Notes: Observations on the First Five Years of the Chinese Anti-monopoly Law' (Remarks delivered at the Competition Committee Meeting of the United States Council for International Business, Washington, DC, 9 May 2013), pp. 8–9; Sokol, 'Merger Control under China's Anti-monopoly Law', 29.

For example, there are complaints that the MOFCOM does not communicate the concerns of consulted third parties (such as other government departments and competitors) about proposed mergers to merging parties, which means that merging parties are not given the opportunity to respond to such concerns.[50] Lengthy merger reviews and delays are also cited as a major problem, although such concerns have been tempered somewhat by the MOFCOM's adoption of a simple merger review process.[51] The US Chamber of Commerce has also argued that the exclusion of foreign legal counsel from participating in merger review proceedings denies merging parties the right to adequate legal representation, even if local counsel are present.[52]

Non-merger investigations made by the NDRC have raised similar concerns. There were reports that the NDRC had, on occasion, used tactics such as forced confessions and intimidation to pressure companies to make admissions that they had breached the AML or to cooperate with investigations, even in situations where the company did not know why they were being investigated.[53] These reports have alarmed many commentators.[54] Critics have also raised concerns regarding the inability of outside legal counsel to be present at dawn raids and/or meetings with the competition agencies during the investigation process.[55]

---

[50] Deng and Huang, 'A Five Year Review', 10; US Chamber of Commerce, *Competing Interests in China's Competition Law Enforcement*, pp. 47–8; US–China Business Council, 'Competition Policy and Enforcement in China', p. 15; Sokol, 'Merger Control under China's Anti-monopoly Law', 30.

[51] US Chamber of Commerce, *Competing Interests in China's Competition Law Enforcement*, pp. 50–3; US–China Business Council, 'Competition Policy and Enforcement in China', pp. 16–17; Deng and Huang, 'A Five Year Review', 5–7; Kuang, 'Celebrating with a Damp Squib', 422–4; O'Connell, 'The Year of the Metal Rabbit', 8; Sokol, 'Merger Control under China's Anti-monopoly Law', 33–5.

[52] US Chamber of Commerce, *Competing Interests in China's Competition Law Enforcement*, p. 49.

[53] Michael Martina, 'Exclusive: Tough-Talking China Pricing Regulator Sought Confessions from Foreign Firms', *Reuters*, 21 August 2013, available at www.reuters.com/article/us-china-antitrust-idUSBRE97K05020130821; Michael Martina and Matthew Miller, '"Mr Confession" and His Boss Drive China's Antitrust Crusade', *Reuters*, 15 September 2014, available at www.reuters.com/article/us-china-antitrust-ndrc-insight-idUSKBN0 HA27X20140915; US–China Business Council, 'Competition Policy and Enforcement in China', p. 14.

[54] European Union Chamber of Commerce in China, 'European Chamber Releases Statement on China AML-related Investigations'; US Chamber of Commerce, *Competing Interests in China's Competition Law Enforcement*, p. 6; O'Connell, 'The Year of the Metal Rabbit', 9.

[55] US–China Business Council, 'Competition Policy and Enforcement in China', pp. 14–15; US Chamber of Commerce, *Competing Interests in China's Competition Law*

Concerns about due process are exacerbated by the limited transparency provided by the Chinese competition authorities in their published decisions. Commentators argue that, despite continuing efforts made by the competition authorities to improve the transparency of decision-making under the AML, both the quantity and the quality of published decisions remains inadequate. Only a small percentage of merger decisions are published, and the NDRC (unlike the SAIC, which has committed to publishing all of its AML decisions) only releases information about some, not all, of its AML investigations. Commentators also believe that the decisions and information published by the competition authorities fail to provide sufficient detail about the competition authority's reasoning.[56]

## 1.3 Competition Law and the Relevance of Context

Many of the concerns voiced by commentators regarding the AML relate to China's local conditions, such as the involvement of SOEs in the economy, or provisions or arrangements that are China-specific and not typically found in other competition laws, such as the prohibition against administrative monopoly. Nonetheless, the AML remains drawn from or significantly influenced by the competition laws of the European Union, Germany and the United States; in this sense the AML has the attributes of a legal transplant.[57]

A legal transplant[58] is 'the moving of a rule or a system of law from one country to another, or from one people to another'.[59] Globally,

---

*Enforcement*, p. 67. In response to these criticisms, the Chinese government committed to allowing local legal counsel and foreign legal counsel to be present at meetings with any of the Chinese competition authorities: US Department of Commerce, Office of Public Affairs, 'Fact Sheet: 25th US–China Joint Commission on Commerce and Trade' (Press Release, 19 December 2014).

[56] Deng and Huang, 'A Five Year Review', 5; US–China Business Council, 'Competition Policy and Enforcement in China', p. 15; Wang and Emch, 'Five Years of Implementation of China's Anti-monopoly Law', 254–6; Fay Zhou, John Eichlin and Xi Liao, 'International Standards of Procedural Fairness and Transparency in Chinese Investigations' [2015] (1) *CPI Antitrust Chronicle* 1 at 9–10; Michael Han and Janet (Jingyuan) Wang, 'Due Process in Chinese Competition Law Regime' [2014] (1) *CPI Antitrust Chronicle* 1 at 8–9.

[57] Zheng, 'Transplanting Antitrust in China', 647–8.

[58] Also known as legal transfers, legal borrowings, legal irritants, legal transpositions, and legal imports.

[59] Alan Watson, *Legal Transplants: An Approach to Comparative Law*, 2nd edn (Athens: University of Georgia Press, 1993), p. 21.

competition law generally is a product of legal transplantation, as it is largely based on the competition (antitrust) laws of the United States and Europe. The United States was the second country in the world to adopt a competition law statute,[60] enacting the Sherman Act in 1890, which codified then existing case law prohibiting restraints of trade and monopolisation.[61] The first competition law statute in Europe was enacted in Germany in 1923.[62] The Treaty of Rome, which contained competition provisions that applied generally to Member States and throughout the European Community, was signed in 1957 and came into effect in 1958.[63] From these origins, competition laws have spread worldwide, and more than 100 jurisdictions have adopted competition laws.[64] The competition laws that have been adopted predominantly follow the prescriptions and enforcement practices of the United States and/or the European Union.[65] While not all competition laws are in the same form, they typically regulate horizontal restraints (such as cartels aimed at price fixing, market sharing or restricting output),[66] vertical restraints,[67] and abuses of dominant position, market power or monopoly. The majority of competition laws also provide for the regulation of mergers and acquisitions.[68]

---

[60] Canada was the first country to enact a competition law statute, but its enforcement was much weaker than the enforcement of the Sherman Act. See Pradeep S. Mehta and S. Chakravarthy, 'Dimensions of Competition Policy and Law in Emerging Economies' (Discussion Paper, CUTS Centre for Competition, Investment & Economic Regulation, Jaipur, 2010), p. 5.

[61] David J. Gerber, 'Constructing Competition Law in China: The Potential Value of European and U.S. Experience' (2004) 3 *Washington University Global Studies Law Review* 315 at 316–17.

[62] *Verordnung gegen Missbrauch wirtschaftlicher Machtstellungen* [Ordinance against Abuse of Economic Power] (Germany) 2 November 1923, [1923] RGB I, 1067.

[63] Treaty Establishing the European Economic Community, Rome, 25 March 1957, in force 1 January 1958, 298 UNTS 11, arts. 81–9.

[64] David J. Gerber, *Global Competition: Law, Markets, and Globalization* (Oxford: Oxford University Press, 2010), p. 85.

[65] Bruce M. Owen, 'Competition Policy in Emerging Economies' (SIEPR Discussion Paper No. 04-10, Stanford Institute for Economic Policy Research, 2005), pp. 3, 6–7; Susan Joekes and Phil Evans, 'Competition and Development: The Power of Competitive Markets' (International Development Research Centre, 2008), p. 14.

[66] Restraints between competitors; that is, parties operating at the same level in the supply chain.

[67] Restraints between parties operating at different levels in the supply chain; for example, a manufacturer and a retailer.

[68] Maher M. Dabbah, *The Internationalisation of Antitrust Policy* (Cambridge: Cambridge University Press, 2003), p. 2.

An important issue that arises when international and foreign rules, institutions and norms are brought into a domestic legal system concerns whether and how they will operate in the domestic context. This issue is widely discussed in comparative law literature and revolves around questions related to the feasibility of legal transplants, how legal change via legal transplantation occurs, and whether and how legal transplants have been accepted or absorbed by the recipient jurisdiction.[69] The common thread underlying these discussions is a debate about the relationship between law and its societal context.

On one view, law and its societal context are largely autonomous.[70] The strongest proponent of this view is Watson, who argues that, because formal legal rules are borrowed frequently and generally survive in the recipient country, this means that they are not tied to or reflective of a particular societal context.[71] Therefore, legal transplants are 'socially easy', even if the legal rules come from a different kind of system.[72] In contrast, other scholars argue that there is a close relationship between law and society.[73] For example, Legrand argues that law is culturally specific, and Teubner contends that a legal transplant 'irritates' the domestic legal and social discourses that are closely related to the law.[74] For these scholars, the inquiry relates to how the societal context shapes the operation of the legal transplant in the domestic context and what changes the legal transplant might engender more broadly.[75]

---

[69] See, e.g., Watson, *Legal Transplants*; Otto Kahn-Freund, 'On Uses and Misuses of Comparative Law' (1974) 37 *The Modern Law Review* 1; Pierre Legrand, 'The Impossibility of "Legal Transplants"' (1997) 4 *Maastricht Journal of European and Comparative Law* 111; Gunther Teubner, 'Legal Irritants: Good Faith in British Law or How Unifying Law Ends Up in New Divergences' (1998) 61 *The Modern Law Review* 11; Daniel Berkowitz, Katharina Pistor and Jean-Francois Richard, 'The Transplant Effect' (2003) 51 *The American Journal of Comparative Law* 163.

[70] Alan Watson, 'Legal Change: Sources of Law and Legal Culture' (1983) 131 *University of Pennsylvania Law Review* 1121 at 1134.

[71] Ibid., 1138–9; Alan Watson, *Society and Legal Change*, 2nd edn (Philadelphia: Temple University Press, 2001), pp. 98, 110, 130. Cf Legrand, 'The Impossibility of "Legal Transplants"', 114.

[72] Watson, *Legal Transplants*, pp. 94–5; Watson, *Society and Legal Change*, p. 130.

[73] Kahn-Freund, 'On Uses and Misuses of Comparative Law'; Legrand, 'The Impossibility of "Legal Transplants"'; Teubner, 'Legal Irritants'.

[74] Legrand, 'The Impossibility of "Legal Transplants"', 123–4; Teubner, 'Legal Irritants', 31.

[75] See, e.g., Kahn-Freund, 'On Uses and Misuses of Comparative Law'; Legrand, 'The Impossibility of "Legal Transplants"'; Teubner, 'Legal Irritants'; John Gillespie, 'Developing a Decentred Analysis of Legal Transfers' in Penelope (Pip) Nicholson and Sarah Biddulph (eds.), *Examining Practice, Interrogating Theory: Comparative Legal Studies in*

Support for the view that there is a close relationship between law and society can be found in competition law literature. A number of authors have demonstrated that a detailed study of the societal context of competition law is essential to understanding its design and enforcement, especially in developing and transitioning countries.[76] They argue that a range of matters such as institutional capabilities, the role of the state, politics and other development and policy goals influence the enforcement of competition law in developing and transitioning countries, if not also its text.[77]

These observations are also relevant to competition law in China because, despite China's size, population and rapid growth since embarking on economic reforms and opening up, China remains a developing country and its market reforms are considered to be incomplete.[78] While there are some aspects – such as the large size of the Chinese economy and population, its substantial economic and political global influence and its long bureaucratic tradition[79] – that differentiate China from many other developing countries, nonetheless China does face some of the challenges that other developing and transition countries encounter in adopting and enforcing the AML, such as limited institutional capabilities. Further, the drafters of the AML themselves

---

*Asia* (Leiden: Martinus Nijhoff Publishers, 2008), p. 30; Berkowitz, Pistor and Richard, 'The Transplant Effect'.

[76] See, e.g., Michal S. Gal, *Competition Policy for Small Market Economies* (Cambridge, MA: Harvard University Press, 2003); William E. Kovacic, 'Designing and Implementing Competition and Consumer Protection Reforms in Transitional Economies: Perspectives from Mongolia, Nepal, Ukraine, and Zimbabwe' (1995) 44 *DePaul Law Review* 1197; Maher M. Dabbah, 'Competition Law and Policy in Developing Countries: A Critical Assessment of the Challenges to Establishing an Effective Competition Law Regime' (2010) 33 *World Competition* 457.

[77] See, e.g., Michal Gal, 'The Ecology of Antitrust: Preconditions for Competition Law Enforcement in Developing Countries' in Ana María Alvarez et al. (eds.), *Competition, Competitiveness and Development: Lessons from Developing Countries* (Geneva: United Nations Conference on Trade and Development, 2004); William E. Kovacic, 'Getting Started: Creating New Competition Policy Institutions in Transition Economies' (1997) 23 *Brooklyn Journal of International Law* 403; Pradeep S. Mehta, Manish Agarwal and V. V. Singh, 'Politics Trumps Economics – Lessons and Experiences on Competition and Regulatory Regimes from Developing Countries' (CUTS International, CUTS Institute for Regulation & Competition and CUTS Centre for Competition, Investment & Economic Regulation, 2007).

[78] 'China Overview', The World Bank, 6 April 2016, available at www.worldbank.org/en/country/china/overview.

[79] Jianfu Chen, *Chinese Law: Context and Transformation*, revised and expanded edn (Leiden: Brill Nijhoff, 2015), p. 22.

recognised that, while it was important to learn from other jurisdictions' experiences on competition law and for the AML to be consistent with international norms, the AML also needed to reflect and suit China's specific needs and circumstances.[80] Therefore, in addition to international standards, the AML needs to be explained and understood by reference to its institutional, economic and political contexts, that is, the Chinese political economy.

### 1.4 Need for a New Analytical Framework for the Anti-monopoly Law

This book argues that a detailed examination of the economic, institutional and political contexts related to the AML is crucial to understanding the making, implementation and enforcement of competition law in China. Such an approach to analysing and understanding the AML has not yet been taken with sufficient depth, scope and rigour.

Overall, the analytical approach to the AML taken by most commentators to date has been to compare the AML to United States antitrust law and European Union competition law, which are regarded as leading competition law jurisdictions, and to prevailing international competition law norms. The legal and economic analytical approaches, decisions and outcomes reached by the Chinese competition authorities under the AML are then compared to those taken or reached (actual or theoretical) in these competition law jurisdictions regarding the same or similar conduct. Analyses, decisions and outcomes that are considered consistent with US, European and international norms are typically thought to raise fewer concerns, whereas those that depart from US, European and international standards attract additional scrutiny, criticism and speculation.

There is some consideration in the existing AML literature of the impact of the Chinese societal context on the AML. There is general recognition that the AML is influenced by its societal context and that this may result in divergence between the AML and the competition laws of other countries.[81] For example, most commentators supported

---

[80] 关于《中华人民共和国反垄断法(草案)》的说明 [An Explanation of China's Anti-monopoly Law (Draft)], 22nd Session of the Tenth Standing Committee of the National People's Congress, 24 June 2006; Zhenguo Wu, 'Perspectives on the Chinese Anti-monopoly Law' (2008) 75 *Antitrust Law Journal* 73 at 77.

[81] See, e.g., Harris et al., *Anti-monopoly Law and Practice in China*, pp. 2–3; Owen, Sun and Zheng, 'Antitrust in China'; Huang, 'Pursuing the Second Best'.

including administrative monopoly within the scope of the AML even though government restraints on competition are typically dealt with by other laws or the constitution in other jurisdictions. This is because they recognise that administrative monopoly is the biggest barrier to the formation of a unified and national Chinese market.[82] There is also a core but small group of commentators, including Gerber, Williams and Huang, who engage in more detailed contextual analyses of the AML.[83]

The existing literature engages with the societal context of the AML to varying degrees of depth and breadth. For example, there is a rich critique concerning the institutional design of administrative enforcement and how it may affect enforcement, practices and effectiveness.[84] The important role that SOEs play in the Chinese economy and the policy tensions involved in enforcing the AML against SOEs, especially those operating in regulated or state-monopolised industries, is also acknowledged. However, there is insufficient consideration of whether and how the broader Chinese governance, regulatory and policy environment might influence enforcement. For example, the distribution of power among government authorities, the role and influence of the CPC, and the lines of accountability and authority between government and political bodies, and how these matters may affect the AML, are hardly discussed in the existing literature. These matters are important to the making, implementation and enforcement of the AML and should be discussed openly and in more detail. Similarly, while commentators speculate that a number of AML enforcement decisions have been motivated by industrial policy or other non-competition matters, there has been minimal discussion on how such concerns might enter the AML decision-making process, and why. As such, these claims are often insufficiently substantiated and some do not move beyond speculation. The existing literature is also limited in its understanding of the actors

---

[82] Wang, 'Highlights of China's New Anti-monopoly Law', 148–9; Fox, 'An Anti-monopoly Law for China'; Sections of Antitrust Law and International Law and Practice, 23–5.

[83] Gerber, 'Constructing Competition Law in China'; David J. Gerber, 'Economics, Law & Institutions: The Shaping of Chinese Competition Law' (2008) 26 *Journal of Law & Policy* 271; Gerber, *Global Competition*, pp. 223–36; Williams, *Competition Policy and Law*; Mark Williams, 'China', in Mark Williams (ed.), *The Political Economy of Competition Law in Asia* (Cheltenham: Edward Elgar Publishing, 2013); Huang, 'Pursuing the Second Best'; Huang, 'Coordination of International Competition Policies'; Huang and Li, 'An Overview of Chinese Competition Policy'.

[84] Zhang, 'The Enforcement of the Anti-monopoly Law in China'; Hao, 'The Multiple Hands'.

involved in the making of AML decisions, in particular actors other than the Chinese competition authorities. For example, while some commentators investigate the interests, capabilities and constraints of the Chinese competition authorities, there is little discussion of their motivations.[85] There is also inadequate consideration of the other actors that are involved with the AML such as industry regulators and competition law experts.

Therefore, whilst there is awareness that the Chinese context is likely to affect the making, implementation and enforcement of the AML, the extent to which this context is examined and drawn upon in the AML literature remains limited.

This book develops the existing literature in two ways. First, it engages in a detailed and empirically informed examination of the legal, institutional, economic and political contexts surrounding the AML and its broader governance, regulatory and policy environment. Second, based on this analysis, it explores why, how and the extent to which these contexts have influenced, and may influence, the AML and its enforcement outcomes. The observations and insights yielded from this analysis go beyond the existing literature, and explain how and why the societal context has shaped the AML. They also provide the basis to confirm, qualify, or refute the concerns and claims made in the existing literature. These findings are especially relevant and important where suggestions for reform of the AML are discussed.

## 1.5 A Political Economy Framework for the Anti-monopoly Law

The analytical framework used in this book is based on Milhaupt and Pistor's political economy framework for understanding the law and its societal context, which they frame in terms of the supply of and demand for law.[86] The supply of law refers to the processes of law production and

---

[85] Exceptions include Gerber, 'Economics, Law & Institutions'; Angela Huyue Zhang, 'Bureaucratic Politics and China's Anti-monopoly Law' (2014) 47 *Cornell International Law Journal* 671 at 689–707.

[86] Curtis J. Milhaupt and Katharina Pistor, *Law and Capitalism: What Corporate Crises Reveal about Legal Systems and Economic Development around the World* (Chicago: University of Chicago Press, 2008). In their book, Milhaupt and Pistor develop an organising concept for legal systems that is based upon insights from political economy as a new way to understand the relationship between law and markets. They argue that an understanding of the interplay between law, markets, and political economy reveals the way in which laws actually operate in support of markets.

enforcement, and the demand for law relates to its desirability and function as a governance device.

Milhaupt and Pistor's conception of the political economy of law is one that is shaped significantly by the actors involved in or impacted by law, on both the supply and demand sides. They believe that the law is a political product both at its inception and in the way it affects and is shaped by the interests of a range of actors.[87] In their view, the balance of power among actors substantially influences the nature of the rights protected by law and how those rights are allocated and balanced.[88] Further, they believe that the law has disparate effects on incumbents and actors who are seeking reforms, which have political consequences.[89] Hence Milhaupt and Pistor's political economy framework is one that centres on understanding the identity, interests, incentives and relative power of actors and the factors that shape them, thus expressly placing these stakeholders and the law within its surrounding context.

Another aspect of Milhaupt and Pistor's analytical approach to understanding legal systems is that it does not prescribe a normative relation between the law and its context. Their aim is to provide informed descriptions of legal systems and to understand legal systems both on their own terms and in terms of what is actually happening.[90]

These features of Milhaupt and Pistor's political economy framework make it especially suited for use in this book to examine the relationship between the societal context and Chinese competition law and policy. For example, if, as speculated in the existing literature, AML decisions are in fact influenced by non-competition concerns or other matters, this actor-focused analysis will help to explain why and how such matters enter the decision-making process and how they are balanced against competition concerns. The framework also highlights the importance of understanding the relationships and interactions between stakeholders and how demand-side and supply-side stakeholders and factors influence each other.[91] Further, by not prescribing a normative relation between law and its context and by emphasising an understanding of legal systems on their own terms, Milhaupt and Pistor's analytical framework enables and necessitates an exploration of the societal context and its relation to the AML which is focused on understanding what is

---

[87] Ibid., p. 40.  [88] Ibid., p. 180.  [89] Ibid., pp. 43–4.  [90] Ibid., p. 10.
[91] Jackie Vandermeulen and Philippe Perron-Savard, 'Law and Capitalism: A Book Review' (2009) 67 *University of Toronto Faculty of Law Review* 327 at 341–2; David A. Skeel Jr, 'Book Review: Governance in Ruins' (2008) 122 *Harvard Law Review* 696 at 699.

actually happening. The use of empirical data gathered from the interviews conducted for this book fits in well with this emphasis on providing an informed description of the law that derives from observations in the real world.

## 1.6 Methodology and Scope

This book is a socio-legal and empirical study of competition law in China and, in particular, the AML. It is not a normative study. It is interdisciplinary in its approach and engages in doctrinal, institutional, economic and political review and analysis of the relevant source materials. Interviews, case studies and English- and Chinese-language primary and secondary documentary sources are used.[92]

While the book analyses the AML in its domestic environment and does not engage in an explicit comparison of the competition laws of various jurisdictions, this study of the AML is nonetheless an implicitly comparative exercise due to the nature of the AML as a legal transplant in China.[93] However, the book will not assess whether the AML is a 'successful' legal transplant, or engage in a traditional comparative black-letter-law analysis of the AML, European competition law, United States antitrust law and/or any other jurisdiction's competition law.

The focus of this book is on the public (administrative) enforcement of the AML. Private enforcement of the AML is not examined in detail. The material in this book is current as of 31 December 2016.

## 1.7 Structure of Book

After this introductory chapter, Chapter 2 engages in legal doctrinal analysis of the AML provisions and of the published administrative enforcement decisions made by the Chinese competition agencies pursuant to the AML. It argues that, while this legal analysis provides informative and useful insights into the AML and its enforcement, the limited transparency and detail provided by the Chinese competition

---

[92] Additional information on the interviews, case studies, and documentary materials used in this book can be found in Appendix A.
[93] Sarah Biddulph and Pip Nicholson, 'Expanding the Circle: Comparative Legal Studies in Transition', in Penelope (Pip) Nicholson and Sarah Biddulph (eds.), *Examining Practice, Interrogating Theory: Comparative Legal Studies in Asia* (Leiden: Martinus Nijhoff Publishers, 2008), pp. 14–15.

authorities in their published decisions means that this analysis may be, in some respects, deficient.

In response, Part II of this book adapts and develops Milhaupt and Pistor's supply and demand framework to formulate a new analytical framework for the AML. Chapters 3 and 4 explore the demand and supply sides of the AML, respectively. The relevant stakeholders are examined in depth by looking at their backgrounds, interests, incentives, powers, constraints, knowledge of and attitudes to competition law and relationships with other actors. SOEs, industry regulators, private businesses and industry associations are identified as actors influencing the demand-side of the AML, whereas the supply-side is shaped by relevant legislative, executive, judicial and administrative bodies; competition law experts; and legal practitioners. The broader legal, institutional, economic and policy environment shaping demand and supply is explored and its relevance for competition policy in China considered.

Part III of this book takes the observations about and insights into these stakeholders and the societal context that were gleaned in Chapters 3 and 4 and applies them to investigate the making and enactment of the AML (Chapter 5) and its public enforcement (Chapter 6). These chapters demonstrate that certain actors and issues have especially influenced both the substance and the dynamics of the drafting and public enforcement of the AML.

Chapter 7 concludes this book by drawing together the key observations about the AML obtained through applying the political economy framework. Struggles among various government authorities for power to enforce the AML and the balancing of the dual roles of the state as a market participant and as competition regulator in China's socialist market economy have significantly influenced the enactment, implementation and enforcement of the AML. Further, the introduction and operation of the AML have been constrained by the consideration of other government laws and policies, the level of competition law expertise and knowledge within the government and business community and the position of the Chinese competition agencies within the broader government bureaucracy. These findings provide insights into how and why certain outcomes are reached under the AML.

Chapter 7 also evaluates the concerns and criticisms of the AML made by commentators in light of the observations and insights drawn from the political economy analysis. This book corroborates many of these criticisms and concerns, and offers explanations for why they may be well founded. It also qualifies or dispels some of the commentators' concerns and claims. For example, concerns that the divided enforcement structure would result in conflicts among the Chinese competition authorities have not generally been borne out. Instead, it has been the industry regulators that have sought to intervene in investigations and enforcement outcomes.

# 2

# Legal Analysis of the Anti-monopoly Law

## 2.1 Introduction

Before embarking on an exploration of the Chinese economic, institutional and political context and how it shapes the making, implementation and enforcement of competition law in China, this book analyses the Anti-monopoly Law (AML) and the decisions made by the Chinese competition authorities pursuant to the AML from a legal doctrinal perspective. The law itself and legal factors provide the structure (both procedural and substantive) within which competition authorities make and justify their decisions. It is therefore important to understand how Chinese competition authorities are interpreting, applying and developing the AML. The legal rules, doctrines and logic underlying these decisions then form the foundation for the political economy analysis to follow in the remainder of the book. It provides points of reference against which to evaluate the decisions made and outcomes reached by competition authorities and helps to identify potential gaps, inconsistencies and situations in which contextual analysis may be especially relevant and useful in explaining decisions and outcomes made under the AML.

This chapter engages in legal doctrinal analysis of the AML provisions and published decisions made by the competition authorities in China pursuant to the AML. This covers merger review, monopoly agreements, abuse of dominance and abuse of administrative power. It does not include private enforcement cases. This chapter undertakes an explanatory analysis of the AML with the aim to explicate; it does not engage in a critical evaluation of the legal principles and analytical approaches adopted by the competition authorities. It should be noted that conduct caught by the AML may also fall under the scope of other laws, such as the Anti-Unfair Competition Law and the Price Law; however, analysis of such laws is beyond the scope of this chapter.

## 2.2 Merger Control

Mergers, acquisitions and other concentrations of business operators (*jizhong*)[1] that reach a particular threshold must be notified to the competition authority.[2] The AML does not only apply to mergers that are implemented within China; mergers outside China that have the effect of eliminating or restricting competition in China's domestic market are also subject to its application.[3] If a merger reaches the notification thresholds but is not notified to the relevant competition authority for review, the parties may be investigated, fined up to RMB 500,000 and/or ordered to adopt measures to restore the pre-merger situation.[4]

The Ministry of Commerce (MOFCOM) is responsible for merger review and enforcement, and its tasks are handled at the central level by the MOFCOM Anti-monopoly Bureau (MOFCOM Bureau). Once a notification is accepted, the MOFCOM has thirty days to conduct a preliminary review of the merger and decide whether it will initiate further review (known as 'Phase 1 review'). If the MOFCOM decides to initiate a further

---

[1] 'Concentration of business operators' is defined in Article 20 of the Anti-monopoly Law, and additional guidance on the meaning of 'control' is provided in Article 3 of the 关于经营者集中申报的指导意见 [Guiding Opinion on Notification of Concentration of Business Operators] (People's Republic of China) Ministry of Commerce, 6 June 2014.

[2] A concentration must be notified where: (i) the combined worldwide turnover of all business operators involved in the concentration exceeded RMB 10 billion in the previous accounting year, and the turnover in China of at least two of the business operators involved exceeded RMB 400 million in the previous accounting year; or (ii) the combined turnover in China of all business operators involved in the concentration exceeded RMB 2 billion in the previous accounting year, and the turnover in China of at least two business operators involved exceeded RMB 400 million in the previous accounting year: 国务院关于经营者集中申报标准的规定 [Regulation of the State Council on the Notification Thresholds for Concentrations of Business Operators] (People's Republic of China) State Council, Order No. 529, 3 August 2008, art. 3.

[3] 中华人民共和国反垄断法 [Anti-monopoly Law of the People's Republic of China] (People's Republic of China) Standing Committee of the National People's Congress, 30 August 2007, art. 2.

[4] 未依法申报经营者集中调查处理暂行办法 [Interim Measure for Investigating and Handling Concentrations of Business Operators Not Notified in Accordance with the Law] (People's Republic of China) Ministry of Commerce, Order No. 6, 30 December 2011.

In the published administrative penalty decisions to date, the MOFCOM determined that the merger constituted a concentration under Article 20 of the AML, that the merger had reached the notification thresholds, and that, by not notifying the merger for review, the parties had violated Article 21 of the AML. The MOFCOM also assessed the competitive impact of the merger and concluded that the merger had no anti-competitive effect. In determining the type and level of sanction to impose on the parties, the MOFCOM considers the nature, degree and duration of the conduct, and the competitive effect of the not previously notified merger.

investigation, it has ninety days to complete its review and make a decision (known as 'Phase 2 review'). The MOFCOM may extend the review period by an additional sixty days (known as 'extended Phase 2 review') under certain circumstances.[5] Thus, the review process can potentially last 180 days from the date that the notification is accepted. In addition to this standard merger review procedure in the AML, the MOFCOM has adopted an expedited review process for mergers that do not raise substantial competition concerns.[6] Mergers classified as 'simple cases'[7] are reviewed under a simple case procedure. This means that the parties have fewer notification materials to submit to the MOFCOM, a public notice on the proposed merger will be published on the MOFCOM's website and the public will have a ten-day period during which to raise objections to

---

[5] Anti-monopoly Law, arts. 25–6. The merger review process is outlined in more detail in 经营者集中审查办法 [Measure on the Review of Concentrations of Business Operators] (People's Republic of China) Ministry of Commerce, Order No. 12, 15 July 2009.

[6] 关于经营者集中简易案件适用标准的暂行规定 [Interim Regulation on the Applicable Standards for Simple Cases of Concentrations of Business Operators] (People's Republic of China) Ministry of Commerce, Order No. 12, 11 February 2014; 关于经营者集中简易案件申报的指导意见(试行) [Guiding Opinion on Notification of Simple Cases of Concentrations of Business Operators (Trial)] (People's Republic of China) Ministry of Commerce, 18 April 2014.

[7] The following mergers will be treated as simple cases:

- Horizontal mergers where the parties' combined market share in the overlap markets is below 15 per cent;
- Vertical mergers where the parties' market share in the relevant upstream and downstream markets is below 25 per cent;
- Conglomerate mergers where the parties' market share is below 25 per cent in their respective markets;
- Offshore joint ventures that will not engage in any economic activities in China; and
- Reductions in the number of controlling shareholders in a joint venture that results in the joint venture being controlled by one or more of the remaining shareholder/s.

However, even if a merger meets the above conditions, it will not be treated as a simple case if:

- The number of controlling shareholders in a joint venture is reduced and the joint venture is controlled by one or more of the remaining shareholder/s, and the remaining controlling shareholder/s competes with the joint venture in the same relevant market;
- The relevant market is difficult to define;
- The merger may have an adverse effect on market entry or technological progress, consumers or other business operators, or China's economic development; or
- In the MOFCOM's view, the merger otherwise adversely affects competition.

See Interim Regulation on the Applicable Standards for Simple Cases of Concentrations of Business Operators, arts. 2–3.

the proposed merger.[8] Although there is no provision in the AML or the relevant regulations that reviews of simple cases will be fast-tracked, in practice most simple cases have been reviewed and approved within thirty days of the acceptance of the notification.[9] Since its introduction in April 2014, a majority of all the mergers notified to the MOFCOM have been reviewed under the simple case procedure.[10]

A merger may be approved either unconditionally or conditionally, or prohibited. A merger will be prohibited if it results or may result in the elimination or restriction of competition.[11] However, a merger may be approved if the parties involved can prove that its positive effects outweigh its negative effects or that the merger is in the public interest.[12] Alternatively, the competition authority may attach restrictive conditions (*xianzhi tiaojian*) to its approval to eliminate or reduce the anticompetitive effects of the merger.[13] The merging parties may submit proposed restrictive conditions to the competition authority to address its concerns.[14] If the merging parties do submit a proposal, a final

---

[8] Guiding Opinion on the Notification of Simple Cases of Concentrations of Business Operators (Trial).

[9] Interviews with Chinese competition law experts and stakeholders; Marc Waha, 'MOFCOM Simple Cases: The First Six Months' [2015] (1) *CPI Antitrust Chronicle* 1, available at www.competitionpolicyinternational.com/mofcom-simple-cases-the-first-six-months. It should be noted that an earlier draft of the regulation (released in May 2012) had stated that the MOFCOM would endeavour to approve simple cases within the first thirty days except in special circumstances. This was deleted from the adopted regulation. See 'MOFCOM Solicits Comments on Draft Rules Regarding "Simple" Transactions', Cleary Gottlieb, 16 April 2013, 3, available at www.clearygottlieb.com/news-and-insights/publication-listing/mofcom-solicits-comments-on-draft-rules-regarding-simple-transactions2; 'MOFCOM Seeks to Streamline and Clarify the Chinese Merger Control Process – Draft Regulations Published' (Briefing Note, Clifford Chance, April 2013) 4, available at www.cliffordchance.com/briefings/2013/04/mofcom_seeks_to_streamlineandclarifyth.html.

[10] A list of the merger reviews made under the simple merger review process is found at 经营者集中简易案件公示 [Announcement of Simple Cases of Concentrations of Business Operators], Ministry of Commerce of the People's Republic of China Antimonopoly Bureau, available at http://fldj.mofcom.gov.cn/article/jyzjzjyajgs. See also Waha, 'MOFCOM Simple Cases'.

[11] Anti-monopoly Law, art. 28. [12] Ibid.

[13] Ibid., art. 29; Measure on the Review of Concentrations of Business Operators, art. 12.

[14] 商务部反垄断局负责人关于《关于经营者集中附加限制性条件的规定(试行)》的解读 [Head of the Ministry of Commerce Anti-monopoly Bureau's Interpretation of the 'Regulation on the Imposition of Restrictive Conditions on Concentrations of Business Operators (Trial)'] (People's Republic of China) Ministry of Commerce Antimonopoly Bureau, 17 December 2014, available at http://fldj.mofcom.gov.cn/article/j/201412/20141200835988.shtml.

proposal must be submitted within twenty days before the end of the relevant review period. If the merging parties fail to submit a proposal within the prescribed period, or if the proposed restrictive conditions are not sufficient to address the anti-competitive effects of the merger, the merger will be prohibited.[15]

Of the 1,657 mergers that the MOFCOM reviewed and concluded as at 31 December 2016, it unconditionally approved 1,627 (98.19 per cent), attached restrictive conditions to the approval of 28 (1.69 per cent) and prohibited 2 (0.12 per cent).

To date, the MOFCOM has published thirty merger review decisions, all of which pertain to conditional approvals and prohibitions. A list is provided in Appendix B. The decision typically sets out the timeline of the key events in the case acceptance, merger review and restrictive condition negotiation process; briefly discusses the MOFCOM's consultation with third parties and the notifying parties; presents its conclusions on relevant market definition and competition assessment; and sets out the restrictive conditions imposed, or states that the merger has been prohibited. The MOFCOM also publishes a list of its unconditionally approved mergers, which is updated on a quarterly basis.[16] It provides the case name, the merging parties and, for cases decided from 1 October 2012 onwards, the date on which the decision was made.

The level of reasoning and analysis in merger decisions has improved remarkably since the MOFCOM published its first decision (*InBev/Anheuser-Busch*) in November 2008. That decision was less than one page in length and contained only two lines of analysis. The MOFCOM stated that 'due to the very large scale of this acquisition, the merged entity will have a large market share and its competitiveness will be clearly enhanced',[17] and that it had decided to attach restrictive conditions to its approval to 'reduce the potential adverse effect on the Chinese beer market in the future'.[18] Since then its decisions have become increasingly

---

[15] 关于经营者集中附加限制性条件的规定（试行）[Regulation on the Imposition of Restrictive Conditions on Concentrations of Business Operators (Trial)] (People's Republic of China) Ministry of Commerce, Order No. 6, 4 December 2014, art. 6.

[16] Anti-monopoly Bureau of the Ministry of Commerce, 反垄断局加强经营者集中案件信息公开 [Anti-monopoly Bureau Enhances Disclosure of Notifications of Concentrations of Business Operators] (News Release, 15 November 2012).

[17] 中华人民共和国商务部公告2008年第95号 [Announcement No. 95 of 2008 of the Ministry of Commerce of the People's Republic of China] (People's Republic of China) Ministry of Commerce, Order No. 95, 18 November 2008.

[18] Ibid.

detailed and sophisticated, and demonstrate a deeper understanding of, and greater comfort and confidence with, merger analysis.[19] For example, in its conditional approval of *Glencore/Xstrata* in April 2013, which was six pages long, the MOFCOM analysed both the horizontal and vertical impacts of the concentration in three separate product markets and considered factors such as market entry and countervailing power.[20]

Before engaging in substantive analysis of the MOFCOM's merger decisions, the following matters should be noted. First, only 30 of the 1,657 (1.81 per cent) merger review decisions made by the MOFCOM have been published. This is because the MOFCOM is required to publish its decision only if it attaches restrictive conditions to a merger or prohibits one.[21] Second, while the quality of the MOFCOM's published decisions has improved significantly over time, they nonetheless provide only limited insight into the MOFCOM's approach to merger analysis. The decisions tend to be relatively brief and the analysis is presented as conclusions. There is little to no discussion or evaluation of competing legal, economic and factual arguments, or of the submissions made by the merging parties and consulted parties. The factors examined vary from decision to decision, and often limited analysis or supporting information is provided on how and why particular anti-competitive effects might arise. The MOFCOM also does not explain how or why the restrictive conditions attached to an approval will address its concerns about the anti-competitive effects of a proposed merger. Hence the robustness of the observations and conclusions (to the extent they can be drawn) about merger analysis in China is necessarily constrained by the information provided, and therefore care must be taken.

### 2.2.1 Relevant Market Definition

Defining the relevant market has been the first analytical step taken in most of the MOFCOM's published decisions. The Market Definition

---

[19] Fei Deng and Cunzhen Huang, 'A Five Year Review of Merger Enforcement in China' [2013] (October) *The Antitrust Source* 1 at 4–5, available at www.americanbar.org/content/dam/aba/directories/antitrust/oct13_deng_10_29f.authcheckdam.pdf.
[20] 关于附加限制性条件批准嘉能可国际公司收购斯特拉塔公司经营者集中反垄断审查决定的公告 [Announcement of the Anti-monopoly Review of Concentrations of Business Operators Decision to Impose Restrictive Conditions to the Approval of Glencore International Acquisition of Xstrata] (People's Republic of China) Ministry of Commerce, Order No. 20, 16 April 2013 (*Glencore/Xstrata*).
[21] Anti-monopoly Law, art. 30.

Guideline,[22] issued by the Anti-monopoly Commission (AMC) and which applies to all three Chinese competition authorities, outlines an approach to market definition that is similar to that followed by competition agencies in other jurisdictions such as the European Union, the United States and Australia. The Chinese competition authorities define the product and geographic dimensions of the market and focus on demand-side substitution and, to a lesser extent, supply-side substitution.[23] The Market Definition Guideline also recognises the relevance to market definition of economic analysis and the hypothetical monopolist test,[24] along with its limitations.[25]

Several observations can be made from the MOFCOM's published decisions about its approach to market definition. The MOFCOM's starting point in market definition is the products and services that are offered by the merging parties and the overlaps between the merging parties' products and services. It has, in various decisions, considered both demand-side and supply-side substitution factors when examining the product market, although, as indicated in the Market Definition Guideline, it has tended to place more emphasis on demand-side considerations. With respect to the geographic market, in nearly all the published decisions to date, the MOFCOM has defined China, Mainland China and global markets, and has examined them either separately or together. There has only been one published decision (*Anheuser Busch InBev/SABMiller*) in which the MOFCOM defined provincial markets, although it also considered the market on a national basis. This may be related to the fact that most of the mergers conditionally approved or prohibited by the MOFCOM thus far have been offshore mergers.[26]

---

[22] 国务院反垄断委员会关于相关市场界定的指南 [Guideline of the Anti-monopoly Commission of the State Council on Defining the Relevant Market] (People's Republic of China) Anti-monopoly Commission of the State Council, 24 May 2009.

[23] Ibid., arts. 3–6.

[24] The hypothetical monopolist test determines the smallest product or group of products and the geographic area in which it is sold or produced, such that a hypothetical profit-maximising firm that was the only present and future producer or seller of those products in that area would be likely to impose at least a small but significant non-transitory increase in price (SSNIP) on at least one product in the market. It is also known as the SSNIP test.

[25] Market Definition Guideline, arts. 7, 10, 11.

[26] Of the published merger decisions to date, one has involved a Chinese state-owned enterprise (*General Electric/Shenhua*); one has involved a joint venture between Chinese companies and foreign companies (*NiMH Battery Joint Venture*); and two mergers relate to Chinese brands – fruit juice (*Coca-Cola/Huiyuan*) and an online shopping platform (*Wal-Mart/Newheight*). All purely domestic mergers reviewed by the MOFCOM under the AML have been approved unconditionally.

The MOFCOM has considered, in various combinations, the geographic scope of the merging parties' operations, how the products or services are usually procured and supplied, transportation costs and customs taxes and other legal and practical barriers in defining the geographic market. The decisions do not indicate whether the MOFCOM has used the hypothetical monopolist test in its market definition exercise.

### 2.2.2 Competition Analysis

The substantive test that the MOFCOM is required to apply when reviewing mergers is whether the proposed merger will or may result in the effect of eliminating or restricting competition.[27] This test does not expressly require that the elimination or restriction of competition be substantial, significant or material. It should be noted that, on at least a few occasions, the MOFCOM engaged a third-party consultant to assess the impact of the proposed merger on competition.[28]

#### 2.2.2.1 Merger Factors

The AML provides that the MOFCOM must, in its assessment of a proposed merger, consider the market share of the business operators involved and their ability to control the market; the degree of market concentration; the effect of the merger on market entry, technological progress, consumers, other business operators and national economic development; and other factors it deems relevant to its merger analysis.[29] In addition, the MOFCOM recognises that mergers may increase economic efficiency, achieve economies of scale and scope, reduce product cost and increase product diversification, all of which have positive impacts on consumer interest.[30]

It is apparent from the MOFCOM's published decisions that market share, the degree of market concentration and market entry are key considerations in its assessment of the competitive impact of a proposed merger. These three factors are examined in nearly every published decision. This is not to say that the MOFCOM has not considered the

---

[27] Anti-monopoly Law, art. 28.
[28] *Seagate/Samsung, Western Digital/Hitachi, MediaTek/MStar, Thermo Fisher/Life, Merck/ AZ Electronics, P3 Shipping Alliance.*
[29] Anti-monopoly Law, art. 27.
[30] 关于评估经营者集中竞争影响的暂行规定 [Interim Provision on the Assessment of the Effect of Concentrations of Business Operators on Competition] (People's Republic of China) Ministry of Commerce, Order No. 55, 29 August 2011, art. 9.

effect of a proposed merger on competitors, customers, innovation or national economic development in its published decisions. Rather, these factors tend to have been considered on an *ad hoc* basis or are embedded within the analysis of market share, concentration and entry.

(i) **Market Share** The MOFCOM looks at the merging parties' market shares and positions before and after the merger, along with the market shares or market positions of their competitors. The decisions do not indicate that there is a particular market share threshold above which competition concerns are triggered or that the MOFCOM adopts a safe harbour for mergers below a particular market share threshold. The MOFCOM has found potential anti-competitive effects arising from a proposed merger at combined post-merger market shares ranging from 9.3 per cent[31] to 18 per cent,[32] 46.7 per cent,[33] 64 per cent[34] and 84 per cent.[35] Small market share increments were also sufficient to find potential anti-competitive effects in *Glencore/Xstrata*, *Novartis/Alcon* and *Marubeni/Gavilon*, particularly with the latter two mergers involving increments of less than 1 per cent.[36] The market position of the merged entity is also an important consideration. In these decisions, the MOFCOM found that the merged entity would, in most cases, be the largest player in the market, with a much larger market share than its competitors or significant advantages over them, even in cases where the market share was relatively low.

(ii) **Market Concentration** The MOFCOM has used the Herfindahl-Hirschman Index (commonly known as the HHI)[37] to examine market

---

[31] One of the relevant markets in *Glencore/Xstrata* (global copper concentrate market).
[32] *Marubeni/Gavilon*.  [33] *P3 Shipping Alliance*.  [34] *Baxter/Gambro*.
[35] *UTC/Goodrich*.
[36] *Glencore/Xstrata*; 公布关于附条件批准诺华股份公司收购爱尔康公司反垄断审查决定的公告 [Announcement of the Anti-monopoly Review Decision to Conditionally Approve Novartis' Acquisition of Alcon] (People's Republic of China) Ministry of Commerce, Order No. 53, 13 August 2010 (*Novartis/Alcon*); 关于附加限制性条件批准丸红公司收购高鸿公司100%股权经营者集中反垄断审查决定的公告 [Announcement of the Anti-monopoly Review of Concentrations of Business Operators Decision to Impose Restrictive Conditions to the Approval of Marubeni's Acquisition of 100 Per cent Equity Interest of Gavilon Holdings] (People's Republic of China) Ministry of Commerce, Order No. 22, 23 April 2013 (*Marubeni/Gavilon*).
[37] The HHI is calculated by adding the sum of the squares of the individual firms' market shares in the relevant market. The HHI therefore places greater weight on higher market shares.

concentration in a number of its decisions.[38] The HHI is a measure of the degree of concentration in a market, and the post-merger HHI and the change in HHI resulting from the merger (known as delta) are quite commonly used by competition agencies worldwide, including in the United States, Australia, the European Union and Japan. While some authorities provide guidance on the HHI thresholds for mergers that are more or less likely to attract greater scrutiny (each competition authority strikes slightly different thresholds), the MOFCOM has not done so in the implementing regulations. Some insight is provided in the *Thermo Fisher/Life* decision, where it calculated the HHI for fifty-nine products where the merging parties had competitive overlaps and decided to further examine only those products where the HHI was over 1,500 and the delta was over 100.[39] In those decisions where the MOFCOM expressly referred to use of the HHI, it has conditionally approved or prohibited mergers with post-merger HHIs of between 2,000 and over 9,000, with a delta of between 300 and nearly 3,500. Generally, however, the MOFCOM has not evaluated or discussed the meaning or implication of such HHI and delta figures.

(iii) **Market Entry**  Market entry features prominently in the MOFCOM's merger analysis. The MOFCOM states that it considers whether the proposed merger would make it more difficult for potential competitors to enter the market due to the merging parties' increased control of production inputs, sales channels, technology, essential infrastructure and other matters.[40] Other frequently identified barriers to entry include research and development costs, capital requirements, lengthy project time periods, access to raw materials, intellectual property rights, distribution and marketing networks, legal and governmental barriers (such as legal restrictions, government approvals, government policies and standards), economies of scale and switching costs for customers. In some of

---

[38] *Pfizer/Wyeth*; *Henkel/Tiande*; *UTC/Goodrich*; *Baxter/Gambro*; *MediaTek/MStar*; *Thermo Fisher/Life*; *P3 Shipping Alliance*; *Abbott Laboratories/St Jude Medical*.

[39] 关于附加限制性条件批准赛默飞世尔科技公司收购立菲技术公司案经营者集中反垄断审查决定的公告 [Announcement of the Anti-monopoly Review of Concentrations of Business Operators Decision to Impose Restrictive Conditions to the Approval of Thermo Fisher Scientific's Acquisition of Life Technologies] (People's Republic of China) Ministry of Commerce, Order No. 3, 15 January 2014 (*Thermo Fisher/Life*).

[40] Interim Provision on the Assessment of the Effect of Concentrations of Business Operators on Competition, art. 7.

these published decisions, the MOFCOM also noted the lack of new entry,[41] unsuccessful attempts at entry[42] and the exit of competitors.[43]

There has been limited discussion or examination of the effect of the proposed merger on barriers to entry. In a majority of the published decisions where market entry was considered, the MOFCOM simply concluded that market entry was (very) difficult. In the handful of cases where this was considered, the MOFCOM found that the merger would lead to higher barriers to entry because the merging parties would have greater control of well-known brands,[44] raw materials sources[45] or distribution channels,[46] or have combined patent advantages[47] or networks.[48]

#### 2.2.2.2 Theories of Harm

The MOFCOM's approach to assessing the potential harm to competition arising from a proposed merger is outlined in the Interim Provision on the Assessment of the Effect of Concentrations of Business Operators on Competition (Interim Merger Guideline).[49] The MOFCOM uses theories of competitive harm that are recognised in antitrust economics that are commonly adopted by other competition law jurisdictions (such as the United States,[50] Australia[51] and Japan[52]) and accepted by the international competition law community.[53] These standard theories of competitive harm have been applied by the MOFCOM in nearly every published decision to date. In these decisions, however, detailed data and analysis to support its use of a particular theory of harm have generally not been provided.

**(i) Unilateral Effects** According to the Interim Merger Guideline, the MOFCOM first examines whether the merger would create or enhance

---

[41] *Glencore/Xstrata* and *Marubeni/Gavilon*.    [42] *Alpha V/Savio*.    [43] *Henkel/Tiande*.
[44] *Coca-Cola/Huiyuan*.    [45] *Glencore/Xstrata* and *Marubeni/Gavilon*.
[46] *Anheuser-Busch InBev/SABMiller*.    [47] *NXP/Freescale*.    [48] *P3 Shipping Alliance*.
[49] 关于评估经营者集中竞争影响的暂行规定 [Interim Provision on the Assessment of the Effect of Concentrations of Business Operators on Competition] (People's Republic of China) Ministry of Commerce, Order No. 55, 29 August 2011.
[50] US Department of Justice and Federal Trade Commission, 'Horizontal Merger Guidelines', 19 August 2010, pp. 20–6.
[51] Australian Competition and Consumer Commission, 'Merger Guidelines' (November 2008), pp. 24–34.
[52] Japan Fair Trade Commission, 'Guidelines to Application of the Antimonopoly Act Concerning Review of Business Combination', 14 June 2011.
[53] See, e.g., International Competition Network Merger Working Group, 'ICN Recommended Practices for Merger Analysis' (2009, rev. 2010).

the ability and incentive of a single operator, acting alone, to eliminate or restrict competition, and the possibility of that occurring.[54] This type of competitive harm is known as the unilateral or non-coordinated effects of a merger.

Unilateral effects analysis has been a focus of a number of the MOFCOM's decisions involving mergers between competitors (also known as horizontal mergers) and, to a lesser extent, mergers between parties that interact on both vertical and horizontal markets. In these decisions, the MOFCOM found that the elimination of a key or close competitor,[55] the lack of incentive for competitors to compete,[56] the lack of countervailing buyer power[57] or the restriction of downstream customers' choice of suppliers[58] meant that competitive constraints were insufficient to limit the increase in the merged entity's control of the relevant market or its dominance. China's dependence on imports of the relevant product was also an important consideration in *Uralkali/Silvinit* and *Marubeni/Gavilon* when examining whether effective competitive restraints on the merged entity existed. Some of the harms potential that the MOFCOM has identified as resulting from unilateral effects include higher prices,[59] harm to customers,[60] reduced research and development and innovation,[61] and higher barriers to entry,[62] as well as the exit of competitors from the market.[63]

The MOFCOM's decisions, however, do not generally consider why the merged entity would have the incentive to, for example, increase prices, other than it having the ability to do so due to market control or dominance and the lack of effective competitive restraint. Similarly, there has been no discussion of why the merged entity would choose to act in such a way. However, in *Microsoft/Nokia*, the MOFCOM did take into account the impact of the proposed merger on the incentives of the seller (Nokia in this case) post-merger. The MOFCOM found

---

[54] Interim Provision on the Assessment of the Effect of Concentrations of Business Operators on Competition, art. 4.
[55] *UTC/Goodrich*; *Baxter/Gambro*; *MediaTek/MStar*; *NXP/Freescale*.
[56] *Panasonic/Sanyo*.   [57] *Marubeni/Gavilon*; *Nokia/Alcatel-Lucent*.
[58] *Panasonic/Sanyo*; *UTC/Goodrich*; *MediaTek/MStar*; *Thermo Fisher/Life*; *Nokia/Alcatel-Lucent*.
[59] *Panasonic/Sanyo*; *MediaTek/MStar*; *Thermo Fisher/Life*; *Abbott Laboratories/St Jude Medical*.
[60] *Thermo Fisher/Life*; *P3 Shipping Alliance*; *Nokia/Alcatel-Lucent*.
[61] *MediaTek/MStar*; *NXP/Freescale*.   [62] *Anheuser-Busch InBev/SABMiller*.
[63] *Nokia/Alcatel-Lucent*.

that the merger would increase Nokia's incentives to license its patents for greater profits, because Nokia would no longer need to obtain cross-licences due to its exit from the downstream device and service market.[64]

(ii) **Coordinated Effects** Where a small number of operators exist in a relevant market, the MOFCOM considers whether the proposed merger will create or enhance the ability and incentive of these operators to act jointly to eliminate or restrict competition, and the possibility that they will do so.[65] This is similar to what are known as the coordinated effects of a merger. Mergers can give rise to coordinated effects by enabling or encouraging implicit or explicit coordination between competitors on pricing, output or other competitive factors.

The MOFCOM has applied the coordinated effects theory of harm in several of its published decisions, though its use has not been as frequent as that of unilateral effects analysis. In these decisions, when evaluating the potential impact of the merger on the ability, likelihood and possibility of coordination among competitors, the MOFCOM appears to consider two key issues, although often not together.

First, it assesses whether the market is likely to be prone to coordination. In *Seagate/Samsung* and *Western Digital/Hitachi*, both of which related to mergers in the hard disk drive market, the MOFCOM examined the degree of market concentration, as well as market transparency, the procurement process, market capacity, buyer power, innovation and market entry. It found that the hard disk drive market is highly concentrated and quite transparent, with homogenous products, low switching costs for downstream customers and little excess capacity. In each decision, the MOFCOM concluded that the merger would eliminate an important competitor and reduce competitive pressure in procurement. As the market is transparent, the remaining competitors would be able to predict their competitors' actions. Therefore, the MOFCOM concluded that the merger would increase the possibility that the hard

---

[64] 关于附加限制性条件批准微软收购诺基亚设备和服务业务案经营者集中反垄断审查决定的公告 [Announcement of the Anti-monopoly Review of Concentrations of Business Operators Decision to Impose Restrictive Conditions to the Approval of Microsoft's Acquisition of Nokia's Device and Service Business] (People's Republic of China) Ministry of Commerce, Order No. 24, 8 April 2014 (*Microsoft/Nokia*).

[65] Interim Provision on the Assessment of the Effect of Concentrations of Business Operators on Competition, art. 4.

disk drive manufacturers would coordinate their actions and eliminate or restrict competition.[66]

Second, the MOFCOM has found that a relationship between one of the merging parties and its major competitor would increase the likelihood that a merger would lead to coordinated effects. That relationship might arise from being counterparties to a pre-existing agreement or from a common shareholder. In *Novartis/Alcon*, the MOFCOM was concerned that an existing exclusive distribution agreement between the acquirer's wholly-owned subsidiary and its largest competitor in the Chinese contact lens care products market would lead to coordination on price, quantity and sales territories for the sale and distribution of contact lens care products in China.[67] Similarly, in *Baxter/Gambro*, an outsourcing production agreement between Baxter and a competitor that covered competitively sensitive information such as production cost and volume was regarded by the MOFCOM as facilitating coordination in the Chinese haemodialysis market.[68] In both cases, the merger would result in the merged entity becoming the second largest player in the market, and therefore the parties to the agreement would be the two largest players in the market. The source of the MOFCOM's concerns in *Alpha V/Savio* was a common shareholder. In addition to acquiring Savio, Alpha V was also the largest shareholder in Savio's competitor, Uster, with a 27.9 per cent interest. Uster and Savio's wholly owned subsidiary were the only two suppliers of electronic yarn cleaners for automatic winders in the world. The MOFCOM was concerned that the two suppliers would, through Alpha V, coordinate their business activities and eliminate or restrict competition, and that Alpha V would use its

---

[66] 关于附条件批准希捷科技公司收购三星电子有限公司硬盘驱动器业务反垄断审查决定的公告 [Announcement of the Anti-monopoly Review Decision to Conditionally Approve Seagate Technology's Acquisition of the Hard Disk Drive Business of Samsung Electronics] (People's Republic of China) Ministry of Commerce, Order No. 90, 12 December 2011 (*Seagate/Samsung*); 关于附加限制性条件批准西部数据收购日立存储经营者集中反垄断审查决定的公告 [Announcement of the Anti-monopoly Review of Concentrations of Business Operators Decision to Impose Restrictive Conditions to the Approval of Western Digital's Acquisition of Hitachi] (People's Republic of China) Ministry of Commerce, Order No. 9, 2 March 2012 (*Western Digital/Hitachi*).

[67] *Novartis/Alcon*.

[68] 关于附加限制性条件批准美国百特国际有限公司收购瑞典金宝公司经营者集中反垄断审查决定的公告 [Announcement of the Anti-monopoly Review of Concentrations of Business Operators Decision to Impose Restrictive Conditions to the Approval of Baxter International's Acquisition of Gambro] (People's Republic of China) Ministry of Commerce, Order No. 58, 13 August 2013 (*Baxter/Gambro*).

influence in both suppliers to coordinate their activities to eliminate or restrict competition.[69] No explanation, however, was given as to why and how Alpha V would exercise such influence.

(iii) **Foreclosure Effects** For mergers between parties that are not actual or potential competitors in the same market (also known as non-horizontal mergers), the MOFCOM will assess whether the merger will have or be likely to have the effect of eliminating or restricting competition in an upstream, downstream or associated market.[70] While there is no additional guidance on how such mergers should be assessed in the Interim Merger Guideline, the AML or other regulations, the MOFCOM's published decisions do provide some insight.

Nearly half of the MOFCOM's published decisions have involved mergers where the merging parties did not compete in the same market. In these mergers, the merger parties operated in markets that were vertically related (usually one party operated in the upstream market and the other in the downstream market) or unrelated, adjacent or complementary (known as conglomerate mergers). Some of these mergers also involved multiple markets, where the merging parties were competitors in one market but not in others.

The focus of the MOFCOM's competitive effects analysis in mergers between non-competitors has been on whether the merger would impede or eliminate actual or potential competitors' access to a market. Such effects are commonly known as foreclosure effects. The MOFCOM has intervened to impose restrictions on or prohibit a non-horizontal merger where a merging party operated in an upstream market and was the largest supplier of the relevant product or service or had a position of dominance or control arising from its market share[71] or ownership of relevant intellectual property.[72] Its concern was that the merged entity would use its strength in the upstream market to restrict competition in the downstream market, where the merged entity was usually faced with greater competition (although this was not always the case). The types of

---

[69] 关于附条件批准佩内洛普有限责任公司收购萨维奥纺织机械股份有限公司反垄断审查决定的公告 [Announcement of the Anti-monopoly Review Decision to Conditionally Approve Alpha V's Acquisition of Savio] (People's Republic of China) Ministry of Commerce, Order No. 73, 31 October 2011 (*Alpha V/Savio*).
[70] Interim Provisions on the Assessment of the Effect of Concentrations of Business Operators on Competition, art. 4.
[71] *NiMH Battery Joint Venture*; *Henkel/Tiande*.
[72] *Google/Motorola Mobility*; *ARM Joint Venture*; *Microsoft/Nokia*.

conduct that the MOFCOM has identified as problematic include the merged entity restricting supply of an important upstream good or service to downstream competitors (and therefore foreclosing access to a key input of downstream competitors),[73] engaging in discriminatory treatment to favour its related downstream business or disfavour downstream competitors[74] or increasing the price of the upstream good or service (and thus increasing downstream competitors' costs).[75]

With conglomerate mergers, in addition to foreclosure effects arising from the leveraging of a competitive advantage in one market to a related market,[76] the MOFCOM has examined the merged entity's ability to bundle and tie related products together as a source of potential anticompetitive harm arising from the merger. In *Merck/AZ Electronics*, it found that the merged entity would be the largest supplier of liquid crystal and photoresist, whereas its competitors only supplied one of the products and had limited production capacity. The merged entity was therefore found to have the ability to bundle sales of liquid crystal and photoresist or engage in cross-subsidisation, potentially harming competition as the merged entity expanded market share and increased profits.[77]

In all of these decisions, the MOFCOM focused on examining the merged entity's ability to engage in the conduct giving rise to the foreclosure effect or tied sales. It did not, however, examine whether the merged entity would have the incentive to engage in such conduct, and how it would do so.

### 2.2.3 Restrictive Conditions

As noted above, the MOFCOM may decide to attach restrictive conditions to its merger approval to eliminate or reduce the anti-competitive effects of a merger. Such restrictive conditions, also known as remedies or commitments, may be structural or behavioural, or a combination of both.[78]

---

[73] *GE/Shenhua*; *NiMH Battery Joint Venture*.
[74] *Henkel/Tiande*; *Google/Motorola Mobility*; *ARM Joint Venture*.   [75] *Microsoft/Nokia*.
[76] *Wal-Mart/Newheight* (advantages in physical stores); *Coca-Cola/Huiyuan* (brand).
[77] 关于附加限制性条件批准默克公司收购安智电子材料公司案经营者集中反垄断审查决定的公告 [Announcement of the Anti-monopoly Review of Concentrations of Business Operators Decision to Impose Restrictive Conditions to the Approval of Merck's Acquisition of AZ Electronics Materials] (People's Republic of China) Ministry of Commerce, Order No. 30, 30 April 2014 (*Merck/AZ Electronics*).
[78] 关于经营者集中附加限制性条件的规定(试行) [Regulation on the Imposition of Restrictive Conditions on Concentrations of Business Operators (Trial)] (People's Republic of China) Ministry of Commerce, Order No. 6, 4 December 2014, art. 3.

The AML and implementing regulations do not define structural or behavioural conditions, although the MOFCOM provides a few examples in its Regulation on the Imposition of Restrictive Conditions on Concentrations of Business Operators (Trial) (Trial Remedy Regulation).[79] The examples provided indicate that the MOFCOM's approach to structural and behavioural remedies appears consistent with the practices of other jurisdictions. Typically, structural remedies are one-off remedies aimed at restoring or maintaining the competitive structure of the market that existed before the merger.[80] The divestiture of tangible or intangible assets, which is the most common type of structural remedy, is provided as an example by the MOFCOM.[81] According to the MOFCOM, divestiture conditions have two objectives: one is to weaken the market control that the merging parties gain or strengthen through the merger, and the other is to enhance the ability of the buyer of the divested business to exert competitive pressure on the merged entity.[82] Behavioural remedies, on the other hand, are generally ongoing remedies designed to modify or constrain the behaviour of the merged firm.[83] The MOFCOM points to the granting of access to infrastructure such as networks or platforms, the licensing of relevant technologies and the termination of exclusive agreements as examples of behavioural conditions.[84] Behavioural remedies usually require a greater level and longer period of ongoing monitoring and compliance than structural remedies.

No specific guidance is provided in the AML or the implementing regulations regarding the situations in which it is appropriate to impose structural conditions as opposed to behavioural conditions, and vice versa. In contrast to a number of other jurisdictions, which express a strong preference for structural over behavioural conditions, there is no

---

[79] Regulation on the Imposition of Restrictive Conditions on Concentrations of Business Operators (Trial) (People's Republic of China) Ministry of Commerce, Order No 6, 4 December 2014.

[80] International Competition Network Merger Working Group: Analytical Framework Subgroup, 'Merger Remedies Review Project' (Report for the Fourth ICN Annual Conference, Bonn, June 2005), p. 7.

[81] Regulation on the Imposition of Restrictive Conditions on Concentrations of Business Operators (Trial), art. 3.

[82] Head of the Ministry of Commerce Anti-monopoly Bureau's Interpretation of the Regulation on the Imposition of Restrictive Conditions in Concentrations of Business Operators (Trial), para. 4.

[83] ICN Merger Working Group, 'Merger Remedies Review Project', 7.

[84] Regulation on the Imposition of Restrictive Conditions on Concentrations of Business Operators (Trial), art. 3.

preference for a particular type of remedy evident in the AML, the implementing regulations or the MOFCOM's public statements.[85] Rather, regardless of the type of condition, the MOFCOM requires that it be sufficient to eliminate the anticompetitive effects of the merger, operational in practice and capable of addressing the competition problem in a timely manner.[86] There are, however, no further criteria provided by the AML, the implementing regulations or the MOFCOM on the evaluation of conditions and whether they sufficiently eliminate or reduce the merger's anti-competitive effect.

In practice, the MOFCOM has attached a range and combination of structural and behavioural conditions to its merger approvals to address a variety of concerns. The MOFCOM has used behavioural conditions more often than structural conditions to address anti-competitive harm arising from both horizontal and non-horizontal mergers.[87] Unfortunately, however, the decisions do not set out any reasons or explanations as to why the MOFCOM believed that the attached conditions would reduce or eliminate the anti-competitive effects of the merger.

#### 2.2.3.1 Structural Conditions

The MOFCOM has imposed structural conditions to address competition concerns in some mergers where there was a horizontal overlap. This includes horizontal mergers[88] and mergers with both horizontal and vertical dimensions.[89] There have been a small number of mergers in which purely structural conditions were imposed,[90] but most of the time a combination of structural and behavioural conditions

---

[85] Fei Deng and Yizhe Zhang, 'Interview with Shang Ming, Director General of the Antimonopoly Bureau under the Ministry of Commerce of the People's Republic of China' [2014] (April) *The Antitrust Source* 1 at 3, available at www.americanbar.org/content/dam/aba/publishing/antitrust_source/apr14_shang_intrvw_4_8f.pdf; ICN Merger Working Group, 'Merger Remedies Review Project', 7.

[86] Head of the Ministry of Commerce Anti-monopoly Bureau's Interpretation of the Regulation on the Imposition of Restrictive Conditions in Concentrations of Business Operators (Trial).

[87] For horizontal mergers, the MOFCOM has imposed structural remedies in six cases, behavioural remedies in eight cases, and a combination of both structural and behavioural remedies in five cases. For non-horizontal mergers, only behavioural remedies were imposed.

[88] E.g. *Pfizer/Wyeth*; *Western Digital/Hitachi*.

[89] *Mitsubishi Rayon/Lucite*; *Glencore/Xstrata*.

[90] *Panasonic/Sanyo*; *Alpha V/Savio*; *UTC/Goodrich*; *NXP/Freescale*; *Anheuser-Busch InBev/SAB Miller*; *Abbott Laboratories/St Jude Medical*.

has been used. Divestiture has been the main structural remedy used by the MOFCOM to date.

The MOFCOM's published decisions have not provided much insight into the specific competition concerns that it has sought to address with the structural conditions. Generally, in mergers where the MOFCOM has imposed structural conditions, the merged entity had a high post-merger market share and/or a position of dominance, there were high barriers to entry and the merger would increase concentration in the market and remove an effective competitive constraint. The remedy in such cases would include the divestiture of an asset to remove the horizontal overlap of concern. However, as will be discussed below, the MOFCOM has also imposed purely behavioural remedies in similar circumstances.

Several categories of assets have been subject to a divestment condition. The most commonly divested asset has been the entire business relating to a particular product.[91] That business might be a subsidiary, branch or department of any of the merging parties.[92] For example, in *Baxter/Gambro*, Baxter was required to divest its global continuous renal replacement therapy business,[93] whereas in *Panasonic/Sanyo*, the three businesses to be divested spanned both Panasonic's and Sanyo's operations.[94] Where an entire business must be divested, the MOFCOM has usually specified that the divested business includes all the tangible and intangible assets that are necessary for its viability and competitiveness.[95] The merging parties have also been required to divest an equity interest in some cases.[96] In *Panasonic/Sanyo*, Panasonic needed to decrease its capital contribution in a joint venture from 40 per cent to 19.5 per cent,[97] and in *Alpha V/Savio*, Alpha V was required to transfer its 27.9 per cent

---

[91] *Pfizer/Wyeth*; *Panasonic/Sanyo*; *Western Digital/Hitachi*; *UTC/Goodrich*; *Baxter/Gambro*; *Thermo Fisher/Life*; *NXP/Freescale*; *Abbott Laboratories/St Jude Medical*.

[92] Regulation on the Imposition of Restrictive Conditions on Concentrations of Business Operators (Trial), art. 4.

[93] *Baxter/Gambro*.

[94] The divested businesses were Sanyo's lithium coin secondary battery business, Sanyo's or Panasonic's nickel metal hydride (ordinary use) battery business at specified locations and Panasonic's nickel metal hydride (automotive use) battery business at its Shonan Japan plant: 关于附条件批准松下公司收购三洋公司反垄断审查决定的公告 [Announcement of the Anti-monopoly Review Decision to Conditionally Approve Panasonic's Acquisition of Sanyo] (People's Republic of China) Ministry of Commerce, Order No. 82, 30 October 2009 (*Panasonic/Sanyo*).

[95] *Pfizer/Wyeth*; *UTC/Goodrich*; *Baxter/Gambro*.

[96] *Panasonic/Sanyo*; *Alpha V/Savio*; *Thermo Fisher/Life*; *Anheuser-Busch InBev/SAB Miller*.

[97] *Panasonic/Sanyo*.

interest in Uster to an independent third party.[98] Other types of assets required to be divested include a specified asset (in *Glencore/Xstrata*, the Las Bambas copper project in Peru) and production capacity (in *Mitsubishi Rayon/Lucite*, 50 per cent of Lucite China's annual production capacity of methyl methacrylate for five years).

The MOFCOM has also required what are commonly known as 'fix-it-first' and 'crown jewel' provisions as part of the divestiture conditions in some decisions. Such provisions are also used by competition authorities in other jurisdictions, and may be required where a competition authority wishes to ensure that there will be a buyer for the business to be divested, so that competition is preserved.[99] Article 14 of the Trial Remedy Regulation provides that the MOFCOM may request that the merging parties identify a buyer and enter into a sales agreement before the proposed merger is implemented in certain circumstances.[100] For example, a fix-it-first remedy was required in *NXP/Freescale*, where NXP voluntarily proposed that it would divest its radio frequency power transistor business to JAC Capital and submitted a signed purchase agreement to that effect. As part of its approval of the merger, the MOFCOM required that NXP sell that business in accordance with the submitted purchase agreement and complete the divestment before completing its acquisition of Freescale.[101] Similarly, the MOFCOM approved the transactions in *Anheuser-Busch InBev/SAB Miller* and *Abbott Laboratories/St Jude Medical* on the condition that the divestitures be completed in accordance with the submitted sale and purchase agreements and within twenty-four hours and twenty days, respectively, of the completion of the notified merger.[102]

---

[98] *Alpha V/Savio*.
[99] See, e.g., US Department of Justice Antitrust Division, 'Antitrust Division Policy Guide to Merger Remedies' (June 2011), p. 9.
[100] Such circumstances are where (i) there is a high risk that the competitiveness and merchantability of the divested business may be compromised prior to the divestiture; (ii) the buyer's identity has a decisive influence upon whether the divested business can restore market competition; or (iii) a third-party claims rights over the divested business.
[101] 关于附加限制性条件批准恩智浦收购飞思卡尔全部股权案经营者集中反垄断审查决定的公告 [Announcement of the Anti-monopoly Review of Concentrations of Business Operators Decision to Impose Restrictive Conditions to the Approval of NXP's Acquisition of Freescale's Entire Share Capital] (People's Republic of China) Ministry of Commerce, Order No. 64, 25 November 2015 (*NXP/Freescale*).
[102] 关于附加限制性条件批准百威英博啤酒集团收购英国南非米勒酿酒公司股权案经营者集中反垄断审查决定的公告 [Announcement of the Anti-monopoly Review of Concentrations of Business Operators Decision to Impose Restrictive Conditions to the

The crown jewel provision was used in both *Mitsubishi Rayon/Lucite* and *Glencore/Xstrata*. A crown jewel provision is stipulated in Article 7 of the Trial Remedy Regulation. It provides that, where there is a risk that the proposed package of assets cannot be divested, the MOFCOM may require that the merging parties submit an alternative package of assets to be divested if the original divestiture is unsuccessful. In *Mitsubishi Rayon/Lucite*, the MOFCOM required the merging parties to sell 100 per cent of Lucite China if they were unable to sell 50 per cent of Lucite China's annual production capacity of methyl methacrylate to one or more independent parties within six months.[103] Similarly, in *Glencore/Xstrata*, if Glencore was unable to sell its entire interest in Las Bambas by certain dates, Glencore would be required to appoint a divestiture trustee to auction its entire interest in one of four other designated assets.[104]

Ancillary conditions have been attached to accompany and support the implementation of the divestiture. The MOFCOM has required the appointment of a trustee to either carry out the divestment[105] or supervise the implementation of the remedies overall.[106] In some cases, the merging parties were required to maintain and operate the business to be divested separately and independently to the remainder of the merged entity pending divestment.[107]

### 2.2.3.2 Behavioural Conditions

While the Trial Remedy Regulation and other AML implementing regulations largely focus on structural conditions (and divestiture in particular), in practice, behavioural conditions have been imposed more frequently. Behavioural conditions have been used in a majority of the

---

Approval of Anheuser-Busch InBev's Acquisition of Shares in SABMiller] (People's Republic of China) Ministry of Commerce, Order No. 38, 29 July 2016 (*Anheuser-Busch InBev/SAB Miller*); 关于附加限制性条件批准雅培公司收购圣犹达医疗公司股权案经营者集中反垄断审查决定的公告 [Announcement of the Anti-monopoly Review of Concentrations of Business Operators Decision to Impose Restrictive Conditions to the Approval of Abbott Laboratories' Acquisition of Shares in St Jude Medical] (People's Republic of China) Ministry of Commerce, Order No. 88, 30 December 2016 (*Abbott Laboratories/St Jude Medical*).

[103] 中华人民共和国商务部公告(2009年第28号) [Announcement of the Ministry of Commerce of the People's Republic of China (No. 28 of 2009)] (People's Republic of China) Ministry of Commerce, Order No. 28, 24 April 2009.
[104] *Glencore/Xstrata*. [105] *Pfizer/Wyeth; Alpha V/Savio; Thermo Fisher/Life*.
[106] *Western Digital/Hitachi; UTC/Goodrich; Glencore/Xstrata; Baxter/Gambro*.
[107] *Mitsubishi Rayon/Lucite; Panasonic/Sanyo; UTC/Goodrich; Baxter/Gambro; Thermo Fisher/Life; NXP/Freescale*.

mergers conditionally approved by the MOFCOM to date. In non-horizontal mergers, only behavioural conditions have been imposed. In contrast to the preferences and enforcement practices of other competition agencies, who generally prefer to use structural over behavioural conditions in horizontal mergers and usually only impose behavioural conditions in vertical mergers, the MOFCOM has often applied purely behavioural conditions to address its concerns in horizontal mergers.[108]

There is little guidance provided in the AML and the implementing regulations on the form and content of behavioural conditions. As noted above, the MOFCOM provides examples such as the granting of access to infrastructure including networks or platforms, the licensing of relevant technologies and the termination of exclusive agreements. In practice, the MOFCOM has imposed a much broader range of conditions modifying the behaviour of the parties concerned. Further, to assist the MOFCOM to monitor the parties' implementation of the conditions, it has increasingly required the merging parties to appoint a monitoring trustee to oversee the performance of the conditions (or reserved its right to appoint such a trustee)[109] and/or to provide periodic reports to the MOFCOM directly or the monitoring trustee on its compliance with the conditions.[110] The duration of the behavioural conditions has ranged from twelve months[111] to ten years,[112] and, in some cases, the conditions seem to apply indefinitely.[113]

(i) **Supply or Access Commitment** The most common type of behavioural remedy imposed by the MOFCOM has required the merged entity to supply or provide customers with access to a particular product, asset or information. This condition has been imposed in both horizontal and

---

[108] *InBev/Anheuser-Busch; Novartis/Alcon; Uralkali/Silvinit; Seagate/Samsung; Marubeni/Gavilon; MediaTek/MStar; NiMH Battery Joint Venture; Nokia/Alcatel-Lucent.*
[109] *Novartis/Alcon; Uralkali/Silvinit; Seagate/Samsung; Henkel/Tiande; Western Digital/Hitachi; Google/Motorola Mobility; Wal-Mart/Newheight; Glencore/Xstrata; Marubeni/Gavilon; Baxter/Gambro; MediaTek/MStar; Thermo Fisher/Life; Microsoft/Nokia; Merck/AZ Electronics; NiMH Battery Joint Venture; NXP/Freescale.*
[110] *General Motors/Delphi; Uralkali/Silvinit; Seagate/Samsung; Henkel/Tiande; Western Digital/Hitachi; Google/Motorola Mobility; Glencore/Xstrata; Marubeni/Gavilon; Baxter/Gambro; MediaTek/MStar; Microsoft/Nokia; Merck/AZ Electronics; NiMH Battery Joint Venture; Nokia/Alcatel-Lucent.*
[111] *Seagate/Samsung.* [112] *Thermo Fisher/Life.*
[113] *InBev/Anheuser-Busch; General Motors/Delphi; Uralkali/Silvinit; General Electric/Shenhua; Henkel/Tiande; Wal-Mart/Newheight; Microsoft/Nokia; NiMH Battery Joint Venture.*

non-horizontal mergers. For example, in *General Motors/Delphi*, Delphi was required to continue supplying auto parts to Chinese automotive manufacturers,[114] and in *Henkel/Tiande*, the merged entity had to supply ethyl cyanoacetate to downstream customers.[115] Other products that merging parties have been required to supply include potassium chloride;[116] copper, lead and zinc concentrate;[117] nickel metal hydride car batteries;[118] and SSP kits and SDS-PAGE protein standards.[119] The supply or access obligation has not been restricted to tangible goods; it has also applied to intellectual property (patents[120] and mobile operating systems[121]) and technology-related information.[122]

The merging parties have often been required to provide such supply or access on particular terms. The most frequent terms are supply or access on a non-discriminatory or fair, reasonable and non-discriminatory (FRAND) basis,[123] or in a manner consistent with current (that is, pre-merger) practice.[124] In a small number of cases, the MOFCOM also constrained the freedom of the merging parties to determine the price, volume or mode of such supply or access. For example, in *Uralkali/Silvinit*, the merged entity was required to continue to supply potassium chloride to China via both rail and sea.[125] The merged firm in *Thermo Fisher/Life* was required to supply SSP kits and SDS-PAGE protein standards to third parties either on an original equipment manufacturer basis or by granting a perpetual and non-exclusive licence to use

---

[114] 关于附条件批准美国通用汽车公司收购德尔福公司反垄断审查决定的公告 [Announcement of the Anti-monopoly Review Decision to Conditionally Approve General Motors' Acquisition of Delphi] (People's Republic of China) Ministry of Commerce, Order No. 76, 28 September 2009 (*General Motors/Delphi*).

[115] 关于附加限制性条件批准汉高香港与天德化工组建合营企业经营者集中反垄断审查决定的公告 [Announcement of the Anti-monopoly Review of Concentrations of Business Operators Decision to Impose Restrictive Conditions to the Approval of the Establishment of a Joint Venture between Hong Kong Henkel and Tiande] (People's Republic of China) Ministry of Commerce, Order No. 6, 9 February 2012 (*Henkel/Tiande*).

[116] *Uralkali/Silvinit*.   [117] *Glencore/Xstrata*.   [118] *NiMH Battery Joint Venture*.
[119] *Thermo Fisher/Life*.   [120] *Microsoft/Nokia*; *Google/Motorola Mobility*.
[121] *Google/Motorola Mobility*.   [122] *ARM Joint Venture*.
[123] *General Motors/Delphi*; *Henkel/Tiande*; *Google/Motorola Mobility*; *ARM Joint Venture*; *Microsoft/Nokia*; *NiMH Battery Joint Venture*.
[124] *General Motors/Delphi*; *Uralkali/Silvinit*; *Google/Motorola Mobility*; *Microsoft/Nokia*.
[125] 关于附条件批准乌拉尔开放型股份公司吸收合并谢尔维尼特开放型股份公司反垄断审查决定的公告 [Announcement of the Anti-monopoly Review Decision to Conditionally Approve Uralkali's Merger with Silvinit] (People's Republic of China) Ministry of Commerce, Order No. 33, 2 June 2011 (*Uralkali/Silvinit*).

the technology relating to these products. The MOFCOM also placed limits on the prices that the merged firm in *Thermo Fisher/Life* could charge for these products in China.[126] Similarly, the merged entity in *Glencore/Xstrata* was required to supply Chinese customers with an annual minimum volume of copper concentrate under long-term contracts, and a portion of that minimum volume had to be priced at a particular benchmark price.[127] In *Microsoft/Nokia*, the royalty rates for the program patent licences could not exceed those that existed prior to the merger or which were stipulated in existing licensing agreements.[128]

The MOFCOM's decisions do not provide information or explain why requiring access or supply would address its concerns about the anticompetitive harm arising from the proposed merger. However, a couple of observations on this matter can be drawn by examining the theories of harm adopted by the MOFCOM in these decisions. Where this condition was imposed in vertical mergers, the common underlying concern was that the merged entity would try to extend its dominance from one market into a vertically-related market by changing the way that it supplied or provided access, or by supplying or providing that access in a way that harmed competitors in that vertically-related market. In contrast, where the condition was imposed in horizontal mergers, the concern seemed to vary. In *Uralkali/Silvinit*, the greater control that the merged entity would have had over imports into China was identified as the anti-competitive harm,[129] whereas in the *NiMH Battery Joint Venture*, the MOFCOM was concerned that the joint venture would not supply nickel metal hydride batteries to automotive manufacturers other than Toyota.[130] No specific supply or access issue leading to competition concerns was raised in the MOFCOM's decision concerning *Thermo Fisher/Life*.

**(ii) Long-term Hold-separate Commitment** The MOFCOM has used a quasi-structural remedy requiring the merged entity to maintain and

---

[126] *Thermo Fisher/Life*. [127] *Glencore/Xstrata*. [128] *Microsoft/Nokia*.
[129] *Uralkali/Silvinit*.
[130] 商务部关于附加限制性条件批准科力远、丰田中国、PEVE、新中源、丰田通商拟设立合营企业案经营者集中反垄断审查决定的公告 [Announcement of the Anti-monopoly Review of Concentrations of Business Operators Decision to Impose Restrictive Conditions to the Approval of the Establishment of a Joint Venture among Hunan Corun New Energy, Toyota China, PEVE, Changshu Sinogy Venture Capital, and Toyota Tsusho] (People's Republic of China) Ministry of Commerce, Order No. 49, 2 July 2014 (*NiMH Battery Joint Venture*).

operate a designated business unit as a separate and independent entity for a period of time. This is commonly referred to as a 'hold-separate' remedy, and other competition agencies have generally used it in conjunction with divestiture to 'prevent interim competitive harm and to preserve the viability and competitiveness of the assets pending divestiture'.[131] The MOFCOM has followed this practice and has required the hold-separate remedy in some cases where divestiture was required, as noted above.[132] In addition, the MOFCOM has imposed the hold-separate remedy as a long-term standalone remedy in cases where it believed that divestiture was not possible and behavioural conditions were unable to fully address the competition concerns arising from the proposed merger.[133] However, the MOFCOM acknowledges that this is an experimental remedy that will not be widely adopted, and that its effects need to be monitored.[134]

The long-term hold-separate remedy has been applied in four horizontal mergers to date. In each of *Seagate/Samsung* and *Western Digital/ Hitachi*, the merging parties were required to maintain their hard disk drive businesses as independent competitors. The acquired hard disk drive business had to be maintained as a separate legal entity with independent pricing, sales, products, research and development and business operations, and the merging parties were required to implement protective measures to prevent the exchange of competitively sensitive information.[135] Similar conditions were attached to the MOFCOM's approval in *Marubeni/Gavilon* and *MediaTek/MStar*. The merging parties in *Marubeni/Gavilon* had to maintain their businesses exporting and selling soybeans to China as separate and independent businesses,[136]

---

[131] 'Frequently Asked Questions about Merger Consent Order Provisions' (Answer to Question 40), US Federal Trade Commission, available at www.ftc.gov/tips-advice/competition-guidance/guide-antitrust-laws/mergers/merger-faq#Hold%20Separate%20Orders.
[132] *Mitsubishi Rayon/Lucite*; *Panasonic/Sanyo*; *Alpha V/Savio*; *UTC/Goodrich*.
[133] 蒋安杰 [Jiang Anjie], 中外专家为反垄断法实施建言献策—第三届中国竞争政策论坛综述 [Chinese and Foreign Experts Offer Advice and Suggestions on Anti-monopoly Law Implementation – The Third Forum on China Competition Policy], 法制日报 [*Legal Daily*], 28 May 2014, available at http://epaper.legaldaily.com.cn/fzrb/content/20140528/Articel09002GN.htm. The MOFCOM Anti-monopoly Bureau Director-General Shang Ming has also stated that the long-term hold separate remedy is designed and imposed after consulting with the merging parties and undertaking legal and economic analysis. He believes that the long-term hold separate remedy is not in conflict with Chinese or other countries' laws, and that it is economically viable.
[134] Ibid.    [135] *Seagate/Samsung*; *Western Digital/Hitachi*.    [136] *Marubeni/Gavilon*.

and, in *MediaTek/MStar*, MStar Taiwan (which retained its liquid crystal display television control chip business) was maintained as a separate competitor and legal entity.[137] The parties were allowed to apply to the MOFCOM for release from the hold-separate requirement after a period of time (twelve months for *Seagate/Samsung*, twenty-four months for *Western Digital/Hitachi* and *Marubeni/Gavilon* and three years for *MediaTek/MStar*). In all of these cases, the independent business reported to a monitoring trustee.

Examining the remedies imposed and competition problems identified in *Seagate/Samsung*, *Western Digital/Hitachi* and *MediaTek/MStar*, it seems that the MOFCOM aimed to preserve the pre-merger market structure and pattern of competition by ensuring that the important competitor – which would otherwise have been eliminated by the merger – remained in existence, while still enabling the merger to occur. In *Marubeni/Gavilon*, the remedy appears to address the MOFCOM's concern that Marubeni would increase its ability to export soybeans to China through integration with Gavilon's abilities in soybean procurement, warehousing and logistics in North America. Unfortunately, the MOFCOM did not discuss or explain why these concerns could not have been adequately addressed with behavioural conditions or why divestiture was not feasible.

(iii) **Terminate an Existing Agreement** A divestment-like behavioural remedy was imposed in *Novartis/Alcon* and *Baxter/Gambro*. In each merger, the merged entity was required to terminate an existing agreement with its main competitor in the relevant market. There was an exclusive distribution agreement between Novartis's subsidiary, Shanghai Ciba Vision Trading, and Hydron, its largest competitor in the contact lens care products market. Baxter had an outsourcing production agreement with Nipro, its main competitor in the Chinese haemodialysis dialyser market. The MOFCOM raised concerns in both decisions that the agreements might facilitate coordination on competition factors between the merged entity and its competitor, and thereby harm competition.[138]

---

[137] 关于附加限制性条件批准联发科技股份有限公司吸收合并开曼晨星半导体公司经营者集中反垄断审查决定的公告 [Announcement of the Anti-monopoly Review of Concentrations of Business Operators Decision to Impose Restrictive Conditions to the Approval of MediaTek's Merger with MStar Semiconductor] (People's Republic of China) Ministry of Commerce, Order No. 61, 26 August 2013 (*MediaTek/MStar*).

[138] *Novartis/Alcon*; *Baxter/Gambro*.

Thus, applying remedial measures in these cases removed that medium for potential coordination.

**(iv) Limit Market Expansion** The MOFCOM has also imposed behavioural conditions constraining the merging parties' ability to expand their market presence in China. The activities that the MOFCOM has sought to restrict include increasing an existing minority equity interest in certain competitors;[139] acquiring certain competitors or manufacturers of a particular product;[140] constructing a factory in China to manufacture a particular product;[141] and entering (or re-entering) specific markets in China.[142] For example, in *Novartis/Alcon*, Novartis was prevented from re-launching a product that it had already decided would exit the Chinese market or from selling the same product under a different brand name in China.[143] In most of these cases, the merged entity was required to obtain the MOFCOM's prior consent before it could undertake the transaction. The exception was *Wal-Mart/Newheight*, where Wal-Mart was prohibited from engaging in a value-added telecommunications services (VATS) business through Newheight without first obtaining the appropriate licence, which is granted by the Ministry for Industry and Information Technology (MIIT).[144]

The MOFCOM has not provided clear grounds or explanations as to why this type of behavioural condition was required to eliminate harm to competition in these mergers. In *Novartis/Alcon*, it seemed that the MOFCOM was concerned about the anti-competitive harm that might result if Novartis did not maintain its strategy of exiting the ophthalmic anti-inflammatory and anti-infective compound product market. It stated that if Novartis had decided to exit the ophthalmic anti-inflammatory and anti-infective compound product market for this merger and, post-merger, it was able to re-launch the product, this could lead to anti-competitive effects in China if its market share then reached

---

[139] *InBev/Anheuser-Busch*.
[140] *InBev/Anheuser-Busch*; *Mitsubishi Rayon/Lucite*; *MediaTek/MStar*.
[141] *Mitsubishi Rayon/Lucite*.     [142] *Novartis/Alcon*; *Wal-Mart/Newheight*.
[143] *Novartis/Alcon*.
[144] 关于附加限制性条件批准沃尔玛公司收购纽海控股33.6%股权经营者集中反垄断审查决定的公告 [Announcement of the Anti-monopoly Review of Concentrations of Business Operators Decision to Impose Restrictive Conditions to the Approval of Wal-Mart's Acquisition of 33.6 Per cent Equity Interest in Newheight (Shanghai)] (People's Republic of China) Ministry of Commerce, Order No. 49, 13 August 2012 (*Wal-Mart/Newheight*).

a certain level.[145] In *Wal-Mart/Newheight*, the remedy did not relate to the market that the MOFCOM had defined as being relevant (which was the business-to-consumer online sales market in China). Rather, the condition was directed at potential harm to competition in the VATS market, which was a market that the MOFCOM found could be related to the merger.[146] In *InBev/Anheuser-Busch*, *Mitsubishi Rayon/Lucite* and *MediaTek/MStar*, no competition problems were raised that specifically related to the merged entity's potential expansion activities in the future.

**(v) Prevent Exclusive Dealing and Tying or Bundling Conduct** The MOFCOM has conditioned some of its merger approvals on requiring the merging parties not to force customers or suppliers into certain transactions or dealings. In effect, the MOFCOM has prevented merging parties from engaging in exclusive dealing or tying or bundling conduct.

Exclusive dealing was relevant in *Seagate/Samsung* and *Western Digital/Hitachi*. The merging parties in both cases were prevented from forcing their customers to exclusively buy their brands of hard disk drive. In addition, Seagate was not allowed to prevent or restrict a specific supplier from selling to others. However, the decisions did not clarify why this was a concern for the MOFCOM, as they centred primarily on the potential coordinated effects arising from each merger.[147] Similarly, in *General Motors/Delphi*, the MOFCOM required Delphi to cooperate with its customers' reasonable requests to switch suppliers. In its decision, the MOFCOM expressly stated its concern that Delphi would not cooperate with requests from Chinese automotive manufacturers to change auto parts suppliers or would delay acting on those requests; hence the condition imposed directly corresponded to this concern.[148]

Tying and bundling conduct was also addressed in some mergers. In *General Electric/Shenhua*, Shenhua was not permitted to condition its supply of coal for coal-water slurry gasification (where Shenhua was the largest supplier) on use of the joint venture's technology,[149] and in *Merck/AZ Electronics*, the MOFCOM required the merged entity not to

---

[145] *Novartis/Alcon*.    [146] *Wal-Mart/Newheight*.
[147] *Seagate/Samsung*; *Western Digital/Hitachi*.    [148] *General Motors/Delphi*.
[149] 关于附条件批准通用电气(中国)有限公司与中国神华煤制油化工有限公司设立合营企业反垄断审查决定的公告 [Announcement of the Anti-monopoly Review Decision to Conditionally Approve the Establishment of a Joint Venture between General Electric (China) and Shenhua] (People's Republic of China) Ministry of Commerce, Order No. 74, 10 November 2011 (*GE/Shenhua*).

bundle sales compelling Chinese customers to purchase liquid crystal products and photoresist at the same time.[150] In both cases, the MOFCOM's theory of harm was based on foreclosure effects, whereby the parties' advantage in one market would be leveraged into another market. The restriction on tying would therefore be directed at eliminating these foreclosure effects. In *Microsoft/Nokia*, where the MOFCOM was concerned that the merger would change the seller's (Nokia) profit incentives, the MOFCOM required Nokia not to tie the licensing of its standard essential patents (SEPs) to the licensing of its patents that were not subject to a FRAND obligation.[151]

(vi) **Constrain the Exercise of Rights** Some behavioural remedies imposed by the MOFCOM have constrained a merging party from exercising its shareholder rights. In *Panasonic/Sanyo*, the MOFCOM was concerned that Panasonic would use its position in its nickel-metal hydride (automotive use) battery joint venture with Toyota to weaken competition. The imposed remedy therefore addressed this concern by requiring that Panasonic waive some of the shareholder rights (voting, appointing directors and veto powers) that it enjoyed in relation to the joint venture.[152] To support the hold-separate remedy, MediaTek was not allowed to exercise its shareholder rights in MStar Taiwan during the hold-separate period, other than to receive dividends, to receive information on the consolidated financial statements of the listed company, and to conditionally appoint directors.[153]

The MOFCOM also limited the situations where a merging party could seek an injunction or exclusion order to enforce intellectual property rights in *Microsoft/Nokia* and *Nokia/Alcatel-Lucent*. Both mergers involved SEPs and non-SEPs in the telecommunications industry. In *Microsoft/Nokia*, Microsoft was prevented from seeking injunctive relief to enforce SEPs on Android phones produced by Chinese manufacturers, and where Microsoft wished to seek an injunction to enforce non-SEPs, it could only do so where the potential licensee did not negotiate for the licence in good faith.[154] In *Nokia/Alcatel-Lucent*, Nokia committed not to enforce SEPs through injunctions to prevent the implementation of FRAND standards, unless the potential licensee did not enter into the licence in good faith or comply with FRAND

---

[150] *Merck/AZ Electronics.*   [151] *Microsoft/Nokia.*   [152] *Panasonic/Sanyo.*
[153] *MediaTek/MStar.*   [154] *Microsoft/Nokia.*

license terms.[155] In terms of the anti-competitive harm that the remedies were designed to eliminate, the remedies appear to be linked to the MOFCOM's concern that, post-merger, the parties would have incentives to increase their patent-licensing fees.

#### 2.2.3.3 Review, Variation and Revocation of Restrictive Conditions

Restrictive conditions may be reviewed, varied or revoked upon application by a party, or initiated by the MOFCOM itself.[156] When reviewing a request for variation or revocation, the Trial Remedy Regulation provides that the MOFCOM will consider whether the merging parties have undergone any material change, whether the competition conditions in the relevant market have substantially changed, whether it is unnecessary or impossible to implement the restrictive conditions and other factors.[157] A decision to vary or revoke a restrictive condition must be published.[158]

To date, the MOFCOM has varied the remedies imposed in three mergers (*Google/Motorola Mobility*, *Seagate/Samsung* and *Western Digital/Hitachi*) and released Wal-Mart from the commitments it made in its 2012 acquisition of Newheight. In *Google/Motorola Mobility*, *Seagate/Samsung* and *Western Digital/Hitachi*, the original conditional approval had stipulated that the merging parties could apply to the MOFCOM for release from the conditions or variation. Whereas Google would be required to show that market conditions had changed or that it had ceased to control Motorola Mobility,[159] no specified grounds were expressly stipulated for either Seagate or Western Digital to apply for variation or release.[160] In contrast, there was no provision for revocation or variation in *Wal-Mart/Newheight*.[161]

---

[155] 关于附加限制性条件批准诺基亚收购阿尔卡特朗讯股权案经营者集中反垄断审查决定的公告 [Announcement of the Anti-monopoly Review of Concentrations of Business Operators Decision to Impose Restrictive Conditions to the Approval of Nokia's Acquisition of Shares in Alcatel-Lucent] (People's Republic of China) Ministry of Commerce, Order No. 44, 19 October 2015 (*Nokia/Alcatel-Lucent*).

[156] Regulation on the Imposition of Restrictive Conditions on Concentrations of Business Operators (Trial), arts. 25–26.

[157] Ibid., art. 27.    [158] Ibid., art. 28.

[159] 关于附加限制性条件批准谷歌收购摩托罗拉移动经营者集中反垄断审查决定的公告 [Announcement of the Anti-monopoly Review of Concentrations of Business Operators Decision to Impose Restrictive Conditions to the Approval of Google's Acquisition of Motorola Mobility] (People's Republic of China) Ministry of Commerce, Order No. 25, 19 May 2012 (*Google/Motorola Mobility*).

[160] *Seagate/Samsung*; *Western Digital/Hitachi*.    [161] *Wal-Mart/Newheight*.

The MOFCOM granted Google's application and released it from the requirement to treat all original equipment manufacturers on a non-discriminatory basis in matters relating to the Android platform. This was because Google had sold Motorola Mobility's smartphone business to Lenovo in October 2014. No further competition analysis was conducted by the MOFCOM in coming to its decision. The MOFCOM noted that, even though Google no longer manufactured smart mobile devices, it nonetheless continued to own Motorola Mobility's communication technology patents and confirmed that Google remained bound by the other conditions attached to its original merger approval.[162]

Seagate and Western Digital each applied for release from their respective hold-separate obligations and from the requirement to determine production capacity according to market conditions.[163] The MOFCOM took a very similar approach when considering both applications. It reviewed each party's compliance with the restrictive conditions and engaged in some competition analysis. The competition analysis consisted of examining changes in market conditions and competition and assessing the reasons for and the effect of releasing the party from the commitments. It also engaged a third-party consultant to conduct economic analysis.

The MOFCOM reached slightly different decisions on both applications. Whereas Seagate's application was granted and it was released from both conditions, the MOFCOM released Western Digital from its hold-separate commitment only insofar as it related to production and research and development activities, but required it to continue maintaining independent product brands and sales. There seemed to be two main reasons for the divergent outcomes. First, the MOFCOM found that, while the competitive landscape had not changed significantly since 2012 – the identity and number of competitors had remained unchanged – Western

---

[162] 关于解除谷歌收购摩托罗拉案部分义务的公告 [Announcement of the Partial Release of Commitments Relating to Google's Acquisition of Motorola Mobility] (People's Republic of China) Ministry of Commerce, Order No. 2, 6 January 2015.

[163] 关于变更希捷科技公司收购三星电子有限公司硬盘驱动器业务经营者集中限制性条件的公告 [Announcement of the Variation to the Restrictive Conditions Imposed on Seagate Technology's Acquisition of the Hard Disk Drive Business of Samsung Electronics] (People's Republic of China) Ministry of Commerce, Order No. 43, 19 October 2015; 关于变更西部数据收购日立存储经营者集中限制性条件的公告 [Announcement of the Variation to the Restrictive Conditions Imposed on Western Digital's Acquisition of Hitachi] (People's Republic of China) Ministry of Commerce, Order No. 41, 19 October 2015.

Digital, HGST (the hard disk drive business acquired by Western Digital) and Seagate were still the key competitors in the storage market, whereas Samsung (whose hard disk drive business was acquired by Seagate) was now relatively weaker. Second, the MOFCOM believed that allowing Western Digital and HGST to integrate production and research and development would help Western Digital reduce its costs and enable its full participation in the market. At the same time, the MOFCOM found that maintaining competition between the independent sales teams and product brands of two of the main competitors in the storage market would help to reduce the anti-competitive effects of the merger.

In deciding to grant Wal-Mart's application, the MOFCOM's main considerations were changes in the competitive conditions in the market and the acquired business. It concluded that the barriers to entry into the VATS market had significantly decreased due to policy and regulatory changes, and that the market was much more competitive in 2016 than it had been in 2012. The MOFCOM also found that the acquired party, Yihaodian, had become less competitive as its revenue growth rate had slowed down, it had not materially increased its market share and it had gradually lost its competitive advantage. On this basis, the MOFCOM determined that an anti-competitive effect would be unlikely if Wal-Mart was released from those conditions.[164]

The MOFCOM has also reviewed a merged firm's compliance with its restrictive conditions. In 2014, the MOFCOM initiated an investigation into Western Digital's compliance with the hold-separate commitments and fined Western Digital RMB 600,000 for breaching the condition in two ways.[165]

### 2.2.4 Merger Prohibition

As noted earlier, a merger will be prohibited if it results in or may result in the elimination or restriction of competition, and the merging parties do not submit remedies that sufficiently eliminate the anti-competitive

---

[164] 关于解除沃尔玛收购纽海控股33.6%股权经营者集中限制性条件的公告 [Announcement of the Release of Restrictive Conditions Imposed on Wal-Mart's Acquisition of 33.6 per cent Equity Interest in Newheight (Shanghai)] (People's Republic of China) Ministry of Commerce, Order No. 23, 30 May 2016.

[165] 商务部行政处罚决定书 [Ministry of Commerce Administrative Penalty Decision] (People's Republic of China) Ministry of Commerce, Order No. 787, 2 December 2014; 商务部行政处罚决定书 [Ministry of Commerce Administrative Penalty Decision] (People's Republic of China) Ministry of Commerce, Order No. 788, 2 December 2014.

effects or do not prove that its positive effects outweigh its negative effects or that the merger is in the public interest. Some examples of mergers that might satisfy the public interest requirement include mergers in national economic lifeline and national security industries that promote development, employment, technological advancement and international competitiveness.[166]

To date, the MOFCOM has prohibited the implementation of two mergers: *Coca-Cola/Huiyuan* and *P3 Shipping Alliance*. In both cases, the MOFCOM found that the proposed remedies submitted by the parties (of which there were several rounds) were insufficient to fully eliminate the anti-competitive effects arising from the proposed merger.[167] In particular, the MOFCOM noted in *P3 Shipping Alliance* that the remedies 'lacked sufficient legal basis and convincing evidentiary support'.[168] However, it did not go on to provide further analysis or explanation as to why the proposed remedies were inadequate. The MOFCOM also held that the parties in each case had not proven that the positive effects of the merger outweighed its negative effects, or that the proposed merger was consistent with public interest. However, the MOFCOM did not discuss what, if any, evidence and arguments were presented by the parties on these points; nor did it provide its analysis or evaluation of such information.

## 2.3 Non-Merger Conduct

Apart from mergers, the AML also prohibits monopoly agreements (*longduanxieyi*, also known as anticompetitive agreements), abuses of dominance (*lanyong shichangzhipei diwei*) and abuses of administrative power (*lanyong xingzhengquanli*, also known as administrative monopoly).

---

[166] 全国人大常委会法制工作委员会经济法室 [Economic Law Division of the Legal Affairs Commission of the Standing Committee of the National People's Congress (ed.)], 中华人民共和国反垄断：法条文说明、立法理由及相关规定 [The Anti-monopoly Law of the People's Republic of China: Explanation of the Articles, Legislative Reasons, and Related Regulations] (北京大学出版社 [Peking University Press], 2007), p. 186.

[167] 关于禁止可口可乐公司收购中国汇源公司审查决定的公告 [Announcement of the Review Decision to Prohibit Coca-Cola's Acquisition of Huiyuan] (People's Republic of China) Ministry of Commerce, Order No. 22, 18 March 2009 (*Coca-Cola/Huiyuan*); 关于禁止马士基、地中海航运、达飞设立网络中心经营者集中反垄断审查决定的公告 [Announcement of the Anti-monopoly Review of Concentrations of Business Operators Decision to Prohibit the Establishment of a Network Centre by AP Møller-Maersk, MSC Mediterranean Shipping Company, and CMA CGM] (People's Republic of China) Ministry of Commerce, Order No. 46, 17 June 2014 (*P3 Shipping Alliance*).

[168] *P3 Shipping Alliance*.

Responsibility for public enforcement of the AML against monopoly agreements and abuse of dominance is divided between the National Development and Reform Commission (NDRC) and the State Administration for Industry and Commerce (SAIC). The NDRC is responsible for the price-related aspects and the SAIC for the non-price-related aspects of such conduct. Where necessary, the NDRC and the SAIC can delegate enforcement responsibilities to their provincial-level authorities. For the abuse of administrative power, it is the superior authority of the relevant administrative organ that is responsible for enforcement; the NDRC's and the SAIC's roles are limited to making a non-binding recommendation to that superior authority on how to handle the case under the AML.[169]

In the first three years of enforcement, the NDRC and the SAIC largely focused on preparing implementing regulations and capacity-building. The cases announced during these initial years tended to involve enforcement actions taken by local authorities against small domestic companies. Since then, the number of non-merger enforcement actions taken by both competition authorities, at the central and local levels, has gradually increased. The NDRC increased its staff numbers at the central level, undertook some high-profile investigations into foreign and Chinese companies and imposed some significant fines. In the period from 2011 to 2015, the NDRC investigated ninety-seven price-related anti-monopoly cases and imposed aggregate sanctions of RMB 10.397 billion. Of these cases, seventy-six involved monopoly agreements, thirteen related to abuse of dominance and eight were administrative monopoly cases.[170] While the SAIC has been generally less active and high-profile than the NDRC in AML enforcement, it too has increased its enforcement activities over time. Since handing down its first decision in January 2011, the SAIC has published forty-eight administrative penalty decisions covering monopoly agreements and abuse of dominance, and it is currently investigating Microsoft for potential AML-related infringements. The SAIC stated that as at 31 December 2015, it had investigated sixty AML cases since the AML came into effect;[171] by October 2015,

---

[169] Anti-monopoly Law, art. 51.
[170] 十二五"期间反价格垄断取得重大进展 [During the Twelfth Five-Year Plan, Anti-Price Monopoly Made Significant Progress] (3 April 2016) 中华人民共和国国家发展和改革委员会 [National Development and Reform Commission] available at www.sdpc.gov.cn/xwzx/xwfb/201603/t20160304_791938.html.
[171] 工商部门迄今查办垄断案60件 [SAIC Investigates 60 Anti-monopoly Cases to Date], 法制日报 [Legal Daily], 27 April 2016, available at http://epaper.legaldaily.com.cn/fzrb/content/20160427/Articel04006GN.htm.

it had completed its investigation in twenty-three of those cases and stopped its investigation in four.[172] It is unclear, however, whether the remaining cases are still under investigation, suspended or closed. While the NDRC has enforced the AML against a range of entities (foreign and domestic, public and private, organisations and individuals), the SAIC has focused its investigations on the activities of industry associations and domestic companies.[173] For investigations where decisions have been published, catalysts for initiating investigations have included media reports, referrals from local government authorities, complaints from customers and competitors, the adoption of regulatory measures by central government authorities and self-reporting from the infringing parties themselves.

At the NDRC, both its central and local authorities have investigated and made decisions under the AML. The NDRC Bureau of Price Supervision and Anti-monopoly (NDRC Bureau), the NDRC department responsible for AML enforcement at the central level, has tended to handle investigations involving conduct that is regional, national or international in scope, whereas the cases handled by the NDRC's provincial-level authorities have generally involved anti-competitive conduct engaged in by local companies or which have local impact. In contrast, most of the SAIC's investigations and decisions have been made by its local offices. The SAIC Antimonopoly and Anti-Unfair Competition Enforcement Bureau (SAIC Bureau), the SAIC department at the central level responsible for the AML, has largely focused on developing and issuing AML implementing regulations and providing enforcement guidance to its local offices.[174] The reliance of the NDRC, and especially the SAIC, on local bureaus to enforce the AML might be, in part, due to the limited resources available at the central level.

---

[172] 陈立彤, 顾正平 [Chen Litong and Gu Zhengping], 工商局首次处罚不配合反垄断调查公司的警示 [First Time SAIC Punishes Company for Non-Cooperation with Antimonopoly Investigation], 财新网 [Caixin], 21 January 2016, available at http://opinion.caixin.com/2016-01-21/100902263.html.

[173] 张晓松 [Zhang Xiaosong], 工商总局副局长谈反垄断法实施5年案件查办等情况 [SAIC Deputy Director Discusses Anti-monopoly Law Investigations and Other Matters in the 5 Years of Implementation], 新华社 [Xinhua News Agency], 29 July 2013, available at www.gov.cn/jrzg/2013-07/29/content_2457600.htm.

[174] Hao Qian, 'The Multiple Hands: Institutional Dynamics of China's Competition Regime' in Adrian Emch and David Stallibrass (eds.), *China's Anti-monopoly Law: The First Five Years* (Alphen aan den Rijn, The Netherlands: Kluwer Law International, 2013), p. 31.

For violations of the monopoly agreement and abuse of dominance provisions of the AML, the NDRC and the SAIC can order the investigated party to stop the illegal conduct and can confiscate illegal gains and impose fines (1–10 per cent of the party's aggregate turnover in the previous year, or a maximum of RMB 500,000 where a monopoly agreement has not been implemented).[175] When determining the fine amount, the AML provides that the competition authority should consider factors such as the nature, seriousness and duration of the illegal conduct.[176] In particular, for monopoly agreements, if a participant to such an agreement reports that conduct to the competition authority and provides important evidence, it may be exempt from penalty or have its penalty reduced.[177] In addition, an industry association involved with the making and/or implementation of a monopoly agreement can be fined up to RMB 500,000.[178] Alternatively, instead of imposing sanctions, the NDRC or the SAIC may decide to suspend an investigation upon the receipt of suitable commitments from the investigated party, and then terminate the investigation after the successful implementation of those commitments.[179]

In practice, enforcement outcomes have included imposing fines, confiscating illegal gains, issuing warnings or cautions, ordering the cessation of illegal conduct, requiring the implementation of corrective measures or suspending or terminating the investigation with the offering of commitments. The relevant factors in determining the type and quantum of sanctions imposed have included the seriousness of the conduct and resultant harm, the party's role in the illegal conduct, whether the party had voluntarily stopped the illegal conduct, the party's level of cooperation with the investigation (including whether it had provided evidence or other information), whether the party voluntarily took measures to rectify the conduct and/or mitigate its effects and how much a party benefited from illegal conduct. Further, apart from the AML, the competition authorities have also referred to the Administrative Penalty Law[180] and the NDRC's Administrative Regulation on Penalties for Pricing Violations[181] in making their decisions.

---

[175] Anti-monopoly Law, arts. 46–47.   [176] Ibid., art. 49.   [177] Ibid., art. 46.
[178] Ibid.   [179] Ibid., art. 45.
[180] 中华人民共和国行政处罚法 [Administrative Penalty Law of the People's Republic of China] (People's Republic of China) National People's Congress, 17 March 1996.
[181] 价格违法行为行政处罚规定 [Administrative Regulation on Penalties for Pricing Violations] (People's Republic of China) State Council, 29 November 2010.

Unlike the MOFCOM, which is required to publish its conditional and prohibition merger decisions, there is no obligation on the NDRC or the SAIC to publish their decisions. Nonetheless, the NDRC and the SAIC have both made some of their decisions publicly available. The SAIC has committed to publishing all AML decisions made by it and its local authorities on an 'anti-monopoly decision publication platform' on its website.[182] As of 31 December 2016, the SAIC had published forty-eight administrative penalty decisions, a list of which is provided in Appendix B. The NDRC has also made some of its AML investigations and decisions public. However, unlike the SAIC, it has not committed to publishing all of its AML decisions; there is no central portal or platform where AML decisions made by the NDRC and its local price authorities are published, and decisions and related information (such as case statistics) seem to be released on an ad hoc basis. A number of the AML decisions have been published on the NDRC's website, while others have been published on the website of the local price authority that conducted the investigation, or announced during presentations at conferences or workshops or during interviews with media outlets. Further, in contrast to the SAIC, most of the NDRC's decisions have been made public via press release and not through the release of the administrative penalty decision. A list of the decisions and investigations believed to have been made by the NDRC, as of 31 December 2016, is provided in Appendix B.

Similar to the MOFCOM's merger decisions, the decisions published by the SAIC and especially the NDRC have been relatively brief and provide limited insight into their analysis and decision-making. Generally, a decision sets out the timeline of the key events in the investigation, the facts of the case (which comprise most of the decision) and the authority's findings. The SAIC (but not the NDRC) also provides a list of the evidence it relied upon in making its decision and has often addressed the defences and arguments for exemption raised by the investigated parties. In the relatively few cases in which the competition authorities have engaged in competition analysis, such analysis has been quite brief. In particular, where the competitive impact of a monopoly agreement has been considered, there is no clarity from the decisions as to where such analysis is most relevant, as consideration of competitive effect has occurred in the context of determining the existence,

---

[182] 张晓松 [Zhang Xiaosong], 工商总局公布12起垄断案件 [SAIC Publishes 12 AML Cases], Xinhua, 29 July 2013, available at http://politics.people.com.cn/n/2013/0729/c70731-22369568.html.

prohibition or exemption of a monopoly agreement. In cases where an investigated party committed to implementing corrective measures, there was no explanation or discussion as to why or how those commitments were able to address competition concerns or mitigate the effect of the anti-competitive conduct. The decisions also do not explain why a particular type or level of sanction was imposed, although the grounds upon which a penalty reduction or exemption was granted are provided. Therefore, caution must be exercised regarding the extent to which findings or conclusions may be elicited from the decisions about the Chinese competition authorities' analytical approach to assessing the competitive effect of non-merger conduct.

### 2.3.1 Monopoly Agreements

The AML prohibits certain categories of monopoly agreements made between competitors (horizontal agreements) and between a business operator and its trading partner (vertical agreements). Article 13 of the AML provides that monopoly agreements that fix or change prices, restrict output or sales volume or allocate sales markets or raw material purchasing markets – examples of what are commonly known as 'hard-core' cartels and also prohibited in other jurisdictions – are prohibited by the AML, along with horizontal monopoly agreements that restrict the purchase of new technology or equipment, restrict the development of new technology or product or collectively boycott. Vertical monopoly agreements that fix the resale price or restrict the minimum resale price (commonly referred to as resale price maintenance in other countries) are prohibited by Article 14 of the AML. Other types of monopoly agreements may also be prohibited by the competition authority.[183] However, agreements entered into for certain objectives may be exempt from the application of Articles 13 and 14 of the AML.[184] To gain the benefit of the exemption, generally the parties to the agreement must also prove that the agreement will not substantially restrict competition in the relevant market and will enable consumers to share in the benefits derived from the agreement.

In enforcement, most of the NDRC's investigations and decisions relating to monopoly agreements have involved price fixing and resale price maintenance conduct, whereas the SAIC has focused on market

---

[183] Anti-monopoly Law, arts. 13(6), 14(3).   [184] Ibid., art. 15.

sharing conduct and has not yet made any decisions relating to vertical monopoly agreements. The different emphasis of these two competition authorities is consistent with the division of responsibility between the NDRC and the SAIC along price-related and non-price-related lines, respectively. Further, whereas price-related vertical monopoly agreements are specifically prohibited by the AML, non-price-related vertical monopoly agreements (for example, exclusive dealing) are not, and neither of the implementing regulations adopted by the NDRC or the SAIC have yet expanded the prohibition of vertical monopoly agreements to cover non-price-related behaviour. It should also be noted that most of the NDRC's and the SAIC's decisions have dealt with horizontal and vertical monopoly agreements separately. However, in its decisions involving manufacturers and dealers in the automobile industry, the NDRC found that the facts gave rise to both horizontal and vertical monopoly agreements.

### 2.3.1.1 Determining Monopoly Agreements

A monopoly agreement is an agreement, decision or other concerted practice that eliminates or restricts competition.[185] A monopoly agreement may be reached among business operators or organised by industry associations, and an agreement or decision may be either written or oral.[186] Notably with respect to industry associations, in addition to organising for their members to reach and/or implement a monopoly agreement, the industry association might itself formulate and issue documents (such as articles of association, rules, decisions, notices or standards) that eliminate or restrict competition.[187] Regarding the requirement that the agreement, decision or concerted practice eliminate or restrict competition, it should be noted that neither the AML nor the implementing regulations expressly specify that such elimination or restriction of competition be significant or substantial.

---

[185] Ibid., art. 13.
[186] 工商行政管理机关禁止垄断协议行为的规定 [Regulation of the Administration for Industry and Commerce on the Prohibition of Monopoly Agreements] (People's Republic of China) State Administration for Industry and Commerce, Order No. 53, 31 December 2010, arts. 2, 9; 反价格垄断规定 [Anti-Price Monopoly Regulation] (People's Republic of China) National Development and Reform Commission, Order No. 7, 29 December 2010, art. 9.
[187] Regulation of the Administration for Industry and Commerce on the Prohibition of Monopoly Agreements, art. 9; Anti-Price Monopoly Regulation, art 9.

To date, the question of what constitutes a monopoly agreement has not yet been examined in great depth by the NDRC or the SAIC in their decisions or enforcement practice. Most decisions have either not addressed the issue at all or have simply concluded that a monopoly agreement had been reached and/or implemented with no further explanation or reference to the facts. In those decisions where the NDRC and the SAIC did consider the issue more closely,[188] the conduct that constituted the agreement, the type of monopoly agreement reached and/or implemented and the restriction and/or elimination of competition arising from the agreement were important factors in the finding of the existence of a monopoly agreement. In addition, in cases involving horizontal agreements, the competition authority made it clear that the monopoly agreement was made between competitors, even in cases where it was the industry association that was ultimately sanctioned and not the participants to the agreements themselves.

(i) **Agreement, Decision and Concerted Practice** Written or oral agreements have been the most common basis upon which the competition authorities have found a monopoly agreement. Typically, these agreements have been formal written agreements reached and signed by the investigated parties, whether organised themselves[189] or through an industry association.[190] Agreed price lists, documents issued by an industry association (for example, notices, rules and guidelines) and oral agreements and understandings made in meetings and via telephone calls have also been sufficient to constitute a monopoly agreement. The mechanisms that the investigated parties had in place to ensure compliance with the monopoly agreement (such as financial penalties, reporting requirements, payment of bond moneys and restricting supply) were also considered.

There have been two cases in which a monopoly agreement was founded on concerted practices. The SAIC defines concerted practices to be 'coordinated conduct, in practice, between parties without express

---

[188] *Yongzhou New Car Insurance Cartel*; *Changde New Car Insurance Cartel*; *Chenzhou New Car Insurance Cartel*; *Yibin Shale Brick Cartel*; *Panyu Animation Expo Cartel*; *Yongzhou Commercial Concrete Cartel*; *Jiangxi Coinsurance Cartel*; *Allopurinol Tablet Cartel*; *Infant Formula RPM*; *Lens Manufacturers RPM*; *Dongfeng Nissan Cartel and RPM*; *Anhui Payment Encryption Device Cartel*.

[189] Examples include cooperation agreements, coinsurance agreements, partnership agreements and distribution agreements.

[190] Examples include self-discipline agreements and conventions.

written or oral agreement or decision'.[191] While the NDRC does not define concerted practices, the two authorities seem to adopt a largely similar approach to determining whether concerted practices exist. Both authorities look at whether there is uniform conduct and intentional contact or information exchange between the parties, as well as the market situation.[192] In addition, the SAIC will take into account whether there is a reasonable explanation for the uniform conduct.[193] In the *Chifeng Fireworks and Firecracker Cartel* case, the SAIC's local authority in Inner Mongolia determined that, in the absence of a written agreement, the investigated parties had engaged in concerted action due to their adoption of similar measures to implement a regulatory framework that divided the wholesale distribution of fireworks and firecrackers into management zones.[194] It concluded that the wholesalers had actively organised and engaged in conduct that divided the wholesale firework and firecracker market in breach of Article 13(3) of the AML and Article 2 of the SAIC's Regulation on the Prohibition of Monopoly Agreements.[195] It should be noted, however, that the decision did not consider whether there was intentional contact among the wholesalers, and the Inner Mongolian authority found that the relevant regulation (which might otherwise have been regarded as a reasonable explanation for the conduct) had not prevented the wholesalers from supplying

---

[191] Regulation of the Administration for Industry and Commerce on the Prohibition of Monopoly Agreements, art. 2.
[192] Ibid., arts. 2–3; Anti-Price Monopoly Regulation, art. 6.
[193] Regulation of the Administration for Industry and Commerce on the Prohibition of Monopoly Agreements, art. 3.
[194] 关于赤峰中心城区烟花爆竹批发企业以行政机关限定为由实施垄断行为的处罚决定 [Administrative Penalty on Fireworks and Firecracker Wholesale Businesses in Chifeng City Centre for Implementing Monopoly Agreement by Reason of Administrative Restriction] (People's Republic of China) Inner Mongolia Autonomous Region Administration for Industry and Commerce, Order No. 1, 27 May 2014 (*Chifeng Fireworks and Firecracker Cartel*). The local production safety supervision and administration bureau divided the district into management zones. One wholesaler was designated as the supplier for each zone; retailers could only purchase products from the designated wholesaler in their area, and wholesalers were prohibited from supplying into other zones. The wholesalers were also delegated responsibility for administering a retailer licensing regime. The wholesalers organised training for retailers, administered the retailers' licensing regime, applied anti-counterfeit labels to their own products, confiscated products from other sources and conducted market investigations. Some wholesalers also imposed unreasonable terms such as requiring the prepayment of orders and minimum purchase requirements.
[195] Regulation of the Administration for Industry and Commerce on the Prohibition of Monopoly Agreements.

retailers in other areas. Similarly, in the *Anhui Payment Encryption Device Cartel* case, the SAIC's local authority in Anhui found that the parties had engaged in concerted conduct by adopting similar measures to implement the market sharing plan organised by the local branch of the People's Bank of China. The authority also determined that there was intentional contact among the parties because they participated in meetings organised by the local People's Bank of China branch where the market sharing plan was agreed upon and discussed.[196]

**(ii) Types of Monopoly Agreements** The decisions also provide insight into the types of pricing and non-pricing behaviour that fall within the Article 13 and 14 prohibitions.

To date, Article 13 of the AML has been enforced mainly to target price fixing and market sharing, with some cases relating to output restriction,[197] bid rigging[198] and collective boycotts.[199] These are all forms of hard-core cartel conduct. As noted above, price fixing, market sharing, output restriction and collective boycotts are specifically and expressly prohibited under Article 13 of the AML, whereas bid rigging is not. Instead, Article 7(4) of the NDRC's Anti-Price Monopoly Regulation may apply to bid rigging. In enforcement, however, bid rigging was held to contravene Article 13 of the AML as price fixing and market sharing conduct,[200] and not Article 7(4) of the Anti-Price Monopoly Regulation.

For price fixing, both the NDRC's Anti-Price Monopoly Regulation and enforcement practice confirm that the AML prohibits not only agreements to directly fix prices at a particular level, but also a wider range of arrangements that directly or indirectly impact on price. According to the Anti-Price Monopoly Regulation, price fixing encompasses agreements that fix or change price levels, ranges of price change and other price-related charges (such as fees or discounts); that set an agreed price as a basis for transacting with third parties; that adopt pricing formulae; and that require consent from a third party to change

---

[196] 安徽信雅达等三家密码器企业垄断协议案 [Three Encryption Device Businesses Monopoly Agreement Case] (People's Republic of China) Anhui Administration for Industry and Commerce, Order No. 9, 4 November 2016.
[197] *Zhejiang Paperboard Cartel*; *Liaoning Cement Clinker Cartel*; *Yibin Shale Brick Cartel*; *Chifeng Fireworks and Firecracker Cartel*; *Mayang Miao Autonomous County Shale Brick Cartel*.
[198] *Roll On/Roll Off Shipping Cartel*; *Allopurinol Tablet Cartel*.
[199] *Panyu Animation Expo Cartel*; *Estazolam Tablet Cartel*.
[200] *Roll On/Roll Off Shipping Cartel*; *Allopurinol Tablet Cartel*.

prices, as well as other forms of disguised price fixes or changes.[201] In enforcement, the NDRC has focused on agreements that set prices (which include commission rates, rebates and discounts) at particular levels (both minimum prices as well as specific prices), keep prices within a particular range (such as specifying suitable deviations from a guidance price) or increase prices by a certain amount.

With respect to market sharing, the prohibition in the AML applies expressly to both sales markets and raw material-purchasing markets.[202] In particular, the SAIC's Regulation on the Prohibition of Monopoly Agreements specifies that the prohibition applies to the division of a market along territory, product, volume, customer or supplier lines, and the purchase of semi-finished products, parts, components, equipment and other raw materials.[203] To date, nearly all of the SAIC's published decisions pertaining to market sharing have related to sales markets, with a majority of those cases involving participants allocating markets according to market shares,[204] and a few cases where allocation was made according to production volume,[205] territory[206] or customer.[207] Further, there is one decision in which the SAIC's local authority in Jiangxi investigated and sanctioned cartel participants for allocating the market according to, *inter alia*, functional level. In the *Taihe Bulk LPG Cartel* case, an agreement was made among seven operators at different levels in the bulk liquefied petroleum gas market. They agreed that one operator would distribute liquefied petroleum gas, one operator would sell bulk liquefied petroleum gas in Taihe and one operator would sell bulk liquefied petroleum gas to the rural areas surrounding Wanhe, and the four remaining operators agreed to stop their liquefied petroleum gas businesses in the county.[208]

---

[201] Anti-Price Monopoly Regulation, art. 7.   [202] Anti-monopoly Law, art. 13(3).
[203] Regulation of the Administration for Industry and Commerce on the Prohibition of Monopoly Agreements, art. 5.
[204] *Cixi Energy Saving Testing Cartel; Yongzhou New Car Insurance Cartel; Changde New Car Insurance Cartel; Jiangshan Commercial Concrete Cartel; Shangyu Commercial Concrete Cartel; Wuhan Coinsurance Cartel; Wuhan New Car Insurance Cartel.*
[205] *Liangyungang Ready-Mix Concrete Cartel; Mayang Miao Autonomous County Shale Brick Cartel; Yongzhou Commercial Concrete Cartel.*
[206] *Taihe Bulk LPG Cartel; Chifeng Fireworks and Firecracker Cartel; Roll On/Roll Off Shipping Cartel.*
[207] *Wuxi Quarry Cartel; Roll On/Roll Off Shipping Cartel; Anhui Payment Encryption Device Cartel.*
[208] 江西省泰和县液化石油气经营者从事垄断协议案 [Jiangxi Province Taihe County Liquified Petroleum Gas Monopoly Agreement Case] (People's Republic of China)

Decisions involving vertical monopoly agreements have all concerned conduct in which manufacturers fixed the resale prices,[209] or restricted or fixed the minimum resale prices,[210] of their distributors or retailers. The prohibition has applied to retail and wholesale prices, recommended prices coupled with punishments for deviation from recommended prices, advertised prices, gross margins, discounts or other promotions and ultimate selling prices. It should be noted that the competition authorities have not yet, in their enforcement practice, extended the prohibition in Article 14 of the AML to cover non-price vertical monopoly agreements, which is consistent with the AML and the implementing regulations. As noted above, the SAIC has not yet taken enforcement action to address vertical monopoly agreements. In the *Wuliangye RPM* case, while the NDRC's local bureau in Sichuan found that Wuliangye had punished distributors for selling below minimum price, across regions and across channels, it regarded the regional and channel restrictions as a means to implement the minimum resale price rather than as standalone breaches of Article 14 of the AML.[211]

### 2.3.1.2 Prohibiting Monopoly Agreements

Whereas the AML distinguishes between horizontal and vertical monopoly agreements, it does not expressly differentiate between those monopoly agreements that are prohibited outright (*per se* prohibitions) and those that will be evaluated by weighing their pro- and anti-competitive effects (also referred to as the 'rule of reason').[212] Instead, the NDRC

---

Jiangxi Province Administration for Industry and Commerce, Order No. 1, 1 April 2011 (*Taihe Bulk LPG Cartel*).

[209] *Tianlu Dairy RPM*; *Shanghai Chrysler Cartel and RPM*; *FAW-Volkswagen and Audi Cartel and RPM*; *Dongfeng Nissan Cartel and RPM*; *Smith & Nephew RPM*.

[210] *Moutai RPM*; *Wuliangye RPM*; *Infant Formula RPM*; *Lens Manufacturers RPM*; *Mercedes-Benz Cartel and RPM*; *Hanook Tire RPM*; *Haier RPM*; *SAIC General Motors RPM*; *Speed Fresh RPM*.

[211] Sichuan Development and Reform Commission, 五粮液公司实施价格垄断被处罚2.02亿元 [Wuliangye Fined RMB 202 Million for Implementing Price Monopoly] (News Release, 22 February 2013).

[212] For agreements between competitors, it is quite common in a number of developed competition law jurisdictions (such as the United States, United Kingdom, European Union, and Australia) to prohibit hardcore cartels *per se* and assess other horizontal agreements for their competitive effects. For vertical agreements, the situation varies across jurisdictions, with some (such as the European Union, Australia and South Africa) prohibiting some vertical restraints (usually resale price maintenance) outright and subjecting other vertical arrangements to a competition test, whereas the United States, for example, adopts a rule of reason test for all vertical arrangements. See Einer

believes that a 'prohibition and exemption' approach to horizontal and vertical monopoly agreements is adopted under the AML.[213] Xu Kunlin, the Director-General of the NDRC Bureau from 2008 to 2015, stated that such an approach gives consideration to both the illegality (through the prohibition) and the reasonableness (through exemptions) of monopoly agreements, and that it was not necessary to apply the labels of 'per se' or 'rule of reason' to monopoly agreements.[214]

The decisions of the NDRC and the SAIC have not provided much clarity on what this 'prohibition and exemption' approach entails. In particular, the authorities have been unclear about the basis upon which a monopoly agreement may be prohibited in practice. In a majority of cases, the fact that a monopoly agreement existed was sufficient to conclude that it was prohibited.

There were a few cases in which the competition authority did engage in an examination (although generally limited and brief) of the impact of the monopoly agreement on competition before concluding that the monopoly agreement was prohibited.[215] In relation to horizontal monopoly agreements, the authorities' concerns tended to centre on three types of harms: to customers, to competitors and their incentives to compete and to competition more broadly. Apart from higher prices and lower quality, the authorities were concerned that horizontal agreements would restrict or deprive customers of their choice of suppliers and of their ability to enjoy the benefits of competition. The competition agencies also found that horizontal agreements may prevent businesses from competing due to the creation of artificial barriers to entry, the limitations placed on the contracting parties' freedom to compete and the exclusion of businesses not party to the agreement from competition. Horizontal agreements also eliminated direct competition between competitors, which might weaken competitors' incentives to compete by

---

Elhauge and Damien Geradin, *Global Competition Law and Economics*, 2nd edn (Oxford: Oxford University Press, 2011), pp 735, 743, 772–3.

[213] 许昆林 [Xu Kunlin], 宽大政策适用于纵向垄断协议 [Leniency Policy Applies to Vertical Monopoly Agreements], 中国经济导报 [China Economic Herald], 31 October 2013, available at www.ceh.com.cn/xwpd/2013/10/255896.shtml.

[214] Ibid.

[215] *Taihe Bulk LPG Cartel*; *Anyang Used Car Service Fees Cartel*; *Yongzhou New Car Insurance Cartel*; *Chenzhou New Car Insurance Cartel*; *Zhangjiajie New Car Insurance Cartel*; *Jiangshan Commercial Concrete Cartel*; *Yibin Shale Brick Cartel*; *Xishuangbanna Tourism Cartel*; *Zhejiang New Car Insurance Cartel*; *Chifeng Fireworks and Firecracker Cartel*; *Mayang Miao Autonomous County Shale Brick Cartel*; *Jiangxi Coinsurance Cartel*; *Estazolam Tablet Cartel*; *Anhui Payment Encryption Device Cartel*.

innovating and improving product quality and service. More generally, horizontal agreements were found to result in the suboptimal allocation of resources, harm to the competitive structure of the market and loss of the 'survival of the fittest' mechanism in competition, and also prevented the healthy development of businesses, the market and the industry.

The competitive effects of vertical monopoly agreements were considered briefly in a few cases involving resale price maintenance. For example, in the *Wuliangye RPM* and *Infant Formula RPM* cases, the elimination of intrabrand competition, the restriction of interbrand competition and the harm to consumer interest resulting from higher prices and no opportunity to purchase lower-priced products were the identified competition concerns that led to the competition authority's conclusion that the monopoly agreement contravened Article 14 of the AML.[216]

### 2.3.1.3 Exempting Monopoly Agreements

The second limb of the 'prohibition and exemption' approach to monopoly agreements under the AML is consideration of whether the monopoly agreement may be exempt under Article 15 of the AML. So far, no party has successfully made the case for exemption of their monopoly agreement.

As noted above, Article 15 of the AML provides that monopoly agreements entered into for certain objectives may be exempt. Such objectives include improving techniques or researching and developing new products; improving product quality, lowering costs, enhancing efficiency, unifying product specifications and standards and implementing competitive advantages; improving the operational efficiency and competitiveness of small- and medium-sized businesses; pursuing public interest objectives such as conserving energy, environmental protection and disaster relief; mitigating severe decreases in sales volume or excessive capacity during economic downturn; and protecting legitimate interests in foreign trade and economic cooperation. For objectives other than protecting legitimate interests in foreign trade and economic cooperation, to gain the benefit of exemption the parties to the agreement must also prove that the agreement will not substantially restrict competition

---

[216] Sichuan Development and Reform Commission, 'Wuliangye Fined RMB 202 Million'; National Development and Reform Commission, 合生元等乳粉生产企业违反《反垄断法》限制竞争行为共被处罚6.6873亿元 [Biostime and Other Infant Formula Producers Restricted Competition and Violated the Anti-monopoly Law, Fined a Total of RMB 668.73m] (News Release, 7 August 2013).

in the relevant market and will enable consumers to share in the benefits derived from the agreement. No further explanation or details on the content of the objectives themselves, or what it means for consumers to share in the benefits derived from the agreement, have been provided in the implementing regulations or other documents issued by the competition authorities.

In practice, the issue of exemption has been considered as a general matter and not on specific grounds. This seems to reflect the fact that, in most of the decisions published to date, the investigated parties have made a general case for exemption under Article 15 rather than arguing that their monopoly agreement was made for a specified purpose under Article 15. In the *Yongzhou New Car Insurance Cartel* and *Chenzhou New Car Insurance Cartel* cases, the parties' arguments bore no real relation to the objectives stated in Article 15 and seemed to be general appeals for a lighter penalty.[217] In the *Liaoning Cement Clinker Cartel* and *Panyu Animation Expo Cartel* cases, the parties argued that the monopoly agreements were made for objectives that were somewhat analogous or related to those listed in Article 15.[218] In the two decisions

---

[217] In the *Yongzhou New Car Insurance Cartel*, the industry association argued that the monopoly agreement had operated only for a short period of time and had not been implemented well: 湖南省永州市保险行业协会组织本行经营者从事垄断协议案 [Hunan Province Yongzhou City Insurance Industry Association Monopoly Agreement Case] (People's Republic of China) Hunan Province Administration for Industry and Commerce, Order No. 1, 30 November 2012 (*Yongzhou New Car Insurance Cartel*). In the *Chenzhou New Car Insurance Cartel*, the industry association argued that there was no intention to act illegally, the monopoly agreement had no adverse effect and the investigation should be handled carefully because of its impact on thousands of families: 湖南省郴州市保险行业协会组织本行经营者从事垄断协议案 [Hunan Province Chenzhou City Insurance Industry Association Monopoly Agreement Case] (People's Republic of China) Hunan Province Administration for Industry and Commerce, Order No. 3, 3 December 2012 (*Chenzhou New Car Insurance Cartel*).

[218] In the *Liaoning Cement Clinker Cartel*, the parties argued that losses had occurred in the entire industry due to malicious competition and dumping by businesses, and that stopping production over winter for maintenance would regulate excess production, save resources and ensure production quality: 关于辽阳冀东水泥有限公司协议垄断经营行为的处罚决定 [Administrative Penalty on Liaoning Jidong Cement Monopoly Agreement Conduct] (People's Republic of China) Liaoning Province Administration for Industry and Commerce, Order No. 2, 13 August 2012 (*Liaoning Cement Clinker Cartel*). In the *Panyu Animation Expo Cartel*, the industry association argued that the purpose of the monopoly agreement was to promote the legitimate and reasonable planning of expos, and that the agreement did not eliminate or restrict competition or have any effect or substantial harm on the industry, industry operators or related operators or businesses: 广州市番禺动漫游艺行业协会垄断协议案 [Guangdong Panyu Animation and Entertainment Industry Association Monopoly Agreement Case]

published to date which have involved a claim for exemption of a monopoly agreement based on a specific ground under Article 15 of the AML (the *Anyang City Used Car Service Fees Cartel* and the *Jiangshan Commercial Concrete Cartel*), the parties relied upon Article 15(3) of the AML (improving the operational efficiency and competitiveness of small- and medium-sized businesses).[219] One reason given by the competition authorities for denying a claim for exemption has been that the investigated party did not sufficiently show that the basis for the claim was valid or justified, although they provided no elaboration or information on how a party might be able to demonstrate the validity of their claim.

The most common reason given for refusing to grant a claim for exemption was that the monopoly agreement restricted competition. This is consistent with the requirement in Article 15 of the AML that the parties must prove that the agreement would not substantially restrict competition even if made for one of the specified objectives. The competition issues considered in the context of exemption have not been substantially different to those looked at when determining whether the monopoly agreement is prohibited. The authorities identified similar adverse effects arising from the monopoly agreement: elimination of competition between businesses in the market and fewer incentives to compete; higher prices for consumers; increased costs for other businesses; damage to the competition mechanism and order; harm to the interests of businesses in related industries; and harm to consumer interest. Additionally, in two published decisions, the SAIC specifically looked at competitive harm in terms of the objectives listed in Article 15. In the *Cixi Energy Saving Testing Cartel*, the SAIC's local authority in Zhejiang concluded that the parties had not innovated or improved their testing techniques, equipment, instruments, efficiency or industry standards.[220]

---

(People's Republic of China) Guangdong Province Administration for Industry and Commerce, Order No. 1, 9 May 2015 (*Panyu Animation Expo Cartel*).

[219] 河南省安阳市旧机动车经营者从事垄断协议案 [Henan Province Anyang City Used Car Operators Monopoly Agreement Case] (People's Republic of China) Henan Province Administration for Industry and Commerce, Order No. 1, 4 January 2012 (*Anyang Used Car Service Fees Cartel*); 浙江省江山市混凝土经营者从事垄断协议案 [Zhejiang Province Jiangshan City Concrete Businesses Monopoly Agreement Case] (People's Republic of China) Zhejiang Province Administration for Industry and Commerce, Order No. 16, 14 December 2012 (*Jiangshan Commercial Concrete Cartel*).

[220] 浙江省慈溪市建设工程检测协会组织本行业经营者从事垄断协议案 [Zhejiang Province Cixi City Construction Quality Assurance Industry Association Monopoly Agreement

Similarly, the SAIC's authority in Hunan stated that the parties had not made significant improvements relating to the objectives listed in Article 15 of the AML in the *Mayang Miao Autonomous County Shale Brick Cartel*.[221] However, despite the express stipulation in Article 15 that a monopoly agreement made for an objective listed in Article 15 of the AML would only lose the benefit of that exemption where it substantially restricted competition, it has been unclear whether substantiality is required in practice. The competition authorities have been inconsistent in their published decisions, with some decisions noting that the restriction of competition was serious,[222] whereas no such mention was made in other decisions.[223]

The requirement that the consumer should be able to share in the benefits derived from the agreement for it to qualify for exemption has not been considered in detail by the competition authorities in their published decisions.

In May 2016, the NDRC released a draft guideline on the exemption of monopoly agreements for public consultation. This draft exemption guideline provides information on the procedures relating to the application and review of exemption requests, the materials to be provided in the exemption application, the factors relevant to whether a monopoly agreement falls within the conditions for exemption, the factors relevant to assessing the competitive impact of the agreement, the types of benefits generated from the agreement that are relevant to whether consumers can share in the benefits arising from the agreement and procedures and requirements surrounding exemption consultations.[224]

---

Case] (People's Republic of China) Zhejiang Province Administration for Industry and Commerce, Order No. 15, 14 March 2013 (*Cixi Energy Saving Testing Cartel*).

[221] See, e.g., 麻阳苗族自治县页岩砖经营者垄断案 [Mayang Miao Autonomous Region Shale Brick Businesses Monopoly Case] (People's Republic of China) Hunan Province Administration for Industry and Commerce, Order No. 1, 5 January 2015 (*Mayang Miao Autonomous County Shale Brick Cartel*).

[222] *Yongzhou New Car Insurance Cartel*; *Changde New Car Insurance Cartel*; *Chenzhou New Car Insurance Cartel*; *Mayang Miao Autonomous County Shale Brick Cartel*.

[223] *Cixi Energy Saving Testing Cartel*; *Zhangjiajie New Car Insurance Cartel*; *Jiangshan Commercial Concrete Cartel*; *Panyu Animation Expo Cartel*.

[224] 国务院反垄断委员会关于垄断协议豁免一般性条件和程序的指南 （征求意见稿） [State Council Anti-monopoly Commission Guideline on General Conditions and Procedures for the Exemption of Monopoly Agreements (Consultation Draft)] (People's Republic of China) National Development and Reform Commission, 12 May 2016, available at http://jjs.ndrc.gov.cn/fjgld/201605/t20160512_801559.html.

Once finalised, the guideline will be adopted by the AMC and will apply to both the NDRC and the SAIC.

#### 2.3.1.4 Leniency Policy

As noted above, a party to a monopoly agreement may be exempt from penalty or have its penalty reduced if it voluntarily reports the conduct to the competition authority and provides important evidence.[225] Important evidence is evidence that plays a key role in the competition authority's determination of the existence of a monopoly agreement,[226] or, in the case of the SAIC, helps it to initiate an investigation.[227] It may include information on the parties to the agreement, the products involved, the form and content of the agreement and specific details about the implementation of the agreement.[228]

The NDRC applies the leniency policy equally to horizontal and vertical agreements.[229] This stands in contrast to the approach taken in a number of other jurisdictions, such as the United States, where leniency is only available in relation to horizontal agreements.[230] In the NDRC's view, parties who voluntarily report vertical monopoly agreements and provide important evidence should also benefit from the leniency policy, because horizontal and vertical agreements are treated the same under the AML, vertical agreements are difficult to detect and it facilitates enforcement.[231] The SAIC, on the other hand, has not definitively stated whether it would use the leniency policy for both horizontal and vertical monopoly agreements. However, as noted above, the prohibition against vertical agreements has not yet been extended to cover non-price conduct and all of the SAIC's published decisions to date involving monopoly agreements have been horizontal agreements.

The NDRC has used the leniency policy in a number of its published decisions relating to horizontal and vertical monopoly agreements.[232]

---

[225] Anti-monopoly Law, art. 46.
[226] Regulation of the Administration for Industry and Commerce on the Prohibition of Monopoly Agreements, art. 11.
[227] Ibid.   [228] Ibid.
[229] Xu, 'Leniency Policy Applies to Vertical Monopoly Agreements'.
[230] In the United States, the leniency policy applies to horizontal agreements only: Scott D. Hammond and Belinda A. Barnett, 'Frequently Asked Questions Regarding the Antitrust Division's Leniency Program and Model Leniency Letters' (US Department of Justice, 19 November 2008) available at www.justice.gov/atr/public/criminal/239583.htm.
[231] Xu, 'Leniency Policy Applies to Vertical Monopoly Agreements'.
[232] *China Paper and Cardboard Box Packaging Cartel*; *Guangdong Sea Sand Cartel*; *Infant Formula RPM*; *Zhejiang New Car Insurance Cartel*; *Lens Manufacturers RPM*; *Japanese*

Some legal practitioners also observe that the NDRC has often used leniency to encourage cooperation from parties in an AML investigation.[233] There were also media reports that the NDRC Bureau actively met with a number of foreign companies to encourage them to voluntarily report violations of the AML.[234] Some commentators speculate that the NDRC's frequent application of the leniency policy is due to its limitations in resources, competition law knowledge, legal analytical capabilities and enforcement capabilities, and that it is easier for the NDRC to enforce the AML with the cooperation of and admissions from investigated parties.[235] The leniency policy has been used with much less frequency by the SAIC. Of its published decisions relating to monopoly agreements to date, only one (concerning a horizontal market sharing agreement) has involved the application of the leniency policy.[236]

Once the conditions of leniency are satisfied, a party may be exempt from penalty or have the penalty reduced. The NDRC's Regulation on Anti-Price Monopoly Administrative Enforcement Procedures provides that the first party to voluntarily report the monopoly agreement to the NDRC and provide important evidence may be exempted from penalty.[237] In its published decisions to date, where the NDRC has used the leniency policy, the first-in-line applicant has generally been exempt from penalty; the exception is the *Guangdong Sea Sand Cartel* case, in which the whistleblower (who was also one of the organisers of the cartel)

---

*Auto Parts Cartel; Japanese Ball Bearings Cartel; FAW-Volkswagen and Audi RPM and Cartel; Mercedes-Benz Cartel and RPM; Roll On/Roll Off Shipping Cartel.*
[233] John Yong Ren and Jet Zhisong Deng, 'Developments in Anti-monopoly Agreement Enforcement and Suggestions Regarding Compliance Programs in China' [2013] (2) *CPI Antitrust Chronicle* 1 at 3; 'China's NDRC and SAIC Intensify Non-Merger Antitrust Enforcement', Freshfields Bruckhaus Deringer, 24 October 2013, available at www.freshfields.com/en/knowledge/China%E2%80%99s_NDRC_and_SAIC_Intensify_Non-merger_Antitrust_Enforcement; David Livdahl et al., 'NDRC's Recent Enforcement of the PRC Anti-monopoly Law: A More Aggressive and Transparent Direction', *China Matters: Paul Hastings' Newsletter for Investing and Operating in the People's Republic of China*, 25 April 2013, 2, available at www.paulhastings.com/publications-items/details?id=9311de69-2334-6428-811c-ff00004cbded.
[234] Michael Martina, 'Exclusive: Tough-Talking China Pricing Regulator Sought Confessions from Foreign Firms', Reuters, 21 August 2013, available at www.reuters.com/article/2013/08/21/us-china-antitrust-idUSBRE97K05020130821.
[235] See, e.g., ibid.   [236] *Yongzhou Commercial Concrete Cartel*.
[237] 反价格垄断行政执法程序规定 [Regulation on Anti-Price Monopoly Administrative Enforcement Procedures] (People's Republic of China) National Reform and Development Commission, Order No. 8, 29 December 2010, art. 14.

was given a 50 per cent penalty reduction.[238] For parties that are the second or subsequent in line to make a leniency application, the NDRC has stated that it may grant the second party a penalty reduction of at least 50 per cent and subsequent parties a maximum penalty reduction of 50 per cent.[239] In practice, the penalty reduction granted to the second-in-line applicant has been 60–90 per cent, and to the third-in-line applicant, 30–45 per cent. The NDRC has also granted penalty exemptions to multiple parties in the same investigation. In the *Infant Formula RPM* case, three of the nine companies investigated were exempt from administrative sanction for voluntarily reporting the monopoly agreement to the NDRC, providing important evidence and voluntarily and actively implementing corrective measures.[240] Similarly, in the *Lens Manufacturers RPM* case, which involved vertical monopoly agreements adopted by two types of lens manufacturers (glasses and contact lenses), two companies were granted exemptions from penalty; one was a glasses lens manufacturer and the other a contact lens manufacturer.[241]

A draft leniency guideline was released by the NDRC in February 2016 for public consultation. Similar to the draft exemption guideline, once finalised, the leniency guideline will be adopted by the AMC and apply to all Chinese competition agencies. This will eliminate some of the inconsistencies between the NDRC and the SAIC in their application of the leniency policy. For example, whereas the NDRC may grant leniency to a party who organised the monopoly agreement, the SAIC will not grant leniency in similar circumstances.[242] The February 2016 draft leniency guideline applies to horizontal monopoly agreements only and covers matters such as the content of and procedure for the leniency

---

[238] National Development and Reform Commission, 广东查处海砂价格垄断案件 确保国家重点工程建设顺利进行 [Guangdong Investigates Sea Sand Price Monopoly Case, Ensures Smooth Progress of Nationally Important Construction Project] (News Release, 26 October 2012).
[239] Regulation on Anti-Price Monopoly Administrative Enforcement Procedures, art. 14.
[240] National Development and Reform Commission, 'Biostime and Other Infant Formula Producers'.
[241] National Development and Reform Commission, 部分眼镜镜片生产企业维持转售价格行为被依法查处 [Resale Price Maintenance Conduct of Some Glass Lens Manufacturers Handled According to Law] (News Release, 29 May 2014).
[242] 工商行政管理机关查处垄断协议、滥用市场支配地位案件程序规定 [Regulation of the Administration for Industry and Commerce on the Procedures Relating to the Investigation of Monopoly Agreement and Abuse of Dominance Cases] (People's Republic of China) State Administration for Industry and Commerce, Order No. 42, 26 May 2009, art. 20.

application, the criteria that the applicant must satisfy to qualify for leniency, the sequencing of applications, guidance on the penalty reductions and confidentiality.[243]

### 2.3.2 Abuse of Dominance

A business operator with a dominant market position is prohibited from engaging in certain conduct that constitutes abuse of dominance. Article 17 of the AML provides that such a business operator must not sell products at unfairly high prices (also known as excessive pricing), buy products at unfairly low prices, sell products at below cost, refuse to deal with trading partners, require trading partners to deal exclusively with it or designated businesses, engage in tying conduct, impose unreasonable conditions or treat similar parties differently with respect to price and other trading conditions. However, for conduct other than unfair high pricing and buying products at unfairly low prices, the business operator will not breach the AML if it has a legitimate reason for engaging in that conduct.

While the number of published decisions relating to abuse of dominance is somewhat less than those relating to monopoly agreements, enforcement activity against conduct amounting to abuse of dominance has increased significantly since 2014. This has been the case especially for the SAIC, which has been more active than the NDRC in publishing decisions in this area. To date, most of the known investigations and published decisions relate to public utilities (water and gas),[244] statutory monopolies (tobacco and salt),[245] the telecommunications industry,[246]

---

[243] 横向垄断协议案件宽大制度适用指南 (征求意见稿) [Guideline on the Application of Leniency in Cases Involving Horizontal Monopoly Agreements (Consultation Draft)] (People's Republic of China) National Development and Reform Commission, 2 February 2016, available at http://jjs.ndrc.gov.cn/fjgld/201602/t20160203_774287.html.

[244] *Yiyuan Purified Water Unreasonable Conditions*; *Chongqing Gas Unreasonable Conditions*; *Dongfang Water Unreasonable Conditions*; *Qingdao Xinao Xincheng Gas Unreasonable Conditions*; *Alxa Zuoqi Water Unreasonable Conditions*; *Hubei Piped Natural Gas Excessive Pricing*; *Urumqi Water Exclusive Dealing*; *Suqian Yinkong Water Exclusive Dealing*.

[245] *Wuchang Salt Tying*; *Jiangsu Salt Tying*; *Chifeng Tobacco Tying*; *Pizhou Tobacco Differential Treatment*; *Fushun Tobacco Tying*; *Chifeng Salt Differential Treatment*; *Yongzhou Salt Tying*.

[246] *China Telecom/China Unicom Abuse of Dominance*; *Quanzhou Cable Television Tying*; *Ningxia Broadband Internet Tying*; *Inner Mongolia Mobile Unreasonable Conditions*; *Inner Mongolia Unicom Tying*; *Xilin Gol Radio and Television Unreasonable Conditions*.

the pharmaceutical industry[247] and intellectual property rights.[248] The SAIC has targeted public utilities and the tobacco industry, whereas the NDRC's earlier decisions relate to the salt industry, although it has more recently focused on intellectual property rights. While the SAIC's enforcement activities have mostly related to tying conduct or the imposition of unreasonable conditions, the NDRC has investigated a range of different conduct. Further, a not insignificant proportion of the published decisions relating to abuse of dominance have been suspension and/or termination decisions.[249]

Both the NDRC and the SAIC adopt a similar analytical approach to abuse of dominance, although the SAIC has been more consistent and detailed in its approach than the NDRC. The competition authorities begin by defining the relevant market, followed by a determination of whether the investigated party has a dominant market position, whether it engaged in conduct amounting to abuse of dominance and whether it had a legitimate reason for engaging in that conduct. The last step in the analysis has been, in most cases, an assessment of the effect of that conduct on competition. Decisions relating to the suspension of an abuse of dominance investigation have been less structured and detailed than decisions where the investigated party was ultimately subject to administrative sanction.

#### 2.3.2.1 Relevant Market Definition

Market definition has generally been the first analytical step taken by the competition authorities in their decisions regarding abuse of dominance. Their approach to market definition is similar to that taken by the MOFCOM in merger decisions, and is consistent with the Market Definition Guideline. The starting points for market definition have been the products, services and geographic scope of the investigated party's operations, and demand and supply-side substitution factors are considered subsequently. Such factors have included constraints imposed by licences, other laws and infrastructure required to deliver the products and services, and the preferences and actual choices made by consumers.

---

[247] *Shandong Reserprine Exclusive Agreements*; *Chongqing Qingyang Pharmaceutical Refusal to Supply*; *Chongqing Southwest Pharmaceutical Refusal to Supply*.
[248] *InterDigital Abuse of Dominance*; *Qualcomm Abuse of Dominance*.
[249] *China Telecom/China Unicom Abuse of Dominance*; *InterDigital Abuse of Dominance*; *Beijing Shankai Sports Tying*; *Ningxia Broadband Internet Tying*; *Inner Mongolia Mobile Unreasonable Conditions*; *Inner Mongolia Unicom Tying*; *Hai'an Electric Power Unreasonable Conditions*.

It should be noted that, unlike mergers, where the geographic market has generally been at least national in scope, the scope of the geographic market in abuse of dominance cases has varied widely. It has ranged from a district within a city,[250] to a city or municipality,[251] to China,[252] and even to the global market.[253] This reflects the mix in the types of business operators and conduct that the competition authorities have pursued. The SAIC has tended to investigate the suspected abuse of dominance conduct of local and domestic businesses, whereas the NDRC has investigated national or multinational businesses.

### 2.3.2.2 Determining a Dominant Market Position

A dominant market position is defined in the AML as the market position that enables a business operator to control the price, volume or other trading condition of a product in the relevant market, or to impede or affect entry into the relevant market by other businesses.[254] In making that determination, the competition authority must take into account the investigated party's market share, ability to control the sales or raw materials purchasing market and financial and technical status; the competition conditions in the market; the dependence of other businesses on the investigated party; the degree of difficulty of market entry; and other relevant factors.[255] A rebuttable presumption of dominance applies if one business operator has a 50 per cent market share, two business operators have a combined market share of 66.67 per cent or three business operators have a combined market share of 75 per cent. However, where a business operator is presumed to have dominance based on a combined market share, the presumption will not apply if its share of the market is less than 10 per cent.[256]

---

[250] *Yiyuan Purified Water Unreasonable Conditions*; *Chifeng Tobacco Tying*; *Qingdao Xinao Xincheng Gas Unreasonable Conditions*; *Alxa Zuoqi Water Unreasonable Conditions*.
[251] *Chongqing Gas Unreasonable Conditions*; *Pizhou Tobacco Differential Treatment*; *Fushun Tobacco Tying*; *Xilin Gol Radio and Television Unreasonable Conditions*.
[252] *Qualcomm Abuse of Dominance*; *Chongqing Qingyang Pharmaceutical Refusal to Supply*; *Tetra Pak Abuse of Dominance*; *Chongqing Southwest Pharmaceutical Refusal to Supply*.
[253] *Qualcomm Abuse of Dominance*.      [254] Anti-monopoly Law, art. 17.
[255] Ibid., art. 18. The SAIC has provided further explanation on each factor in its regulations: 工商行政管理机关禁止滥用市场支配地位行为的规定 [Regulation of the Administration for Industry and Commerce on the Prohibition of Abuse of Dominance Conduct] (People's Republic of China) State Administration for Industry and Commerce, Order No. 54, 31 December 2010, art. 10.
[256] Anti-monopoly Law, art. 19.

It is quite evident from the published decisions that market share, the ability to control the market and market entry are key factors that competition authorities examine when determining whether an investigated party has a position of market dominance. The authorities have also looked at the dependence of downstream customers on the investigated party, but usually as part of considering whether the investigated party has the ability to control the market.[257] There has, however, been no mention in the decisions of whether the market dominance presumptions were relied upon or whether any investigated party had tried to rebut those presumptions.

(i) **Market Share**   A majority of the published decisions have involved monopolists. As noted above, a number of the cases involved public utilities and statutory monopolies. In these cases, the competition authority found that the investigated party was either a natural monopoly or the only licensed operator in the market. Monopolists have been found to exist in other markets and situations as well.[258] For example, in the *Qualcomm Abuse of Dominance* case, the NDRC Bureau, having defined one of the relevant markets to be the licensing of SEPs for wireless communication technology standards, held that Qualcomm had a 100 per cent market share for each wireless communication technology SEP that it held.[259] Market dominance has also been found at market share levels of 53.9 per cent,[260] 64.08 per cent[261] and over 90 per cent.[262] In *Tetra Pak Abuse of Dominance*, for example, the SAIC Bureau found that, despite Tetra Pak's declining market share in two of the three relevant markets, this market share nonetheless amounted to at least 50 and 60 per cent, respectively.[263]

---

[257] An exception is the SAIC Bureau's *Tetra Pak Abuse of Dominance* decision, where it expressly considered other businesses' dependence on Tetra Pak as a separate factor in its assessment of whether Tetra Pak was in a position of market dominance.

[258] *Qualcomm Abuse of Dominance*; *Quanzhou Cable Television Tying*; *Chongqing Qingyang Pharmaceutical Refusal to Supply*.

[259] 行政处罚决定书 [Administrative Penalty Decision] (People's Republic of China) National Development and Reform Commission, Order No. 1, 9 February 2015 (*Qualcomm Abuse of Dominance*).

[260] *Qualcomm Abuse of Dominance* (in relation to the WCDMA baseband chip market).

[261] *Inner Mongolia Mobile Unreasonable Conditions*.

[262] *Qualcomm Abuse of Dominance* (in relation to the CDMA baseband chip and LTE baseband chip markets), *Xilin Gol Radio and Television Unreasonable Conditions*.

[263] 国家工商行政管理总局行政处罚决定书 [State Administration for Industry and Commerce Administrative Penalty Decision] (People's Republic of China) State

There have also been cases involving joint or collective dominance. In the *Shandong Reserprine Exclusive Agreements* case, for example, the NDRC Bureau found that the two investigated parties had together monopolised the supply of promethazine hydrochloride in China by entering into exclusive distribution agreements with the only two manufacturers of that product in China.[264] Other collective dominance cases include the *China Telecom/China Unicom Abuse of Dominance* and *Ningxia Broadband Internet Tying* cases.

(ii) **Ability to Control the Market** The ability to control the market is an important factor in the NDRC's and the SAIC's assessment of whether the investigated party has a position of dominance. This is consistent with the definition of a dominant market position, which is a market position that enables a business operator to control the price, volume or other trading condition of a product in the relevant market. Other trading conditions are factors other than price and volume that can substantially affect market transactions, which include product quality, payment terms, delivery methods, after-sales services, transaction options and technical constraints.[265]

In enforcement, an investigated party's ability to determine whether to supply, how to supply and the conditions upon which to supply (including the price), along with a high degree of customer dependence, were crucial to finding that it had the ability to control the market. Another relevant factor was whether customers have countervailing power to constrain the investigated party's ability to control the market.[266]

As most of the cases involved a monopolist, the competition authorities found that the investigated party was able to unilaterally determine whether and how to supply, and the terms of supply, meaning that it controlled the market. Further, as customers had no alternative sources of supply, they were therefore highly (and in some cases completely) dependent on the investigated party. This was especially the case if the

---

Administration for Industry and Commerce, Order No. 1, 9 November 2016 (*Tetra Pak Abuse of Dominance*).

[264] National Development and Reform Commission, 两医药公司垄断复方利血平原料药收到严厉处罚 [Two Pharmaceutical Companies Strictly Punished for Monopolising Compound Reserpine Raw Materials] (News Release, 15 November 2011).

[265] Anti-Price Monopoly Regulation, art. 17; Regulation of the Administration for Industry and Commerce on the Prohibition of Abuse of Dominance Conduct, art. 3.

[266] *Qualcomm Abuse of Dominance*; *Chongqing Qingyang Pharmaceutical Refusal to Supply*; *Tetra Pak Abuse of Dominance*.

investigated party was a natural monopoly (as was the case for public utilities), because its services were regarded by the competition authority as irreplaceable, non-selective and in the public interest.

In cases where the investigated party did not have a 100 per cent market share, the relative market shares of the market participants and any competitive advantage that the investigated party had over its competitors were also considerations. For example, in *Qualcomm Abuse of Dominance*, the NDRC found that Qualcomm had held a leading position in the baseband chip markets for a long period of time, that the market shares of Qualcomm's competitors were significantly lower and that Qualcomm had significant competitive advantages in terms of the technology, function and branding of its baseband chip products over other market participants. These factors meant that Qualcomm was found to have the ability to control the baseband chip markets and that downstream manufacturers were highly dependent on Qualcomm's supply of baseband chips.[267] Similarly, in *Tetra Pak Abuse of Dominance*, in relation to the Mainland China packaging materials market, the SAIC Bureau found that Tetra Pak had a clear commercial advantage because it was the only competitor able to source kraft paperboard, which is an important input that has strength, toughness and cost advantages over other inputs.[268]

**(iii) Market Entry** Another way in which a business operator may be found to have a position of market dominance is if it occupies a market position that enables it to impede or affect other businesses' market entry.[269] Further, both the SAIC and the NDRC provide that a business operator impedes or affects market entry if it eliminates or delays entry by other businesses or substantially increases entry costs for potential entrants, making it impossible or difficult for them to compete effectively, although entry is possible.[270]

In enforcement, the competition authorities have tended to focus on the existence of high barriers to entry, rather than on the investigated party's ability to impact market entry, in assessing dominance. The authorities have identified legal and regulatory requirements (such as licensing and qualification requirements), access to networks and related

---

[267] *Qualcomm Abuse of Dominance*.    [268] *Tetra Pak Abuse of Dominance*.
[269] Anti-monopoly Law, art. 17.
[270] Anti-Price Monopoly Regulation, art. 17; Regulation of the Administration for Industry and Commerce on the Prohibition of Abuse of Dominance Conduct, art. 3.

infrastructure, substantial investment costs, long cost recovery cycles, strict quality and safety processes and limited natural resources as limiting entry into the market by potential competitors. These factors are similar to those usually identified in merger decisions. In a few decisions, there was some discussion of the investigated party's impact on market entry. In the *Yiyuan Purified Water Unreasonable Conditions*,[271] *Dongfang Water Unreasonable Conditions*[272] and *Alxa Zuoqi Water Unreasonable Conditions* cases,[273] all of which involved the supply of water services, the competition authority found that the possibility of new entry was low as an entrant would need the cooperation of the investigated party to enter the market, because the water pipeline network and related infrastructure were owned by the investigated party. In *Tetra Pak Abuse of Dominance*, the SAIC Bureau determined that Tetra Pak had increased the barriers to entry into the technical services for paper-based aseptic liquid food-packaging equipment market by providing training sessions only to those customers that purchased its equipment, meaning that other equipment manufacturers and maintenance services providers were unable to receive such training.[274]

### 2.3.2.3 Abuse of Dominance Conduct

Article 17 of the AML has been enforced mainly to address tying conduct and the imposition of unreasonable conditions, both of which are prohibited under Article 17(5). Excessive pricing,[275] refusal to supply,[276]

---

[271] 广东惠州大亚湾溢源净水有限公司滥用市场支配地位案 [Guangdong Huizhou Daya Bay Yiyuan Purified Water Company Abuse of Dominance Case] (People's Republic of China) Guangdong Province Administration for Industry and Commerce, Order No. 2, 16 December 2013 (*Yiyuan Purified Water Unreasonable Conditions*).

[272] 海南省东方市自来水公司垄断案 [Hainan Province Dongfang Water Company Monopoly Case] (People's Republic of China) Hainan Province Administration for Industry and Commerce, Order No. 2, 9 January 2015 (*Dongfang Water Unreasonable Conditions*).

[273] 内蒙古自治区阿拉善左旗城市给排水公司滥用市场支配地位案 [Inner Mongolia Autonomous Region Alxa Zuoqi Water Supply and Drainage Company Abuse of Dominance Case] (People's Republic of China) Inner Mongolia Autonomous Region Province Administration for Industry and Commerce, Order No. 1, 22 April 2016 (*Alxa Zuoqi Water Unreasonable Conditions*).

[274] *Tetra Pak Abuse of Dominance*.

[275] *Qualcomm Abuse of Dominance*; *InterDigital Abuse of Dominance*; *Hubei Piped Natural Gas Excessive Pricing*.

[276] *Chongqing Qingyang Pharmaceutical Refusal to Supply*; *Chongqing Southwest Pharmaceutical Refusal to Supply*.

exclusive dealing[277] and engaging in differential treatment[278] have also been considered, but those published decisions have been substantially fewer in number. The SAIC has also considered loyalty discounts as 'other types of abuse of dominance conduct' under Article 17(7) of the AML.[279]

According to the SAIC's Regulation on the Prohibition of Abuse of Dominance Conduct, the forced tying or bundling of different products that is contrary to business practices, consumer preferences or product function is prohibited under the AML.[280] In enforcement, tying conduct has typically been found in circumstances where customers had no choice but to purchase the tied products and services in order to secure supply of another product or service (the tying product or service). For example, in the *Chifeng Tobacco Tying*[281] and *Fushun Tobacco Tying* cases,[282] retailers purchased cigarettes that they did not want because the wholesaler tied the order volume of popular or bestselling cigarettes to the order volume of other cigarettes. Similarly, in *Qualcomm Abuse of Dominance*, manufacturers of wireless communications devices had licensed wireless communications technology-related non-SEPs from Qualcomm (which they did not need, because they could design around non-SEPs or obtain non-SEPs from Qualcomm's competitors), in order to obtain licences for Qualcomm's wireless communications technology-related SEPs (which they did need).[283] In these cases, the competition authorities determined that customers had no choice but to purchase the tied product or service because the investigated party was dominant in the tying product or service. The relevant local SAIC authorities in the *Chifeng Tobacco Tying* and *Fushun Tobacco Tying* cases found that the

---

[277] *Shandong Reserprine Exclusive Agreements*; *Urumqi Water Exclusive Dealing*; *Tetra Pak Abuse of Dominance*; *Suqian Yinkong Water Exclusive Dealing*.
[278] *Pizhou Tobacco Differential Treatment*; *Chifeng Salt Differential Treatment*.
[279] *Tetra Pak Abuse of Dominance*.
[280] Regulation of the Administration for Industry and Commerce on the Prohibition of Abuse of Dominance Conduct, art. 6.
[281] 内蒙古自治区烟草公司赤峰市公司滥用市场支配地位案 [Inner Mongolia Tobacco Company Chifeng Subsidiary Abuse of Dominance Case] (People's Republic of China) Inner Mongolia Autonomous Region Province Administration for Industry and Commerce, Order No. 2, 4 July 2014 (*Chifeng Tobacco Tying*).
[282] 辽宁省烟草公司抚顺市公司滥用市场支配地位案 [Liaoning Tobacco Company Fushun Subsidiary Abuse of Dominance Case] (People's Republic of China) Liaoning Province Administration for Industry and Commerce, Order No. 2, 1 June 2015 (*Fushun Tobacco Tying*).
[283] *Qualcomm Abuse of Dominance*.

investigated parties were able to enforce their sales policy because they were statutory monopolies and had dominance in the cigarette wholesale market.[284] Similarly, the NDRC Bureau concluded that wireless communications device manufacturers had no choice but to comply with Qualcomm's licensing policy, because Qualcomm held a number of SEPs that formed part of the wireless communications technology standards and there was no competition.[285]

With respect to the imposition of unreasonable conditions, the SAIC's Regulation on the Prohibition of Abuse of Dominance Conduct stipulates that unreasonable conditions are unreasonable restrictions relating to contract term, payment methods, transportation of products, mode of delivery of products or services, sales territory, target customers or after-sales services, or conditions that are irrelevant to the transaction.[286] In addition, the NDRC's Anti-Price Monopoly Regulation provides that unreasonable conditions are unreasonable charges imposed on top of the price.[287] Examples of unreasonable conditions that have been targeted in enforcement include: requiring customers to pay a security deposit or make a prepayment;[288] charging users based not on actual consumption volume but on an adjusted volume;[289] requiring licensees to promise not to challenge the patent licensing agreement;[290] and not allowing the rollover of unused mobile phone data.[291] Tying conduct has also been treated as an imposed unreasonable condition.[292] As such, the distinction between tying conduct and imposing unreasonable conditions has been somewhat blurred in enforcement.

For excessive pricing, according to the NDRC, relevant considerations in finding an unfairly high price are whether the sale price is clearly higher than the sale price charged by other business operators for similar products; whether the sale price increase is abnormal, in circumstances where costs have remained stable; whether the sale price increase is clearly larger than the cost increase; and other

---

[284] *Chifeng Tobacco Tying; Fushun Tobacco Tying.*   [285] *Qualcomm Abuse of Dominance.*
[286] Regulation of the Administration for Industry and Commerce on the Prohibition of Abuse of Dominance Conduct, art. 6.
[287] Anti-Price Monopoly Regulation, art. 15.
[288] *Dongfang Water Unreasonable Conditions; Alxa Zuoqi Water Unreasonable Conditions; Hai'an Electric Power Unreasonable Conditions.*
[289] *Chongqing Gas Unreasonable Conditions.*   [290] *Qualcomm Abuse of Dominance.*
[291] *Inner Mongolia Mobile Unreasonable Conditions.*
[292] *Yiyuan Purified Water Unreasonable Conditions; Alxa Zuoqi Water Unreasonable Conditions; Xilin Gol Radio and Television Unreasonable Conditions.*

relevant factors.²⁹³ In the *Hubei Piped Natural Gas Excessive Pricing* decision, the NDRC Bureau held that the fees charged by the investigated parties were unfairly high because they were significantly greater than the incurred costs and the parties' fees and profits were substantially higher than those of similar businesses.²⁹⁴ By contrast, the NDRC Bureau seemed to have focused more on unfairness and less on the level of the fee in its *Qualcomm Abuse of Dominance* decision. The NDRC Bureau concluded that the licence fees charged by Qualcomm were unfairly high because Qualcomm had included expired patents in its patent licensing portfolio (and therefore charged license fees for expired patents), unfairly required licensees to cross-license their patents to Qualcomm at no cost and based the royalty rate on the net wholesale price of wireless communications devices.²⁹⁵

Nearly all published decisions have involved only one type of abuse of dominance conduct. The exceptions are the NDRC's decisions in *Qualcomm Abuse of Dominance* and *InterDigital Abuse of Dominance*, both which involved tying conduct, the imposition of unreasonable conditions and excessive pricing,²⁹⁶ and the SAIC's *Tetra Pak Abuse of Dominance* decision, which involved tying conduct, exclusive dealing and loyalty discounts.²⁹⁷

### 2.3.2.4 Legitimate Reasons for Engaging in Abuse of Dominance Conduct

As noted above, for conduct other than excessive pricing or purchasing goods at unfairly low prices, if a business operator in a position of market dominance has a legitimate reason for engaging in that conduct, it will not breach Article 17 of the AML. Both the NDRC and the SAIC give some guidance on what constitutes a legitimate reason in their implementing regulations. The NDRC's Anti-Price Monopoly Regulation provides a few examples of legitimate reasons for selling below cost, refusing to supply (through the setting of excessively high sales prices or

---

[293] Anti-Price Monopoly Regulation, art. 11.
[294] 湖北省物价局对5家天然气公司价格垄断行为进行处罚 [Hubei Price Bureau Punishes Five Natural Gas Companies' Price Monopoly Conduct] (News Release, 12 July 2016).
[295] *Qualcomm Abuse of Dominance*.
[296] National Development and Reform Commission, 国家发展改革委对美国IDC公司涉嫌价格垄断案中止调查 [NDRC Stops Investigation of InterDigital Suspected Price Monopoly Case] (News Release, 22 May 2014); *Qualcomm Abuse of Dominance*.
[297] *Tetra Pak Abuse of Dominance*.

excessively low purchase prices) and requiring trading partners to deal exclusively with it or designated businesses.[298] Although the SAIC does not similarly provide examples of legitimate reasons, it does give general guidance. For the SAIC, relevant factors include whether the conduct was taken in the normal course of operations and for normal profits, and the effect of the conduct on economic efficiency, public interest and economic development.[299]

Legitimate reasons for imposing unreasonable conditions, tying, refusing to supply, exclusive dealing and engaging in differential treatment have been considered by competition authorities in their published decisions. One of the more typical justifications given by investigated parties for engaging in different types of abuse of dominance conduct has been compliance with legal requirements and obligations.[300] For example, compliance with local regulations was cited as a reason for engaging in tying conduct in the *Quanzhou Cable Television Tying*[301] and *Yiyuan Purified Water Unreasonable Conditions* cases,[302] and in the *Chongqing Qingyang Pharmaceutical Refusal to Supply* case, the investigated party argued that it would breach its exclusive sales agent agreement if it supplied allopurinol active pharmaceutical ingredients to third parties in China during the grace period provided for in that agreement.[303] Another relatively common reason given by investigated parties, especially in the context of tying conduct, was that customers were not forced into the transaction.[304] Other reasons that have been put forth by

---

[298] Anti-Price Monopoly Regulation, arts. 12–14.
[299] Regulation of the Administration for Industry and Commerce on the Prohibition of Abuse of Dominance Conduct, art. 8.
[300] *Yiyuan Purified Water Unreasonable Conditions*; *Quanzhou Cable Television Tying*; *Chongqing Qingyang Pharmaceutical Refusal to Supply*; *Chifeng Salt Differential Treatment*; *Urumqi Water Exclusive Dealing*; *Suqian Yinkong Water Exclusive Dealing*.
[301] 限制竞争还是技术局限—泉州广电捆绑销售机顶盒、智能卡案件追踪 [Restriction of Competition or Technical Limitations – Following the Quanzhou Radio and Television Set-Top Box and Smart Card Tying Case], 中国工商报 [China Industry & Commerce News], 21 May 2014, available at www.saic.gov.cn/zt/jg/fldybzdjz/201405/t20140521_219942.html.
[302] *Yiyuan Purified Water Unreasonable Conditions*.
[303] 重庆青阳药业有限公司涉嫌滥用市场支配地位拒绝交易案 [Chongqing Qingyang Pharmaceutical Company Suspected Abuse of Dominance Refusal to Deal Case] (People's Republic of China) Chongqing Administration for Industry and Commerce, Order No. 15, 28 October 2015 (*Chongqing Qingyang Pharmaceutical Refusal to Supply*).
[304] *Yiyuan Purified Water Unreasonable Conditions*; *Quanzhou Cable Television Tying*; *Qualcomm Abuse of Dominance*; *Urumqi Water Exclusive Dealing*; *Suqian Yinkong Water Exclusive Dealing*. This reason was also put forth in *Dongfang Water*

investigated parties include mitigating against the risk that customers would delay or not make payments,[305] protecting against losses arising from equipment measurement errors,[306] and liquidity or commercial pressures,[307] as well as ensuring quality and safety.[308]

So far, no investigated party has successfully shown that they had a legitimate reason for engaging in the abuse of dominance conduct. These reasons have been rejected by the competition authorities on the basis that the conduct was not a common business practice,[309] the conduct was aimed solely at furthering the investigated party's own interests,[310] customers had entered into the transaction against their will[311] or were deprived of choice,[312] or there was no legal basis for its conduct.[313]

#### 2.3.2.5 Competitive Effect of the Abuse of Dominance Conduct

An examination of the impact of the abuse of dominance conduct on competition is not expressly required by the AML or the implementing regulations. In enforcement, however, the competition authorities will usually consider the competitive effect of the conduct, albeit briefly. This may be done in the context of determining whether the investigated party

---

*Unreasonable Conditions* (arguing that payment of a security deposit by new customers was voluntary).

[305] *Dongfang Water Unreasonable Conditions; Qingdao Xinao Xincheng Gas Unreasonable Conditions.*

[306] *Chongqing Gas Unreasonable Conditions; Alxa Zuoqi Water Unreasonable Conditions.*

[307] *Qingdao Xinao Xincheng Gas Unreasonable Conditions; Alxa Zuoqi Water Unreasonable Conditions.*

[308] *Yiyuan Purified Water Unreasonable Conditions; Urumqi Water Exclusive Dealing; Tetra Pak Abuse of Dominance; Chongqing Southwest Pharmaceutical Refusal to Supply; Suqian Yinkong Water Exclusive Dealing.*

[309] *Yiyuan Purified Water Unreasonable Conditions; Tetra Pak Abuse of Dominance.*

[310] *Chongqing Gas Unreasonable Conditions; Chongqing Qingyang Pharmaceutical Refusal to Supply.*

[311] *Yiyuan Purified Water Unreasonable Conditions; Dongfang Water Unreasonable Conditions; Qualcomm Abuse of Dominance; Urumqi Water Exclusive Dealing; Suqian Yinkong Water Exclusive Dealing.*

[312] *Alxa Zuoqi Water Unreasonable Conditions; Qingdao Xinao Xincheng Gas Unreasonable Conditions.*

[313] *Yiyuan Purified Water Unreasonable Conditions; Chongqing Gas Imposition of Unreasonable Conditions; Quanzhou Cable Television Tying Conduct; Dongfang Water Imposition of Unreasonable Conditions; Urumqi Water Exclusive Dealing; Chongqing Southwest Pharmaceutical Refusal to Supply; Suqian Yinkong Water Exclusive Dealing.*

has engaged in abuse of dominance conduct,[314] or whether there is a legitimate reason for engaging in such conduct,[315] or as a separate analytical step. The latter has been the more typical approach.

The competition concerns identified by the competition authorities in abuse of dominance decisions have mostly related to harm to the interests of downstream customers and consumers, the impact on competitors and the harm to competition in general. These concerns are similar to those identified by the authorities in monopoly agreement decisions. Here, the competition authorities have been concerned that the abuse of dominance conduct had restricted choices available to customers and consumers, increased their economic burden and/or deprived them of the benefits of competition, such as lower-priced and better-quality products and services.[316] For example, in *Qualcomm Abuse of Dominance*, the NDRC Bureau was concerned that the imposition of unreasonable conditions on the supply of baseband chips had reduced the competitiveness of Qualcomm's competitors and limited their opportunity to compete.[317] In terms of harm to competition, the competition authorities pointed out that the investigated party had limited the role of supply and demand in the market, and had therefore damaged the market competition order.[318]

### 2.3.3 Abuse of Administrative Power

Article 8 of the AML provides that administrative authorities must not abuse their administrative power to eliminate or restrict competition.[319] This is commonly referred to as administrative monopoly. The types of administrative conduct prohibited by the AML are detailed in its Chapter V. This conduct covers both industry monopoly (where government departments impede entry into particular industries) and regional monopoly (acts of local protectionism). Administrative authorities are prohibited from requiring businesses to purchase or use products

---

[314] *Qualcomm Abuse of Dominance*; *Xilin Gol Radio and Television Unreasonable Conditions*.
[315] *Yiyuan Purified Water Unreasonable Conditions*; *Qualcomm Abuse of Dominance*.
[316] See, e.g., *Yiyuan Purified Water Unreasonable Conditions*; *Fushun Tobacco*; *Chongqing Qingyang Pharmaceutical Refusal to Supply*; *Qingdao Xinao Xincheng Gas Unreasonable Conditions*; *Urumqi Water Exclusive Dealing*; *Tetra Pak Abuse of Dominance*; *Suqian Yinkong Water Exclusive Dealing*.
[317] *Qualcomm Abuse of Dominance*.
[318] See, e.g., *Pizhou Tobacco Tying*; *Chongqing Qingyang Pharmaceutical Refusal to Supply*.
[319] This includes organisations authorised by law to engage in public administration.

provided by designated businesses;[320] engaging in conduct that prevents the free movement of products between regions;[321] preventing or restricting non-local businesses from participating in tenders, investing locally, or establishing local branches;[322] or compelling businesses to engage in monopoly conduct that is prohibited under the AML.[323] Further, administrative authorities must not formulate or adopt administrative regulations that have provisions restricting or eliminating competition.[324] Relatedly, the SAIC makes it clear that businesses must not enter or implement monopoly agreements or engage in abuse of dominance conduct, even if that conduct is administratively restricted or authorised, or pursuant to an administrative regulation.[325]

Of the four categories of anti-competitive conduct prohibited by the AML, enforcement relating to the abuse of administrative power has been the least active, although activity has significantly increased since the second half of 2014. In July 2013, the SAIC reported that it had conducted thirty investigations into administrative monopoly conduct.[326] However, to date, the SAIC has publicly released information on one investigation only,[327] and the outcomes of its other administrative monopoly investigations are not publicly known. Whereas the NDRC did not publish its first administrative monopoly decision until September 2014, it has made publicly available the outcomes of the twelve cases it investigated in the period 2011–2016. The publicly-known investigations mostly involved sectors related to transportation[328] and pharmaceutical

---

[320] Anti-monopoly Law, art. 32.   [321] Ibid., art. 33.   [322] Ibid., arts. 34–35.
[323] Ibid., art. 36.   [324] Ibid., art. 37.
[325] 工商行政管理机关制止滥用行政权利排除，限制竞争行为的规定 [Regulation of the Administration for Industry and Commerce on the Prohibition of Abuse of Administrative Power to Restrict or Eliminate Competition] (People's Republic of China) State Administration for Industry and Commerce, Order No. 55, 31 December 2010, art. 5.
[326] 反垄断法实施5年：公平竞争市场环境的有力维护者 [Five Years of Implementing Anti-monopoly Law: Strong Protectors of a Fair Market Competition Environment] 工商总局 [State Administration for Industry and Commerce] 29 July 2013, available at www.gov.cn/gzdt/2013-07/31/content_2458835.htm.
[327] 会议纪要指定经营者,工商机关首次行使建议权《反垄断法》剑指地方政府排除限制竞争—广东省工商局调查滥用行政权力排除、限制竞争案纪实 [Minutes of Meeting Designate Operators, SAIC Authorities Target Their Recommendation Powers under Anti-monopoly Law at Local Governments that Eliminate or Restrict Competition for the First Time – Case Report of the Guangdong AIC's Investigation of Abuse of Administrative Power to Eliminate or Restrict Competition], 中国工商报 [China Business News], 27 July 2011, available at www.saic.gov.cn/zt/jg/fldybzdjz/201209/t20120918_219847.html.
[328] *Heyuan GPS Platform Administrative Monopoly*; *Hebei Toll Road Administrative Monopoly*; *Shandong GPS Platform Administrative Monopoly*; *Wuwei Car Maintenance Fees*

procurement.³²⁹ The division of responsibility along price-related and non-price-related lines for the NDRC and the SAIC, respectively, does not appear to have been as strictly applied in practice with respect to administrative monopoly investigations. Many of the NDRC's administrative monopoly cases relate to price and non-price-related conduct, and the NDRC's investigations into drug procurement by the Sichuan Health and Family Commission and the Zhejiang Health and Family Planning Commission concerned measures that discriminated against the participation of non-local drug manufacturers or certain products in tenders, but did not expressly involve price-related measures.³³⁰

Generally, the administrative monopoly decisions have focused on identifying and classifying administrative monopoly conduct. None of the administrative monopoly decisions cover market definition, and they tend not to consider the competitive effects of the administrative measures.

In terms of the types of administrative monopoly conduct investigated and reported in the published decisions, nearly all types of administrative monopoly conduct outlined in Chapter V of the AML have been targeted by the competition authorities, the exception being conduct that limits local investment by non-local businesses. The most common types of administrative monopoly conduct investigated were requirements that businesses purchase or use products provided by designated suppliers,³³¹ and the organisation and enforcement of cartel conduct.³³²

---

*Administrative Monopoly; Gansu GPS Platform Administrative Monopoly; Huangpu River Cruise Operators Administrative Monopoly.*

³²⁹ *Bengbu Health and Planning Commission Drug Procurement Administrative Monopoly; Sichuan and Zhejiang Health and Planning Commissions Drug Procurement Administrative Monopoly.*

³³⁰ National Development and Reform Commission, 四川、浙江省卫生和计划生育委员会及时纠正药品集中采购中违反《反垄断法》、排除限制竞争行为 [Sichuan Province and Zhejiang Province Health and Planning Commissions Promptly Corrects Anti-Competitive Conduct Violating the Anti-monopoly Law in Centralised Drug Procurement] (News Release, 2 November 2015).

³³¹ *Heyuan GPS Platform Administrative Monopoly; Shandong GPS Platform Administrative Monopoly; Bengbu Health and Family Planning Commission Drug Procurement Administrative Monopoly; Sichuan and Zhejiang Health and Planning Commissions Drug Procurement Administrative Monopoly; Gansu GPS Platform Administrative Monopoly.*

³³² *Yunnan Communications Authority Administrative Monopoly; Wuwei Car Maintenance Fees Administrative Monopoly; Huangpu River Cruise Operators Administrative Monopoly; Beijing Concrete Quality Control Administrative Monopoly; New Residential Area Electricity Supply Equipment Administrative Monopoly.*

A majority of the published decisions also involved multiple types of administrative monopoly conduct.[333]

The NDRC engaged in limited consideration of the competitive effect of the conduct in a few cases.[334] The *Shandong GPS Platform Administrative Monopoly* and *Gansu GPS Platform Administrative Monopoly* cases involved the administrative authority designating a particular monitoring services platform and device, issuing relevant regulations and placing a price cap on global positioning system devices. In both cases, the competition authority found that the conduct had deprived road transport users of their right to choose a monitoring services platform and global positioning system device, which completely eliminated competition in the market and led to an unreasonable increase in the price of global positioning system devices.[335] Similarly, in the *Beijing Concrete Quality Control Administrative Monopoly* case, the NDRC determined that the administrative agency had interfered with the ability of the concrete businesses to determine their own prices, which restricted competition in the market.[336]

Responsibility for enforcing the prohibition against administrative monopoly lies with the superior authority of the administrative organ, not the competition authorities. The competition authority's role is limited to making recommendations to the superior authority on how

---

[333] *Bengbu Health and Family Planning Commission Drug Procurement Administrative Monopoly; Sichuan and Zhejiang Health and Planning Commissions Drug Procurement Administrative Monopoly; Shandong GPS Platform Administrative Monopoly; Gansu GPS Platform Administrative Monopoly.*

[334] *Shandong GPS Platform Administrative Monopoly; Gansu GPS Platform Administrative Monopoly; Beijing Concrete Quality Control Administrative Monopoly.*

[335] 国家发展改革委办公厅关于建议纠正山东省交通运输厅滥用行政权力排除限制竞争有关行为的函 [National Development and Reform Commission General Office Letter Recommending that Shandong Province Department of Transportation Correct Its Abuse of Administrative Power Conduct Restricting Competition] (People's Republic of China) National Development and Reform Commission, Order No. 501, 9 March 2015 (*Shandong GPS Platform Administrative Monopoly*); 甘肃省发改和改革委员会关于建议纠正甘肃省道路运输管理局滥用行政权利排除，限制竞争有关行为的涵 [Gansu Province Development and Reform Commission Letter Recommending that the Gansu Province Road Transport Authority Correct its Abuse of Administrative Power Conduct Eliminating or Restricting Competition] Gansu Province Development and Reform Commission, Order No. 7, 26 November 2015 (*Gansu GPS Platform Administrative Monopoly*).

[336] 北京市住建委纠正混凝土行业管理中滥用行政权力排除限制竞争行为 [Beijing Municipal Commission of Housing and Urban–Rural Development Corrects Conduct that Abuses Administrative Power to Eliminate or Restrict Competition in Its Management of the Concrete Industry] (News Release, 29 December 2016).

to handle the case under the AML.[337] Such recommendations may include stopping the administrative authority from compelling businesses to engage in monopoly conduct, repealing regulations with provisions that eliminate or restrict competition, disciplining relevant persons or adopting other measures to rectify the abuse of administrative power conduct.[338] In practice, the recommendations made by the competition authorities have ranged from the very general (such as requiring the administrative authority to adopt measures to rectify the administrative monopoly conduct or to encourage market prices)[339] to the specific (for example, returning fees held in escrow).[340]

In most of the published cases, the recommendation, if one is given, has been addressed to the provincial government as the superior authority.[341] A few cases have deviated from this pattern. In *Yunnan Communications Authority Administrative Monopoly*, the NDRC's local bureau in Yunnan did not make its recommendation to the Yunnan Provincial Government. Instead, the Yunnan bureau directly urged the Yunnan Communications Authority to stop and rectify its conduct. Further, the NDRC discussed the investigation with the MIIT, which is the relevant line ministry for the Yunnan Communications Authority at the central level, and the MIIT responded that it would guide its provincial-level authorities to improve their awareness and understanding of the AML and to rectify similar conduct within their jurisdictions.[342] In the two transport-related administrative monopoly cases investigated by the NDRC's local authority in Gansu, in which a division of the local transport department was investigated, the recommendation was

---

[337] Anti-monopoly Law, art. 51; Regulation of the Administration for Industry and Commerce on the Prohibition of Abuse of Administrative Power to Restrict or Eliminate Competition, art. 6; Regulation on Anti-Price Monopoly Administrative Enforcement Procedures, art. 19.
[338] Regulation on Anti-Price Monopoly Administrative Enforcement Procedures, art. 19.
[339] See, e.g., *Heyuan GPS Platform Administrative Monopoly*; *Hebei Toll Road Administrative Monopoly*; *Shandong GPS Platform Administrative Monopoly*; *Yunnan Communications Authority Administrative Monopoly*.
[340] *Wuwei Car Maintenance Fees Administrative Monopoly*.
[341] *Heyuan GPS Platform Administrative Monopoly*; *Hebei Toll Road Administrative Monopoly*; *Shandong GPS Platform Administrative Monopoly*; *Bengbu Health and Planning Commission Drug Procurement Administrative Monopoly*.
[342] National Development and Reform Commission, 云南省通信管理局违反《反垄断法》滥用行政权力排除限制竞争被依法纠正 [Yunnan Province Communications Authority's Abuse of Administrative Power to Eliminate or Restrict Competition in Violation of the Anti-monopoly Law Has Been Corrected] (News Release, 2 June 2015).

addressed to that local transport department.[343] There have also been cases in which it seems that the investigated authority undertook corrective measures without the involvement of their superior authorities.[344] For example, in the NDRC Bureau's investigation of the health and family planning commissions in Sichuan and Zhejiang, the decisions stated that the health and family planning commissions undertook corrective measures, but made no mention of whether any recommendation had been made to a superior authority such as the relevant provincial-level government.[345]

## 2.4 Conclusion

The preceding legal analysis of the AML and the enforcement decisions made by the Chinese competition agencies demonstrates that, overall, the AML is being interpreted and applied in a manner that is increasingly analytically sophisticated, from both a legal and economic perspective.

Merger enforcement, in particular, appears to be developing in a manner that is broadly consistent with what is regarded as prevailing international practice. The MOFCOM's merger analysis considers factors and uses theories of harm that are adopted by mature competition law jurisdictions such as the United States and the European Union. The MOFCOM's adoption of a simplified merger review process also demonstrates that it is receptive to suggestions from the practitioner and business community regarding how to improve its merger review procedures. Interestingly, it is in relation to the attachment of conditions to merger approvals that the MOFCOM appears to have been less concerned about following international practices and norms and more focused on tailoring the conditions to address competition concerns in China. The range of commitments required by the MOFCOM has been very broad, encompassing both structural and behavioural conditions,

---

[343] *Wuwei Car Maintenance Fees Administrative Monopoly*; *Gansu GPS Platform Administrative Monopoly*.

[344] *Sichuan and Zhejiang Health and Planning Commissions Drug Procurement Administrative Monopoly*; *Huangpu River Cruise Operators Administrative Monopoly*; *Beijing Concrete Quality Control Administrative Monopoly*; *Shenzhen Primary and High School Supplies Procurement Administrative Monopoly*; *New Residential Area Electricity Supply Equipment Administrative Monopoly*.

[345] National Development and Reform Commission, 'Sichuan Province and Zhejiang Province Health and Planning Commissions'.

and in some cases the reach of those conditions into the operations of the merging parties has been significant.

Non-merger enforcement, however, appears to have developed at a slower pace and with less clarity than merger enforcement. While the conduct targeted by the NDRC and the SAIC has been conduct typically addressed by other competition agencies, the manner in which those conclusions are reached has been more difficult to determine. One of the main challenges has been the lack of consistency across decisions involving monopoly agreement or abuse of dominance conduct, especially in relation to competition assessment of the conduct in question. Also, the use of price-related and non-price-related conduct to divide enforcement responsibility between the NDRC and the SAIC seems to have been effective in monopoly agreement cases, but less so in abuse of dominance and administrative monopoly cases.

It is also imperative to acknowledge that the limited transparency provided by all of the competition agencies in their published decisions presents challenges to the utility and soundness of a legal doctrinal approach to the AML. As discussed, not all decisions made by the authorities pursuant to the AML are released to the public. Although the level of detail and analysis provided in published decisions has improved significantly in the past few years, the decisions remain relatively brief and focus on presenting conclusions rather than on providing reasons for those conclusions or on evaluating arguments, and the analytical approach taken by the authorities has, at times, lacked consistency and rigour. Thus, it can be rather difficult to draw concrete conclusions from this legal doctrinal analysis on how the AML is being interpreted and applied by the Chinese competition agencies. This is not to say that a legal doctrinal approach to the AML is not useful or relevant – however, it should be recognised that there are some deficiencies and limitations associated with such an approach.

Therefore, this book argues that a detailed exploration of the Chinese economic, institutional and political contexts will help to overcome the issues associated with the lack of transparency and detail. Contextual analysis looks behind and beyond the published decisions. A detailed analysis of the actors involved in the making, implementation and enforcement of the AML will help to provide insights into the decision-making process that are not disclosed in the decisions themselves. Further, empirical research that gathers information on the AML which is not otherwise publicly available will provide valuable additional information and insights.

# PART II

A Political Economy Framework for the Anti-monopoly Law

# 3

# Demand-Side Analysis of the Anti-monopoly Law

## 3.1 Introduction

As discussed in Chapter 1, the analytical framework used in this book to examine the political economy of China's competition law is framed in terms of demand and supply. The following chapter develops this framework by exploring the stakeholders and dynamics that shape demand for the Anti-monopoly Law (AML) as a governance device.

Through lobbying, pursuing private legal proceedings or other actions, stakeholders on the demand-side can influence the type and content of laws that are developed by law-makers and the courts. They can also constitute major obstacles to law enforcement and legal reforms. Whether demand-side actors support or undermine the AML will depend on their interests, incentives and understanding of the AML and their attitudes towards compliance. Their level of influence will be shaped by their relationship to other stakeholders, on both the demand and supply-sides, and the broader policy environment. Other factors that shape demand include the existence of effective, lower-cost, non-legal alternatives to the AML for the governance of economic and market activity; the extent to which demand-side stakeholders participate in the supply of the AML; and the size and complexity of markets and the diversity of market actors.[1]

This chapter is structured as follows. Section 3.2 examines the interests, powers, incentives, and knowledge and attitude to competition law of the major stakeholders on the demand-side of the AML, and their relationships with each other and stakeholders involved in the supply of the AML. It also considers the extent to which demand-side stakeholders

---

[1] Curtis J. Milhaupt and Katharina Pistor, *Law and Capitalism: What Corporate Crises Reveal about Legal Systems and Economic Development around the World* (Chicago: University of Chicago Press, 2008), pp. 40–4. See also Curtis J. Milhaupt, 'Beyond Legal Origin: Rethinking Law's Relationship to the Economy – Implications for Policy' (2009) 57 *American Journal of Comparative Law* 831 at 839.

participate in the making and implementation of the AML. Section 3.3 considers the growing demand for the AML that was created by economic reforms and the perceived gap in economic and market governance. It also examines how the existence of alternatives to the AML might affect demand for AML enforcement. The broader governance, regulatory and policy environment that shapes the demand-side dynamics of the AML is discussed in Section 3.4.

## 3.2 Key Stakeholders on the Demand-Side of the Anti-monopoly Law

A variety of government, quasi-government and private actors constitute demand-side stakeholders and groups who influence, or seek to influence, the supply of the AML. They include Chinese businesses (state-owned enterprises (SOEs) and private businesses), foreign businesses, various government authorities and industry associations. These demand-side actors have incentives to support and oppose the AML, depending on the issues involved. SOEs, private Chinese businesses and foreign businesses are likely enforcement targets of the AML; industry regulators are the government authorities whose powers might be eroded by the AML; and industry associations have traditionally coordinated the business activities of their members to maintain industry self-discipline. The interests of SOEs, industry regulators and the State-owned Assets Supervision and Administration Commission (SASAC), the government authority that represents the state's ownership interest in SOEs, are likely to be aligned as they all have incentives to protect the interests of SOEs.

This section examines the powers, interests, incentives, relationships, and knowledge and attitudes to competition law of SOEs, industry regulators, private Chinese companies, foreign companies and industry associations. It also considers the extent to which these demand-side actors participate in the supply of the AML.

### 3.2.1 State-owned Enterprises

SOEs are major economic and political actors in China. Many of the largest Chinese companies are SOEs. In 2012, 310 of the 500 largest Chinese enterprises were SOEs, and the top thirty enterprises were all SOEs.[2] Some large SOEs have also become economically powerful and significant

---

[2] Wei Tan, 'SOEs and Competition', *CPI Asia Column*, 10 December 2012, 3, available at www.competitionpolicyinternational.com/soes-and-competition-policy-in-china.

globally. For example, in 2015, three central SOEs – China Petrochemical Corporation (Sinopec), China National Petroleum Corporation (CNPC) and State Grid Corporation – were in the top ten of the Fortune Global 500.[3] Although SOEs' share of the economy has declined in recent years and private enterprises now play an increasingly important role in the economy,[4] SOEs continue to provide a significant portion of China's domestic goods and services, and they account for a not insubstantial share of the total assets of enterprises in China.[5] SOEs operate in a wide variety of industries (strategically important, regulated or competitive), including natural resources, utilities, property development and hotel management.[6] In particular, SOEs are dominant in industries that are considered key to the national economy (so-called 'lifeline industries') and national security. For example, in 2010, central SOEs controlled more than 90 per cent of assets in the oil, electric power, telecommunications and shipping industries, and more than 75 per cent of assets in the aviation, defence and coal industries.[7] SOEs also have social functions and responsibilities such as providing employment, housing and health care.[8]

---

[3] 'Global 500 – 2015', *Fortune*, available at http://fortune.com/global500/2015.
[4] Office of the Leading Group of the State Council for the Second National Economic Census, 'Communiqué on Major Data of the Second National Economic Census (No. 1)', National Bureau of Statistics of China, 25 December 2009, available at www.stats.gov.cn/english/NewsEvents/200912/t20091225_26264.html; Office of the Leading Group of the State Council for the First National Economic Census, 'Communiqué on Major Data of the First National Economic Census of China (No. 1)', National Bureau of Statistics of China, 6 December 2005, available at www.stats.gov.cn/english/NewsEvents/200603/t20060301_25734.html. See generally Nicholas R. Lardy, *Markets Over Mao: The Rise of Private Business in China* (Washington, DC: Peterson Institute for International Economics, 2014).
[5] See, e.g., 'Communiqué on Major Data of the Second National Economic Census (No. 1)'.
[6] Cheng Li, 'China's Midterm Jockeying: Gearing Up for 2012 (Part 4: Top Leaders of Major State-owned Enterprises)' [2011] (34) *China Leadership Monitor* 1 at 27–8.
[7] 李荣融: 以朱镕基为榜样 以普京为偶像 [Li Rongrong: Zhu Rongji as a Role Model, Putin as an Idol], 人民日报海外版 [People's Daily Overseas Edition], 8 September 2010, available at http://cpc.people.com.cn/GB/64093/64102/12672016.html; 中国中央企业国有资本超过2万亿元 [Total Assets of the SASAC Companies Exceed 2 Trillion Yuan], 新华网 [Xinhuanet], 12 August 2010, available at http://finance.eastmoney.com/news/1350,201008 1289688835.html.
[8] 胡鞍钢 [Hu Angang], 国有企业是中国经济崛起的"领头羊"—基于历史和国际两个视角的分析 [State-owned Enterprises are the 'Leaders' in the Rise of China's Economy – Analysis from Historical and International Perspectives] [2012] (19) 红旗文稿 [Red Flag Manuscript], available at www.qstheory.cn/hqwg/2012/201219/201210/t20121011_185632.htm; Hon S. Chan, 'Politics over Markets: Integrating State-owned Enterprises into Chinese Socialist Market' (2009) 29 *Public Administration and Development* 43 at 46; Margaret Pearson, 'The Business of Governing Business in China: Institutions and Norms of the Emerging Regulatory State' (2005) 57 *World Politics* 296 at 313–14.

SOEs are owned either by the central government or local governments. Central SOEs account for only a very small proportion of SOEs in China, and a vast majority of SOEs in China are controlled by local governments.[9] For example, the SASAC estimated that, as of 2010, there were around 114,500 SOEs in China;[10] as at the end of 2010, there were 120 central SOEs.[11] Though relatively few in number, central SOEs are believed to be, on average, much larger than SOEs under the control of local governments.[12] Central SOEs also typically operate in industries that are dominated by SOEs, such as petroleum, electricity, telecommunications and aviation, or which are considered important to the national economy and national security. In contrast, local SOEs often operate in competitive sectors and compete with private companies.[13] Nonetheless, local SOEs can also be leading national and multinational companies, in addition to being important to the local economy.[14]

A significant majority of SOEs are shareholding companies registered under China's Company Law and operate through a corporate structure, with the state as the ultimate controlling shareholder.[15] Like other companies, a number of SOEs (but not all) have a board of directors and a supervisory board,[16] with reforms having been made to separate the management of SOEs from their ownership and administration.

For SOEs owned and administered directly by the central government, the state's ownership interest is held either by the SASAC, the China

---

[9] Andrew Szamosszegi and Cole Kyle, 'An Analysis of State-owned Enterprises and State Capitalism in China' (Research Report, US–China Economic and Security Review Commission, 2011), p. 26.

[10] 'Li Rongrong: Zhu Rongji as a Role Model, Putin as an Idol'.

[11] 中央企业2010年度总体以及分行业运行情况 [Operations of Central SOEs in 2010, Overall and by Sector], State-owned Assets Supervision and Administration Commission, 14 October 2011, available at www.gov.cn/gzdt/2011-10/14/content_1970139.htm.

[12] Szamosszegi and Kyle, 'An Analysis of State-owned Enterprises', 26.

[13] Angela Huyue Zhang, 'Antitrust Regulation of Chinese State-owned Enterprises' in Benjamin L. Liebman and Curtis J. Milhaupt (eds.), *Regulating the Visible Hand?: The Institutional Implications of Chinese State Capitalism* (New York: Oxford University Press, 2016), p. 89.

[14] Ibid.

[15] Chenxia Shi, 'Recent Ownership Reform and Control of Central State-owned Enterprises in China: Taking One Step at a Time' (2007) 30 *UNSW Law Journal* 855 at 857; 'SOE Reform Essential to a Stable Economy', Xinhua, 9 November 2013, available at www.chinadaily.com.cn/china/2013cpctps/2013-11/09/content_17093214.htm; Szamosszegi and Kyle, 'An Analysis of State-owned Enterprises', 72.

[16] Li-Wen Lin and Curtis J. Milhaupt, 'We Are the (National) Champions: Understanding the Mechanisms of State Capitalism in China' (2013) 65 *Stanford Law Review* 697 at 738–9.

Banking Regulatory Commission (CBRC), the China Securities Regulatory Commission (CSRC), the China Insurance Regulatory Commission (CIRC) or other individual ministries, commissions or agencies under the State Council. In particular, the SASAC, a central ministerial-level agency, was established in 2003 to represent the state's ownership interest in state-owned assets and exercise its rights as shareholder.[17] The SASAC has both ownership and regulatory roles; for example, approving major decisions of SOEs such as mergers, bankruptcy, the issuance of new securities, restructuring and share transfers.[18] In particular, it has been decreasing the number of central SOEs under its control (from 198 in 2003 to 102 at the end of 2016)[19] by restructuring and consolidating SOEs, privatising small and medium-sized SOEs and closing down loss-making and inefficient SOEs.[20] Lin and Milhaupt also observe that there are personnel exchanges between the SASAC and SOEs, as SOE managers are seconded to the SASAC for one-year periods, and vice versa.[21] For SOEs owned and administered by local governments, lower-level governments have established local-level SASAC authorities to represent their ownership interests in, and supervise, local SOEs.[22]

SOEs also have administrative ranks (also known as bureaucratic ranks). An SOE may be equal in rank to a government minister or vice

---

[17] 企业国有资产监督管理暂行条例 [Provisional Regulation on the State-owned Assets Supervision and Administration Commission] (People's Republic of China) State Council, Order No. 378, 27 May 2003, art 12; 中华人民共和国企业国有资产法 [State-owned Assets Law of the People's Republic of China] (People's Republic of China) Standing Committee of the National People's Congress, Order No. 5, 28 October 2008, art. 11.
[18] State-owned Assets Law, arts. 31, 40, 53.
[19] 央企名录 [Central SOE Directory], State-owned Assets Supervision and Administration Commission of the State Council, available at www.sasac.gov.cn/n2588035/n2641579/n2641645/index.html.
[20] 推进国有资本调整和国有企业重组指导意见的通知 [Guiding Opinion on Promoting the Adjustment of State-owned Assets and Reorganisation of State-owned Enterprises] (People's Republic of China) State Council, Order No. 97, 5 December 2006, art. 1(2); Xiaofei Mao, 'An Overview of the Anti-monopoly Practice in the People's Republic of China' in Hassan Qaqaya and George Lipimile (eds.), *The Effects of Anti-Competitive Business Practices on Developing Countries and Their Development Prospects* (New York: United Nations Conference on Trade and Development, 2008), p. 523; Yingyi Qian and Jinglian Wu, 'China's Transition to a Market Economy: How Far across the River?' in Nicholas C. Hope, Dennis Tao Yang and Mu Yang Li (eds.), *How Far across the River? Chinese Policy Reform at the Millennium* (Stanford: Stanford University Press, 2003), pp. 45–6.
[21] Lin and Milhaupt, 'We Are the (National) Champions', 726–7.
[22] Barry Naughton, 'The State Asset Commission: A Powerful New Government Body' [2003] (8) *China Leadership Monitor* 1 at 3; Chan, 'Politics over Markets', 48.

minister, or the head or deputy of a department, bureau or section.[23] That rank is dependent on the ownership of the SOE and its strategic importance and size. For example, it is believed that central SOEs regarded as 'important backbone SOEs' (there were sixty-eight such central SOEs in 2015) have a vice-ministerial rank, a very small number of central SOEs have a ministerial rank and other central SOEs have a departmental rank.[24]

The state exercises substantial power and control over SOEs, despite having undertaken reforms to give SOEs much more autonomy and control over their operation and management. The approval of certain government ministries and agencies is required before SOEs can embark on major business activities. For example, major overseas investments by SOEs require the approval of the National Development and Reform Commission (NDRC), the Ministry of Commerce (MOFCOM), the State Administration of Foreign Exchange and the SASAC.[25] SOEs may also be subject to sector-specific laws and regulations. For example, central SOEs such as China Mobile and China Telecom are accountable to the SASAC and subject to laws and regulations concerning the telecommunications industry that are administered by industry regulators. The relationship between SOEs and industry regulators is discussed in more detail in Section 3.2.2 below.

Most importantly, the Communist Party of China (CPC) and the SASAC control the appointment and removal of senior executives at SOEs.[26] The CPC controls the appointment of many senior positions across a range of government organisations, including SOEs, through the *nomenklatura* system. While the SASAC holds the formal appointment authority for senior executives at SOEs, in reality it is the CPC that makes the appointment.[27] Pei estimates that, in 2006, the CPC appointed

---

[23] 央企"一把手"行政级别有多高 [How High Are the Administrative Ranks of Central SOE Leaders?], finance.ifeng.com, available at http://finance.ifeng.com/news/special/gqybs.

[24] "国有重要骨干"有企哪些? [Which are the 'Important Backbone SOEs'?], 新华网 [Xinhuanet], 30 January 2015, available at http://news.xinhuanet.com/video/sjxw/2015-01/30/c_127440169.htm; 方乐迪 [Fang Ledi], 央企行政级别有门道 国资委hold不住央企 [There's a Knack to Central SOE Administrative Ranks, SASAC Cannot Hold onto Central SOEs], 大公报 [Ta Kung Pao], 1 July 2013, available at http://news.takungpao.com/mainland/focus/2013-07/1727688.html; Wendy Leutert, 'Challenges Ahead in China's Reform of State-owned Enterprises' (2016) 21 *Asia Policy* 83 at 87.

[25] Szamosszegi and Kyle, 'An Analysis of State-owned Enterprises', 89–90.

[26] Lin and Milhaupt, 'We Are the (National) Champions', 737–43.

[27] Chan, 'Politics over Markets', 50.

81 per cent of chief executives and more than half of all senior executives at SOEs.[28] It is understood that the Organisation Department of the Central Committee of the CPC (Organisation Department) directly appoints the top positions at more than fifty of the largest central SOEs, and the SASAC, in consultation with the Organisation Department, appoints the remaining senior positions at these SOEs.[29] The SASAC also decides the appointment and removal of all senior executive positions at the remaining central SOEs under its administration and supervises executive compensation at all central SOEs.[30] Similarly, the major personnel decisions at local SOEs are managed by local SASAC authorities.[31] The people appointed to senior positions within SOEs tend to be CPC members, and often the same person holds the position of party secretary (which is the most senior party position within the SOE) and the top management position.[32] Therefore, as the remuneration and career prospects of senior SOE executives are determined by either the Organisation Department or the SASAC, such executives have personal incentives to follow and advance CPC and government policies and directives in addition to growing corporate profits.[33]

According to interviewees who have advised SOEs on AML-related matters, the level of knowledge and awareness of the AML at SOEs tends to be relatively limited, but is improving.[34] In the first few years of enforcement, interviewees observed that most SOEs' attitude towards AML compliance was one of avoidance.[35] Such avoidance may have been due to any of the following: a lack of awareness of competition law; a view that competition law did not apply to them; a lack of concern

---

[28] Minxin Pei, 'The Dark Side of China's Rise', Foreign Policy, 17 February 2006, available at www.foreignpolicy.com/articles/2006/02/17/the_dark_side_of_chinas_rise.
[29] Kjeld Erik Brødsgaard, 'Politics and Business Group Formation in China: The Party in Control?' (2012) 211 The China Quarterly 624 at 633–4; Lin and Milhaupt, 'We Are the (National) Champions', 737–8.
[30] Lin and Milhaupt, 'We Are the (National) Champions', 737–43; Szamosszegi and Kyle, 'An Analysis of State-owned Enterprises', 75.
[31] Szamosszegi and Kyle, 'An Analysis of State-owned Enterprises', 75.
[32] Li, 'China's Midterm Jockeying (Part 4)', 21. See also Brødsgaard, 'Politics and Business Group Formation in China', 634; Pei, 'The Dark Side of China's Rise'.
[33] Susan V. Lawrence and Michael F. Martin, 'Understanding China's Political System' (Congressional Research Service, 31 January 2013), p. 35.
[34] Interviews with Chinese competition law experts and stakeholders. See also John Yong Ren and Jet Zhisong Deng, 'Developments in Anti-monopoly Agreement Enforcement and Suggestions Regarding Compliance Programs in China' [2013] (2) CPI Antitrust Chronicle 1 at 6.
[35] Interviews with Chinese competition law experts and stakeholders.

about the potential consequences; a belief that competition law issues could be dealt with by extra-legal means; or an aversion to engaging with the legal system and legal compliance more generally.[36] However, interviewees believe that SOEs' awareness and understanding of the AML have improved in the past three to four years. Over the past few years, visible enforcement of the AML against SOEs, high-profile AML investigations involving foreign companies, ongoing anti-corruption campaigns and the increasing importance attached to SOEs' AML compliance by the Chinese government have generally enhanced SOEs' awareness of, and willingness to comply with, the AML.[37] For example, Ren and Deng observe that some SOEs have introduced AML compliance programs, launched cooperation projects with universities or sought legal advice on AML compliance.[38] Further, SOEs with overseas operations or which have had exposure to foreign competition law regimes (such as filing merger notifications or being involved in competition law investigations or legal proceedings) are likely to have greater knowledge and awareness of the AML, in contrast to SOEs that concentrate primarily on the Chinese market.[39]

As SOEs may be dominant or important competitors in their industry, especially central SOEs operating in strategic and pillar industries, they are among the natural targets of the AML. During the drafting process, SOEs sought an exemption from the AML, but they were unsuccessful. They also argued that the AML should be incorporated into their existing regulatory arrangements; that is, the relevant industry regulators should have authority to enforce the AML. Their views were supported by industry regulators, and together they significantly influenced the drafting of the AML. These matters are examined in detail in Chapter 5. In addition, the relationship between SOEs and other government authorities and the status of SOEs in the socialist market economy might

---

[36] Interviews with Chinese competition law experts and stakeholders; Ren and Deng, 'Developments in Anti-monopoly Agreement Enforcement', 5.
[37] Interviews with Chinese competition law experts and stakeholders. Further, for example, in 2009, the SASAC issued rules stipulating that where anti-monopoly approval is required for transactions involving SOEs, the transaction agreement may only come into effect after such approval has been obtained: 企业国有产权交易操作规则 [Operational Rule on Transactions Involving State-owned Assets] (People's Republic of China) State-owned Assets Supervision and Administration Commission of the State Council, Order No. 120, 15 June 2009, art. 37.
[38] Ren and Deng, 'Developments in Anti-monopoly Agreement Enforcement', 6.
[39] Interviews with Chinese competition law experts and stakeholders. See also Ren and Deng, 'Developments in Anti-monopoly Agreement Enforcement', 5.

pose challenges to AML enforcement. For example, as explored further in Chapter 6, it appears that industry regulators have intervened in some investigations involving SOEs, and merger enforcement activity involving SOEs appears to be disproportionately low. Moreover, while SOEs have incentives to minimise the impact of the AML on their status and activities, they might also see the AML as a means to further their own interests.[40] For example, Huang and Li observe that, during the drafting of the AML, SOEs argued that foreign companies held positions of market dominance and therefore foreign monopolists should be the true targets of the AML, not SOEs.[41] Moreover, SOEs also participated in the formulation of the AML, having been directly consulted in its drafting; additionally, during a merger review, the MOFCOM consults with the competitors and downstream customers of the merging parties, which may include SOEs. In addition, as the SASAC and relevant industry regulators have incentives to protect and advance the interests of SOEs, SOEs may be able to influence the SASAC and industry regulators to support their views and positions. The participation of SOEs on the supply-side of the AML, and how they have influenced the enactment, implementation and enforcement of the AML, is explored further in Chapters 5 and 6.

### 3.2.2 Industry Regulators

Industry regulators are key players in decision-making and policy implementation in their areas of responsibility. They have the power to issue administrative rules and regulations to implement national laws and policies.[42] They can exercise substantial political influence as they have discretion in how they implement those national laws and policies, and can use that power to set and influence policy and expand their scope of authority.[43] This often results in overlapping spheres of authority

---

[40] Yong Huang and Richean Zhiyan Li, 'An Overview of Chinese Competition Policy: Between Fragmentation and Consolidation', in Adrian Emch and David Stallibrass (eds.), *China's Anti-monopoly Law: The First Five Years* (Alphen aan den Rijn, The Netherlands: Kluwer Law International, 2013), p. 5.
[41] Ibid.
[42] 中华人民共和国宪法 [Constitution of the People's Republic of China] art. 90.
[43] Lawrence and Martin, 'Understanding China's Political System', 30; Hao Qian, 'The Multiple Hands: Institutional Dynamics of China's Competition Regime' in Adrian Emch and David Stallibrass (eds.), *China's Anti-monopoly Law: The First Five Years* (Alphen aan den Rijn, The Netherlands: Kluwer Law International, 2013), p. 20.

between industry regulators.[44] A number of regulatory authorities are likely to have power over various issues in regulated industries, especially strategic industries.[45] An example is the telecommunications industry, where the Ministry of Industry and Information Technology (MIIT), the NDRC, the State Administration for Industry and Commerce (SAIC), the Ministry of Finance, the State Administration of Press, Publication, Radio, Film and Television (SAPPRFT) and the Ministry of Public Security, among others, have jurisdiction. Moreover, Jiang argues that, as the State Council's ministries and commissions draft a majority of the laws considered by the Chinese legislative bodies, industry regulators can also use this process to prepare a draft favouring their interests.[46]

One of the most important industry regulators is the MIIT, which was established in 2008 through the merging of the former Ministry for Information Industry, the Commission for Science, Technology, and Industry for National Defence, the State Council Informatisation Office and the State Tobacco Monopoly Bureau.[47] It also assumed the NDRC's industry regulation and information technology powers.[48] The MIIT has a very broad mandate, as it is both a general and a specific industry regulator. It formulates policies for industries that are not subject to sector-specific regulation, and regulates specific sectors including information technology (which includes electronics, information technology manufacturing, software and the internet), telecommunications, national defence, radio and television transmission and post. It also approves industry projects.[49] Other industry regulators include the Ministry of Transport, which regulates roads, water traffic and air transportation; the CBRC, the CSRC and the CIRC, which regulate the banking, securities and insurance industries, respectively; the National Energy Administration, which regulates the energy sector; and the SAPPRFT, which regulates the press, publication, radio, film and television industries.

The actions of industry regulators can be a source of industry monopoly, which is a type of administrative monopoly that exists in China.

---

[44] Hao, 'The Multiple Hands', 20.
[45] Pearson, 'The Business of Governing Business in China', 313.
[46] 江涌 [Jiang Yong], 警惕部门利益膨胀 [Be Wary of the Expansion of Industry and Sector Interests] [2006] (41) 瞭望新闻周刊 [Outlook] 33 at 33.
[47] 工业和信息化部主要职责内设机构和人员编制规定 [Regulation on the Major Duties, Internal Structure, and Staffing Requirements of the Ministry of Industry and Information Technology] (People's Republic of China) State Council, Order No. 72, 11 July 2008, art. 1.
[48] Ibid.    [49] Ibid., arts. 1–2.

As noted in Chapter 1, administrative monopoly is the abuse of administrative power to restrict competition, and includes exercises of administrative power to impede competition in or market entry into particular industries or sectors. The aim of industry monopoly is to protect favoured companies, which are typically SOEs, government-affiliated businesses or incumbents. Industry monopoly usually exists in industries where SOEs are dominant.[50] For example, Wu and Liu observe that industry monopoly is common in the public utilities, railway, civil aviation, telecommunications and postal industries, which are dominated by SOEs.[51] The issue of whether the AML would prohibit administrative monopoly was significant throughout the drafting of the AML. It is thought that pressure from industry regulators led to both the deletion of the administrative monopoly prohibition from the draft AML and the narrowed scope of that prohibition when it was reinstated a few months later.[52] This issue is explored in more detail in Chapter 5.

There is a close relationship and alignment of interests between industry regulators and SOEs. Industry regulators generally regulate industries where SOEs are the major or only players in the industry. Even though reforms have tried to separate administration and management of SOEs, a number of commentators believe that industry regulators continue to protect the SOEs within their purview from competition, or use their power to gain economic advantages for these SOEs.[53] There is also a practice, as noted by Lin and Milhaupt, for substantive management rights in nationally important SOEs to be granted to the relevant industry

---

[50] Bruce M. Owen, Su Sun and Wentong Zheng, 'China's Competition Policy Reforms: The Anti-monopoly Law and Beyond' (2008) 75 *Antitrust Law Journal* 231 at 242–3, 255; Eleanor M. Fox, 'An Anti-monopoly Law for China – Scaling the Walls of Government Restraints' (2008) 75 *Antitrust Law Journal* 173 at 173; Gordon Y. M. Chan, 'Administrative Monopoly and the Anti-monopoly Law: An Examination of the Debate in China' (2009) 18 *Journal of Contemporary China* 263 at 266.
[51] Changqi Wu and Zhicheng Liu, 'A Tiger without Teeth? Regulation of Administrative Monopoly under China's Anti-monopoly Law' (2012) 41 *Review of Industrial Organisation* 133 at 136.
[52] Xiaoye Wang, 'The New Chinese Anti-monopoly Law: A Survey of a Work in Progress' (2009) 54 *Antitrust Bulletin* 577 at 596; Interviews with Chinese competition law experts and stakeholders.
[53] *OECD Reviews of Regulatory Reform: China: Defining the Boundary between the Market and the State* (Organisation for Economic Co-Operation and Development, 2009), p. 99; Chan, 'Administrative Monopoly and the Anti-monopoly Law', 265; Yong, 'Be Wary of the Expansion of Industry and Sector Interests', 35; Shen Jia, 'The Invisible Obstacle', *News China Magazine* (January 2011).

regulator.[54] Further, Pearson observes that the relationship between regulatory authorities and SOEs tends to be closer than arm's-length, especially in strategic and pillar industries.[55] As strategic and pillar industries are considered economically and politically important to the state, and as SOEs in these industries carry out state policies, Pearson argues that this has resulted in a regulatory preference for controlled, orderly competition among a limited number of firms.[56] Other authors agree and note that SOEs often compete against other SOEs in the same industry, thereby providing to the state the dual benefit of control over the industry and competition.[57]

The relationship between industry regulators and SOEs is reflected in the enactment and enforcement of the AML, with industry regulators tending to voice positions that echo and support those taken by SOEs. For example, during the drafting of the AML, industry regulators argued that SOEs should be exempt from the AML and that, if SOEs were subject to the AML, SOEs should remain within the purview of industry regulators as per the existing arrangements.[58] These views were influential during the drafting process and are explored in further detail in Chapter 5. Similarly, industry regulators are thought to have played a role in some of the public enforcement investigations involving SOEs, which are discussed in Chapter 6.

Industry regulators also have incentives to protect their regulatory turf.[59] Some of the laws and regulations administered by industry regulators also contain competition-related provisions. Examples include the

---

[54] Lin and Milhaupt, 'We Are the (National) Champions', 726.
[55] Pearson, 'The Business of Governing Business in China', 308–9.  [56] Ibid., 314–5.
[57] See, e.g., Deng Fei and Gregory K. Leonard, 'The Role of China's Unique Economic Characteristics in Antitrust Enforcement' in Adrian Emch and David Stallibrass (eds.), *China's Anti-monopoly Law: The First Five Years* (Alphen aan den Rijn, The Netherlands: Kluwer Law International, 2013), pp. 61–2; Deng Feng, 'Indigenous Evolution of SOE Regulation' in Benjamin L. Liebman and Curtis J. Milhaupt (eds.), *Regulating the Visible Hand?: The Institutional Implications of Chinese State Capitalism* (New York: Oxford University Press, 2016), p. 23.
[58] Yong Huang, 'Coordination of International Competition Policies: An Anatomy Based on Chinese Reality' in Andrew T. Guzman (ed.), *Cooperation, Comity, and Competition Policy* (New York: Oxford University Press, 2011), p. 247; Mark Williams, *Competition Policy and Law in China, Hong Kong, and Taiwan* (Cambridge: Cambridge University Press, 2005) pp. 174, 192; 王毕强 [Wang Biqiang], 《反垄断法》草案二审: 反垄断前路漫漫 [Anti-monopoly Law Draft Second Review: A Long Road Ahead for Anti-monopoly Law], 经济观察网 [Economic Observer Online], 2 July 2007, available at www.eeo.com.cn/2007/0702/74098.shtml; Interviews with Chinese competition law experts and stakeholders.
[59] Interviews with Chinese competition law experts and stakeholders.

Telecommunications Regulation, the Commercial Banking Law, the Electric Power Law, the Insurance Law and the Postal Law. It is thought that concerns regarding which government authority would have power to enforce the AML against SOEs, as well as the relationship between the AML and sector-specific laws, delayed the drafting and enactment of the AML significantly. This is examined in more detail in Chapter 5.

In addition to influencing demand for competition law, industry regulators also participate on the supply-side in several ways. The views of industry regulators were solicited during the drafting of the AML. Relevant industry regulators also provide input into AML investigations and reviews conducted by the Chinese competition agencies. In particular, industry regulators are believed to have used the merger consultation procedure to exert pressure on the MOFCOM to have their views reflected in merger outcomes. Further, a number of industry regulators have been appointed to the Anti-monopoly Commission (AMC), and therefore they have a formal voice in competition policy and other higher-level AML-related matters.[60] Their involvement in the supply-side of the AML, and how that has shaped the enactment, implementation and enforcement of the AML, is investigated in Chapters 5 and 6.

### 3.2.3 Chinese Private Businesses and Foreign Companies

Private Chinese companies and foreign companies are an important part of the Chinese economy. According to the most recent national economic census, as at year-end 2013, Chinese private businesses and foreign businesses accounted for more than 70 per cent of all companies registered in China.[61] China began to open its economy to foreign investment in 1979,[62] and the private sector was officially recognised in

---

[60] Industry regulators appointed to the AMC are the MIIT, the Ministry of Transport, the CBRC, the CSRC, the CIRC and the State Electricity Regulatory Commission: 国务院办公厅关于国务院反垄断委员会主要职责和组成人员的通知 [Notice of the General Office of the State Council on the Primary Duties and Composition of the Anti-monopoly Commission of the State Council] (People's Republic of China) State Council, Order No. 104, 28 July 2008.

[61] Office of the Leading Group of the State Council for the Third National Economic Census, 'Communiqué on Major Data of the Third National Economic Census (No. 1)', National Bureau of Statistics of China, 16 December 2014, available at www.stats.gov.cn/english/PressRelease/201412/t20141216_653982.html.

[62] Yingyi Qian, 'The Process of China's Market Transition (1978–1998): The Evolutionary, Historical, and Comparative Perspectives' (2000) 156 *Journal of Institutional and Theoretical Economics* 151 at 152–3.

1988, when the Chinese Constitution was amended to recognise that 'the private economy is a supplement to the socialist public economy'.[63] Now, the non-public economy is regarded as an important component of the socialist market economy, and is encouraged, supported and guided by the state.[64]

There are formal links between China's private sector, on the one hand, and the government and the CPC, on the other. Since the ban on private entrepreneurs joining the CPC was officially lifted in July 2001, private entrepreneurs have been formally allowed to join the CPC as members,[65] and in November 2002 private entrepreneurs (seven in total) were delegates to the 16th Party Congress of the CPC for the first time.[66] In 2012, more than thirty private entrepreneurs were elected as delegates to the 18th Party Congress of the CPC.[67] Similarly, a number of private entrepreneurs are delegates to the National People's Congress (NPC) and the Chinese People's Political Consultative Conference (CPPCC).[68] Party units are also established in private enterprises in China. As of 2012, party units existed in about 983,000 private enterprises, including 47,000 foreign-funded companies.[69]

Chinese private companies and foreign companies lobby the government. They interact with the ministries, commissions and agencies under

---

[63] 中华人民共和国宪法修正案 (1988年) [Amendment to the Constitution of the People's Republic of China (1988)] (People's Republic of China) National People's Congress, 12 April 1988, art. 1.

[64] Constitution of the People's Republic of China, art. 11.

[65] Private entrepreneurs have been CPC members since the 1980s, but were only officially welcomed into the CPC after 2001. See, e.g., Lardy, *Markets over Mao*, 119; Cheng Li, *Chinese Politics in the Xi Jinping Era: Reassessing Collective Leadership* (Washington: Brookings Institution Press, 2016), pp. 172–3.

[66] Bruce J. Dickson, *Wealth into Power: The Communist Party's Embrace of China's Private Sector* (New York: Cambridge University Press, 2008), p. 78; Li, *Chinese Politics in the Xi Jinping Era*, 171–3.

[67] 'Entrepreneurs' Presence Grows at CPC Congress', Xinhua, 12 November 2012, available at www.chinadaily.com.cn/china/2012cpc/2012-11/12/content_15919473.htm.

[68] Li, *Chinese Politics in the Xi Jinping Era*, 173. The Chinese People's Political Consultative Conference is a united front organisation under the leadership of the CPC. Its members include the CPC, other political parties and mass organisations. Its functions are political consultation, democratic supervision and participation in the deliberation and administration of state affairs. It can make suggestions about various aspects of public policy, but the CPC is not obliged to act upon those suggestions. See 'Nature and Position', The National Committee of the Chinese People's Political Consultative Conference, available at www.cppcc.gov.cn/zxww/2012/07/03/ARTI1341301557187103.shtml; Lawrence and Martin, 'Understanding China's Political System', 32.

[69] 'Entrepreneurs' Presence Grows at CPC Congress'.

the State Council, the NPC, the CPPCC and local governments, although smaller companies tend to engage with local governments more often than national bodies.[70] According to Deng and Kennedy, who conducted a survey of elite businesses in China, all companies – whether state or privately owned, Chinese or foreign – engage in similar lobbying behaviour.[71] Lobbying activities typically centre on providing company and industry information to the government, public relations and building trust and *guanxi* with the government.[72] Chinese private companies and foreign companies might do the lobbying themselves, or might go through an intermediary such as an industry association or a law firm.[73]

The level of competition law knowledge and awareness amongst Chinese private companies is similar to that of SOEs. Overall, competition law awareness and knowledge is relatively low, and companies that are more active overseas or have had exposure to foreign competition laws are likely to have a greater level of knowledge and awareness of the AML than those companies that focus primarily on the Chinese market.[74] Also, according to some interviewees, while AML compliance is not generally a high priority for Chinese private companies, such companies tend to be more active than SOEs with respect to AML compliance – although this gap is narrowing.[75] As an illustration that awareness of the AML is increasing within the Chinese private sector, there have been a small but significant and growing number of private AML cases filed before the courts by Chinese companies and individuals against other Chinese companies (including SOEs) and government authorities.[76]

---

[70] Guosheng Deng and Scott Kennedy, 'Big Business and Industry Association Lobbying in China: The Paradox of Contrasting Styles' (2010) 63 *The China Journal* 101 at 110.
[71] Ibid., 112.
[72] Ibid., 112. See also generally Yongqiang Gao and Zhilong Tian, 'How Firms Influence the Government Policy Decision-Making in China' (2006) 28 *Singapore Management Review* 73.
[73] Deng and Kennedy, 'Big Business and Industry Association Lobbying in China', 112; *Conducting Government Affairs in China: Best Practices* (The US–China Business Council, 2008) 13.
[74] Interviews with Chinese competition law experts and stakeholders; Ren and Deng, 'Developments in Anti-monopoly Agreement Enforcement', 5.
[75] Interviews with Chinese competition law experts and stakeholders; Ren and Deng, 'Developments in Anti-monopoly Agreement Enforcement', 5; Yuni Yan Sobel, 'Domestic-to-Domestic Transactions (2014–2015) – A Narrowing Gap in China's Merger Control Regime' [2016] (February) *The Antitrust Source* 1 at 4, available at www.americanbar.org/content/dam/aba/publishing/antitrust_source/feb16_sobel_2_12f.authcheckdam.pdf.
[76] For example, *Susheng v. Shanda*; *Renren v. Baidu*. There has also been a complaint filed against the General Administration of Quality Supervision, Inspection, and Quarantine for administrative monopoly.

Between 1 August 2008, when the AML first came into effect, and the end of 2012, courts handled 116 AML cases at first instance, and more than 300 AML cases have been brought before the courts since then.[77] Further, a few administrative proceedings (reconsideration or review) have been brought by investigated parties to review or have set aside decisions made by the NDRC or the SAIC under the AML, although these cases were ultimately unsuccessful.[78] Chinese companies have also complained to the NDRC or the SAIC about the anti-competitive conduct of other companies.[79] These actions indicate that there is a certain level of awareness of, and demand for, the AML within the Chinese private sector.

With respect to foreign companies, the consensus among interviewees is that foreign companies are generally knowledgeable about competition law in China, and that they take compliance seriously.[80] This is largely due to foreign companies' knowledge and exposure to competition law in their home jurisdictions, and also reflects their attitude towards legal compliance more generally.[81] Some interviewees do note, however, that sometimes a foreign company might be prevented from complying with competition law under the influence of their Chinese partner.[82] Ren and Deng observe that, in their experience, legal advice on competition law compliance has mainly been provided to foreign companies rather than Chinese companies.[83] This view is corroborated by interviewees who have experience advising Chinese and foreign companies on AML compliance.[84]

---

[77] 杨维汉、陈菲 [Yang Weihan and Chen Fei], 最高人民法院公布中国首部反垄断审判司法解释 [Supreme People's Court Announces China's First Judicial Interpretation on Anti-monopoly Trials], 新华网 [Xinhuanet], 8 May 2012, available at www.china.com.cn/policy/txt/2012-05/09/content_25337524.htm; 田兴春 [Tian Xingchun], 最高法通报近年来人民法院审理商标和不正当竞争案件有关情况2012年法院审理商标民事案19815件 年增长率超50% [Supreme People's Court Reports on Trademark and Unfair Competition Cases Heard by the People's Courts, Court Hears 19815 Trademark Civil Cases in 2012, Annual Growth Rate of Over 50 per cent], 人民网 [people.cn] 28 March 2013, available at http://legal.people.com.cn/n/2013/0328/c42510-20950833.html; Zhan Hao and Song Ying, 'At the Cutting Edge of PRC AML Private Litigation' [2016] (1) *CPI Antitrust Chronicle* 1.

[78] See, e.g., NDRC Bureau of Price Supervision and Anti-monopoly, 江苏省两家混凝土企业不服反垄断处罚败诉 [Two Concrete Enterprises in Jiangsu Province Not Satisfied with Anti-monopoly Punishment, Lose Lawsuit] (News Release, 8 December 2014).

[79] Ren and Deng, 'Developments in Anti-monopoly Agreement Enforcement', 6; Interviews with Chinese competition law experts and stakeholders.

[80] Interviews with Chinese competition law experts and stakeholders.

[81] Interviews with Chinese competition law experts and stakeholders.

[82] Interviews with Chinese competition law experts and stakeholders.

[83] Ren and Deng, 'Developments in Anti-monopoly Agreement Enforcement', 5.

[84] Interviews with Chinese competition law experts and stakeholders.

Foreign companies are concerned about AML enforcement due to increasing enforcement activity by the Chinese competition agencies and a number of high-profile cases in the past few years, especially against foreign companies. For example, according to a survey conducted by the US–China Business Council in 2014, 86 per cent of US companies are at least somewhat concerned about China's AML legal and enforcement environment.[85] In response, interviewees note that foreign companies have stepped up their compliance efforts (such as compliance training, increasing the number of compliance officers within the company, reviewing and revising business practices and conducting audits), and some have increased their proactive engagement with the Chinese competition agencies.[86]

In addition to being potential targets of AML enforcement, as well as influencing the level of demand for the AML as a governance device, Chinese private companies and foreign companies also participate on the supply-side of the AML. As noted above, in the merger review process, the MOFCOM consults with a number of third parties, including businesses that are competitors or downstream customers of the merging parties.[87] Foreign companies were consulted during the drafting of the AML.[88] They were particularly concerned that the AML might be used to specifically target them and their activities, invalidate their intellectual property rights or compel them to license their intellectual property rights to Chinese companies.[89]

---

[85] *USCBC 2014 China Business Environment Survey Results: Growth Continues Amidst Rising Competition, Policy Uncertainty* (US–China Business Council, 2014), pp. 20–1.
[86] Interviews with Chinese competition law experts and stakeholders.
[87] 经营者集中审查办法 [Measure on the Review of Concentrations of Business Operators] (People's Republic of China) Ministry of Commerce, Order No. 12, 15 July 2009, arts. 6–7.
[88] H. Stephen Harris, Jr, 'The Making of an Antitrust Law: The Pending Anti-monopoly Law of the People's Republic of China' (2006) 7 *Chicago Journal of International Law* 169 at 182; John Yong Ren and Ning Yang, 'The Imminent Release of China's Anti-monopoly Law – What to Expect' [2005] (7) *China Law & Practice* 26; Lillian Yang, 'Anti-monopoly Bill for Review', *South China Morning Post*, 7 November 2006, available at www.scmp.com/node/570629; Interviews with Chinese competition law experts and stakeholders.
[89] H. Stephen Harris, Jr, 'An Overview of the Draft China Antimonopoly Law' (2005) 34 *Georgia Journal of International and Comparative Law* 131 at 134, 140–1; Nathan Bush, 'Chinese Competition Policy: It Takes More Than a Law' (May/June 2005) 32(3) *China Business Review* 30; Ren and Yang, 'The Imminent Release of China's Anti-monopoly Law'.

### 3.2.4 Industry Associations

Industry associations have a long history of organising and coordinating the business activities of their members to fix prices, maintain minimum prices and allocate markets.[90] According to Zhang and Zhang, many industry associations believe that it is part of their duty to help members determine the right price.[91] However, this is precisely the type of conduct that the AML now prohibits. Some industry associations did not appear to be aware of this change, and continued to engage in the same conduct after the AML came into effect. This is reflected in enforcement actions taken by the NDRC and the SAIC under the AML, with many of their published decisions relating to the conduct of industry associations in arranging for their members to engage in price fixing, market sharing or output restriction. It is believed that cartels organised by industry associations are often more harmful than those organised by the businesses themselves.[92]

The Chinese government started to form industry associations in the 1980s to help the economic reform process. The role of industry associations is to provide industry coordination, maintain industry self-discipline, promote the development of the industry and mediate the relationship between the government and business. Industry associations are organised by membership and/or by industry, and typically have both national-level and local-level organisations.[93]

Overall, industry associations are quasi-governmental in nature. Most industry associations were established by the relevant ministry or, in industries where the government had abolished its formal regulatory role, emerged from the former supervisory ministry. Other industry associations include those organised by the government with the support of businesses and those founded by the members themselves, with the latter type being in

---

[90] H. Stephen Harris, Jr et al., *Anti-monopoly Law and Practice in China* (New York: Oxford University Press, 2011), p. 201; Zhenguo Wu, 'Perspectives on the Chinese Anti-monopoly Law' (2008) 75 *Antitrust Law Journal* 73 at 110; Xinzhu Zhang and Vanessa Yanhua Zhang, 'New Wine into Old Wineskins: Recent Developments in China's Competition Policy against Monopolistic/Collusive Agreements' (2012) 41 *Review of Industrial Organization* 53 at 54.

[91] Zhang and Zhang, 'New Wine into Old Wineskins', 54.

[92] Wu, 'Perspectives on the Chinese Anti-monopoly Law', 110.

[93] Harris et al., *Anti-monopoly Law and Practice in China*, 202; Chenxia Shi, 'Self-Regulation of Business Associations and Companies' (2010) 2 *Peking University Journal of Legal Studies* 182 at 195.

the minority.[94] All industry associations are registered with the Ministry of Civil Affairs and must be sponsored by a government department (usually the ministry or agency that directly supervises their industry) or a CPC institution (such as the All-China Federation of Industry and Commerce, which is a people's group and chamber of commerce established by the CPC).[95] The sponsoring institution is involved in the submission of the registration application and is responsible for the industry association's conduct; therefore it is likely to have substantial power and influence over the industry association.[96] Further, it is common for current or former government officials to work in or be involved with the everyday operations of industry associations; some industry associations might even rely on the government for resources such as office space.[97] Due to the quasi-governmental nature of industry associations, Harris and colleagues note that it may be unclear whether anti-competitive conduct organised or coordinated by industry associations can be attributed to individual businesses or the industry association, or regarded as having been encouraged or authorised by government bodies.[98] This was illustrated by a case where four Chinese vitamin C producers were sued for price fixing and output restriction in New York. The vitamin C producers were members of an industry association, which the plaintiffs argued had organised for the defendants to meet and agree on prices. The defendants argued that their actions were compelled by the Chinese government, and the MOFCOM submitted an amicus brief in support of the defendants' position.[99]

---

[94] Deng and Kennedy, 'Big Business and Industry Association Lobbying in China', 108. See also Harris et al., *Anti-monopoly Law and Practice in China*, 201.

[95] 社会团体登记管理条例 [Regulation on the Registration and Management of Social Organisations] (People's Republic of China) State Council, Order No. 250, 25 October 1998.

[96] Shi, 'Self-Regulation of Business Associations and Companies', 188.

[97] Ibid., 189; Hao Qian, 'Trade Associations and Private Antitrust Litigation in China' [2013] (1) *CPI Antitrust Chronicle* 1 at 1.

[98] Harris et al., *Anti-monopoly Law and Practice in China*, 203.

[99] The defendants and the MOFCOM argued that the industry association was established by the MOFCOM to regulate exports and imports, and that one of its tasks was to coordinate the vitamin C market and export prices. To obtain the necessary customs approval for export, vitamin producers had to submit their export contracts to the industry association to verify that the contract complied with the MOFCOM's export price requirements: 沈丹阳 [Shen Danyang], 商务部召开例行新闻发布会 (2013年3月19日) [Regular Press Conference of the Ministry of Commerce (19 March 2013)] Ministry of Commerce, 19 March 2013, available at www.mofcom.gov.cn/article/ae/ah/diaocd/201303/20130300059439.shtml; Brett Kendall, 'US Court Throws Out Price-Fixing Judgment Against Chinese Vitamin C Makers', The Wall Street Journal, 20 September 2016, available at www.wsj.com/articles/u-s-court-throws-out-price-fixing-judgment-against-chinese-vitamin-c-manufacturers-1474391092.

Industry associations have varying degrees of influence on and independence from the state.[100] Some industry associations effectively act as extensions of their sponsoring institution, while others have a greater degree of independence and act more as associations advancing their members' interests. While the quasi-governmental nature of industry associations means that they might be restricted by the policies of or be subject to directives from their sponsoring government department or the CPC, they derive much of their capacity to influence the government from their close connection to government, and from their knowledge of the policy and decision-making process.[101] They tend to engage with ministries, commissions and agencies under the State Council and local governments.[102] In a survey conducted by Deng and Kennedy, a majority of the industry associations surveyed reported that they had successfully lobbied the central or local government to adopt a policy, with just under half claiming to have persuaded the central or local government to revise or abandon a policy.[103]

### 3.3 Shaping the Demand for Competition Law in China: Economic Reforms and the Governance Gap

The adoption of a competition law was necessitated by the process of economic reform and opening up. This created a growing demand for competition law, leading eventually to the adoption of the AML in 2008.

The Chinese government and law-makers believed that competition law was an important component of a legal system required to support the functioning of a market economy and further economic reforms.[104] They understood that a competition law, popularly referred to as an 'economic constitution',[105] would help to establish competitive market

---

[100] Harris et al., *Anti-monopoly Law and Practice in China*, 201.
[101] Shi, 'Self-Regulation of Business Associations and Companies', 196–7.
[102] Deng and Kennedy, 'Big Business and Industry Association Lobbying in China', 113.
[103] Ibid., 116.
[104] 关于《中华人民共和国反垄断法 (草案)》的说明 [An Explanation of China's Anti-monopoly Law (Draft)], 22nd Session of the Standing Committee of the Tenth National People's Congress, 24 June 2006; 发言摘登: 反垄断法草案 [Speech Excerpts: Draft of the Anti-monopoly Law], 22nd Session of the Standing Committee of the Tenth National People's Congress, 27 June 2006; Ming Shang, 'Antitrust in China – A Constantly Evolving Subject' (2009) 3 *Competition Law International* 4 at 4.
[105] The term 'economic constitution' is associated with German ordoliberalism. According to Gerber, ordoliberals believed that a political constitution must also establish the

structures, promote and ensure competitive conduct and guide the direction of China's economic reforms.[106] A competition law regime existed prior to the AML; however, it was criticised as being fragmented, incomplete and lacking in deterrent effect and effective enforcement.[107] The Chinese government and law-makers realised that the pre-existing competition law regime no longer suited the needs of China's socialist market economy and that China needed to implement a more complete competition law regime.[108] Hence, there was a demand for legal regulation that was not being met by the pre-existing competition law regime.

Prior to enactment of the AML, competition-related provisions were scattered throughout various laws, regulations, administrative rules and regulatory documents, including sector-specific laws and regulations that were administered by industry regulators.[109] The primary laws and regulations regulating anti-competitive conduct within China prior to the AML were the Anti-Unfair Competition Law (AUCL),[110] the Price Law,[111] and the Regulation on Mergers with and Acquisitions of Domestic Enterprises by Foreign Investors.[112] There were also regulations that

---

characteristics of its economic system and that economic systems are formed through political and legal decision-making: David J. Gerber, *Law and Competition in Twentieth Century Europe: Protecting Prometheus* (New York: Oxford University Press, 1998), p. 245.

[106] An Explanation of China's Anti-monopoly Law (Draft), 24 June 2006; Speech Excerpts: Draft of the Anti-monopoly Law, 27 June 2006.

[107] Shang, 'Antitrust in China', 5; Wu, 'Perspectives on the Chinese Anti-monopoly Law', 76; Xiaoye Wang, 'The Prospect of Antimonopoly Legislation in China' (2002) 1 *Washington University Global Studies Law Review* 201 at 222–3.

[108] An Explanation of China's Anti-monopoly Law (Draft), 24 June 2006; Wu, 'Perspectives on the Chinese Anti-monopoly Law', 76.

[109] Shang, 'Antitrust in China', 5. For a list of the Chinese laws and regulations with competition-related provisions, see Maher M. Dabbah, 'The Development of Sound Competition Law and Policy and China: An (Im)Possible Dream?' (2007) 30 *World Competition* 341 at 346–7.

[110] 中华人民共和国反不正当竞争法 [Anti-Unfair Competition Law of the People's Republic of China] (People's Republic of China) Standing Committee of the National People's Congress, 2 September 1993.

[111] 中华人民共和国价格法 [Price Law of the People's Republic of China] (People's Republic of China) Standing Committee of the National People's Congress, 29 December 1997.

[112] 关于外国投资者并购境内企业的规定 [Regulation on Mergers with and Acquisitions of Domestic Enterprises by Foreign Investors] (People's Republic of China) Ministry of Commerce, State Assets Supervision and Administration Commission of the State Council, State Administration of Taxation, State Administration for Industry and Commerce, China Securities Regulatory Commission, and State Administration of

dealt with administrative monopolies, such as the Provisional Regulation on the Development and Protection of Socialist Competition,[113] which was enacted by the State Council in 1980 and is considered the first rule pertaining to competition issues in China.[114] These laws and regulations were enacted on an ad hoc basis at various stages of China's legal and economic development process to deal with issues as they arose or were deemed to be important at the time.

Although the Chinese government pointed to a governance gap that was not being filled by the existing competition law regime, many of these competition-related laws and regulations have not been repealed and remain in effect alongside the AML.[115] The existence of these alternatives to the AML – especially the AUCL, Price Law and sector-specific laws and regulations – may reduce the demand for AML enforcement, especially in situations where the same conduct is caught by multiple competition-related laws.

There are overlaps between the AUCL, the Price Law and the AML. For example, predatory pricing conduct is prohibited by all three laws; price fixing falls within the scope of both the AML and the Price Law; and tying conduct is regulated by both the AUCL and the AML, although there are differences in the requirements for breach and scope in each case.[116] In such circumstances, as discussed further in Chapter 4, the NDRC (responsible for enforcing the Price Law) or the SAIC (responsible for enforcing the AUCL) may choose to handle the case under the Price Law or the AUCL instead of the AML, especially as the departments within the NDRC and the SAIC that

---

Foreign Exchange, Order No. 10, 8 August 2006. Interim provisions were in force from 2003, before the final regulations were enacted in 2006.

[113] 关于开展和保护社会主义竞争的暂行规定 [Provisional Regulation on the Development and Protection of Socialist Competition] (People's Republic of China) State Council, 17 October 1980.

[114] Ibid., arts. 3, 6.

[115] The main exception is the competition review of mergers and acquisitions under the Regulation on Mergers with and Acquisitions of Domestic Enterprises by Foreign Investors, which was repealed in June 2009, with the result that the competition review of mergers and acquisitions is now consolidated under the AML: 关于外国投资者并购境内企业的规定 [Regulation on Mergers with and Acquisitions of Domestic Enterprises by Foreign Investors] (People's Republic of China) Ministry of Commerce, Order No. 6, 22 June 2009.

[116] Much of the overlap between the AUCL and the AML is likely to be removed soon, as the AUCL is currently being amended. See 中华人民共和国反不正当竞争法(修订草案送审稿) [Anti-Unfair Competition Law (Draft Amendment for Review)] Legislative Affairs Office of the State Council, 25 February 2016.

are responsible for enforcing the AML are also responsible for enforcing the Price Law and the AUCL, respectively. This has been borne out to a limited extent in AML enforcement, especially during its early stages. The NDRC has used both the AML and the Price Law and, in some cases, just the Price Law as grounds for investigating and/or sanctioning price-related anti-competitive conduct. This is explored further in Chapter 6.

A similar issue arises with respect to sector-specific laws and regulations and the AML. As noted in Section 3.2.2, some sector-specific laws and regulations contain competition-related provisions. The relationship between the AML and sector-specific laws and regulations is unclear, as the AML is silent on which laws or regulations apply in the event of conflict or overlap. Some general principles relevant to this issue are found in the Law on Legislation.[117] According to the Law on Legislation, national laws prevail over administrative regulations (which are issued by the State Council), local regulations and rules; administrative regulations prevail over local regulations and rules; specific laws prevail over general laws; and newer laws prevail over older laws.[118] Further, there is no priority between departmental rules, or between departmental rules and local government rules.[119] Therefore, in theory, the AML should have priority over sector-specific administrative regulations such as the Telecommunications Regulation, but ambiguity remains over whether the AML – as a newer general law – prevails over older sector-specific laws such as the Commercial Banking Law, the Electric Power Law, the Insurance Law, the Railway Law and the Postal Law.[120]

In practice, the relationship between sector-specific laws and regulations and the AML will probably depend on where boundaries are drawn vis-à-vis the competition agency and the ministry or government department implementing the sector-specific law or regulation, and their relative degree of power. This has been reflected in AML enforcement, where industry regulators appear to have intervened in a few cases involving the anti-competitive conduct of businesses operating in regulated industries. This is examined further in Chapter 6.

---

[117] 中华人民共和国立法法 [Law on Legislation of the People's Republic of China] (People's Republic of China) National People's Congress, 15 March 2000.
[118] Ibid., arts. 88, 89, 92. [119] Ibid., art. 91.
[120] Interviews with Chinese competition law experts and stakeholders.

## 3.4 Broader Policy Environment Influencing Demand-Side Dynamics

This section examines some of the matters relating to the broader policy environment in China that influences the demand-side dynamics of the AML. Concerns about foreign companies, foreign investment and economic security were some of the main impetuses behind the adoption of the AML and have continued to shape its enforcement. In addition, the SOE policy environment is complex and implicates a multitude of government and CPC policies, of which competition policy is but one. Policy tensions have influenced how the AML applies to SOEs and are likely to continue to do so.

### 3.4.1 Foreign Companies and Foreign Investment

Attitudes towards foreign companies and foreign investment have influenced – and are likely to continue to influence – demand for the AML as a governance device. One of the main impetuses behind the enactment of the AML was the concern held by Chinese law-makers, and reportedly the general public, that foreign companies were dominating Chinese markets, engaging in anti-competitive conduct, and threatening China's national economic security.[121]

Since China began to open up its economy in 1978, many foreign businesses and individuals have invested in China, making it one of the largest recipients of foreign investment worldwide. Foreign investment has brought financial capital, technology, know-how and expertise into China, all of which are viewed as crucial to its economic reforms.[122] China's integration into the global economy, enhanced by its accession

---

[121] An Explanation of China's Anti-monopoly Law (Draft), 24 June 2006. See also Wang, 'The Prospect of Antimonopoly Legislation in China', 230–1; Owen, Sun and Zheng, 'China's Competition Policy Reforms', 252; 'Laws Necessary to Counter Monopoly', People's Daily, 15 November 2004, available at www.chinadaily.com.cn/english/doc/2004-11/15/content_391618.htm; Fu Jing, 'Foreign Firms' Monopolies Cause Concern', China Daily, 8 December 2005, available at www.chinadaily.com.cn/english/doc/2005-12/08/content_501524.htm.

[122] 胡锦涛 [Hu Jintao], 讲话 [Speech] (Speech delivered at the 纪念党的十一届三中全会召开30周年大会 [Thirtieth Anniversary Ceremony Commemorating the Third Plenum of the Eleventh Chinese Communist Party Central Committee], Beijing, 18 December 2008) available at http://cpc.people.com.cn/GB/64093/64094/8544901.html; David J. Gerber, 'Economics, Law & Institutions: The Shaping of Chinese Competition Law' (2008) 26 Journal of Law & Policy 271 at 278–9.

to the WTO, also strengthened its desirability as a destination for foreign investment and promoted economic development. However, according to Huang and Li, when the AML was being drafted, there was a widespread belief that foreign companies were dominating Chinese markets with their superior financial and technological capabilities, and that these foreign companies – not the SOEs – were the true monopolies in China and were engaging in anti-competitive conduct.[123] For example, foreign companies were seen as relying on their intellectual property, technology and other expertise to compete, and there were concerns that foreign companies had used their intellectual property rights to engage in anti-competitive behaviour against Chinese companies, particularly in the granting of licences to Chinese companies.[124] Concerns such as these increased demand for enactment of the AML, with competition law viewed as a means of preventing foreign companies from monopolising Chinese markets and abusing their positions of dominance.[125]

These concerns were intensified by the publication of a SAIC report in 2004 entitled Competition Restricting Conduct of Multinational Companies in China and Countermeasures (the SAIC Report), in which it advocated for the adoption of a competition law.[126] It was released in response to research conducted by Professor Sheng Jiemin of Peking University on the competition-restricting conduct of multinational companies in China. In the report, the SAIC claimed that multinational companies such as Microsoft and Tetra Pak had enjoyed competitive advantages or monopoly positions, and that they had abused their competitive advantage to restrict competition.[127] The MOFCOM

---

[123] Huang and Li, 'An Overview of Chinese Competition Policy', p. 5.
[124] Speech Excerpts: Draft of the Anti-monopoly Law, 27 June 2006; 跨国公司滥用知识产权是典型违法垄断 [Abuse of Intellectual Property by Multinational Companies Is a Typical Example of Illegal Monopoly Conduct], 法制日报 [*Legal Daily*], 20 May 2005, available at http://finance.sina.com.cn/roll/20050520/09321606527.shtml.
[125] 王晓玲 [Wang Xiaoling], 《反垄断法》:把立法难题留到执法中解决—访中国社科院规制与竞争研究中心主任张昕竹 [Anti-monopoly Law: Defers Resolution of Difficult Legislative Issues to Enforcement – Interview with Director of Chinese Academy of Social Sciences Centre for Regulation and Competition Zhang Xinzhu] [2005] (17) 商务周刊 [Business Watch Magazine] 47 at 47; 'Laws Necessary to Counter Monopoly'.
[126] Fair Trade Bureau and Anti-monopoly Division of the State Administration for Industry and Commerce, 在华跨国公司限制竞争行为表现及对策 [Competition Restricting Conduct of Multinational Companies in China and Countermeasures] (2004) 5 工商行政管理 [Biweekly of Industry and Commerce Administration] 42.
[127] Ibid.

disagreed with the SAIC's opinion.[128] Nonetheless, according to some media reports, the SAIC Report generated interest from businesses, academics and the general public, and reignited public discussion on the AML.[129] Some interviewees who were involved in the drafting process believed that the report helped to increase demand for the AML and push for its enactment.[130]

Concerns about China's economic security and foreign investment also strengthened the demand for enactment of the AML. Chinese government officials were worried about foreign companies acquiring stakes in Chinese companies.[131] For example, foreign companies had acquired interests in SOEs, companies that owned famous brands and companies operating in high-tech industries that other countries regarded as extremely sensitive.[132] A number of commentators believed that such interests fuelled fears that China's key technologies and strategic industries would be controlled by foreign companies, and thus compromise the Chinese government's control over the national economy.[133] Chinese law-makers and the general public had

---

[128] 商务部报告: 中国尚无行业真正被外资垄断 [MOFCOM Report: No Real Foreign Monopolies in Chinese Industries Yet], 中国新闻网 [China News Online], 9 September 2007, available at http://finance.people.com.cn/GB/6236466.html.

[129] 张黎明 [Zhang Liming], 中央三部委争立《反垄断法》今年出台无望 [Three Central Ministries Fight for the Anti-monopoly Law, No Hope for Enactment This Year], 北京晨报 [Beijing Morning News], 11 January 2005, available at www.southcn.com/news/china/zgkx/200501110126.htm; 反垄断法的19年风雨历程 [Anti-monopoly Law's Stormy 19-Year Journey] (2006) 358 中国经济周刊 [China Economic Weekly] 20.

[130] Interviews with Chinese competition law experts and stakeholders.

[131] 全国人大法律委员会关于《中华人民共和国反垄断法 (草案)》修改情况的汇报 [Report of the Law Committee of the National People's Congress on the Revision of the Anti-monopoly Law of the People's Republic of China (Draft)], 28th Session of the Standing Committee of the Tenth National People's Congress, 24 June 2007; Speech Excerpts: Draft of the Anti-monopoly Law, 27 June 2006.

[132] Report of the Law Committee of the National People's Congress on the Revision of the Anti-monopoly Law of the People's Republic of China (Draft), 24 June 2007; Speech Excerpts: Draft of the Anti-monopoly Law, 27 June 2006; R. Hewitt Pate, 'What I Heard in the Great Hall of the People – Realistic Expectations of Chinese Antitrust' (2008) 75 *Antitrust Law Journal* 195 at 205; Thomas R. Howell et al., 'China's New Anti-monopoly Law: A Perspective from the United States' (2009) 18(1) *Pacific Rim Law & Policy Journal* 53 at 91–2.

[133] Yong Huang, 'Pursuing the Second Best: The History, Momentum, and Remaining Issues of China's Anti-monopoly Law' (2008) 75 *Antitrust Law Journal* 117 at 129; Pate, 'What I Heard in the Great Hall of the People', 205; Wu, 'Perspectives on the Chinese Anti-monopoly Law', 100; Qihua Feng, 'Anti-monopoly Legislation Urged', *China Daily*, 16 March 2002, available at www.chinadaily.com.cn/en/doc/2002-03/16/content_111189.htm; Fu, 'Foreign Firms' Monopolies Cause Concern'.

also become more aware of how other countries dealt with foreign investment and national security issues, due largely to the media coverage of CNOOC's unsuccessful 2005 bid to take over Unocal, a US oil company, which raised national security concerns.[134] Consequently, enacting the AML was regarded as a way to help China protect its economic security from concerns arising from foreign investment.[135]

The conduct of foreign companies continues to be subject to scrutiny.[136] In particular, there has been widespread media coverage of growing public dissatisfaction that the prices of imported or foreign-branded goods, ranging from luxury goods to everyday items such as coffee and ice cream, are more expensive in China than overseas.[137] Chinese authorities have also initiated high-profile investigations into the conduct of foreign companies in relation to bribery and national security issues.[138]

---

[134] 'US Lawmakers Meddle in CNOOC's Unocal Bid', *China Daily*, 6 July 2005, available at www.chinadaily.com.cn/english/doc/2005-07/06/content_457677.htm; Dai Yan, 'Foreign Takeover Controversial', *China Daily*, 11 April 2006, available at www.chinadaily.com.cn/china/2006-04/11/content_565382.htm.

[135] Speech Excerpts: Draft of the Anti-monopoly Law, 27 June 2006; Wang, 'The Prospect of Antimonopoly Legislation in China', 230–1; Dai, 'Foreign Takeover Controversial'; interviews with Chinese competition law experts and stakeholders.

[136] See, e.g., Tom Mitchell, 'China Dream Sours for Foreign Companies', *The Financial Times*, 10 August 2013, 10; Adam Jourdan, 'Starbucks under Media Fire in China for High Prices', Reuters, 21 October 2013, available at www.reuters.com/article/2013/10/21/starbucks-china-pricing-idUSL3N0IB4BG20131021; 'China Vows Tough Regulation after Apple's Disputed Repair Policies', Xinhua, 28 March 2013, available at www.china.org.cn/china/Off_the_Wire/2013-03/28/content_28390858.htm.

[137] Laurie Burkitt, 'In China, Veil Begins to Lift on High Consumer Prices', *The Wall Street Journal*, 4 September 2013, B1; Ernest Kao, 'Luxury Brands Still Reaping Big Rewards in China', *South China Morning Post*, 18 February 2013, available at www.scmp.com/news/china/article/1153131/luxury-brands-still-reaping-big-margins-china-market; Zhou Xiaoyuan, 'Why Are Chinese Goods More Expensive at Home Than Abroad?', *People's Daily* Overseas Edition, 9 April 2012, available at http://english.people.com.cn/90780/7781053.html.

[138] Laurie Burkitt and Jeanne Whalen, 'China Targets Big Pharma', *The Wall Street Journal*, 16 July 2013, A1; Liang Fei, 'More Drug Firms Receive Govt "Visits"', *Global Times*, 2 August 2013, available at http://en.people.cn/90778/8350806.html; 'AstraZeneca Probed in China amid GSK Scandal', *People's Daily*, 23 July 2013, available at http://english.people.com.cn/90778/8338450.html; Pete Sweeney and Paul Carsten, 'China Seen Probing IBM, Oracle, EMC after Snowden Leaks', Reuters, 16 August 2013, available at www.reuters.com/article/2013/08/16/us-china-ioe-idUSBRE97F02720130816; 'China Investigating Foreign Companies Over Security', Xinhua, 21 August 2013, http://english.peopledaily.com.cn/90778/8371655.html.

The concerns regarding foreign companies appear to have supported demand for AML enforcement, and are reflected in AML enforcement activities. The NDRC has undertaken a number of high profile investigations into the conduct of foreign companies (some cases of which are discussed in Chapter 6). It estimates that around 10 per cent of its AML investigations involve the conduct of foreign companies.[139] The SAIC has fined Tetra Pak for abuse of dominance, and is investigating Microsoft for possible breaches of the AML.[140]

### 3.4.2 State-owned Enterprises and Their Policy Environment

As noted above, the policy environment relating to SOEs is complex and involves a wide range of government and CPC policies and priorities, of which competition policy is but one. The leading role of SOEs in China is recognised, protected and enhanced by policy measures, and SOEs are instrumental in helping the state implement and achieve policy goals. At the same time, the state has undertaken a number of SOE reforms, as such reform is considered key to the development of China's socialist market economy. Therefore, tensions and conflicts between competition policy and other government and CPC policies and priorities might arise where SOEs are concerned, especially in circumstances where SOEs are carrying out government and CPC policies and directives, or where the conduct occurs in an important, strategic, sensitive or regulated industry.

Public ownership is the foundation of China's socialist economic system, and its leading role in the economy is recognised in the Chinese Constitution.[141] The dominant role of public ownership in China's economic system and the leading role of the SOEs were recently

---

[139] 单素敏 [Dan Sumin], 许昆林: 亲历重大反垄断案 [Xu Kunlin: Personally Experienced a Major Anti-monopoly Case], 瞭望东方周刊 [*Oriental Outlook*], 25 June 2015, available at www.lwdf.cn/article_1473_1.html.

[140] 国家工商行政管理总局行政处罚决定书 [State Administration for Industry and Commerce Administrative Penalty Decision] (People's Republic of China) State Administration for Industry and Commerce, Order No. 1, 9 November 2016; 国家工商总局专案组对微软公司进行反垄断调查询问 [SAIC Special Investigation Team Makes Enquiries of Microsoft on Its Anti-monopoly Investigation] State Administration for Industry and Commerce, 5 January 2016, available at www.saic.gov.cn/fldyfbzdjz/gzdt/201601/t20160105_205359.html.

[141] Constitution of the People's Republic of China, arts. 6–7.

reaffirmed by the Third Plenum of the 18th Central Committee of the CPC (Third Plenum), which was held in November 2013,[142] and in the Thirteenth Five-Year Plan for National Economic and Social Development (Thirteenth Five-Year Plan), which applies from 2016 to 2020.[143] Relevantly, the dominance of SOEs in China's strategic and important industries is protected by the state. The central government has declared that the state will maintain sole ownership or absolute control of strategic industries and strong control of pillar industries.[144] Strategic industries in China are the defence, electric power and grid, petroleum and petrochemical, telecommunications, coal, civil aviation and shipping industries, while pillar industries are the equipment manufacturing, automobile, information technology, construction, iron and steel, non-ferrous metals, chemicals and survey and design industries.[145]

SOEs are provided with a range of fiscal and policy support by the state. SOEs have soft budget constraints and benefit from grants, capital injections, favourable tax treatment, and favourable treatment from state-owned banks such as below-market interest rates on loans, preferential access to loans and debt forgiveness (including SOEs that are technically bankrupt).[146] Since the mid-1990s, the central government has expressly supported the creation and promotion of national champions.[147] The central government is committed to fostering and developing a 'national team' of internationally competitive Chinese SOEs. These national champions are supported by favourable government policies and encouraged to list on domestic

---

[142] 中共中央关于全面深化改革若干重大问题的决定 [Decision of the Central Committee of the Communist Party of China on Some Major Issues Concerning Comprehensively Deepening Reform] (People's Republic of China) Third Plenary Session of the 18th Central Committee of the Communist Party of China, 12 November 2013.

[143] 中华人民共和国国民经济和社会发展第十三个五年规划纲要 [Outline of the 13th Five-Year Plan for National Economic and Social Development] (People's Republic of China) National People's Congress, 16 March 2016, ch. 11.

[144] 我国明确七大行业将由国有经济保持绝对控制力 [China Clarifies Seven Industries Where the State-owned Economy Will Have Absolute Control], 新华社 [Xinhua News Agency], 18 December 2006, available at http://finance.people.com.cn/GB/1037/5184638.html.

[145] Ibid.

[146] Szamosszegi and Kyle, 'An Analysis of State-owned Enterprises', 44–8, 51–3.

[147] Wang, 'The New Chinese Anti-monopoly Law', 614–15; Shang, 'Antitrust in China', 7; Xinzhen Lan, 'State Seeks Control of Critical Industries', *Beijing Review*, 9 January 2007, available at www.bjreview.com.cn/print/txt/2007-01/09/content_52480.htm.

and international stock exchanges.[148] For example, industrial, informational, financial and fiscal support was provided to SOEs and other Chinese companies in the telecommunications industry to aid their overseas expansion efforts.[149]

The state views and uses SOEs as important instruments to implement and achieve policy goals. For example, during the financial crisis in 2008 and 2009, state-owned banks were used to finance China's RMB 4 trillion economic stimulus package, lending money to, *inter alia*, local governments to finance an array of public infrastructure projects, many of which were undertaken by SOEs. At the same time, SOEs were asked by the government to accept loans and invest to support the government's economic stimulus policy.[150] In 2012, a number of local governments announced new stimulus projects, which were funded by state-owned banks.[151] SOEs also have important roles in implementing and reaching targets under Five-Year Plans. For example, under the Thirteenth Five-Year Plan, a group of key SOEs with innovation capabilities that are internationally competitive will be fostered, and more state capital will be invested in key industries relating to national security and the national economy – industries that are already dominated by SOEs.[152] SOEs are also critical to the Chinese government's 'going global' strategy.[153] The major goals of the 'going global' strategy are to enlarge the market for Chinese products, to secure the supply of natural resources, to obtain more advanced technologies and to enhance Chinese brands.[154] SOEs account for a substantial majority of Chinese foreign direct investment, with the biggest Chinese overseas investors being large

---

[148] Brødsgaard, 'Politics and Business Group Formation in China', 628; Lin and Milhaupt, 'We Are the (National) Champions', 714; Li, 'China's Midterm Jockeying (Part 4)', 11–13.
[149] Li, 'China's Midterm Jockeying (Part 4)', 13.
[150] Yongheng Deng and Bernard Yeung, 'China's Stimulus May Be a Curse in Disguise', *Forbes*, 25 August 2010, available at www.forbes.com/2010/08/25/china-soe-real-estate-property-markets-economy-stimulus.html.
[151] Chris Oliver, 'Can China's Stimulus Plans Really Help?' MarketWatch, 23 August 2012, available at http://cbonds.com/news/item/591863.
[152] Outline of the 13th Five-Year Plan for National Economic and Social Development, ch. 11.
[153] Hu Angang, 'State-owned Enterprises are the "Leaders" in the Rise of China's Economy'.
[154] 'State Owned Enterprises in China: Reviewing the Evidence' (Occasional Paper, OECD Working Group on Privatisation and Corporate Governance of State Owned Assets, 26 January 2009), p. 9; Szamosszegi and Kyle, 'An Analysis of State-owned Enterprises', 85.

SOEs such as Sinopec, CNOOC and CITIC Group.[155] Many SOEs have made overseas investments in or secured the supply of resources considered essential to economic development, such as minerals and natural resources.[156] SOEs have also been integral to the government's plans to improve the technological level of Chinese businesses, and have formed joint ventures with foreign companies or acquired technology overseas.[157]

At the same time, China has progressively reformed SOEs and industries that are dominated by SOEs, as such reform is considered essential to the development of China's socialist market economy. So far, SOE reforms have largely focused on the commercialisation, corporatisation and consolidation of SOEs, all of which were intended to encourage SOEs to perform more efficiently.[158] However, many SOEs are, on average, less efficient and profitable than private companies.[159] They also continue to receive favourable treatment from the state, which makes it difficult for new businesses to compete successfully against SOEs.[160] There are also complaints about the high prices and low quality of the goods and services delivered by SOEs operating in industries where SOEs are dominant.[161] For example, in 2009, the NDRC initiated an investigation into China

---

[155] 'State Owned Enterprises in China', 10.
[156] Szamosszegi and Kyle, 'An Analysis of State-owned Enterprises', 85–7.
[157] Ibid., 66–8.
[158] Qian, 'The Process of China's Market Transition', 163–4; Donald C. Clarke, 'Corporate Governance in China: An Overview' (2003) 14 *China Economic Review* 494 at 496; Shi, 'Recent Ownership Reform and Control of Central State-owned Enterprises in China', 857–8; Mao, 'An Overview of the Anti-monopoly Practice in the People's Republic of China', 523; Qian and Wu, 'China's Transition to a Market Economy', 45–6.
[159] The World Bank and the Development Research Center of the State Council, the People's Republic of China, *China 2030: Building a Modern, Harmonious, and Creative Society* (Washington, DC: The World Bank, 2013), p. 105.
[160] Jijian Yang, 'Market Power in China: Manifestations, Effects and Legislation' (2002) 21 *Review of Industrial Organization* 167 at 174; Williams, *Competition Policy and Law*, p. 115; Fox, 'An Anti-monopoly Law for China', 178–9; Bruce M. Owen, Su Sun and Wentong Zheng, 'Antitrust in China: The Problem of Incentive Compatibility' (2005) 1 *Journal of Competition Law and Economics* 123 at 131.
[161] 对滥用市场支配地位行为的认定—分组审议反垄断法草案发言摘登 (二) [Identifying Abuse of Dominant Market Position Conduct—Speech Excerpts of the Group Deliberations of the Draft Anti-monopoly Law (2)], 29th Session of the Standing Committee of the Tenth National People's Congress, 24 August 2007; 程刚, 崔丽 [Cheng Gang and Cui Li], 反垄断法草案: 严禁国企和公用事业借垄断自肥 [Anti-monopoly Law Draft: State-owned Enterprises and Public Enterprises Strictly Prohibited from Relying on Monopoly to Fatten Themselves], 中国青年报 [*China Youth Daily*],

Telecom and China Unicom in response to complaints from customers about the high prices and low quality of the internet services provided.[162]

The government committed to a new round of SOE reforms at the Third Plenum. The Third Plenum adopted a blueprint for wide-ranging reforms and aims to have achieved results in key sectors by 2020. The intended SOE reforms centre upon allowing more private capital to be invested into SOEs (resulting in SOEs with mixed ownership) and improving the corporate governance and enterprise management of SOEs, rather than introducing or increasing competition in industries where SOEs are dominant.[163] To implement the reforms put forward by the Third Plenum, leading small groups have been established by the CPC (led by General Secretary Xi Jinping), by the State Council and at the local-party level.[164] The establishment of these leading small groups signals the CPC's and the Chinese government's commitment to the reforms.[165] It is likely that they will also help to overcome resistance to the reforms, as leading small groups are believed to be more important and powerful than ministries on matters of policy.[166] These leading small groups will be particularly important to implementing the intended SOE reforms, because SOEs are an area in which there are a number of entrenched interests (such as the SASAC) that are likely to

---

25 August 2007, available at www.sznews.com/news/content/2007-08/25/content_1457259.htm; Wu, 'Perspectives on the Chinese Anti-monopoly Law', 99.

[162] 于华鹏, 沈建缘, 张向东 [Yu Huapeng, Chen Jianyuan, and Zhang Xiangdong], 电信业风起反垄断 [Anti-monopoly Trend Blows through the Telecommunications Industry], 经济观察网 [Economic Observer Online], 12 November 2011, available at www.eeo.com.cn/2011/1112/215612.shtml.

[163] Bao Chang, 'SOE Reforms to Be Launched after Plenum', *China Daily*, 11 November 2013, available at www.chinadaily.com.cn/china/2013cpctps/2013-11/11/content_17094060.htm.

[164] 'President Xi to Lead Overall Reform', *China Daily*, 30 December 2013; 'China's Reform Leading Group Holds First Meeting', *China Daily*, 22 January 2014, available at www.chinadaily.com.cn/china/2014-01/22/content_17252345.htm; Barry Naughton, '"Deepening Reform": The Organization and the Emerging Strategy' [2014] (44) *China Leadership Monitor* 1; Barry Naughton, 'Reform Agenda in Turmoil: Can Policy-Makers Regain the Initiative?' [2015] (48) *China Leadership Monitor* 1 at 5.

[165] 'President Xi to Lead Overall Reform'; Cary Huang, 'How Leading Small Groups Help Xi Jinping and Other Party Leaders Exert Power', *South China Morning Post*, 20 January 2014, available at www.scmp.com/news/china/article/1409118/how-leading-small-groups-help-xi-jinping-and-other-party-leaders-exert.

[166] 'President Xi to Lead Overall Reform'; Huang, 'How Leading Small Groups Help Xi Jinping'.

resist or stall reforms.[167] SOE reforms outlined at the Third Plenum have been reiterated and supported in the Thirteenth Five-Year Plan. In addition, the Thirteenth Five-Year Plan includes reforms such as allowing commercial SOEs to operate independently, introducing competition into public benefit SOEs and reforming the SOE share-capital system.[168] However, Naughton observes that these SOE reforms have stalled somewhat, and seem to have been subsumed into general supply-side structural reforms that were announced in November 2015.[169]

The implementation and enforcement of the AML will need to be balanced against the state's leading position in the socialist market economy and the roles of SOEs in carrying out various policies of the state. This balance is reflected in Article 7, which recognises and protects the state's controlling position in national economic lifeline, national security and state-granted monopoly industries, but also confirms that SOEs in these industries must not abuse their dominance to harm consumers. The circumstances that led to the inclusion of Article 7 in the AML reflect this policy tension and are examined in Chapter 5. Where the balance is struck in the implementation and enforcement of the AML may depend on the state's broader agenda and policy priorities, its commitment to reforming SOEs and the relative power of the government agencies involved, and may be coordinated by more senior government officials or CPC leaders, such as those at the AMC or State Council levels.

In particular, there is potential tension between industrial policy and competition policy where SOEs are involved. As discussed above, a number of SOEs are dominant or important competitors in their industry, considered as national champions, and/or participate in or

---

[167] Philip Wen, 'China's Xi Jinping Compared to Deng Xiaoping as His Power Base Grows', The Age, 18 November 2013, available at www.theage.com.au/world/chinas-xi-jinping-compared-to-deng-xiaoping-as-his-power-base-grows-20131117-2xp3y.html; Chris Buckley, 'Chinese Leader's Economic Plan Tests Goal to Fortify Party Power', New York Times, 6 November 2013, available at www.nytimes.com/2013/11/07/world/asia/a-clash-of-goals-for-chinas-leader.html; Shen, 'The Invisible Obstacle'; Yong, 'Be Wary of the Expansion of Industry and Sector Interests', 35.

[168] Outline of the 13th Five-Year Plan for National Economic and Social Development, ch. 11.

[169] Barry Naughton, 'Two Trains Running: Supply-Side Reform, SOE Reform and the Authoritative Personage' [2015] (50) China Leadership Monitor 1 at 6–8. Supply-side reforms have five main elements: eliminating excess capacity; reducing excess housing stock; de-leveraging; reducing costs; and strengthening weak points.

play leading roles in developing industries that are essential to the government's industrial policy. For example, in the merger context, tensions may arise where the SASAC is restructuring and consolidating central SOEs pursuant to various industrial policies. Mergers involving SOEs that meet the notification thresholds are legally required to be notified to the MOFCOM and are subject to anti-monopoly merger review. Such mergers would have already been approved by the SASAC; they may even have been orchestrated by the SASAC as part of restructuring efforts. The question here is whether these mergers would still be notified to the MOFCOM for anti-monopoly review and, if so, whether the SASAC's approval of the merger would be relevant to such a review. Some of these matters appear to have had an effect on merger enforcement and are discussed in Chapter 6.

In addition, the AML and the introduction of competition into industries where SOEs operate are regarded by the Chinese government as necessary to continue SOE reforms and help SOEs increase their efficiency and improve their performance.[170] A competition law is also seen as a means to improve the distribution of benefits and profits generated by SOEs within society.[171] The media has reported, and law-makers believe, that the public is dissatisfied with SOEs in part because it sees or receives little benefit associated with having SOEs, as the profits and benefits generated by SOEs remain within the SOEs and are not distributed to the nation as a whole.[172] Huang notes that there is a general perception that the elimination of monopolies will result in greater opportunities for consumers and businesses.[173] Thus, the implementation and enforcement of the AML may be impacted by the extent to which the AML fits into the SOE reforms proposed by the Chinese government and the CPC.

---

[170] Speech Excerpts: Draft of the Anti-monopoly Law, 27 June 2006; Wu, 'Perspectives on the Chinese Anti-monopoly Law', 99–100.

[171] Huang, 'Pursuing the Second Best', 120; Zhengxin Huo, 'A Tiger without Teeth: The Antitrust Law of the People's Republic of China' (2008) 10 *Asian-Pacific Law & Policy Journal* 32 at 49–50; David J. Gerber, *Global Competition: Law, Markets, and Globalization* (Oxford: Oxford University Press, 2010), p. 226.

[172] Speech Excerpts: Draft of the Anti-monopoly Law, 27 June 2006; Gang and Li, 'Anti-monopoly Law Draft'; Xiaoying Qin, 'Law to Protect Public Interests from Monopoly', *China Daily*, 13 July 2006, available at www.chinadaily.com.cn/chinagate/doc/2006-07/13/content_640069.htm.

[173] Huang, 'Pursuing the Second Best', 124.

## 3.5 Conclusion

The detailed analysis of the AML's demand-side dynamics undertaken in this chapter reveals that SOEs and industry regulators are the most powerful and influential demand-side stakeholders. They have a close relationship with one another and their interests are often aligned on competition law matters. For SOEs, the AML poses a threat to their leading positions and potentially restricts their activities, and industry regulators have little incentive to share their authority over regulated industries with the competition authorities. Further, their government and insider status enhances their ability to influence supply-side actors. Chapters 5 and 6, examine how, and the extent to which, SOEs and industry regulators have challenged or resisted the adoption or enforcement of the AML, and their impact on the law-making and decision-making process.

The broader governance, regulatory and policy environment that shapes the demand-side dynamics of the AML is complex and marked by tension and potential conflict between competition policy on the one hand, and the leading role of the state and industrial policy on the other. The balance struck between these policies depends in part on the state's political commitment to furthering economic and SOE reforms at a particular point in time, and the perceived role of the AML in advancing those interests. Similarly, perceptions about and attitudes towards foreign companies and foreign investment also shape the AML. These factors helped to create demand for a competition law in China that maintains and promotes competition and supports the development of the market; their continued relevance in enforcement is explored in Chapter 6. The coordination and balancing of various policy interests suggests that one of the main functions of the AML is to manage relationships between actors and interests.

These observations about and insights into demand-side stakeholders and their broader policy environment are used to explore the AML drafting process in Chapter 5 and public enforcement of the AML in Chapter 6.

# 4

# Supply-Side Analysis of the Anti-monopoly Law

## 4.1 Introduction

With Chapter 3 having explored the stakeholders and the broader economic and policy environment shaping the demand-side dynamics of the Anti-monopoly Law (AML), this chapter further develops the analytical framework used in this book by examining the key actors involved in the production, enforcement and implementation – that is, the supply – of the AML, and the various factors that shape their actions and decisions.

An investigation of the actors involved in the supply of the AML is especially important in the Chinese context as policy, law and decision-making in China is achieved largely through consensus. Many actors are consulted and involved in the process of consensus-building, and action is taken only once agreement is reached.[1] Any policy, law or decision is the result of, and reflects, a complex process of negotiation, bargaining, exchange and balancing of competing interests that occurs predominantly behind the scenes.[2] Moreover, there is no separation of powers in China, at least not in the way that this is typically understood in Western liberal democracies; instead, China adopts the principle of unity of deliberation and execution.[3] In practice, this means that all powers (legislative, executive and judicial) are subsumed into one administrative system, which is based upon the separation of functions, coordination and mutual restriction.[4] As such, examining the interests, incentives,

---

[1] Susan L. Shirk, *The Political Logic of Economic Reform in China* (Berkeley: University of California Press, 1993), pp. 116–17.

[2] Angela Huyue Zhang, 'Bureaucratic Politics and China's Anti-monopoly Law' (2014) 47 *Cornell International Law Journal* 671 at 674, 685–6.

[3] Jianfu Chen, *Chinese Law: Context and Transformation*, revised and expanded edn (Leiden: Brill Nijhoff, 2015), p. 135.

[4] Ibid; Ronald C. Keith and Zhiqiu Lin, 'Judicial Interpretation of China's Supreme People's Court as "Secondary Law" with Special Reference to Criminal Law' (2009) 23(2) *China Information* 223 at 229, 246.

relative powers and interrelationships of the actors involved in the supply of the AML promotes understanding of why and how a particular outcome is reached.

This chapter is structured as follows. Section 4.2 examines the interests, powers, incentives and knowledge of and attitude towards competition law of the main actors involved in the supply of the AML, and their relationships with other AML stakeholders. Section 4.3 considers how, why and the extent to which aspects of the institutional design structure of AML enforcement present potential challenges to enforcement. The broader governance, regulatory and policy environment of China and how this might shape the incentives of and relationships between actors is explored in Section 4.4. Following this chapter, these observations about and insights into the supply-side dynamics of the AML are then applied to explore the processes of making and enacting the AML in Chapter 5, and of public enforcement of the AML in Chapter 6.

## 4.2 Key Stakeholders on the Supply-Side of the Anti-monopoly Law

A wide range of actors – government and non-government, Chinese and foreign – participate in the supply of the AML. They include central-level Chinese law-making and enforcement institutions, provincial and local government authorities, Chinese and foreign competition law experts and legal practitioners. Many of the actors who were involved in the drafting of the AML continue to participate in its implementation. For example, in addition to enforcing the AML, the three Chinese competition agencies were all involved, to varying degrees, in its drafting. Similarly, the views of Chinese and foreign competition law experts were sought during the drafting process, and many of these experts continue to be involved in the drafting of implementing regulations and providing training and other capacity-building assistance.

This section examines the powers, interests, incentives, relationships and knowledge of and attitude towards competition law of the actors involved on the supply-side of the AML. These actors are the National Development and Reform Commission (NDRC), the Ministry of Commerce (MOFCOM) and the State Administration for Industry and Commerce (SAIC), who are the administrative bodies responsible for enforcing the AML; the Anti-monopoly Commission (AMC), which is the government authority created under the AML to organise, coordinate and supervise AML-related work; the Standing Committee of the National People's Congress (SCNPC); the State Council; provincial and lower-level governments; the courts; competition law experts, including Chinese academics, foreign competition law experts and economists; and legal practitioners.

### 4.2.1 Chinese Competition Authorities

As discussed in Chapter 2, the State Council designated that the administrative enforcement of the AML be divided among three enforcement agencies: the NDRC, the MOFCOM and the SAIC. The MOFCOM is responsible for merger enforcement and the NDRC and the SAIC share the responsibility for enforcing the AML against non-merger conduct,[5] with the NDRC responsible for the price-related aspects and the SAIC for the non-price-related aspects of non-merger conduct.[6] The enforcement agencies have the power to conduct investigations, determine liability and impose sanctions on investigated parties,[7] or they may accept commitments from the investigated parties and suspend an investigation without making a finding or imposing a penalty.[8] Their decisions are subject to administrative review.[9]

This tripartite enforcement arrangement reflects the enforcement of China's pre-AML competition-related laws. It is a compromise struck by

---

[5] Note that, in relation to administrative monopoly, the power of the NDRC and the SAIC is limited to making recommendations to the relevant superior authority, and it is the relevant superior authority that has the power to enforce that prohibition: 中华人民共和国反垄断法 [Anti-monopoly Law of the People's Republic of China] (People's Republic of China) Standing Committee of the National People's Congress, 30 August 2007, art. 51.

[6] 反价格垄断规定 [Anti-Price Monopoly Regulation] (People's Republic of China) National Development and Reform Commission, Order No. 7, 29 December 2010, arts. 7–8, 11–16; 工商行政管理机关禁止垄断协议行为的规定 [Regulation of the Administration for Industry and Commerce on the Prohibition of Monopoly Agreements] (People's Republic of China) State Administration for Industry and Commerce, Order No. 53, 31 December 2010, arts. 4–7; 工商行政管理机关禁止滥用市场支配地位行为的规定 [Regulation of the Administration of Industry and Commerce on the Prohibition of Abuse of Dominance Conduct] (People's Republic of China) State Administration for Industry and Commerce, Order No. 54, 31 December 2010, arts. 4–7.

[7] Anti-monopoly Law, ch. VI.   [8] Ibid., art. 45.

[9] Ibid., art. 53. Administrative litigation for merger decisions is available only after the party has applied for administrative reconsideration and remains dissatisfied, whereas in other decisions made by a Chinese competition agency pursuant to the AML, the availability of administrative litigation is not conditional on having applied for and received a decision under administrative reconsideration.

the State Council as both the MOFCOM and the SAIC, who were the agencies that were most involved in the drafting of the AML, wished to be the primary AML enforcement agency and the NDRC wanted to preserve its authority over certain pricing practices.[10] The dynamics of the drafting process that led to this administrative enforcement structure are analysed in Chapter 5.

#### 4.2.1.1 National Development and Reform Commission

The NDRC is a ministry-level agency directly under the State Council. It is one of the most politically powerful agencies in the central government, deriving its power from its broad mandate and its legacy as the successor to the State Planning Commission, which was the government body that was responsible for managing the planned economy and price control prior to 1978.[11] It is also referred to as the 'mini State Council' and is one of the largest ministries within the Chinese government.[12] Nonetheless, Naughton notes that the NDRC's power has decreased significantly since the 1980s with the increasing marketisation of China's economy.[13] Despite being one of the most powerful central government authorities, the NDRC can still face bureaucratic pressure and resistance from other government authorities, such as industry regulators, in their AML enforcement activities. This is examined further in Chapter 6.

Its mandate covers industrial policy, economic restructuring, pricing, infrastructure and energy projects, sustainable development, climate change, foreign investment, developing the agriculture and high-tech industries and managing the state's reserves of important resources.[14] In particular, the NDRC is China's macroeconomic planning body, and is responsible for formulating and implementing national economic and

---

[10] Yong Huang, 'Pursuing the Second Best: The History, Momentum, and Remaining Issues of China's Anti-monopoly Law' (2008) 75 *Antitrust Law Journal* 117 at 125–6.

[11] Nathan Bush and Yue Bo, 'Adding Antitrust to NDRC's Arsenal' [2011] (2) *CPI Antitrust Chronicle* 1 at 2; *OECD Reviews of Regulatory Reform: China: Defining the Boundary between the Market and the State* (Organisation for Economic Co-Operation and Development, 2009), p. 96.

[12] Hao Qian, 'The Multiple Hands: Institutional Dynamics of China's Competition Regime' in Adrian Emch and David Stallibrass (eds.), *China's Anti-monopoly Law: The First Five Years* (Alphen aan den Rijn, The Netherlands: Kluwer Law International, 2013), p. 28.

[13] Barry Naughton, 'Strengthening the Center, and Premier Wen Jiabao' [2007] (21) *China Leadership Monitor* 1 at 4–5.

[14] National Development and Reform Commission, 'Main Functions of the NDRC', available at http://en.ndrc.gov.cn/mfndrc.

development policies. It prepares national economic development plans that are submitted to the National People's Congress (NPC) on behalf of the State Council, has authority over economic and industrial policies and manages the transition of China's economy from a planned economy to a socialist market economy.[15] It is also China's price regulator and administers the Price Law.[16] Under the Price Law, the NDRC regulates the price of certain key commodities that are considered to be vital to the development of the Chinese economy and the Chinese people, scarce resources, natural monopolies, important public utilities and important public welfare services.[17] It also controls and stabilises the general level of prices.[18] Further, as noted in Chapter 3, the Price Law contains some competition provisions and prohibits unfair pricing conduct,[19] some of which overlaps with the AML. The potential tension between the NDRC's price regulation role and its competition enforcement activities is discussed in Section 4.3.3.

Within the NDRC, the Bureau of Price Supervision and Anti-monopoly (NDRC Bureau) is responsible for enforcing the AML at the central level.[20] It was formed from the NDRC's Department of Price Supervision, which was in charge of guiding price supervision and inspection and ensuring compliance with the Price Law.[21] The NDRC Bureau has ten divisions, four of which deal with AML-related matters. The Anti-Price Monopoly Investigation Division 1, the Anti-Price Monopoly Investigation Division 2 and the Competition Policy and International Cooperation Division are divisions that deal solely with AML-related matters, and the Legal Affairs Division handles both Price

---

[15] Ibid.
[16] 中华人民共和国价格法 [Price Law of the People's Republic of China] (People's Republic of China) Standing Committee of the National People's Congress, 29 December 1997.
[17] Ibid., art. 18. This is administered by the Department of Price at the NDRC.
[18] Ibid., art. 26.     [19] Ibid., art. 14.
[20] 国家发展和改革委员会主要职责内设机构和人员编制规定 [Regulation on the Major Duties, Internal Structure, and Staffing Requirements of the National Development and Reform Commission] (People's Republic of China) National Development and Reform Commission, 25 August 2008, art. 3(23).
[21] The Department of Price of the NDRC is responsible for setting the prices of regulated goods and services, setting and adjusting the prices and fees administered by the central government and recommending objectives, policies and reform plans for price adjustment: National Development and Reform Commission, 'Main Functions of Departments of the NDRC: Department of Price', available at http://en.ndrc.gov.cn/mfod/200812/t20081218_252212.html.

Law and AML-related matters.[22] It is believed that around fifty officials work at the NDRC Bureau, about half of whom work on AML matters.[23] These officials generally have a law or economics background.[24] Interviewees with experience working with the NDRC also observe that the NDRC Bureau might consult with academics or other experts in more complex AML enforcement cases, particularly to undertake economic analysis; however, this does not happen very often.[25] The NDRC has also delegated its AML enforcement authority to provincial-level price authorities.[26] At the provincial level, there are about 150 officials working on AML-related matters.[27]

#### 4.2.1.2 Ministry of Commerce

The MOFCOM is a ministerial-level agency that sits below the State Council. It was formed in 2003 when the State Council restructured the government and merged the State Economic and Trade Commission and the Ministry of Foreign Trade and Economic Cooperation.[28] The MOFCOM's portfolio includes domestic and foreign trade, international economic cooperation, foreign investment and market regulation.[29]

---

[22] 机构设置 [Institutional Arrangements], National Development and Reform Commission Bureau of Price Supervision and Anti-monopoly, available at http://jjs.ndrc.gov.cn/jgsz; Li Qing, 'New Developments in the Enforcement of Anti-monopoly Law by NDRC' (Speech delivered at Asian Competition Association Conference, Beijing, 21 October 2012).

[23] Zhao Yinan, 'Antitrust Office Beefs Up Price Fixing Squad', *China Daily*, 12 December 2013, available at http://usa.chinadaily.com.cn/business/2013-12/12/content_17170067.htm; 原金 [Yuan Jin], 发改委谈反垄断困境: 有协会上来就拍桌子 [NDRC Talks about Anti-monopoly Dilemmas: An Industry Association Approached and Pounded the Table], 每经网 [nbd.com.cn], 27 August 2013, available at www.nbd.com.cn/articles/2013-08-27/768536.html.

[24] Jessica Su and Xiaoye Wang, 'China: The Competition Law System and the Country's Norms' in Eleanor M. Fox and Michael J. Trebilcock (eds.), *The Design of Competition Law Institutions: Global Norms, Local Choices* (Oxford: Oxford University Press, 2013), p. 226.

[25] Interviews with Chinese competition law experts and stakeholders.

[26] 反价格垄断行政执法程序规定 [Regulation on Anti-Price Monopoly Administrative Enforcement Procedures] (People's Republic of China) National Reform and Development Commission, Order No. 8, 29 December 2010, art. 3.

[27] 单素敏 [Dan Sumin], 许昆林: 亲历重大反垄断案 [Xu Kunlin: Personally Experienced a Major Anti-monopoly Case], 瞭望东方周刊 [*Oriental Outlook*], 25 June 2015, available at www.lwdf.cn/article_1473_1.html.

[28] H. Stephen Harris, Jr et al., *Anti-monopoly Law and Practice in China* (New York: Oxford University Press, 2011), p. 270.

[29] Ministry of Commerce, 'Mission', 7 December 2010, available at http://english.mofcom.gov.cn/column/mission2010.shtml; Harris et al., *Anti-monopoly Law and Practice in China*, pp. 270–1.

Together with the SAIC, it is also responsible for administering the Regulation on Mergers with and Acquisitions of Domestic Enterprises by Foreign Investors (Foreign M&A Rules),[30] which was China's merger control system prior to the AML coming into effect. The regulation applied only to mergers and acquisitions by foreign investors and provided for both a competition review and a national economic security review.

The MOFCOM formed the Anti-monopoly Bureau (MOFCOM Bureau) in 2008 to be its responsible department for the AML.[31] The MOFCOM Bureau is divided into seven divisions: the General Office, the Competition Policy Division, the Investigation Division 1, the Investigation Division 2, the Investigation Division 3, the Supervision and Law Enforcement Division and the AMC Coordination Division.[32] The MOFCOM Bureau conducts anti-monopoly consultations; accepts, reviews and investigates notifications of concentrations; drafts AML implementing regulations; guides Chinese entities in defending competition law claims overseas;[33] and coordinates bilateral and multilateral international cooperation on competition policy issues.[34] The MOFCOM Bureau is also the secretariat office for the AMC and undertakes the daily

---

[30] 关于外国投资着并购境内企业的规定 [Regulation on Mergers with and Acquisitions of Domestic Enterprises by Foreign Investors] (People's Republic of China) Ministry of Commerce, State Assets Supervision and Administration Commission of the State Council, State Administration of Taxation, State Administration for Industry and Commerce, China Securities Regulatory Commission, and State Administration of Foreign Exchange, Order No. 10, 8 August 2006. See also Hao, 'The Multiple Hands', pp. 20–1; Peter J. Wang, 'Chinese Merger Control' [2006] *The Asia-Pacific Antitrust & Trade Review* 29.

[31] 商务部主要职责内设机构和人员编制规定 [Regulation on the Major Duties, Internal Structure, and Staffing Requirements of the Ministry of Commerce] (People's Republic of China) Ministry of Commerce, 24 August 2008, art. 3(11).

[32] 内设机构 [Internal Structure], Anti-monopoly Bureau of the Ministry of Commerce, 13 March 2010, available at http://fldj.mofcom.gov.cn/article/gywm/200811/20081105868495.shtml.

[33] For example, the MOFCOM filed an amicus brief in a case where four Chinese vitamin C producers were sued in New York for price fixing. The MOFCOM stated that the Chinese producers' actions were compelled by the Chinese government and performed in compliance with Chinese law and regulations: 沈丹阳 [Shen Danyang], 商务部召开例行新闻发布会 (2013年3月19日) [Regular Press Conference of the Ministry of Commerce (19 March 2013)] Ministry of Commerce, 19 March 2013, available at www.mofcom.gov.cn/article/ae/ah/diaocd/201303/20130300059439.shtml.

[34] H. Stephen Harris, Jr and Keith D. Shugarman, 'Interview with Shang Ming, Director General of the Anti-monopoly Bureau under the Ministry of Commerce of the People's Republic of China' [2009] (February) *The Antitrust Source* 1 at 3, available at www.americanbar.org/content/dam/aba/publishing/antitrust_source/Feb09_ShangIntrvw2_26f.authcheckdam.pdf.

work of the AMC. There are currently around thirty staff assigned to the MOFCOM Bureau and they generally have a law or economics background.[35] In particular, the Economic Analysis Division at the MOFCOM Bureau is headed by a PhD economist and consists of five economists.[36] From time to time the MOFCOM Bureau also consults with legal academics, economists, law firms and other experts when drafting AML implementing regulations or in its merger review.[37] The MOFCOM has not delegated its AML enforcement powers to any local MOFCOM authorities; therefore, AML enforcement work for the MOFCOM is centralised.[38] In some cases, however, the MOFCOM Bureau might ask local MOFCOM authorities to help verify local facts.[39]

The consensus among stakeholders and experts interviewed for this book is that, of the three Chinese competition authorities, the MOFCOM Bureau is the most knowledgeable about competition law and has, within a relatively short period of time, greatly advanced its competition law knowledge. They agree that it adopts a professional and positive attitude to competition law enforcement and learning.[40] A number of interviewees also believe that the MOFCOM Bureau is the most open of the three competition authorities.[41] The MOFCOM Bureau is also

---

[35] 商务部反垄断局局长尚明谈 推进反垄断执法工作 维护市场公平竞争 [MOFCOM Anti-monopoly Bureau Director-General Shang Ming Talks, Advance Anti-monopoly Enforcement Work and Maintain Fair Market Competition] (5 December 2008) 访谈—中国政府网 [Interview – Chinese Government Website], available at www.gov.cn/zxft/ft155/wz.htm; Huang Yong and Richean Zhiyan Li, 'An Overview of Chinese Competition Policy: Between Fragmentation and Consolidation' in Adrian Emch and David Stallibrass (eds.), *China's Anti-monopoly Law: The First Five Years* (Alphen aan den Rijn, The Netherlands: Kluwer Law International, 2013), p. 9; Fei Deng and Cunzhen Huang, 'A Five Year Review of Merger Enforcement in China' [2013] (October) *The Antitrust Source* 1 at 6, available at www.americanbar.org/content/dam/aba/directories/antitrust/oct13_deng_10_29f.authcheckdam.pdf; Su and Wang, 'China: The Competition Law System', p. 226.

[36] Fei Deng, H. Stephen Harris, Jr and Yizhe Zhang, 'Interview with Shang Ming, Director General of the Anti-monopoly Bureau under the Ministry of Commerce of the People's Republic of China' [2011] (February) *The Antitrust Source* 1 at 4, available at www.americanbar.org/content/dam/aba/migrated/2011_build/antitrust_law/feb11_shang_intrvw2_23f.pdf; Deng and Huang, 'A Five Year Review', 11; Xinzhu Zhang and Vanessa Yanhua Zhang, 'New Wine into Old Wineskins: Recent Developments in China's Competition Policy against Monopolistic/Collusive Agreements' (2012) 41 *Review of Industrial Organization* 53 at 68.

[37] Interviews with Chinese competition law experts and stakeholders.

[38] Harris et al., *Anti-monopoly Law and Practice in China*, p. 272.

[39] Deng, Harris and Zhang, 'Interview with Shang Ming', 4.

[40] Interviews with Chinese competition law experts and stakeholders.

[41] Interviews with Chinese competition law experts and stakeholders.

the only competition authority to have a dedicated division handling economic analysis issues.

### 4.2.1.3 State Administration for Industry and Commerce

The SAIC is a ministry-level agency that sits directly under the State Council. The SAIC is responsible for market regulation and supervision and protecting the rights and interests of businesses and consumers.[42] It administers the registration of businesses and trademarks, is responsible for consumer protection, investigates business fraud, regulates advertising and direct marketing and regulates food distribution.[43] In particular, the SAIC enforces the Anti-Unfair Competition Law (AUCL). Its enforcement activities under the competition-related provisions of the AUCL have focused on administrative monopolies and the anti-competitive conduct of enterprises in monopoly industries such as telecommunications, post, insurance, banking, electricity supply, water supply, gas supply, oil, tobacco, salt, tourism, railways and transportation.[44] The SAIC, together with the MOFCOM, is also responsible for enforcing the Foreign M&A Rules, although its level of activity pursuant to those rules has been relatively low.[45]

At the central level, the SAIC has sixteen divisions and approximately 300 staff.[46] It has provincial, sub-provincial and local-level Administrations for Industry and Commerce (AICs) in nearly every city and county in China, with a reported 70,000 enforcement officers who have knowledge and expertise in policing market conduct.[47]

Within the SAIC, the Anti-monopoly and Anti-Unfair Competition Enforcement Bureau (SAIC Bureau) is responsible for AML enforcement

---

[42] State Administration for Industry and Commerce, 'Mission', available at www.saic.gov.cn/english/aboutus/Mission/index.html.
[43] Ibid.
[44] 周萍 [Zhou Ping], 破除市场垄断、倡导公平竞争—全国工商机关反垄断执法综述 [Break Monopolies, Promote Fair Competition – A Review of Anti-monopoly Enforcement by the SAIC] (17 September 2008) 中国工商报 [China Industry & Commerce News], available at www.saic.gov.cn/zt/jg/fldybzdjz/200809/t20080917_219814.html.
[45] Harris et al., *Anti-monopoly Law and Practice in China*, p. 274.
[46] State Administration for Industry and Commerce, 机构 [Organisation], available at www.saic.gov.cn/jggk; Richean Zhiyan Li, 'Unraveling the Jurisdictional Riddle of China's Antitrust Regime' [2011] (2) *CPI Antitrust Chronicle* 1 at 2–3.
[47] Harris et al., *Anti-monopoly Law and Practice in China*, p. 273; Zhang Xian-Chu, 'An Anti-monopoly Legal Regime in the Making in China as a Socialist Market Economy' (2009) 43 *The International Lawyer* 1469 at 1478; Li, 'Unraveling the Jurisdictional Riddle', 2–3.

at the central level.[48] It was formed in 2008 to replace the former Fair Trade Bureau, which was responsible for enforcing the AUCL.[49] It has eight divisions, three of which have AML-related responsibilities, namely the Anti-monopoly Law Guidance Division, Anti-monopoly Enforcement Division 1 and Anti-monopoly Enforcement Division 2.[50] About 1,000 government officials at the national and provincial levels are involved in AML enforcement.[51] However, of the three competition enforcement agencies, the SAIC has the fewest resources at the central level, with approximately ten officials working on AML-related matters at the SAIC Bureau; these officials are believed to have either a law or economics background.[52] The SAIC delegates its AML enforcement authority to provincial-level AICs on a case-by-case basis, with the exception of administrative monopolies, where provincial-level AICs automatically have authority to handle such cases.[53] If authority has been delegated to a provincial-level AIC, that AIC must report to the SAIC prior to making a final decision to either suspend or terminate an investigation, or to impose sanctions.[54]

---

[48] 国家工商总局主要职责内设机构和人员编制规定 [Notice on the Major Duties, Internal Structure, and Staffing Requirements of the State Administration for Industry and Commerce] (People's Republic of China) State Council, Order No. 88, 11 July 2008, art. 3(3).

[49] Hao, 'The Multiple Hands', p. 30.

[50] SAIC Anti-monopoly and Anti-Unfair Competition Enforcement Bureau, 司局介绍 [Introduction to the Bureau], available at www.saic.gov.cn/fldyfbzdjz/sjjs.

[51] Fei Deng, H. Stephen Harris, Jr and Yizhe Zhang, 'Interview with Ning Wanglu, Director General of the Anti-monopoly and Anti-Unfair Competition Enforcement Bureau under the State Administration for Industry and Commerce of People's Republic of China' [2011] (February) *The Antitrust Source* 1 at 1, available at www.americanbar.org/content/dam/aba/migrated/2011_build/antitrust_law/feb11_ningintrvw2_23f.pdf.

[52] Hao, 'The Multiple Hands', p. 31; John Yong Ren and Jet Zhisong Deng, 'Developments in Anti-monopoly Agreement Enforcement and Suggestions Regarding Compliance Programs in China' [2013] (2) *CPI Antitrust Chronicle* 1 at 3; Su and Wang, 'China: The Competition Law System', 226.

[53] 工商行政管理机关查处垄断协议、滥用市场支配地位案件程序规定 [Regulation of the Administration for Industry and Commerce on the Procedures Relating to the Investigation of Monopoly Agreement and Abuse of Dominance Cases] (People's Republic of China) State Administration for Industry and Commerce, Order No. 42, 26 May 2009, art. 2; 工商行政管理机关制止滥用行政权力排除、限制竞争行为程序规定 [Regulation of the Administration for Industry and Commerce on Procedures Relating to the Prevention of the Abuse of Administrative Power to Eliminate or Restrict Competition] (People's Republic of China) State Administration for Industry and Commerce, 5 June 2009, art. 2.

[54] Regulation of the Administration for Industry and Commerce on the Procedures Relating to the Investigation of Cases Involving Monopoly Agreements and Abuse of Market Dominance, art. 23.

Of the three competition authorities, the SAIC is the least politically powerful and has the lowest status.[55] Prior to 2001, the SAIC was a vice-ministerial level agency, meaning that it had a lower bureaucratic rank than a ministry such as the NDRC and the MOFCOM.[56] Its status limited its ability to effectively enforce the AUCL, especially against SOEs and government agencies.[57] Although the State Council upgraded the SAIC to a ministry-level agency in 2001 to boost its enforcement authority and effectiveness,[58] Jung and Hao note that the upgrade had little impact on AUCL enforcement, and suggest that the formal elevation in status did not translate to an actual increase in political power.[59] The SAIC's relatively weak position might impact on its ability to assert authority over anti-competitive conduct. For example, in the dispute between Qihoo 360 and Tencent that is discussed in Chapter 6, both the SAIC and the Ministry of Industry and Information Technology (MIIT) could have asserted authority over the dispute. However, it was the MIIT, not the SAIC, which led the Chinese government's intervention to resolve the dispute and investigation.

The SAIC had built up some knowledge of competition law from its enforcement of the competition-related provisions of the AUCL.[60] However, as its enforcement of the AUCL was relatively opaque,[61] it is

[55] Hao, 'The Multiple Hands', p. 30.
[56] 耿振淞 [Geng Zhensong], 国家工商局换牌称总局 晋级为正部 [SAIC Changes Its Nameplate to General Administration, Upgraded to Ministry], 北京青年报 [Beijing Youth Daily], 11 April 2001, available at www.people.com.cn/GB/jinji/32/180/20010411/439009.html; Xinzhu Zhang and Vanessa Yanhua Zhang, 'The Antimonopoly Law in China: Where Do We Stand?' (2007) 3(2) *Competition Policy International* 185 at 189.
[57] Chenxia Shi and Dong Kaijun, 'The Proposed Antitrust Law and the Problem of Administrative Monopolies in China' (2004) 12 *Trade Practices Law Journal* 106 at 108; Youngjin Jung and Qian Hao, 'The New Economic Constitution in China: A Third Way for Competition Regime?' (2003) 24 *Northwestern Journal of International Law & Business* 107 at 130.
[58] Geng, 'SAIC Changes Its Nameplate to General Administration'; Min Wei, 'State Monopoly Too Hard a Nut to Crack', *China Daily*, 17 April 2001, available at www.chinadaily.com.cn/en/doc/2001-04/17/content_51654.htm.
[59] Jung and Hao, 'The New Economic Constitution in China', 130.
[60] The AUCL prohibits public enterprises and monopolists from restricting competition by constraining buyers from purchasing products other than from specified suppliers, engaging in below-cost pricing for anti-competitive purposes, imposing unreasonable conditions or forcing tie-in sales against customers' wishes and bid rigging: 中华人民共和国反不正当竞争法 [Anti-Unfair Competition Law of the People's Republic of China] (People's Republic of China) National People's Congress, 2 September 1993, arts. 6, 11, 12, 15.
[61] Mark Williams, *Competition Policy and Law in China, Hong Kong and Taiwan* (Cambridge: Cambridge University Press, 2005), pp. 167–9.

unclear how much competition law knowledge the SAIC had accrued through its AUCL enforcement activities prior to the adoption of the AML. Some indication of that knowledge is contained in its 2004 report on the anti-competitive conduct of multinational companies in China (discussed in Chapter 3). In its report, the SAIC noted that predatory pricing, discriminatory pricing and exclusionary conduct could be abuses of market dominance.[62] However, it also seems to have conflated competitive advantage with market power, the accumulation of market share with actual or potential abuse of dominance, and having lower prices than competitors with below-cost pricing.[63]

### 4.2.2 Anti-monopoly Commission

In addition to the competition enforcement agencies, the AML established the AMC to be responsible for the organisation, coordination and supervision of AML-related work. The AMC studies and formulates competition policies; organises the research, assessment and preparation of reports regarding the overall competitive condition of markets; drafts and promulgates AML guidelines; and coordinates AML enforcement.[64] The AMC has designated the MOFCOM to be its secretariat office to handle its day-to-day administrative work.[65]

The AMC comprises twenty-one government officials. The Chairman of the AMC is a Vice-Premier of the State Council, and the four Vice-Chairmen are the heads of the MOFCOM, the NDRC and the SAIC, as well as the Deputy Secretary-General of the State Council. The remaining members of the AMC are representatives from government ministries and agencies, including the NDRC, the MIIT, the Ministry of Supervision, the Ministry of Finance, the Ministry of Transport, the MOFCOM,

---

[62] Fair Trade Bureau and Anti-monopoly Division of the State Administration for Industry and Commerce, 在华跨国公司限制竞争行为表现及对策 [Competition Restricting Conduct of Multinational Companies in China and Countermeasures] (2004) 5 工商行政管理 [Biweekly of Industry and Commerce Administration] 42 at 42–3.
[63] For critique, see Williams, *Competition Policy and Law*, pp. 213–14.
[64] 国务院办公厅关于国务院反垄断委员会主要职责和组成人员的通知 [Notice of the General Office of the State Council on the Primary Duties and Composition of the Anti-monopoly Commission of the State Council] (People's Republic of China) State Council, Order No. 104, 28 July 2008.
[65] 商务部反垄断局将承担反垄断委员会的具体工作 [MOFCOM Anti-monopoly Bureau Assumes the Specific Work of the Anti-monopoly Commission], 中国新闻网 [China News], 1 August 2008, available at www.chinanews.com/cj/gncj/news/2008/08-01/1333119.shtml.

the State-owned Assets Supervision and Administration Commission (SASAC), the SAIC, the State Intellectual Property Office, the State Council Legislative Affairs Office (LAO), the People's Bank of China, the National Bureau of Statistics, the China Banking Regulatory Commission, the China Securities Regulatory Commission, the China Insurance Regulatory Commission and the State Electricity Regulatory Commission (which has now been merged into the National Energy Administration, and is directly under the NDRC).[66]

There is an expert group (the AMC Expert Group) that advises the AMC on competition policy matters. Each member of the AMC nominated an expert to be part of the AMC Expert Group, which comprises experts such as academics, economists and former senior government officials.[67] The inclusion of former government officials as experts in the AMC Expert Group brings industry, technical and other knowledge into the group, although some interviewees have expressed concerns about their level of competition law knowledge.[68] In addition to advising the AMC on competition law and policy matters, the AMC Expert Group also advises the State Council and the competition enforcement agencies on competition policy matters.[69]

The AMC appears to have several functions. First, it can help coordinate the interests of government ministries and agencies with a stake in competition law matters.[70] Members of the AMC include not only the enforcement agencies but also industry regulators and the SASAC. As explored further in Chapter 5, some of the most hotly debated issues during the drafting of the AML related to the relationship between the AML and regulated sectors and SOEs; these issues remain relevant in the enforcement of the AML. The AMC might operate as a forum where such issues are discussed and perhaps resolved at a policy-level. Second, the AMC can help to reduce inconsistency or divergence among

---

[66] Notice of the General Office of the State Council on the Primary Duties and Composition of the Anti-monopoly Commission of the State Council; 国务院反垄断委员会关于印发《关于相关市场界定的指南》的通知 [Notice Regarding the Issue of the 'Guidelines on the Definition of the Relevant Market' by the Anti-monopoly Commission of the State Council] (People's Republic of China) Anti-monopoly Commission, Order No. 3, 6 July 2009. The People's Bank of China and the National Bureau of Statistics were not originally members of the AMC and were added subsequently.
[67] Interviews with Chinese competition law experts and stakeholders.
[68] Interviews with Chinese competition law experts and stakeholders.
[69] Interviews with Chinese competition law experts and stakeholders.
[70] Interviews with Chinese competition law experts and stakeholders. See also Zhang, 'Bureaucratic Politics and China's Anti-monopoly Law', 686–7.

the three enforcement agencies in enforcement, especially where they face common issues.[71] To that end, in addition to its guideline on relevant market definition,[72] the AMC will soon issue guidelines on leniency, commitments, exemptions for anti-competitive agreements, determination of illegal gains and fines, abuse of intellectual property rights and the automotive industry. These guidelines will apply to all three enforcement agencies. Third, there were concerns that the anti-monopoly departments within the competition authorities might be too low in the Chinese administrative hierarchy to be able to effectively investigate or make decisions against other government agencies, or against large SOEs that are of higher bureaucratic rank. The AMC, with its chairman being a high-ranking and politically influential Chinese leader, might help to overcome these enforcement challenges.

### 4.2.3 Standing Committee of the National People's Congress

The AML was enacted by the SCNPC. The SCNPC is the permanent body of the NPC, which is the highest organ of state power and exercises the legislative power of the state.[73] Basic laws are enacted by the NPC and other laws are enacted by the SCNPC.[74] Apart from legislative power, the NPC has a wide range of other powers and functions such as appointing and removing the President, the Premier and the President of the Supreme People's Court (SPC).[75] The SCNPC exercises the powers of the NPC when the NPC is not in session.[76] As the NPC only meets annually, in March, for two to three weeks, most of the work (and therefore most of the legislation enacted) is undertaken by the SCNPC, which meets once every two months for around two weeks at a time.[77] The NPC's legislative role is hampered somewhat by the fact that it only meets once a year for a short period of time;[78] however, it is taking an

---

[71] Harris et al., *Anti-monopoly Law and Practice in China*, p. 269.
[72] 国务院反垄断委员会关于相关市场界定的指南 [Guideline of the Anti-monopoly Commission of the State Council on Defining the Relevant Market] (People's Republic of China) Anti-monopoly Commission of the State Council, 24 May 2009.
[73] 中华人民共和国宪法 [Constitution of the People's Republic of China] arts. 57–8.
[74] Ibid., arts. 62(2), 67(2).     [75] Ibid., arts. 62–3.     [76] Ibid., art. 67.
[77] 中华人民共和国全国人民代表大会组织法 [Organic Law of the National People's Congress of the People's Republic of China] (People's Republic of China) National People's Congress, 10 December 1982, art. 29.
[78] Constitution of the People's Republic of China, art. 61.

increasingly active role in law-making, and is no longer considered to be a 'rubber-stamp' institution.[79]

The SCNPC also has its own powers, including supervising the work of the State Council and the SPC and appointing the judges to the SPC.[80] It has exclusive power to interpret the Chinese Constitution and the statutes that have been enacted by the NPC and itself.[81] The SCNPC has delegated part of this interpretation power to the SPC, the Supreme People's Procuratorate, the State Council and local governments,[82] and rarely exercises its superior power of interpretation.[83]

The SCNPC has around 175 members (compared to the entire NPC, which has about 3,000 members), and consists of the Chairman, the Vice Chairmen, the Secretary-General and other members.[84] The Chairman's Council, which is composed of the Chairman, the Vice Chairmen and the Secretary-General, handles the important daily work of the SCNPC, including setting the NPC's legislative agenda.[85] Members of the SCNPC are supposed to work full-time for the SCNPC and are not allowed to hold a position in any administrative, judicial or procuratorial body during their term in office.[86] SCNPC members are generally former senior officials of the central or local government or the Communist Party of China (CPC), most of whom do not have a legal background and will have come from a variety of different backgrounds such as industry regulators or monopoly industries.[87] Some interviewees noted that,

---

[79] Randall Peerenboom, *China's Long March toward Rule of Law* (Cambridge: Cambridge University Press, 2002), pp. 12–13, 215, 239; Murray Scot Tanner, 'The National People's Congress', in Merle Goldman and Roderick MacFarquhar (eds.), *The Paradox of China's Post-Mao Reforms* (Cambridge, MA.: Harvard University Press, 1999); Young Nam Cho, 'From "Rubber Stamps" to "Iron Stamps": The Emergence of Chinese Local People's Congresses as Supervisory Powerhouses' (2002) 171 *The China Quarterly* 724.

[80] Constitution of the People's Republic of China, art. 67.   [81] Ibid., arts. 67(1), (4).

[82] 关于加强法律解释工作的决议 [Resolution on Strengthening Legal Interpretation Work] (People's Republic of China) Standing Committee of the National People's Congress, 10 June 1981.

[83] Keith and Lin, 'Judicial Interpretation of China's Supreme People's Court', 229–30.

[84] Constitution of the People's Republic of China, art. 65; Susan V. Lawrence and Michael F. Martin, 'Understanding China's Political System' (Congressional Research Service, 31 January 2013), pp. 30–1. A list of the SCNPC members is available at www.npc.gov.cn/npc/cwhhy/12jcwh/node_31314.htm.

[85] Constitution of the People's Republic of China, art. 68.

[86] Ibid., art. 65. Non-SCNPC members of the NPC are not paid and do not work full-time for the NPC.

[87] Lawrence and Martin, 'Understanding China's Political System', p. 31; Qianlan Wu, *Competition Laws, Globalization and Legal Pluralism: China's Experiences* (Oxford: Hart

because of their previous experience, SCNPC members tend to consider broader issues, such as industrial policy and national security, when deliberating draft laws.[88] This was reflected in the drafting of the AML, where the members of the SCNPC added articles relating to industrial policy, national security and the leading role of the state in the economy. This is examined in detail in Chapter 5.

Draft laws placed on the agenda of the SCNPC session are generally deliberated three times by the SCNPC before being voted upon.[89] While the SCNPC almost always approves the draft legislation put before it, such approval is not necessarily a 'rubber stamp'.[90] Some members might withhold support and request revisions to work reports, draft legislation or the budget; opposition voting, however, is relatively rare.[91]

Two NPC institutions were particularly relevant and important to the drafting of the AML. The first institution is the Law Committee, which assists the NPC and the SCNPC in reviewing and drafting legislation.[92] It, along with eight other specialised committees,[93] provides the NPC and the SCNPC with the relevant policy expertise. Draft laws are generally reviewed by both the Law Committee and the relevant specialised committee.[94] In the case of the AML, the draft was

---

Publishing, 2013), p. 131; Interviews with Chinese competition law experts and stakeholders.

[88] Interviews with Chinese competition law experts and stakeholders.

[89] 中华人民共和国立法法 [Law on Legislation of the People's Republic of China] (People's Republic of China) National People's Congress, 15 March 2000, art. 27. There is no time limit on the three deliberations stipulated in the law.

[90] Peerenboom, *China's Long March toward Rule of Law*, pp. 12–13, 215, 239; Tanner, 'The National People's Congress'.

[91] 王毕强, 郑猛 [Wang Biqiang and Zheng Meng], 今年人大预算报告反对票数创记录 审议频遭冷场 [Opposing Votes for the Budget Report at this Year's NPC Set a Record: Review Frequently Meets with Awkward Silence] [2012] (9) *Caijing*, available at http://news.hexun.com/2012-03-26/139730819.html; Tony Saich, *Governance and Politics of China*, 3rd edn (Houndmills, Basingstoke: Palgrave McMillan, 2011), pp. 156–8.

[92] Law on Legislation, art. 34.

[93] The other special committees of the NPC are the Ethnic Affairs Committee; Internal and Judicial Affairs Committee; Financial and Economic Affairs Committee; Education, Science, Culture and Public Health Committee; Foreign Affairs Committee; Overseas Chinese Affairs Committee; Environment Protection and Resources Conservation Committee; and the Agriculture and Rural Affairs Committee. See The National People's Congress of the People's Republic of China, 'Special Committees', available at www.npc.gov.cn/englishnpc/Organization/node_2849.htm.

[94] Chien-Min Chao, 'The National People's Congress Oversight Power and the Role of the CCP' (2003) 17 *The Copenhagen Journal of Asian Studies* 6 at 12–13.

reviewed by both the Law Committee and the Financial and Economic Affairs Committee of the NPC (FEA Committee).[95] Committee members tend to be former high-ranking government or CPC officials who have recently retired, or who are specialists in the field, such as academics or representatives from mass organisations such as the Chinese Women's Federation.[96] Of the NPC's special committees, the Law Committee has the most influence over law-making. It generally reviews all draft laws submitted to the NPC and SCNPC for consideration and collates the comments on the draft law made by other special committees, members of the NPC or the SCNPC or government bodies. The Law Committee can decide to incorporate these comments into the draft law or bring them to the attention of the NPC or the SCNPC.[97] Also, while every specialised committee has the power to draft legislation, in practice the Law Committee usually takes the lead in drafting legislation initiated by the NPC or the SCNPC. For example, during the drafting of the AML, the Law Committee (together with the FEA Committee) conducted research and made recommendations on revisions to the draft AML to address concerns raised by members of the SCNPC and other relevant parties, and then provided the SCNPC with reports on such work.[98]

The other important NPC institution is the Legislative Affairs Commission, which is one of the working and administrative bodies of

---

[95] 全国人大法律委员会关于《中华人民共和国反垄断法(草案)》修改情况的汇报 [Report of the Law Committee of the National People's Congress on the Revision of the Anti-monopoly Law of the People's Republic of China (Draft)], 28th Session of the Standing Committee of the Tenth National People's Congress, 24 June 2007; Interviews with Chinese competition law experts and stakeholders.

[96] Chao, 'The National People's Congress Oversight Power', 11; Murray Scot Tanner, 'How a Bill Becomes a Law in China: Stages and Processes in Lawmaking' (1995) 141 *The China Quarterly* 39 at 57–8.

[97] Chao, 'The National People's Congress Oversight Power', 13–14.

[98] Report of the Law Committee of the National People's Congress on the Revision of the Anti-monopoly Law of the People's Republic of China (Draft), 24 June 2007; 全国人大法律委员会关于《中华人民共和国反垄断法 (草案二次审议稿)》审议结果的报告 [Report of the Law Committee of the National People's Congress on the Outcome of Anti-monopoly Law of the People's Republic of China (Second Deliberation Draft) Deliberations], 29th Session of the Standing Committee of the Tenth National People's Congress, 24 August 2007; 全国人大法律委员会关于《中华人民共和国反垄断法 (草案三次审议稿)》修改意见的报告 [Report of the Law Committee of the National People's Congress on Views Regarding the Revision of the Anti-monopoly Law of the People's Republic of China (Third Deliberation Draft)], 29th Session of the Standing Committee of the Tenth National People's Congress, 29 August 2007.

the SCNPC.[99] The Legislative Affairs Commission is responsible for doing the daily work relating to the drafting and reviewing of draft laws.[100] During the drafting of the AML, the Economic Law Division of the Legislative Affairs Commission was responsible for managing and coordinating the SCNPC's review of the draft AML on a day-to-day basis.[101]

There is substantial overlap between the work of the Legislative Affairs Commission and the Law Committee. However, unlike the Law Committee, the Legislative Affairs Commission is an administrative body and is staffed with government officials rather than NPC members. It also handles the more technical aspects of the law and legal drafting.[102] The Chairman and Vice Chairman of the Legislative Affairs Commission are both members of the Law Committee. This arrangement helps to improve communication and coordination between the two bodies, as well as increase the consistency of legislative drafting across them and reduces the competition for power and control over legislative drafting activities within the SCNPC.

The Law Committee and the Legislative Affairs Commission also need to balance and resolve the different and potentially competing interests of various interested parties during the drafting process. In particular, as many members of the SCNPC and the special committees are retired former high-ranking government officials, they come to the drafting process with different industry backgrounds, expertise and interests. This does not mean, however, that these SCNPC members necessarily agree with, adopt the position of or champion the interests of their former government agency in SCNPC deliberations over draft legislation.[103] What it does mean is that the members may consider different matters when deliberating and making suggestions on the proposed legislation. The SCNPC members can also act as informal channels of communication between the SCNPC and the State Council

---

[99] The other working and administrative offices of the SCNPC are the General Office, Budgetary Affairs Commission, Credentials Committee, Hong Kong Special Administrative Region Basic Law Committee and Macao Special Administrative Region Basic Law Committee. See The National People's Congress of the People's Republic of China, 'Working and Administrative Bodies of the Standing Committee', available at www.npc.gov.cn/englishnpc/Organization/node_2850.htm.
[100] Law on Legislation, art. 34.
[101] Interviews with Chinese competition law experts and stakeholders.
[102] Interviews with Chinese competition law experts and stakeholders.
[103] Tanner, 'How a Bill Becomes a Law in China', 58.

as they generally retain ties to their former government agencies, thus supplementing the formal relationship and channels of communication between the State Council and the SCNPC.

These dynamics played out during the drafting of the AML at the SCNPC. The AML touches upon and overlaps with a number of policies, including industrial policy, trade, foreign investment and national security. The relationship between competition policy and other policies featured in the deliberations between SCNPC members, especially as many of these members came to the AML from an industry or government background rather than a legal one.[104] These matters are explored further in Chapter 5.

### 4.2.4 State Council

The State Council is regarded as China's most powerful and active law-making institution.[105] It and its constituents issue a large number of administrative rules and regulations and initiate (often drafting) a majority of the laws that are considered by the NPC or the SCNPC.[106] The State Council also serves as the forum in which much of the political bargaining over policy-making and law-making occurs.[107] As demonstrated in Chapter 5, the State Council was significantly involved in the drafting of the AML, during which it coordinated and balanced the various opinions on the AML held by its constituents, especially industry regulators and enforcement agencies.

The State Council is the executive body of the NPC and the highest organ of state administration.[108] It is responsible and reports on its work to the NPC and, when the NPC is not in session, the SCNPC.[109] The State Council comprises the Premier, Vice Premiers, State Councillors, the heads of the ministries and commissions, the Secretary-General and the Auditor-General.[110] Ministries are responsible for a particular

---

[104] Interviews with Chinese competition law experts and stakeholders.
[105] Chen, *Chinese Law*, pp. 135, 243–4; Stanley Lubman, 'Looking for Law in China' (2006) 20 *Columbia Journal of Asian Law* 1 at 28. The State Council's legislative power is supplemented with several open-ended delegations of legislative power from the NPC and the SCNPC.
[106] Chen, *Chinese Law*, 243; Jean-Pierre Cabestan, 'The Relationship between the National People's Congress and the State Council in the People's Republic of China: A Few Checks but No Balances' (2001) 19(3) *American Asian Review* 35 at 62.
[107] Tanner, 'How a Bill Becomes a Law in China'.
[108] Constitution of the People's Republic of China, art. 85.     [109] Ibid., art. 92.
[110] Ibid., art. 87.

industry or sector, whereas commissions take a more comprehensive, national view of matters and integrate policy with other facets of the economy.[111] The Premier has overall responsibility for the State Council. The State Council makes decisions through executive meetings (held every week and attended by the Premier, Vice Premiers and State Councillors) and full meetings (held every six months).[112]

Some of the State Council's roles and responsibilities include submitting proposals to the NPC and the SCNPC, devising and implementing the national economic and social development plan and state budget and supervising the administrative work of its ministries and commissions, special organisations, organisations, administrative offices and institutions.[113] The State Council issues administrative rules and regulations to implement national laws and policies.[114] In particular, its ministries and commissions are key players in decision-making and policy implementation in their areas of responsibility.[115] Further, the State Council has some powers of interpretation, having been delegated that power by the SCNPC. The State Council (including its ministries and commissions) can interpret questions of law arising from the specific application of law outside judicial proceedings and procuratorial work.[116] The State Council, ministries and commissions can also interpret their own administrative rules and regulations.[117]

The State Council LAO plays an important role as it drafts the government's annual legislative agenda and works with the relevant government ministries and agencies to implement that agenda. It also often supervises and guides the drafting of laws and regulations, and serves as a mechanism to coordinate and balance competing interests within the State Council.[118] As shown in Chapter 5, the LAO played an important role in drafting the AML and coordinating the various comments and opinions of the relevant interests within the State Council.

---

[111] There are also administrations and bureaus under the ministries and commissions: 'State Council Organization Chart', english.gov.cn (The Chinese Government's Official Web Portal), available at http://english.gov.cn/state_council/2014/09/03/content_281474985533579.htm.

[112] Cheng Li, 'China's Midterm Jockeying: Gearing Up for 2012 (Part 2: Cabinet Ministers)' [2010] (32) China Leadership Monitor 1 at 3.

[113] Constitution of the People's Republic of China, art. 89.   [114] Ibid., art. 89(1).

[115] Li, 'China's Midterm Jockeying (Part 2)', 4.

[116] Resolution on Strengthening Legal Interpretation Work, art. 3.

[117] Chen, Chinese Law, 268.

[118] Lawrence and Martin, 'Understanding China's Political System', p. 30.

### 4.2.5 Provincial and Lower-Level Government Authorities

Both the incentive and the ability of provincial[119] and lower-level government authorities to investigate and enforce the AML vis-à-vis businesses in their region are likely to impact the enforcement of the AML. As noted in Section 4.2.1, the NDRC has delegated, and the SAIC may delegate, its AML enforcement authority to provincial-level price authorities and AICs, respectively. This delegation of authority has been relied upon by the NDRC and SAIC to enforce the AML. To date, a majority of the AML enforcement decisions published by the SAIC, and most of the NDRC's publicly-known investigations and decisions, have been made by provincial authorities. Provincial and lower-level government authorities may also be involved in investigating and sanctioning administrative monopolies as the superior authority of the administrative organ whose conduct is in question.[120] Private enforcement might also be affected because, as discussed in Section 4.2.6, judges and courts are not independent from the government at the same level.

Below the central government there are three levels of government. The lowest level of government is the township, town or district; the intermediate level is the county, city or district; and the highest level is the province and its equivalents.[121] At each of these levels, there is a people's congress and a people's government. The three levels of government below the centre are structured in essentially the same way as the central government, and local-level institutions have similar powers to their central-level counterparts. Provinces have significant representation in NPC and CPC institutions, and provincial leaders have the equivalent bureaucratic rank to a ministry.[122] Provincial leaders often go on to hold national leadership positions in the government and the CPC, and many senior central government and CPC officials have significant provincial management experience.[123] Provincial and

---

[119] Any reference to 'province' or 'provincial' includes provinces, autonomous regions and municipalities that are directly under the central government.
[120] Anti-monopoly Law, art. 51.
[121] There are twenty-three provinces (including Taiwan), five autonomous regions (Guangxi, Inner Mongolia, Ningxia, Tibet and Xinjiang), four municipalities directly under the central government (Shanghai, Beijing, Tianjin and Chongqing) and two special administrative regions (Hong Kong and Macau).
[122] Lawrence and Martin, 'Understanding China's Political System', p. 8; Saich, *Governance and Politics of China*, pp. 184–5.
[123] Cheng Li, 'China's Midterm Jockeying: Gearing Up for 2012 (Part 1: Provincial Chiefs)' [2010] (31) *China Leadership Monitor* 1 at 2–4; Saich, *Governance and Politics of China*, 185.

municipal people's congresses can adopt local regulations, and local governments at and above the county level can issue decisions and orders.[124] The SCNPC has also delegated some interpretation power to local governments, and local governments can interpret questions of law arising from the specific application of their local laws and decrees.[125]

While all provinces and municipalities carry the same bureaucratic rank on paper, some are in fact more powerful and influential than others.[126] Those provinces and municipalities that are more economically prosperous and developed have more political power than less developed provinces.[127] The more powerful provinces and municipalities tend to be along the coast (such as Shanghai and Guangdong), as they have been able to take advantage of the preferential policies that were implemented by the central government earlier in the economic reform process.[128] For example, the central government established Special Economic Zones and Coastal Economic Open Areas as free-trade zones for the purpose of general development and opening up to foreign trade and investment, and these zones have enjoyed lower tax rates and a special institutional and policy environment.[129] Poorer provinces are typically interior provinces that, due to factors such as lack of financial resources and skilled personnel and geography, have faced difficulties in developing their local economies.[130] Since the early 2000s, the central government has emphasised the economic development of the western and north-eastern regions of China.[131]

Since beginning economic reforms in 1978, the central government has encouraged local governments to experiment with reforms and take responsibility for their region's economic development. In 1980, the central government implemented the fiscal contracting system (FCS),[132]

---

[124] Constitution of the People's Republic of China, arts. 100, 107.
[125] Resolution on Strengthening Legal Interpretation Work, art. 4.
[126] Saich, *Governance and Politics of China*, p. 182. [127] Ibid., pp. 182–3.
[128] Kenneth Lieberthal, *Governing China: From Revolution through Reform*, 2nd edn (New York: W. W. Norton, 2004), p. 182.
[129] Gabriella Montinola, Yingyi Qian and Barry R. Weingast, 'Federalism, Chinese Style: The Political Bias for Economic Success in China' (1995) 48 *World Politics* 50 at 62–3.
[130] Yongnian Zheng, 'Central–Local Relations: The Power to Dominate', in Joseph Fewsmith (ed.), *China Today, China Tomorrow: Domestic Politics, Economy, and Society* (Lanham, MD: Rowman & Littlefield Publishers, 2010), p. 199; Saich, *Governance and Politics of China*, pp. 190–1.
[131] Saich, *Governance and Politics of China*, p. 193.
[132] Prior to the implementation of the FCS, all government revenue and expenditure went through the central government (unified revenue and unified expenditure). The FCS is

which was a revenue-sharing system between local and central governments, with the contractual sharing rates varying from province to province.[133] The FCS strengthened the link between local revenue and local expenditures and provided financial incentives for local governments to develop the local economy, as the revenue they were able to retain was linked to local economic prosperity.[134] The central government also devolved decision-making power to local governments, making local governments responsible for the provision of services such as education, health, housing and local infrastructure, and for the administrative supervision of SOEs.[135]

There is considerable competition between provinces and between lower-level governments. As a result of the economic reforms and devolution of economic power from the central government to provincial and local governments, provincial and lower-level governments are highly dependent on the financial performance of businesses in their region.[136] Promotions of provincial and local government officials are also partially based on local economic performance.[137] Provincial and local government leaders therefore have economic, political and personal incentives to develop their own region's economy and protect local businesses, and there is little incentive to distribute wealth to or coordinate with other

---

also known as 'eating from separate kitchens'. Under the FCS, budgetary revenue (central fixed revenue and local revenue) was subject to sharing between the local and central governments, while extra-budgetary revenue (tax surcharges and user fees levied by the central and local government agencies and earnings from SOEs) and off-budget revenue (revenue not incorporated into the budgetary process) were retained by the local government and not shared with the central government. See, e.g., Yingyi Qian and Barry R. Weingast, 'China's Transition to Markets: Market Preserving Federalism, Chinese Style' (1996) 1 *Journal of Policy Reform* 149 at 162–3.

[133] Yingyi Qian, 'How Reform Worked in China' (William Davidson Working Paper No. 473, The William Davidson Institute at the University of Michigan Business School, June 2002), p. 28.

[134] Qian and Weingast, 'China's Transition to Markets', 162–3; Qian, 'How Reform Worked in China', pp. 27–31.

[135] William A. Byrd, *The Market Mechanism and Economic Reforms in China* (Armonk, NY: M. E. Sharpe, 1991), p. 5.

[136] Qian and Weingast, 'China's Transition to Markets', 162–3.

[137] R Hewitt Pate, 'What I Heard in the Great Hall of the People – Realistic Expectations of Chinese Antitrust' (2008) 75 *Antitrust Law Journal* 195 at 202–3; Youngjin Jung and Qian Hao, 'The New Economic Constitution in China: A Third Way for Competition Regime?' (2003) 24 *Northwestern Journal of International Law & Business* 107 at 115; Eun Kyong Choi, 'Patronage and Performance: Factors in the Political Mobility of Provincial Leaders in Post-Deng China' (2012) 212 *The China Quarterly* 965 at 967.

provinces or localities.[138] Provinces compete with one another to attract foreign investment and other capital inflows. They might also adopt laws, regulations and policies to foster and protect local businesses, increase the local revenue base and prevent businesses from other provinces doing business in their province.[139] Such actions might constitute regional monopoly, which is a main form of administrative monopoly in China.

Regional monopolies are protected through various acts of protectionism engaged in by local or provincial governments.[140] Such acts of local protectionism 'discriminate against and burden the flow of goods from one province or locality into another',[141] typically creating barriers to entry and restricting the inflow of products from other areas into local markets and the outflow of products, especially raw materials and technology, from local markets.[142] The most common acts of local protectionism are regional blockades and the abuse of government approval and licensing powers.[143] Poor transportation and communication networks also help to protect regional monopolies.[144] This has resulted in relatively little interregional competition and a low level of industrial concentration in most sectors.[145] The manner in which economic reforms have been pursued has contributed to the existence of regional monopolies.[146]

---

[138] Zheng, 'Central–Local Relations: The Power to Dominate', 200–1.
[139] Pate, 'What I Heard in the Great Hall of the People', 202–3; Jung and Hao, 'The New Economic Constitution in China', 115.
[140] Xiaoye Wang, 'The Prospect of Antimonopoly Legislation in China' (2002) 1 *Washington University Global Studies Law Review* 201 at 211.
[141] Eleanor M. Fox, 'An Anti-monopoly Law for China – Scaling the Walls of Government Restraints' (2008) 75 *Antitrust Law Journal* 173 at 173.
[142] Ibid., 173; Bruce M. Owen, Su Sun and Wentong Zheng, 'China's Competition Policy Reforms: The Anti-monopoly Law and Beyond' (2008) 75 *Antitrust Law Journal* 231 at 255; Gordon Y. M. Chan, 'Administrative Monopoly and the Anti-monopoly Law: An Examination of the Debate in China' (2009) 18 *Journal of Contemporary China* 263 at 266; Shi and Kaijun, 'The Proposed Antitrust Law', 110.
[143] Bing Song, 'Competition Policy in a Transitional Economy: The Case of China' (1995) 31 *Stanford Journal of International Law* 387 at 407, 418; Jung and Hao, 'The New Economic Constitution in China', 114.
[144] Song, 'Competition Policy in a Transitional Economy', 405–6.
[145] The World Bank and the Development Research Center of the State Council, the People's Republic of China, *China 2030: Building a Modern, Harmonious, and Creative Society* (Washington, DC: The World Bank, 2013), pp. 105–6.
[146] Yong Guo and Angang Hu, 'The Administrative Monopoly in China's Economic Transition' (2004) 37 *Communist and Post-Communist Studies* 265 at 273–4; Wang, 'The Prospect of Antimonopoly Legislation in China', 210; Chan, 'Administrative Monopoly and the Anti-monopoly Law', 265–6; Wentong Zheng, 'Transplanting Antitrust in China: Economic Transition, Market Structure, and State Control' (2010) 32

Concerns about administrative monopoly were a significant factor influencing demand for the enactment of the AML. However, support for the inclusion of a prohibition against administrative monopoly in the AML fluctuated throughout the drafting process and was one of the main reasons for delays in the process. This is examined in Chapter 5. Enforcement of the prohibition on administrative monopoly will also likely face challenges, given the weak enforcement mechanism and the support of vested interests for protective measures that give rise to administrative monopoly. This is reflected in the relatively small number of publicly-known investigations involving administrative monopoly under the AML, as discussed in Chapter 2.

More broadly, provincial and local governments have an interest in AML cases that involve or affect their local businesses or economy, and they might seek to influence the outcome of an investigation or merger review. As provinces have the same bureaucratic rank as ministries and are generally politically powerful entities themselves, provincial governments have not only the incentive but also the ability to assert such influence.[147] For example, a provincial government might make a complaint to the MOFCOM Bureau about a proposed merger involving a local company if the merger will lead to unemployment in the province or involve relocation of the merged entity's headquarters to another province, and seek to have conditions attached to the merger or the merger prohibited. It might refuse to cooperate with an investigation or place pressure on the competition agencies, their local authorities or the court to stop or suspend an investigation, to refrain from publicising an investigation or to refrain from imposing fines or other sanctions. In these situations, the provincial-level competition authorities will need to balance and coordinate the interests of both their superior agencies; that is, the central-level competition authority on the one hand, and the provincial government on the other. This tension between central and local interests is examined further in Section 4.4.3. The competition authorities and courts might also encounter difficulties when trying to implement enforcement decisions in circumstances where the cooperation of lower-level governments is required.

---

*University of Pennsylvania Journal of International Law* 643 at 657–8; Williams, *Competition Policy and Law*, p. 109.

[147] Harris et al., *Anti-monopoly Law and Practice in China*, p. 276.

### 4.2.6 Courts

Business operators that engage in monopoly conduct in breach of the AML will be responsible for civil liabilities for any loss caused by such conduct.[148] A private party can bring an action before the court without first having to file a complaint with a competition authority.[149] Further, if a party is dissatisfied with a decision made by a competition authority under the AML, they can apply to the court for review of the administrative decision.[150] For example, several of the accounting firms sanctioned in the *Linyi Accounting Firm Cartel* case instituted administrative proceedings to set aside a penalty decision made by the SAIC's local authority in Shandong; they were ultimately unsuccessful.[151]

There are four levels of courts in China. The SPC is the highest judicial organ in China.[152] It is headquartered in Beijing and has six circuit court divisions (situated in Shenzhen, Shenyang, Nanjing, Zhengzhou, Chongqing and Xi'an) to handle major administrative, civil and commercial cases in the provinces within each circuit court's jurisdiction.[153] At the next level are the high people's courts, which are the highest-level courts in provinces, autonomous regions and municipalities that fall under the direct control of the central government. Intermediate people's courts are established at the city and

---

[148] Anti-monopoly Law, art. 50.
[149] 最高人民法院关于审理因垄断行为引发的民事纠纷案件应用法律若干问题的规定 [Provision of the Supreme People's Court on Several Issues Regarding the Application of Law in the Hearing of Civil Dispute Cases Caused by Monopolistic Conduct] (People's Republic of China) Supreme People's Court, Legal Interpretation No. 5, 30 January 2012, arts. 1–2.
[150] Anti-monopoly Law, art. 53.
[151] 山东省济南市历下区人民法院一审维持山东省局行政处罚决定 [Shandong Jinan Lixia District People's Court First Instance Hearing Maintains Shandong AIC's Administrative Penalty Decision], 6 September 2016, available at www.saic.gov.cn/fldyfbzdjz/gzdt/201609/t20160906_205297.html.
[152] Constitution of the People's Republic of China, art. 127.
[153] 最高人民法院关于巡回法庭审理案件若干问题的规定 [Provision of the Supreme People's Court on Several Issues Regarding the Trial of Cases in Circuit Court Divisions] (People's Republic of China) Supreme People's Court, Legal Interpretation No. 3, 28 January 2015; 习近平: 全面贯彻党的十八届六中全会精神 [Xi Jinping: Comprehensively Implement the Spirit of the Sixth Plenum of the 18th CPC Central Committee], 11 November 2016, available at www.court.gov.cn/zixun-xiangqing-29261.html; 'China Inaugurates its 3rd, 4th Circuit Courts', *China Daily*, 28 December 2016, available at www.chinadaily.com.cn/china/2016-12/28/content_27805067.htm; 'More SPC Circuit Courts Start Business', *Shanghai Daily*, 31 December 2016, available at www.shanghaidaily.com/nation/More-SPC-circuit-courts-start-business/shdaily.shtml.

prefecture levels, and the lowest-level courts are the basic people's courts, which are established at the district and county levels.

Other than simple civil cases and minor criminal cases, which may be heard by a single judge, other cases are heard by a collegiate panel of judges and layperson assessors.[154] In addition, adjudication committees composed of senior judges and heads of divisions are established by courts at all levels, and are responsible for discussing major or difficult cases and adjudication experiences.[155]

The courts of first instance for civil disputes and administrative cases involving AML matters are the intermediate people's courts of the capital cities of provinces and their equivalents, municipalities with independent planning status[156] and others as designated by the SPC.[157] The SPC may also approve certain basic people's courts as courts of first instance in AML matters.[158] As the SPC has included AML disputes under the scope of intellectual property disputes, the intellectual property tribunal, which sits within the civil division of courts, is responsible for hearing AML cases.[159] The SPC has also created specialised intellectual property courts in Beijing, Shanghai and Guangzhou. These are the courts of first instance for technically complex civil and administrative intellectual

---

[154] 中华人民共和国人民法院组织法 [Organic Law of the People's Courts of the People's Republic of China] (People's Republic of China) National People's Congress, 1 July 1979, art. 9. On the requirements for layperson assessors, see 全国人大常委会关于完善人民陪审员制度的决定 [Decision of the Standing Committee of the National People's Congress on Perfecting the Layperson Assessors System] (People's Republic of China) Standing Committee of the National People's Congress, 28 August 2004, arts. 4–6.

[155] Organic Law of the People's Courts, 1 July 1979, art. 10.

[156] Dalian, Ningbo, Qingdao, Shenzhen and Xiamen.

[157] Provision on Several Issues Regarding the Application of Law in the Hearing of Civil Dispute Cases Caused by Monopolistic Conduct, art. 3; 中华人民共和国行政诉讼法 [Administrative Procedure Law of the People's Republic of China] (People's Republic of China) National People's Congress, 4 April 1989, art. 14(1).

[158] Provision on Several Issues Regarding the Application of Law in the Hearing of Civil Dispute Cases Caused by Monopolistic Conduct, art. 3.

[159] 民事案件案由规定 [Provision on the Causes of Action for Civil Cases] (People's Republic of China) Supreme People's Court, Order No. 11, 29 October 2007, pt. 5 s. 16, as amended by 最高人民法院关于修改《民事案件案由规定》的决定 [Decision of the Supreme People's Court to Amend the Provisions on the Causes of Action for Civil Cases] (People's Republic of China) Supreme People's Court, Order No. 41, 18 February 2011; 最高人民法院关于认真学习和贯彻《中华人民共和国反垄断法》的通知 [Notice of the Supreme People's Court on the Study and Implementation of the Antimonopoly Law] (People's Republic of China) Supreme People's Court, Order No. 23, 28 July 2008.

property cases such as patents, new plant varieties, integrated circuit designs, technological secrets and computer software; administrative cases relating to copyright, trademark and unfair competition; and civil cases involving well-known trademarks. They also hear appeals from civil and administrative copyright, trademark and unfair competition cases.[160] The intellectual property courts have also heard AML cases. For example, the Beijing Intellectual Property Court has received six AML cases since its establishment in November 2014.[161]

Only a limited number of decisions and rulings made by courts are published and made available to the public. Court decisions are generally difficult to access, unless the parties to the case have made such decisions available or the media has reported on the case.[162] These difficulties have been reflected in the reporting and disclosure of the AML-related court cases. For example, as at the end of 2012, although courts had handled 116 AML cases at the first instance,[163] publicly available information on these cases was available only for a portion of those cases. Formal decisions are released publicly on a seemingly ad hoc basis, and there is no central portal where AML-related court decisions are published. Further, to date, there has been no information released on the aggregate number of AML-related appeals that have been handled by the courts. Some steps have been taken to improve judicial transparency. For example, in November 2013, the SPC issued a regulation that required people's courts throughout China to submit their decisions and rulings for publication on a central website, which is to be established and

---

[160] 最高人民法院关于北京、上海、广州知识产权法院案件管辖的规定 [Provision on the Jurisdiction of the Intellectual Property Courts in Beijing, Shanghai, and Guangzhou] (People's Republic of China) Supreme People's Court, Order No. 12, 31 October 2014.

[161] Lisha Zhou, 'Beijing IP Court Has Handled Six Antitrust Lawsuits since Inception' (The Fifth China Competition Policy Forum: PaRR Special Report, October 2016), p. 4.

[162] Benjamin L. Liebman, 'China's Courts: Restricted Reform' (2007) 21 *Columbia Journal of Asian Law* 1 at 26.

[163] 杨维汉、陈菲 [Yang Weihan and Chen Fei], 最高人民法院公布中国首部反垄断审判司法解释 [Supreme People's Court Announces China's First Judicial Interpretation on Antimonopoly Trials], 新华网 [Xinhuanet], 8 May 2012, available at www.china.com.cn/policy/txt/2012-05/09/content_25337524.htm; 田兴春 [Tian Xingchun], 最高法通报近年来人民法院审理商标和不正当竞争案件有关情况2012年法院审理商标民事案19815件 年增长率超50% [Supreme People's Court Reports on Trademark and Unfair Competition Cases Heard by the People's Courts, Court Hears 19815 Trademark Civil Cases in 2012, Annual Growth Rate of Over 50 Per cent], 人民网 [people.cn] 28 March 2013, available at http://legal.people.com.cn/n/2013/0328/c42510-20950833.html.

maintained by the SPC.[164] The SPC has also emphasised that non-publication of court decisions will be the exception, not the rule.[165]

According to Chinese constitutional theory and administrative practice, the power to interpret legislation is characterised as a legislative rather than a judicial function, and courts do not have the power to conduct constitutional judicial review.[166] Nonetheless, Chen observes that the SPC is the most active and important interpretative authority.[167] As noted in Section 4.2.3, the SCNPC has delegated some interpretation power to the SPC.[168] The SPC (but not lower-level courts)[169] can interpret questions of law arising from the specific application of law in judicial proceedings.[170] Further, although the SPC's powers of interpretation are technically limited to that which is required to decide issues that have arisen or are likely to arise in specific cases, some scholars note that the SPC has at times pushed the limits of its delegated authority by issuing a number of general interpretations of key laws or interpretations that appear to go beyond the text of the statute.[171]

It is important to note that the courts are not independent of the government, and judges may be vulnerable to pressure from or interference by local government or people's congresses to decide cases in a

---

[164] 最高人民法院关于人民法院在互联网公布裁判文书的规定 [Provision of the Supreme People's Court Regarding the Publication of the Judgments and Rulings of the People's Courts on the Internet] (People's Republic of China) Supreme People's Court, Legal Interpretation No. 26, 13 November 2013.

[165] 最高人民法院印发《关于推进司法公开三大平台建设的若干意见》的通知 [Notice of the Supreme People's Court on the Issuance of the Several Opinions on the Establishment of Three Major Platforms to Promote Judicial Transparency] (People's Republic of China) Supreme People's Court, 21 November 2013, art. 11.

[166] Stanley Lubman, 'Introduction: The Future of Chinese Law' (1995) 141 *The China Quarterly* 1 at 4; Peerenboom, *China's Long March toward Rule of Law*, pp. 281, 317.

[167] Chen, *Chinese Law*, p. 269.

[168] Constitution of the People's Republic of China, arts. 67(1), (4); Resolution on Strengthening Legal Interpretation Work.

[169] The SPC has not delegated the power to issue interpretations to the lower courts: 最高人民法院发布关于司法解释工作的规定 [Regulation Concerning Judicial Interpretation Work] (People's Republic of China) Supreme People's Court, 23 March 2007, arts. 6, 10; 关于地方各级人民法院不应制定司法解释性文件的批复 [A Reply from the Supreme People's Court that Local People's Courts at Various Levels Shall Not Make Judicial Interpretation Documents] (People's Republic of China) Supreme People's Court, 31 March 1987. See Keith and Lin, 'Judicial Interpretation of China's Supreme People's Court', 239.

[170] Resolution on Strengthening Legal Interpretation Work, art. 2.

[171] Peerenboom, *China's Long March toward Rule of Law*, p. 317; Liebman, 'China's Courts', 33; Keith and Lin, 'Judicial Interpretation of China's Supreme People's Court'.

certain way.[172] Courts are accountable to the people's congress that created them.[173] Judges are appointed by the people's congress or its standing committee at the corresponding level.[174] Further, although the central government provides funding to lower-level courts, they remain substantially funded by the government at the same level.[175] As judges are appointed and remunerated by the people's congresses and governments in the jurisdictions in which they serve, they may be subject to pressure and interference from local officials to decide cases in favour of local interests.[176] The people's congresses may also use their power of supervision to intervene in judicial decision-making.[177] Since 2012, a number of reforms have been proposed by the government and the SPC to increase the courts' independence from local government. For example, new judges will be selected by a judicial selection committee at the provincial level, and the appointment and removal of judges will be made according to statutory procedures. Funding for local courts below the provincial level will also be fully guaranteed by the central and provincial governments, with provincial fiscal departments responsible for managing the funding of local courts below the provincial level.[178]

As the courts are part of China's bureaucratic system, its decisions are not necessarily binding on other government actors or in other geographic locations. This may hinder the enforcement of judgments, especially where the cooperation of other administrative agencies might be

---

[172] Peerenboom, *China's Long March toward Rule of Law*, pp. 309–12; Cabestan, 'The Relationship between the National People's Congress and the State Council', 56.
[173] Constitution of the People's Republic of China, art. 128.
[174] 中华人民共和国法官法 [Law on Judges of the People's Republic of China] (People's Republic of China) National People's Congress, 28 February 1995, art. 11.
[175] Constitution of the People's Republic of China, art. 128. See also Chen, *Chinese Law*, pp. 189–90; Peerenboom, *China's Long March toward Rule of Law*, pp. 280–1.
[176] Stanley Lubman, 'Bird in a Cage: Chinese Law Reform after Twenty Years' (2000) 20 *Northwestern Journal of International Law & Business* 383 at 395.
[177] Yuwen Li, 'Judicial Independence: Applying International Minimum Standards to Chinese Law and Practice' (2001) 15(1) *China Information* 67 at 96–7.
[178] Supreme People's Court of the People's Republic of China, 'Judicial Reform of Chinese Courts', 3 March 2016, ch. II, available at http://english.court.gov.cn/2016-03/03/content_23724636.htm; 最高人民法院关于全面深化人民法院改革的意见—人民法院第四个五年改革纲要(2014–2018) [Opinion of the Supreme People's Court on the Comprehensive Reform of People's Courts – Outline of the Fourth Five-Year Reform Plan of the People's Court (2014–2018)] (People's Republic of China) Supreme People's Court, 4 February 2015, Order No. 3, art. 50.

required for their implementation.[179] Thus the enforcement of court decisions is variable and will likely depend on the relative power of the court and government agencies involved. These factors might affect AML cases before the courts, especially for cases brought against important companies or individuals within a court's jurisdiction or that relate to protectionist measures adopted by local governments, or in circumstances where a party is from outside the jurisdiction. Further, it is thought that the evaluation of a judge's performance is based on factors such as rank, number of cases completed, number of errors and the number of appeals or petitions lodged against their decisions.[180] This gives judges another incentive to decide cases in favour of local interests and influential businesses, with a view to minimising complaints about or appeals from their decisions.[181]

Moreover, the CPC has substantial influence over the courts and judges.[182] The appointment and promotion of judges is controlled by the CPC,[183] and many judges are members of the CPC.[184] Members of the adjudication committee are usually CPC members, and Wang notes that the president is always the party secretary of the court.[185] Further, politico-legal committees (which are part of party committees) exist within courts. These committees, which are CPC institutions, help the CPC provide ideological and political leadership and policy guidance to the courts, as well as supervises and exercises control over the courts from within.[186] Liebman observes that CPC officials have intervened in politically sensitive court cases, such as those involving the state's financial interests, individuals with ties to the state, high-profile companies or

---

[179] Peerenboom, *China's Long March toward Rule of Law*, pp. 287–8; Liebman, 'China's Courts', 15–16; Saich, *Governance and Politics of China*, p. 162.
[180] Benjamin L. Liebman, 'Assessing China's Legal Reforms' (2009) 23 *Columbia Journal of Asian Law* 17 at 27; Liebman, 'China's Courts', 23; Peerenboom, *China's Long March toward Rule of Law*, p. 294; Randall Peerenboom, 'Judicial Independence in China: Common Myths and Unfounded Assumptions' in Randall Peerenboom (ed.), *Judicial Independence in China: Lessons for Global Rule of Law Promotion* (Cambridge: Cambridge University Press, 2009), p. 77.
[181] Peerenboom, *China's Long March toward Rule of Law*, pp. 311–12.
[182] Ibid., pp. 302–9, 320–2.    [183] Ibid., pp. 305–6.
[184] There are no statistics on how many judicial personnel are CPC members: Chen, *Chinese Law*, pp. 1010–11. Cohen estimates that more than 90 per cent of judicial personnel are CPC members: Jerome A. Cohen, 'Reforming China's Civil Procedure: Judging the Courts' (1997) 45 *The American Journal of Comparative Law* 793 at 797.
[185] Yuhua Wang, *Tying the Autocrat's Hands: The Rise of the Rule of Law in China* (New York: Cambridge University Press, 2015), p. 44.
[186] Chen, *Chinese Law*, pp. 181–7.

a large number of potential plaintiffs, together with high-profile cases that receive extensive media coverage.[187] In these cases, he notes that judges might balance political interests and pressures against legal requirements.[188] However, Fu notes that, as the focus of politico-legal committees is mainly on criminal justice matters, the decreasing importance of criminal trials within the court system and the rise of civil and commercial court cases has resulted in the influence of these committees diminishing somewhat.[189] Nonetheless, while politico-legal committees may be less involved in the day-to-day handling of cases, Chen believes that the CPC will continue to be integrated with the courts.[190]

### 4.2.7 Competition Law Experts

One of the guiding principles adopted by the drafters of the AML was that it should be consistent with prevailing international competition law norms and practices.[191] Consistent with this, throughout the drafting process, a number of Chinese and foreign competition law experts were consulted. They included academics, economists, foreign competition authorities and international organisations. These experts' influence on the drafting of the AML is investigated in detail in Chapter 5.

#### 4.2.7.1 Chinese Competition Law Academics

A core group of Chinese competition law academics was deeply involved in the AML drafting process, especially while the State Council had responsibility for preparing the draft AML.[192] This group consisted of Professors Wang Xiaoye, Wang Xianlin, Shi Jianzhong, Huang Yong and Sheng Jiemin. Professor Wang Xiaoye was the first Chinese competition law academic involved in the drafting of the AML, having participated in the AML drafting group established by the LAO in August 1994. Professors Wang Xianlin, Shi, Huang and Sheng became involved in

---

[187] Liebman, 'China's Courts', 15.    [188] Ibid.
[189] Hualing Fu, 'Autonomy, Courts, and the Politico-Legal Order in Contemporary China' in Liqun Cao, Ivan Y. Sun and Bill Hebenton (eds.), *The Routledge Handbook of Chinese Criminology* (London: Routledge, 2013), pp. 80–1.
[190] Chen, *Chinese Law*, pp. 186–7.
[191] 关于《中华人民共和国反垄断法 (草案)》的说明 [An Explanation of China's Antimonopoly Law (Draft)], 22nd Session of the Standing Committee of the Tenth National People's Congress, 24 June 2006; Zhenguo Wu, 'Perspectives on the Chinese Antimonopoly Law' (2008) 75 *Antitrust Law Journal* 73 at 78.
[192] Interviews with Chinese competition law experts and stakeholders.

the drafting of the AML at a later stage, when efforts to enact a Chinese competition law escalated, around the time China joined the World Trade Organization. They participated in the expert group that was convened by the LAO to advise the LAO and the State Council on the drafting of the AML.[193] Throughout the drafting process, in addition to providing advice and comments on various drafts of the AML, this group of Chinese competition law academics organised domestic and international conferences to discuss and solicit comments on the draft AML from government officials and experts, and they acted as intermediaries between the Chinese government officials responsible for preparing the draft AML and the foreign competition law experts who were consulted.[194]

The Chinese competition law academics held similar views on the AML. They believed that there should be an independent, single and unified ministry-level enforcement agency;[195] that the AML should prohibit administrative monopoly;[196] and that the AML should apply to all industries.[197] They also recognised that the AML would differ from the competition laws of advanced market economies, because China is a developing country in economic transition and the government has a higher level of involvement in the economy.[198] The influence of Chinese competition law experts during the drafting of the AML, the different views of Chinese and foreign competition law experts and how such matters affected the content of the AML are explored in more detail in Chapter 5.

Chinese competition law academics continue to play an important role in the implementation of the AML. Several Chinese competition law academics, including Professors Wang Xiaoye, Wang Xianlin,

---

[193] Interviews with Chinese competition law experts and stakeholders; 黄小伟 [Wang Xiaowei], 反垄断法二审: 良法仍有希望 [Second Review of the Anti-monopoly Law: There Is Still Hope for a Good Law], 南方周末 [Southern Weekend], 4 July 2007, available at www.infzm.com/content/7581; 吴晓锋 [Wu Xiaofeng], 反垄断法是反'垄断的行为'而非'垄断的状态' [Anti-monopoly Law Opposes 'Monopoly Conduct' and Not 'Monopoly Status'] (26 November 2007) 中国人大新闻—人民网 [National People's Congress of China News – www.people.com.cn], available at http://npc.people.com.cn/GB/6574653.html.
[194] John Yong Ren and Ning Yang, 'The Imminent Release of China's Anti-monopoly Law – What to Expect' [2005] (7) *China Law & Practice* 26.
[195] Xiaoye Wang, 'Highlights of China's New Anti-monopoly Law' (2008) 75 *Antitrust Law Journal* 133 at 144–5; Huang, 'Pursuing the Second Best', 125.
[196] Wang, 'The Prospect of Antimonopoly Legislation in China', 228.
[197] Huang, 'Pursuing the Second Best', 126–7.
[198] Yong Huang, 'Coordination of International Competition Policies: An Anatomy Based on Chinese Reality' in Andrew T. Guzman (ed.), *Cooperation, Comity, and Competition Policy* (New York: Oxford University Press, 2011), pp. 255–6.

KEY STAKEHOLDERS ON THE SUPPLY-SIDE

Huang and Shi, have been appointed to the expert group that advises the AMC.[199] The AMC and the Chinese enforcement authorities also outsource some of their research projects to competition law academics (as well as economists and legal practitioners).[200] Such research projects may relate to the drafting of implementing regulations, or they might be studies of how competition law applies in particular sectors.[201] More generally, the views of competition law academics are sought on drafts of AML implementing regulations prepared by the Chinese enforcement agencies and the AMC.[202]

It should be noted that, in addition to competition law academics, a number of Chinese experts from related fields such as civil law, administrative law and commercial law also participated in discussions on the AML during the drafting process, in order to ensure that the AML would not conflict with relevant Chinese laws.[203]

### 4.2.7.2 Foreign Competition Law Experts

The views of foreign competition law experts were obtained throughout the AML drafting process, and continue to be sought in the drafting of the implementing regulations.[204] These experts include competition authorities,[205] international organisations,[206] professional and business organisations and academics.[207] They were involved in international conferences and seminars held by the Chinese government to discuss,

---

[199] Interviews with Chinese competition law experts and stakeholders.
[200] Interviews with Chinese competition law experts and stakeholders.
[201] Interviews with Chinese competition law experts and stakeholders. For example, Professor Wang Xianlin was closely involved in the SAIC's drafting of its regulation on the application of the AML to the abuse of intellectual property rights.
[202] Interviews with Chinese competition law experts and stakeholders.
[203] Interviews with Chinese competition law experts and stakeholders.
[204] An Explanation of China's Anti-monopoly Law (Draft), 24 June 2006; Wu, 'Perspectives on the Chinese Anti-monopoly Law', 78; Wu, *Competition Laws, Globalization and Legal Pluralism*, 137; Interviews with Chinese competition law experts and stakeholders.
[205] For example, the US Department of Justice, the US Federal Trade Commission, the Directorate-General for Competition of the European Commission, Germany's Bundeskartellamt, the Japan Fair Trade Commission, the Korea Fair Trade Commission, Russia's Federal Antimonopoly Service and the Australian Competition and Consumer Commission.
[206] For example, the Organisation for Co-operation and Economic Development, the World Bank, the United Nations Conference on Trade and Development and the Asia-Pacific Economic Cooperation.
[207] For example, the American Bar Association, the International Bar Association and the American Chamber of Commerce.

comment and make suggestions on the draft AML.[208] Chinese government officials involved in the drafting of the AML also visited the United States, Europe, Japan, Australia and other jurisdictions to learn from their experiences with competition law and policy.[209]

Foreign competition law experts are mainly focused on whether the AML and the implementing regulations are consistent with what they regard as prevailing competition law norms, which are those competition law norms and practices adopted in mature competition law jurisdictions such as the United States and the European Union.[210] When commenting on the draft AML, they provided detailed comments and suggestions on technical competition law issues such as the definition of key concepts, including 'market', 'business operator' and 'control', and on the types of conduct that should be prohibited under the AML.[211] They were also concerned with some broader policy issues. In particular, they were concerned that the AML would be used to pursue policies that they considered contrary to competition law norms, such as industrial or foreign investment policies.[212] In addition to recommending that the objectives of the AML should be limited to consumer welfare and economic efficiency, they recommended the establishment of a single, independent and unified enforcement authority.[213] If the

---

[208] 张穹 [Zhang Qiong], 国务院法制办公室张穹副主任在反垄断立法国际研讨会闭幕式上的讲话 [Closing Remarks of Deputy Director of the Legislative Affairs Office of the State Council Zhang Qiong at the International Symposium on the Anti-monopoly Legislation] (Closing Remarks, Beijing, 9 October 2005), available at http://tfs.mofcom.gov.cn/article/bc/200510/20051000525406.shtml; Harris et al., *Anti-monopoly Law and Practice in China*, p. 15, 17–18; H. Stephen Harris, Jr, 'The Making of an Antitrust Law: The Pending Antimonopoly Law of the People's Republic of China' (2006) 7 *Chicago Journal of International Law* 169 at 181; OECD, *Governance in China* (Paris: OECD Publishing, 2005), p. 362; Wang, 'The Prospect of Antimonopoly Legislation in China', 224; Xiaoye Wang, 'Issues Surrounding the Drafting of China's Anti-monopoly Law' (2004) 3 *Washington University Global Studies Law Review* 285 at 285; Interviews with Chinese competition law experts and stakeholders.

[209] Wang, 'The Prospect of Antimonopoly Legislation in China', 224. See, e.g., H. Stephen Harris Jr and Kathy Lijun Yang, 'China: Latest Developments in Anti-monopoly Law Legislation' (2005) 19(2) *Antitrust* 89 at 89.

[210] Harris et al., *Anti-monopoly Law and Practice in China*, p. 22; Harris and Yang, 'China: Latest Developments', 89; Pate, 'What I Heard in the Great Hall of the People', 195.

[211] See, e.g., Sections of Antitrust Law and International Law and Practice, American Bar Association, 'Joint Submission to the Ministry of Commerce of the People's Republic of China', 15 July 2003, 10–23.

[212] Ibid., pp. 2, 7–10; Harris et al., *Anti-monopoly Law and Practice in China*, pp. 22, 37; Harris and Yang, 'China: Latest Developments', 90.

[213] Sections of Antitrust Law and International Law and Practice, 4–5, 26; Sections of Antitrust Law, Intellectual Property Law and International Law, American Bar

enforcement authority was to be established under an existing ministry or department, foreign experts tended to prefer the MOFCOM over the SAIC because they believed that the MOFCOM had more experience dealing with a broader range of businesses (including foreign and multinational companies) and was more open, more conversant in the economic analysis of markets and better able to weigh up domestic and international interests.[214] They also supported the prohibition of administrative monopolies in the AML, as they agreed with the principle that SOEs and other businesses should be treated equally under the law.[215] Foreign competition law experts also opposed provisions that would undermine the protection of intellectual property rights.[216] Chapter 5 examines how the views of foreign competition law experts influenced the content of the AML.

Chinese competition authorities might need to cooperate with other competition authorities in enforcement. Globalisation and increasingly global markets has meant that transactions and anti-competitive conduct often have cross-border impacts. Cooperation of this nature may be conducted pursuant to formal channels of consultation and cooperation, such as the bilateral or multilateral agreements that the Chinese competition agencies have signed with other competition agencies. The Chinese competition authorities have signed memoranda of understanding on competition law with a number of other competition authorities, such as the United States, the European Commission, the United Kingdom, South Korea, Australia, Brazil, Russia, India and South Africa.

Foreign competition authorities and international organisations also provide technical and capacity-building assistance to the Chinese competition authorities, the SPC and other higher-level courts and universities.[217] Wong observes that the United States and the European Union have been the major providers of technical assistance to China, with

---

Association, 'Joint Submission to the Ministry of Commerce of the People's Republic of China', 19 May 2005, 4, 9; Harris and Yang, 'China: Latest Developments', 91.

[214] Harris and Yang, 'China: Latest Developments', 91.
[215] Sections of Antitrust Law and International Law and Practice, 4, 24; Sections of Antitrust Law, Intellectual Property Law and International Law, 4, 28.
[216] Pate, 'What I Heard in the Great Hall of the People', 206; Harris, 'The Making of an Antitrust Law', 227–8.
[217] Stanley Wong, 'Effectiveness of Technical Assistance in Capacity Building on Competition Law and Policy: The Case of China' in Adrian Emch and David Stallibrass (eds.), *China's Anti-monopoly Law: The First Five Years* (Alphen aan den Rijn, The Netherlands: Kluwer Law International, 2013), pp. 364–5.

172    SUPPLY-SIDE ANALYSIS OF THE ANTI-MONOPOLY LAW

Germany, Japan, South Korea, the United Kingdom, the Organisation for Co-operation and Economic Development and the United Nations Conference on Trade and Development also active in providing such assistance.[218] For example, the European Union has held seminars and workshops on various aspects of mergers and anti-competitive conduct, including investigative techniques, remedies and judging cases, as well as organising study tours for Chinese government officials to visit or engage in internships at the European Commission and the competition authorities of member states of the European Union.[219]

#### 4.2.7.3   Economists

Several Chinese economists with expertise in regulation, industrial organisation and macroeconomics were consulted during the drafting of the AML by the government officials in charge of the drafting process. The NPC asked Professors Zhang Xinzhu and Zhang Weiying to conduct research on various economic issues related to anti-monopoly law,[220] and Professors Zhang Xinzhu, Qi Yudong and Wu Hanhong were members of the expert group organised by the LAO to advise it and the State Council on drafting the AML.[221] Economists have also been appointed to the AMC Expert Group to advise the AMC on matters of competition law and policy, and are involved in the drafting of implementing regulations.[222] In particular, the views of economists were solicited

---

[218] Ibid., pp. 364–5.
[219] EU–China Competition Cooperation, 'EU-China Competition Policy: Competition Weeks', available at www.euchinacomp.org/index.php/competition-weeks; Wong, 'Effectiveness of Technical Assistance in Capacity Building', 366–7.
[220] 王晓玲 [Wang Xiaoling],《反垄断法》：把立法难题留到执法中解决—访中国社科院规制与竞争研究中心主任张昕竹 [Anti-monopoly Law: Defers Resolution of Difficult Legislative Issues to Enforcement – Interview with Director of Chinese Academy of Social Sciences Centre for Regulation and Competition Zhang Xinzhu] [2005] (17) 商务周刊 [Business Watch Magazine] 47 at 47.
[221] 谢晓冬 [Xie Xiaodong],《反垄断法》草案减负"反行政垄断"被整体删除 [Draft Anti-monopoly Law Reduces Its Burden, 'Administrative Monopoly Prohibition' Is Entirely Deleted], 新京报 [Beijing News], 11 January 2006, available at http://finance1.people.com.cn/GB/1037/4017283.html; Wang, 'Second Review of the Anti-monopoly Law'; Wu, 'Anti-monopoly Law Opposes "Monopoly Conduct"'; 反垄断法短期内难见效 [Difficult for Anti-monopoly Law to Be Effective within the Short Term], 华夏时报 [China Times], 27 June 2006, available at www.china.com.cn/chinese/news/1256769.htm.
[222] Interviews with Chinese competition law experts and stakeholders; 商务部"反垄断工作"专题新闻发布会 [MOFCOM 'Anti-monopoly Work' Special Press Conference] (Ministry of Commerce, 27 February 2014), available at www.mofcom.gov.cn/article/ae/slfw/201402/20140200502174.shtml.

KEY STAKEHOLDERS ON THE SUPPLY-SIDE          173

in the preparation of regulations relating to the definition of the relevant market and merger notification thresholds.[223]

Economists play a role in both public and private enforcement. In addition to having in-house economists, the MOFCOM may consult with external economists in some particularly significant, difficult or complex merger cases.[224] For example, external economists were engaged to conduct competition assessments in the MOFCOM's review of the *Seagate/Samsung, Western Digital/Hitachi, MediaTek/MStar, Microsoft/ Nokia, Merck/AZ Electronics* and *P3 Shipping Alliance* transactions. The SAIC Bureau has also engaged economists to help review evidence in its investigation into Tetra Pak for abuse of dominance.[225] The NDRC will also engage external economists to undertake case analysis, or seek their opinions.[226] However, the level of involvement of economists in review and investigations, the type of economic analysis undertaken and the analytical frameworks adopted by the enforcement authorities are unclear.[227] In actions brought before the courts by private parties, economists can give expert testimony before the court or be engaged to conduct market research or produce economic analysis reports on specific issues in the case.[228] For example, this occurred in Qihoo 360's action against Tencent for abuse of dominance before the Guangdong High People's Court and the SPC on appeal, and in Rainbow's action

---

[223] Interviews with Chinese competition law experts and stakeholders.
[224] Interviews with Chinese competition law experts and stakeholders; Fei Deng and Yizhe Zhang, 'Interview with Shang Ming, Director General of the Anti-monopoly Bureau under the Ministry of Commerce of the People's Republic of China' [2014] (April) *The Antitrust Source* 1 at 3, available at www.americanbar.org/content/dam/aba/publishing/antitrust_source/apr14_shang_intrvw_4_8f.pdf.
[225] 周锐 [Zhou Rui], 工商总局披露利乐案调查内情：恢复一些被删邮件 [SAIC Discloses Inside Details of Its Tetra Pak Investigation: Restored Some Deleted Emails], 中国新闻网 [China News Online], 31 July 2013, available at www.chinanews.com/gn/2013/07-31/5108197.shtml.
[226] Fei Deng and Yizhe Zhang, 'Interview with Xu Kunlin, Director General of the Bureau of Price Supervision and Anti-monopoly under the National Development and Reform Commission of the People's Republic of China' [2014] (August) *The Antitrust Source* 1 at 4, available at www.americanbar.org/content/dam/aba/publishing/antitrust_source/aug14_xu_intrvw_7_23f.pdf.
[227] Elizabeth Xiao-Ru Wang and Sharon Pang, 'A Discussion of MOFCOM's Competitive Analysis in 2012 from an Economic Perspective' [2013] (2) *CPI Antitrust Chronicle* 1 at 1; Deng and Huang, 'A Five Year Review', 11.
[228] Provision on Several Issues Regarding the Application of Law in the Hearing of Civil Dispute Cases Caused by Monopolistic Conduct, arts. 12–13.

against Johnson & Johnson for vertical price fixing. Both sides engaged economists to prepare evidence and testify before the court.[229]

It is important to note that the role of economists in AML enforcement is still developing. Applying economics to analyse competition law issues is a new area of specialisation in China, and there are not many economists who specialise in competition analysis in China. Much of this knowledge within the Chinese competition authorities has been developed through on-the-job training and more formalised training sessions.[230] It will take time for this expertise to develop within the enforcement agencies, industry and academia in China.

### 4.2.8   Legal Practitioners

Chinese and foreign law firms are active in the provision of competition law advice in China. They are also active in the drafting of AML implementing regulations.[231]

A large number of foreign law firms have representative offices in China, such as Clifford Chance, Freshfields, Allen & Overy, Linklaters, Jones Day, Hogan Lovells and Baker & McKenzie. Foreign lawyers are allowed to interpret and advise on foreign and international law, and to advise on the impact of the Chinese legal environment.[232] Strictly speaking, foreign lawyers are not allowed to interpret or advise on any Chinese laws. However, Godwin observes that many foreign law firms operate in a grey area.[233] In practice, foreign law firms do advise on matters related

---

[229] 陈凯 [Chen Kai], 腾讯案的关键: 是否滥用市场支配地位 [Key in Tencent's Case: Whether It Abused Its Dominant Market Position], 经济参考报 [*Economic Information Daily*], 8 May 2012, available at http://jjckb.xinhuanet.com/opinion/2012-05/08/content_373844.htm. For a discussion of the economic evidence and analysis in these cases, see Fang Qi, Marshall Yan and Yan Luo, 'Consideration of Economic Evidence by Chinese Courts in Antitrust Litigation' [2014] (1) *CPI Antitrust Chronicle* 1; David S. Evans, Vanessa Yanhua Zhang and Howard H. Chang, 'Analyzing Competition among Internet Players: Qihoo 360 v. Tencent' [2013] (1) *CPI Antitrust Chronicle* 1; Chunfai Lui, 'A Landmark Court Ruling in China: Resale Price Maintenance as Examined in the Johnson & Johnson Case' [2013] (2) *CPI Antitrust Chronicle* 1.
[230] Su and Wang, 'China: The Competition Law System', p. 226.
[231] Interviews with Chinese competition law experts and stakeholders.
[232] 外国律师事务所驻华代表机构管理条例 [Regulation on the Administration of Foreign Law Firms' Representative Offices in China] (People's Republic of China) State Council, Order No. 338, 19 December 2001, art. 15.
[233] Andrew Godwin, 'The Professional "Tug of War": The Regulation of Foreign Lawyers in China, Business Scope Issues and Some Suggestions for Reform' (2009) 33 *Melbourne University Law Review* 132 at 142–3.

to Chinese law, but they engage and instruct Chinese lawyers, on behalf of their clients, to issue legal opinions on matters of Chinese law and to represent clients in proceedings before the Chinese courts and government authorities.[234] With respect to AML matters, however, the Chinese government has recently stated that foreign lawyers may accompany their clients to attend meetings at the enforcement agencies.[235]

In addition to acting as intermediaries between foreign lawyers, on the one hand, and the Chinese courts and government agencies, on the other, a growing number of Chinese law firms have developed expertise in competition law and are advising clients directly on competition law matters. Such firms include AnJie Law Firm, Broad & Bright, Dacheng Law Offices, Fangda Partners, Grandall, Jun He, King & Wood Mallesons, T&D Associates and Zhong Lun Law Firm. According to interviewees who have been involved in enforcement cases, Chinese lawyers are generally less likely than foreign lawyers to challenge the views put forth by the competition agencies.[236]

## 4.3 Institutional Design Issues Influencing Supply-Side Dynamics

This section considers the institutional design issues relating to the enforcement of the AML which are likely to affect enforcement and implementation. Such issues include the resource and knowledge constraints faced by the Chinese competition authorities and the judiciary, the coordination issues arising from the divided administrative enforcement structure, the broader roles and responsibilities held by each competition authority outside the AML and the influence of bureaucratic rank.

### 4.3.1 Resource and Knowledge Constraints

One of the biggest challenges facing the Chinese competition agencies is the lack of resources. As noted above, there are fewer than 100 staff across the three competition authorities at the central level and, as AML

---

[234] Ibid., 142; Sida Liu, 'Client Influence and the Contingency of Professionalism: The Work of Elite Corporate Lawyers in China' (2006) 40 *Law and Society Review* 751 at 759.
[235] 'Fact Sheet: 25th US–China Joint Commission on Commerce and Trade', United States Department of Commerce, 19 December 2014, available at www.commerce.gov/news/fact-sheets/2014/12/19/fact-sheet-25th-us-china-joint-commission-commerce-and-trade.
[236] Interviews with Chinese competition law experts and stakeholders.

enforcement is only part of the work of the NDRC Bureau and the SAIC Bureau, the number of staff actually working on AML-related matters is lower.[237] This number is unlikely to be sufficient to enforce a competition law in a country of China's size – one with a population of 1.3 billion people and the second largest economy in the world, which is the largest recipient of foreign direct investment funds globally and is experiencing rapid economic growth. In contrast, more than 800 people work at the European Commission Directorate-General for Competition, more than 800 people work at the Antitrust Division of the US Department of Justice, and nearly 300 people work at the Bureau of Competition at the US Federal Trade Commission.[238]

These limitations are particularly relevant for the MOFCOM as its AML enforcement is centralised, whereas the NDRC and the SAIC delegate enforcement duties to their provincial-level authorities and have relied on these local authorities in most of their enforcement activities to date. Further, as notification of concentrations is mandatory once the notification thresholds are met, the MOFCOM has little control over the number of cases it must review and investigate. This stands in contrast to the NDRC and the SAIC, which can decide which cases to investigate. The MOFCOM's workload has also increased significantly since the AML came into effect in 2008. In 2009, which was the first full year of enforcement of the AML, the MOFCOM accepted seventy-seven notifications for review; in 2016, it accepted 360 notifications for review.[239] There are also specific deadlines which the MOFCOM must meet in its merger review. While this timetable is largely in line with international norms, it becomes much harder to meet it if fewer than thirty staff are

---

[237] 国新办就反垄断执法工作情况举行吹风会 [State Council Information Office Briefing on Anti-monopoly Law Enforcement Activities] (11 September 2014), State Council Information Office, available at www.china.com.cn/zhibo/2014-09/11/content_33487367.htm.

[238] 'HR Key Figures Card – Staff Members' (European Commission, 2016), available at http://ec.europa.eu/civil_service/docs/hr_key_figures_en.pdf; 'FY 2016 Budget Request at a Glance' (Antitrust Division, US Department of Justice, 30 January 2015), available at www.justice.gov/sites/default/files/jmd/pages/attachments/2015/01/30/19_bs_section_ii_chapter_-_atr.pdf; 'Inside the Bureau of Competition', Federal Trade Commission, available at www.ftc.gov/about-ftc/bureaus-offices/bureau-competition/inside-bureau-competition.

[239] Ministry of Commerce Information Office, 2016 年商务工作年终综述之十二: 全面推进反垄断工作 营造法治化营商环境 [Summary of the MOFCOM's 2016 Work (Part 12): Comprehensively Promote Anti-monopoly Work, Create a Legalised Business Environment], 11 January 2017, available at www.mofcom.gov.cn/article/ae/ai/201701/20170102499312.shtml.

assigned to review mergers. As discussed in Chapter 6, many legal practitioners in China have expressed dissatisfaction about the length of time it takes for mergers to be reviewed and cleared by the MOFCOM.

Another challenge faced by the Chinese competition authorities is that knowledge of competition law and economics is limited within these agencies. China only decided to embark on economic reform and opening up in December 1978. Economic reforms were carried out within the then-existing central planning framework until 1993, when China decided formally to adopt a socialist market economy. Therefore, the concepts of competition, markets and their associated laws are quite new. Competition law and economics as academic disciplines are also fairly new in China. A number of interviewees believe that the technical capacity of the Chinese competition authorities to conduct competition and economic analysis is limited, despite each authority having enforced competition-related laws for some years prior to the enactment of the AML.[240] Although there are some in-house economists at the MOFCOM Bureau, a number of interviewees believe that these economists have limited experience in applying economics to competition-specific issues, especially with respect to sophisticated economic methodologies and analyses.[241] Neither the NDRC nor the SAIC have specialised economists for AML enforcement.[242]

However, knowledge and awareness of competition law is increasing at the Chinese enforcement agencies. A growing number of officials at the competition enforcement authorities have law or economic degrees and have received training on competition law and economics, particularly at the MOFCOM Bureau.[243] Each competition agency runs training sessions and seminars for its officials at both the central and local levels, often in conjunction with competition law academics, economists, foreign competition agencies and international organisations.[244] For example, the SAIC ran a nationwide 'AML knowledge contest' for its employees in July 2009 to raise awareness and knowledge of the AML.[245]

---

[240] Interviews with Chinese competition law experts and stakeholders.
[241] Interviews with Chinese competition law experts and stakeholders.
[242] Zhang and Zhang, 'New Wine into Old Wineskins', 68.
[243] Su and Wang, 'China: The Competition Law System', p. 226.
[244] Deng, Harris and Zhang, 'Interview with Ning Wanglu', 2; Deng, Harris and Zhang, 'Interview with Shang Ming', 3-4.
[245] 反垄断法律知识竞赛开赛 [Anti-monopoly Law Knowledge Contest] (30 July 2009) State Administration for Industry and Commerce, available at www.saic.gov.cn/fldyfbzdjz/gzdt/200909/t20090927_205502.html.

The Chinese competition agencies have sent delegations to overseas competition agencies to learn more about their enforcement practices and attend training sessions, and some officials from the MOFCOM Bureau and the NDRC Bureau have been seconded to work at foreign competition agencies.[246] The consensus among interviewees is that the government officials at the Chinese competition authorities are eager to learn about competition law and have already learnt a great deal in a very short period of time.[247] A number of interviewees described these officials as professional, well-intentioned and ethical.[248] However, some interviewees also note that, in their experience, there is pressure on investigated parties to cooperate with investigations, make admissions and offer commitments or rectification measures, in part due to the resource and knowledge constraints faced by the competition agencies.[249] The increasing level of competition law knowledge has been reflected in some of the more recent published decisions, especially those relating to mergers. As noted in Chapter 2, the level of reasoning, analysis and disclosure provided in published decisions has generally improved over time. Nonetheless, there is still some difficulty retaining competition law knowledge within the Chinese competition authorities. As part of Chinese government practice, government officials are often rotated to other central or local-level government agencies for a period of a few years, and such knowledge is often lost during that time.[250]

Similarly, one of the most significant factors affecting private enforcement of the AML is the judges' level of knowledge, competence and professionalism. Although the level of legal knowledge and competence of Chinese judges has greatly improved since the implementation of judicial reforms beginning in 1999, and the SPC has taken steps to improve the quality of court decisions,[251] the professionalism and

---

[246] 'EU–China Competition Policy'; Wong, 'Effectiveness of Technical Assistance in Capacity Building', pp. 366–7; 'MOFCOM 'Anti-monopoly Work' Special Press Conference'.
[247] Interviews with Chinese competition law experts and stakeholders. See also 'MOFCOM 'Anti-monopoly Work' Special Press Conference'.
[248] Interviews with Chinese competition law experts and stakeholders.
[249] Interviews with Chinese competition law experts and stakeholders. See also Michael Martina, 'Exclusive: Tough-Talking China Pricing Regulator Sought Confessions from Foreign Firms', Reuters, 21 August 2013, available at www.reuters.com/article/2013/08/21/us-china-antitrust-idUSBRE97K05020130821.
[250] Kjeld Erik Brødsgaard, 'Politics and Business Group Formation in China: The Party in Control?' (2012) 211 *The China Quarterly* 624 at 634; Interviews with Chinese competition law experts and stakeholders.
[251] Chen, *Chinese Law*, pp. 192–94.

competence of judges remains of concern to private litigants.[252] The quality and experience of judges is unbalanced across China and varies according to the court level and its location.[253] Judges are called upon to apply economic concepts, undertake economic analysis and understand economic and other expert evidence which might be presented to them in AML-related legal proceedings.[254] This might be a challenge for judges, especially if AML proceedings are brought before courts that are not well resourced or where judges are less accustomed to dealing with legal issues that require interdisciplinary analysis. To help alleviate these challenges, the SPC has held AML training sessions for judges. The judges sitting on intellectual property tribunals are more used to handling technical issues and expert evidence, and are regarded by some commentators as the most professional and competent of Chinese judges.[255] Lower-level courts are also required to report AML cases that are considered to be important or which raise new situations, issues or research outcomes to the SPC.[256]

### 4.3.2 Cooperation and Coordination

As noted in Chapter 2, the administrative enforcement of the AML is divided between the MOFCOM, the NDRC and the SAIC, with the AMC coordinating AML enforcement. The AMC issues guidelines that apply to all Chinese competition authorities, which helps to reduce inconsistency across the authorities. So far, the AMC has issued a guideline on relevant market definition and is currently drafting a suite of six guidelines on other AML-related matters. Beyond the issuance of guidelines, it is unclear whether the AMC has helped to

---

[252] Peerenboom, *China's Long March toward Rule of Law*, pp. 289–95.
[253] Harris et al., *Anti-monopoly Law and Practice in China*, p. 270; Weixia Gu, 'The Judiciary in Economic and Political Transformation: *Quo Vadis* Chinese Courts?' (2013) 1 *The Chinese Journal of Comparative Law* 303 at 313; Interviews with Chinese competition law experts and stakeholders.
[254] Provision on Several Issues Regarding the Application of Law in the Hearing of Civil Dispute Cases Caused by Monopolistic Conduct, arts. 12–13.
[255] Nathan Bush, 'Constraints on Convergence in Chinese Antitrust' (2009) 54 *Antitrust Bulletin* 87 at 109; Lester Ross and Kenneth Zhou, 'Administrative and Civil Litigation under the Anti-monopoly Law' in Adrian Emch and David Stallibrass (eds.), *China's Anti-monopoly Law: The First Five Years* (Alphen aan den Rijn, The Netherlands: Kluwer Law International, 2013), p. 322.
[256] Notice of the Supreme People's Court on the Study and Implementation of the Anti-monopoly Law.

coordinate the AML implementation and enforcement work of the Chinese competition authorities.[257]

Coordination and cooperation among the Chinese competition agencies, especially between the NDRC and the SAIC, will be required to avoid potential conflict or inconsistent enforcement. Whereas the scope of the MOFCOM's responsibility is clearly defined and distinct, the division of responsibility between the NDRC and the SAIC is not so clear-cut. Formally, the NDRC and the SAIC are each responsible for enforcing the price-related and non-price-related non-merger provisions of the AML, respectively. However, this division between price and non-price-related conduct might not be so easy to implement in practice, especially in cases where conduct has both price and non-price elements. The NDRC and the SAIC acknowledge this difficulty and have agreed that, in cases where there is an overlap in jurisdiction and both authorities could undertake an investigation, the authority who first discovers the case will initiate the investigation, retain the case and notify the other of its investigation.[258] They might also jointly investigate some high-profile cases.[259] Chapter 6 examines whether this arrangement has been implemented and/or is effective in practice.

The NDRC and the SAIC have cooperated with each other in the issuance of implementing regulations.[260] Li comments that the regulations reflect good coordination between the NDRC and the SAIC, as they are largely consistent and, when read together, provide a full picture of the division of responsibilities between the NDRC and the SAIC.[261] Nonetheless, there are some inconsistences in the regulations. One such example is leniency. As discussed in Chapter 2, according to the SAIC's

---

[257] Hao, 'The Multiple Hands', p. 33.
[258] 马红丽 [Ma Lihong], 许昆林: 反垄断维护市场竞争秩序保护公众利益 [Xu Kunlin: Anti-monopoly Maintains Market Competition Order and Protects the Public Interest], 经济日报 [Economy], 27 September 2013; Harris et al., *Anti-monopoly Law and Practice in China*, pp. 269–70; James H. Jeffs, 'A Short Comparison of Certain Provisions of the New NDRC and SAIC Regulations' [2011] (2) *CPI Antitrust Chronicle* 1 at 2–3.
[259] Deng, Harris and Zhang, 'Interview with Ning Wanglu', 3; Fei Deng, H. Stephen Harris, Jr and Yizhe Zhang, 'Interview with Xu Kunlin, Director General of the Department of Price Supervision under the National Development and Reform Commission of People's Republic of China' [2011] (February) *The Antitrust Source* 1 at 3, available at www.americanbar.org/content/dam/aba/migrated/2011_build/antitrust_law/feb11_xuintrvw2_23f.authcheckdam.pdf.
[260] Deng, Harris and Zhang, 'Interview with Xu Kunlin', 3.
[261] Li, 'Unraveling the Jurisdictional Riddle', 6–7.

INSTITUTIONAL DESIGN ISSUES        181

regulation, leniency is unavailable to ringleaders, even if they voluntarily report the conduct to the SAIC and provide important evidence.[262] In contrast, the NDRC does not address this issue in its regulation and has, in practice, reduced the fine imposed on a ringleader because it was the first to report the case to the NDRC.[263] This inconsistency will be resolved with the AMC's issuance of a guideline on leniency, which is currently being drafted, and which will apply to all Chinese competition authorities.

As the power to enforce the AML has been decentralised, to an extent, to the provincial-level authorities of the NDRC and the SAIC, this presents additional coordination challenges. Both the NDRC and the SAIC have issued regulations that delineate the enforcement authority between central and provincial authorities. The NDRC Bureau and the SAIC Bureau are responsible for enforcing the AML where the conduct has significant impact throughout the country, whereas provincial-level authorities investigate conduct that occurs within their region.[264] Further, provincial AICs are required to notify the SAIC Bureau prior to making a decision to suspend or terminate an investigation or to impose a fine, and they are required to file final decisions with the SAIC Bureau.[265] This facilitates consistency in enforcement and coordination between provincial AICs. As the SAIC Bureau delegates authority to provincial AICs to investigate potential breaches of the AML on a case-by-case basis, this will also help it ensure coordination and consistency in enforcement by provincial AICs.[266] In addition, interviewees note that,

---

[262] Regulation of the Administration for Industry and Commerce on the Procedures Relating to the Investigation of Cases Involving Monopoly Agreements and Abuse of Market Dominance, art. 20.

[263] This occurred in the *Guangdong Sea Sand Cartel* case, where the ringleader and whistleblower received a 50 per cent penalty reduction (discussed in Chapter 2). See National Development and Reform Commission, 广东查处海砂价格垄断案件 确保国家重点工程建设顺利进行 [Guangdong Investigates Sea Sand Price Monopoly Case, Ensures Smooth Progress of Nationally Important Construction Project] (News Release, 26 October 2012); Clare Gaofen Ye, 'Combating Monopoly Agreements under China's Anti- Monopoly Law: Recent Developments and Challenges' [2014] (1) *CPI Antitrust Chronicle* 1 at 8–9.

[264] Regulation of the Administration for Industry and Commerce on the Procedures Relating to the Investigation of Cases Involving Monopoly Agreements and Abuse of Market Dominance, art. 3; Regulation on Anti-Price Monopoly Administrative Enforcement Procedures, art. 3.

[265] Regulation of the Administration for Industry and Commerce on the Procedures Relating to the Investigation of Cases Involving Monopoly Agreements and Abuse of Market Dominance, art. 23.

[266] Harris et al., *Anti-monopoly Law and Practice in China*, p. 276.

in some cases, the NDRC Bureau and the SAIC Bureau will work with local officials.[267] Having said that, central authority coordination of the enforcement activities of provincial authorities may be affected by the relationship between central and provincial authorities (discussed in Section 4.4.3), the power dynamics between provincial governments and their incentives to cooperate with central authorities (examined in Section 4.2.5).

### 4.3.3 Multiple Roles and Responsibilities

As noted in Section 4.2.1, the NDRC Bureau, the MOFCOM Bureau and the SAIC Bureau each sit within a broader ministry that is responsible for the administration of a number of laws and policies apart from the AML. Such laws and policies relate to, *inter alia*, industrial policy, price regulation and stabilisation, trade policy, foreign investment policy, national security, consumer protection and unfair competition. The competition authorities continue to carry out their responsibilities under the competition regime that existed prior to the enactment of the AML, which remains largely in force. Relevant laws include the Price Law (the NDRC), the AUCL (the SAIC) and the Foreign M&A Rules (the MOFCOM and the SAIC). Huang and Li believe that the multiple responsibilities and roles of the Chinese competition authorities will result in an 'identity problem' for them, which is not conducive to the development of a clear competition policy for China.[268] This issue is especially relevant to the NDRC and the SAIC, because the NDRC Bureau and the SAIC Bureau have non-AML responsibilities, whereas the MOFCOM Bureau focuses on the AML and competition policy issues.

With respect to the NDRC, its roles as economic planner, industrial development organiser and price regulator are the most relevant to AML enforcement, given the potential for overlap in these roles.[269] In particular, as part of the NDRC's mandate as price regulator, it is also responsible for stabilising the general level of prices. Controlling inflation and maintaining price stability has been one of the Chinese government's top

---

[267] Interviews with Chinese competition law experts and stakeholders.
[268] Huang and Li, 'An Overview of Chinese Competition Policy', 6–8; Huang, 'Coordination of International Competition Policies', pp. 237–8.
[269] Huang and Li, 'An Overview of Chinese Competition Policy', 6–7; Huang, 'Coordination of International Competition Policies', pp. 237–8.

priorities over the past few years.[270] The NDRC regards the AML as a component of the legal system on price regulation, and its investigations into price-related monopoly conduct are viewed as helping it to strengthen price regulation, maintain overall price stability and curb inflation.[271] This is reinforced by the fact that the NDRC allocated its AML enforcement powers to the department originally responsible for price supervision.[272] Some of the NDRC's enforcement activities suggest that it has used the AML as an instrument to help it carry out its price supervisory role to stabilise prices.[273] This is examined in greater detail in Chapter 7.

Whether the NDRC will apply the Price Law or the AML depends on the circumstances of each case.[274] Some interviewees believe that the NDRC might be more inclined to use the Price Law instead of the AML in cases where both laws could apply, as the NDRC has enforced the Price Law since 1998 and is likely to be more familiar and comfortable with it.[275] Price fixing, predatory pricing and price discrimination are covered by both the AML and the Price Law,[276] although the legal requirements to establish a breach under the AML and the Price Law are different.[277] The Price Law requires looking at whether the conduct

---

[270] Barry Naughton, 'Inflation, Welfare, and the Political Business Cycle' [2011] (35) *China Leadership Monitor* 1.

[271] 李镭 [Li Lei], 总结经验，继往开来，开创制止价格垄断工作新局面 [Lessons Learned, Continue Opening Up, Create a New Situation to Stop Price Monopoly] (22 July 2008) National Development and Reform Commission, available at www.sdpc.gov.cn/fzgggz/jggl/zhdt/200808/t20080829_248411.html; 坚持稳中求进，锐意改革创新，促进经济持续健康发展和社会和谐稳定—全国发展和改革工作会议在京召开 [Insist on Progress Whilst Maintaining Stability, Commit to Reform and Innovation, Promote Sustained and Healthy Economic Development and a Harmonious and Stable Society – National Development and Reform Commission Work Conference Held in Beijing], 15 December 2013, available at www.sdpc.gov.cn/xwzx/xwfb/201312/t20131215_570441.html; Deng, Harris and Zhang, 'Interview with Xu Kunlin', 3–4.

[272] Hao, 'The Multiple Hands', p. 28.

[273] Bush and Bo, 'Adding Antitrust to NDRC's Arsenal'.

[274] Deng, Harris and Zhang, 'Interview with Xu Kunlin', 4.

[275] Interviews with Chinese competition law experts and stakeholders.

[276] The Price Law prohibits unfair pricing conduct, which includes colluding or manipulating prices, predatory pricing, fabricating and spreading price information to drive up prices, using misleading or deceptive pricing tactics, price discrimination, disguising the increase or decrease in price by changing the grade of the good or service and profiteering in breach of laws and regulations: Price Law, art. 14.

[277] For example, the fact of price discrimination or predatory pricing is sufficient to find a breach under the Price Law whereas, under the AML, a precondition to finding a breach is that the company has a dominant market position and no valid justification for

itself complies with the law, whereas under the AML an assessment of the impact of the conduct on competition and economic analysis are required.[278] The consequences flowing from taking action under the Price Law as compared to the AML also differ in at least two respects. Under the Price Law, a company can be fined up to five times the illegal gain, whereas under the AML the maximum fine a company faces is 10 per cent of the previous year's turnover.[279] Parties can apply to the NDRC for suspension of an investigation conducted pursuant to the AML; this is not an option under the Price Law.[280] However, penalty reductions are available under both the AML[281] and the Price Law,[282] although the conditions to qualify for such reductions are slightly different.[283]

Enforcement of the AML and the AUCL is carried out by SAIC. Of the competition-related laws that were in place prior to the enactment of the AML, the AUCL was the broadest and most comprehensive with respect to competition-related matters. The AML and the AUCL are closely related.[284] It was originally intended that China's competition law would cover both anti-monopoly and unfair competition conduct; however, a law covering unfair competition conduct (the AUCL) was enacted first due to the lack of consensus over whether an anti-monopoly law was needed at the time.[285] Both laws share a common stated objective – to

engaging in such conduct: Li Qing, 'The Relationship between the Anti-monopoly Law and the Price Law' in Adrian Emch and David Stallibrass (eds.), *China's Anti-monopoly Law: The First Five Years* (Alphen aan den Rijn, The Netherlands: Kluwer Law International, 2013), pp. 79–80.

[278] Deng, Harris and Zhang, 'Interview with Xu Kunlin', 4; Interviews with Chinese competition law experts and stakeholders.
[279] Li, 'The Relationship between the Anti-monopoly Law and the Price Law', pp. 79–81.
[280] Deng, Harris and Zhang, 'Interview with Xu Kunlin', 4.
[281] Anti-monopoly Law, art. 2.
[282] 规范价格行政处罚权的若干规定 [Several Provisions on Regulating Price-Related Administrative Penalty Power] (People's Republic of China) National Development and Reform Commission, Order No. 1223, 7 June 2014, art. 4.
[283] Nate Bush, 'Weathervanes, Lightning Rods, and Pliers: The NDRC's Competition Enforcement Program' [2014] (August) *The Antitrust Source* 1 at 5–8, available at www.americanbar.org/content/dam/aba/publishing/antitrust_source/aug14_bush_7_23f.pdf.
[284] 王晓晔 [Wang Xiaoye], 我国反垄断立法宗旨 [The Legislative Purpose of China's Anti-monopoly Law] [2008] (2) 华东政法大学校报 [Journal of East China University of Political Science and Law] 37 at 41.
[285] 反对垄断和不正当竞争暂行条例草案 [Anti-monopoly and Anti-Unfair Competition Draft Interim Regulation]. See Wang, 'The Prospect of Antimonopoly Legislation in China', 225; *OECD Reviews of Regulatory Reform*, p. 126; 反垄断法的19年风雨历程

maintain fair competition – and are complementary in nature.[286] Wang observes that, whereas the AML protects the rights of entities to compete and participate in the market, the AUCL ensures that the competitive environment is fair.[287] Some of the unfair competition practices targeted by the AUCL, such as predatory pricing and tying conduct, also fall within the scope of the AML.[288] However, some of the overlaps between the AML and the AUCL are likely to be removed with the upcoming revision of the AUCL.[289] The compatibility and overlap between the AML and the AUCL may result in the SAIC enforcing the AML in a manner that also furthers, or is consistent with, its unfair competition mandate under the AUCL.

### 4.3.4 Bureaucratic Rank

In China, bureaucratic and individual ranks are associated with power and prestige. Each government and CPC organisation, such as SOEs, the courts, universities and research institutes, has a bureaucratic rank, while government and CPC officials hold individual ranks.[290] An organisation's authority is based upon its bureaucratic rank and the status of the individuals that lead it.[291] An official's authority derives from his or her formal government and/or CPC title, civil service grade and CPC rank.[292]

---

[Anti-monopoly Law's Stormy 19-Year Journey] (2006) 358 中国经济周刊 [China Economic Weekly] 20.

[286] The purpose of the AUCL is to 'promote the development of the socialist market economy, encourage and maintain fair competition, stop unfair competition, and protect the legal interests of operators and consumers': Anti-Unfair Competition Law, art. 1.

[287] Wang, 'The Legislative Purpose of China's Anti-monopoly Law', 41.

[288] The AUCL prohibits eleven types of unfair competition practices, five of which overlap with anti-competitive conduct: exclusionary conduct by public utilities or other monopolies; administrative monopoly; predatory pricing; tying conduct or otherwise imposing unreasonable trading conditions; and bid rigging: Anti-Unfair Competition Law, arts. 6, 7, 11, 12, 15. See also Harris et al., *Anti-monopoly Law and Practice in China*, pp. 333–44.

[289] According to the draft amendment circulated for public comment in February 2016, the existing provisions relating to administrative monopoly, predatory pricing and tying conduct (which is conduct also regulated under the AML) will be deleted from the AUCL. However, the draft amendment also introduced a new provision that regulates abuses of a 'relatively advantageous position', which might overlap somewhat with abuse of dominant position under the AML. See 中华人民共和国反不正当竞争法 (修订草案送审稿) [Anti-Unfair Competition Law (Draft Amendment for Review)] Legislative Affairs Office of the State Council, 25 February 2016.

[290] Kenneth Lieberthal and Michel Oksenberg, *Policy Making in China: Leaders, Structure, and Processes* (Princeton: Princeton University Press, 1988), pp. 142–5.

[291] Ibid.   [292] Ibid., pp. 145–6.

The ranking system enables government and CPC organisations and officials to evaluate their status and position vis-à-vis other entities.

The ranking system influences the relationship between and interaction of actors within the State Council and the CPC and between central and local governments, the courts and litigants and SOEs and government authorities.[293] Higher-ranked entities can issue binding orders to, and compel cooperation from, lower-ranked entities. Lower-ranked entities cannot issue binding orders to higher-ranked authorities and might face difficulties when trying to cooperate with higher-ranked entities. To liaise with higher-ranked entities, the lower-ranked entity will need to seek the help of a higher-ranked entity to secure cooperation. Further, entities of the same rank cannot issue binding orders to each other or compel cooperation.[294] As such, the place of a government agency in the administrative hierarchy, and therefore its political power and enforcement clout, is very important. Zhang and Zhang note that 'administrative power is traditionally considered more important than the power of the legal authorities'.[295]

The position of Chinese competition authorities in the administrative hierarchy may influence the enforcement of the AML, especially if the enforcement target is an SOE or a company operating in a regulated industry. The responsible authorities actually enforcing the AML within the MOFCOM, the NDRC and the SAIC are bureaus within a ministry; therefore their ranks are below the ministry level. SOEs, depending on whether they are locally or centrally owned, their level of importance and the individual rank of their leaders, might have a higher bureaucratic rank than the responsible bureaus within the Chinese competition authorities. If that is the case, the responsible bureaus might have difficulties enforcing the AML against these SOEs because of their lower rank. Similar issues and considerations arise if the responsible bureaus seek to enforce the AML against companies in regulated industries. The industry regulator, which might have ministerial or vice-ministerial rank, might step in to either assert authority over the matter itself or interfere with the AML investigation or review. In these situations, the responsible bureau might need to elevate the issue within its ministry and seek the assistance of higher-ranked authorities or individuals to be able

---

[293] Brødsgaard, 'Politics and Business Group Formation in China', 627–8; Lawrence and Martin, 'Understanding China's Political System', 14.
[294] Lawrence and Martin, 'Understanding China's Political System', p. 15.
[295] Zhang and Zhang, 'The Antimonopoly Law in China', 189.

to enforce the AML against SOEs or in regulated industries. Whether this assistance is provided would likely depend on ministerial or broader priorities. These issues appear to have posed some challenges to Chinese competition authorities seeking to enforce the AML against SOEs, and are discussed in Chapter 6.

## 4.4 Broader Governance and Policy Environment Influencing Supply-Side Dynamics

This section considers some of the matters relating to the broader governance, regulatory and policy environment in China which potentially affect the production and implementation of law, including the relationships between key stakeholders. The CPC's role in governance was discussed briefly in Chapter 4, and is explored more generally in this section. The overriding macroeconomic control of the state, whether through maintaining control over certain industries via SOEs and sector-specific regulation, intervening to coordinate outcomes or guiding development through the use of five-year plans, may also influence and restrict the way in which administrative enforcement agencies approach competition regulation under the AML. Further, this section examines how the dynamics of the relationship between central and local governments may impact interactions between actors involved in the production and implementation of the AML and those who are subject to its regulation.

### 4.4.1 Role of the Communist Party of China

The CPC is the dominant party in China and has control over state affairs.[296] It is led by the General Secretary, who is also the President and the Chairman of the Central Military Commission, the highest state military organ. Formally, the National Party Congress (and the Central Committee of the CPC, which takes over the functions of the National Party Congress when it is not in session) is the leading body of the CPC.[297] In reality, however, the Standing Committee of the Political Bureau of the Central Committee (Standing Committee of the Politburo) is the most powerful and core decision-making body of the CPC, and its

---

[296] Chen, *Chinese Law*, p. 121.
[297] 中国共产党章程 [Constitution of the Communist Party of China] (People's Republic of China) National Congress of the Communist Party of China, 21 October 2007, art. 10.

members (currently seven) are the most senior leaders in China. They are all members of the Political Bureau of the Central Committee (Politburo), which comprises twenty-five members and is the second most powerful decision-making organ of the CPC; they are, in turn, members of the Central Committee of the CPC.

Even though the CPC and the Chinese government are organisationally distinct and the role of the CPC is not clearly defined in the Chinese Constitution or laws, in reality the CPC has authority over and is involved in governance.[298] This influence is believed to be strong, despite some observations that there is a growing separation between the CPC and the government.[299] However, both the means through which the CPC achieves this control, and to what extent this is the case, are unclear as relatively little information is available to outsiders, within and outside China, on this matter.[300] What scholars do know is that the CPC has some mechanisms to exercise control over government institutions, including the courts.

It is understood that the CPC controls the appointment of a wide range of senior government positions through the *nomenklatura*.[301] The *nomenklatura* system consists of 'lists of leading positions over which party committees exercise the power of appointment, lists of reserve cadre for the available positions, and the institutions and processes for making the appropriate personnel changes'.[302] The scope of the *nomenklatura* is wide. It is implemented by the central secretariat of the CPC together with organisation bureaus in lower-level party committees.[303] As noted in Chapter 4, the CPC, through its organisation department, controls the senior appointments at the largest and important SOEs and the judiciary.

---

[298] Peerenboom, *China's Long March toward Rule of Law*, p. 214; Chen, *Chinese Law*, 121–2, pp. 180–81; Shirk, *The Political Logic of Economic Reform in China*, p. 55; Manuél E. Delmestro, 'The Communist Party and the Law: An Outline of Formal and Less Formal Linkages between the Ruling Party and Other Legal Institutions in the People's Republic of China' (2010) 43 *Suffolk University Law Review* 681 at 682–90.

[299] Peerenboom, *China's Long March toward Rule of Law*, pp. 188–226; Chen, *Chinese Law*, pp. 256–61; Lieberthal and Oksenberg, *Policy Making in China*, p. 146.

[300] Chen, *Chinese Law*, p. 256.

[301] John P. Burns, 'China's *Nomenklatura* System' (1987) 36(5) *Problems of Communism* 36; Hon S. Chan, 'Cadre Personnel Management in China: The Nomenklatura System, 1990–1998' (2004) 179 *The China Quarterly* 703; Melanie Manion, 'When Communist Party Candidates Can Lose, Who Wins? Assessing the Role of Local People's Congresses in the Selection of Leaders in China' (2008) 195 *The China Quarterly* 607.

[302] Burns, 'China's *Nomenklatura* System', 36.

[303] Ibid., 48; Manion, 'When Communist Party Candidates Can Lose', 612.

In addition to the SOEs and the courts, the CPC also controls the appointment of senior positions at, *inter alia*, the NPC, the State Council, ministries and commissions under the State Council, the procuratorate, provincial governments, research institutes, universities and mass organisations.[304] The CPC can install its members in these positions to ensure the implementation of CPC policies and directives. In particular, the top government officials also hold leading positions in the CPC.[305] For example, the Premier and the Chairman of the NPC are both members of the Standing Committee of the Politburo. Hence there is less incentive for senior government officials to implement government policies that are contrary to party policies because, being members of the CPC, they are required to follow party policy and directives, they are subject to party discipline and their careers and advancement prospects are dependent on pleasing CPC leaders.[306] Even if the CPC appoints non-CPC members to these senior government positions, there is nonetheless little incentive for appointees to fall foul of the CPC's policies and directives.

The CPC also has a presence in government organisations, which allows them to supervise government work from within. There are two main types of CPC supervisory organs. The top CPC members within a government institution, who are typically also the top government officials, are organised into a party committee.[307] Party committees are subordinate to higher-level party committees, therefore replicating the hierarchy of government institutions.[308] Party groups also exist within government institutions. The main differences between party groups and party committees are that party groups are appointed, are not elected and have control over the non-CPC members in their

---

[304] Chan, 'Cadre Personnel Management in China', 719–34.
[305] Lawrence and Martin, 'Understanding China's Political System', p. 28.
[306] Shirk, *The Political Logic of Economic Reform in China*, p. 69; Murray Scot Tanner, 'The Erosion of Communist Party Control over Lawmaking in China' (1994) 138 *The China Quarterly* 381 at 389.
[307] Typically consists of the Secretary, Deputy Secretaries, a Secretary of the Discipline Inspection Commission (an anti-corruption office), and other members: Li-Wen Lin and Curtis J. Milhaupt, 'We Are the (National) Champions: Understanding the Mechanisms of State Capitalism in China' (2013) 65 *Stanford Law Review* 697 at 737.
[308] Benjamin van Rooij, 'China's System of Public Administration' in Jianfu Chen, Yuwen Li and Jan Michael Otto (eds.), *Implementation of Law in the People's Republic of China* (The Hague: Kluwer Law International, 2002), pp. 332–3; Carol Lee Hamrin, 'The Party Leadership System' in Kenneth G. Lieberthal and David M. Lampton (eds.), *Bureaucracy, Politics, and Decision Making in Post-Mao China* (Berkeley: University of California Press, 1992), p. 97.

government institution.[309] Together, they ensure the implementation of CPC policies and principles, discuss and make decisions on important issues facing the institution, supervise the behaviour of CPC members, uphold and enforce party discipline and run party life.[310] This system of party committees and party groups inside state institutions creates a *de facto* parallel system of government composed of CPC institutions.[311] Some scholars argue that this blurs the distinction between the CPC and the government.[312]

By controlling the appointment of top government leaders and internally supervising the government, the CPC can help to ensure that the policies set and coordinated through 'leading small groups' established under the Central Committee of the CPC are followed and implemented.[313] For example, as discussed in Chapter 4, leading small groups, led by General Secretary Xi Jinping, have been established by the CPC to implement the reforms put forward by the Third Plenum of the 18th Central Committee of the CPC (Third Plenum). Leading small groups are also established within government institutions.[314]

Although relatively little information is known about leading small groups, scholars believe that each leading small group is led by a member of the Politburo or the Standing Committee of the Politburo, and reports directly to the Standing Committee of the Politburo and the Secretariat of the Central Committee.[315] Leading small groups are also replicated

---

[309] van Rooij, 'China's System of Public Administration', pp. 332–3; Shirk, *The Political Logic of Economic Reform in China*, pp. 59–60.

[310] Constitution of the Communist Party of China, arts. 29–32. See also Hon S. Chan, 'Politics over Markets: Integrating State-owned Enterprises into Chinese Socialist Market' (2009) 29 *Public Administration and Development* 43 at 50; Lieberthal, *Governing China*, pp. 239–40.

[311] Shirk, *The Political Logic of Economic Reform in China*, p. 58; Delmestro, 'The Communist Party and the Law', 694.

[312] Lieberthal, *Governing China*, pp. 239–40; Shirk, *The Political Logic of Economic Reform in China*, pp. 59–62.

[313] Alice Miller, 'The CPC Central Committee's Leading Small Groups' [2008] (26) *China Leadership Monitor* 1 at 1, 3; Lieberthal, *Governing China*, p. 217; 周望 [Zhou Wang], 中国'小组'政治模式解析 [China's 'Small Group' Political Model Analysed] [2010] (3) 云南社会科学 [Social Sciences in Yunnan] 14 at 16–17.

[314] Alice Miller, 'More Already on the Central Committee's Leading Small Groups' [2014] (44) *China Leadership Monitor* 1 at 1.

[315] Constitution of the Communist Party of China, art. 22. See also Saich, *Governance and Politics of China*, p. 118; Miller, 'The CPC Central Committee's Leading Small Groups', 1.

in lower-level party committees.[316] These leading small groups are organised into major functional areas or systems and link the top leadership of the CPC with the government, CPC and other bodies within that functional area.[317] They are thought to be responsible for policy formulation, coordination and implementation in key policy areas such as foreign affairs; however, they have no formal power or authority and are largely hidden from public view.[318] Scholars believe that the leading small group system allows the CPC to guide government policy from within its top leadership and plays an important role in defining how political power is organised in the CPC and government.[319]

The control and supervision of the CPC might be relevant in the enforcement of the AML. The types of cases pursued and the sectors targeted for enforcement action might be determined by the broader priorities and policies set by the CPC.

### 4.4.2 Macroeconomic Regulation and Control

Economic reforms to move China away from a centrally-planned economy to a socialist market economy have led to decreasing state control over the economy and increasing reliance on market forces to allocate and distribute resources. Nonetheless, the state continues to play a leading role in the economy in at least two ways. First, it maintains control over strategic or important industries through SOEs and sector-specific regulation. In particular, the state exercises substantial control over SOEs and their activities, and SOEs are used to implement and achieve policy goals. The tension between the AML and the leading role of SOEs was discussed in Chapter 3, and Chapter 5 will examine how this tension and balance is reflected in the AML.

Second, while the market mechanism is important in the socialist market economy, it is nonetheless subject to the macroeconomic control of the socialist state.[320] One SAIC official describes China's economy as 'government-guided', where, in addition to the market coordinating

---

[316] Miller, 'The CPC Central Committee's Leading Small Groups', 1; Hamrin, 'The Party Leadership System', pp. 96, 99.
[317] Lieberthal, *Governing China*, pp. 215–16.
[318] Miller, 'The CPC Central Committee's Leading Small Groups', 1, 3; Lieberthal, *Governing China*, p. 217; Zhou, 'China's "Small Group" Political Model Analysed', 16–17.
[319] Lieberthal, *Governing China*, p. 216.
[320] Jiang Zemin, 江泽民在中国共产党第十四次全国代表大会上的报告 [Report of Jiang Zemin at the Meeting of the Fourteenth National Congress of the Communist Party of

outcomes, the state might also intervene to achieve particular outcomes.[321] The CPC recognises that it needs to strike a balance between the role of the market and the role of the government in the economy. At the Third Plenum held in November 2013, the CPC stated its intention to undertake reforms to allow the market to play the decisive (though not a complete) role in allocating resources, and that government's role in directly allocating resources would be reduced.[322] However, it is important to note that, at the same time, the CPC stated that the government's role is to, *inter alia*, strengthen oversight of the market, maintain market order and intervene and remedy market failures.[323] The relevance of both the market and government in the socialist market economy and the different nature of their roles have also been confirmed by CPC General Secretary Xi Jinping.[324]

Since 1953, the CPC has used a series of five-year plans to guide China's economic, social and technological development as part of its macroeconomic control of the state. Each five-year plan provides a national blueprint for the economy over a five-year cycle. It contains guidelines, policy frameworks and targets for industry regulators and government officials at all levels of government, who are responsible for its implementation. In addition to five-year goals, annual targets are set through the annual government work reports.

China], 12 October 1992, available at http://cpc.people.com.cn/GB/64162/64168/64567/65446/4526308.html.

[321] Xue Zheng Wang, 'Challenges/Obstacles Faced by Competition Authorities in Achieving Greater Economic Development through the Promotion of Competition – Contribution from China – Session II' (Note Submitted by China at the OECD Global Forum on Competition, 9 January 2004), p. 1. See also Williams, *Competition Policy and Law*, p. 144.

[322] 中共中央关于全面深化改革若干重大问题的决定 [Decision of the Central Committee of the Communist Party of China on Some Major Issues Concerning Comprehensively Deepening Reform] (People's Republic of China) Third Plenary Session of the 18th Central Committee of the Communist Party of China, 12 November 2013; 习近平 [Xi Jinping], 关于《中共中央关于全面深化改革若干重大问题的决定》的说明 [An Explanation of 'Decision of the Central Committee of the Communist Party of China on Some Major Issues Concerning Comprehensively Deepening Reform'], Third Plenary Session of the 18th Central Committee of the Communist Party of China, 15 November 2013.

[323] 'Decision of the Central Committee of the Communist Party of China on Some Major Issues Concerning Comprehensively Deepening Reform'.

[324] Xi, 'An Explanation of "Decision of the Central Committee of the Communist Party of China on Some Major Issues Concerning Comprehensively Deepening Reform"'.

Five-year plans are the product of complex interactions between stakeholders in the government and the CPC. The NDRC takes the lead throughout the drafting process, which spans several years and involves multiple stages. It solicits, collates and coordinates input from the Central Committee of the CPC; the Politburo; the State Council; various ministries, commissions and agencies under the State Council; local governments; the Chinese People's Political Consultative Conference, the NPC, former officials, the Special Administrative Regions; local people's congresses; experts; business people; workers; and farmers. The NDRC puts together an outline which is then approved by the State Council and the Politburo before being submitted to the NPC for ratification. This ratified outline is the document widely referred to as the 'five-year plan' and represents the consensus of many stakeholders. Based on this five-year plan, ministries and provinces will formulate specific outlines and detailed policies (known as 'special plans') to tailor the national five-year plan to the needs of their industry, issue or province. Various departments at the local level will issue more detailed documents to specify how the special plan will be implemented. Policy initiatives, special plans and outlines are reviewed and revised throughout the five-year cycle.[325]

Five-year plans are important because they set China's industrial policy, reform priorities and economic, demographic and social targets for the following five-year period.[326] They are authoritative, having been approved by the top echelons of the CPC, the government and the NPC, and having involved the input of many stakeholders. As such, achievement of the goals and targets in five-year plans is taken seriously. The career advancement prospects of government and CPC officials are closely tied to the meeting of certain targets in the plan, and therefore the incentive to meet plan targets is quite strong.[327] The implementation of five-year plans is likely to impact the AML, especially in situations where the enforcement of the AML would detract from the achievement of plan goals and targets or the implementation of plan policies.

---

[325] 胡鞍钢详解"十二五"规划制定过程: 大体11个步骤 [Hu Angang Details the Process of Formulating the 12th Five-Year Plan: Roughly 11 Steps], 新华网 [Xinhuanet], 29 October 2010, available at www.china.com.cn/economic/txt/2010-10/29/content_21228169.htm.
[326] Lawrence and Martin, 'Understanding China's Political System', p. 12.
[327] Willy C. Shih, 'Prepared Statement' (Prepared Statement for the US–China Economic and Security Review Commission Hearing on 'China's Twelfth Five-Year Plan, Indigenous Innovation and Technology Transfers, and Outsourcing', Washington, DC, 15 June 2011), p. 29; 'China's 12th Five-Year Plan: How It Actually Works and What's in Store for the Next Five Years' (APCO Worldwide, 10 December 2010), p. 11.

The most recent five-year plan is the Thirteenth Five-Year Plan for National Economic and Social Development (Thirteenth Five-Year Plan), which applies from 2016 to 2020. Five principles underlie development under the Thirteenth Five-Year Plan: innovation, coordination, green, openness and inclusiveness.[328] The plan also emphasises the importance of deepening reforms (such as improving market mechanisms, restructuring SOEs and streamlining administration) and law-based governance to development.[329] For example, competition law and policy is included as part of efforts to improve the market system, with the implementation of a fair competition review system, improvement of anti-monopoly and market regulation laws and the combatting of administrative monopolies.[330] At the same time, the state's leading role in achieving development outcomes remains strong, with state intervention and regulation being the primary means through which goals under the plan will be achieved.[331] Further, the Thirteenth Five-Year Plan expressly provides that the CPC has a leadership and coordination role in the implementation of the plan, and that the role of the CPC should be strengthened.[332] Kennedy and Johnson believe that, while there is a rebalancing of the economy under the plan, there will be little change in the relationship between the state and the market.[333]

### 4.4.3 Central–Local Relations

Both public and private enforcement of the AML have been somewhat decentralised. As previously discussed, the NDRC has, and the SAIC may, delegate AML enforcement authority to its provincial authorities. These provincial authorities are accountable both to the central-level NDRC and the central-level SAIC, as the case may be, and the relevant provincial government. This system of dual accountability is known as the *tiao kuai* system, whereby *tiao* refers to the vertical line of responsibility over the sector originating from the relevant central government

---

[328] 中华人民共和国国民经济和社会发展第十三个五年规划纲要 [Outline of the 13th Five-Year Plan for National Economic and Social Development] (People's Republic of China) National People's Congress, 16 March 2016, ch. 4.
[329] Ibid., ch. 2.   [330] Ibid., ch. 13.
[331] Scott Kennedy and Christopher K. Johnson, 'Perfecting China, Inc.: The 13th Five-Year Plan' (Center for Strategic and International Studies, 2016), p. 33.
[332] Outline of the 13th Five-Year Plan for National Economic and Social Development, ch. 79.
[333] Kennedy and Johnson, 'Perfecting China, Inc.', 33.

ministry, and *kuai* refers to the horizontal line of responsibility from the relevant regional government at the provincial or local level.[334] Similarly, the SPC has designated the intermediate people's courts of provinces and municipalities to be the courts of first instance for AML-related matters. Intermediate people's courts are subject to the supervision of higher-level courts and are accountable to their corresponding people's congress.[335]

This dual system of accountability means that the provincial-level authorities will need to balance and coordinate the interests of both their superior agencies; that is, the central-level competition authority or SPC on the one hand, and the provincial government on the other. This is complicated by the fact that the leaders of the Chinese competition authorities and provincial governments all carry the same bureaucratic rank of ministry, and there is no priority established in the Law on Legislation between departmental rules issued by ministries and local government rules enacted by provincial governments.[336] Li argues that enforcement of the AML might be compromised if the interests of the central ministries or the SPC conflict with the provincial government's agenda.[337] This issue is compounded by the incentives for provincial governments to engage in administrative monopoly. While conflicts or other problems that arise from dual accountability are supposed to be resolved by the CPC as the unifying authority, Schroeder notes that, in reality, the resolution of such issues depends on the relative power of the central and local authorities and the issue at hand.[338]

Overall, provincial governments (and their equivalents) have substantial economic and political power vis-à-vis the central government. Practically speaking, the central government cannot effectively govern or manage a country the size of China without relying on the cooperation of provincial governments to, for example, implement national laws and policies, undertake national construction projects and deliver goods and services to the general public. Provincial and local governments have been largely responsible for developing their local economy, and the central government has devolved administrative power to local governments. Provincial and local governments approve, undertake or oversee a

---

[334] Paul E. Schroeder, 'Territorial Actors as Competitors for Power: The Case of Hubei and Wuhan' in Kenneth G. Lieberthal and David M. Lampton (eds.), *Bureaucracy, Politics, and Decision Making in Post-Mao China* (Berkeley: University of California Press, 1992), pp. 286–7.
[335] Peerenboom, *China's Long March toward Rule of Law*, pp. 280–1.
[336] Law on Legislation, art. 91.  [337] Li, 'Unraveling the Jurisdictional Riddle', 2–3.
[338] Schroeder, 'Territorial Actors as Competitors for Power', pp. 286–7.

substantial majority of the investment projects in China.[339] They are also responsible for the provision of services such as education, health, housing and local infrastructure and for the supervision of local SOEs, and are empowered to draft and implement their own laws and regulations (although such laws and regulations are not to conflict with national laws and regulations).[340] Further, provincial governments have significant discretion in implementing and adapting national laws and policies to suit local conditions.[341]

While the devolution of economic and administrative power has been instrumental to the success of China's economic reforms, it has diminished central political control.[342] Some commentators note that it has become more difficult for the central government to implement unified policies due to increasing resistance from provincial and local governments.[343] This has occurred despite efforts by the central government to reassert fiscal and administrative control by implementing selective reforms to recentralise decision-making through measures such as banking, tax, SOE and legal reforms and increasingly centralising legislative power.[344] Further, as discussed in Section 4.2.5, the manner in which economic reforms have been pursued has promoted administrative monopoly, which is considered to be the main barrier to furthering China's economic reforms and creating a national market.

---

[339] Andrew Szamosszegi and Cole Kyle, 'An Analysis of State-owned Enterprises and State Capitalism in China' (Research Report, US–China Economic and Security Review Commission, 2011), p. 32.

[340] Byrd, *The Market Mechanism*, p. 5; Lawrence and Martin, 'Understanding China's Political System', pp. 8–9.

[341] Chen, *Chinese Law*, pp. 245–8; Lawrence and Martin, 'Understanding China's Political System', pp. 8–9.

[342] Montinola, Qian and Weingast, 'Federalism, Chinese Style'; Merle Goldman and Roderick MacFarquhar, 'Dynamic Economy, Declining Party-State' in Merle Goldman and Roderick MacFarquhar (eds.), *The Paradox of China's Post-Mao Reforms* (Cambridge, MA: Harvard University Press, 1999), p. 9; Lubman, 'Bird in a Cage', 402.

[343] Kenneth G. Lieberthal, 'The "Fragmented Authoritarianism" Model and Its Limitations' in Kenneth G. Lieberthal and David M. Lampton (eds.), *Bureaucracy, Politics, and Decision Making in Post-Mao China* (Berkeley: University of California Press, 1992), pp. 20–1; Lubman, 'Bird in a Cage', 408–9; Zheng, 'Central–Local Relations', 199–201.

[344] Laura Paler, 'China's Legislation Law and the Making of a More Orderly and Representative Legislative System' (2005) 182 *The China Quarterly* 301 at 305–7; Zheng, 'Central-Local Relations', 201–3, 208–12.

## 4.5 Conclusion

The examination of the supply-side dynamics of the AML in this chapter shows that the interactions and relationships of the Chinese competition authorities with each other and with other stakeholders will likely have had a significant influence on the drafting and implementation of the AML, and will continue to do so. Each competition enforcement authority had a role under the pre-AML competition law regime, and during the drafting of the AML they haved incentives to protect their regulatory authority and ensure that the adoption of the AML did not erode these powers. The resulting division of AML enforcement authority between three ministries might also lead to conflicts of authority in enforcement. The dynamics of the interaction between the Chinese competition authorities and other supply-side actors, in particular the lower-level governments, will also likely have an impact on the AML. Another factor that is likely to shape AML outcomes is the relationship between the Chinese competition authorities and stakeholders on the demand side, especially industry regulators and SOEs. As discussed in Chapter 3, SOEs and industry regulators are likely to challenge and oppose the application of the AML to SOEs and regulated industries. The ability of Chinese competition authorities to assert their authority over anti-competitive conduct in regulated industries and SOEs will depend, in part, on the power relations between these actors, which are also shaped by the constraints posed on the Chinese competition authorities by limited resources and bureaucratic ranks. Whether, and how, these relationships influence the making and enactment of the AML and its public enforcement are explored in Chapters 5 and 6, respectively.

The institutional and political arrangements underlying the supply of the AML indicate that decisions and actions taken pursuant to the AML will involve the coordination of various interests, actors and policies, with the AML serving as a conduit for such coordination. Such coordination appears to occur at several levels. The first is within the Chinese competition authorities themselves, as each holds other roles and responsibilities, some of which overlap or may conflict with the AML. The second is among the Chinese competition authorities, due to the division of administrative enforcement authority between three ministries. The third is between the Chinese competition authorities and other government authorities, especially industry regulators and provincial and lower-level governments. Fourth, in finding a balance between the market mechanism and the leading role of the state in the socialist market economy, this will likely involve consideration of how markets, competition and the AML fit with the macroeconomic control exercised by the state over the economy. Broader government priorities and commitments will also influence these interactions and outcomes.

While this coordination does not mean that the actors involved on the supply-side of the AML will disregard the AML as a means to promote and protect competition and support the development of the market, it does suggest that competition policy in China is broader than competition law; that is, it includes consideration of other government policies and laws that constrain its operation. This is consistent with the observation made in Chapter 3 that the broader policy environment affecting the demand for the AML as a governance device implicates multiple policy interests. While a macro view of competition policy is not unique to China,[345] this observation helps to explain aspects of the AML's development and enforcement experience to date, and is explored in Chapters 5 and 6.

---

[345] For example, in Australia, see 'National Competition Policy', National Competition Council, available at http://ncp.ncc.gov.au/pages/overview.

# PART III

Understanding the Anti-monopoly Law in Its Context

# 5

# The Making of the Anti-monopoly Law

## 5.1 Introduction

The analytical framework developed in Chapters 3 and 4, which examined the supply and demand-sides of the Anti-monopoly Law (AML), provides the foundation upon which to explore how the political economy influences China's competition law. This analysis has produced several key insights into Chinese political economy that are likely to have some bearing on the enactment, implementation and enforcement of the AML. The relationships and interactions of the Chinese competition agencies, both among themselves and with other actors on the supply and demand-sides (especially industry regulators and state-owned enterprises (SOEs)), and the extent to which their interests and incentives are compatible will be important in determining the issues that might be contentious and how they might be resolved. Further, there may be potential tensions and conflicts in the broader policy and governance environment, such as between the market and economic reform on the one side, and the leading role of the state and industrial policy on the other. Such matters will likely influence decisions made and actions taken in relation to the drafting and enforcement of the AML. Consequently, the coordination of various interests, actors and policies will be vital to the AML.

This chapter investigates the process through which the AML was discussed, drafted and adopted. The following analysis focuses on examining the actors and issues that significantly influenced the drafting process or the text of the AML itself, with a view to understanding how the political economy shaped the making and adoption of the AML. These insights will shed light on how the AML might be interpreted and enforced, especially as many of the actors that participated in the drafting of the AML continue to be involved in its enforcement.

This chapter is structured as follows. The background to the AML drafting process is provided in Section 5.2, with a brief legislative history and discussion of the level of political will and commitment required to adopt the AML, the evolution of the issues discussed as drafting progressed and which significantly shaped the drafting process and/or outcomes, and the special role and influence of competition law experts in the drafting process. Section 5.3 examines the key issues that were discussed during the drafting of the AML. In particular, the focus is on understanding how specific actors and events influenced the debate and resolution of these issues, and whether and how the dynamics changed throughout the drafting process. Section 5.4 concludes.

It is important to note that, while the drafting process was relatively open – with drafters consulting quite widely outside the Chinese government, including with a number of foreign experts – it was nonetheless not entirely transparent or open to the general public. Most drafts of the AML were only circulated to members of the relevant drafting groups and other individuals and organisations consulted during the drafting process. Therefore, this analysis relies on excerpts of or references to these drafts made in secondary materials. Also, there is a limited amount of publicly available information on the views of and arguments made by government actors and institutions on various issues related to the AML, the extent of their participation in the drafting process and their influence. Publicly available information on these matters is limited because it is rare for information about disagreements between government agencies to be disclosed publicly. To overcome such issues, this chapter draws on empirical data obtained from interviews conducted with people who were involved in the drafting process to supplement the publicly available information.

## 5.2 The Anti-monopoly Law Drafting Process

Discussions about the possible enactment of a competition law in China had been ongoing since the mid-1980s.[1] In August 1987, the State Council Legislative Affairs Office (LAO) established a group to draft legislation that covered both competition law and unfair competition law and, in 1988, it produced the draft Interim Regulations Against Monopoly and Unfair Competition. However, the draft interim regulations were not adopted due to a lack of consensus over whether a

---

[1] H. Stephen Harris, Jr et al., *Anti-monopoly Law and Practice in China* (New York: Oxford University Press, 2011), p. 11.

competition law was needed at that time.[2] Instead, the Anti-Unfair Competition Law (AUCL) was enacted in 1993.

In 1994, shortly after the enactment of the AUCL, the AML was placed on the legislative agenda of the Eighth National People's Congress (NPC), and again on the legislative agendas of the Ninth and Tenth NPCs in 1998 and 2004, respectively.[3] In May 1994, the LAO established a group with responsibility for drafting the AML (Ministry Drafting Group). This group was led by the State Economic and Trade Commission (SETC) and the State Administration for Industry and Commerce (SAIC), and included representatives from relevant government ministries and departments and the NPC's Legislative Affairs Commission.[4] Drafting work stalled during the enactment of the Price Law in 1997, due to concerns that a competition law would impede the growth of SOEs.[5] In 1999, drafting of the AML progressed as Cheng Siwei, the Vice Chairman of the Standing Committee of the National People's Congress (SCNPC), organised several legal and economic experts from the Chinese Academy of Social Sciences (CASS) to conduct research on competition law; several outline drafts of the AML were produced from this initiative.[6] In March 2001, drafting work was reinvigorated when the SCNPC announced that China would draft and adopt a competition law in preparation for its accession to the World Trade Organization (WTO).[7] Subsequently, drafting work proceeded more consistently and with greater purpose.

[2] 反对垄断和不正当竞争暂行条例草案 [Anti-monopoly and Anti-Unfair Competition Draft Interim Regulation]. See Xiaoye Wang, 'The Prospect of Antimonopoly Legislation in China' (2002) 1 *Washington University Global Studies Law Review* 201 at 225; *OECD Reviews of Regulatory Reform: China: Defining the Boundary between the Market and the State* (Organisation for Economic Co-Operation and Development, 2009), p. 126; Harris et al., *Anti-monopoly Law and Practice in China*, p. 11; 反垄断法的19年风雨历程 [Anti-monopoly Law's Stormy 19-Year Journey] (2006) 358 中国经济周刊 [China Economic Weekly] 20 at 20.
[3] *OECD Reviews of Regulatory Reform*, p. 126.
[4] Wang, 'The Prospect of Antimonopoly Legislation in China', 224; Mark Williams, *Competition Policy and Law in China, Hong Kong and Taiwan* (Cambridge: Cambridge University Press, 2005), p. 173; 'Anti-monopoly Law's Stormy 19-Year Journey'.
[5] H. Stephen Harris, Jr, 'The Making of an Antitrust Law: The Pending Anti-monopoly Law of the People's Republic of China' (2006) 7 *Chicago Journal of International Law* 169 at 176; Harris et al., *Anti-monopoly Law and Practice in China*, p. 13.
[6] 发言摘登: 反垄断法草案 [Speech Excerpts: Draft of the Anti-monopoly Law], 22nd Session of the Standing Committee of the Tenth National People's Congress, 27 June 2006; Wang, 'The Prospect of Antimonopoly Legislation in China', 224; *OECD Reviews of Regulatory Reform*, p. 126.
[7] *OECD Reviews of Regulatory Reform*, p. 126; 'China Busy Preparing for WTO Entry', Xinhua, 9 March 2001.

Between 2001 and 2004, the Ministry Drafting Group prepared and revised several drafts of the AML and submitted them to the LAO for review. From the second half of 2004 onward, the State Council took the lead in preparing the draft AML, and the AML was included on the State Council's legislative agenda in February 2005. In April 2005, the LAO formed a leading small group (LAO Drafting Group) to lead drafting efforts and to coordinate the interests of various parties.[8] It was composed of representatives from the Financial and Economic Affairs Committee of the NPC (FEA Committee), the Law Committee of the NPC, the Supreme People's Court (SPC), the National Development and Reform Commission (NDRC), the Ministry of Commerce (MOFCOM), the SAIC, the State Council Development Research Centre of the State Council and CASS. The LAO also appointed a group of experts to advise on the draft law.[9]

In June 2006, the State Council submitted a draft of the AML to the SCNPC for its consideration. The SCNPC reviewed the draft three times (June 2006, June 2007 and August 2007). The AML was promulgated on 31 August 2007 and came into effect on 1 August 2008.

Overall, the AML drafting process was divided into three broad stages: (i) preparation of the draft by the SETC, the MOFCOM (which replaced the SETC after a government restructuring in 2003) and the SAIC, during the period between 1994 and mid-2004 (the Ministry Stage); (ii) review and drafting by the State Council, led by the LAO, which occurred from mid-2004 to 2006 (the State Council Stage); and (iii) review and revision of the draft by the SCNPC, administered by the Legislative Affairs Commission and with substantial input from the FEA Committee and the Law Committee of the NPC, from 2006 to 2007 (the SCNPC Stage). A number of actors were consulted throughout the drafting process, including relevant government authorities (typically industry

---

[8] 关于《中华人民共和国反垄断法（草案）》的说明 [An Explanation of China's Anti-monopoly Law (Draft)], 22nd Session of the Standing Committee of the Tenth National People's Congress, 24 June 2006; 王晓玲 [Wang Xiaoling],《反垄断法》: 把立法难题留到执法中解决—访中国社科院规制与竞争研究中心主任张昕竹 [Anti-monopoly Law: Defers Resolution of Difficult Legislative Issues to Enforcement – Interview with Director of Chinese Academy of Social Sciences Centre for Regulation and Competition Zhang Xinzhu] [2005] (17) 商务周刊 [Business Watch Magazine] 47 at 49.

[9] Xiaoye Wang, *The Evolution of China's Anti-monopoly Law* (Cheltenham: Edward Elgar, 2014) p. xviii. Experts involved in this group included Wang Xiaoye, Shi Jianzhong, Wang Xianlin, Sheng Jiemin, Huang Yong, Shi Jichun, Zhang Xinzhu, Qi Yudong, Wu Hanhong and some recently retired government officials.

regulators and local governments), competition law experts, foreign competition authorities, international organisations, lawyers, businesses and industry associations.[10] As discussed in Chapters 3 and 4, each of these actors had different opinions on and interests in the draft AML, and on competition law more generally. In particular, the views of industry regulators and Chinese and foreign competition law experts were influential in shaping not only the substance of the AML, but also the dynamics and progress of the drafting process.

A more detailed timeline of the drafting process can be found in Appendix C.

### 5.2.1 Political Will to Adopt the Anti-monopoly Law

Political consensus on the necessity and desirability of a competition law and the accompanying political will to adopt and implement that law waxed and waned throughout the long period of time it took to enact the AML. This was reflected in the intermittent nature of the drafting efforts undertaken during the early years of the drafting process. As noted above, Chinese law-makers and scholars had been in discussions about the enactment of a competition law in China since the mid-1980s, a working group was established in 1993 to work on a draft competition law and a competition law was placed on the legislative agenda of each of the Eighth, Ninth and Tenth NPCs. However, efforts to progress a draft competition law languished due to the lack of consensus on whether China needed a competition law, given its level of economic development. Arguments against the adoption of a competition law at that time included that China's economy was still in the relatively early stages of development, that Chinese businesses were relatively small in scale compared to large multinational corporations and had not developed economies of scale and that horizontal alliances were just beginning to develop.[11] In 1988, the SETC and the SAIC conducted an investigation into China's market conditions and concluded that competition issues were neither typical nor widespread, whereas the problem of unfair competition was more serious.[12] Therefore it was thought that a competition law, in particular one that included a merger control regime which

---

[10] Ibid., pp. xvi, xvii–xix.
[11] Wang, 'The Prospect of Antimonopoly Legislation in China', 226; *OECD Reviews of Regulatory Reform*, p. 126; Williams, *Competition Policy and Law*, pp. 162–3.
[12] 'Anti-monopoly Law's Stormy 19-Year Journey', 20.

might prevent Chinese businesses from developing economies of scale, would have negative effects on China's industrial policy and economic development.[13] Williams also notes that there was division in the Chinese government, with some believing that competition and free markets would deliver economic benefits and industrial development more quickly and efficiently than a more active and interventionist policy with the government playing a major role in the economy, which was preferred by others.[14]

China's accession to the WTO rejuvenated efforts to draft and adopt a competition law in China.[15] Even though China's accession to the WTO was not conditional on the adoption of a competition law, membership would oblige China to provide non-discriminatory treatment to all WTO members and all foreign individuals and companies.[16] Therefore, in the period leading up to China's accession to the WTO, the Chinese government committed to drafting and enacting a competition law as it was considered compatible with China's WTO obligations.[17] In its Tenth Five-Year Plan for National Economic and Social Development, which was adopted in 2001 and introduced prior to China's accession to the WTO, the Chinese government emphasised the need to prepare for its entry into the WTO and to 'establish a system of foreign trade and economic co-operation compatible with international norms and suitable to domestic conditions [and] step up the work of revising relevant laws and regulations'.[18] This commitment was reaffirmed by the NPC

---

[13] Zhenguo Wu, 'Perspectives on the Chinese Anti-monopoly Law' (2008) 75 *Antitrust Law Journal* 73 at 77; Wang, 'The Prospect of Antimonopoly Legislation in China', 226; Williams, *Competition Policy and Law*, p. 175; Interviews with Chinese competition law experts and stakeholders.

[14] Williams, *Competition Policy and Law*, p. 175.

[15] Wang, 'The Prospect of Antimonopoly Legislation in China', 228–9; Qihua Feng, 'Antimonopoly Legislation Urged', *China Daily*, 16 March 2002, available at www.chinadaily.com.cn/en/doc/2002-03/16/content_111189.htm.

[16] World Trade Organisation, 'WTO Successfully Concludes Negotiations on China's Entry' (Press Release, Press/243, 17 September 2001), p. 1.

[17] 'China Busy Preparing for WTO Entry'; 'NPC to Continue Making Laws to Comply to WTO Rules: Li Peng', *China Daily*, 9 March 2002, available at www.chinadaily.com.cn/en/doc/2002-03/09/content_110119.htm.

[18] Zhu Rongji, 'Report on the Outline of the Tenth Five-Year Plan for National Economic and Social Development' (Address delivered at the Fourth Session of the Ninth National People's Congress, Beijing, 5 March 2001) available at http://en.people.cn/features/lianghui/zhureport.html.

in 2002 after China joined the WTO.[19] A number of commentators believed that the enactment of the AML was viewed by the Chinese government as a way to reassure and signal to other WTO members and foreign companies that China was serious about its WTO commitments and would be able to comply with the WTO's requirements of transparency and non-discrimination.[20] Further, Wu believes that China's accession to the WTO and the competition law norms generated by the WTO provided the Chinese government with the opportunity and impetus to push through the enactment of a competition law.[21]

### 5.2.2 The Influence of Policy on the Drafting Process

As drafting progressed from stage to stage, the matters discussed evolved from the detailed and technical nature of the competition law provisions to greater consideration of the policy issues. During the Ministry Stage, drafting efforts focused primarily on competition-related and/or technical matters such as the substantive legal rules on monopoly agreements, abuse of dominance and mergers; the basic structure of the AML was also determined during this stage.[22] The Ministry Drafting Group also considered matters relating to the scope of the AML's application, such as exemptions for certain types of anti-competitive agreements, businesses and industries; exemptions for SOEs; and the relationship between the AML and intellectual property law.[23] Some of these issues

---

[19] 曾建徽: 适应入世要求, 及时修改制定有关法律 [Zeng Jianhui: To Comply with WTO Requirements, Promptly Revise and Formulate Relevant Laws], 人民网 [People's Daily Online], 4 March 2002, available at www.people.com.cn/GB/shizheng/7501/7507/20020304/678785.html.

[20] Harris, 'The Making of an Antitrust Law', 176–7; David J. Gerber, 'Economics, Law & Institutions: The Shaping of Chinese Competition Law' (2008) 26 Journal of Law & Policy 271 at 281, 297; Yongzhe Huo, 'Nation Poised to Hammer Out Anti-monopoly Law', Business Weekly, China Daily, 28 January 2003, available at www.chinadaily.com.cn/en/doc/2003-01/28/content_154221.htm.

[21] Qianlan Wu, Competition Laws, Globalization and Legal Pluralism: China's Experiences (Oxford: Hart Publishing, 2013), pp. 126–7.

[22] Interviews with Chinese competition law experts and stakeholders.

[23] The Section of Antitrust Law and the Section of International Law and Practice of the American Bar Association, 'Joint Submission to the Ministry of Commerce of the People's Republic of China', 15 July 2003, 20–3, 31–2; Youngjin Jung and Qian Hao, 'The New Economic Constitution in China: A Third Way for Competition Regime?' (2003) 24 Northwestern Journal of International Law & Business 107 at 131–68; H. Stephen Harris, Jr and Kathy Lijun Yang, 'China: Latest Developments in Anti-monopoly

were resolved during the Ministry Stage;[24] others continued to be discussed at later stages of the drafting process.[25]

Several interviewees believed that the draft AML produced by the State Council reflected a compromise struck between the interests of the various ministries and departments under the State Council.[26] While many of the issues discussed at the State Council related to substantive competition-related matters,[27] because the State Council represents a wide range of interests and issues, the points that it considered and needed to weigh up were necessarily broader than those considered during the Ministry Stage.[28] Therefore, while the draft AML prepared by the State Council in large part related to competition law matters, there were also some articles that reflected ministerial and departmental interests.[29] For example, as discussed in Section 5.3.1.2 below, the draft AML submitted by the State Council to the SCNPC provided that industry regulators had the authority to enforce the AML in regulated industries or sectors, with only a minor role left for the competition agencies. It was these ministerial and departmental issues, rather than competition law considerations, which impeded the progress of the drafting of the AML.

The SCNPC's review of the draft AML took into account even broader matters such as industrial policy, national security, the role of the state with respect to the AML and socialist market economy and how the AML relates to the reality of the situation in China.[30] As outlined in Chapter 4, the SCNPC members come from a variety of backgrounds, few of which include law, and their level of competition law knowledge is generally fairly low. Given the members' backgrounds, some interviewees commented that the SCNPC's consideration of broader issues such as

---

Law Legislation' (2005) 19(2) *Antitrust* 89 at 91; Interviews with Chinese competition law experts and stakeholders.

[24] For example, exemption for certain businesses, industries and SOEs under the AML.
[25] For example, individual exemption for anti-competitive agreements and the relationship between intellectual property rights and the AML.
[26] Interviews with Chinese competition law experts and stakeholders.
[27] For example, the issue of whether to include a form of the essential facilities doctrine in the AML was discussed during the State Council Stage.
[28] Interviews with Chinese competition law experts and stakeholders.
[29] Interviews with Chinese competition law experts and stakeholders.
[30] 全国人大法律委员会关于《中华人民共和国反垄断法(草案)》修改情况的汇报 [Report of the Law Committee of the National People's Congress on the Revision of the Anti-monopoly Law of the People's Republic of China (Draft)], 28th Session of the Standing Committee of the Tenth National People's Congress, 24 June 2007.

industrial policy and national security was perhaps inevitable.[31] In addition to addressing technical issues such as making the presumption of dominance rebuttable and amending the administrative review provisions,[32] the SCNPC added several articles to the AML. These additions caused quite a bit of controversy, as they related to policy concerns not typically considered appropriate for competition law. As will be discussed further in this chapter, the articles reflected topical issues at the time, as well as industrial policy issues, the role of the state in the economy and concerns that the AML needed to be China-specific. Some interviewees who were involved in the drafting of the AML believed that these articles were added as part of a compromise to ease the concerns held by some SCNPC members regarding the need for and role of competition law and to increase their support for the AML, otherwise the enactment of the AML might have been further delayed or perhaps not have happened at all.[33] One interviewee commented that it was likely that leaders high up in the Chinese political hierarchy had required the addition of the new articles.[34]

### 5.2.3 *Role and Influence of Competition Law Experts and International Competition Law Norms and Practices*

A notable and significant characteristic of the AML drafting process was the substantial influence that competition law experts had on technical and broader policy issues.[35] The opinions and suggestions of competition law experts were sought and carefully considered by the drafters, as one of their guiding drafting principles was to ensure that the AML was consistent with prevailing international competition law norms and practices.[36]

---

[31] Interviews with Chinese competition law experts and stakeholders.
[32] 全国人大法律委员会关于《中华人民共和国反垄断法 （草案二次审议稿）》审议结果的报告 [Report of the Law Committee of the National People's Congress on the Results of the Deliberations over the Anti-monopoly Law of the People's Republic of China (Second Deliberation Draft)], 29th Session of the Standing Committee of the Tenth National People's Congress, 24 August 2007; Report of the Law Committee of the National People's Congress on the Revision of the Anti-monopoly Law of the People's Republic of China (Draft), 24 June 2007.
[33] Interviews with Chinese competition law experts and stakeholders.
[34] Interviews with Chinese competition law experts and stakeholders.
[35] David J. Gerber, *Global Competition: Law, Markets, and Globalization* (Oxford: Oxford University Press, 2010) pp. 227–8.
[36] An Explanation of China's Anti-monopoly Law (Draft), 24 June 2006; Wu, 'Perspectives on the Chinese Anti-monopoly Law', 78.

A core group of Chinese competition law academics consisting of Professors Wang Xiaoye, Wang Xianlin, Shi Jianzhong, Huang Yong and Sheng Jiemin had a definite influence on the drafting process. They advised drafters on competition law issues throughout the drafting process (in addition to providing advice informally, they were also formally appointed as experts to advise the LAO Drafting Group), undertook research projects, made comments and suggestions on the content of the law and helped facilitate exchanges between the officials responsible for preparing the draft AML and foreign competition law experts.[37] While not all of their suggestions were adopted,[38] the Chinese competition law academics were influential on some particularly contentious matters. As discussed in Section 5.3.2, Chinese competition law scholars had advocated strongly for inclusion of the prohibition of administrative monopoly in the AML. They provided government officials involved in the drafting of the AML with a better understanding of the harms to competition associated with administrative monopolies and raised public discourse and awareness about administrative monopolies in the media, especially in the aftermath of the deletion of the chapter on administrative monopolies from the draft AML in late 2005/early 2006.[39] Their strong opposition to exemptions for certain regulated or monopoly industries also led to the deletion of an article in the draft AML which provided for such an exemption. Similarly, in the face of strong opposition from foreign experts, their support helped to secure the inclusion of Article 55, which concerns the application of the AML to the exercise of intellectual property rights.

---

[37] 谢晓冬 [Xie Xiaodong],《反垄断法》草案减负 "反行政垄断"被整体删除 [Draft Anti-monopoly Law Reduces Its Burden, 'Administrative Monopoly Prohibition' Is Entirely Deleted], 新京报 [Beijing News], 11 January 2006, available at http://finance1.people.com.cn/GB/1037/4017283.html; Interviews with Chinese competition law experts and stakeholders.

[38] For example, the essential facilities doctrine in the April 2005 draft AML was included at the suggestion of Professor Xiaoye Wang. However, it was deleted from the draft AML by the State Council. See Xiaoye Wang, 'Issues Surrounding the Drafting of China's Anti-monopoly Law' (2004) 3 *Washington University Global Studies Law Review* 285 at 288–9; 王晓晔 [Wang Xiaoye], 入世与中国反垄断法的制定 [Accession to the WTO and the Drafting of the Anti-monopoly Law] [2003] (2) 法学研究 [CASS Journal of Law] 122 at 137–8. Cf The Section of Antitrust Law, the Section of Intellectual Property Law and the Section of International Law of the American Bar Association, 'Joint Submission to the Ministry of Commerce of the People's Republic of China', 19 May 2005, 4–5.

[39] Wang, *The Evolution of China's Anti-monopoly Law*, p. xvii.

In contrast, it seems that Chinese economists had limited influence on the drafting of the AML. According to some interviewees involved in the drafting process, the main role of Chinese economists was to improve the drafters' understanding and awareness of competition law economic theories.[40] Economists also provided input on matters relating to mergers (such as notification thresholds), market shares and the presumption of dominance.[41]

The drafters also learnt from the experiences of other jurisdictions. For example, earlier drafts of the AML provided that businesses could apply for exemptions of monopoly agreements on a case-by-case basis. Foreign competition law experts argued that this arrangement should be deleted from the AML, citing the experiences of the European Commission in administering its individual exemption regime, which it eventually decided to abandon.[42] The LAO deleted the exemption regime from the draft AML in July 2005, having learnt from the European Commission's experience.[43] A leniency policy[44] and a system for the competition authority to accept remedial or corrective commitments[45] were also incorporated into the AML. This was in part based on the experiences of other jurisdictions, as leniency is also consistent with Chinese administrative law principles, under which a party will have its penalty reduced if it, *inter alia*, voluntarily cooperates with the investigation or mitigates the effect of the illegal conduct.[46] Foreign competition law experts also weighed in on technical competition law matters and concepts such as market definition, the concept of a dominant market position, the

---

[40] Interviews with Chinese competition law experts and stakeholders.
[41] Interviews with Chinese competition law experts and stakeholders.
[42] Xiaoye Wang, 'The New Chinese Anti-monopoly Law: A Survey of a Work in Progress' (2009) 54 *Antitrust Bulletin* 577 at 601; Harris, 'The Making of an Antitrust Law', 193.
[43] Wang, 'The New Chinese Anti-monopoly Law', 601; Jessica Su and Xiaoye Wang, 'China: The Competition Law System and the Country's Norms' in Eleanor M. Fox and Michael J. Trebilcock (eds.), *The Design of Competition Law Institutions: Global Norms, Local Choices* (Oxford: Oxford University Press, 2013), p. 209; Harris et al., *Anti-monopoly Law and Practice in China*, p. 11; Interviews with Chinese competition law experts and stakeholders.
[44] 中华人民共和国反垄断法 [Anti-monopoly Law of the People's Republic of China] (People's Republic of China) Standing Committee of the National People's Congress, 30 August 2007, art. 46.
[45] Anti-monopoly Law, art. 45.
[46] Harris, 'The Making of an Antitrust Law', 219; Harris et al., *Anti-monopoly Law and Practice in China*, pp. 47–8; Wu, 'Perspectives on the Chinese Anti-monopoly Law', 108; Nate Bush, 'Weathervanes, Lightning Rods, and Pliers: The NDRC's Competition Enforcement Program' [2014] (August) *The Antitrust Source* 1 at 5–6, available at www.americanbar.org/content/dam/aba/publishing/antitrust_source/aug14_bush_7_23f.pdf.

distinction between horizontal and vertical agreements and their competitive effects and merger review.[47]

Although foreign experiences and international competition law norms were considered by the drafters and a number of concepts and practices from other jurisdictions were incorporated into the AML, such views and experiences were nonetheless balanced against another guiding principle adopted by the drafters, which was that the AML needed to reflect and suit China's specific needs and circumstances.[48] Throughout the drafting process, the drafters emphasised that the AML needed to be tailored to suit China's national conditions, including its stage of economic development and industrial policy concerns.[49]

For example, against advice from US antitrust law experts, the drafters of the AML decided to include Article 55 in the AML. Under Article 55, the AML does not apply to the exercise of intellectual property rights in accordance with relevant intellectual property laws and administrative regulations, but it does apply to the abuse of intellectual property rights to eliminate or restrict market competition. US antitrust law experts argued that the lack of guidance as to what constitutes 'abuse' and the consequences flowing from such abuse might discourage innovation and render intellectual property laws ineffective.[50] Deng and Fei suspect that such views might stem from concerns regarding the diffusion of intellectual property and technology from foreign companies to Chinese competitors in China, which resulted from the weak protection of intellectual

---

[47] Harris, 'The Making of an Antitrust Law', 188–9, 195, 210; William Blumenthal, 'Presentation to the International Symposium on the Draft Anti-monopoly Law of the People's Republic of China' (Speech delivered at the Legislative Affairs Office of the State Council, Beijing, 24–25 May 2005), pp. 4–5.

[48] Wu, 'Perspectives on the Chinese Anti-monopoly Law', 77; Xiaoye Wang, 'Highlights of China's New Anti-monopoly Law' (2008) 75 *Antitrust Law Journal* 133 at 134–5; Interviews with Chinese competition law experts and stakeholders.

[49] An Explanation of China's Anti-monopoly Law (Draft), 24 June 2006; 反垄断法二审稿更加符合我国国情—分组审议反垄断法草案发言摘登 (一) [Anti-monopoly Law Second Deliberation Draft More Compatible with Our National Conditions – Speech Excerpts of the Group Deliberations of the Draft Anti-monopoly Law (1)], 28th Session of the Standing Committee of the Tenth National People's Congress, 25 June 2007; Wu, 'Perspectives on the Chinese Anti-monopoly Law', 77.

[50] The Section of Antitrust Law and the Section of International Law and Practice of the American Bar Association, 31; The Section of Antitrust Law, the Section of Intellectual Property Law and the Section of International Law of the American Bar Association, 34; Harris, 'The Making of an Antitrust Law', 227–8; H. Stephen Harris, Jr and Rodney H. Ganske, 'The Monopolization and IP Abuse Provisions of China's Anti-monopoly Law: Concerns and a Proposal' (2008) 75 *Antitrust Law Journal* 213 at 221–8.

property rights in China and the requirement, in many cases, that a foreign company transfer technology to its Chinese partner.[51] US antitrust law experts also believed that it was unnecessary, at that time, to address the interface between the AML and intellectual property law.[52]

In contrast, the drafters held the view that foreign companies occupied positions of competitive advantage or dominance in many Chinese industries, and that they relied on their intellectual property rights to impose unreasonable conditions and harm competition and consumer interests in China.[53] Therefore, they thought that the AML needed to address this issue as Chinese companies had been harmed by the abuse of intellectual property rights by foreign companies.[54] They also believed that the inclusion of Article 55 was consistent with prevailing international practice.[55]

## 5.3 Major Issues Considered in the Drafting of the Anti-monopoly Law

During the drafting process, several important – and contentious – issues dominated discussions and had a significant impact not only on the

---

[51] Deng Fei and Gregory K. Leonard, 'The Role of China's Unique Economic Characteristics in Antitrust Enforcement' in Adrian Emch and David Stallibrass (eds.), *China's Antimonopoly Law: The First Five Years* (Alphen aan den Rijn, The Netherlands: Kluwer Law International, 2013), p. 68.

[52] The Section of Antitrust Law and the Section of International Law and Practice of the American Bar Association, 31; The Section of Antitrust Law, the Section of Intellectual Property Law and the Section of International Law of the American Bar Association, 34.

[53] An Explanation of China's Anti-monopoly Law (Draft)], 24 June 2006; 王晓晔 [Wang Xiaoye], 中华人民共和国反垄断法详解 [Detailed Explanation of the Anti-monopoly Law of the People's Republic of China], (知识产权出版社 [Intellectual Property Publishing House], 2008), pp. 273–4; 商思林 [Shang Silin], 反垄断法: 化解知识产权国际压力的中国利器? [Anti-monopoly Law: China's Weapon to Resolve International Pressure on Intellectual Property Rights?], 南方周末 [Southern Weekend], 6 July 2006, available at http://finance.sina.com.cn/roll/20060706/1449784438.shtml.

[54] An Explanation of China's Anti-monopoly Law (Draft), 24 June 2006; Wang, 'Detailed Explanation of the Anti-monopoly Law of the People's Republic of China', 273–4; Shang, 'Anti-monopoly Law'.

[55] An Explanation of China's Anti-monopoly Law (Draft), 24 June 2006; Economic Law Division of the Legal Affairs Commission of the Standing Committee of the National People's Congress (ed.), 中华人民共和国反垄断: 法条文说明、立法理由及相关规定 [The Anti-monopoly Law of the People's Republic of China: Explanation of the Articles, Legislative Reasons, and Related Regulations] (北京大学出版社 [Peking University Press], 2007), p. 346; Wu, 'Perspectives on the Chinese Anti-monopoly Law', 96–7; Shang, 'Anti-monopoly Law'.

content of the AML, but also on the progress and dynamics of the drafting process. The issues concerned matters of enforcement authority and the scope of the AML, the abuse of administrative (as opposed to private) power, the state's leading role in the economy and other policy issues that are traditionally regarded as external to competition law.

This section examines and explores these debates, focusing on the actors involved, their interests and positions, the development of the draft AML in response to these discussions and the resolution of these debates by those responsible for preparing the draft and/or ultimately adopting the AML.

### 5.3.1 Jurisdiction: Enforcement and Scope Issues

Some of the most contentious and bottleneck-inducing issues discussed during the drafting process concerned matters of enforcement authority and scope.[56] Which government agency would have power to enforce the AML and how the AML would apply in regulated industries were issues that emerged as key concerns. These issues were always contentious and were never fully resolved in the drafting process. In fact, the solutions presented became less and less certain as drafting progressed, leaving room for discretion, and ultimately the real resolution of these issues was deferred until after enactment of the AML.

#### 5.3.1.1 Power to Enforce the Anti-monopoly Law

From the beginning of the drafting process, there was a tussle between several State Council ministries for power to enforce the AML. The MOFCOM, the SAIC and the NDRC all vied for enforcement authority. Their claims to jurisdiction[57] were largely based on their existing competition-related experience and responsibilities.[58] The existing competition law regime and the roles of the NDRC, the MOFCOM and the SAIC in enforcing that regime are discussed in Chapters 3 and 4. As the AML would overlap with these existing responsibilities, there was a risk that these ministries would lose some of their existing power after the

---

[56] Wang, 'Anti-monopoly Law: Defers Resolution of Difficult Legislative Issues to Enforcement', 47, 49.
[57] The term 'jurisdiction' is used to refer to the issues relating to enforcement authority and scope. This is because Chinese law-makers, academics and media use the term 管辖权 when discussing these issues, which is translated as 'jurisdiction' in English.
[58] Interviews with Chinese competition law experts and stakeholders.

enactment of the AML. Therefore, it was in their interests to advocate for jurisdiction under the AML to protect their regulatory turf.

From the beginning of the drafting process, the MOFCOM and the SAIC were the frontrunners in the race to act as the competition enforcement agency. As discussed above, both ministries were involved in the preparation of the draft AML throughout the entire drafting process, including jointly leading drafting efforts during the Ministry Stage. Despite initial intentions for the two ministries to work together, over time they undertook the drafting work separately, including submitting separate drafts of the AML to the State Council, where they each nominated themselves as the sole government agency responsible for enforcing the AML.[59] Each ministry also engaged in other actions to demonstrate that it should be the AML enforcement agency. For example, the MOFCOM publicly claimed primary responsibility for drafting the AML, pointing out that it had consulted other ministries and departments under the State Council as well as experts throughout its drafting process, had conducted research with the LAO and SCNPC and had submitted a draft to the State Council for its review.[60] It also established an anti-monopoly investigation office in September 2004 to be responsible for anti-monopoly investigations, legislative work and international cooperation activity,[61] and established a competition policy dialogue with the Directorate-General for Competition of the European Commission in May 2004.[62] With respect to the SAIC, it undertook a nationwide

---

[59] Interviews with Chinese competition law experts and stakeholders; Wang, *The Evolution of China's Anti-monopoly Law*, p. xvii; Wang, 'Anti-monopoly Law: Leaves the Difficult Legislative Issues to Be Resolved in Enforcement', 49; Hao Qian, 'The Multiple Hands: Institutional Dynamics of China's Competition Regime' in Adrian Emch and David Stallibrass (eds.), *China's Anti-monopoly Law: The First Five Years* (Alphen aan den Rijn, The Netherlands: Kluwer Law International, 2013), p. 16.

[60] Ministry of Commerce, 商务部条法司有关负责人介绍反垄断立法情况 [MOFCOM Department of Treaty and Law Responsible Person Introduces the Anti-monopoly Law Situation] (Press Release, 11 January 2005); 张琼 [Zhang Qiong], 国务院法制办公室张琼副主任在反垄断立法国际研讨会闭幕式上的讲话 [Closing Remarks of Deputy Director of the Legislative Affairs Office of the State Council Zhang Qiong at the International Symposium on the Anti-monopoly Legislation] (Closing Remarks, Beijing, 9 October 2005); David Fang, 'Bureaucrats Stall Anti-monopoly Law', *South China Morning Post*, 12 January 2005, available at www.scmp.com/article/485151/bureaucrats-stall-anti-monopoly-law.

[61] Ministry of Commerce, Press Release, 11 January 2005.

[62] Ministry of Commerce of China and the Directorate-General for Competition of European Commission, *Terms of Reference of the EU–China Competition Policy Dialogue*, 6 May 2004, available at http://ec.europa.eu/competition/international/bilateral/china_tor_en.pdf.

campaign in 2001 to combat administrative monopolies and maintain fair competition,[63] and in 2004 it released a report on the anti-competitive conduct of multinationals in China, which is discussed in Chapters 3 and 4. In that report, the SAIC firmly asserted itself as the government agency in charge of enforcing competition laws and regulations and advocated for the enactment of the AML.[64] It also attended the OECD Global Forum on Competition held in February 2003 as China's representative, and it publicly lobbied to be the enforcement agency under the AML and requested the support of the international community in this.[65]

From 2003 onwards, and especially when the drafting of the AML progressed to the State Council Stage, the issue of which agency would enforce the AML became more complex as the NDRC entered the fray. In June 2003, the NDRC released the Price Monopoly Interim Provisions,[66] which Bush and Bo note 'read like a rough draft of the AML'.[67] It also began to publicly advocate for the enactment of the AML and slated it as one of its six key focal points in 2005.[68] Even though the NDRC had

---

[63] 'Breaking Administrative Monopoly Benefits All', *China Daily*, 24 December 2002, available at www.chinadaily.com.cn/chinagate/doc/2002-12/24/content_249316.htm; 'Market Says Goodbye to Foul Play', *China Daily*, 9 January 2002, available at www.chinadaily.com.cn/en/doc/2002-01/09/content_101213.htm.

[64] 国家工商总局公平交易局和反垄断处 [Fair Trade Bureau and Anti-monopoly Division of the State Administration for Industry and Commerce], 在华跨国公司限制竞争行为表现及对策 [The Competition Restricting Conduct of Multinational Companies in China and Countermeasures] (2004) 5 工商行政管理 [Biweekly of Industry and Commerce Administration] 42 at 43.

[65] 'The Objectives of Competition Law and Policy and the Optimal Design of a Competition Agency – China' (Note submitted by China at the OECD Global Forum on Competition, 9 January 2003), p. 4.

[66] 制止价格垄断行为暂行决定 [Interim Provision on Preventing Price-Related Monopoly Conduct] (People's Republic of China) National Development Reform Commission, Order No. 3, 18 June 2003.

[67] Nathan Bush and Yue Bo, 'Adding Antitrust to NDRC's Arsenal' [2011] (2) *CPI Antitrust Chronicle* 1 at 3.

[68] Economic Situation Analytical Taskforce of the Macroeconomic Research Institute of the National Development and Reform Commission, 发改委专家: 明年增长降到8% 调控力度难办 [NDRC Expert: Next Year's Growth to Drop to 8 per cent, Difficult to Control], 瞭望新闻周刊 [*Outlook Weekly*] 1 November 2004, available at http://news.sina.com.cn/c/2004-11-01/19144107872s.shtml; Economic Situation Analytical Taskforce of the Macroeconomic Research Institute of the National Development and Reform Commission, 当前经济形势及2005年的政策取向 [Current Economic Situation and Policy Direction for 2005] (7 January 2005) 中国中小企业信息网 [www.sme.gov.cn] available at www.sme.gov.cn/cms/news/100000/0000000223/2005/1/7/ycqywyuytmhwghxskfw1104366671998.shtml.

MAJOR ISSUES CONSIDERED IN DRAFTING                217

the lowest level of involvement in the drafting process of the three ministries, and its price-related enforcement activities focused more on misrepresentation, unfair charges and price regulation matters rather than competition matters such as price fixing or predation,[69] it is the most politically powerful of the three ministries and hence was able to effectively exert pressure and lobby for jurisdiction.

This three-way struggle for jurisdiction affected the drafting of the AML in at least two ways. First, it delayed the progress of drafting.[70] While the three ministries each promoted the enactment of the AML, the lack of clarity and consensus over the identity of the enforcement agency is seen as the major reason why the adoption of the AML was delayed.[71] Professor Sheng Jiemin, who was a member of the LAO Expert Group, commented that it was difficult to select one government authority to be the enforcement agency, as the NDRC had experience with respect to major bidding projects and macroeconomic policy, whereas the SAIC and the MOFCOM had experience regulating businesses, markets and industries.[72] This issue continued to prove intractable at the SCNPC stage.[73]

Second, it significantly changed the administrative enforcement structure of the AML. During the Ministry Stage and the first part of the State Council Stage, the enforcement structure options fluctuated from an independent, new, ministry-level 'anti-monopoly administration authority' established under the State Council, to an authority established under 'the competent authority in charge of commerce under the State Council', to, at one point, dividing enforcement between the MOFCOM (merger review and administrative monopolies), the SAIC (monopoly agreements and abuse of dominance) and the NDRC (price collusion and

---

[69] OECD Reviews of Regulatory Reform, p. 143.
[70] Wang, 'The New Chinese Anti-monopoly Law', 587; Zhao Yong, 'Will Protectionists Hijack China's Competition Law?' (2004) 23 International Financial Law Review 21 at 21; Wei Min, 'State Monopoly Too Hard a Nut to Crack', China Daily, 17 April 2001, avaliable at www.chinadaily.com.cn/en/doc/2001-04/17/content_51654.htm; Interviews with Chinese competition law experts and stakeholders.
[71] 张黎明 [Zhang Liming], 中央三部委争立《反垄断法》今年出台无望 [Three Central Ministries Fight for the Anti-monopoly Law, No Hope for Enactment This Year], 北京晨报 [Beijing Morning News], 11 January 2005, available at www.southcn.com/news/china/zgkx/200501110126.htm.
[72] Ibid.
[73] 反垄断法暂无望二审 [Currently No Hope for Second Review of the Anti-monopoly Law], 经济观察网 [Economic Observer Online], 13 October 2006, available at www.eeo.com.cn/2006/1013/41491.shtml.

bid rigging).[74] In November 2005, the State Council decided to adopt a two-tiered enforcement structure.[75] The Anti-monopoly Commission (AMC) would be responsible for leading, organising and coordinating AML enforcement work, and a competition enforcement authority would be responsible for the day-to-day enforcement work.[76] This dual-layer enforcement structure was contrary to the advice of domestic and foreign competition law experts, who argued that effective enforcement of the AML required an independent, single and unified enforcement authority.[77] Instead, it reflected a political compromise struck by the State Council amongst its ministries and departments in order to progress the drafting of the AML and have a draft submitted to the SCNPC for deliberation.[78] In fact, after the specific enforcement arrangements were confirmed, the Director-General of the NDRC Bureau commented that, had there been insistence on a single competition enforcement agency, the enactment of the AML might have been delayed by several years.[79] As one interviewee who participated in the drafting process pointed out, despite the disagreements between the ministries and departments and the tussle for jurisdiction, they nonetheless recognised that they needed to reach a compromise to progress the law because political leaders and the public demanded the enactment of the AML.[80] The general nature of the administrative enforcement arrangements under the AML provided the State Council with both the necessary discretion to work out the specific enforcement arrangements after the adoption of the AML and the sufficient specificity to appease the various interested parties. It would have helped to facilitate the progress of the AML even though, in reality, the resolution of the issue was merely

[74] Williams, *Competition Policy and Law*, p. 185; Jung and Hao, 'The New Economic Constitution in China', 159; Harris, 'The Making of an Antitrust Law', 178–9; Harris and Yang, 'China: Latest Developments', 91; *OECD Reviews of Regulatory Reform*, p. 140.
[75] Harris et al., *Anti-monopoly Law and Practice in China*, p. 45.
[76] 中华人民共和国反垄断法 (草案) (全国人大第一次审议稿) [Anti-monopoly Law of the People's Republic of China (Draft) (First Deliberation Draft of the National People's Congress)] (People's Republic of China) arts. 5, 33–4.
[77] Interviews with Chinese competition law experts and stakeholders.
[78] Su and Wang, 'China: The Competition Law System', pp. 227–8; Interviews with Chinese competition law experts and stakeholders.
[79] 国新办就反垄断执法工作情况举行吹风会 [State Council Information Office Briefing on Anti-monopoly Law Enforcement Activities] (11 September 2014), State Council Information Office, available at www.china.com.cn/zhibo/2014-09/11/content_ 33487367.htm.
[80] Interviews with Chinese competition law experts and stakeholders.

deferred. By deferring the resolution of the issue to a later stage, the State Council and the SCNPC also acknowledged that it was a complex issue, which required more time to resolve than was permitted by the more pressing need to enact the AML. Further, establishing a commission that spans across ministries and departments to act as a coordination and negotiation mechanism is regarded as a common strategy used by the State Council to achieve consensus where multiple State Council bodies participate or have an interest in enforcement.[81] It also signalled that political considerations and other policy concerns would likely play a role in the AML.[82]

As discussed in Chapter 4, the administrative enforcement structure that was ultimately adopted by the State Council reflected the existing competition enforcement arrangements, and the AMC comprised representatives from a variety of ministries and government authorities, each with an interest in competition policy. During his explanation of the draft AML to the SCNPC before that body's first review, Cao Kangtai, Director of the LAO, strongly hinted that the State Council preferred to maintain the existing enforcement arrangements, at least in the early stages of AML enforcement.[83] This preference for the status quo was confirmed after the enactment of the AML. Earlier drafts of the AML prepared by the State Council also showed that it was likely that the AMC would consist of leaders of relevant government ministries, departments and agencies, and certain experts.[84]

### 5.3.1.2 Application of the Anti-monopoly Law in Regulated Industries

Similarly, the issue of jurisdiction over regulated industries was very contentious throughout the drafting process.[85] Matters involving regulated industries are particularly complex because of the many government interests and actors involved. Industry regulators, regulated businesses (including SOEs) and the State-owned Assets Supervision and Administration Commission all have an interest in how the AML

---

[81] Speech Excerpts: Draft of the Anti-monopoly Law, 27 June 2006.
[82] Harris et al., *Anti-monopoly Law and Practice in China*, p. 45.
[83] An Explanation of China's Anti-monopoly Law (Draft), 24 June 2006; Wang, 'The New Chinese Anti-monopoly Law', 583–7.
[84] Anti-monopoly Law, First Deliberation Draft, art. 33.
[85] Yong Huang, 'Coordination of International Competition Policies: An Anatomy Based on Chinese Reality' in Andrew T. Guzman (ed.), *Cooperation, Comity, and Competition Policy* (New York: Oxford University Press, 2011), p. 247.

might apply in regulated industries, and all voiced their opinions and concerns about the AML throughout the drafting process.[86] A number of interviewees and commentators observed that industry regulators have incentives to protect their regulatory turf, and regulated businesses, in particular SOEs, prefer to be subject to sector-specific laws and regulations and under the supervision of industry regulators, as those arrangements are generally regarded as being favourable to their interests.[87] As such, negotiation and coordination among relevant industry regulators is usually one of the main challenges to overcome when drafting a law in China, and it can be a long and complex process.[88]

During the drafting process, discussions regarding regulated industries and the AML centred on several issues: first, whether regulated industries would be exempt from the application of the AML; second, if regulated industries were subject to the AML, which government authority would have power to enforce the AML in regulated industries; and third, what would the relationship be between the AML and other laws, in particular sector-specific laws.[89]

**(i) Exemption for Regulated Industries** The issue of whether regulated industries would be exempt from the AML was discussed and resolved at the Ministry Stage.[90] Industry regulators and SOEs operating in regulated industries had pressed strongly for a blanket exemption for regulated industries from the AML, or for special treatment under the AML.[91] For example, the Ministry of Railways and the Civil Aviation Administration of China argued that railways and airports should be exempt from the AML as they were natural monopolies.[92] These views were, for a time,

---

[86] Ibid. Lillian Yang, 'Anti-monopoly Bill for Review', *South China Morning Post*, 7 November 2006, available at www.scmp.com/node/570629; Interviews with Chinese competition law experts and stakeholders.

[87] Interviews with Chinese competition law experts and stakeholders; 李莫言 [Li Moyan], 让反垄断法少些遗憾 [Let Anti-monopoly Law Have Fewer Defects] [2006] (7) 大经贸 [Foreign Business] 24 at 24; Philip Wen, 'China's Xi Jinping Compared to Deng Xiaoping as His Power Base Grows', The Age, 18 November 2013, available at www.theage.com.au/world/chinas-xi-jinping-compared-to-deng-xiaoping-as-his-power-base-grows-20131117-2xp3y.html.

[88] Wu, *Competition Laws, Globalization and Legal Pluralism*, p. 122.

[89] Interviews with Chinese competition law experts and stakeholders.

[90] Interviews with Chinese competition law experts and stakeholders.

[91] Huang, 'Coordination of International Competition Policies', p. 247; Williams, *Competition Policy and Law*, pp. 174, 192; Interviews with Chinese competition law experts and stakeholders.

[92] Williams, *Competition Policy and Law*, p. 192.

persuasive. A draft prepared by the Ministry Drafting Group in November 1999 provided that the AML would not apply to certain conduct of natural monopolies or public utilities (such as those operating in the post, railroads, electricity, gas and water industries) for five years after the adoption of the AML.[93] However, that provision was deleted from a draft dated February 2002 (the reasons for this deletion have not been made public).[94] The LAO and the State Council did not revisit the issue of exemption for regulated industries,[95] and they noted that a majority of the domestic and foreign experts consulted believed that exemptions should not apply to industries as a whole.[96]

**(ii) Jurisdiction in Regulated Industries** While the issue of exemption for regulated industries was settled at a relatively early stage in the AML drafting process, the question of who would have jurisdiction over regulated industries under the AML remained hotly debated. On one side, industry regulators and SOEs argued that jurisdiction should remain with industry regulators, as per existing arrangements.[97] On the other side, the competition law experts who were consulted called for the unification of AML jurisdiction under one independent competition authority.[98] They pointed out that other laws which divided enforcement between the enforcement agency and industry regulators, such as the AUCL, had been ineffectively enforced by industry regulators.[99] These views were shared by some SCNPC members.[100]

The State Council agreed with the view put forward by industry regulators and SOEs. In the draft AML that the State Council submitted

---

[93] Wang, 'The Prospect of Antimonopoly Legislation in China', 225; Wang, 'Highlights of China's New Anti-monopoly Law', 135; Williams, *Competition Policy and Law*, p. 190.
[94] Wang, 'Issues Surrounding the Drafting of China's Anti-monopoly Law', 286.
[95] Interviews with Chinese competition law experts and stakeholders.
[96] Zhang, 'Closing Remarks of Deputy Director of the Legislative Affairs Office of the State Council'.
[97] 王毕强 [Wang Biqiang], 《反垄断法》草案二审: 反垄断前路漫漫 [Second Review of the Anti-monopoly Law: A Long Road Ahead for Anti-monopoly Law], 经济观察网 [Economic Observer Online], 2 July 2007, available at www.eeo.com.cn/2007/0702/74098.shtml.
[98] 'Currently No Hope for Second Review of the Anti-monopoly Law'; 反垄断法月底三审, 垄断国企拒绝交易等纳入监管 [Anti-monopoly Law Third Review at the End of the Month, State-owned Monopolies Refuse to be Subject to Regulation], 21世纪经济报道 [*21st Century Business Herald*], 21 August 2007, available at www.china.com.cn/policy/txt/2007-08/21/content_8718921.htm.
[99] 'Currently No Hope for Second Review of the Anti-monopoly Law'.
[100] Speech Excerpts: Draft of the Anti-monopoly Law, 27 June 2006.

to the SCNPC for review, it stated that the relevant industry regulator would handle cases of anti-competitive conduct in regulated industries, with only a minor role left for the competition authority.[101] The industry regulator would need to notify the AMC of the results of such investigations, and the competition authority would have power to investigate and handle any monopolistic conduct that was not being investigated or handled by the industry regulator.[102] It is not surprising that the State Council decided to preserve the jurisdiction of industry regulators in relation to anti-competitive conduct in regulated industries. As discussed in Chapters 3 and 4, industry regulators are key players within their areas of responsibility and important constituents of the State Council. Thus, their influence over the draft law produced by the State Council was not insubstantial, with the resulting draft reflecting the bargains and compromises struck by the State Council as it sought to build consensus and support for the draft AML.

However, this article was deleted by the SCNPC during its second review of the draft AML in June 2007. Some members of the SCNPC thought that the issue of AML jurisdiction over regulated industries was part of the broader issue of which government body would enforce the AML. As such, they believed that the State Council should consider the related issues together when it determined which government authority would be the competition agency.[103] The SCNPC's deletion of this article sent a positive signal to competition law academics and others who had advocated for a single enforcement agency for all industries that their concerns had been heard and acknowledged. However, deletion of the article did not preclude industry regulators and other government departments with regulatory responsibilities from having anti-monopoly jurisdiction, as there was nothing in the draft AML that expressly denied them that enforcement power.[104] This vague solution was probably adopted to progress the drafting of the AML. Despite the SCNPC's addition of Article 7 to the AML during its first review – a provision which protected the state's controlling position in certain industries – industry regulators continued to press for additional provisions to

---

[101] Anti-monopoly Law, First Deliberation Draft, art. 44.   [102] Ibid.
[103] Report of the Law Committee of the National People's Congress, Anti-monopoly Law, Second Deliberation Draft.
[104] Wang, 'Highlights of China's New Anti-monopoly Law', 148; Harris et al., *Anti-monopoly Law and Practice in China*, p. 26; Interviews with Chinese competition law experts and stakeholders.

protect the status quo and the state-owned economy.[105] It is reported that this debate was one of the main reasons why a year lapsed between the SCNPC's first and second reviews, and it had threatened to further delay or jeopardise the enactment of the AML.[106]

### (iii) Relationship between the Anti-monopoly Law and Sector-Specific-Laws

A related question that was debated during the drafting process was that of the relationship between the AML and other laws, especially sector-specific laws, and which law would have priority over the other.[107] As the AML would overlap with sector-specific laws, Wang believes that industry regulators opposed the AML due to concerns that they would lose some of their powers.[108] Both industry regulators and SOEs argued that sector-specific laws should apply in preference over the AML in regulated industries, whereas Chinese competition law experts argued that the AML should apply in these industries, pointing out that existing sector-specific laws and regulations had not been effective in addressing anti-competitive conduct in regulated industries.[109]

Like the issue of jurisdiction in regulated industries, the State Council decided this matter in favour of regulated industries and businesses. In the AML draft submitted by the State Council to the SCNPC for review, its Article 2(2) provided that, where conduct regulated by the AML falls within the scope of other laws and regulations, those other laws and regulations would apply.[110] However, this provision was not in the final enacted version of the AML, and there is no information on the public record as to why this provision was deleted from the final AML. One interviewee involved in the drafting process believed that the deletion could be ascribed to the broader issue of whether the competition authority would be a single, unified authority, the resolution of which was to be deferred until after the enactment of the AML.[111] As a result, the AML is unclear on the relationship between the AML and other laws and regulations; this matter will therefore be determined and developed

---

[105] Wang, 'The Second Review of the Anti-monopoly Law'.
[106] 'Currently No Hope for Second Review of the Anti-monopoly Law'.
[107] Interviews with Chinese competition law experts and stakeholders.
[108] Wang, 'Issues Surrounding the Drafting of China's Anti-monopoly Law', 295; Interviews with Chinese competition law experts and stakeholders.
[109] 'Currently No Hope for Second Review of the Anti-monopoly Law'.
[110] Anti-monopoly Law First Deliberation Draft, art. 2(2).
[111] Interviews with Chinese competition law experts and stakeholders.

through the implementation and enforcement of the AML. This relationship is explored further in Chapter 6.

### 5.3.2 Administrative Monopoly

Administrative monopoly was one of the most controversial and debated issues raised during the AML drafting process. As explained in Chapters 3 and 4, administrative monopoly is the abuse of administrative power to restrict competition. It includes regional monopoly, which is a form of local protectionism where the local governments prevent the free flow of goods and services between regions, and industry monopoly, where government departments or industry regulators impede competition or entry into specific industries or sectors, typically to protect businesses operating in that industry. Administrative monopoly is widely considered by Chinese law-makers and the general public to be the main barrier to furthering China's economic reforms and creating a national market.[112] The nature of administrative monopolies makes them hard to regulate, punish and prevent. In particular, they involve many governmental and business interests (especially those of SOEs), which hampers efforts to reform the area, given the benefit derived by such interests from administrative monopoly.

During the drafting of the AML, debate did not focus on whether administrative monopoly should be combatted, as the consensus reflected that it was an extremely serious issue facing the Chinese economy and one that needed to be eradicated.[113] The real debate was over whether it was appropriate for the AML to address the issue.[114] Related issues discussed during the drafting process included the definition of administrative monopoly (including the conduct that would be prohibited as an abuse of administrative power) and how the prohibition would be enforced.

Those opposing the inclusion of administrative monopoly provisions in the AML believed that administrative monopoly was not a proper

---

[112] Speech Excerpts: Draft of the Anti-monopoly Law, 27 June 2006; Dai Yan, 'Making of Anti-Trust Law Is Speeded Up', *China Daily*, 28 October 2004, available at www.chinadaily.com.cn/english/doc/2004-10/28/content_386300.htm.

[113] Xie Xiaodong, 'Draft Anti-monopoly Law Reduces Its Burden'; 赵杰 [Zhao Jie], 反垄断法草案删除关于行政性垄断章节 [Anti-monopoly Law Draft Deletes Administrative Monopoly Chapter], 第一财经日报 [First Financial Daily], 8 June 2006, available at http://finance.people.com.cn/GB/1037/4448654.html.

[114] Xie, 'Draft Anti-monopoly Law Reduces Its Burden'.

subject for the AML.[115] Some people argued that the AML should be a competition law for a market economy, and thus consistent with prevailing international practices. In their view, as the competition laws of the United States and other established competition law jurisdictions did not deal with government restraints (which are instead addressed in other laws or the constitution), the AML should not address administrative monopolies either.[116] Others, in particular administrative law scholars, believed that administrative monopoly was an issue to be addressed by administrative law and not economic law.[117] Other people, including some leaders and academics, believed that the problem required economic and political reform, and that it was beyond the abilities of the AML to deal with it.[118]

In contrast, those advocating for the inclusion of a prohibition on administrative monopoly in the AML argued that the AML should reflect the real market situation in China.[119] Supporters of this position included competition law academics, a number of SCNPC members and a number of foreign experts who were consulted.[120] They argued that administrative monopoly is the most obvious, and biggest, barrier to furthering China's economic development and to forming a national, unified market; it therefore needed to be addressed by the AML, even if it was not possible for the AML to solve the problem on its own.[121] They also

---

[115] Yong Huang, 'Pursuing the Second Best: The History, Momentum, and Remaining Issues of China's Anti-monopoly Law' (2008) 75 *Antitrust Law Journal* 117 at 131; Interviews with Chinese competition law experts and stakeholders.

[116] 刘娜 [Liu Na], 反垄断法如期初审, 行政性垄断内容再写入草案 [Initial Review of the Anti-monopoly Law as Planned, Administrative Monopoly Content Restored in Draft], 经济观察报 [Economic Observer Online], 24 June 2006, available at http://finance.sina.com.cn/g/20060624/22332678790.shtml; Harris et al., *Anti-monopoly Law and Practice in China*, p. 44; Interviews with Chinese competition law experts and stakeholders.

[117] Liu, 'Initial Review of the Anti-monopoly Law'; Interviews with Chinese competition law experts and stakeholders.

[118] Wu, 'Perspectives on the Chinese Anti-monopoly Law', 93–4; Wang, 'Issues Surrounding the Drafting of China's Anti-monopoly Law', 293; Harris et al., *Anti-monopoly Law and Practice in China*, p. 44; Xie, 'Draft Anti-monopoly Law Reduces Its Burden'; Interviews with Chinese competition law experts and stakeholders.

[119] Harris et al., *Anti-monopoly Law and Practice in China*, p. 44; Wu, 'Perspectives on the Chinese Anti-monopoly Law', 94; Xie, 'Draft Anti-monopoly Law Reduces Its Burden'.

[120] Speech Excerpts: Draft Anti-monopoly Law, 27 June 2006; Wang, *The Evolution of China's Anti-monopoly Law*, p. xvii; The Section of Antitrust Law and the Section of International Law and Practice of the American Bar Association, 4, 24; The Section of Antitrust Law, the Section of Intellectual Property Law and the Section of International Law of the American Bar Association, 4, 28.

[121] Speech Excerpts: Draft Anti-monopoly Law, 27 June 2006; Liu, 'Initial Review of the Anti-monopoly Law'; Interviews with Chinese competition law experts and stakeholders.

referred to the competition laws of Russia and Ukraine, both of which include administrative monopoly provisions, as examples that are particularly relevant to China's situation, given that those countries' economies are also undergoing transition.[122] This was the mainstream view during the drafting process, and one that was said to have had public support.[123]

This debate persisted throughout the drafting process and was finely balanced.[124] The draft AML had, from the very beginning, included the abuse of administrative power in the definition of 'monopolistic conduct', a provision on administrative monopoly in the general provisions and a chapter that specifically dealt with administrative monopoly.[125] However, there was a period of time during which it appeared that the minority view would prevail. In July 2005, the LAO removed the abuse of administrative power from the definition of 'monopolistic conduct' and some key provisions from the chapter on administrative monopoly, and in late 2005 it deleted the chapter on administrative monopoly in its entirety (although the article in the general provisions remained).[126] The draft AML that was approved in principle by an executive meeting of the State Council in early June 2006 did not have a chapter on administrative monopoly.[127] The deletion of this chapter came as a surprise; it was controversial and attracted attention domestically and internationally.[128] In particular, Chinese competition law academics vocally opposed the deletion of this chapter and, in response, raised public discourse and awareness about administrative monopolies in the media.[129] It was

---

[122] Xie, 'Draft Anti-monopoly Law Reduces Its Burden'.
[123] Wu, 'Perspectives on the Chinese Anti-monopoly Law', 94; Wang, 'The New Chinese Anti-monopoly Law', 596; Wang, 'Anti-monopoly Law: Leaves the Difficult Legislative Issues to Be Resolved in Enforcement', 48; Interviews with Chinese competition law experts and stakeholders.
[124] Harris, 'The Making of an Antitrust Law', 170; Xie, 'Draft Anti-monopoly Law Reduces Its Burden'.
[125] Xie, 'Draft Anti-monopoly Law Reduces Its Burden'; Zhengxin Huo, 'A Tiger without Teeth: The Antitrust Law of the People's Republic of China' (2008) 10 *Asian-Pacific Law & Policy Journal* 32 at 50–1.
[126] Huo, 'A Tiger without Teeth', 50–1; Harris, 'The Making of an Antitrust Law', 187.
[127] Xie, 'Draft Anti-monopoly Law Reduces Its Burden'; Zhao, 'Anti-monopoly Law Draft Deletes Administrative Monopoly Chapter'; Harris, 'The Making of an Antitrust Law', 170.
[128] Interviews with Chinese competition law experts and stakeholders.
[129] 时建中 [Shi Jianzhong], 反垄断法修改审查组专家: 反行政垄断不能删除 [Anti-monopoly Law Review and Deliberation Group Expert: Prohibition on Administrative Monopoly Cannot be Deleted], 新京报 [*The Beijing News*], 9 July 2006, available at

MAJOR ISSUES CONSIDERED IN DRAFTING    227

reported that one of the main reasons why the LAO had deleted this chapter was concern over the enforceability of its provisions and issues of legal liability.[130] Wang also speculates that pressure from central and local government departments may have led to the deletion of the chapter, because they have economic and political incentives to engage in administrative monopoly conduct.[131]

However, the chapter on administrative monopoly was restored in late June 2006, when it re-appeared in the draft AML that was being reviewed for the first time by the SCNPC.[132] The reasons for and circumstances surrounding the reinstatement of this chapter are unclear, although some commentators speculated that it was largely in response to public pressure.[133] When the State Council approved its draft AML in early June 2006, it did state that the draft would undergo further revision before submitting it to the SCNPC for consideration.[134] Therefore the change could have been made by the State Council during this intervening period. An interviewee involved in the drafting process believed that the draft submitted by the State Council to the SCNPC did not contain the chapter on administrative monopoly; however, the SCNPC sent the draft back to the State Council because it was dissatisfied with the fact that it did not deal with what the members believed was a form of monopoly that was very harmful to the Chinese economy and which the public was said to be very concerned about.[135] Regardless, it was clear that the members of the SCNPC believed administrative monopoly to be an important issue that the AML needed to address. It continued to be a topic of discussion at the SCNPC Stage, with a number of SCNPC members recognising the economic harm caused by administrative monopolies, their impediment to China's economic development and

---

www.southcn.com/news/china/zgkx/200607100074.htm; Xie, 'Draft Anti-monopoly Law Reduces Its Burden'; Zhao, 'Anti-monopoly Law Draft Deletes Administrative Monopoly Chapter'.

[130] Xie, 'Draft Anti-monopoly Law Reduces Its Burden'; Harris et al., *Anti-monopoly Law and Practice in China*, p. 44.
[131] Wang, 'The New Chinese Anti-monopoly Law', 596.
[132] Liu, 'Initial Review of the Anti-monopoly Law'.
[133] 陈欢 [Chen Huan], 反垄断法审议再起波折，行政垄断条款仍存争议 [Setbacks Again in the Review of Anti-monopoly Law, Administrative Monopoly Provisions Remain Controversial], 21世纪经济报道 [*21st Century Business Herald*] 15 June 2006, available at www.ce.cn/law/shouye/fzgc/200606/15/t20060615_7352556.shtml; Huo, 'A Tiger without Teeth', 50–1.
[134] Zhao, 'Anti-monopoly Law Draft Deletes Administrative Monopoly Chapter'.
[135] Interviews with Chinese competition law experts and stakeholders.

formation of a unified market and the public's concern.[136] Hence the SCNPC adopted the AML with a chapter on the abuse of administrative power.

The scope of the prohibition on administrative monopoly changed as drafting progressed, focusing more on regional monopolies and less on industry monopolies. Various drafts during the Ministry Stage had prohibited both regional monopolies and industry monopolies,[137] but this was changed by the LAO Drafting Group in July 2005. The LAO Drafting Group expanded the prohibition on regional monopolies but deleted the prohibition on industry monopolies.[138] While regional monopolies involve local governments, industry monopolies often involve ministries and government departments under the State Council and industries that are regulated or considered to be important to the Chinese economy. Therefore, these ministries and government departments have incentives to oppose the prohibition on industry monopolies. Two interviewees noted that such opposition may have constrained the ability of the State Council to maintain the prohibition on industry monopoly, whereas it is easier for the State Council to address regional monopolies.[139] The administrative monopoly chapter that was reinstated in June 2006 was substantially similar to the administrative monopoly chapter in the July 2005 draft, and also largely focused on regional, not industry, monopolies (although there is at least one article that specifically addresses industry monopoly).[140] Further, the only revision made by the SCNPC to the administrative monopoly chapter concerned regional monopoly, where it added a catch-all provision for conduct that prevents the free flow of goods between regions.[141]

---

[136] Speech Excerpts: Draft of the Anti-monopoly Law, 27 June 2006; Wu, 'Perspectives on the Chinese Anti-monopoly Law', 94; Interviews with Chinese competition law experts and stakeholders.

[137] Wang, 'The Prospect of Antimonopoly Legislation in China', 224; Wang, 'Issues Surrounding the Drafting of China's Anti-monopoly Law', 290–1; Jung and Hao, 'The New Economic Constitution in China', 134; The Section of Antitrust Law and the Section of International Law and Practice of the American Bar Association, 24; Harris and Yang, 'China: Latest Developments', 93.

[138] Harris et al., Anti-monopoly Law and Practice in China, p. 41.

[139] Interviews with Chinese competition law experts and stakeholders.

[140] Harris et al., Anti-monopoly Law and Practice in China, p. 27. Article 32 of the AML prohibits administrative agencies from requiring the purchase or use of products provided by designated businesses.

[141] 全国人大法律委员会关于《中华人民共和国反垄断法(草案三次审议稿)》修改意见的报告 [Report of the Law Committee of the National People's Congress on Views Regarding the Revision of the Anti-monopoly Law of the People's Republic of China

The mechanism for enforcing the prohibition against administrative monopoly also changed during the drafting process. At the Ministry Stage, and during part of the State Council Stage, the draft stipulated that the competition authority had power to directly enforce the provisions on administrative monopoly.[142] However, in September 2005, the LAO Drafting Group significantly limited the competition authority's power in administrative monopoly cases. The power to enforce the prohibition against administrative monopoly shifted to the 'superior authority' of the administrative organ whose conduct was in question, and the competition authority's role was limited to making recommendations to that superior authority on the enforcement action that should be taken.[143] As the superior authority shares in the benefit derived from administrative monopoly, it is questionable whether it would have the incentive to enforce that prohibition, which would render the prohibition on administrative monopoly largely ineffective.

As noted above, the State Council reportedly had concerns about the effectiveness of this enforcement mechanism, and it was one of the reasons for deleting the administrative monopoly chapter in late 2005. However, when the administrative monopoly chapter was reinstated in June 2006, the enforcement mechanism was unchanged and the superior authority still had enforcement power. This suggests that, while the reinstatement of the administrative monopoly chapter acknowledges the opposition to and economic harm caused by administrative monopoly, nonetheless the prohibition might remain largely symbolic and ineffectively enforced, as it is coupled with a weak enforcement mechanism.[144]

### 5.3.3 Role of the State in the Economy

During the SCNPC's first review of the AML draft, two articles were added to the AML which reflected the members' concern that the AML should recognise and protect the leading role of the state in the economy.[145]

---

(Third Deliberation Draft)], 29th Session of the Standing Committee of the Tenth National People's Congress, 29 August 2007.
[142] Jung and Hao, 'The New Economic Constitution in China', 140; Harris et al., *Anti-monopoly Law and Practice in China*, p. 43.
[143] Harris et al., *Anti-monopoly Law and Practice in China*, pp. 43–4. [144] Ibid., p. 45.
[145] Report of the Law Committee of the National People's Congress on the Revision of the Anti-monopoly Law of the People's Republic of China (Draft), 24 June 2007.

Article 4 was added to recognise the strong guiding and supervisory role of the state in the economy and market. It provides that the state 'establishes and implements competition rules that are compatible with the socialist market economy, strengthens and perfects macroeconomic supervision and control, and develops a unified, open, competitive and orderly market system'.[146] According to the Legislative Affairs Commission, Article 4 establishes the basic principles that should be followed by the AML.[147] It was added to the draft in response to concerns held by some members of the SCNPC, NPC representatives, local governments and central government departments.[148] They believed that the AML should reflect China's national conditions, suit the socialist market economy, coordinate the relationship between industrial policy and other economic policies under the guidance of national macroeconomic control and maintain and promote fair and orderly market competition.[149] As such, they regarded competition and the AML as ways to allow the state (acting through SOEs and local and central governments) to achieve economic and other goals.[150]

Similarly, Article 7 was added to the draft because some SCNPC members and NPC representatives believed that the AML should protect the state's controlling position in certain industries.[151] Article 7 recognises and protects the state's controlling position in national economic lifeline, national security and state-granted monopoly industries, and confirms that businesses in these industries must not abuse their position.[152] The state's control over these industries, which are considered to be strategic or important to the Chinese government and are dominated by SOEs, is regarded as important to economic development and political

---

[146] Anti-monopoly Law, art. 4.
[147] Economic Law Division, *The Anti-monopoly Law of the People's Republic of China*, p. 14.
[148] Report of the Law Committee of the National People's Congress on the Revision of the Anti-monopoly Law of the People's Republic of China (Draft), 24 June 2007.
[149] Ibid.
[150] Economic Law Division, *The Anti-monopoly Law of the People's Republic of China*, p. 15.
[151] Report of the Law Committee of the National People's Congress on the Revision of the Anti-monopoly Law of the People's Republic of China (Draft), 24 June 2007.
[152] Article 7 states: 'The state will, in industries that relate to the national economic lifeline and national security that are controlled by the state-owned economy or which are subject to exclusive operations and sales according to the law, protect the lawful business activities of such operators, supervise and regulate the conduct and price of goods and services of those operators according to the law, protect consumer interest, and promote technological progress. Operators in these industries must operate their business according to law, act in good faith, engage in strict self-discipline, accept public supervision, and not use their controlling position or monopoly status to harm consumer interest.'

stability in China.[153] As such, the government has incentives to protect these industries and SOEs operating in these industries, and it is not surprising that these industries were singled out for protection by the SCNPC in Article 7. It is also consistent with one of the State Council's guiding principles when it prepared the draft AML, which was to protect China's national interests and products related to the people's livelihood.[154]

This article was added against the backdrop of opposition to the AML from SOEs and industry regulators, as well as concerns on the part of a number of SCNPC members and, reportedly, the public about anti-competitive conduct in industries where SOEs are dominant.[155] Article 7 therefore served to smooth the concerns of both sides: on the one hand, it reassures SOEs in these industries that it is not illegal to have a controlling or monopoly position as long as that position is acquired legally, and that only conduct that constitutes abuse of that controlling or monopoly position to harm consumers is prohibited;[156] on the other, it helps to allay concerns about anti-competitive conduct by SOEs in these industries by providing that the state will supervise and regulate the price of products and services of businesses in these industries and safeguard consumer interest. In fact, it appears that, by requiring participants in these industries to act in good faith and be self-disciplined, Article 7(2) has imposed a positive obligation on the SOEs operating in these industries. This was the position taken by the NDRC's local authority in Hubei province in its decision in the *Wuchang Salt Tying* case, in which it found that the state-owned salt supplier had breached Article 7(2) of the AML.[157] Therefore, contrary to the concerns of some commentators (which were discussed in Chapter 1), it

---

[153] Wu, 'Perspectives on the Chinese Anti-monopoly Law', 98.
[154] An Explanation of China's Anti-monopoly Law (Draft), 24 June 2006.
[155] 'Currently No Hope for Second Review of the Anti-monopoly Law'; 对滥用市场支配地位行为的认定—分组审议反垄断法草案发言摘登 (二) [Identifying Abuse of Dominant Market Position Conduct – Speech Excerpts of the Group Deliberations of the Draft Anti-monopoly Law (2)], 29th Session of the Standing Committee of the Tenth National People's Congress, 24 August 2007; 程刚，崔丽 [Cheng Gang and Cui Li], 反垄断法草案有望通过，严禁国企和公用事业借垄断自肥 [Anti-monopoly Law Draft: State-owned Enterprises and Public Enterprises Strictly Prohibited From Relying on Monopoly to Fatten Themselves], 中国青年报 [*China Youth Daily*], 25 August 2007, available at www.sznews.com/news/content/2007-08/25/content_1457259.htm; Wu, 'Perspectives on the Chinese Anti-monopoly Law', 99.
[156] Interviews with Chinese competition law experts and stakeholders.
[157] National Development and Reform Commission, 湖北省物价局依法查处武昌盐业分公司强制搭售案件 [Hubei Price Bureau Investigates the Wuhan Salt Industry Group Branch Forced Tying Case According to Law] (News Release, 15 November 2010).

does not appear that SOEs or other businesses operating in these industries are exempt from the AML or will receive special treatment.[158]

### 5.3.4 Industrial Policy

One of the key concerns for some members of the SCNPC was the inability of most Chinese businesses to compete with better resourced, more technologically advanced and more sophisticated foreign companies.[159] There was a perception that Chinese businesses are small and inefficient, operate at a local or provincial level only and lack economies of scale and scope.[160] In their view, the AML should be conducive to helping Chinese businesses grow bigger and stronger, develop economies of scale, increase industrial concentration and strengthen competitiveness through mergers.[161] This concern was shared by local governments, central government departments, industry associations and businesses that were consulted during the SCNPC Stage.[162] Similarly, according to Huang, SOEs argued that the AML should not prevent SOEs from merging with their competitors in order to grow bigger and stronger.[163]

The phrase 'become bigger and stronger' (*zuoda zuoqiang*) often appears in Chinese government documents and is mentioned by Chinese government officials. It encapsulates the government's policy and emphasis on developing large companies and conglomerates, and on encouraging the development of economies of scale.[164] As noted in Chapter 3, the central government is focused on creating and fostering national champions, aiming to have thirty to fifty internationally competitive SOEs. Provincial and local governments are also supporting Chinese businesses to become bigger and stronger.[165] Coordinating

---

[158] Harris et al., *Anti-monopoly Law and Practice in China*, p. 25.
[159] Economic Law Division, *The Anti-monopoly Law of the People's Republic of China*, p. 17; Speech Excerpts: Draft Anti-monopoly Law, 27 June 2006.
[160] Jijian Yang, 'Market Power in China: Manifestations, Effects and Legislation' (2002) 21 *Review of Industrial Organization* 167 at 169–71.
[161] Report of the Law Committee of the National People's Congress on the Revision of the Anti-monopoly Law of the People's Republic of China (Draft), 24 June 2007.
[162] Ibid.   [163] Huang, 'Pursuing the Second Best', 128–9.
[164] Shang Ming, 'Antitrust in China – A Constantly Evolving Subject' (2009) 3 *Competition Law International* 4 at 7; Wu, 'Perspectives on the Chinese Anti-monopoly Law', 97.
[165] See, e.g., 关于促进工业企业做大做强若干奖励政策 [Some Incentives on Promoting Industrial Enterprises to Become Bigger and Stronger] (People's Republic of China) Luyang Government, Order No. 12, 23 May 2007; Sichuan Provincial People's Government, 2007年做大做强煤炭产业 [Coal Industry Becoming Bigger and Stronger in

competition policy and encouraging businesses to become bigger and stronger were guiding principles followed by the State Council during its preparation of the draft AML.[166] Likewise, some SCNPC members believe it is important that Chinese businesses be allowed and encouraged to grow.[167] The SCNPC believes that one of the most important ways for businesses to expand their business scope and increase competitiveness is through mergers, and thus it wanted to ensure that the AML did not affect businesses' ability to do so, subject to the overriding consideration that such merger did not eliminate or restrict competition.[168] Therefore, in response to these concerns, Article 5 – which states that businesses are allowed, through fair competition and voluntary alliances, to implement mergers, expand their business scale and improve their market competitiveness according to law – was added to the draft AML after the SCNPC's first review.

A related concern was the distinction between the possession of a position of market dominance and the abuse of that position. Earlier drafts of the AML prepared by the Ministry Drafting Group had prohibited monopolies. Some foreign competition law experts pointed out that competition laws generally do not prohibit the possession of a monopoly position, but rather the abuse of that position.[169] Following these comments, the LAO changed the draft AML to prohibit 'monopolistic conduct' but not 'monopolies'.[170] This distinction was noted and

---

2007] Sichuan Yearbook 2008, 14 May 2009, available at www.sc.gov.cn/scgk1/jj/gy/mtgy/200905/t20090514_735500.shtml; 关于做大做强民营经济的意见 [Opinion on the Private Economy Becoming Bigger and Stronger] (People's Republic of China) Suzhou Provincial Government, Order No. 24, 13 February 2004; 孟斌 [Meng Bin], 王文超在全市要求加强党建工作做大做强国企 [Wang Wenchao Calls for the Strengthening of Party Building Work and for SOEs to Become Bigger and Stronger], 郑州日报 [Zhengzhou Daily], 22 June 2007, available at www.zynews.com/2007-06/22/content_454693.htm.

[166] An Explanation of China's Anti-monopoly Law (Draft), 24 June 2006.
[167] Speech Excerpts: Draft Anti-monopoly Law, 27 June 2006; 反垄断法热点问题聚焦—全国人大常委会法工委有关负责人谈反垄断法热点问题 [Focus on Anti-monopoly Law Hot Spot Issues – Legal Affairs Commission of the Standing Committee of the National People's Congress Responsible Person Talks about Anti-monopoly Law Hot Spot Issues], 新华网 [Xinhuanet], 9 September 2007, available at www.npc.gov.cn/npc/xinwen/lfgz/lfdt/2007-09/30/content_372832.htm; Wu, 'Perspectives on the Chinese Anti-monopoly Law', 97.
[168] Economic Law Division, *The Anti-monopoly Law of the People's Republic of China*, p. 16.
[169] The Section of Antitrust Law and the Section of International Law and Practice of the American Bar Association, 3, 7, 11–12.
[170] Blumenthal, 'Presentation to the International Symposium on the Draft Anti-monopoly Law', 2; Harris, 'The Making of an Antitrust Law', 184.

made even clearer during the SCNPC Stage when the SCNPC added Article 6, which provides that businesses with positions of market dominance must not abuse that position to eliminate or restrict competition.[171] However, the reasons which the SCNPC members gave for adding Article 6 to the AML demonstrated that they were motivated more by industrial policy considerations and a desire to protect the leading role of the state in the economy than by a desire to be consistent with international competition law norms.[172] They believed that, by making sure that the AML did not prohibit businesses from becoming dominant, domestic businesses would be helped to become bigger and stronger and that it would strengthen the state's control of the national security and national lifeline industries and other important sectors.[173] Hence their main concern was not to restrict the illegal conduct of monopolies *per se* but to remove barriers to Chinese businesses, in particular SOEs, becoming bigger and stronger.[174]

The SCNPC's concern to find the right balance between preventing the abuse of dominant positions and ensuring that Chinese businesses were not restricted from growing bigger and stronger also manifested in its discussion of the merger notification thresholds during its second review of the draft AML. The draft submitted to the SCNPC by the State Council contained specific merger notification thresholds. SCNPC members, local governments, central government departments, industry associations and businesses were worried that Chinese companies would be prevented from becoming bigger and stronger through mergers if the notification threshold was set too low, as this would result in too many mergers being notified and run the risk of not being approved.[175] On the other hand, they were concerned that mergers would result in monopolies if the bar for notification was set too high.[176] As no consensus was reached on the level or type of threshold to be used, the SCNPC believed that the State

---

[171] Report of the Law Committee of the National People's Congress on the Revision of the Anti-monopoly Law of the People's Republic of China (Draft), 24 June 2007; Speech Excerpts: Draft of the Anti-monopoly Law, 27 June 2006; Wu, 'Perspectives on the Chinese Anti-monopoly Law', 84–5.
[172] Speech Excerpts: Draft Anti-monopoly Law, 27 June 2006.
[173] Report of the Law Committee of the National People's Congress on the Revision of the Anti-monopoly Law of the People's Republic of China (Draft), 24 June 2007.
[174] Interviews with Chinese competition law experts and stakeholders.
[175] Report of the Law Committee of the National People's Congress on the Revision of the Anti-monopoly Law of the People's Republic of China (Draft), 24 June 2007.
[176] Ibid.

Council should determine the thresholds at a later date and deleted this provision after its second review.[177] Further, SCNPC members believed that having the State Council determine the notification thresholds would be more flexible, as it would allow the thresholds to be adjusted in accordance with economic development needs and other changing conditions.[178] It would be easier for the State Council to change the threshold by issuing an amended or new regulation than for the SCNPC to amend the statute.[179]

### 5.3.5 Industry Associations

Industry associations were a focus of deliberations during the SCNPC's third and final review of the draft AML at the end of August 2007. This was due to a price fixing case involving an industry association that was widely reported in the media in the weeks leading up to the SCNPC's final review of the draft.

Towards the end of July 2007, a spokesperson for the China branch of the World Instant Noodles Association publicly announced that its members, which together accounted for 95 per cent of the Chinese instant noodle market, were to increase the price of instant noodles by an average of 20 per cent.[180] This announcement, along with strong negative public reaction to it, was widely reported in the media as instant noodles are a popular food in China.[181] The China Consumer Association made a complaint to the NDRC and urged the NDRC to take action.[182] On 16 August 2007, the NDRC issued a decision finding that the China branch of the World Instant Noodles Association had

---

[177] Ibid.; Speech Excerpts: Draft Anti-monopoly Law, 27 June 2006.
[178] Report of the Law Committee of the National People's Congress on the Revision of the Anti-monopoly Law of the People's Republic of China (Draft), 24 June 2007; Interviews with Chinese competition law experts and stakeholders.
[179] Report of the Law Committee of the National People's Congress on the Revision of the Anti-monopoly Law of the People's Republic of China (Draft), 24 June 2007; Interviews with Chinese competition law experts and stakeholders.
[180] 'Lawyer Appeals to Gov't over Instant Noodle Price Hike', *China Daily*, 31 July 2007, available at www.chinadaily.com.cn/china/2007-07/31/content_5446492.htm.
[181] Zhang Hao, 'Price Noodling Turns Spotlight on Food Cartels', Caijing, 31 July 2007, available at http://english.caijing.com.cn/2007-07-31/100025733.html; Gordon Bell, 'Instant Noodle Makers Illegally Fix Price', *China Daily*, 17 August 2007, available at www.chinadaily.com.cn/china/2007-08/17/content_6031382.htm.
[182] 'Lawyer Appeals to Gov't over Instant Noodle Price Hike'.

organised, planned and coordinated for its members to engage in price collusion in breach of the Price Law.[183] The NDRC's decision, which was published after the SCNPC's second review of the draft AML, was widely reported in the media.[184]

During the SCNPC's third review of the draft AML, which was carried out just over a week after the NDRC handed down its instant noodles cartel decision, some members stated that the draft was not clear enough on how the AML applies to industry associations and suggested that industry associations be expressly prohibited from organising the collusion of businesses in the industry or engaging in other anti-competitive conduct, and they should also be held legally liable.[185] At the time, there were two articles in the draft AML concerning industry associations. One article stated that the AML applies to industry associations engaging in conduct that eliminates or restricts competition,[186] and another recognised the role of industry associations in strengthening industry self-discipline, guiding the industry to compete lawfully and maintaining the order of market competition.[187] The instant noodle cartel put the spotlight on industry associations, their conduct and how the AML might apply to them.[188] This case showed that, in addition to their role in guiding the development of the industry and encouraging self-discipline, there was a possibility that industry associations could organise for members to engage in cartels or other anti-competitive conduct and result in harm to consumers. In response, a number of SCNPC members raised concern about the conduct of industry associations and wanted to

---

[183] National Development and Reform Commission, 国家发展改革委对方便面价格串通案调查情况的通报 [National Development and Reform Commission's Report on its Instant Noodle Price Collusion Investigation] (News Release, 16 August 2007).

[184] 发改委拿方便面开刀? 政府价格监管风暴正升级 [NDRC to Use Instant Noodles as a Weapon? The Government Price Regulation Storm Upgraded], 华夏时报 [*China Times*], 18 August 2007, available at http://news.enorth.com.cn/system/2007/08/19/001830080.shtml; 方便面涨价被调查始末: 三次会议助推涨价 [Instant Noodle Price Increases Investigated: Three Meetings Helped Increase Prices], 新京报 [*The Beijing News*], 17 August 2007, available at www.chinanews.com/cj/xfsh/news/2007/08-17/1004121.shtml.

[185] Report of the Law Committee of the National People's Congress on Views Regarding the Revision of the Anti-monopoly Law of the People's Republic of China (Third Deliberation Draft), 29 August 2007.

[186] Anti-monopoly Law, First Deliberation Draft, art. 53.

[187] Report of the Law Committee of the National People's Congress on the Revision of the Anti-monopoly Law of the People's Republic of China (Draft), 24 June 2007.

[188] Interviews with Chinese competition law experts and stakeholders.

ensure that the AML applied to their conduct and reflected the reality of the situation.[189]

Further, the instant noodle cartel related to the government's more general concern about rising food prices. As outlined in Chapter 4, one of the government's priorities is controlling inflation and stabilising prices, and it is especially concerned with rising food prices. China's inflation rate was at a ten-year high in July 2007 and food prices were increasing rapidly, with the price of staple foods such as eggs, meat, poultry and cooking oil increasing by more than 30 per cent, and that of fresh vegetables by more than 15 per cent.[190] In addition to instant noodles, there were also reports of a number of other food-related cartels during that time.[191] Substantial pressure was put on the government to take action to stabilise prices and, in response, the NDRC embarked on a campaign to target food producers, wholesalers and retailers to stabilise the prices of staple foods such as grains, meat, cooking oil, eggs, milk and poultry.[192] Therefore, at the time of the SCNPC's third review of the draft AML in August 2007, the SCNPC members are likely to have been concerned about inflation and the media reports reflecting public pressure to tackle inflation. In this context, two new provisions were added to the AML: Article 16, which expressly prohibits industry associations from organising business operators in the industry from engaging in conduct prohibited by Chapter II of the AML; and a third paragraph to Article 46, which provides that an industry association may be fined a maximum of RMB 500,000, or have its registration cancelled in serious cases.[193] By directly addressing the issue of industry associations and

---

[189] Economic Law Division, *The Anti-monopoly Law of the People's Republic of China*, p. 93; Interviews with Chinese competition law experts and stakeholders.

[190] 'China Makes New Anti-Inflation Move', *China Daily*, 14 January 2008, available at www.chinadaily.com.cn/bizchina/2008-01/14/content_6393131.htm; Li Fangchao, 'Food Group Slammed for Price Collusion', *China Daily*, 17 August 2007, available at www.chinadaily.com.cn/cndy/2007-08/17/content_6030552.htm; Bell, 'Instant Noodle Makers Illegally Fix Price'.

[191] Zhang, 'Price Noodling Turns Spotlight on Food Cartels'; Interviews with Chinese competition law experts and stakeholders.

[192] Liu Jie, 'Rising Costs Prompt Calls for Action on Prices', *China Daily*, 14 August 2007, available at www.chinadaily.com.cn/cndy/2007-08/14/content_6025017.htm; Bell, 'Instant Noodle Makers Illegally Fix Price'; Fu Jing, 'Stiff Penalties for Price Rigging', *China Daily*, 29 August 2007, available at www.chinadaily.com.cn/cndy/2007-08/29/content_6063449.htm.

[193] Report of the Law Committee of the National People's Congress on Views Regarding the Revision of the Anti-monopoly Law of the People's Republic of China (Third Deliberation Draft), 29 August 2007.

cartels in the AML, the SCNPC signalled to the general public that it was taking action to address concerns in the area.

### 5.3.6 National Security

According to an interviewee involved in the AML drafting process, the issue of national security had not been considered seriously prior to the SCNPC's review of the draft AML.[194] It was generally thought that national security concerns were separate to competition concerns.[195] However, national security became a central issue at the SCNPC Stage.[196]

A number of high-profile cross-border deals, such as the joint venture between Danone and Wahaha (one of China's largest beverage producers and best known brands), Lenovo's acquisition of the personal computer business of International Business Machines (which had been subject to US national security review), Carlyle's acquisition of Xuzhou Construction Machinery (China's largest construction machinery manufacturer) and Group SEB's acquisition of Supor (a large Chinese home appliance manufacturer), had highlighted the national security issues relating to mergers between Chinese and foreign businesses.[197] Particularly controversial was CNOOC's unsuccessful takeover bid for Unocal, a US oil and gas company, which occurred less than a year prior to the SCNPC's first review of the draft AML. In June 2005, CNOOC, a Chinese SOE and oil and gas producer, made an unsolicited bid to acquire Unocal, the latter having already agreed to a merger with Chevron in April 2005. CNOOC's takeover bid was met with substantial political opposition in the United States, based on national security concerns.[198] For example, the US House of Representatives passed measures which declared that allowing the CNOOC–Unocal deal would threaten to impair the national security of the United States, called for President Bush to review the deal

---

[194] Interviews with Chinese competition law experts and stakeholders.
[195] Interviews with Chinese competition law experts and stakeholders.
[196] Report of the Law Committee of the National People's Congress on the Revision of the Anti-monopoly Law of the People's Republic of China (Draft), 24 June 2007; Speech Excerpts: Draft Anti-monopoly Law, 27 June 2006.
[197] Huang, 'Pursuing the Second Best', 123; Harris et al., *Anti-monopoly Law and Practice in China*, p. 41; 王毕强 [Wang Biqiang], 三大修改尘埃落定《反垄断法》有望八月通过 [Dust Settles After the Third Major Amendments to the Anti-monopoly Law, Expected to be Passed in August], 经济观察网 [Economic Observer Online] 24 August 2007, available at www.eeo.com.cn/2007/0824/81095.shtml.
[198] 'The Way of the Dragon', *The Economist*, 23 June 2005, available at www.economist.com/node/4102015.

MAJOR ISSUES CONSIDERED IN DRAFTING 239

and would have delayed any Chinese acquisition of a US oil company by at least 120 days.[199] Although CNOOC's offer was higher than Chevron's, the board of Unocal recommended Chevron's offer over CNOOC's due to the political risks associated with the CNOOC deal.[200] In August 2005, CNOOC withdrew its offer, citing the US political environment and political risk as reasons for its withdrawal.[201] This case was covered widely by the Chinese media and generated substantial debate in China, as it not only involved a strategic national resource and one of the largest SOEs in China, but also highlighted the potentially political nature of mergers between foreign and domestic businesses, the manner in which other countries deal with such issues and the need for the AML.[202] One interviewee suggests that the memory of the CNOOC–Unocal deal and its related national security and political issues would have been relatively fresh in the minds of the SCNPC members when they began their review of the AML draft.[203]

Some SCNPC members, NPC representatives and central government departments were concerned about the growing number of foreign acquisitions of Chinese businesses.[204] The Legal Affairs Commission noted that foreign acquisitions of Chinese businesses had increased from 5 per cent of foreign direct investment in China in 2004 to nearly 20 per cent in 2005, with approximately 70 per cent of such acquisitions being in the manufacturing sector.[205] A number of SCNPC members were concerned that foreign companies were entering the Chinese market, acquiring leading and key businesses and obtaining monopoly positions.[206] The CNOOC–Unocal deal showed Chinese law-makers that

---

[199] Steve Lohr, 'Unocal Bid Opens Up New Issues of Security', *New York Times*, 13 July 2005, available at www.nytimes.com/2005/07/13/business/worldbusiness/13unocal.html; 'CNOOC Withdraws Unocal Bid', Xinhua, 3 August 2005, available at www.china.org.cn/english/2005/Aug/137165.htm.
[200] 'CNOOC Withdraws Unocal Bid'.
[201] CNOOC Limited, 'CNOOC Limited to Withdraw Unocal Bid' (Press Release, 2 August 2005).
[202] Interviews with Chinese competition law experts and stakeholders.
[203] Interviews with Chinese competition law experts and stakeholders.
[204] Report of the Law Committee of the National People's Congress on the Revision of the Anti-monopoly Law of the People's Republic of China (Draft), 24 June 2007; Speech Excerpts: Draft Anti-monopoly Law, 27 June 2006.
[205] Economic Law Division, *The Anti-monopoly Law of the People's Republic of China*, p. 208.
[206] Speech Excerpts: Draft Anti-monopoly Law, 27 June 2006; 关于法律规定的三个垄断行为一分组审议反垄断法草案发言摘登 (四) [About the Three Types of Monopolistic Conduct Regulated by the Law – Speech Excerpts of Group Deliberations on the Draft

China, like the United States, could use national security review to prevent harm to its national security and economic interests.[207] While national security review and competition review are different, they are both triggered by a merger or acquisition of one business by another. A couple of interviewees suggested that this commonality underlay some SCNPC members' belief that the AML would be an appropriate vehicle to signal the Chinese government's stance on Chinese/foreign mergers that involve national security issues.[208] Therefore, the SCNPC wanted to make sure that the AML expressly provided that Chinese/foreign mergers were subject to both competition review and national security review, even though the two reviews are separate and conducted under different legal regimes and standards.[209] Further, in China, the concept of national security not only covers matters relating to national defence, but also includes national economic security.[210] Therefore, Article 31,[211] which confirms that mergers are subject to review under both the AML and the relevant national security regulations, was added to the AML to signal that the Chinese government was aware of and concerned about the national security issues relating to foreign mergers with domestic businesses.

## 5.4 Conclusion

Drawing upon the political economy analysis undertaken in Chapters 3 and 4, this chapter investigated the law-making process behind the enactment of the AML. This examination has yielded several key observations about the drafting process.

---

Anti-monopoly Law (4)], 28th Session of the Standing Committee of the Tenth National People's Congress, 25 June 2007.
[207] Speech Excerpts: Draft Anti-monopoly Law, 27 June 2006; About the Three Types of Monopolistic Conduct Regulated by the Law – Speech Excerpts of Group Deliberations on the Draft Anti-monopoly Law (4), 25 June 2007; Interviews with Chinese competition law experts and stakeholders.
[208] Interviews with Chinese competition law experts and stakeholders.
[209] Report of the Law Committee of the National People's Congress on the Revision of the Anti-monopoly Law of the People's Republic of China (Draft), 24 June 2007; Speech Excerpts: Draft Anti-monopoly Law, 27 June 2006.
[210] Huang, 'Coordination of International Competition Policies', p. 240.
[211] Article 31 of the AML states that, 'in addition to reviews of concentrations pursuant to this law, acquisitions of or other concentrations involving domestic companies by foreign investors that concern national security will also undergo national security review pursuant to relevant laws and regulations of the state'.

Many of the issues discussed during the drafting of the AML, especially those that were contentious and resulted in delays and bottlenecks, reflected the interests, incentives and understanding of competition law of the actors involved at different stages of the drafting process. Those responsible for preparing the draft consulted widely throughout the drafting process, seeking the views of central and local government organs, Chinese and foreign experts, businesses and industry associations. Two groups of actors in particular significantly influenced the debate and final text of the AML. First, the opinions and suggestions of Chinese and foreign competition law experts were sought and carefully considered by the drafters, and these views were persuasive on many technical issues and on some broader policy issues such as administrative monopoly. Second, demand-side actors, especially industry regulators and SOEs, were able to exert substantial pressure during the drafting process, hampering its progress and bringing about the addition of articles reflecting their interests.

Some of the most discussed issues throughout the drafting process revolved around struggles for enforcement authority under the AML. The MOFCOM, the SAIC and the NDRC, each with responsibilities enforcing a particular aspect of the pre-AML competition law regime, all vied for jurisdiction to enforce the AML. This three-way struggle resulted in the current tripartite administrative enforcement structure. Industry regulators also weighed in on these debates and argued that they should retain jurisdiction over regulated industries. The debates were driven by stakeholder incentives to protect the scope of their regulatory authority and, in the case of industry regulators, the interests of SOEs.

The addition of two articles by the SCNPC, which recognise and protect the leading role of the state in the economy, both as a regulator and as a participant, demonstrates the political importance attached to these matters by the Chinese government. Moreover, it indicates that the balance of competition policy and other government policies and laws, especially the leading role of SOEs in the economy and the macroeconomic control exercised by the state, will likely be relevant factors in the enforcement of the AML. This is explored further in Chapter 6.

These observations about the drafting process demonstrate that the AML is the product of coordination. In order to achieve the political consensus required to enact the AML and not delay its enactment, those responsible for preparing the AML at different stages of the drafting process were required to coordinate and balance different views and objectives, which included tussles over jurisdiction resulting from vested interests; the desire to have a competition law in line with international competition law norms while also ensuring that the law remains tailored to China's needs and national conditions; the relationship between competition law and other policies and laws; and the participatory and regulatory roles of the state in the economy and the role of the market. Given that the AML is a reflection of these interests, this suggests that one of the main functions of the AML will be to coordinate these same interests in its implementation and enforcement. Similarly, the AML was used as a means for law-makers to signal to the public that they were responsive to the public's concerns. The articles concerning industry associations, national security review and abuse of administrative power were included as a response to the demand that the AML address issues relating to inflation, foreign investment and administrative monopoly.

# 6

# The Public Enforcement of the Anti-monopoly Law

## 6.1 Introduction

Drawing on the political economy framework set out in Chapters 3 and 4, and the insights into the drafting of the Anti-monopoly Law (AML) obtained in Chapter 5, this chapter investigates the administrative enforcement of the AML. It seeks to understand why, how and the extent to which stakeholders, issues and dynamics have influenced AML enforcement outcomes and decision-making processes. Many of the stakeholders and issues that significantly influenced the AML drafting process are likely to remain relevant to its administrative enforcement, especially as the resolution of a few key issues that had delayed the drafting process was ultimately deferred or vaguely addressed in order to facilitate the enactment of the AML. These matters will need to be addressed in enforcement and implementation.

This chapter is set out as follows. Section 6.2 examines the impact that the division of enforcement power among the three Chinese competition authorities has had on public enforcement. It also considers the role and influence of other government departments in the investigation and merger review processes. Section 6.3 considers how the AML has been coordinated with other government policies. The relevance of the relationship between the state and the market to AML enforcement is examined in Section 6.4. Section 6.5 concludes.

It should be noted that – as raised in Chapter 2 – the competition agencies provide a limited degree of transparency concerning their decision-making processes and investigation outcomes, although this has improved over time. The competition authorities do not provide publicly available information on all their investigations, outcomes or decisions, and sometimes investigated parties request that competition authorities refrain from disclosing investigations.[1] This chapter aims to overcome this limitation

---

[1] 单素敏 [Dan Sumin], 许昆林: 亲历重大反垄断案 [Xu Kunlin: Personally Experienced a Major Anti-monopoly Case], 瞭望东方周刊 [*Oriental Outlook*], 25 June 2015, available at www.lwdf.cn/article_1473_1.html.

through the use of interviews with legal practitioners, academics, economists and government officials involved in AML enforcement. Their experiences and observations are used in this chapter to provide a more complete picture of public enforcement under the AML. More information on the interviews is provided in Appendix A.

## 6.2 Jurisdiction: Enforcement and Scope Issues

As explored in Chapter 5, issues regarding the application of the AML in regulated industries were contentious throughout the drafting of the AML. Industry regulators argued that they should retain jurisdiction to enforce the AML in regulated industries,[2] whereas competition law experts and some members of the Standing Committee of the National People's Congress believed that the competition authorities should have that power across all industries. Similarly, the contest for the power to enforce the AML among the Ministry of Commerce (MOFCOM), the National Development and Reform Commission (NDRC) and the State Administration for Industry and Commerce (SAIC) resulted in the divided enforcement structure that currently exists. These tussles for jurisdiction continue to be relevant in, and influence, the administrative enforcement of the AML to varying degrees.

### 6.2.1 Division of Enforcement Responsibilities among Competition Authorities

One of the most debated – and bottleneck – issues during the drafting of the AML was the identity of the government body that would have power to enforce it. While the tussle for jurisdiction between the MOFCOM, the SAIC and the NDRC was strong during the *drafting* of the AML, to date a similar contest has not been evident in enforcement following the AML's enactment, at least not among the anti-monopoly bureaus within the ministries that carry out the enforcement work. The purview of the MOFCOM Anti-monopoly Bureau (MOFCOM Bureau) is merger enforcement, which is largely distinct from the enforcement responsibilities of the NDRC Bureau of Price Supervision and Anti-monopoly (NDRC Bureau), the SAIC Anti-monopoly and Anti-Unfair Competition Enforcement Bureau (SAIC Bureau) and their local authorities. There is

---

[2] As noted in Chapter 5, in the Chinese law context, 'jurisdiction' 管辖权 refers to enforcement scope or authority.

greater potential for jurisdictional conflict between the NDRC and the SAIC, as they share non-merger responsibilities, albeit divided along price-related and non-price-related lines, respectively. However, in practice, it appears that the NDRC and the SAIC have not interfered with the other's investigations and are pragmatic about the implementation of their respective scopes of authority. As discussed in Chapter 4, they have agreed upon the 'first to discover, first to investigate' coordination mechanism, whereby if conduct involves both price-related and non-price-related elements, each authority will retain jurisdiction over cases it discovers and notify the other of its investigation. Indeed, it seems that, apart from the adoption of this coordination mechanism, there is limited coordination or communication between the SAIC and the NDRC in enforcement. For example, the NDRC and the SAIC separately investigated anti-competitive conduct relating to allopurinol,[3] with the NDRC initiating its investigation less than two weeks before the SAIC published its decision in October 2015. One plausible explanation for the apparent lack of communication and coordination between the authorities, which is illustrated by this example, is that – as commented by one interviewee – the NDRC and the SAIC may lack the incentive to interfere with each other's AML enforcement activities or fight for jurisdiction over a case because they do not have sufficient resources.[4]

In enforcement, as noted in Chapter 2, the NDRC and the SAIC have largely followed the division between price-related and non-price-related conduct in their monopoly agreement actions. The NDRC focuses on price fixing and resale price maintenance, whereas the SAIC primarily investigates market sharing arrangements. Nonetheless, a few cases reflect the overlapping jurisdiction of the authorities. The NDRC and the SAIC have investigated monopoly agreements involving both price-related and non-price-related conduct. The SAIC has investigated monopoly agreements that involve price-fixing in addition to market sharing or joint boycott,[5] and the NDRC's price fixing investigations have also involved output restriction, market sharing, or joint boycott.[6] They have also undertaken separate inquiries into monopoly agreements involving

---

[3] *Chongqing Qingyang Pharmaceutical Refusal to Supply* (SAIC), *Allopurinol Tablet Cartel* (NDRC).
[4] Interviews with Chinese competition law experts and stakeholders.
[5] *Anyang Used Car Service Fees Cartel*; *Jiangshan Commercial Concrete Cartel*; *Xishuangbanna Tourism Cartel*.
[6] *Zhejiang Paperboard Cartel*; *Loudi New Car Insurance Cartel*; *Allopurinol Tablet Cartel*; *Estazolam Tablet Cartel*.

similar conduct in the same industry in the same province; this occurred in relation to the new car insurance industry in Hunan province[7] and the tourism industry in Yunnan province.[8] For these cases, there is no indication in the published decisions that the authorities cooperated in their investigations. Rather, this indicates that the 'first to discover, first to investigate' coordination mechanism is being implemented.

The use of this coordination mechanism can also be seen in the enforcement actions taken in respect to abuse of dominance and administrative monopoly. For abuse of dominance, the SAIC's enforcement actions have generally remained within the ambit of its jurisdiction, with most of its published decisions relating to tying conduct or unreasonable conditions that are not, on their face, related to price (even if the ultimate effect may have been to increase prices).[9] In contrast, the majority of the NDRC's publicly known abuse of dominance cases – including its most high-profile – involved a combination of price-related and non-price-related conduct,[10] and one of its earlier decisions concerned non-price abuse of dominance conduct only.[11] Similarly, the administrative monopoly actions investigated by both competition authorities have nearly all covered a combination of price-related and non-price-related measures. These cases suggest that it may be more difficult to separate abuse of dominance and administrative monopoly conduct into their respective price and non-price components, and that adoption of the 'first to discover, first to investigate' principle has been especially helpful to the NDRC, in this context, in avoiding tussles over jurisdiction.

---

[7] *Yongzhou New Car Insurance Cartel*; *Changde New Car Insurance Cartel*; *Chenzhou New Car Insurance Cartel*; *Zhangjiajie New Car Insurance Cartel*; *Loudi New Car Insurance Cartel*.

[8] 云南省西双版纳州旅游协会, 西双版纳州旅行社协会组织本行业经营者从事垄断协议案 [Yunnan Province Xishuangbanna Tourism Association, Xishuangbanna Travel Agency Association Organise for Industry Operators to Implement Monopoly Agreements Case] (People's Republic of China) Yunnan Province Administration for Industry and Commerce, Order No. 1, 7 April 2013; National Development and Reform Commission, 一批扰乱旅游市场秩序的价格违法案件受到严肃查处 [Some Illegal Price-Related Conduct Cases that Disrupted Market Order in the Tourism Market Severely Punished] (News Release, 29 September 2013).

[9] The exception being the *Chongqing Gas Unreasonable Conditions* case, where the SAIC's local authority in Chongqing determined that a provision in a gas supply contract relating to the basis upon which gas users would be charged was an unreasonable condition.

[10] The high-profile cases being *China Telecom/China Unicom Abuse of Dominance*, *Inter-Digital Abuse of Dominance* and *Qualcomm Abuse of Dominance*. *Shandong Reserprine Exclusive Arrangements* also involved price-related and non-price-related conduct.

[11] *Wuchang Salt Tying*.

Enforcement activity under the AML is also coordinated between central and local authorities. As discussed in Chapter 4, the NDRC has made a general delegation of AML enforcement power to its provincial price authorities, whereas the SAIC authorises its provincial authorities' investigations either on a case-by-case basis (for abuses of dominance or monopoly agreements) or outright (for administrative monopoly conduct). Thus, in theory, the SAIC's approach to decentralising AML enforcement, whereby the local authority must receive authorisation from the SAIC Bureau before taking a formal investigation, provides a greater level of oversight and coordination between local and central authorities than that of the NDRC. Indeed, in each of the SAIC's published decisions, the local authority refers to the fact that it received authorisation from the SAIC Bureau before initiating a formal investigation (though often a local authority will have conducted preliminary investigations before requesting authorisation). In practice, interviewees observe that, for both the NDRC and the SAIC, local authorities are quite closely supervised by the central authorities. They believe that local authorities are required to provide periodic reports on their investigations to the central authorities, and that the NDRC Bureau and the SAIC Bureau often assign their officials to work with local authorities on important cases, to provide input and to issue directions.[12]

### 6.2.2 Involvement of Other Government Departments in Competition Enforcement

While the contest for jurisdiction between the competition authorities appears to be limited other government departments, especially industry regulators, have sought to exercise some degree of influence and authority in AML enforcement activities. This reflects a continuation of dynamics from the drafting process.

#### 6.2.2.1 Merger Review

In merger enforcement, contests for AML enforcement authority have played out in the MOFCOM's consultation with other government departments to obtain their views on a proposed merger. During merger review, the MOFCOM is required to consult with relevant government departments (and other third parties) to verify data and other information

---

[12] Interviews with Chinese competition law experts and stakeholders.

provided by the notifying parties, and to understand the relevant products, market definition, market structure, and particular characteristics, trends and future development of the industry.[13] This practice of consulting other government departments to obtain their comments or views on a particular matter is also part of the normal decision-making process at central-level ministries.[14]

(i) Consultation and Decision-Making by Consensus   Consultation with other government departments brings consideration of industrial policy, regulatory concerns and other matters (which might be regarded by some as 'non-competition concerns') into the decision-making process.[15] Although the MOFCOM does not disclose the identities of the consulted government departments (interviewees note that even the merging parties themselves and their lawyers are not told this information), interviewees who have been involved with merger review believe that – depending on the industry, products and parties involved in a merger – industry regulators, foreign investment regulators and local government bodies are usually consulted.[16] In particular, the most frequently consulted government departments are thought to be the NDRC (that is, those bureaus and departments that do not enforce the AML) and the Ministry of Industry and Information Technology (MIIT), due to their broad regulatory scopes.[17] Other government departments that might be consulted include the SAIC, other departments within the MOFCOM, local foreign investment approval authorities and other local government authorities.[18] The competencies, focuses and incentives of consulted

---

[13] 经营者集中审查办法 [Measure on the Review of Concentrations of Business Operators] (People's Republic of China) Ministry of Commerce, Order No. 12, 15 July 2009, arts. 6–7.

[14] Angela Huyue Zhang, 'Bureaucratic Politics and China's Anti-monopoly Law' (2014) 47 *Cornell International Law Journal* 671 at 687–8. See also 国务院工作规则 [State Council Work Rules] (People's Republic of China) State Council, Order No. 16, 23 March 2013, art. 23.

[15] See also Wendy Ng, 'The Independence of Chinese Competition Agencies and the Impact on Competition Enforcement in China' (2016) 4 *Journal of Antitrust Enforcement* 188 at 202–4.

[16] Interviews with Chinese competition law experts and stakeholders.

[17] Interviews with Chinese competition law experts and stakeholders. See also Susan Ning et al., 'Review of Merger Control and Merger Remedies Regime in China: From 2008–2013', China Law Insight: Antitrust & Competition, 23 August 2013, available at www.chinalawinsight.com/2013/08/articles/corporate/antitrust-competition/review-of-merger-control-and-merger-remedies-regime-in-china-from-2008-2013.

[18] Interviews with Chinese competition law experts and stakeholders; Ning et al., 'Review of Merger Control and Merger Remedies Regime in China'.

government departments are likely to revolve around their industry, sector or region, and their primary concern might not be competition policy. For example, a number of interviewees believe that industry regulators, especially the NDRC and the MIIT, use the consultation procedure to inject industrial policy or regulatory considerations into the decision-making process.[19] This is not surprising, as the NDRC has a broad mandate which includes overseeing the development and implementation of industrial policy in certain industries, sectors or regions. Therefore, the NDRC will likely look at a proposed merger through an industrial policy lens, rather than one of competition. Some industry regulators also administer laws and regulations that contain competition-related provisions which overlap with the AML, such as the Railway Law or Telecommunications Regulation. Thus, they have incentives to protect their regulatory turf and provide input into the AML to reflect their own regulatory interests.

While the consulted government departments need to agree and sign off on the outcome of the MOFCOM's merger review, this does not necessarily mean that their views will be incorporated or reflected in the MOFCOM's final decision.[20] On the one hand, the MOFCOM cannot simply ignore the views of these government departments because, as Zhang notes, the legitimacy of a merger decision made by the MOFCOM without the proper consultation of other government departments could be challenged within the government bureaucracy.[21] On the other hand, matters such as the identity of the government department consulted, the strength of its concerns, whether the MOFCOM agrees with those concerns, the political and power dynamics between the agencies and the views of the merging parties are also important inputs into the decision-making process.[22] Interviewees note that the MOFCOM has often successfully pushed back against other government departments' concerns to focus on merger-specific and competition issues.[23]

---

[19] Interviews with Chinese competition law experts and stakeholders. See also Michael Martina, 'Insight: Flexing Antitrust Muscle, China is a New Merger Hurdle', Reuters, 2 May 2013, available at www.reuters.com/article/2013/05/02/us-mergers-regulation-china-insight-idUSBRE94116920130502.

[20] Zhang, 'Bureaucratic Politics and China's Anti-monopoly Law', 688–9.

[21] Ibid., 688.

[22] Interviews with Chinese competition law experts and stakeholders; D. Daniel Sokol, 'Merger Control under China's Anti-monopoly Law' (2013) 10 *New York University Journal of Law & Business* 1 at 26; Zhang, 'Bureaucratic Politics and China's Anti-monopoly Law', 689.

[23] Interviews with Chinese competition law experts and stakeholders. See also Sokol, 'Merger Control under China's Anti-monopoly Law', 26.

Sometimes, however, the other government department's oppositions to or concerns about a merger might be so strong that the MOFCOM has little choice but to address them.[24] Either way, the MOFCOM – through negotiating, bargaining and compromising with the consulted government departments and merging parties – will need to find a solution that is satisfactory to all parties concerned before it can reach a final, formal decision.[25] As such, from a practical perspective, the MOFCOM's consultation with other government departments goes beyond mere consultation;[26] to build consensus to support a merger outcome, sometimes the MOFCOM's merger enforcement powers are partially shared with the consulted government departments.

One way in which the views of consulted government departments are manifest in merger outcomes is in the conditions attached by the MOFCOM to its merger approval. Those conditions may be directed towards addressing the concerns of the consulted government departments. Some interviewees also note that, to their knowledge, there were some cases during the early years of merger enforcement in which merging parties provided informal commitments – typically in the form of side letters relating to matters such as competition concerns, foreign investment issues, regulatory issues or the transfer of technology to Chinese firms – to the MOFCOM or another government department to secure merger approval.[27] It was thought that such commitments provided consulted government departments with a sufficient degree of comfort that their concerns were being addressed and, at the same time, the informal nature of these commitments enabled the MOFCOM to approve such mergers unconditionally.[28] However, the use of informal commitments was not common or widely known. Interviewees with knowledge of these cases note that informal commitments are no longer used, perhaps reflecting the MOFCOM's growing confidence in its merger review analysis and decision-making.[29]

---

[24] Interviews with Chinese competition law experts and stakeholders; Sokol, 'Merger Control under China's Anti-monopoly Law', 33.
[25] Interviews with Chinese competition law experts and stakeholders; Zhang, 'Bureaucratic Politics and China's Anti-monopoly Law', 689; Sokol, 'Merger Control under China's Anti-monopoly Law', 33.
[26] Interviews with Chinese competition law experts and stakeholders; Sokol, 'Merger Control under China's Anti-monopoly Law', 33.
[27] Interviews with Chinese competition law experts and stakeholders; Sokol, 'Merger Control under China's Anti-monopoly Law', 21.
[28] Interviews with Chinese competition law experts and stakeholders.
[29] Interviews with Chinese competition law experts and stakeholders.

(ii) **Lengthy Merger Reviews and Delays** Delays are widely cited as a major problem in merger review, even for mergers with few or no discernible competition concerns, or which are eventually approved unconditionally.[30] For example, of the 161 mergers approved by the MOFCOM during the January–October 2013 period, 157 were approved unconditionally, and more than 80 per cent of these unconditional approvals were approved during Phase 2 review, which ranges from 31 to 120 days.[31] For conditionally approved or prohibited mergers, the MOFCOM has taken an average of nearly 150 calendar days to review such mergers and come to a decision. Its reviews of the *Western Digital/ Hitachi*, *Glencore/Xstrata*, *Marubeni/Gavilon*, *MediaTek/MStar* and *P3 Shipping Alliance* mergers were especially lengthy.

Consultation with government departments is believed to be one of the main reasons for lengthy merger reviews and delays.[32] During the consultation process, the MOFCOM acts as a conduit for the exchange and coordination of views between the consulted government departments and the merging parties.[33] As a result, this process can take some time, especially when consultations raise industrial policy, political or other concerns.[34] Interviewees point out that it may take a long time for consulted government departments to respond to the MOFCOM's consultation requests, and that they may raise questions or concerns late in the merger review process.[35] The fact that the consulted government

---

[30] Interviews with Chinese competition law experts and stakeholders; François Renard and Michael Edwards, 'China Merger Control Practice: A Comparative Analysis' in Adrian Emch and David Stallibrass (eds.), *China's Anti-monopoly Law: The First Five Years* (Alphen aan den Rijn, The Netherlands: Kluwer Law International, 2013), p. 174; Sokol, 'Merger Control under China's Anti-monopoly Law', 33–4; US–China Business Council, 'Competition Policy and Enforcement in China' (September 2014), pp. 16–17, available at www.uschina.org/reports/competition-policy-and-enforcement-china; Michael Han and Richard Hughes, 'Merger Control in China: Developments in 2012' [2013] (2) *CPI Antitrust Chronicle* 1 at 4.

[31] Ministry of Commerce, 2013 年商务工作年终述评之三: 努力做好经营者集中反垄断审查 维护公平竞争秩序 [MOFCOM's Review of 2013 Work (Part 3): Improve Review of Concentrations of Business Operators, Protect the Fair Competition Order] (Press Release, 4 December 2013).

[32] Interviews with Chinese competition law experts and stakeholders; Sokol, 'Merger Control under China's Anti-monopoly Law', 33–4; US–China Business Council, 'Competition Policy and Enforcement in China', 16–17. See also Ng, 'The Independence of Chinese Competition Agencies', 204–5.

[33] Interviews with Chinese competition law experts and stakeholders.

[34] Interviews with Chinese competition law experts and stakeholders. See also Sokol, 'Merger Control under China's Anti-monopoly Law', 33.

[35] Interviews with Chinese competition law experts and stakeholders.

departments' views and the merging parties' responses to questions are filtered through the MOFCOM can also contribute to the delay, as it is not always clear whether the merging parties have sufficiently responded to and addressed the consulted government departments' questions.[36]

The consensus among interviewees is that adoption of the simple merger review process has improved merger review. They observe that mergers which do not raise substantial competition concerns are approved more quickly once accepted, and that the procedure provides more certainty and predictability for merging parties.[37] As most notified mergers are classified as 'simple cases' and are thus reviewed under the simple merger review process, these improvements have real and substantial practical implications.[38] Interviewees note, however, that there has been little or no change to the time taken by the MOFCOM to accept a notification as complete; in their experience, it can take between one and two months, which is comparable to the pre-acceptance period under the standard merger review process.[39] Another aspect of the merger review process that they believe remains largely unchanged by the adoption of the simple merger review process is the transparency of merger review.[40]

In addition, the use of the simple merger review process seems to have reduced both the involvement of other government departments and, as a corollary, the consideration of industrial policy and other 'non-competition' matters in merger review. In contrast to the standard merger review process, here the MOFCOM does not necessarily approach and solicit the opinion of other government departments. Instead, public notices relating to proposed mergers are published on the MOFCOM's website, and third parties have a ten-day period during which to raise objections to proposed mergers.[41] Interviewees

---

[36] Interviews with Chinese competition law experts and stakeholders. See also Sokol, 'Merger Control under China's Anti-monopoly Law', 33; Lei Kuang, 'Celebrating with a Damp Squib: China's Public Competition Enforcement' (2016) 4 *Journal of Antitrust Enforcement* 411 at 425.

[37] Interviews with Chinese competition law experts and stakeholders.

[38] Interviews with Chinese competition law experts and stakeholders; Marc Waha, 'MOFCOM Simple Cases: The First Six Months' [2015] (1) *CPI Antitrust Chronicle* 1 at 3, available at www.competitionpolicyinternational.com/mofcom-simple-cases-the-first-six-months; 'Competition Law in East Asia: A Month in Review' (Norton Rose Fulbright, January 2017), pp. 3–4.

[39] Interviews with Chinese competition law experts and stakeholders. See also Waha, 'MOFCOM Simple Cases', 3.

[40] Interviews with Chinese competition law experts and stakeholders.

[41] 关于经营者集中简易案件申报的指导意见 (试行) [Guiding Opinion on the Notification of Simple Cases of Concentrations of Business Operators (Trial)] (People's Republic of China) Ministry of Commerce, 18 April 2014.

observe that, like other third parties, it is up to other government departments to raise their concerns about a proposed merger with the MOFCOM.[42] While one interviewee notes that the MOFCOM may nonetheless solicit the views of other government departments, overall, consultation with other government departments occurs much less frequently in simple merger review than in standard merger review.[43] The limited involvement of other government departments in simple merger review may, in part, explain why the MOFCOM is able to assess and make decisions more quickly in relation to simple mergers.

#### 6.2.2.2 Investigations of Non-Merger Conduct

Unlike the MOFCOM, which is required under the AML to consult with relevant government departments during merger review, there is no such obligation imposed on the NDRC or the SAIC in their AML investigations of non-merger conduct. However, pursuant to the State Council Work Rules, a ministry or commission must, inter alia, consult with relevant central and local government departments before submitting an important matter to the State Council for consideration and decision.[44] Thus the NDRC and the SAIC will need to consult with other government departments in some situations, but they have some discretion. According to interviewees, the NDRC and the SAIC are much less likely than the MOFCOM to consult with other government departments during their investigations.[45] Interviewees also observe that the SAIC, and especially the NDRC, will resist attempts by other government departments to interfere with their investigations. As such, the NDRC and the SAIC typically run AML investigations with little third party input and influence.[46]

Nonetheless, the involvement of other government departments seems to have influenced the outcome of a small number of non-merger investigations that were taken (or that should have been taken) by the NDRC or the SAIC during the first few years of enforcement. In these cases – *China Telecom/China Unicom Abuse of Dominance*, *TravelSky Cartel* and *Tencent/Qihoo 360* – industry regulators reportedly either opposed the investigation, which then resulted in the competition

---

[42] Interviews with Chinese competition law experts and stakeholders.
[43] Interviews with Chinese competition law experts and stakeholders.
[44] State Council Work Rules, art. 23.
[45] Interviews with Chinese competition law experts and stakeholders.
[46] Interviews with Chinese competition law experts and stakeholders.

authority's investigation being settled or terminated, or intervened directly and usurped the competition authority's jurisdiction.

In *China Telecom/China Unicom Abuse of Dominance*, the NDRC investigated China Telecom and China Unicom, two of the largest telecommunications companies in China and both powerful state-owned enterprises (SOEs), for potentially abusing their dominance. The NDRC investigated China Telecom for refusing to deal with China Mobile Tietong (another Chinese telecommunications SOE and competitor), and both China Telecom and China Unicom for engaging in price discrimination vis-à-vis Internet service providers.[47] According to Xinhua, the state's news agency, the NDRC intended to impose fines on China Telecom and China Unicom for abusing their dominance.[48] When the NDRC announced its investigation (which was run by its central-level authority, NDRC Bureau) on national television in November 2011, it clearly stated that if the companies were found to have abused their dominance, they faced a fine ranging from 1 to 10 per cent of their turnover for the previous year.[49] It also refuted claims that the investigation would be settled or terminated, and confirmed that even if the investigation was suspended, it could still impose fines.[50] However, instead of imposing fines, the NDRC accepted the parties' commitments to adopt corrective measures and expand their bandwidth, reduce prices and improve interoperability; in February 2014, the Director-General of the NDRC Bureau confirmed that both companies had submitted reports on the implementation of those measures and that it was in the process of assessing whether the two companies had fully fulfilled their commitments.[51]

---

[47] 国家发改委就价格监管与反垄断工作情况举行新闻发布会 [NDRC Holds News Conference on Price Supervision and Anti-monopoly Work] (19 February 2014) available at www.china.com.cn/zhibo/2014-02/19/content_31502397.htm.

[48] 新华社调查电信联通涉嫌垄断案, 称系"神仙战" [Xinhua Investigates China Telecom/China Unicom Suspected Monopoly Case, Calls It the "Battle of the Gods"], 新华网 [Xinhuanet], 11 November 2011, available at www.dezhoudaily.com/news/folder1004/2011/11/2011-11-17305760.html.

[49] China Central Television, 新闻30分 [News 30'], 9 November 2011 (李青 [Li Qing]) available at http://news.cntv.cn/program/C20692/20111109/107411.shtml.

[50] 发改委否认宽带垄断案和解, 称已获得核心证据 [NDRC Denies Settling Broadband Monopoly Case, Says It has Already Gathered Core Evidence], 新京报 [*The Beijing News*], 22 November 2011, available at http://finance.sina.com.cn/g/20111122/075410857808.shtml.

[51] China Telecom Corporation Limited, 'Announcement' (Hong Kong Stock Exchange Announcement, 2 December 2011); China Unicom (Hong Kong) Limited, 'Announcement' (Hong Kong Stock Exchange Announcement, 2 December 2011); 'NDRC Holds News Conference on Price Supervision and Anti-monopoly Work', 19 February 2014.

Wang suggests that the NDRC's decision to accept commitments rather than impose fines might be the result of strong opposition from other government bodies, especially the MIIT, to its investigation.[52] According to Xinhua, the NDRC consulted with the State Council Legislative Affairs Office, the Supreme People's Court (SPC) and the MIIT after it had made its preliminary findings and decided to impose a fine. However, there were reportedly significant differences in the views of these government authorities, and the NDRC agreed to consult further with the MIIT and the State-owned Assets Supervision and Administration Commission (SASAC) before making its report to the State Council.[53] These differences came to light shortly after the investigation was announced, when two newspapers administered by the MIIT published claims that the NDRC's announcement had misled the public and was full of mistakes, and that there was no basis for stating that the two telecommunications companies were dominant or had abused their dominance.[54] Such a public display of disagreement between government departments is rare in China, and there was speculation that this reflected a power struggle between the NDRC and the MIIT.[55] The unconventional manner in which the NDRC announced its investigation also hinted at the political dynamics underlying the investigation. Normally, central government policies are announced through Xinhua and then later broadcast on the national broadcaster's evening news.[56]

---

[52] Xiaoye Wang, 'The China Telecom and China Unicom Case and the Future of Chinese Antitrust' in Adrian Emch and David Stallibrass (eds.), *China's Anti-monopoly Law: The First Five Years* (Alphen aan den Rijn, The Netherlands: Kluwer Law International, 2013), p. 485. See also interviews with Chinese competition law experts and stakeholders.
[53] 'Xinhua Investigates China Telecom/China Unicom Suspected Monopoly Case', 12 November 2011; 赵谨, 李蕾 [Zhao Jin and Li Lei], 工信部下属两家媒体驳电信联通涉嫌垄断报道 [Two Media Outlets under the MIIT Refute Reports of Alleged Monopolisation by China Telecom/China Unicom], 新京报 [*The Beijing News*], 12 November 2011, available at www.chinanews.com/it/2011/11-12/3455659.shtml; 'Editorial: Antimonopoly Investigations Should Be Conducted Openly and Independently', *News China Magazine* (January 2012).
[54] Zhao and Li, 'Two Media Outlets under the MIIT'; 叶逗逗 [Ye Doudou], 工信部主管媒体痛批央视 称其电信反垄断报道混淆视听 [MIIT Controlled Media Criticises CCTV, Says that the Telecommunications Anti-monopoly Report Misled the Public], 财新 [Caixin], 11 November 2011, available at http://china.caixin.com/2011-11-11/100324903.html.
[55] Wang Xiangwei, 'Beijing Must Back NDRC in Probe of Telecoms Giants', *South China Morning Post*, 14 November 2011, available at www.scmp.com/article/984757/beijing-must-back-ndrc-probe-telecoms-giants.
[56] Ibid.

However, the NDRC announced the investigation on the afternoon news program, reportedly without first notifying any of the relevant ministries, China Telecom or China Unicom.[57] This suggests that the announcement was made, in part, in order for the NDRC to assert ownership over the investigation and generate public support.[58] The Director-General of the NDRC Bureau also alluded to the strong pressure that it faced during the investigation, when he commented that the NDRC Bureau had been subject to pressure from all sides during its investigation.[59]

There are also indications that the NDRC faced some opposition from the industry regulator during its *TravelSky Cartel* investigation. In that case, the NDRC investigated TravelSky – which is the ticketing website of the Civil Aviation Administration of China (CAAC) (China's aviation industry regulator) and issues the tickets for major Chinese airlines – and several state-owned Chinese airlines for alleged price fixing.[60] In March 2009, nearly all Chinese airlines simultaneously announced a price increase in their airfares, and TravelSky adjusted its discount policies and effectively increased the price of airfares offered by all the airlines in its network. During the NDRC's investigation, the CAAC made a public statement in support of the airlines' conduct, stating that they had independently adjusted their prices and had not entered into an agreement to fix prices.[61] Unfortunately, it is not known whether the NDRC made any findings or issued any orders or sanctions, because it never made any formal announcements about the progress or outcome of its investigation. However, some commentators believe that the

---

[57] 'Xinhua Investigates China Telecom/China Unicom Suspected Monopoly Case', 12 November 2011.
[58] Wang Xiangwei, 'Beijing Must Back NDRC in Probe of Telecoms Giants'; 'Xinhua Investigates China Telecom/China Unicom Suspected Monopoly Case', 12 November 2011.
[59] 发改委反垄断局: 继续督促电信联通反垄断整改 限期3-5年[NDRC Anti-monopoly Bureau: Continues to Urge China Telecom and China Unicom to Undertake Antimonopoly Rectification, Time Limit of 3-5 Years], 证券时报 [Securities Times], 25 September 2013, available at www.cs.com.cn/xwzx/hg/201309/t20130925_4153920.html.
[60] 王毕强, 刘伟勋 [Wang Biqiang and Liu Weixun], 涉操纵机票涨价 发改委调查中航信 [Suspected Manipulation of Airfare Price Increases, NDRC Investigates TravelSky], 经济观测网 [Economic Observer Online], 17 May 2009, available at www.eeo.com.cn/finance/other/2009/05/16/137823.shtml.
[61] 林红梅 [Lin Hongmei], 中国民航局澄清: 中国民航运价政策没有发生变化 [Civil Aviation Administration of China Clarifies: China's Civil Aviation Pricing Policy Has Not Changed], 新华社 [Xinhua News Agency], 21 April 2009, available at www.gov.cn/fwxx/ly/2009-04/21/content_1291265.htm.

NDRC was behind the airlines' decision to revert to old discount policies six months after the announced price increase.[62]

Although the involvement of industry regulators in *China Telecom/ China Unicom Abuse of Dominance* and *TravelSky Cartel* seems to have constrained the NDRC's ability to investigate and sanction the companies, the investigations were nonetheless effective in delivering benefits to consumers in the form of reduced prices and/or improved services.[63] Indeed, the Director-General of the NDRC Bureau has stated that the aim of AML investigations is not to impose fines but to 'create a competitive market and fair order'.[64] Further, while the industry regulators opposed the investigation and probably influenced the enforcement outcome, control of the investigation nonetheless remained with the NDRC.

In contrast, with the *Tencent/Qihoo 360* dispute, it was the MIIT – as the industry regulator – that intervened to resolve the dispute, not the SAIC, which also had jurisdiction.[65] Tencent and Qihoo 360 are both large Chinese internet companies. Tencent operates QQ, a popular instant-messaging software service in China, and Qihoo 360 provides leading antivirus software. In September 2010, Qihoo 360 accused Tencent of violating the privacy of QQ users and released privacy protection software. In response, Tencent stated that Qihoo 360's privacy protection software caused QQ to malfunction and, in October 2010, it launched legal proceedings against Qihoo 360 for breaching the Anti-Unfair Competition Law (AUCL).[66] On 3 November 2010, Tencent announced that it would stop providing QQ to users who

---

[62] 'Domestic Aviation Companies' Price Alliance Collapses', *People's Daily* Online, 21 September 2009, available at http://english.people.com.cn/90001/90778/90857/90860/6763625.html; Liao Jiehua, 'Controversial Air Ticket Pricing System Collapses', *Economic Observer*, 22 September 2009, available at www.eeo.com.cn/ens/Politics/2009/09/22/152023.shtml.

[63] Xiaoye Wang, 'The China Telecom and China Unicom Case', 484.

[64] Dan, 'Xu Kunlin'.

[65] Nate Bush and Yue Bo, 'Disentangling Industrial Policy and Competition Policy in China' [2011] (February) *The Antitrust Source* 1 at 11–12, available at www.americanbar.org/content/dam/aba/migrated/2011_build/antitrust_law/feb11_bush2_23f.authcheckdam.pdf; Qianlan Wu, *Competition Laws, Globalization and Legal Pluralism: China's Experiences* (Oxford: Hart Publishing, 2013), p. 155; Meng Yanbei, 'The Uneasy Relationship between Antitrust Enforcement and Industry-Specific Regulation in China' in Adrian Emch and David Stallibrass (eds.), *China's Anti-monopoly Law: The First Five Years* (Alphen aan den Rijn, The Netherlands: Kluwer Law International, 2013), pp. 259–60.

[66] In October 2010, Tencent filed a claim before the Beijing Chaoyang District People's Court alleging that Qihoo 360 had breached the AUCL. The Court accepted the claim on 3 November 2010, and handed down its decision in April 2011. It ruled in favour of

had installed Qihoo 360.[67] At around the same time, lawyers based in Beijing petitioned the SAIC to investigate Tencent for abuse of dominance.[68]

Both the MIIT and the SAIC had jurisdiction over the dispute. The MIIT is the regulator of the information technology and internet industries and the SAIC enforces the AUCL and the AML (non-price-related infringements), which were the laws that potentially applied in the dispute. However, it was the MIIT that led the Chinese government's intervention to resolve the dispute and investigate Tencent's and Qihoo 360's conduct.[69] On 20 November 2010, the MIIT issued a notice criticising Tencent's and Qihoo 360's conduct and ordered that they issue public apologies, stop attacking one another and cooperate to ensure software compatibility.[70] Further, in December 2011, the MIIT issued

---

Tencent and ordered Qihoo 360 to pay RMB 400,000 in compensation and costs. See 腾讯诉360不正当竞争 北京朝阳法院正式受理该案 [Tencent Sues 360 for Unfair Competition, Beijing Chaoyang District Court Formally Accepts the Case], 中国经济网 [China Economic News], 3 November 2010, available at www.ce.cn/cysc/tech/07hlw/guonei/201011/03/t20101103_20536304.shtml; 腾讯诉360案宣判: 奇虎停止发行360隐私保护器 赔偿腾讯40万 [Decision in Tencent vs 360 Case: Qihoo to Stop Issuing Its 360 Privacy Protection Tool, Pay Tencent 400,000 Compensation], 财经网 [Caijing], 26 April 2011, available at www.caijing.com.cn/2011-04-26/110702615.html.

[67] Juliet Ye, 'QQ-360 Battle Escalates into War', *The Wall Street Journal*, 5 November 2010, available at http://blogs.wsj.com/chinarealtime/2010/11/05/qq-360-battle-escalates-into-war; 腾讯宣布装有360软件电脑将停止运行QQ [Tencent Announces that Computers Installed with 360 Software Will Stop Running QQ], 财经网 [Caijing], 3 November 2010, available at www.caijing.com.cn/2010-11-03/110558875.html.

[68] 律师上书国家工商局申请对腾讯展开反垄断调查 [Lawyers Petition SAIC to Launch an Anti-monopoly Investigation into Tencent], 每日经济新闻 [Daily Economic News], 5 November 2010, available at www.ce.cn/cysc/tech/07hlw/guonei/201011/05/t20101105_20538202.shtml; 反垄断局紧急约见提交对腾讯反垄断调查律师 [Anti-monopoly Bureau Has Urgent Meeting with Lawyers Requesting Anti-monopoly Investigation of Tencent], 每日经济新闻 [Daily Economic News], 9 November 2010, available at http://tech.sina.com.cn/i/2010-11-09/01024841632.shtml.

[69] 刘菊花 [Liu Juhua], 李毅中: 工信部正抓紧处理360与QQ纠纷事件 [Liu Yizhong: MIIT Currently Handling 360/QQ Dispute], 新华网 [Xinhuanet], 10 November 2010, available at www.yicai.com/news/595608.html; 李斌 [Li Bin], 多部门出面"叫暂停" "3Q之战" 中场休息. [Many Departments Call for a "Time Out", Intermission in the "3Q War"], 京华时报 [Beijing Times], 5 November 2010, available at http://media.people.com.cn/GB/13134342.html; Wang Xing and Chen Limin, 'Minister: Internet Companies' Spat Immoral, Irresponsible', *China Daily*, 10 November 2010, available at www.chinadaily.com.cn/business/2010-11/10/content_11526774.htm.

[70] 关于批评北京奇虎科技有限公司和深圳市腾讯计算机系统有限公司的通报 [Notice on Criticising Beijing Qihoo Technology Co., Ltd. and Shenzhen Tencent Computer System Co., Ltd.] (People's Republic of China) Ministry of Industry and Information Technology, Order No. 536, 20 November 2010.

sector regulations to protect against the risks that were exposed by the dispute and to prevent a similar dispute from occurring in the future.[71] As noted in Chapter 3, the MIIT is one of the most important and powerful industry regulators, whereas the SAIC is the weakest of the three competition authorities. This disparity in power may have been a reason why the MIIT and not the SAIC was able to successfully assert jurisdiction over the *Tencent/Qihoo 360* dispute. Reflecting this, Bush and Bo believe that the MIIT's release of sector regulations in December 2011 was an effort to strengthen its authority in the internet industry, at the expense of the competition authorities and competition policy.[72] Another pressing concern was the need to resolve the dispute quickly. At the time, the Minister of the MIIT noted that China's leaders were aware of the dispute and that they hoped the situation would be resolved soon.[73] A regulatory intervention by the MIIT, rather than an investigation by the SAIC, might have been regarded as the quickest way to settle the dispute and deliver what the Chinese leaders and the public demanded.

## 6.3 Anti-monopoly Law and Other Government Policies

Discussions of the AML are often linked to the government's broader policies, priorities and reform and development agenda. While the Chinese government regards the AML as helping to establish competitive market structures, promote and ensure competitive conduct and maintain market competition, it also believes that the AML can coordinate competition law and policy with other policies and priorities to jointly promote and achieve economic, development and other outcomes. As shown in Chapter 5, this was a theme underlying discussions during the AML drafting process, and is reflected in some of the AML provisions.

The enforcement activity to date suggests that, in some cases – in addition to addressing concerns about anti-competitive conduct such as higher prices, reduced consumer choices and harms to the competitive process – the AML has been enforced in a manner that is also consistent with promoting and achieving other government policy aims and concerns. This is not to suggest that anti-competitive harm is not the main reason for taking enforcement action, that there are cases in which

---

[71] 规范互联网信息服务市场秩序若干规定 [Several Provisions on Regulating Internet Information Services Market Order] (People's Republic of China) Ministry of Industry and Information Technology, Order No. 20, 29 December 2011.
[72] Bush and Bo, 'Disentangling Industrial Policy and Competition Policy in China', 12–13.
[73] Wang and Chen, 'Minister: Internet Companies' Spat Immoral, Irresponsible'.

limited or no justification exists to apply the AML or that the AML is being applied to pursue industrial policy or other goals without regard to their implications for competition law and policy. The fact that the Chinese competition authorities have particular enforcement priorities is also not unique to China. The reality for competition authorities worldwide is that they have limited resources but are faced with a broad range of potentially anti-competitive conduct, and thus they need to prioritise particular types of conduct or industries for enforcement.

Rather, these cases suggest that, consistent with the intention of the legislators that the AML coordinate industrial policy and other economic policies, competition policy and other government policies are coordinated and balanced via the AML.[74] Formal and informal mechanisms exist within the AML that allow for such coordination. For example, as discussed in Chapter 4, the Anti-monopoly Commission (AMC) is a forum in which the interests of various government departments and entities with an interest in competition law matters can be discussed, coordinated and balanced, although it has not been very active to date. The involvement of other government departments during merger reviews and non-merger investigation processes, which is examined in Section 6.2.2, can bring other policy considerations that require resolution into the AML decision-making process. Further, on a more general level, there are coordination mechanisms and incentives within the governance environment which help to ensure that the policies and priorities set by the Chinese leadership are followed and implemented by all levels of government.

Section 6.3.1 considers how AML enforcement appears to have been coordinated with other government policies, namely, industrial policy and regulation, foreign investment policy and the people's wellbeing and livelihood.

### 6.3.1 Innovation and Innovation-Driven Development

The complementary relationship between competition and innovation forms part of discussions regarding competition law and policy in China. The Chinese government recognises that competition plays a fundamental role in encouraging innovation by providing incentives for

---

[74] See, e.g., 价格监督检查与反垄断工作取得新成绩 [Price Supervision and Inspection and Anti-monopoly Work Achieves New Results] (13 February 2013) National Development and Reform Commission, available at www.ndrc.gov.cn/xwzx/xwfb/201502/t20150213_664544.html.

businesses to innovate, which in turn promotes economic development and transformation.[75] Competition law is viewed as part of the institutional environment that fosters innovation.[76]

Further, innovation is integral to China's reform and development strategy. The Chinese government has made it a priority to transform China's economic development model into one of sustainable development, and China's economy into an innovation economy. The emphasis on innovation is part of the Chinese government's goal to move China from traditional, low-tech and low value-added activities into more innovative, knowledge-intensive, high-tech and high value-added activities.[77] To that end, a major fifteen-year program to develop science and technology and promote innovation was launched by the Chinese government in 2006.[78] More recently, the Communist Party of China (CPC) adopted a wide-ranging reform blueprint at the Third Plenum of the 18th Central Committee of the CPC (Third Plenum) in which the importance of innovation to deepening science and technology structural reform was reconfirmed;[79] subsequently, the CPC and the State Council jointly adopted an innovation-driven development strategy that, *inter alia*, aims

---

[75] Xu Kunlin, 'Gradually Establishing the Fundamental Status of Competition Policy' (2015) 2 *International Antitrust Bulletin* 12 at 12–13; 俞岚, 周锐 [Yu Lan and Zhou Rui], 中国反价格垄断获突破性进展 已调查案件49起 [Breakthrough Developments in Anti-Price Monopoly in China, Already Investigated 49 Cases], 中国新闻网 [China News Online], 4 January 2013, available at http://finance.chinanews.com/cj/2013/01–04/4454595.shtml.

[76] 中共中央国务院关于深化体制机制改革加快实施创新驱动发展战略的若干意见 [Some Opinions of the Central Committee of the Communist Party of China and the State Council on Deepening Institutional Reforms and Accelerating the Implementation of the Innovation-Driven Development Strategy] (People's Republic of China) Central Committee of the Communist Party of China and the State Council, 13 March 2015; 'State Council Policy Briefing' (State Council Information Office, 27 March 2015), available at http://english.gov.cn/news/policy_briefings/2015/03/27/content_281475078591808.htm.

[77] 中华人民共和国国民经济和社会发展第十二个五年规划纲要 [Outline of the 12th Five-Year Plan for National Economic and Social Development] (People's Republic of China) National People's Congress, 14 March 2011, ch. 2.

[78] 国家中长期科学和技术发展规划纲要 (2006–2020) 年 [Outline of the National Medium- and Long-Term Plan for the Development of Science and Technology (2006–2020)] (People's Republic of China) State Council, 9 February 2006; *OECD Review of Innovation Policy: China* (Organisation for Economic Co-operation and Development and the Chinese Ministry of Science and Technology, 2007), p. 12; Sylvia Schwaag Serger and Magnus Breidne, 'China's Fifteen-Year Plan for Science and Technology: An Assessment' (2007) 4 *Asia Policy* 135.

[79] 中共中央关于全面深化改革若干重大问题的决定 [Decision of the Central Committee of the Communist Party of China on Some Major Issues Concerning Comprehensively

to create an institutional environment conducive to innovation.[80] Innovation is also a key principle underlying the Thirteenth Five-Year Plan for National Economic and Social Development (Thirteenth Five-Year Plan), with innovation-driven development taking a leading role.[81]

In particular, indigenous innovation is a key aspect of China's science and technology strategy.[82] Since economic reform and opening up, China has relied on foreign intellectual property and technology to help develop its economy, and foreign companies have generally controlled core technologies in key sectors – a situation that, according to Xi Jinping, has not undergone any fundamental change.[83] By the end of 2020, China aims to decrease its reliance on imported intellectual property and technology by at least 30 per cent, and to narrow the technology gap between China and developed countries.[84] Accordingly, the Chinese government encourages Chinese businesses to develop their own technology and products.[85] However, the Chinese government also recognises that indigenous innovation is built upon a foundation provided by foreign intellectual property and technology.[86]

#### 6.3.1.1 Intellectual Property Rights

Consistent with the importance placed on innovation and its interaction with competition law and policy, a number of AML enforcement

---

Deepening Reform] (People's Republic of China) Third Plenary Session of the 18th Central Committee of the Communist Party of China, 12 November 2013.

[80] Some Opinions of the Central Committee of the Communist Party of China and the State Council on Deepening Institutional Reforms and Accelerating the Implementation of the Innovation-Driven Development Strategy, 13 March 2015.

[81] 中华人民共和国国民经济和社会发展第十三个五年规划纲要 [Outline of the 13th Five-Year Plan for National Economic and Social Development] (People's Republic of China) National People's Congress, 16 March 2016, pt. I ch. 4, pt. II generally.

[82] Outline of the National Medium- and Long-Term Plan for the Development of Science and Technology (2006–2020).

[83] 习近平 [Xi Jinping], 为建设世界科技强国而奋斗 [Striving to Build a World Power in Science and Technology] (Speech delivered at National Science and Technology Innovation Conference, Biennial Conference of the Chinese Academy of Sciences and Chinese Academy of Engineering, and Ninth National Congress of the China Association for Science and Technology, Beijing, 30 May 2016) available at http://news.xinhuanet.com/politics/2016-05/31/c_1118965169.htm; 'OECD Review of Innovation Policy: China', p. 12.

[84] Outline of the National Medium- and Long-Term Plan for the Development of Science and Technology (2006–2020) ch. 1, ch. 2 art. 2.

[85] Ibid., ch. 2 art. 1.

[86] Indigenous innovation is defined as enhancing original innovation through integrated innovation and re-innovation based on the assimilation and absorption of imported technologies: Ibid., ch. 1 art. 1.

investigations and decisions have dealt with intellectual property rights (IPRs) as their key concern. Chinese competition authorities regard IPRs as essential for innovation and technological advancement, and consider the abuse of IPRs to eliminate or restrict competition as stifling innovation.[87] They also view high IPR licensing fees as not conducive to encouraging research and development or the sustainable development of businesses.[88] Further, as noted above, Chinese companies have generally relied on IPRs held by foreign companies, and the notion of indigenous innovation is based upon the use of foreign technologies. Therefore, the ability to access IPRs, along with the price and other terms of that access, are relevant considerations for innovation and innovation-driven development, in addition to competition. The cases taken in relation to IPRs, which have involved mergers and abuse of dominance, address both these matters.

In the merger context, the MOFCOM has looked at IPR licensing issues in its conditional approvals of *Google/Motorola Mobility*, *Microsoft/Nokia* and *Nokia/Alcatel-Lucent*. These mergers occurred in the communications and technology industry, where the main barrier to entry is access to IPRs, and the parties in these mergers all held key IPRs. In *Google/Motorola Mobility*, the IPRs related to smart mobile device operating systems (Google's Android) and mobile phones (Motorola Mobility's patents); in *Microsoft/Nokia*, Nokia held communications technology standard essential patents (SEPs) and Microsoft had a program of Android-related patents (which include SEPs and non-SEPs); and in *Nokia/Alcatel-Lucent*, both parties held wireless communications standard SEPs. In each case, the MOFCOM was concerned about the terms upon which IPR licences would be granted to smart mobile device manufacturers and other downstream businesses. As IPRs are essential for entry into the relevant markets, the MOFCOM believed that changes to the parties' IPR licensing strategies and practices could harm competition. The MOFCOM believed that the parties would have the ability and

---

[87] 解读《关于禁止滥用知识产权排除、限制竞争行为的规定》 [Interpretation of 'Regulation on the Prohibition of Abuse of Intellectual Property Rights to Eliminate or Restrict Competition'] (3 August 2015) State Administration for Industry and Commerce, available at www.saic.gov.cn/fldyfbzdjz/zcfg/xzgz/201508/t20150803_233534.html.

[88] 关于附加限制性条件批准微软收购诺基亚设备和服务业务案经营者集中反垄断审查决定的公告 [Announcement of the Anti-monopoly Review of Concentrations of Business Operators Decision to Impose Restrictive Conditions to the Approval of Microsoft's Acquisition of Nokia's Device and Service Business] (People's Republic of China) Ministry of Commerce, Order No. 24, 8 April 2014 (*Microsoft/Nokia*).

incentive post-merger to increase licensing fees and/or impose unreasonable licensing conditions, whereas potential licensees had limited bargaining power to counter these changes. To address these concerns, in *Google/Motorola Mobility* and *Microsoft/Nokia*, the MOFCOM required the merging parties to, *inter alia*, license certain IPRs on a fair, reasonable and non-discriminatory (FRAND) basis and to maintain existing licensing practices (including licensing fees) for other IPRs.[89] In *Nokia/Alcatel-Lucent*, the MOFCOM required Nokia to confirm that it would not seek injunctions to prevent the use of SEPs granted on a FRAND basis and to make certain commitments to its licensees and potential licensees in China when transferring a SEP to a third party.[90]

The abuse of IPRs is one of the NDRC's stated AML enforcement priorities.[91] Like the MOFCOM, IPR licensing fees and practices have been targeted by the NDRC in the *Qualcomm Abuse of Dominance* and *InterDigital Abuse of Dominance* investigations. Both companies hold wireless communication standards patents. The NDRC was concerned that the companies had abused their dominance by, *inter alia*, charging unfairly high licensing fees and tying the licensing of non-SEPs to SEPs.[92] Both Qualcomm and InterDigital offered commitments to address the NDRC's concerns, including not tying the licensing of SEPs with non-SEPs or requiring Chinese licensees to cross-license their patents free of

---

[89] 关于附加限制性条件批准谷歌收购摩托罗拉移动经营者集中反垄断审查决定的公告 [Announcement of the Anti-monopoly Review of Concentrations of Business Operators Decision to Impose Restrictive Conditions to the Approval of Google's Acquisition of Motorola Mobility] (People's Republic of China) Ministry of Commerce, Order No. 25, 19 May 2012; *Microsoft/Nokia*.

[90] 关于附加限制性条件批准诺基亚收购阿尔卡特朗讯股权案经营者集中反垄断审查决定的公告 [Announcement of the Anti-monopoly Review of Concentrations of Business Operators Decision to Impose Restrictive Conditions to the Approval of Nokia's Acquisition of Shares in Alcatel-Lucent] (People's Republic of China) Ministry of Commerce, Order No. 44, 19 October 2015.

[91] 林远 [Lin Yun], 反垄断执法新目标: 知识产权滥用 [New Target of Anti-monopoly Enforcement: Abuse of Intellectual Property Rights], 经济参考报 [*Economic Information Daily*], 24 March 2015, available at http://jjckb.xinhuanet.com/2015-03/24/content_541963.htm; 国家发展改革委价监局 [NDRC Bureau of Price Supervision and Anti-monopoly], 2016年价格监管与反垄断工作要点 [Key Points of NDRC Bureau of Price Supervision and Anti-monopoly's Work in 2016] [2016] (2) 中国价格检查与反垄断 [*Price Supervision and Anti-monopoly in China*] 5 at 5.

[92] 行政处罚决定书 [Administrative Penalty Decision] (People's Republic of China) National Development and Reform Commission, Order No. 1, 9 February 2015 (*Qualcomm Abuse of Dominance*); National Development and Reform Commission, 国家发展改革委对美国IDC公司涉嫌价格垄断案中止调查 [NDRC Stops Investigation of InterDigital Suspected Price Monopoly Case] (News Release, 22 May 2014).

charge.[93] They also made commitments relating to licensing fees: Qualcomm would charge patent royalties based on 65 per cent of the net selling price for devices sold in China (representing a reduction in its royalty rate) and InterDigital would not charge Chinese businesses discriminatorily high licensing fees.[94] In the end, Qualcomm was fined RMB 6.088 billion (equal to 8 per cent of its 2013 sales in China), whereas the investigation into InterDigital was suspended on the basis of its commitments.[95]

It is also interesting to note that both the MOFCOM's and the NDRC's IPR-related reviews and investigations have involved the communications and technology industry, in particular smart mobile devices and wireless communication standards. Development and innovation in the communications and technology industry is a priority for the Chinese government, with the next-generation information technology industries (which includes smart mobile devices and 5G mobile communications) designated as 'strategic emerging industries' whose development is supported and fostered in both the Twelfth Five-Year Plan for National Economic and Social Development and the Thirteenth Five-Year Plan.[96] China is also the world's largest producer and consumer of smartphones.[97] Therefore, the ability of Chinese smartphone manufacturers to obtain relevant IPR licenses, the level of IPR licensing fees (the cost of which may ultimately be borne by Chinese consumers) and the licensing practices of IPR holders are likely to impact China's ability to develop

---

[93] National Development and Reform Commission, 'NDRC Stops Investigation of InterDigital Suspected Price Monopoly Case'; Qualcomm, 'Qualcomm and China's National Development and Reform Commission Reach Resolution' (Press Release, 10 February 2015) available at www.qualcomm.com/news/releases/2015/02/09/qualcomm-and-chinas-national-development-and-reform-commission-reach.

[94] National Development and Reform Commission, 'NDRC Stops Investigation of InterDigital Suspected Price Monopoly Case'; Qualcomm, 'Qualcomm and China's National Development and Reform Commission Reach Resolution'. Qualcomm also committed to providing licensees with a patent list and agreed not to condition the supply of baseband chips on the signing of a patent license agreement containing unreasonable terms (including that the licensee cannot challenge the license). InterDigital also stated that it would not directly seek to force Chinese companies to accept unfair licensing conditions through litigation.

[95] *Qualcomm Abuse of Dominance*; National Development and Reform Commission, 'NDRC Stops Investigation of InterDigital Suspected Price Monopoly Case'.

[96] Outline of the 12th Five-Year Plan for National Economic and Social Development, ch. 10; Outline of the 13th Five-Year Plan for National Economic and Social Development, ch. 23.

[97] *Microsoft/Nokia*.

these strategic industries, in addition to affecting Chinese manufacturers and consumers. These IPR-related investigations and outcomes have, however, attracted some controversy, as discussed in Chapter 1.

IPR-related issues have also been addressed in the AML implementing regulations. In April 2015, the SAIC issued regulations on the anti-competitive abuse of IPRs,[98] which took nearly six years to prepare. Two months later, the Chinese government announced that the AMC would adopt an antitrust guideline on the anti-competitive abuse of IPRs.[99] This signals the importance attached to this issue by the Chinese government, as the AMC's antitrust guideline will bind all three competition agencies (in contrast, the SAIC's regulation applies only to the SAIC). All three competition agencies, plus the State Intellectual Property Office, are preparing their own draft antitrust guidelines on the abuse of IPRs for submission to the AMC.[100]

### 6.3.1.2 Brands

Brands are an important consideration in merger review, with the MOFCOM having looked at brands in at least two ways. First, brands can be key factors influencing competition in markets. This was illustrated in the MOFCOM's prohibition of *Coca-Cola/Huiyuan*. In that case, the proposed acquisition would have resulted in Coca-Cola controlling two well-known fruit juice brands (Huiyuan and Coca-Cola's Minute Maid) in China. The MOFCOM stated that, in the beverage market, brands are key factors influencing competition because they signal quality, price and trustworthiness; customers are loyal to brands; and brands are a barrier to entry. As Coca-Cola would be controlling two of the most important fruit juice brands in China, the MOFCOM determined that Coca-Cola's control over the fruit juice market would be enhanced by the proposed acquisition, which would in turn significantly increase barriers to entry to the fruit juice market.[101]

---

[98] 关于禁止滥用知识产权排除，限制竞争行为的规定 [Regulation on the Prohibition of Abuse of Intellectual Property Rights to Eliminate or Restrict Competition] (People's Republic of China) State Administration for Industry and Commerce, Order No. 74, 7 April 2015.

[99] 'Drafting Work Begins on Drafting Auto Industry Antitrust Guidelines, Preliminary Draft in One Year', *Economic Information Daily*, 18 June 2015, available at http://news.xinhuanet.com/finance/2015-06/18/c_127928081.htm.

[100] Susan Ning et al., 'NDRC's Enforcement in 2016' [2017] (3) *CPI Antitrust Chronicle* 1 at 9.

[101] 关于禁止可口可乐公司收购中国汇源公司审查决定的公告 [Announcement of the Review Decision to Prohibit Coca-Cola's Acquisition of Huiyuan] (People's Republic of China) Ministry of Commerce, Order No. 22, 18 March 2009; 商务部就可口可乐收购汇源反垄断审查决定答问 [MOFCOM Q&A on Anti-monopoly Review Decision of

Second, according to some interviewees, the MOFCOM considers a merger's impact on the future development and continuing viability of a brand when reviewing acquisitions of Chinese brands by foreign companies.[102] This observation is consistent with the MOFCOM's unconditional approvals of *Nestlé/Yinlu*, *Nestlé/Hsu Fu Chi*, *Yum! Brands/Little Sheep* and *Diageo/Shui Jing Fang*, where the acquiring parties' commitment to brand development was likely a key factor in securing the MOFCOM's unconditional approval. Nestlé made public commitments to develop the local brands it acquired in *Nestlé/Yinlu* and *Nestlé/Hsu Fu Chi*,[103] and its commitment to develop the Yinlu brand and business model was key to the MOFCOM's decision to unconditionally approve *Nestlé/Yinlu*.[104] Similarly, Yum! Brands publicly committed to building and developing the Little Sheep brand and business model when it announced the MOFCOM's approval.[105] Diageo's ability to expand and promote the Shui Jing Fang brand overseas seemed relevant in *Diageo/Shui Jing Fang*.[106] After the acquisition, Diageo upgraded Shui Jing Fang's production facilities, developed new products and expanded the marketing of Shui Jing Fang outside of

---

Coca-Cola's Acquisition of Huiyuan] (24 March 2009) available at www.gov.cn/gzdt/2009-03/24/content_1267595.htm.

[102] Interviews with Chinese competition law experts and stakeholders. See also David Stallibrass and Jenny Xiaojin Huang, 'Brands, Consumer Protection, and Antitrust – Why China is Special' [2012] (2) *CPI Antitrust Chronicle* 1 at 3–4.

[103] Nestlé SA, 'Nestlé to Enter Partnership with Chinese Food Company Yinlu' (Press Release, 18 April 2011) available at www.nestle.com.au/media/pressreleases/nestletoenterpartnershipwithchinesefoodcompanyyinlu; Nestlé SA, 'Nestlé to Enter Partnership with Chinese Confectionery Company Hsu Fu Chi' (Press Release, 11 July 2011) available at www.nestle.com/media/pressreleases/allpressreleases/nestle-to-enter-partnership-with-chinese-confectionery-company-hsu-fu-chi.

[104] 沈丹阳 [Shen Danyang], 商务部召开例行新闻发布会 (2011年9月20日) [Regular Press Conference of the Ministry of Commerce (20 September 2011)] Ministry of Commerce, 20 September 2011, available at www.mofcom.gov.cn/article/ae/ah/diaocd/201109/20110907748307.shtml.

[105] Yum! Brands Inc., 'Proposed Privatization of Little Sheep at HK$6.50 Per Scheme Share' (Press Release, 13 May 2011) available at www.yum.com/press-releases/proposed-privatization-of-little-sheep-at-hk6-50-per-scheme-share; Yum! Brands Inc., 'China's Ministry of Commerce Approves Yum! Brands Proposal to Acquire China's Little Sheep Restaurants' (Press Release, 7 November 2011) available at www.yum.com/press-releases/chinas-ministry-of-commerce-approves-yum-brands-proposal-to-acquire-chinas-little-sheep-restaurants.

[106] Deng Fei and Gregory K. Leonard, 'The Role of China's Unique Economic Characteristics in Antitrust Enforcement' in Adrian Emch and David Stallibrass (eds.), *China's Anti-monopoly Law: The First Five Years* (Alphen aan den Rijn, The Netherlands: Kluwer Law International, 2013), p. 73.

China; reportedly, these were commitments made by Diageo to the Chinese government at the time of the acquisition.[107]

Deng and Fei note that the concern to ensure the continued development of Chinese brands in merger analysis is consistent with the emphasis on brand creation and development in industrial policy.[108] As noted above, the Chinese government wishes to move China from traditional, low-tech and low value-added activities into more innovative, knowledge-intensive, high-tech and high value-added activities. The creation, building and development of Chinese brands is viewed as a way to help Chinese manufacturers accomplish this goal.[109] Brands are also linked to product quality, which the Chinese government aims to improve.[110] Further, the Chinese government encourages leading Chinese manufacturing businesses to undertake foreign investment to create famous brands.[111] Fostering the emergence of a number of internationally renowned brands by 2013 was also a past strategic objective of China's intellectual property policy.[112]

### 6.3.2 Regulatory Policy

A number of published decisions relate to mergers in regulated industries such as agriculture,[113] food and beverage,[114] information and communications technology,[115] and health (including pharmaceuticals and life

---

[107] James Quinn, 'Diageo's Paul Walsh Cracks China', The Telegraph, 24 March 2013, available at www.telegraph.co.uk/finance/newsbysector/retailandconsumer/9950082/Diageos-Paul-Walsh-cracks-China.html.
[108] Deng and Leonard, 'The Role of China's Unique Economic Characteristics in Antitrust Enforcement', p. 71.
[109] Outline of the 12th Five-Year Plan for National Economic and Social Development, pt. III ch. 9 s. 4.
[110] Outline of the 13th Five-Year Plan for National Economic and Social Development, pt. V s. 4.
[111] Outline of the 12th Five-Year Plan for National Economic and Social Development, pt. XII ch. 52 s. 2.
[112] 国家知识产权战略纲要 [State Intellectual Property Strategic Guideline] (People's Republic of China) State Council, Notice No. 18, 5 June 2008, art. 2(2)(7).
[113] Uralkali/Silvinit; Marubeni/Gavilon.
[114] InBev/Anheuser-Busch; Coca-Cola/Huiyuan; Marubeni/Gavilon; Anheuser-Busch InBev/SABMiller.
[115] Seagate/Samsung; Western Digital/Hitachi; Google/Motorola Mobility; Wal-Mart/Newheight; ARM Joint Venture; MediaTek/MStar; Microsoft/Nokia; Nokia/Alcatel-Lucent; NXP/Freescale.

sciences).[116] As discussed in Section 6.2.2.1, industry regulators are typically consulted on mergers in industries or in relation to activities that fall within their regulatory scope; thus sector-specific concerns and policies might enter into merger review and be reflected in the outcomes of these cases.[117]

The *Wal-Mart/Newheight* acquisition, in particular, is an example of AML enforcement reinforcing sector-specific policies.[118] The conditions imposed by the MOFCOM on that acquisition prevented the merging parties from circumventing the MIIT's e-commerce policies. The acquisition, which occurred in 2012, would have allowed Wal-Mart to indirectly control one of Newheight's subsidiaries, Yishiduo, which operated what was then China's largest online supermarket. Yishiduo's business included direct sales of its own goods online and providing business-to-consumer e-commerce platform services to third parties; the latter was classified as a value-added telecommunications service (VATS) business under the telecommunications regulations that are administered by the MIIT.[119] However, at the time that the merger was being reviewed, Wal-Mart's control of Yishiduo's VATS business was not permitted under telecommunications regulations. According to these regulations, foreign investors could only engage in a VATS business through a joint venture with a Chinese partner where the level of foreign investment did not exceed 50 per cent,[120] and VATS business

---

[116] *Pfizer/Wyeth*; *Novartis/Alcon*; *Baxter/Gambro*; *Thermo Fisher/Life*; *Abbott Laboratories/ St Jude Medical*.

[117] Interviews with Chinese competition law experts and stakeholders.

[118] Zhuowei Li and Ying Zhou, 'MOFCOM's Wal-Mart Decision and its Wider Implications' [2013] (2) *CPI Antitrust Chronicle* 1 at 7–8; 符迎曦, 史怀特 [Yingxi Fu-Tomlinson and Steven R. Wright], 商务部附条件批准沃尔玛收购案—它对沃尔玛、1号店以及VIE结构的未来意味着什么? [MOFCOM's Conditional Approval of Wal-Mart's Acquisition – What Does It Mean for Wal-Mart and Yihaodian and for the Future of the VIE Structure?] (2012) 64 中国法律透视 [China Legal Review], available at http://hk.lexiscnweb.com/clr/view_article.php?clr_id=70&clr_article_id=888#eng.

[119] 电信业务分类目录 (2003 版) [Telecommunications Services Classification Catalogue (2003 Version)] (People's Republic of China) Ministry of Industry and Information Technology, 1 April 2003, art. 2(5).

[120] 外商投资电信企业管理规定 [Provision on the Administration of Foreign-Invested Telecommunications Enterprises] (People's Republic of China) State Council, Order No. 333, 11 December 2001, amended by 国务院关于修改《外商投资电信企业管理规定》的决定 [State Council Decision on Revising the 'Provision on the Administration of Foreign-Invested Telecommunications Enterprises'] (People's Republic of China) State Council, Order No. 534, 10 September 2008, art. 6.

operators required a licence issued by the MIIT.[121] Consistent with these regulations, the conditions that the MOFCOM imposed on the acquisition carved out Newheight's VATS business from Wal-Mart's acquisition, and prohibited Newheight from engaging in a VATS business without first obtaining a VATS licence.[122] Some interviewees believe that these restrictive conditions were heavily driven by the MIIT's policy concerns.[123]

Further, the MOFCOM's decision to grant Wal-Mart's application for release from these conditions reflects the change in the MIIT's policy towards foreign investment in e-commerce. In June 2015, the MIIT issued a new circular that removed the restriction on foreign investment in e-commerce businesses; foreign investors are now allowed to own up to 100 per cent of a company operating an e-commerce business.[124] A month after the change came into effect, Wal-Mart applied to the MOFCOM for release from the conditions in *Wal-Mart/Newheight*. In its decision to grant Wal-Mart's application, the MOFCOM stated that the market competition conditions had substantially changed, and one reason was the adoption of the new MIIT circular, which decreased barriers to entry into the VATS market.[125]

Other examples include the NDRC's and the SAIC's actions in the salt and pharmaceutical industries, which are consistent with and facilitate reforms in those industries to, *inter alia*, liberalise prices and enable them to be determined according to market mechanisms.

---

[121] 中华人民共和国电信条例 [Telecommunications Regulation of the People's Republic of China] (People's Republic of China) State Council, Order No. 291, 25 September 2000, ch. 2.

[122] 关于附加限制性条件批准沃尔玛公司收购纽海控股33.6%股权经营者集中反垄断审查决定的公告 [Announcement of the Anti-monopoly Review of Concentrations of Business Operators Decision to Impose Restrictive Conditions to the Approval of Wal-Mart's Acquisition of 33.6 Per cent Equity Interest in Newheight (Shanghai)] (People's Republic of China) Ministry of Commerce, Order No. 49, 13 August 2012 (*Wal-Mart/Newheight*).

[123] Interviews with Chinese competition law experts and stakeholders.

[124] 关于放开在线数据处理与交易处理业务(经营类电子商务)外资股比限制的通告 [Circular on Removing Restrictions on Foreign-Owned Equity Interests in Online Data Processing and Transaction Processing Services (Operating E-commerce Business)] (People's Republic of China) Ministry for Industry and Information Technology, Order No. 196, 19 June 2015.

[125] 关于解除沃尔玛收购纽海控股33.6%股权经营者集中限制性条件的公告 [Announcement of the Release of Restrictive Conditions Imposed to Wal-Mart's Acquisition of 33.6 Per cent Equity Interest in Newheight (Shanghai)] (People's Republic of China) Ministry of Commerce, Order No. 23, 30 May 2016.

In May 2016, the State Council formally announced reforms to the salt industry, which took effect on 1 January 2017.[126] Table salt has been subject to a government monopoly in China for more than 2,600 years, and reform discussions have been ongoing since about 2001.[127] Prior to these reforms, the China National Salt Industry Corp, a central SOE, and its local branches set salt production levels and prices, restricted distribution channels (it was the only wholesaler of table salt, sales occurred within exclusive territories and cross-territory sales were not allowed) and issued licenses.[128] As of 1 January 2017, salt businesses set their own prices and decided their own sales regions and distribution channels.[129] The NDRC's and the SAIC's abuse of dominance investigations in the salt industry, which relate to tying[130] and discriminatory treatment,[131] appear to be part of the broader conversation about reforms to break up the state's salt monopoly and to introduce market mechanisms into the industry.

Similarly, AML enforcement actions taken in the pharmaceutical industry form part of wider reforms within the industry. From 1 June 2015, government price controls on drugs, which had set maximum prices and profit margins, were removed (except for anaesthetics and grade-one psychiatric medications) and most drug prices are now determined by market mechanisms.[132] However, there were concerns that

---

[126] 盐业体制改革方案 [Salt Industry System Reform Plan] (People's Republic of China) State Council, Order No. 25, 22 April 2016.
[127] 盐业改革方案获发改委通过 2016年将废止盐业专营 [Salt Industry Reform Plan Approved by NDRC, Salt Industry Franchise Abolished in 2016], 证券日报 [Securities Daily], 30 October 2014, available at http://finance.people.com.cn/n/2014/1030/c1004-25934904.html.
[128] See generally Wan Zhe, 'End of Salt Monopoly Opportunity for Private Firms', *Global Times*, 5 January 2017, available at www.globaltimes.cn/content/1027370.shtml; Adrian Emch, 'Taking It With a Grain of Salt – China's Commitment to Breaking Up Monopolies', Kluwer Competition Law Blog, 30 May 2016, available at http://kluwercompetitionlawblog.com/2016/05/30/taking-grain-salt-chinas-commitment-breaking-monopolies; Zi Yang, 'Why China Decided to Abolish its State Salt Monopoly', *The Diplomat*, 12 November 2014, available at http://thediplomat.com/2014/11/why-china-decided-to-abolish-its-state-salt-monopoly.
[129] Salt Industry System Reform Plan.
[130] *Wuchang Salt Tying*; *Jiangsu Salt Tying*; *Yongzhou Salt Tying*.
[131] *Chifeng Salt Differential Treatment*.
[132] 推进药品价格改革意见 [Opinion on Promoting Drug Price Reform] (People's Republic of China) National Development and Reform Commission, National Health and Family Planning Commission, Ministry of Human Resources and Social Security, Ministry of Industry and Information Technology, Ministry of Finance, Ministry of Commerce, and China Food and Drug Administration, Order No. 904, 4 May 2015.

drug prices would increase with the removal of the price and profit margin caps.[133] To address these concerns, when the pricing reform was announced, the NDRC also ordered its local authorities to conduct a six-month inspection campaign to ensure that drug producers, medical organisations, disease prevention and control centres, blood banks and centralised drug procurement platforms did not take advantage of the reforms and engage in collusion, fix prices or charge unfairly high prices, all of which are prohibited under the AML.[134] A similar follow-up campaign ran from May 2016 to November 2016, this time also specifically targeting active pharmaceutical ingredients producers and industry associations that organise the making and/or implementation of monopoly agreements.[135] A new round of drug pricing reforms was initiated in July 2016, which are planned to remove hospital drug price mark-ups by 2020, as part of reforms to improve the public healthcare system.[136]

The SAIC's and the NDRC's AML investigations in the pharmaceutical industry fit within and support this change in regulatory policy. Since at least 2013, the pharmaceutical industry has been a stated AML enforcement priority for both competition authorities.[137] The NDRC has taken a variety of AML actions in the pharmaceutical industry, most of which were published after the drug pricing reform was announced in May 2015 and resulted from its inspection campaign. It investigated

---

[133] Yin Pumin, 'Medicine Price Reforms', *Beijing Review*, 23 June 2015, available at www.bjreview.com.cn/nation/txt/2015-06/23/content_693280.htm.
[134] 关于加强药品市场价格行为监管的通知 [Notice on Strengthening Supervision of Market Prices of Drugs] (People's Republic of China) National Development and Reform Commission, Order No. 930, 4 May 2015.
[135] 关于在全国开展药品价格专项检查的通知 [Notice on Carrying Out National Drug Price Inspections] (People's Republic of China) National Development and Reform Commission, Order No. 1101, 22 May 2016.
[136] 推进医疗服务价格改革的意见 [Opinion on Promoting Medical Service Price Reform] (People's Republic of China) National Development and Reform Commission, National Health and Family Planning Commission, Ministry of Human Resources and Social Security, and Ministry of Finance, Order No. 1431, 1 July 2016.
[137] 王晔君 [Wang Yejun], 航空汽车电信医药纳入发改委反垄断视野 [Aviation, Auto, Telecommunications and Pharmaceuticals Included Within NDRC's Anti-monopoly Field of Vision], 北京商报 [Beijing Business Today], 25 November 2013, available at http://finance.eastmoney.com/news/1355,20131125340227256.html; 张晓松 [Zhang Xiaosong], 工商总局确定2014年市场监管重点 力促公平竞争 [SAIC Determines the Focus of Market Regulation in 2014, Promotes Fair Competition], Xinhua, 26 December 2013, available at www.gov.cn/zhuanti/2013-12/26/content_2594573.htm; 'Key Points of NDRC Bureau of Price Supervision and Anti-monopoly's Work in 2016', 5.

abuse of dominance conduct relating to reserprine active pharmaceutical ingredients,[138] cartels relating to allopurinol tablets and estazolam active pharmaceutical ingredients and tablets,[139] and abuse of administrative power in drug procurement by hospitals and other public health institutions.[140] The SAIC's local authority in Chongqing also investigated and sanctioned companies for refusing to supply allopurinol active pharmaceutical ingredients and phenol active pharmaceutical ingredients.[141] The increased scrutiny of conduct in the pharmaceutical industry is consistent with the Chinese government's intention to strengthen its supervisory role and prevent drug price increases in the aftermath of government price controls being lifted.

### 6.3.3 Foreign Investment Policy

As noted in Section 6.2.2.1, foreign investment government departments at the central and local levels may be consulted during the merger review process. Concerns relating to foreign investment might therefore enter the merger review process.

One of China's main foreign investment policy instruments is the Foreign Investment Industry Guidance Catalogue (Foreign Investment Catalogue).[142] It classifies foreign investment into certain industries, sectors and activities as 'encouraged', 'restricted' or 'forbidden', with those industries, sectors and activities not expressly included in the catalogue therefore being 'permitted'.[143] Since 2000, foreign investors

---

[138] *Shandong Reserprine Exclusive Agreements.* This case was published in 2011.
[139] *Allopurinol Tablet Cartel; Estazolam Tablet Cartel.* Both cases were published in 2016.
[140] *Bengbu Health and Planning Commission Drug Procurement Administrative Monopoly; Sichuan and Zhejiang Health and Planning Commissions Drug Procurement Administrative Monopoly.* Both cases were published in 2015.
[141] *Chongqing Qingyang Pharmaceutical Refusal to Supply; Chongqing Southwest Pharmaceutical Refusal to Supply.*
[142] The latest version was issued in 2015: 外商投资产业指导目录 (2015 年修订) [Foreign Investment Industry Guidance Catalogue (2015 Revised Edition)] (People's Republic of China) National Reform and Development Commission and the Ministry of Commerce, Order No. 22, 10 March 2015.
[143] Ibid. Under revisions to the foreign investment regime adopted in October 2016, foreign investment will need to go through an online filing procedure with the MOFCOM, unless, *inter alia*, that foreign investment occurs in the restricted or prohibited category; in that case, such investment will require approval by the MOFCOM: 全国人民代表大会常务委员会关于修改《中华人民共和国外资企业法》等四部法律的决定 [Decision to Revise Four Laws Including the Law of the People's Republic of China on Wholly Foreign-Owned Enterprises] (People's Republic of China) Standing Committee of the

have used variable interest entities (VIEs) to bypass China's foreign investment restrictions and invest in restricted sectors.[144] This structure typically involves an offshore company that owns a wholly foreign-owned entity in China. That wholly foreign-owned entity, through a series of contractual arrangements, has *de facto* control over a wholly Chinese-owned company which holds the licence or approval required to conduct the restricted activity. However, the legality and enforceability of VIEs is unclear, and the business community generally assumes that the Chinese government tolerates their use.[145] This position may be changing, however, as some central government authorities have issued notices and regulations which suggest that the Chinese government's tacit non-objection to the use of VIEs by foreign investors is under review.[146]

The MOFCOM's decision in *Wal-Mart/Newheight* is part of the Chinese government's evolving attitude towards VIEs. As discussed in Section 6.3.2, part of Wal-Mart's acquisition of Newheight involved the VATS business that Yishiduo operated. Newheight's ownership of Yishiduo was through a VIE structure, as foreign investment in telecommunications companies operating a VATS business was restricted and could not exceed 50 per cent under the Foreign Investment Catalogue in operation at that time.[147] The acquisition would have allowed Wal-Mart to indirectly control Yishiduo's VATS business via the VIE structure. However, the MOFCOM, as part of its conditional approval, prevented Wal-Mart from using the VIE structure to engage in the VATS businesses operated by Yishiduo.[148] By acknowledging and disallowing the use of a VIE in *Wal-Mart/Newheight*, this decision supports the overall message that the Chinese government is sending to foreign investors

National People's Congress, 3 September 2016; 国家发展改革委 商务部公告2016年第22号 [NDRC and MOFCOM Order No. 22, 2016] (People's Republic of China) National Development and Reform Commission and Ministry of Commerce, Order No. 22, 8 October 2016.

[144] Li and Zhou, 'MOFCOM's Wal-Mart Decision and Its Wider Implications', 2–3; Zeng Xianwu and Bai Lihui, 'Variable Interest Entity Structure in China', King & Wood Mallesons, 9 February 2012, available at www.chinalawinsight.com/2012/02/articles/corporate/foreign-investment/variable-interest-entity-structure-in-china.

[145] Shen Wei, 'Will the Door Open Wider in the Aftermath of Alibaba? Placing (or Misplacing) Foreign Investment in a Chinese Public Law Frame' (2012) 42 *Hong Kong Law Journal* 561 at 570.

[146] Ibid., 571–9; Zeng and Bai, 'Variable Interest Entity Structure in China'.

[147] 外商投资产业指导目录 (2011年修订) [Foreign Investment Industry Guidance Catalogue (2011 Revised Edition)] (People's Republic of China) National Reform and Development Commission and the Ministry of Commerce, Order No. 12, 24 December 2011.

[148] *Wal-Mart/Newheight*.

about the use of VIE structures to circumvent foreign investment restrictions, which is that its long assumed tolerance for such arrangements is under reconsideration.[149] Indeed, just a couple of months after the *Wal-Mart/Newheight* decision, the SPC handed down a decision that invalidated the contractual arrangements underlying a VIE structure which had enabled a foreign company to invest in a Chinese financial institution.[150] Further, the draft Foreign Investment Law released by the MOFCOM for public comment in January 2015 rendered ineffective the use of VIEs to avoid foreign investment restrictions.[151] Although this draft was not ultimately enacted and the foreign investment revisions adopted in October 2016 do not really address foreign investment through VIEs, it demonstrates the Chinese government's awareness of the operation and use of VIEs, and that this remains under scrutiny.

The MOFCOM's decision to release Wal-Mart from the conditions in *Wal-Mart/Newheight* reflects changes to foreign investment policy regarding e-commerce. Under the March 2015 revisions to the Foreign Investment Catalogue, while foreign investment in telecommunications companies engaging in VATS business is still restricted to a maximum of 50 per cent, there is an express carve-out for e-commerce.[152] This revision is consistent with changes adopted by the MIIT in the sector (discussed in Section 6.3.2), and means that foreigners wishing to invest more than 50 per cent in an e-commerce business can do so directly, rather than through a VIE. Hence there is no longer a need for the MOFCOM to prevent Wal-Mart from engaging in the e-commerce business operated by Yishiduo.

### 6.3.4 People's Wellbeing and Livelihood

The Chinese government expressly relates competition law and policy to the improvement of people's wellbeing and livelihood. The SAIC has

---

[149] Li and Zhou, 'MOFCOM's Wal-Mart Decision and Its Wider Implications', 7–8; Neil Gough, 'In China, Concern About a Chill on Foreign Investments', *New York Times*, 2 June 2013, available at http://dealbook.nytimes.com/2013/06/02/in-china-concern-of-a-chill-on-foreign-investments.
[150] Gough, 'In China, Concern About a Chill on Foreign Investments'.
[151] 中华人民共和国外国投资法 (草案征求意见稿) [Foreign Investment Law of the People's Republic of China (Consultation Draft)] (People's Republic of China) Ministry of Commerce, 19 January 2015. For a discussion, see, e.g., 'Draft New Foreign Investment Law', Freshfields Bruckhaus Deringer, 26 January 2015, available at http://knowledge.freshfields.com/en/global/r/1159/draft_new_foreign_investment_law.
[152] Foreign Investment Industry Guidance Catalogue (2015 Revised Edition).

stated that its AML enforcement efforts are focused on industries related to the people's livelihood, especially industries concerning consumer goods and public utilities.[153] Similarly, the NDRC has stated that its enforcement actions are aimed at industries related to people's well-being.[154] It has also stated that its enforcement aims are to, *inter alia*, stabilise the market, protect the people's livelihood and maintain social harmony and stability.[155] This is consistent with one of the Chinese government's top priorities, which is the maintenance of social stability.

To date, many non-merger cases have been taken in sectors relating to essential goods and services such as food and beverages,[156] public utilities (water, gas and power),[157] telecommunications,[158] pharmaceuticals and

---

[153] See, e.g., 张晓松 [Zhang Xiaosong], 案件数量逐年递增，民生领域成为重点—工商总局副局长孙鸿志谈反垄断法实施五年案件查办等情况 [Cases Are Increasing Each Year, Emphasis to Be on Sectors Related to the People's Livelihood – SAIC Deputy Director Sun Hongzhi Talks About the Investigation of Cases in the Five Years of Implementing the Anti-monopoly Law], 新华社 [Xinhua News Agency], 29 July 2013, available at www.gov.cn/jrzg/2013-07/29/content_2457600.htm; 2015年全国工商系统消费者权益保护报告 [2015 Report on Consumers' Rights and Interests Protection by the SAIC] 16 March 2016, 中国工商报网 [China Industry & Commerce News] available at www.cicn.com.cn/zggsb/2016-03/16/cms83461article.shtml.

[154] See, e.g., 'NDRC Holds Press Conference on Price Supervision and Anti-monopoly Work', 19 February 2014; 服务群众服务发展 [Serve the Public, Serve Development] (21 April 2015) National Development and Reform Commission, available at www.ndrc.gov.cn/xwzx/xwfb/201504/t20150421_688874.html.

[155] See, e.g., 全国价格监督检查与反垄断工作会议日前召开 [National Price Supervision and Anti-monopoly Work Conference Recently Held] (9 January 2013) National Development and Reform Commission, available at www.sdpc.gov.cn/fzggz/jgjdyfld/jjszhdt/201301/t20130109_522664.html; 江国成 [Jiang Guocheng], 发改委价格监督检查与反垄断局局长谈反价格垄断 [Director-General of the NDRC Price Supervision and Anti-monopoly Bureau Talks About Anti-Price Monopoly], 新华网 [Xinhuanet], 4 August 2013, available at http://finance.qq.com/a/20130804/003640.htm; 王子约, 马晓华 [Wang Ziyue and Ma Xiaohua], 中国掀反垄断风暴 央企无豁免权 [China Whips Up an Anti-monopoly Storm, Central SOEs Are Not Exempt], 第一财经日报 [First Financial Daily], 16 August 2013, available at www.yicai.com/news/2013/08/2942628.html.

[156] See, e.g., *Guangxi Rice Noodle Cartel*; *Wuchang Salt Tying*; *Infant Formula RPM*; *Qinghai Tianlu Dairy RPM*; *Chifeng Salt Differential Treatment*; *Yongzhou Salt Tying*; *Speed Fresh RPM*.

[157] See, e.g., *Taihe Bulk LPG Cartel*; *Yiyuan Purified Water Unreasonable Conditions*; *Chongqing Gas Unreasonable Conditions*; *Hubei Piped Natural Gas Excessive Pricing*; *Hai'an Electric Power Unreasonable Conditions*; *Urumqi Water Exclusive Dealing*; *New Residential Area Electricity Supply Administrative Monopoly*.

[158] *China Telecom/China Unicom Abuse of Dominance*; *InterDigital Abuse of Dominance*; *Qualcomm Abuse of Dominance*; *Ningxia Broadband Internet Tying*; *Yunnan Telecommunications Cartel*; *Yunnan Communications Authority Administrative Monopoly*; *Inner Mongolia Mobile Unreasonable Conditions*; *Inner Mongolia Unicom Tying*.

health[159] and transportation.[160] More recently, the SAIC implemented a national competition law enforcement campaign targeting public enterprises in the water, electricity, gas, public transportation and funeral services industries which ran from April to October 2016,[161] and, as discussed in Section 6.3.2, the NDRC is focusing on pricing conduct in pharmaceuticals and health. The authorities have also conducted several investigations in the construction sector,[162] which is a sector that is also relevant to people's wellbeing and livelihood. In addition to building public infrastructure and services, the construction industry is a large employer, especially of migrant workers, who are typically poor, from rural areas and leave their hometowns to work in other places for most of the year. In 2013, the total number of such migrant workers in China was 166.10 million;[163] it is believed that, generally, one third of migrant workers are employed in the construction industry.[164]

## 6.4 The Relationship between the State and the Market

One of the key economic reform issues to emerge from the Third Plenum is the management of the relationship between the state and the market. That relationship has two important and distinct dimensions, as the state is both a participant and the regulator. In its role as

---

[159] See, e.g., *Shandong Reserprine Exclusive Agreements*; *Bengbu Health and Planning Commission Drug Procurement Administrative Monopoly*; *Chongqing Qingyang Pharmaceutical Refusal to Supply*; *Estazolam Tablet Cartel*; *Medtronic RPM*; *Smith & Nephew RPM*.
[160] See, e.g., *TravelSky Cartel*; *Heyuan GPS Platform Administrative Monopoly*; *Hebei Toll Road Administrative Monopoly*; *Roll On/Roll Off Shipping Cartel*.
[161] 关于公用企业限制竞争和垄断行为突出问题的公告 [Announcement on Prominent Issues Relating to Anti-competitive and Monopolistic Conduct of Public Enterprises] (People's Republic of China) State Administration for Industry and Commerce, Order No. 54, 7 April 2016.
[162] See, e.g., *Lianyungang Ready-Mix Concrete Cartel*; *Guangdong Sea Sand Cartel*; *Jiangshan Commercial Concrete Cartel*; *Yiyuan Purified Water Unreasonable Conditions*; *Hainan Aerated Bricks Cartel*; *Wuxi Quarry Cartel*; *Urumqi Water Exclusive Dealing*; *Beijing Concrete Quality Control Administrative Monopoly*.
[163] 'Statistical Communiqué of the People's Republic of China on the 2013 National Economic and Social Development', National Bureau of Statistics of China, 24 February 2014, available at www.stats.gov.cn/english/PressRelease/201402/t20140224_515103.html.
[164] Sarah Swider, 'Building China: Precarious Employment among Migrant Construction Workers' (2015) 29 *Work, Employment and Society* 41 at 41.

market participant, it acts through SOEs in a variety of sectors; in some sectors, such as those considered key to the national economic lifeline and national security, SOEs are dominant, whereas in others they compete against private businesses, both domestic and foreign. Although the conduct of SOEs is subject to the AML, as discussed in Chapter 3, competition law and policy is but one consideration within the multitude of policy interests relevant to SOEs. As such, the application of the AML to the market activities of SOEs to ensure that they behave in a competitive manner, especially in important and sensitive industries, may be constrained; this will be explored further in Section 6.4.1. In its role as regulator, the state exercises macroeconomic control over the market. This means that the government will, as discussed in Chapter 4, supervise and oversee the market to ensure that market order is maintained, and intervene if necessary to correct market failures. However, the state needs to find a balance between allowing market mechanisms to discipline the market and stepping in to ensure the proper functioning of the market. In particular, through the issuance of regulations, the government itself can impede competition, much like private actors. The use of the AML to assist with finding that balance between state and market regulation will be considered further in Sections 6.4.2 and 6.4.3 below.

### 6.4.1 Enforcement of the Anti-monopoly Law against State-owned Enterprises

Despite initial concerns that SOEs would be exempt from the AML, the Chinese competition agencies have taken a number of investigations and decisions against SOEs under the AML. Nearly all these investigations and decisions have involved SOEs owned and controlled by local governments, although the high-profile *China Telecom/China Unicom Abuse of Dominance* case involved two prominent central SOEs. Investigations have occurred in sectors which are largely dominated by SOEs (such as gas, water, telecommunications, tobacco and salt), and also in competitive industries in which SOEs compete with private enterprises (such as cement, liquor, auto and gold). However, the Chinese competition authorities have faced challenges when seeking to enforce the AML against SOEs, reflecting the complex policy environment and the various vested interests relating to SOEs.

These challenges and dynamics are evident in the way in which some non-merger investigations involving central SOEs were handled and resolved.¹⁶⁵ As discussed in Chapter 3, central SOEs tend to be larger and more powerful SOEs and operate in important and strategic sectors of the economy, where the interests of the SASAC and relevant industry regulators are likely to be implicated. These factors were present in the two publicly known AML cases involving central SOEs (*China Telecom/ China Unicom Abuse of Dominance* and *TravelSky Cartel*, both of which were investigated by the NDRC). Both investigations involved powerful central SOEs and industry regulators who vocally supported the SOEs and opposed the investigations. For example, in *China Telecom/China Unicom Abuse of Dominance*, the MIIT opposed the NDRC's investigation, whereas China Mobile Tietong and the State Administration of Radio, Film, and Television (as it was then known) reportedly supported it.¹⁶⁶ Further, according to the Director-General of the NDRC Bureau, China Telecom and China Unicom did not begin to take the NDRC's investigation seriously or show a real awareness of the AML until after the NDRC announced its investigation on television, even though the investigation had been ongoing since April 2011.¹⁶⁷ In *TravelSky Cartel*, as noted in Section 6.2.2.2, the CAAC denied any wrongdoing on the part of TravelSky and the Chinese SOE airlines being investigated. The involvement of these interests, and the political and economic stature of the investigated parties, is likely to have influenced the handling and result of the investigations. In addition to industry regulators, the NDRC may have faced pressure from other government bodies, highly ranked officials within the NDRC or even the State Council itself to resolve the investigations in a particular way.¹⁶⁸ Further, the SOEs being investigated had a higher bureaucratic rank than the NDRC Bureau, which was running the investigations. China Telecom, China Unicom and some of the investigated SOE airlines are classified as important backbone SOEs, which means they have at least vice-ministerial rank;¹⁶⁹ in contrast, the

---

[165] Xiaoye Wang and Adrian Emch, 'Five Years of Implementation of China's Antimonopoly Law – Achievements and Challenges' (2013) 1 *Journal of Antitrust Enforcement* 247 at 267.
[166] 郎朗 [Lang Lang], 电信联通反垄断调查或搁浅 [China Telecom/China Unicom Antimonopoly Investigated or Stranded], *21st Century Business Herald*, 21 November 2011, available at http://tech.sina.com.cn/t/2011-11-21/23596361616.shtml.
[167] Dan, 'Xu Kunlin'; Zhao and Li, 'Two Media Outlets under the MIIT'.
[168] See, e.g., Wang and Emch, 'Five Years of Implementation of China's Anti-monopoly Law', 267.
[169] "国有重要骨干"有企哪些? [Which Are the "Important Backbone SOEs"?], 新华网 [Xinhuanet], 30 January 2015, available at http://news.xinhuanet.com/video/sjxw/ 2015-01/30/c_127440169.htm.

NDRC Bureau is ranked at (at least) the next level down. This difference in bureaucratic rank would have made it more difficult for the NDRC Bureau to compel cooperation from the SOEs and to resist political pressure, unless more highly ranked officials within the NDRC weighed in. In the end, both *China Telecom/China Unicom Abuse of Dominance* and *TravelSky Cartel* were apparently settled behind the scenes, as no formal decisions or announcements on the outcome were made public.[170] These cases show that even the NDRC, which is one of the most politically powerful agencies in the central government and the most powerful of the three Chinese competition authorities, may face some difficulty when seeking to enforce the AML against large and powerful SOEs.[171]

Non-merger cases involving local SOEs also demonstrate some of these dynamics, providing insight into why it is generally easier to enforce the AML against local SOEs than central SOEs. While most investigations of local SOEs are undertaken by the competition authorities' local offices, in practice, as discussed in Section 6.2.1, they are quite closely supervised by – and have the backing of – the central authority (and in the case of the SAIC, the SAIC Bureau must authorise investigations taken by their local authorities). This helps to overcome issues relating to bureaucratic rank that arise in investigations of central SOEs, as the NDRC Bureau and the SAIC Bureau are likely to have equal or higher bureaucratic ranks than the local SOEs that their local offices are investigating. Also, even though local SOEs can nevertheless be important players in the locality or region and have the support of local government, in most cases the visibility and power of local SOEs is generally less than central SOEs, and local regulators may be less likely to interfere. Zhang notes that most of the cases conducted at the local level tend to involve small rather than large local SOEs.[172]

As a result, enforcement action is taken more frequently against local SOEs than central SOEs. The SAIC, for example, has published nearly twenty decisions relating to its local offices' investigations into the conduct of local SOEs in the gas, power, water, tobacco and salt industries,

---

[170] Wang and Emch, 'Five Years of Implementation of China's Anti-monopoly Law', 267.
[171] See also Angela Huyue Zhang, 'Antitrust Regulation of Chinese State-owned Enterprises' in Benjamin L. Liebman and Curtis J. Milhaupt (eds.), *Regulating the Visible Hand? The Institutional Implications of Chinese State Capitalism* (New York: Oxford University Press, 2016), pp. 100–3.
[172] Ibid., 105.

among others. The NDRC has also investigated a few local SOEs operating in the salt, liquor, gold, telecommunications, gas and auto industries. There also seems to be a higher degree of transparency when local SOEs, rather than central ones, are the targets of investigations. As noted above, the SAIC has published a number of formal decisions relating to enforcement actions taken vis-à-vis local SOEs, and the NDRC has also issued press releases or made other announcements regarding the outcomes of its local SOE investigations. This has been the case even where the investigation was suspended and/or terminated. Local SOEs may be fined, have their illegal gains confiscated or be required to implement corrective measures, which may or may not lead to the suspension and/or termination of the investigation. In contrast, the investigations of *China Telecom/China Unicom Abuse of Dominance* and *TravelSky Cartel* resulted in the acceptance of commitments and settlement. Unfortunately, as the NDRC and the SAIC are not required to publish their decisions, it is difficult to state with certainty that they have not, in fact, investigated a greater number of central and local SOEs than is publicly known.

This does not mean, however, that investigations against local SOEs are without challenges. The actions of local SOEs may be protected by the local government. For example, in the *Shanghai Gold and Platinum Jewellery Cartel*, Zhang points out that the NDRC's Shanghai bureau had been aware of the local SOEs' price fixing arrangement for more than a decade. It had tried to take action under the Price Law in 2001, but the local SOEs' actions were supported by the local government and the Shanghai bureau's actions were rendered ineffective. However, in 2013, the Shanghai bureau was able to successfully investigate and sanction this price fixing arrangement with the support of the NDRC Bureau, which had directed the Shanghai bureau to initiate the AML investigation.[173] Further, most of the investigations that have been suspended and/or terminated have involved local SOEs rather than private companies.[174]

---

[173] Angela Huyue Zhang, 'Taming the Chinese Leviathan: Is Antitrust Regulation a False Hope?' (2015) 51 *Stanford Journal of International Law* 195 at 223–5. See 上海黄金饰品行业协会及部分金店实施价格垄断被依法查处 [Price Monopoly Agreement Implemented by the Shanghai Gold Jewellery Industry Association and Some Jewellery Stores Investigated According to Law] (News Release, 13 August 2013).

[174] See, e.g., *Wuchang Salt Tying*; *Ningxia Broadband Internet Tying*; *Inner Mongolia Mobile Unreasonable Conditions*; *Inner Mongolia Unicom Tying*; *Hai'an Electric Power Unreasonable Conditions*.

This suggests that, in some cases involving local SOEs, the local competition authority may nonetheless face constraints which make seeking corrective measures, rather than imposing fines or other sanctions, a more realistic outcome of the investigation.

The MOFCOM also seems to have encountered challenges in merger enforcement involving SOEs, as merger enforcement activity involving SOEs appears to be disproportionately low. Mergers involving SOEs constitute only a small proportion of the total number of mergers reviewed by the MOFCOM.[175] However, SOEs have been active in mergers since the AML came into effect in August 2008. For example, in 2012, SOEs accounted for 86 per cent of the 1,111 reported mergers of the top 500 enterprises in China.[176] The Chinese government has also been restructuring and consolidating central SOEs to reduce their number to fewer than 100 and to create 30–50 internationally competitive, large SOEs.[177] To this end, from 1 August 2008 to 31 December 2016, the number of SASAC-owned central SOEs was reduced from 149 to 102 through mergers, acquisitions and other restructuring activities.[178] As merger notification thresholds in China are relatively low, a number of mergers involving SOEs, especially those involving central SOEs, are likely to have reached the notification thresholds.[179] However, only nine of the mergers involving central

---

[175] According to Sobel, during the period 1 August 2008 to 31 December 2015, at least 77 of the 151 purely domestic mergers notified for anti-monopoly review involved at least one party that was an SOE, which represents just over 6 per cent of the total number of mergers approved during that period: Yuni Yan Sobel, 'Domestic-to-Domestic Transactions – A Gap in China's Merger Control Regime?' [2014] (February) *The Antitrust Source* 1 at 4, available at www.americanbar.org/content/dam/aba/publishing/antitrust_source/feb14_sobel_2_20f.pdf; Yuni Yan Sobel, 'Domestic-to-Domestic Transactions (2014–2015) – A Narrowing Gap in China's Merger Control Regime' [2016] (February) *The Antitrust Source* 1 at 4, available at www.americanbar.org/content/dam/aba/publishing/antitrust_source/feb16_sobel_2_12f.authcheckdam.pdf.

[176] Wei Tan, 'SOEs and Competition', *CPI Asia Column*, 23 October 2012, available at www.competitionpolicyinternational.com/assets/Columns/cpi-asia-antitrust-column-tan FINAL.pdf.

[177] 'Mergers Reduce China's Central SOEs to 123', Xinhua, 5 August 2010, available at www.chinadaily.com.cn/bizchina/2010-08/06/content_11107199.htm.

[178] 中央变更 [Central SOE Changes], State-owned Assets Supervision and Administration Commission, available at www.sasac.gov.cn/n2588035/n2641579/n2641660/index.html; 央企名录 [Central SOE Directory], State-owned Assets Supervision and Administration Commission of the State Council, available at www.sasac.gov.cn/n2588035/n2641579/n2641645/index.html.

[179] Sobel, 'Domestic-to-Domestic Transactions – A Gap in China's Merger Control Regime?,' 5–6.

SOEs have been notified to the MOFCOM for anti-monopoly review.[180] Therefore, the MOFCOM's merger enforcement statistics do not appear to reflect the actual level of SOE-related merger activity.

According to interviewees, one explanation for this disparity is that SOEs prefer not to, and generally do not, notify their mergers to the MOFCOM for anti-monopoly review.[181] As discussed in Chapter 3, the level of knowledge and awareness of the AML at SOEs tends to be relatively limited, although it is improving. In relation to mergers, SOEs tend to believe that the notification requirements do not apply to them, that the MOFCOM's anti-monopoly approval is unnecessary because they already have the approval of other government departments to undertake their merger and/or that the risk of investigation by the MOFCOM for failing to file is low.[182] Interviewees also comment that, if a SOE does notify a merger, it is usually because a foreign joint venture partner insists upon making the notification.[183]

This situation is getting better, however, in part because the MOFCOM is taking enforcement action against companies for non-compliance with the AML notification requirements. As noted in Chapter 2, the MOFCOM has the power to investigate, fine or order parties, including SOEs, to undertake certain measures if their merger reaches the notification thresholds but is not notified to the MOFCOM for AML review.[184] To date, the MOFCOM has published nine administrative penalty decisions in which merging parties were fined for not notifying their merger for

---

[180] *General Electric/Shenhua; Anshan Iron and Steel/Panzhihua Iron and Steel; China Power Investment/State Nuclear Power Technology; China North Locomotive & Rolling Stock/China South Locomotive & Rolling Stock; China Minmetals/China Metallurgical; Baosteel/Wuhan Iron and Steel; China National Travel Service/CITS; China National Building Materials/Sinoma; COFCO/Chinatex.*

[181] Interviews with Chinese competition law experts and stakeholders. See also Sokol, 'Merger Control under China's Anti-monopoly Law', 21–2.

[182] Interviews with Chinese competition law experts and stakeholders. See also 王华强 [Wang Biqiang], 国资委人士称央企重组不需商务部反垄断审查 [SASAC Official Says MOFCOM Anti-monopoly Review Not Required in Central SOE Restructuring], 经济观察网 [Economic Observer Online], 2 August 2008, available at http://finance.sina.com.cn/roll/20080802/09455160451.shtml; Sokol, 'Merger Control under China's Anti-monopoly Law', 22.

[183] Interviews with Chinese competition law experts and stakeholders; Sokol, 'Merger Control under China's Anti-monopoly Law', 22.

[184] 未依法申报经营者集中调查处理暂行办法 [Interim Measure for Investigating and Handling Concentrations of Business Operators Not Notified in Accordance with the Law] (People's Republic of China) Ministry of Commerce, Order No. 6, 30 December 2011.

AML review, although reportedly the MOFCOM has investigated more than fifty such cases and imposed penalties on a number of those companies.[185] Notably, of the nine published decisions, five relate to mergers involving SOEs, which include local SOEs[186] and subsidiaries of central SOEs.[187] These enforcement actions appear to have increased Chinese companies' awareness of the notification requirements, including that of SOEs, which is resulting in more SOE-related mergers being notified to the MOFCOM for review.[188]

Nevertheless, the MOFCOM may still face challenges investigating and sanctioning SOEs for not complying with AML notification requirements, which are not dissimilar to those faced by the NDRC and the SAIC in their actions involving SOEs. First, there is a lack of resources at the MOFCOM to deal with AML-related matters. As noted in Chapter 4, AML-related work performed by the MOFCOM is centralised at the MOFCOM Bureau, which is staffed by about thirty officials. Their workload is heavy, as the notification thresholds are relatively low, which results in a large number of transactions being filed for review. The MOFCOM Bureau might not have sufficient resources to devote to discovering and investigating SOEs for failing to notify their mergers. In the MOFCOM's publicly known investigations of non-compliance with notification requirements to date, it has become aware of non-notified mergers because merging parties have subsequently voluntarily notified it of their merger,[189] during review of the merging parties' later and related merger,[190] or as a result of third party complaints.[191]

Second, it may be difficult for the MOFCOM to penalise an SOE for implementing a merger that has already been approved by another

---

[185] American Bar Association Section of International Law, 'Seven Years in Beijing: China's Merger Reviews under the Anti-monopoly Law' (Teleconference, 23 September 2015); 'China's Anti-monopoly Law: The Story So Far – And What's Next?' (Freshfields Bruckhaus Deringer, September 2015) available at http://knowledge.freshfields.com/m/Global/r/882/china_s_anti-monopoly_law_-_the_story_so_far___and_what_s.
[186] *Tsinghua Unigroup/RDA Microelectronics*; *BesTV/Microsoft*; *Fujian Electronics/Shenzhen Zhongnuo*.
[187] *CSR Nanjing Puzhen/Bombardier Transportation*; *Beijing CNR/Hitachi*.
[188] Interviews with Chinese competition law experts and stakeholders; Sobel, 'Domestic-to-Domestic Transactions (2014–2015)', 4.
[189] *CSR Nanjing Puzhen/Bombardier Transportation*; *Dade Holdings/Jilin Sichang Pharmaceutical*; *Beijing CNR/Hitachi*.
[190] *Fujian Electronics/Shenzhen Zhongnuo*; *Shanghai Fosun/Suzhou Erye*; *Canon/Toshiba Medical Systems*.
[191] *BesTV/Microsoft*.

government body. The SASAC, other government departments such as industry regulators and even the State Council may have approved mergers involving SOEs. A MOFCOM investigation into an SOE for failing to notify a merger might be perceived as an unwelcome intrusion on regulatory turf by industry regulators who, as discussed in Chapter 3, have incentives to protect SOEs within their jurisdiction, or it might be contrary to broader government directives. For example, China Netcom and China Unicom, which are two leading telecommunications central SOEs, merged in October 2008.[192] According to China Unicom, it obtained the relevant government approvals to undertake the merger, including from the China Securities Regulatory Commission, the securities regulator.[193] However, the MOFCOM advised that the merger had not been notified for anti-monopoly review, despite reaching the notification thresholds, and it indirectly warned China Unicom that its merger with China Netcom had violated the AML.[194] Despite this, the MOFCOM did not subsequently investigate or sanction China Unicom for non-compliance with the AML. It may have been politically difficult for the MOFCOM to take such action, as the merger had been approved by the State Council and completed pursuant to a restructuring of the telecommunications industry undertaken by the MIIT, the NDRC and the Ministry of Finance.[195]

---

[192] 王毕强 [Wang Biqiang], 联通网通合并涉嫌违法 [China Unicom/China Netcom Merger Suspected Illegal], 经济观察网 [Economic Observer Online], 30 April 2009, available at www.eeo.com.cn/industry/it_telecomm/2009/05/01/136645.shtml; Xiaoye Wang and Jessica Su, 'China's Anti-monopoly Law: Agent of Competition Enhancement or Engine of Industrial Policy?' in Daniel Zimmer (ed.), *The Goals of Competition Law* (Cheltenham, UK: Edward Elgar, 2012), pp. 391–3.

[193] 灵戈 [Ling Ge], 联通网通合并案涉嫌违法? 追究责任要全面彻底 [China Unicom/China Netcom Merger Suspected Illegal? Quest for Accountability Must Be Complete and Thoroughly], 人民网 [*People's Daily* Online], 4 May 2009, available at http://it.people.com.cn/GB/42891/42895/9232735.html.

[194] 姜伯静 [Jiang Bojing], 商务部警示联通网通合并涉嫌违法凸显中国法制进步 [MOFCOM Warns China Unicom/China Netcom Merger Might Be Illegal, Highlights Progress in China's Legal System], 人民网 [*People's Daily* Online], 4 May 2009, available at http://it.people.com.cn/GB/42891/42895/9229575.html.

[195] 中国联通与中国网通重组 国资委监管企业调整为141户 [China Unicom and China Netcom Reorganises, SASAC Supervised Businesses Adjusts to 141 Units] (7 January 2009) State-owned Assets Supervision and Administration Commission, available at www.sasac.gov.cn/n2588035/n2641579/n2641660/c3753973/content.html; China Unicom, 'The Red Chip Companies of China Unicom and China Netcom Are Successfully Merged and China Unicom Telecommunications Corporation Limited Is Established in Beijing' (News Release, 15 October 2008).

Third, like the NDRC Bureau and the SAIC Bureau, the MOFCOM Bureau might be ranked lower than the SOEs that it is seeking to investigate and take enforcement action against. As discussed in Chapter 4, it can be difficult for a lower-ranked entity to compel a higher-ranked authority to cooperate. To overcome these difficulties and thus enforce the AML against SOEs, the MOFCOM Bureau could elevate the issue within the MOFCOM (or perhaps even to the State Council) and seek the assistance of higher-ranked authorities or individuals. However, whether such assistance is forthcoming is likely to be dependent on the priorities of the MOFCOM as a whole, or on those of the wider State Council.

### 6.4.2 Anti-monopoly Law and Macroeconomic Regulation and Control

At the same time as prohibiting anti-competitive conduct and maintaining the market competition order, the Chinese competition authorities have also used the AML to help further the macroeconomic control of the state. Many of the conditions imposed by the MOFCOM in its conditional merger approvals have been regulatory in nature, thus enabling the MOFCOM to monitor the merging parties' conduct over a longer period of time and to intervene where necessary. A number of the NDRC's investigations illustrate that the AML is one of a suite of laws relating to price supervision and regulation. Further, the NDRC seems to be applying the AML to help it transition from relying predominantly on interventionist measures to resolve economic problems, to employing a regulatory approach that embraces more of the government's supervisory role in the economy.

#### 6.4.2.1 Regulatory Nature of Merger Conditions

As examined in Chapter 4, the Chinese government believes that its role in the market is one of oversight, market order maintenance and intervention where necessary to prevent and remedy market failure. This approach to market regulation is reflected in the types of conditions imposed by the MOFCOM in its conditional merger approvals. In addition to resolving concerns about the potential anti-competitive effects arising from a merger, many of the merger conditions are also regulatory in nature. They allow the MOFCOM to monitor the conduct of a merged firm over a long-term period and provide it with grounds to intervene after the completion of the merger, where necessary, to ensure compliance with the conditions. The Chinese government's view of its role in the market also helps to explain why the MOFCOM, unlike the competition agencies in many other jurisdictions, has not expressed a preference for structural over behavioural remedies. Other competition agencies are generally reluctant to monitor and supervise the merged firm on an ongoing basis to ensure compliance with behavioural conditions. In contrast, given that the Chinese government believes its role is one of market supervision, it is comfortable with imposing conditions that enable it to carry out that role.

The merger conditions required by the MOFCOM, which were discussed in Chapter 2, can be grouped into several categories. First, some conditions seek to preserve the competitive structure of the market that existed before the merger. In addition to the structural conditions imposed by the MOFCOM – namely, requiring the merging parties to divest a business, equity interest, specific asset, or production capacity; such conditions do not require ongoing monitoring – some behavioural conditions also fall into this category due to their practical effect. Terminating an existing agreement, for example, is akin to a divestment remedy.[196] Another example is the long-term hold-separate commitment, as it maintains the pre-merger market structure for a certain period after the merger is completed.[197] Unlike terminating an existing agreement, however, this remedy requires monitoring during the hold-separate period.

Some merger conditions aim to control market outcomes. The MOFCOM has required merged firms to supply or provide access to certain products, assets or information.[198] It often also sets the parameters of the terms upon which such supply or access is to be provided, such as price or volume; sometimes the conditions also cover the negotiation process.[199] Such conditions help to ensure that the merger does not disrupt supply or access to existing customers or the market more generally, or that the merger does not result in less favourable terms and conditions for customers.

Other conditions constrain the merging parties' ability to engage in certain types of conduct. The MOFCOM has imposed conditions limiting the merging parties' ability to expand their business within China, to exercise their rights as shareholders or to enforce their IPRs.[200]

---

[196] *Novartis/Alcon*; *Baxter/Gambro*.
[197] *Seagate/Samsung*; *Western Digital/Hitachi*; *Marubeni/Gavilon*; *MediaTek/MStar*.
[198] See, e.g., *Henkel/Tiande*; *Glencore/Xstrata*; *Microsoft/Nokia*.
[199] See, e.g., *Uralkali/Silvinit*; *Google/Motorola Mobility*; *Glencore/Xstrata*; *Thermo Fisher/Life*; *Microsoft/Nokia*.
[200] See, e.g., *InBev/Anheuser-Busch*; *Panasonic/Sanyo*; *Nokia/Alcatel-Lucent*.

These conditions enable the MOFCOM to monitor the merging parties' conduct in areas of concern, regardless of the MOFCOM's power to do so under the AML or other laws and regulations.

Moreover, some conditions pre-empt a potential breach of the AML by effectively regulating the conduct *ex ante* and providing the MOFCOM with grounds to directly intervene. By requiring merging parties to provide a supply/access commitment or to promise not to engage in exclusive dealing or tying and bundling conduct, the MOFCOM is preventing the merging parties from engaging in potential abuse of dominance conduct after the completion of the merger. To protect against potential cartel conduct, the MOFCOM has required merging parties to terminate an agreement with a competitor, because that agreement might facilitate coordination. In the absence of these conditions, if such conduct were to occur post-merger, it might be caught as abuse of dominance or monopoly agreement conduct under the AML. However, the potential breach would first need to be detected (which may be difficult), and the competition authority would need to conduct an investigation, which could take some time. In contrast, the merger conditions require merging parties to provide periodic reports to the MOFCOM, which enables the MOFCOM to intervene directly and probably more quickly.

### 6.4.2.2 Price Supervision and Regulation

The Chinese government regards price supervision and regulation as important aspects of market regulation more generally.[201] As noted in Chapter 4, the NDRC considers the AML as part of a set of laws relating to price regulation and supervision. It views improving and increasing the level of implementation and enforcement of the AML as a means of enhancing price regulation and supervision, as well as maintaining fair competition.[202] In addition, under the Price Law, the NDRC is tasked with controlling and stabilising general price levels.[203]

Several investigations and decisions made by the NDRC demonstrate that, in addition to maintaining competition and addressing anticompetitive conduct, it is using the AML to help it supervise and regulate

---

[201] 关于建立完善价格监管机制的意见 [Opinion on Establishing and Perfecting the Price Supervision Mechanism] (People's Republic of China) National Development and Reform Commission, Order No. 2099, 22 October 2013.
[202] Ibid.
[203] 中华人民共和国价格法 [Price Law of the People's Republic of China] (People's Republic of China) Standing Committee of the National People's Congress, 29 December 1997, art. 26.

prices.[204] This was apparent in the inspection campaigns it conducted in the pharmaceutical industry, discussed in Section 6.3.2, where the AML was used to help the NDRC supervise prices in the wake of, and to support, the government's drug pricing reforms. In other cases, the NDRC has applied both the AML and the Price Law as grounds to investigate and/or sanction price-related monopoly agreements,[205] thus illustrating the overlap and complementarity of the two laws that form part of the price regulation and supervision legal system. It should be noted that, while the NDRC regards the Price Law and the AML as instruments to help it control and maintain the stability of general price levels, it is aware that, despite an overlap in the conduct that may be caught under both the AML and the Price Law, the two laws have different legal requirements and capture different types of conduct. For example, in January 2013, the NDRC announced that it had investigated six liquid crystal display manufacturers for engaging in price fixing. It noted that, as the conduct had occurred from 2001 to 2006, the AML did not apply as it came into effect on 1 August 2008 and did not apply retroactively. It therefore relied on the Price Law instead and imposed sanctions accordingly.[206] Another example is the NDRC's *Hainan and Yunnan Tourism Cases*. In that decision, which covered four different types of conduct, the NDRC clearly distinguished between the conduct that fell under the Price Law and the conduct that was caught under the AML.[207]

The NDRC's enforcement of the AML to facilitate price supervision also fits with the Chinese government's broader view that its role in the market economy is evolving from one based on direct intervention to achieve specified outcomes, to one of supervision. Given the NDRC's history and background as the state's economic planner, it tends to rely on direct government intervention to deal with most economic

---

[204] Nathan Bush and Yue Bo, 'Adding Antitrust to NDRC's Arsenal' [2011] (2) *CPI Antitrust Chronicle* 1 at 4; Hao Qian, 'The Multiple Hands: Institutional Dynamics of China's Competition Regime' in Adrian Emch and David Stallibrass (eds.), *China's Antimonopoly Law: The First Five Years* (Alphen aan den Rijn, The Netherlands: Kluwer Law International, 2013), p. 28. See also Ng, 'The Independence of Chinese Competition Agencies', 199–202.

[205] *Guangxi Rice Noodle Cartel*; *Zhejiang Paperboard Cartel*; *Hainan and Yunnan Tourism Cases*; *Xiamen Courier Cartel*; *Wuhan BMW Pre-Delivery Inspection Fee Cartel*.

[206] National Development and Reform Commission, 六家境外企业实施液晶面板价格垄断被依法查处 [Six Overseas Businesses Investigated and Punished for Implementing LCD Panel Price Monopoly] (News Release, 4 January 2013).

[207] National Development and Reform Commission, 'Some Illegal Price-Related Conduct Cases'.

problems.[208] For example, to tackle inflation, it might freeze prices, restrict exports, pressure businesses and directly ask businesses to refrain from increasing prices.[209] However, with the Chinese leadership's emphasis on change regarding the government's role in the market, it is likely that the NDRC is also adapting its approach to market regulation. Naughton believes that the NDRC wants to demonstrate and ensure that it has an important and continuing role to play in deepening market reform.[210]

This adjustment from intervention to supervision can be seen in the NDRC's handling of rising prices and supply shortages of imported infant formula. Since 2008, the price of imported infant formula has increased substantially, due to a loss of consumer confidence in Chinese milk powder products.[211] The initial measures taken by the NDRC in response to these price increases were interventionist. For example, it ordered its local authorities to adopt interventionist measures such as restricting profit margins and prices to prevent unreasonable price increases,[212] and it was reported that the NDRC had met with a number of foreign infant formula producers to have an 'informal talk' about prices, specifically costs.[213]

---

[208] Barry Naughton, 'Since the National People's Congress: Personnel and Programs of Economic Reform Begin to Emerge' [2013] (41) *China Leadership Monitor* 1 at 2; Zhang, 'Bureaucratic Politics and China's Anti-monopoly Law', 695.

[209] 张向东 [Zhang Xiangdong], 发改委有请 [NDRC Has a Request], 经济观察网 [Economic Observer Online], 30 April 2011, available at www.eeo.com.cn/eobserve/Politics/beijing_news/2011/04/30/200332.shtml; Gordon G. Chang, 'China Imposes Price Controls, Informally', *Forbes*, 8 May 2011, available at www.forbes.com/sites/gordonchang/2011/05/08/china-imposes-price-controls-informally; 发改委"出手"康师傅联合利华暂缓涨价 [NDRC Acts, Master Kong and Unilever Suspend Price Increases], 财经网 [Caijing], 1 April 2011, available at www.caijing.com.cn/2011-04-01/110680850.html; Barry Naughton, 'Inflation, Welfare, and the Political Business Cycle' [2011] (35) *China Leadership Monitor* 1 at 3–4.

[210] Naughton, 'Since the National People's Congress', 2.

[211] See, e.g., Dai Lian, 'Food Safety Regulators Reshuffled', Caixin, 18 November 2011, available at www.caixinglobal.com/2011-11-18/101016303.html; Edward Wong, 'Contaminated Milk Is Destroyed in China', *New York Times*, 26 December 2011, available at www.nytimes.com/2011/12/27/world/asia/contaminated-milk-is-destroyed-in-china.html; 'Infant Formula Found Contaminated', *China Daily*, 22 July 2012, available at http://usa.chinadaily.com.cn/china/2012-07/22/content_15606682.htm.

[212] 国家发展改革委发出紧急通知 要求切实加强婴幼儿奶粉价格监管 [NDRC Issues Emergency Notice, Requests Strengthening of Infant Formula Price Supervision] (News Release, 19 September 2008) available at http://www.ndrc.gov.cn/xwtt/200809/t20080919_236575.html.

[213] 发改委约谈六家"洋奶粉"企业表示属例行工作 [NDRC Talks with Six Foreign Infant Formula Businesses, States that it is Routine], 广州日报 [Guangzhou Daily], 9 May 2011, available at www.chinanews.com/cj/2011/05-09/3024728.shtml.

However, these measures were not effective in halting the price increases of imported infant formula.[214] Later, in March 2013, the NDRC initiated an investigation of nine domestic and foreign infant formula producers for suspected breaches of the AML, with news of the investigation becoming public in July 2013.[215] The investigation had at least two direct effects. First, shortly after the investigation was publicised but before the NDRC made its decision, some of the investigated infant formula producers voluntarily announced price decreases.[216] Second, when the NDRC found that the infant formula producers had engaged in resale price maintenance in breach of the AML, the investigation resulted in a total fine of RMB 669 million and the investigated parties committed to reviewing their sales and business practices, undoing the consequences of the illegal conduct and taking action to benefit consumers.[217] The NDRC claims that its investigation resulted in a benefit to consumers of more than RMB 2.4 billion, in the form of reduced prices.[218] Thus, the *Infant Formula RPM* case enabled the NDRC to demonstrate that it could address concerns about high prices and deliver results by using the AML to carry out its price supervision role, rather than by relying upon direct intervention.

---

[214] 李丽 [Li Li], 惠氏、雅培奶粉提价10% 众多品牌不跟风 [Wyeth and Abbott Increase Prices by 10 per cent, Many Brands Do Not Follow], 经济观察网 [Economic Observer Online], 5 July 2011, available at www.eeo.com.cn/2011/0705/205356.shtml.

[215] China Central Television, 发展改革委对合生元等乳粉企业反垄断调查 [NDRC's Anti-monopoly Investigation of Biostime and Other Infant Formula Businesses] 新闻直播间 [News Broadcast] 1 July 2013, available at http://tv.cntv.cn/vodplay/015c07df1972448e915602c6c74c20b2/860010-1102010100; 朱剑红 [Zhu Jianhong], 发改委: 多家奶粉企业涉嫌价格垄断被调查 [NDRC: A Number of Infant Formula Producers Suspected of Price Monopoly are Being Investigated], 新华网 [Xinhuanet], 2 July 2013, available at http://news.hexun.com/2013-07-02/155693324.html.

[216] 惠氏奶粉最高降价二成 洋奶粉反垄断调查效应初现 [Wyeth's Maximum Price Decrease of 20 Per cent, Foreign Infant Formula Anti-monopoly Investigation Sees Initial Effects], 南方日报 [*Southern Daily News*], 4 July 2013, available at http://finance.chinanews.com/cj/2013/07-04/5001321.shtml; 叶碧华 [Ye Bihua], 发改委释疑惠氏免遭重罚: 首先降价率队认错 [NDRC Explains Why Wyeth Was Exempt from Penalty: First to Reduce Price and Make Admissions], 21世纪经济报道 [*21st Century Business Herald*], 8 August 2013, available at http://finance.sina.com.cn/chanjing/gsnews/20130808/022816379184.shtml.

[217] National Reform and Development Commission, 合生元等乳粉生产企业违反《反垄断法》限制竞争行为共被处罚6.6873亿元 [Biostime and Other Infant Formula Producers Restricted Competition and Violated the Anti-monopoly Law, Fined a Total of RMB 668.73m] (News Release, 7 August 2013).

[218] National Development and Reform Commission, 顺利实现价格预期调控目标,价格改革和监管工作取得积极成效 [Price Control Targets Successfully Reached, Price Reform and Supervision Work Achieved Positive Results] (News Release, 24 January 2014) available at www.sdpc.gov.cn/xwzx/xwfb/201401/t20140124_576928.html.

This observation is supported by the NDRC's series of AML decisions in the auto industry. According to reports, imported cars in China are among the highest-priced in the world, and several times the price of similar cars sold overseas.[219] Since 2011, the NDRC has paid close attention to anti-competitive conduct relating to cars and auto parts.[220] In 2012, it asked the China Automobile Dealers Association to conduct research into anti-competitive conduct in the auto industry on its behalf, focusing on vehicle retail prices, after-sales services, auto parts, minimum retail prices and sales territories.[221] As a result, the NDRC initiated a number of high-profile AML investigations against car manufacturers, their local dealers and auto parts manufacturers.[222] Like the *Infant Formula RPM* case, a number of car manufacturers reduced their prices in response to the NDRC's AML investigation before the NDRC made any decisions.[223] In addition to undertaking investigations, the NDRC is currently preparing an antitrust guideline for the auto industry, which will be adopted by the AMC.[224]

---

[219] 发改委彻查进口豪车"低价设限" 车价全球最高被疑垄断 [NDRC Thoroughly Investigates Imported Luxury Cars 'Minimum Price Restrictions', Car Prices Are Highest Globally, Suspected Monopoly], 人民网 [people.cn], 19 August 2013, available at http://news.ifeng.com/gundong/detail_2013_08/19/28768765_0.shtml; 百万豪车国外只卖30多万 价格差巨大谁在获取暴利 [Million Dollar Luxury Cars Only Sell for 300,000 Overseas, Who Is Profiteering from the Huge Price Differences], 新华网 [Xinhuanet], 29 July 2013, available at http://finance.people.com.cn/n/2013/0729/c70846-22364060.html.

[220] 发改委就发展生产性服务业促进产业结构升级召开新闻发布会 [NDRC Holds Press Conference on Developing and Promoting the Structural Upgrade of Producer Service Industries] (6 August 2014) available at www.china.com.cn/zhibo/2014-08/06/content_33139708.htm.

[221] 卢延纯: 反垄断法要促进行业经济发展 [Lu Yanchun: Anti-monopoly Law Needs to Promote Industry Economic Development], auto.sina.com.cn, 29 November 2012, available at http://auto.sina.com.cn/news/2012-11-29/12241071631.shtml; 'NDRC Thoroughly Investigates Imported Luxury Cars "Minimum Price Restrictions"'.

[222] *Shanghai Chrysler Cartel and RPM*; *Japanese Auto Parts Cartel*; *Japanese Ball Bearings Cartel*; *FAW-Volkswagen and Audi Cartel and RPM*; *Mercedes-Benz Cartel and RPM*; *Dongfeng Nissan Cartel and RPM*; *Hanook Tire RPM*; *SAIC General Motors RPM*.

[223] Li Fangfang and Li Fusheng, 'Automakers Lower Prices Following Monopoly Concerns', *China Daily*, 29 July 2014, available at http://usa.chinadaily.com.cn/epaper/2014-07/29/content_18206559.htm; Samuel Shen and Pete Sweeney, 'Japanese Car Makers Cut Parts Prices in China after Anti-monopoly Probe', Reuters, 9 August 2014, available at www.reuters.com/article/us-china-autos-antitrust-idUSKBN0G90H520140809.

[224] 《关于汽车业的反垄断指南》(征求意见稿) 公开征求意见 [Public Consultation for 'Anti-monopoly Guideline for the Auto Industry (Consultation Draft)'] (23 March 2016) National Development and Reform Commission, available at www.sdpc.gov.cn/fzgggz/jgjdyfld/fjgld/201603/t20160323_795741.html.

### 6.4.3 Anti-monopoly Law and the Fair Competition Review System

The Chinese government recognises that its actions might adversely impact the market. It could impede the free flow of goods and services between regions (known as local or regional protectionism), or restrict competition in or prevent entry into certain markets (known as industry monopoly). Such actions are considered inimical to the creation of a unified national market and as distorting the allocation of market resources.[225] These actions – known as abuses of administrative power or administrative monopolies – are not only prohibited under the AML,[226] but are also subject to review under the fair competition review system.[227] Whereas the AML provides for *ex post* examination of government actions for their impact on competition, the fair competition review system largely provides for *ex ante* review. The fair competition review system requires policy-making bodies and the State Council to evaluate proposed regulations and policies against specific criteria[228] before adoption to ensure that they do not eliminate or restrict competition or impede the creation of a unified national market.[229] As such, the fair competition review system operates alongside, and complements, the AML in regulating anti-competitive government behaviour. Both mechanisms might be considered relatively weak, as competition agencies are limited to making recommendations under the AML, and the fair competition review system requires only self-assessment and provides no specific consequences for non-compliance. However, when viewed together, they help to determine the bounds of appropriate government regulation of market activities.[230]

---

[225] Vanessa Yanhua Zhang, 'CPI Talks ... Interview with Mr Handong Zhang, Director General of the National Development and Reform Commission (NDRC) of PR China' [2017] (3) *CPI Antitrust Chronicle* 1 at 1.
[226] 中华人民共和国反垄断法 [Anti-monopoly Law of the People's Republic of China] (People's Republic of China) Standing Committee of the National People's Congress, 30 August 2007, arts. 8, 32–37.
[227] 关于在市场体系建设中建立公平竞争审查制度的意见 [Opinion on Establishing a Fair Competition Review System in the Construction of a Market System] (People's Republic of China) State Council, Order No. 34, 1 June 2016.
[228] Policy-making bodies are administrative authorities and organisations authorised by law to engage in public administration: Ibid., art. 3(1). The eighteen review criteria are grouped into four main categories: market entry and exit; free movement of goods and production factors; impact on production and operating costs; and effect on production and operating conduct: Ibid., art. 3(3).
[229] Ibid., art. 3.   [230] Zhang, 'Interview with Mr Handong Zhang', 2.

The noticeable uptick in AML enforcement activity against administrative monopoly since the latter half of 2014 can be explained, in part, by the adoption of the fair competition review system. As noted in Chapter 2, enforcement relating to abuse of administrative power was negligible in the first few years after the AML came into effect. However, in September 2014, the NDRC – one of the key ministries promoting fair competition review – published its first administrative monopoly recommendation, and has since published a total of twelve recommendations and outcomes arising from its investigations into administrative monopoly. This increase in activity coincides with the Chinese leadership's decision to undertake further reforms enabling the market to play a decisive role in allocating resources, to rebalance the government's role in the economy and to establish a unified, fair, open and competitive market. Following the Third Plenum held in November 2013, the State Council released an opinion in June 2014 on improving the market regulation system and promoting fair competition, in which it called for, *inter alia*, the breaking up of local protectionism and industry monopoly;[231] the fair competition review system was then adopted in June 2016. The Chinese government sees a clear link between fair competition review and the regulation of administrative monopoly under the AML: it believes that AML enforcement promotes fair competition review, and that fair competition review ensures compliance with the AML.[232] Hence the increased focus on fair competition review has likely contributed to greater enforcement of the AML against administrative monopoly.

## 6.5 Conclusion

In this chapter, the examination of the public enforcement of the AML has been informed by, and furthers, the political economy analysis undertaken in the previous chapters. Many of the contentious issues that shaped the progress, dynamics and outcome of the AML drafting process are also highly relevant in enforcement, namely, enforcement authority and scope, the relationship between the state and the market and broader

---

[231] 关于促进市场公平竞争维护市场正常秩序的若干意见 [Some Opinions on Promoting Fair Market Competition and Maintaining Normal Market Order] (People's Republic of China) State Council, Order No. 20, 4 June 2014.

[232] Opinion on Establishing a Fair Competition Review System. See also Zhang, 'Interview with Mr Handong Zhang', 2–3.

government policies and priorities. This study has elicited key observations that explain why, how and the extent to which the legal, institutional, economic and political contexts influence AML investigations and enforcement outcomes.

Consistent with the dynamics of the drafting process, issues relevant to jurisdiction have been a prominent feature of AML enforcement, although perhaps not entirely in the way that was initially expected. The practices of consulting other government departments and decision-making by consensus have enabled industry regulators to use the merger consultation process to have their views reflected in enforcement outcomes, bringing industrial, regulatory and other policies and considerations into the decision-making process. Although industry regulators are less frequently involved in non-merger investigations, there are nevertheless cases in which they were able to intervene and protect their regulatory turf and regulated constituents. In both cases, the nature of the relationship between the competition authority and the industry regulator, the type and responsiveness of the resolution required and the government's other policy priorities and goals were relevant to determining the level of influence that the industry regulators could exert over AML enforcement outcomes. In contrast, the contest for jurisdiction between the NDRC, the MOFCOM and the SAIC that was evident during the drafting of the AML has not really featured in enforcement. There have been some overlaps in and encroachments upon AML enforcement activity among the competition authorities but, generally speaking, they do not interfere with one another's investigations. In particular, the delineation of jurisdiction between the NDRC and the SAIC along price-related and non-price-related lines has worked quite well in practice, in large part because they adopt a pragmatic approach to coordination.

The importance and relevance of the leading and supervisory role of the state in the market economy, and the role that the AML plays in mediating that relationship and its potential tensions, have also shaped enforcement. The two dimensions of that relationship – that of participant and regulator – have resulted in quite different enforcement dynamics. On the one hand, SOEs present challenges to AML enforcement. Public enforcement of the AML against SOEs has been constrained not only by the SOEs themselves (for example, their attitudes towards AML compliance and their political and economic stature), but also by their relationships with the competition authorities and other government bodies and their roles within the broader policy environment. In contrast, the state's supervisory role has enhanced AML enforcement, as the competition agencies have applied the AML in a manner that is compatible with and facilitates macroeconomic control and regulation. Further, while the Chinese government has long recognised that the state itself can hinder competition, the renewed commitment to breaking up administrative monopolies – as demonstrated by the fair competition review system – has resulted in greater and more effective enforcement of the AML prohibition against abuse of administrative power, which is a prohibition that was previously criticised as largely symbolic and toothless.

The experience of public enforcement of the AML to date also supports the hypothesis postulated earlier in this book that the AML is likely to involve, and serve as a conduit for, the coordination of various interests, stakeholders and policies. This corroborates the observation made in Chapter 4 that a macro approach to competition policy – that is, one that is broader than the AML and incorporates other laws and policies which may restrict or affect competition – is taken in China.

# 7

# Conclusion

## 7.1 Introduction

The legal and economic analysis of the Anti-monopoly Law (AML) and its enforcement decisions that was undertaken in Chapter 2 is useful to understand the ways in which the AML enables and constrains the competition authorities in their interpretation and application of the AML. This analysis shows that the AML is being interpreted and applied in a manner that is increasingly analytically sophisticated and largely consistent with international competition law norms and practices. It also reveals that there are some aspects of enforcement practice – for example, concerning merger remedies, the use of the leniency policy, and approach to monopoly agreements – that depart from these norms. Such an analysis, however, does not shed light on why these differences exist. For example, there are provisions in the AML relating to industry policy and the leading role of the state in the economy, but they are not referenced in any of the published decisions; therefore their relevance, if any, to decision-making under the AML is not explored in this doctrinal analysis. Nor does this analysis explain some of the observed enforcement patterns or legal and practice developments in the AML. Thus, recourse must be had to matters beyond legal and economic analysis and the text of the AML itself to explicate the AML more fully.

This book argues that it is essential to examine the AML in the institutional, economic and political context from which it was developed, and in which it is now enforced and implemented. The analytical framework used in this book is based on Milhaupt and Pistor's political economy framework for understanding the law and its societal context. By investigating the stakeholders and dynamics that shape the demand and supply-sides of the AML, this framework, informed by empirical research, is invaluable in enabling a rigorous and systematic analysis of the Chinese context and how it relates to and shapes the AML. It also looks behind and beyond the published decisions, which have been characterised by limited transparency and detail. The insights into the dynamics of competition law and policy in China that result from undertaking this political economy analysis, together with their implications for the observations and criticisms of the AML made by commentators, are discussed in the remainder of this concluding chapter.

## 7.2 Findings

The application of the political economy framework developed in this book to examine the AML has elicited four key observations and insights into competition law and policy in China. These relate to the contests for power among government agencies, the coordination and balancing of the AML and other government laws and policies, the roles of the state and the market in the socialist market economy and knowledge and capacity constraints.

### 7.2.1 Contestations for Enforcement Power among Government Agencies

The dynamics of the AML drafting process were marked substantially by tussles for power to enforce the AML among various government agencies, some of which persist in the enforcement stage. Such contests for enforcement authority have occurred both among the competition authorities themselves and between the competition authorities on the one hand and industry regulators on the other.

As discussed in Chapter 5, during the drafting process, the Ministry of Commerce (MOFCOM), the National Development and Reform Commission (NDRC) and the State Administration for Industry and Commerce (SAIC) vied to be the government authority responsible for enforcing the AML. Their claims for enforcement power largely rested on their responsibilities and experiences enforcing the existing competition-related laws and regulations. Not only was this three-way struggle for enforcement power one of the main causes of delays in the drafting process, but it also resulted in the two-tiered and divided administrative enforcement structure that exists today. This enforcement structure was adopted despite the advice of, and strong opposition from, competition law experts who believed that, as explained in Chapter 1, effective enforcement of the AML required the establishment of a single, unified enforcement authority.

Although the competition authorities competed for enforcement power during the drafting process, this has not translated into significant conflicts or disagreements over authority in enforcement. As shown in Chapters 2 and 6, the price/non-price distinction has worked well for allocating enforcement against monopoly agreements, although it seems harder to apply in abuse of dominance and administrative monopoly cases, which suggests that it may be more difficult to separate the price-related and non-price-related aspects of such conduct. Nevertheless, the price/non-price distinction has been workable in practice, in large part because the NDRC and the SAIC have adopted a pragmatic coordination mechanism whereby the first authority to discover a case will investigate the case. This has meant that, in situations where an investigation involves both price and non-price-related conduct, or even where an authority has actually encroached upon the other's enforcement scope, the NDRC and the SAIC have not interfered with the other's enforcement activities.

The issue of which government authority would have power to enforce the AML in regulated industries was contentious throughout the drafting process. As pointed out in Chapter 5, industry regulators, with the support of state-owned enterprises (SOEs), pressed strongly for regulated industries to be exempt from the AML, for power to enforce the AML in regulated industries and for sector-specific laws to have priority over the AML in regulated industries. While industry regulators were unsuccessful in obtaining an exemption for regulated industries, they significantly delayed the drafting process through continued pressure regarding the latter two issues, so much so that it was thought they would derail enactment of the AML. These dynamics have carried over to enforcement, as industry regulators have tried to influence AML enforcement outcomes. Chapter 6 discussed the ways in which the involvement of industry regulators – whether invited or not – in AML enforcement has affected outcomes. In merger enforcement, industry regulators are typically consulted as part of the MOFCOM's consultation with other government departments during merger review. They might use that process to bring industrial policy, regulatory concerns or other matters into the decision-making process, which, depending on the circumstances, might then be reflected in the conditions that the MOFCOM imposes on a merger. Such consultation is also believed to be a major cause of delay in merger review. Similarly, although industry regulators are less likely to be consulted in non-merger investigations, Chapter 6 discussed the few cases in which industry regulators opposed or interfered in the competition authority's investigation. In *China Telecom/China Unicom Abuse of Dominance* and *TravelSky Cartel*, the industry regulator's objection to the AML investigation seemed to resolve with a behind-the-scenes compromise that resulted in commitments and not fines. In *Tencent/Qihoo 360*, the industry regulator successfully asserted jurisdiction over the dispute, in part because of the disparity in political power between the industry regulator and the competition authority, and also because it is likely that a regulatory intervention, rather than an investigation under the AML, was regarded as the quickest way to resolve the dispute.

### 7.2.2 Coordinating the Anti-monopoly Law with Other Government Policies

The intention for the AML to act as a conduit to coordinate industrial policy and other economic policies is reflected in Article 4 of the AML, discussions surrounding the AML and enforcement outcomes. The AML is often linked to the government's wider policies, priorities and reform agenda, and the outcomes of a number of cases are consistent with promoting and achieving other government policy aims and concerns. These cases were discussed and analysed in Chapter 6. For example, several cases in the areas of mergers and abuse of dominance focus on issues relating to the licensing of intellectual property and brands, which are important facets of China's industrial policy, and reflect the government's view that competition, innovation and development are closely related. AML enforcement actions have been taken as part of broader reforms in the salt and pharmaceutical industries to liberalise prices and introduce market mechanisms, thereby helping to prevent businesses from taking advantage of the reforms by engaging in anticompetitive conduct. The *Wal-Mart/Newheight* merger provides another example of a merger decision echoing and reinforcing another government policy, in this case the government's telecommunications and foreign investment policies. Specifically, the MOFCOM's conditions effectively prevented the merging parties from avoiding compliance with the telecommunications regulations and foreign investment restrictions, and the subsequent decision to release the merged firm from the conditions reflected the Chinese government's change of policy towards foreign investment in e-commerce. The NDRC and the SAIC have also focused their enforcement efforts on industries relating to people's wellbeing and livelihood, such as public utilities and health, which is consistent with the broader government imperative to maintain social and political stability.

These cases illustrate that competition policy in China is broader than the AML, and includes consideration of other laws and policies that may constrain its operation. These other laws and policies are brought into decision-making under the AML via internal and external mechanisms. For example, the AML requires the MOFCOM to (and the MOFCOM does) consult with third parties such as other government departments during merger review. It is this consultation process, together with the practice requiring consulted government departments to sign off on the final decision, which enables the consideration of other government policies and priorities during a merger review. The competition authorities have multiple roles and responsibilities beyond enforcement of the AML and competition policy; this influence is evident in the way in which the NDRC, which also takes on the role of price supervision, has enforced the AML. The Anti-monopoly Commission (AMC), though not very active to date, was established to facilitate coordination and negotiation among various ministries and government bodies with an interest in competition policy. More broadly, as outlined in Chapter 4, there are mechanisms across the government and within the party that help to ensure policies and priorities determined by the central leadership are followed and implemented by all levels of government.

### 7.2.3 The State and the Market in the Socialist Market Economy

The relationship and tension between the dual roles of the state in China's socialist market economy have shaped both the text of the AML and the enforcement outcomes under it. As discussed in Chapter 4, public ownership is regarded as the bedrock of China's economy and the Chinese government believes that, while the market is important in the socialist market economy, it remains subject to the state's macroeconomic control. In accordance with this view, during the last phase of the drafting process, articles were added that protected the state's controlling position in national economic lifeline, national security and state-sanctioned monopoly industries, and which recognised the supervisory role of the state in the market and economy more generally. This was examined in Chapter 5.

Chapter 6 demonstrated that the state's roles as both participant in and regulator of the market have influenced enforcement outcomes under the AML, albeit in quite different ways. The competition authorities face challenges enforcing the AML against SOEs, which are the state's vehicles for direct participation in the economy. As SOEs are part of the political structure, this constrains the competition authorities' ability to enforce the AML against them. SOEs, especially those that are more likely to attract scrutiny under the AML, may be powerful political actors that can challenge or resist AML enforcement efforts. For example, central SOEs might have a higher bureaucratic rank than the ministry bureaus responsible for enforcing the AML, which restricts the enforcement agencies' ability to compel cooperation or compliance from central SOEs. Further, as discussed in Chapter 3, SOEs often have the support of the relevant industry regulators and the State Assets Supervision and Administration Commission, which can add to the political weight opposing AML enforcement. This was demonstrated in both *China Telecom/China Unicom Abuse of Dominance* and *TravelSky Cartel*. In addition, many SOEs are either not sufficiently aware of the AML and their obligations or have limited regard for compliance. These factors can make it difficult for competition authorities to investigate or impose sanctions on SOEs, which, in some cases, has resulted in compromise resolutions.

In contrast, the state's role in exercising macroeconomic control and supervision over the market has facilitated enforcement of the AML, and vice versa. As discussed in Chapter 6, the majority of conditions imposed by the MOFCOM on conditionally approved mergers have been regulatory in nature. Some of these conditions aim to control market outcomes, others constrain the ability of the merging parties to engage in certain types of activities, and some effectively pre-empt a potential breach of the AML after the merger is completed. Consistent with the state's supervisory role and the intention underlying Article 4 of the AML, such merger conditions allow the MOFCOM to monitor the merging parties' conduct over a longer period of time and provide it with grounds to directly intervene where necessary, in addition to addressing concerns about the potentially anti-competitive effects of a proposed merger. Similarly, the NDRC has applied the AML in a manner that reflects its view of the AML as one of a set of laws relating to price supervision and regulation. As argued in Chapter 6, the AML's relevance to the NDRC's price supervision role can be seen in its joint application of the AML and the Price Law to investigate and sanction price-related monopoly agreements, and in the inspection campaigns in the pharmaceutical industry that support the government's recent drug pricing reforms. Further, in situations where the NDRC might have otherwise relied on interventionist measures to achieve particular outcomes, its enforcement of the AML in the *Infant Formula RPM* case and the auto industry suggests that it is increasingly relying on the AML as a means to adapt its approach to market regulation in response to the Chinese leadership's emphasis on adjusting the government's role in the market from direct intervention to supervision.

Further, the Chinese government's focus on ensuring and creating a market environment conducive to fair competition seems to have fostered greater enforcement of the AML against abuses of administrative power. As noted in Chapter 6, the fair competition review system aims to prevent the government itself from impeding competition through the adoption of regulations or policies that eliminate or restrict competition. Thus, the fair competition review system and the AML prohibition against administrative monopoly address the same type of conduct and help to manage the relationship between the government and the market by establishing parameters in relation to the government regulation of market activities.

### 7.2.4 Knowledge and Capacity Constraints

The AML is constrained by the limited competition law knowledge and awareness of both the competition authorities and those who are subject to its application, as well as the general attitude towards legal compliance. As explained in Chapters 3 and 4, the concepts of markets and competition, along with the laws that regulate them, are relatively new in China; therefore, knowledge and awareness of competition law within the government, business community and general public are limited. During the drafting of the AML, this knowledge deficit was addressed by the close involvement of Chinese and international competition law experts. As discussed in Chapter 5, they helped to significantly improve the drafters' knowledge of competition law and ensure that the AML was consistent with international competition law norms while taking into account the specific needs and circumstances of China. However, AML enforcement has been affected by limited competition law knowledge and awareness. For example, Chinese businesses generally have a low level of knowledge and awareness regarding the AML and do not place much importance on competition law compliance, which appears to have resulted in the under-notification of mergers involving Chinese businesses to the MOFCOM for anti-monopoly review. The competition authorities' published decisions, as observed in Chapter 2, are generally quite brief and tend to be limited in their analytical rigour, technical nous and consistency. The effects of the knowledge constraints have been compounded by the competition authorities' limited resources. The MOFCOM's limited resources are believed to be one of the main reasons for delays in merger review. The NDRC and the SAIC rely on their local authorities to undertake most of the investigations, despite the latter generally having less competition law knowledge than the central-level bureaus.

This situation is improving, however, as competition agencies accrue enforcement experience and improve their technical capacity to conduct competition and economic analysis. In addition, competition law experts are involved in implementation; for example, Chinese competition law academics advise the AMC, participate in research projects for the competition authorities and comment on draft regulations, and experts also provide training for Chinese competition officials at both the central and local levels. The increasing level of competition law knowledge among competition authorities is reflected in some of the more recent published decisions, especially those relating to mergers, and the level of reasoning, analysis and disclosure provided in published decisions has improved over time across all three competition authorities. Similarly, Chinese businesses have greater awareness and knowledge of the AML and their obligations due to increased AML enforcement, including the pursuit of high-profile cases by competition authorities, and the exposure of more Chinese companies to overseas competition law regimes. This has resulted in, for example, a greater number of mergers involving Chinese businesses being notified to the MOFCOM for review and an increase in AML compliance programs being implemented by Chinese businesses.

The positioning of competition authorities within the broader government bureaucracy has also influenced enforcement. In particular, it has posed challenges to AML enforcement against SOEs. As discussed in Chapters 4 and 6, although the competition authorities are ministries and have the corresponding bureaucratic rank, the government bodies actually carrying out the day-to-day enforcement work of the AML are bureaus within the ministries, which are not as highly ranked. They may be outranked by the SOEs that they are seeking to investigate. If this is the case, the SOE being investigated will not be required to cooperate with the investigation or follow instructions or orders. To compel such cooperation, the competition authority will have to elevate the issue within the ministry to an entity that has a higher bureaucratic rank than the investigated SOE, which may be difficult.

## 7.3 Implications for Current Evaluations of the Anti-monopoly Law

Having identified and drawn out some important findings and observations about the making, enforcement and implementation of the AML, it is now useful to return to the evaluations and critique of the AML outlined in Chapter 1 and consider whether the insights provided by the political economy analysis support these views, or show that they need to be reconsidered, qualified or revised.

### 7.3.1 Consideration of Non-Competition Factors

The inclusion of provisions in the AML that allow or require the consideration of public interest, national economic development, industrial policy and other 'non-competition' factors has drawn criticism from commentators. There is also speculation that industrial policy and the protection of Chinese companies have been driving factors behind some enforcement investigations and outcomes.

The political economy analysis undertaken in this book supports the view that the AML has been enforced in a manner that is consistent with promoting and achieving other government policy aims and concerns. This does not mean, however, that such enforcement activity has not also addressed concerns about anti-competitive conduct. As demonstrated in Chapter 2, the competition authorities have interpreted and applied the AML in a manner that is broadly consistent with prevailing international norms and practice, with the main exceptions being greater use of behavioural remedies in the merger context and the application of the leniency policy to both horizontal and vertical anti-competitive agreements. The political economy analysis additionally provides insights into how, where and why non-competition considerations may arise. Such concerns might be brought into enforcement of the AML through the competition authority's consultation with other government departments – as a natural consequence of the practice of decision-making by consensus, or because of the state's exercise of macroeconomic control and supervision. The pursuit of other government policies and priorities also reflects the Chinese government's intention that the AML operate as a means to coordinate competition policy with other government policies. Overall, this approach is consistent with the Chinese government's adoption of a macro view of competition policy that extends beyond the AML. While this perspective is not unique to China, this helps to explain some aspects of the AML's development and enforcement experience.

### 7.3.2 Protection of State-owned Enterprises

As discussed in Chapter 1, commentators are concerned that SOEs are afforded protection or special treatment under the AML. Even though there is now little doubt that the AML applies to SOEs, commentators point to the low level of AML enforcement activity involving SOEs, especially in merger enforcement, as well as investigations of SOEs where the competition authorities opted for 'soft remedies' (remedial commitments rather than fines) as evidence of such bias. Some commentators speculate that policy tensions and other government authorities might be reasons for weak enforcement against SOEs, but most offer little evidence to ground such claims.

This book agrees that enforcement of the AML against SOEs is limited, but demonstrates that this is not necessarily due to intentional protection of SOEs by the competition authorities. Rather, the political economy analysis and empirical research show that competition authorities face institutional and political constraints which can render enforcement against SOEs difficult. The low level of merger enforcement activity relating to SOEs can be explained by the fact that many SOEs place limited importance on AML compliance and tend not to notify their mergers to the MOFCOM for anti-monopoly review, although this situation is improving, with the MOFCOM having fined SOEs for not complying with the notification requirements. The MOFCOM's limited resources and bureaucratic rank also restrict its ability to take action against SOEs for non-compliance. The NDRC and the SAIC face similar constraints when investigating SOEs. This was clearly demonstrated in the NDRC's *China Telecom/China Unicom Abuse of Dominance* and *TravelSky Cartel* investigations, which involved large, powerful central SOEs and industry regulators who opposed the investigations. In light of the power dynamics inherent to relationships between the NDRC, industry regulators and investigated central SOEs, accepting remedial commitments may have been regarded as the most realistic and beneficial outcome. These constraints may, in part, explain why most non-merger investigations have involved smaller local SOEs, where the competition authorities are less likely to encounter such challenges.

### 7.3.3 Discrimination against Foreign Companies

There are concerns that the AML is being used to protect Chinese businesses from foreign competition or is being enforced disproportionately against foreign businesses. As support for that proposition, commentators point to the MOFCOM's enforcement record, which shows that a significant majority of the mergers reviewed by the MOFCOM involve foreign companies, that no purely domestic mergers have been conditionally approved or prohibited and that nearly all the MOFCOM's conditional or prohibition decisions involve mergers between foreign companies only. They also speculate that some merger decisions have been motivated by nationalism or foreign investment, rather than competition, concerns. Similarly, commentators are concerned that foreign companies are unfairly targeted in non-merger enforcement. Even though the NDRC and the SAIC have investigated and sanctioned domestic companies for abuse of dominance and monopoly agreement conduct, such instances have tended to involve smaller and local SOEs, whereas the cases that have attracted greater levels of fines have been large, multinational companies.

This study corroborates some of these concerns. As shown in Chapters 3 and 5, some of the rhetoric surrounding the enactment of the AML was protectionist. Both the government and the general public wanted to protect Chinese businesses and consumers from the anti-competitive conduct of dominant foreign companies in China and from foreign takeovers of Chinese companies and brands – therefore there is some basis to the commentators' concerns. Chapter 6 used the example of the MOFCOM's decision to impose and subsequently release conditions in *Wal-Mart/Newheight* to illustrate how foreign investment concerns may be a factor in merger review.

More importantly, however, this research suggests that the high incidence of merger enforcement involving foreign companies is largely due to the fact that more mergers involving foreign companies are being notified to the MOFCOM for review in the first place. As discussed in Chapter 3, foreign businesses tend to have a higher level of competition law awareness and knowledge, attach more importance to competition law compliance and are more likely than Chinese businesses to notify their mergers to the MOFCOM for review. Therefore, the comparatively low level of enforcement against mergers involving Chinese companies could be the result of the weak competition culture within the Chinese business community. This is slowly changing, with an increasing awareness of the AML by Chinese businesses and with the MOFCOM investigating and sanctioning companies for non-compliance with notification requirements.

Similarly, in relation to non-merger enforcement, the findings of this book suggest that the competition authorities' focus on the behaviour of foreign companies, especially in the realm of abuse of dominance, might be, in part, a corollary of the power dynamics of AML enforcement. As pointed out in Chapter 3, foreign companies and SOEs are natural targets of the AML. SOEs may be dominant or major competitors in a number of important and strategic industries, and some foreign companies have leading positions and competitive advantages, especially in technology-related industries. In contrast, even though many large Chinese private businesses have strong market positions, overall they remain smaller and weaker than foreign companies. As discussed in Section 7.3.2, because the competition authorities face institutional and political barriers when seeking to enforce the AML against SOEs, it may be easier for them to investigate foreign companies. This is not to suggest that foreign companies are weak players who do not have political connections; rather, it reflects the fact that competition authorities are less likely to face opposition from other government departments when investigating foreign companies, and they are more likely to have greater power vis-à-vis foreign companies. Therefore, the impression of an enforcement bias against foreign companies may be better explained by the institutional, political and economic realities of AML enforcement.

### 7.3.4 Issues Relating to the Administrative Enforcement Structure

The divided administrative enforcement structure has been criticised as costly, inefficient and likely to give rise to conflicts and inconsistencies in enforcement. Commentators are especially concerned that the competition authorities' lack of independence and low bureaucratic rank hinders enforcement, especially against SOEs and in regulated industries. There are also doubts about the effectiveness of enforcement against the abuse of administrative power. They argue that administrative enforcement of the AML should be handled by a single, unified, ministry-level and independent administrative agency.

The political economy analysis conducted in this book concurs with the view that the lack of independence, the constraints imposed by bureaucratic rank and limited resources are factors currently hindering enforcement. This was discussed above and demonstrated in Chapter 6. There are also relatively few cases relating to administrative monopoly, although the adoption of the fair competition review mechanism has coincided with more investigations being taken against abuse of administrative power, and this is likely to continue.

In contrast, this book also finds that concerns suggesting that the divided enforcement structure would give rise to conflicts and friction among the competition authorities, especially between the NDRC and the SAIC, have not come to fruition. The division of enforcement power along price-related and non-price-related lines, as discussed in Chapters 2 and 6, has been largely workable in practice. While there are situations in which both authorities have investigated similar conduct in the same industry, or where one authority has encroached upon the other's scope of enforcement authority, this has not resulted in apparent conflicts over or attempts to interfere with enforcement. Further, the division of enforcement power has not resulted in obviously inconsistent decision-making or analysis among the three authorities, although it should be recognised that it is difficult to make definitive conclusions on this matter, as the published decisions and announcements contribute to the limited transparency that characterises the decision-making process. Instead of the conflict or friction among the competition authorities that was anticipated, it has been the turf wars between the competition authorities and the industry regulators that have hindered enforcement and significantly shaped the dynamics and outcomes of AML enforcement.

Further, this study demonstrates that the reform proposal advocated by many commentators – that the three competition authorities be consolidated into one enforcement agency – solves only some of the institutional problems currently hindering enforcement of the AML. In particular, the political economy analysis undertaken in this book suggests that the issue of independence is a broader matter than merely extracting the competition authorities from their hosting ministries; it suggests that wider administrative and political reforms are required to ensure their independence from the various mechanisms and conventions within the broader governance system that tie the competition authorities to other government and political bodies. While a single, unified, ministry-level enforcement agency will be better suited to addressing the challenges in enforcement arising from bureaucratic rank and insufficient resources, it is unrealistic to expect that it will be a panacea for the problems associated with the current institutional arrangements for the public enforcement of the AML.[1]

### 7.3.5 Lack of Due Process and Transparency

The lack of due process and transparency in AML enforcement is among commentators' biggest concerns. A common complaint is that merging or investigated parties and their lawyers do not receive sufficient information about the progress of the review or investigation, or about the competition authorities' or other government departments' concerns. Commentators are also critical of the NDRC placing pressure on investigated parties to make admissions, inadequate access to legal representation before and during investigations and the insufficient disclosure of decisions made by the competition authorities. It should also be noted that limited transparency and due process has exacerbated commentators' concerns about other aspects of enforcement, such as the consideration of non-competition factors in AML enforcement, the protection of SOEs and discrimination against foreign companies.

This book shares the commentators' concerns and offers some explanations for the limited transparency and due process in AML investigations and enforcement. As noted in Chapter 4, decision-making in China is achieved largely through consensus; negotiating, coordinating and bargaining occur behind closed doors. It is also uncommon for differences in opinion or conflict between government bodies to be made known to outside parties. In this context, it is understandable why merging or investigated parties and their lawyers receive limited information from the competition authorities during the review or investigation. Further, combined with the fact that Chinese administrative agencies are not accustomed to providing detailed reasons for decisions, this helps to explain why the competition authorities' published decisions are, as noted in Chapter 2, generally quite brief and focus on presenting conclusions rather than on providing reasons, evaluating arguments or discussing the various factors or inputs into their decision-making process. Although limited transparency and due process is quite typical of broader governance practice in China, the competition authorities have nonetheless been responsive to these concerns and made some

---

[1] See generally Wendy Ng, 'The Independence of Chinese Competition Agencies and the Impact on Competition Enforcement in China' (2016) 4 *Journal of Antitrust Enforcement* 188.

improvements. For example, the MOFCOM adopted a simple merger review process to address concerns about delays, the SAIC committed to publishing all of its decisions on a central portal and the NDRC is now publishing some of its decisions in the form of administrative decisions as opposed to press releases. Further, in response to outcry from the international business community, the Chinese government has confirmed that foreign lawyers can attend meetings at the competition agencies with their clients. The NDRC has been criticised for pressuring parties to make admissions during its investigations. This tactic is reminiscent of the interventionist measures that the NDRC is accustomed to relying upon when dealing with economic problems, as discussed in Chapter 6. Another possible explanation is that it reflects and is a consequence of the NDRC's limited resources, competition law knowledge and AML enforcement capabilities, as it is easier to enforce the AML with the cooperation of, and admissions from, investigated parties.

## 7.4 Final Thoughts

Applying the political economy framework developed in this book to analyse the AML has elicited insights into how, why and the extent to which the broader context has influenced the enactment, implementation and enforcement of the AML. This understanding of the AML, which is rooted in its context and incorporates empirical research, has corroborated a number of the observations made and concerns voiced by commentators. Further, and more importantly, it has gone a step further to explain and substantiate why and how these observations and concerns exist. In some cases, the insights provided by the political economy analysis have shown that the existing critique needs to be qualified or is unfounded.

This detailed reading of the context is particularly important where suggestions for reform of the AML are discussed. Comparative analysis of laws, practices and enforcement outcomes with those of other jurisdictions is helpful to identify potential points of weakness and to learn from the experiences of other jurisdictions, especially as the AML is a relatively new competition law and the stakeholders involved are inexperienced compared to their counterparts in countries with a longer history of competition law enforcement. While reform proposals based on these comparative analyses are useful, the question of whether they can be successfully introduced and implemented in China will depend on their fit with the political economy and on acceptance by stakeholders on the supply and demand-sides of the AML. For example, reform proposals may not be feasible or effective in addressing the perceived problem due to a lack of demand for such change or the constraints imposed by the institutional or political context, among other factors. A political economy approach helps to identify appropriate stakeholders where advocacy efforts should be directed, to devise strategies for overcoming resistance from relevant constituencies and to ensure that viable reform proposals are developed which maximise the effectiveness of the AML within its constraints.

# Appendix A

## Research Methods, Materials and Sources

This book is a socio-legal and empirical study of competition law in China and, in particular, the Anti-monopoly Law (AML). It is interdisciplinary in its approach and engages in doctrinal, institutional, economic and political review and analysis of the relevant source materials. Interviews, case studies and English- and Chinese-language primary and secondary documentary sources are used.

This book draws heavily upon qualitative data gathered from interviews. I conducted interviews with twenty-three academics, legal practitioners, economists and government officials who were or are currently involved in the enactment and/or enforcement of the AML. The majority of these interviews were conducted in 2012, while I was based in Beijing; follow-up interviews were conducted in China in 2015 with a number of the original interviewees. The interviews were qualitative in nature and semi-structured, and focused on the interviewees' experiences and opinions relating to the process of drafting the AML, the enforcement experience to date and its associated challenges and likely experiences in the future. The aim of these interviews was to obtain information on the drafting and enforcement of the AML that was not already in the public domain, and to provide additional insight on observations made and concerns voiced in the existing literature. In particular, interviewees were asked about the actors or issues that significantly influenced the AML, their experiences with the enforcement authorities and the enforcement process, attitudes towards competition law compliance and the level of competition law knowledge held by actors involved with the AML. The interviews were conducted in either English or Chinese, in accordance with the wishes of each interviewee. The interviews were conducted on the basis that interviewees would remain anonymous, given the sensitive nature of some of the matters discussed, in order to encourage full and frank disclosure, and in accordance with the requests of a number of the interviewees. Further, it was understood that responses would not be attributed to specific interviewees, and that interviewees would not be directly quoted. Thus, interviewees are not referred to individually (whether by name or by pseudonym), no personal or identifying information is provided, no interviewee has been directly quoted in the book and the identities of all interviewees and the interview records have been kept confidential.

Detailed case studies that examine the drafting process behind the enactment of the AML and the investigations and decisions made by administrative authorities in their enforcement of the AML are also central to this book. These case studies integrate analysis of stakeholders, law-making and decision-making processes and the societal context, and rely upon empirical data gathered from the interviews and the information gathered from, and detailed analysis of, English and Chinese primary and secondary documentary sources.

This book also relies upon English and Chinese-language primary and secondary documentary sources. The primary documentary sources used in the book include Chinese laws, regulations and other government policy and regulatory documents; policy documents of the Communist Party of China; the determinations of Chinese administrative authorities; legislative and regulatory drafting documents; and records of legislative debates and speeches. The secondary documentary sources referred to in the book include Chinese and English-language books, journal articles, magazines, newspapers, speeches, conference materials and other commentaries. Care has been taken to ensure that reputable and credible secondary sources are used. For example, with respect to Chinese-language newspapers and other periodicals, state-sanctioned media sources (such as *Xinhua*, *People's Daily* or *China Daily*) and newspapers and media outlets that have a reputation for credible business reporting (such as *Caijing*, the *21st Century Business Herald* or the *Economic Observer*) are used. It is important to note that there are some challenges associated with relying on Chinese primary documentary sources, as only limited information on the drafting of laws, regulations and policies is publicly available and administrative agencies are generally not accustomed to providing detailed reasons for decisions. In particular, not all decisions made under the AML are released to the public, and the decisions that are released tend to contain limited discussion of the legal and economic analysis and reasoning undertaken, although this is gradually improving.

Unless otherwise noted, all English translations from Chinese-language documentary sources and interviews conducted in Chinese are my own.

# Appendix B

# Published Anti-monopoly Law Administrative Enforcement Decisions as at 31 December 2016

## B.1 Ministry of Commerce

| Date of decision | Merger name | Merger type | Outcome |
|---|---|---|---|
| **Merger reviews** | | | |
| 11 August 2009 | InBev/Anheuser-Busch | Horizontal | Conditional approval (behavioural) |
| 18 March 2009 | Coca-Cola/Huiyuan | Conglomerate | Prohibition |
| 24 April 2009 | Mitsubishi Rayon/Lucite | Horizontal and vertical | Conditional approval (structural and behavioural) |
| 28 September 2009 | General Motors/Delphi | Vertical | Conditional approval (behavioural) |
| 29 September 2009 | Pfizer/Wyeth | Horizontal | Conditional approval (structural and behavioural) |
| 30 October 2009 | Panasonic/Sanyo | Horizontal | Conditional approval (structural) |
| 13 August 2010 | Novartis/Alcon | Horizontal | Conditional approval (behavioural) |
| 2 June 2011 | Uralkali/Silvinit | Horizontal | Conditional approval (behavioural) |
| 31 October 2011 | Alpha V/Savio | Horizontal | Conditional approval (structural) |

(*cont.*)

| Date of decision | Merger name | Merger type | Outcome |
| --- | --- | --- | --- |
| 10 November 2011 | General Electric/Shenhua | Vertical | Conditional approval (behavioural) |
| 12 December 2011 | Seagate/Samsung | Horizontal | Conditional approval (behavioural) |
| 10 February 2012 | Henkel/Tiande | Vertical | Conditional approval (behavioural) |
| 2 March 2012 | Western Digital/Hitachi | Horizontal | Conditional approval (structural and behavioural) |
| 19 May 2012 | Google/Motorola Mobility | Vertical | Conditional approval (behavioural) |
| 16 June 2012 | UTC/Goodrich | Horizontal | Conditional approval (structural) |
| 13 August 2012 | Wal-Mart/Newheight | Conglomerate | Conditional approval (behavioural) |
| 6 December 2012 | ARM joint venture | Vertical | Conditional approval (behavioural) |
| 16 April 2013 | Glencore/Xstrata | Horizontal and vertical | Conditional approval (structural and behavioural) |
| 22 April 2013 | Marubeni/Gavilon | Horizontal | Conditional approval (behavioural) |
| 8 August 2013 | Baxter/Gambro | Horizontal | Conditional approval (structural and behavioural) |
| 26 August 2013 | MediaTek/MStar | Horizontal | Conditional approval (behavioural) |

*(cont.)*

| Date of decision | Merger name | Merger type | Outcome |
| --- | --- | --- | --- |
| 14 January 2014 | Thermo Fisher/Life | Horizontal | Conditional approval (structural and behavioural) |
| 8 April 2014 | Microsoft/Nokia | Vertical | Conditional approval (behavioural) |
| 30 April 2014 | Merck/AZ Electronics | Conglomerate | Conditional approval (behavioural) |
| 17 June 2014 | P3 Shipping Alliance | Horizontal | Prohibition |
| 2 July 2014 | NiMH battery joint venture | Horizontal (with vertical aspects) | Conditional approval (behavioural) |
| 19 October 2015 | Nokia/Alcatel-Lucent | Horizontal | Conditional approval (behavioural) |
| 25 November 2015 | NXP/Freescale | Horizontal | Conditional approval (structural) |
| 29 July 2016 | Anheuser-Busch InBev/SABMiller | Horizontal | Conditional approval (structural) |
| 30 December 2016 | Abbott Laboratories/St Jude Medical | Horizontal | Conditional approval (structural) |
| **Review, variation or revocation of merger conditions** | | | |
| 2 December 2014 | Western Digital/Hitachi | Horizontal | Imposed fine for non-compliance with conditions (2 violations) |
| 9 January 2015 | Google/Motorola Mobility | Vertical | Partial release from conditions |
| 25 August 2015 | InBev/Anheuser-Busch | Horizontal | Approval granted pursuant to conditions |
| 19 October 2015 | Western Digital/Hitachi | Horizontal | Partial release and revision of conditions |

*(cont.)*

| Date of decision | Merger name | Merger type | Outcome |
|---|---|---|---|
| 22 October 2015 | Seagate/Samsung | Horizontal | Partial release from conditions |
| 8 June 2016 | Wal-Mart/Newheight | Conglomerate | Full release from conditions |
| **Failure to notify** | | | |
| 8 December 2014 | Tsinghua Unigroup/RDA Microelectronics | N/A | Imposed fine |
| 16 September 2015 | BesTV/Microsoft | N/A | Imposed fine |
| 16 September 2015 | CSR Nanjing Puzhen/Bombardier Transportation | N/A | Imposed fine |
| 16 September 2015 | Fujian Electronics/Shenzhen Zhongnuo | N/A | Imposed fine |
| 16 September 2015 | Shanghai Fosun/Suzhou Erye | N/A | Imposed fine |
| 21 April 2016 | Beijing CNR/Hitachi | N/A | Imposed fine |
| 21 April 2016 | Dade Holdings/Jilin Sichang Pharmaceutical | N/A | Imposed fine |
| 21 April 2016 | New United Group/Bombardier Transportation | N/A | Imposed fine |
| 16 December 2016 | Canon/Toshiba Medical Systems | N/A | Imposed fine |

## B.2 National Development and Reform Commission

| Date of decision | Case | Investigating authority | Conduct investigated | Outcome |
|---|---|---|---|---|
| 21 April 2009 | TravelSky Cartel | NDRC Bureau | Monopoly agreement (price fixing) | Outcome unknown |
| 30 March 2010 | Guangxi Rice Noodle Cartel | NDRC Bureau Guangxi Price Bureau Nanning Municipal Government Liuzhou Municipal Government Other relevant departments | Monopoly agreement (price fixing) | Imposed fines Issued warnings Issued caution letters |
| 2 September 2010 | Book Publishers RPM | NDRC | Monopoly agreement (RPM) | Requested rectification of conduct |
| 15 November 2010 | Wuchang Salt Tying | Hubei Price Bureau | Abuse of dominance (tying) | Issued warning Accepted commitments to implement corrective measures Terminated investigation |
| 6 December 2010 | Jiangsu Salt Tying | Jiangsu Price Bureau | Abuse of dominance (tying) | N/A |
| 6 December 2010 | Civil Explosives Industry Association Cartel | Liaoning Province Price Bureau | Monopoly agreement (price fixing) | N/A |
| 6 December 2010 | Zhaoqing Badminton Association | Guangdong Price Bureau | Monopoly agreement | N/A |
| 6 December 2010 | Zhuhai Insurance Industry Association | Guangdong Price Bureau | Monopoly agreement | N/A |
| 6 December 2010 | Internet Cafes Cartel | Jiangsu Province Zhenjiang City | Monopoly agreement (price fixing) | N/A |

## (cont.)

| Date of decision | Case | Investigating authority | Conduct investigated | Outcome |
|---|---|---|---|---|
| 6 December 2010 | Tea Industry Association Cartel | Jiangsu Province Zhenjiang City | Monopoly agreement (price fixing) | N/A |
| 6 December 2010 | Dairy Products Businesses Cartel | Xinjiang | Monopoly agreement (price fixing) | N/A |
| 2011 | China Paper and Cardboard Box Packaging Cartel | NDRC Bureau Shanghai Price Bureau Zhejiang Price Bureau Tianjin Price Bureau Liaoning Price Bureau Chongqing Price Bureau | Monopoly agreement (price fixing) | Imposed fines |
| 4 January 2011 | Zhejiang Paperboard Cartel | Zhejiang Price Bureau | Monopoly agreement (price fixing, output restriction) | Imposed fines |
| 9 November 2011 | China Telecom/ China Unicom Abuse of Dominance | NDRC Bureau | Abuse of dominance | Accepted commitments |
| 14 November 2011 | Shandong Reserprine Exclusive Agreements | NDRC Bureau | Abuse of dominance (exclusive agreements) | Ordered the termination of agreements Confiscated illegal gains Imposed fines |
| 2012 | Hubei Hydrosulfite Cartel | Hubei Price Bureau | Monopoly agreement (price fixing) | Confiscated illegal gains Imposed fines |
| 26 October 2012 | Guangdong Sea Sand Cartel | Guangdong Price Bureau NDRC Bureau | Monopoly agreement (price fixing) | Imposed fines Applied leniency policy Issued warnings |
| 28 December 2012 | Loudi New Car Insurance Cartel | Hunan Price Bureau | Monopoly agreement (price fixing, market sharing) | Imposed fines Exempted five companies |

*(cont.)*

| Date of decision | Case | Investigating authority | Conduct investigated | Outcome |
|---|---|---|---|---|
| 22 February 2013 | Moutai RPM | Guizhou Price Bureau | Monopoly agreement (RPM) | Imposed fine |
| 22 February 2013 | Wuliangye RPM | Sichuan DRC | Monopoly agreement (RPM) | Imposed fine |
| 7 August 2013 | Infant Formula RPM | NDRC Bureau | Monopoly agreement (RPM) | Imposed fines Exempted three companies Committed to implement corrective measures |
| 13 August 2013 | Shanghai Gold and Platinum Jewellery Cartel | Shanghai Price Bureau (upon NDRC Bureau's request) | Monopoly agreement (price fixing) | Imposed fines Committed to implement corrective conduct |
| 29 September 2013 | Hainan and Yunnan Tourism Cases | NDRC Bureau Hainan Price Bureau Yunnan DRC Price Bureaus provinces of other popular tourist attractions | Artificial prices Illegal dumping Monopoly agreement (price fixing) | Imposed fines Exempted one business |
| 23 December 2013 | Nanjing Concrete Industry Association Thirty-seven companies | Jiangsu Price Bureau | Monopoly agreement (price fixing) | Imposed fine Unsuccessful administrative litigation |
| 4 December 2013 | Qinghai Tianlu Dairy RPM | Qinghai DRC | Monopoly agreement (RPM) | Suspended investigation Required rectification measures |
| 30 December 2013 | Zhejiang New Car Insurance Cartel | NDRC Bureau | Monopoly agreement (price fixing) | Imposed fines Applied leniency policy |

*(cont.)*

| Date of decision | Case | Investigating authority | Conduct investigated | Outcome |
|---|---|---|---|---|
| 14 January 2014 | Guangdong Driving School Cartel | Guangdong Price Bureau | Monopoly agreement (price fixing) | Imposed fines |
| 3 April 2014 | Xiamen Courier Cartel | Xiamen Price Bureau | Monopoly agreement (price fixing) | Held meeting to order companies to stop implementing the agreement, conduct internal investigations and provide a report |
| 22 May 2014 | InterDigital Abuse of Dominance | NDRC Bureau | Abuse of dominance (unfairly high prices, unreasonable conditions tying) | Suspended investigation Offered commitments |
| 29 May 2014 | Lens Manufacturers RPM | NDRC Bureau Local offices in Beijing, Shanghai and Guangzhou | Monopoly agreement (RPM) | Imposed fines Commitment to continue to implement corrective measures Applied leniency policy |
| 17 July 2014 | Hainan Aerated Bricks Cartel | Hainan Price Bureau | Monopoly agreement (price fixing) | Imposed fines |
| 13 August 2014 | Wuhan BMW Pre-Inspection Fee Cartel | Hubei Price Bureau | Monopoly agreement (price fixing) | Imposed fines |
| 18 August 2014 | Shanghai Chrysler Cartel and RPM | Shanghai Price Bureau | Monopoly agreement (RPM, price fixing) | Imposed fines |
| 20 August 2014 | Japanese Auto Parts Cartel | NDRC Bureau | Monopoly agreement (price fixing) | Imposed fines Applied leniency policy Commitment to implement corrective measures |

## APPENDIX B

*(cont.)*

| Date of decision | Case | Investigating authority | Conduct investigated | Outcome |
|---|---|---|---|---|
| 20 August 2014 | Japanese Ball Bearings Cartel | NDRC Bureau | Monopoly agreement (price fixing) | Imposed fines<br>Applied leniency policy<br>Commitment to implement corrective measures |
| 9 September 2014 | Jilin Cement Cartel | Jilin Price Bureau | Monopoly agreement (price fixing) | Imposed fines |
| 11 September 2014 | FAW-Volkswagen and Audi Cartel and RPM | Hubei Price Bureau | Monopoly agreement (RPM, price fixing) | Imposed fines<br>Applied leniency policy |
| 26 September 2014 | Hebei Toll Road Administrative Monopoly | NDRC Bureau | Administrative monopoly (preferential treatment) | Made recommendation to the Hebei Provincial Government |
| November/ December 2014 | Ningxia Courier Cartel | Ningxia Price Bureau | Monopoly agreement (price fixing) | Imposed fines<br>Ordered to undertake corrective measures<br>Unsuccessful application for administrative reconsideration |
| 10 February 2015 | Qualcomm Abuse of Dominance | NDRC Bureau | Abuse of dominance (tying, unreasonable conditions, refusal to provide information) | Imposed fine<br>Accepted commitments |
| 9 March 2015 | Shandong GPS Platform Administrative Monopoly | NDRC Bureau | Administrative monopoly (designated supplier) | Made recommendation to the Shandong Province People's Government |
| 23 April 2015 | Mercedes-Benz Cartel and RPM | Jiangsu Price Bureau | Monopoly agreement (RPM, price fixing) | Imposed fines<br>Applied leniency policy |

(cont.)

| Date of decision | Case | Investigating authority | Conduct investigated | Outcome |
|---|---|---|---|---|
| 2 June 2015 | Yunnan Telecommunications Cartel<br><br>Yunnan Communications Authority Administrative Monopoly | Yunnan DRC | Administrative monopoly (cartel)<br><br>Monopoly agreement (price fixing) | Imposed fines<br>Urged the Yunnan Province Communications Authority to rectify and stop its conduct and restore fair competition<br>NDRC communicated with the MIIT |
| 17 August 2015 | Bengbu Health and Planning Commission Drug Procurement Administrative Monopoly | NDRC Bureau | Administrative monopoly (procurement) | Made recommendation to the Anhui Provincial Government |
| 19 September 2015 | Dongfeng Nissan Cartel and RPM | Guangdong DRC | Monopoly agreement (RPM, price fixing) | Imposed fines |
| 25 September 2015 | Wuwei Car Maintenance Fees Cartel | Gansu DRC | Monopoly agreement (price fixing) | Imposed fines |
| 2 November 2015 | Sichuan and Zhejiang Health and Planning Commissions Drug Procurement Administrative Monopoly | NDRC Bureau | Administrative monopoly (procurement) | Monitored implementation of corrective measures |
| 5 November 2015 | Wuwei Car Maintenance Fees Administrative Monopoly | Gansu DRC | Administrative monopoly (cartel) | Made recommendation to the Wuwei Transport Bureau |
| 26 November 2015 | Gansu GPS Platform Administrative Monopoly | Gansu DRC | Administrative monopoly (designated supplier) | Made recommendation to the Gansu Transport Department |

*(cont.)*

| Date of decision | Case | Investigating authority | Conduct investigated | Outcome |
| --- | --- | --- | --- | --- |
| 15 December 2015 | Roll On/Roll Off Shipping Cartel | NDRC Bureau | Monopoly agreement (price fixing, bid rigging) | Imposed fine Applied leniency policy |
| 15 January 2016 | Allopurinol Tablet Cartel | NDRC Bureau | Monopoly agreement (price fixing, market sharing, bid rigging) | Imposed fines |
| 13 April 2016 | Shaanxi Motor Vehicle Inspection Fees cartel | Shaanxi Price Bureau | Monopoly agreement (price fixing) | Imposed fines |
| 13 April 2016 | Hanook Tire RPM | Shanghai Price Bureau | Monopoly agreement (RPM) | Imposed fines Ordered to stop illegal conduct |
| 12 July 2016 | Hubei Piped Natural Gas Excessive Pricing | Hubei Price Bureau | Abuse of dominance (unfairly high prices) | Imposed fines |
| 22 July 2016 | Estazolam Tablet Cartel | NDRC Bureau | Monopoly agreement (price fixing, joint boycott) | Imposed fines Ordered to stop illegal conduct |
| 8 August 2016 | Haier RPM | Shanghai Price Bureau | Monopoly agreement (RPM) | Imposed fines Ordered to stop illegal conduct |
| 7 December 2016 | Medtronic RPM | NDRC Bureau | Monopoly agreement (RPM) | Imposed fine Ordered to stop illegal conduct |
| 19 December 2016 | SAIC General Motors RPM | Shanghai Price Bureau | Monopoly agreement (RPM) | Imposed fine |
| 27 December 2016 | Speed Fresh RPM | Shanghai Price Bureau | Monopoly agreement (RPM) | Imposed fine |
| 29 December 2016 | Smith & Nephew RPM | Shanghai Price Bureau | Monopoly agreement (RPM) | Imposed fine Ordered to stop illegal conduct |
| 29 December 2016 | Huangpu River Cruise Operators Administrative Monopoly | NDRC Bureau Shanghai Municipal DRC | Administrative monopoly (cartel) | Urged the implementation of corrective measures |

(cont.)

| Date of decision | Case | Investigating authority | Conduct investigated | Outcome |
|---|---|---|---|---|
| 29 December 2016 | Beijing Concrete Quality Control Administrative Monopoly | NDRC Bureau Beijing Municipal Commission of Development and Reform | Administrative monopoly (cartel) | Urged the implementation of corrective measures |
| 29 December 2016 | Shenzhen Primary and High School Supplies Procurement Administrative Monopoly | NDRC Bureau Guangdong DRC | Administrative monopoly (procurement) | Urged the implementation of corrective measures |
| 29 December 2016 | New Residential Area Electricity Supply Equipment Administrative Monopoly | NDRC Bureau Local authorities in Chongqing, Guizhou, Shanxi, Jiangxi, Liaoning, Jilin, Hebei, Heilongjiang, Gansu, Tianjin, Guangxi, Qinghai | Administrative monopoly (designated supplier, cartel) | All twelve local governments rectified conduct |

## B.3 State Administration for Industry and Commerce

| Date of decision | Case | Investigating authority | Conduct investigated | Outcome |
|---|---|---|---|---|
| 26 January 2011 | Lianyungang Ready-Mix Concrete Cartel | Jiangsu AIC | Monopoly agreement (market sharing) | Ordered to stop illegal conduct Imposed fines |
| 1 April 2011 | Taihe Bulk LPG Cartel | Jiangxi AIC | Monopoly agreement (market sharing) | Confiscated illegal gains Imposed fine Ordered to stop the illegal conduct |
| 27 July 2011 | Heyuan GPS Platform Administrative Monopoly | Guangdong AIC | Administrative monopoly (designated supplier) | Made recommendation to the Guangdong Provincial Government Heyuan Government issued administrative review decision finding breach of AML |
| 7 November 2011 14 March 2013 | Cixi Energy Saving Testing Cartel | Zhejiang AIC | Monopoly agreement (market sharing) | Terminated investigation after fulfilment of commitments |
| 4 January 2012 | Anyang Used Car Service Fees Cartel | Henan AIC | Monopoly agreement (price fixing, market sharing) | Ordered to stop illegal conduct Imposed fines Confiscated illegal gains |
| 6 March 2012 to 13 August 2012 | Liaoning Cement Clinker Cartel | Liaoning AIC | Monopoly agreement (output restriction) | Ordered to stop illegal conduct Imposed fines |
| 30 November 2012 | Yongzhou New Car Insurance Cartel | Hunan AIC | Monopoly agreement (market sharing) | Imposed fines |
| 3 December 2012 | Changde New Car Insurance Cartel | Hunan AIC | Monopoly agreement (market sharing) | Imposed fines |

*(cont.)*

| Date of decision | Case | Investigating authority | Conduct investigated | Outcome |
|---|---|---|---|---|
| 3 December 2012 | Chenzhou New Car Insurance Cartel | Hunan AIC | Monopoly agreement (market sharing) | Imposed fines |
| 3 December 2012 | Zhangjiajie New Car Insurance Cartel | Hunan AIC | Monopoly agreement (market sharing) | Imposed fines |
| 14 December 2012 | Jiangshan Commercial Concrete Cartel | Zhejiang AIC | Monopoly agreement (price fixing, market sharing) | Imposed fines |
| 6 March 2013 | Yibin Shale Brick Cartel | Sichuan AIC | Monopoly agreement (output restriction, market sharing) | Ordered to rectify conduct Imposed fines |
| 7 April 2013 | Xishuangbanna Tourism Cartel | Yunnan AIC | Monopoly agreement (joint boycott, price fixing) | Imposed fines |
| 16 December 2013 | Yiyuan Purified Water Unreasonable Conditions | Guangdong AIC | Abuse of dominance (tying) | Ordered to stop illegal conduct Confiscated illegal gains Imposed fine |
| 28 April 2014 | Chongqing Gas Unreasonable Conditions | Chongqing AIC | Abuse of dominance (tying) | Imposed fine |
| 27 May 2014 | Chifeng Fireworks and Firecracker Cartel | Inner Mongolia AIC | Monopoly agreement (market sharing) | Imposed fines |
| 3 June 2014 2 January 2015 | Beijing Shankai Sports Tying | SAIC | Abuse of dominance (tying) | Terminated investigation after fulfilment of commitments |
| 13 June 2014 (news report) | Quanzhou Cable Television Tying | Quanzhou AIC | Abuse of dominance (tying) | Imposed fines Unsuccessful application for administration reconsideration |

APPENDIX B

*(cont.)*

| Date of decision | Case | Investigating authority | Conduct investigated | Outcome |
|---|---|---|---|---|
| 4 July 2014 | Chifeng Tobacco Tying | Inner Mongolia AIC | Abuse of dominance (tying) | Imposed fine Ordered to stop illegal conduct |
| 18 August 2014 | Wuxi Quarry Cartel | Chongqing AIC | Monopoly agreement (market sharing) | Imposed fines |
| 5 September 2014 | Shangyu Commercial Concrete Cartel | Zhejiang AIC | Monopoly agreement (market sharing) | Imposed fines |
| 29 September 2014 | Pizhou Tobacco Differential Treatment | Jiangsu AIC | Abuse of dominance (differential treatment) | Imposed fine |
| 28 January 2015 | Dongfang Water Unreasonable Conditions | Hainan AIC | Abuse of dominance (unreasonable conditions) | Confiscated illegal gains Imposed fine Ordered to stop illegal conduct |
| December to January 2015 | Mayang Miao Autonomous County Shale Brick Cartel | Hunan AIC | Monopoly agreement (price fixing) | Imposed fines Ordered to stop the illegal conduct |
| 14 May 2015 9 December 2016 | Ningxia Broadband Internet Tying | Ningxia AIC | Abuse of dominance (tying) | Terminated investigation after fulfilment of commitments |
| 1 June 2015 | Fushun Tobacco Tying | Liaoning AIC | Abuse of dominance (tying) | Imposed fine |
| 3 June 2015 | Wuhan Coinsurance Cartel | Hubei AIC | Monopoly agreement (market sharing) | Ordered to stop illegal conduct Confiscated illegal gains Imposed fines |
| 9 July 2015 | Panyu Animation Expo Cartel | Guangdong AIC | Monopoly agreement (collective boycott) | Imposed fine Ordered to stop illegal conduct |
| 1 September 2015 | Inner Mongolia Mobile | Inner Mongolia AIC | Abuse of dominance | Suspended investigation |

(cont.)

| Date of decision | Case | Investigating authority | Conduct investigated | Outcome |
|---|---|---|---|---|
| 28 October 2015 | Chongqing Qingyang Pharmaceutical Refusal to Supply | Chongqing AIC | Unreasonable Conditions (unreasonable conditions) Abuse of dominance (refusal to supply) | Offered commitments Ordered to stop illegal conduct Imposed fine |
| 28 October 2015 | Inner Mongolia Unicom Tying | Inner Mongolia AIC | Abuse of dominance (tying) | Suspended investigation Offered commitments |
| 3 November 2015 | Yongzhou Commercial Concrete Cartel | Hunan AIC | Monopoly agreement (market sharing) | Imposed fines Applied leniency policy |
| 28 December 2015 | Jiangxi Coinsurance Cartel | Jiangxi AIC | Monopoly agreement (market sharing) | Imposed fines Ordered to stop illegal conduct |
| 21 March 2016 | Linyi Accounting Firm Cartel | Shandong AIC | Monopoly agreement (market sharing) | Imposed fine Ordered to stop illegal conduct Unsuccessful administrative litigation |
| 21 March 2016 | Qingdao Xinao Xincheng Gas Unreasonable Conditions | Shandong AIC | Abuse of dominance (unreasonable conditions) | Ordered to stop illegal conduct Imposed fine Confiscated illegal gains |
| 22 April 2016 | Alxa Zuoqi Water Unreasonable Conditions | Inner Mongolia AIC | Abuse of dominance (unreasonable conditions) | Ordered to stop illegal conduct Imposed fine Confiscated illegal gains |
| 6 May 2016 | Wuhan New Car Insurance Cartel | Hubei AIC | Monopoly agreement (market sharing) | Imposed fine |
| 7 June 2016 | Xilin Gol Radio and Television Unreasonable Conditions | Inner Mongolia AIC | Abuse of dominance (unreasonable conditions) | Ordered to stop illegal conduct Imposed fine Confiscated illegal gains |

APPENDIX B 331

*(cont.)*

| Date of decision | Case | Investigating authority | Conduct investigated | Outcome |
| --- | --- | --- | --- | --- |
| 16 August 2016 | Chifeng Salt Differential Treatment | Inner Mongolia AIC | Abuse of dominance (differential treatment) | Imposed fine Confiscated illegal gains |
| 19 August 2016 | Hai'an Electric Power Unreasonable Conditions | Jiangsu AIC | Abuse of dominance (unreasonable conditions) | Terminated investigation after fulfilment of commitments |
| 18 September 2016 | Anhui Payment Encryption Device Cartel | Anhui AIC | Monopoly agreement (market sharing) | Imposed fines Confiscated illegal gains |
| 12 October 2016 | Urumqi Water Exclusive Dealing | Xinjiang AIC | Abuse of dominance (full/third line forcing) | Imposed fine Ordered to stop illegal conduct |
| 26 October 2016 | Yongzhou Salt Tying | Hunan AIC | Abuse of dominance (unreasonable conditions) | Imposed fine Confiscated illegal gains Ordered to stop illegal conduct |
| 9 November 2016 | Tetra Pak Abuse of Dominance | SAIC Bureau | Abuse of dominance (tying, unreasonable conditions, other conduct) | Imposed fine Ordered to stop illegal conduct |
| 24 November 2016 | Chongqing Southwest Pharmaceutical Refusal to Supply | Chongqing AIC | Abuse of dominance (refusal to supply) | Imposed fine Confiscated illegal gains |
| 28 November 2016 | Suqian Yinkong Water Exclusive Dealing | Jiangsu AIC | Abuse of dominance (exclusive dealing) | Imposed fine Confiscated illegal gains |

# Appendix C

# Timeline of the Anti-monopoly Law Drafting Process

| Date | Action |
| --- | --- |
| 1987 | |
| August | The State Council Legislative Affairs Office (LAO) establishes a drafting group for competition legislation. |
| 1988 | The Anti-monopoly and Anti-Unfair Competition Draft Interim Regulation is released by the drafting group. |
| 1993 | |
| September | The Anti-Unfair Competition Law is enacted. |
| 1994 | |
| May | The LAO establishes a group to prepare a draft of the Anti-monopoly Law (AML). This group (the Ministry Drafting Group) is led by the State Economic and Trade Commission (SETC) and the State Administration for Industry and Commerce (SAIC). |
| 1997 | |
| July | First draft outline of the AML is finished. |
| December | Price Law is enacted. |
| 1998 | |
| November | Second draft outline of the AML is finished. |
| | The Ministry Drafting Group and the Organisation for Economic Cooperation and Development (OECD) jointly organise a conference in Beijing to discuss the draft AML. |
| 1999 | Vice Chairman of Standing Committee of the National People's Congress (SCNPC) arranges for experts from the Chinese Academy of Social Sciences (CASS) to conduct research on competition law. |
| | The Ministry Drafting Group produces several outlines of the draft AML. |
| November | Draft outline of the AML released. |
| December | Ministry Drafting Group and OECD jointly organise a seminar in Shanghai to discuss the draft AML. |

*(cont.)*

| Date | Action |
|---|---|
| 2000 | |
| June | A consultation draft of the AML is distributed to relevant government departments. |
| 2001 | |
| March | China announces that it will enact a competition law in preparation for accession into the World Trade Organization. |
| 2002 | |
| April | Revised draft AML released. |
| July | Revised draft AML released. |
| October | Revised draft AML released. |
| | The SETC submits a draft AML to the LAO for review. |
| 2003 | An unofficial draft AML is widely circulated outside China. |
| January | Regulation on Mergers with and Acquisitions of Domestic Enterprises by Foreign Investors implemented. |
| September | Revised draft AML released. |
| | The LAO, the Ministry of Commerce (MOFCOM) and the SAIC solicit comments on revised draft AML from foreign governments and non-governmental organisations. |
| October | The MOFCOM holds a conference outside Beijing to discuss September 2003 draft with foreign experts. |
| 2004 | The American Bar Association holds round-table program for the MOFCOM and American experts to discuss the draft AML. |
| | The MOFCOM, the LAO and relevant SCNPC institutions jointly study the enactment and implementation experiences of the United States, European Union, Norway, Japan and Mexico, and produce a report and recommendations. |
| February | Revised draft AML released. |
| March | The MOFCOM and the SAIC submit draft AML to LAO for review. |
| May | The SAIC's Competition Restricting Conduct of Multinational Companies in China and Countermeasures report released. |
| July | An unofficial draft AML is circulated widely. |
| August | The MOFCOM holds seminar to discuss the draft AML with experts. |
| September | The MOFCOM sets up the Anti-monopoly Office. |

*(cont.)*

| Date | Action |
|---|---|
| October 2005 | The MOFCOM submits draft AML to the LAO for review. |
| February | The AML is included on the State Council's legislative agenda. |
| March | Revised draft AML released. |
| April | Revised draft AML released. |
| | State Council forms a leading small group to be responsible for reviewing and revising the draft AML. |
| May | The LAO holds a conference in Beijing to discuss the draft AML with foreign experts. |
| July | Revised draft AML released. |
| | The LAO holds a conference in Beijing to discuss the revised draft AML with Chinese scholars, government officials and legal counsel from multinational corporations. |
| September | Revised draft AML released. |
| November | Revised draft AML released. |
| | The US Council for International Business, US–China Business Council and US Chamber of Commerce hold a panel discussion in New York to discuss the AML with Chinese government officials and law-makers. |
| 2006 | |
| June | The State Council approves the draft AML in principle on 7 June. |
| | The State Council submits the draft AML to the SCNPC after making further revisions. |
| | The Law Committee of the National People's Congress (Law Committee) holds a conference to discuss the draft AML on an article-by-article basis on 12 and 19 June. |
| | The SCNPC begins first review of the draft AML on 24 June. |
| 2007 | |
| June | The SCNPC conducts second review of the draft AML on 24 and 25 June. |
| August | The SCNPC conducts third review of the draft AML on 24 and 29 August. |
| | The Law Committee holds a conference to discuss the draft AML on 26 August. |
| | The AML is promulgated on 31 August. |
| 2008 | |
| August | The AML comes into effect. |

# BIBLIOGRAPHY

中央企业2014年度经营情况 [2014 Business Operations of Central State-owned Enterprises], State-owned Assets Supervision and Administration Commission of the State Council, 23 January 2015, available at www.sasac.gov.cn/n2588035/n2588330/n2588360/c3777325/content.html

2015年全国工商系统消费者权益保护报告 [2015 Report on Consumers' Rights and Interests Protection by the SAIC], 16 March 2016, 中国工商报网 [China Industry & Commerce News], available at www.cicn.com.cn/zggsb/2016-03/16/cms83461article.shtml

关于法律规定的三个垄断行为—分组审议反垄断法草案发言摘登 (四) [About the Three Types of Monopolistic Conduct Regulated by the Law – Speech Excerpts of Group Deliberations on the Draft Anti-Monopoly Law (4)], 28th Session of the Standing Committee of the Tenth National People's Congress, 25 June 2007

跨国公司滥用知识产权是典型违法垄断 [Abuse of Intellectual Property by Multinational Companies is a Typical Example of Illegal Monopoly Conduct], 法制日报 [*Legal Daily*], 20 May 2005, available at http://finance.sina.com.cn/roll/20050520/09321606527.shtml

Allen, Franklin, Jun Qian and Meijun Qian, 'Law, Finance, and Economic Growth in China' (2005) 77 *Journal of Financial Economics* 57–116

American Bar Association Section of International Law, 'Seven Years in Beijing: China's Merger Reviews under the Anti-Monopoly Law' (Teleconference, 23 September 2015)

关于《中华人民共和国反垄断法 (草案)》的说明 [An Explanation of China's Anti-Monopoly Law (Draft)], 22nd Session of the Standing Committee of the Tenth National People's Congress, 24 June 2006

经营者集中简易案件公示 [Announcement of Simple Cases of Concentrations of Business Operators], Ministry of Commerce of the People's Republic of China Anti-Monopoly Bureau, available at http://fldj.mofcom.gov.cn/article/jyzjzjyajgs

反垄断局紧急约见提交对腾讯反垄断调查律师 [Anti-Monopoly Bureau Has Urgent Meeting with Lawyers Requesting Anti-monopoly Investigation of Tencent], 每日经济新闻 [*Daily Economic News*], 9 November 2010, available at http://tech.sina.com.cn/i/2010-11-09/01024841632.shtml

Anti-Monopoly Bureau of the Ministry of Commerce, 反垄断局加强经营者集中案件信息公开 [Anti-Monopoly Bureau Enhances Disclosure of Notifications of Concentrations of Business Operators] (News Release, 15 November 2012)

反垄断法律知识竞赛开赛 [Anti-Monopoly Law Knowledge Contest] (30 July 2009), State Administration for Industry and Commerce, available at www.saic.gov.cn/fldyfbzdjz/gzdt/200909/t20090927_205502.html

反垄断法二审稿更加符合我国国情—分组审议反垄断法草案发言摘登 (一) [Anti-Monopoly Law Second Deliberation Draft More Compatible with Our National Conditions – Speech Excerpts of the Group Deliberations of the Draft Anti-Monopoly Law (1)], 28th Session of the Standing Committee of the Tenth National People's Congress, 25 June 2007

反垄断法月底三审，垄断国企拒绝交易等纳入监管 [Anti-Monopoly Law Third Review at the End of the Month, State-owned Monopolies Refuse to be Subject to Regulation], 21世纪经济报道 [*21st Century Business Herald*], 21 August 2007, available at www.china.com.cn/policy/txt/2007-08/21/content_8718921.htm

反垄断法的19年风雨历程 [Anti-Monopoly Law's Stormy 19-Year Journey] (2006) 358 中国经济周刊 [China Economic Weekly] 20–1

'AstraZeneca Probed in China amid GSK Scandal', *People's Daily*, 23 July 2013, available at http://english.people.com.cn/90778/8338450.html

Bell, Gordon, 'Instant Noodle Makers Illegally Fix Price', *China Daily*, 17 August 2007, available at www.chinadaily.com.cn/china/2007-08/17/content_6031382.htm

Berkowitz, Daniel, Katharina Pistor and Jean-Francois Richard, 'The Transplant Effect' (2003) 51 *The American Journal of Comparative Law* 163–203

Biddulph, Sarah and Pip Nicholson, 'Expanding the Circle: Comparative Legal Studies in Transition' in Penelope (Pip) Nicholson and Sarah Biddulph (eds.), *Examining Practice, Interrogating Theory: Comparative Legal Studies in Asia* (Leiden: Martinus Nijhoff Publishers, 2008) 9–23

Blumenthal, William, 'Presentation to the International Symposium on the Draft Anti-Monopoly Law of the People's Republic of China' (Speech delivered at the Legislative Affairs Office of the State Council, Beijing, 24–25 May 2005)

'Breaking Administrative Monopoly Benefits All', *China Daily*, 24 December 2002, available at www.chinadaily.com.cn/chinagate/doc/2002-12/24/content_249316.htm

Brødsgaard, Kjeld Erik, 'Politics and Business Group Formation in China: The Party in Control?' (2012) 211 *The China Quarterly* 624–48

Buckley, Chris, 'Chinese Leader's Economic Plan Tests Goal to Fortify Party Power', New York Times, 6 November 2013, available at www.nytimes.com/2013/11/07/world/asia/a-clash-of-goals-for-chinas-leader.html

Buckman, Rebecca, 'China Hurries Antitrust Law', The Wall Street Journal, 11 June 2004, available at http://online.wsj.com/news/articles/SB108689271342233967

Burkitt, Laurie, 'In China, Veil Begins to Lift on High Consumer Prices', The Wall Street Journal, 4 September 2013, B1
Burkitt, Laurie and Jeanne Whalen, 'China Targets Big Pharma', The Wall Street Journal, 16 July 2013, A1
Burns, John P., 'China's *Nomenklatura* System' (1987) 36(5) *Problems of Communism* 36–51
Bush, Nate, 'Weathervanes, Lightning Rods, and Pliers: The NDRC's Competition Enforcement Program' [2014] (August) *The Antitrust Source* 1–10, available at www.americanbar.org/content/dam/aba/publishing/antitrust_source/aug14_bush_7_23f.authcheckdam.pdf
Bush, Nathan, 'Chinese Competition Policy: It Takes More Than a Law' (May/June 2005) 32(3) *China Business Review* 30–5
Bush, Nathan, 'Constraints on Convergence in Chinese Antitrust' (2009) 54 *Antitrust Bulletin* 87–155
Bush, Nathan, 'The PRC Antimonopoly Law: Unanswered Questions and Challenges Ahead' [2007] (October) *The Antitrust Source* 1–13, available at www.americanbar.org/content/dam/aba/publishing/antitrust_source/Oct07_Bush10_18f.authcheckdam.pdf
Bush, Nathan and Yue Bo, 'Adding Antitrust to NDRC's Arsenal' [2011] (2) *CPI Antitrust Chronicle* 1–11
Bush, Nate and Yue Bo, 'Disentangling Industrial Policy and Competition Policy in China' [2011] (February) *The Antitrust Source* 1–14, available at www.americanbar.org/content/dam/aba/migrated/2011_build/antitrust_law/feb11_bush2_23f.authcheckdam.pdf
Byrd, William A., *The Market Mechanism and Economic Reforms in China* (Armonk, NY: M. E. Sharpe, 1991)
Cabestan, Jean-Pierre, 'The Relationship between the National People's Congress and the State Council in the People's Republic of China: A Few Checks but No Balances' (2001) 19(3) *American Asian Review* 35–73
中央变更 [Central SOE Changes], State-owned Assets Supervision and Administration Commission, available at www.sasac.gov.cn/n2588035/n2641579/n2641660/index.html
央企名录 [Central SOE Directory], State-owned Assets Supervision and Administration Commission of the State Council, available at www.sasac.gov.cn/n2588035/n2641579/n2641645/index.html
Chan, Gordon Y. M., 'Administrative Monopoly and the Anti-monopoly Law: An Examination of the Debate in China' (2009) 18 *Journal of Contemporary China* 263–83
Chan, Hon S., 'Cadre Personnel Management in China: The Nomenklatura System, 1990–1998' (2004) 179 *The China Quarterly* 703–34
Chan, Hon S., 'Politics over Markets: Integrating State-owned Enterprises into Chinese Socialist Market' (2009) 29 *Public Administration and Development* 43–54

Chang, Bao, 'SOE Reforms to Be Launched After Plenum', *China Daily*, 11 November 2013, available at www.chinadaily.com.cn/china/2013cpctps/2013-11/11/content_17094060.htm

Chang, Gordon G., 'China Imposes Price Controls, Informally', *Forbes*, 8 May 2011, available at www.forbes.com/sites/gordonchang/2011/05/08/china-imposes-price-controls-informally

Chang, Gordon G., 'China Mugs Foreign Companies with Price Investigations', *Forbes*, 7 July 2013, available at www.forbes.com/sites/gordonchang/2013/07/07/china-mugs-foreign-companies-with-price-investigations

Chao, Chien-Min, 'The National People's Congress Oversight Power and the Role of the CCP' (2003) 17 *The Copenhagen Journal of Asian Studies* 6–30

陈欢 [Chen Huan], 反垄断法审议再起波折，行政垄断条款仍存争议 [Setbacks Again in the Review of Anti-monopoly Law, Administrative Monopoly Provisions Remain Controversial], 21世纪经济报道 [*21st Century Business Herald*] 15 June 2006, available at www.ce.cn/law/shouye/fzgc/200606/15/t20060615_7352556.shtml

Chen, Jianfu, *Chinese Law: Context and Transformation*, revised and expanded edn (Leiden: Brill Nijhoff, 2015)

陈凯 [Chen Kai], 腾讯案的关键：是否滥用市场支配地位 [Key in Tencent's Case: Whether It Abused Its Dominant Market Position], 经济参考报 [*Economic Information Daily*], 8 May 2012, available at http://jjckb.xinhuanet.com/opinion/2012-05/08/content_373844.htm

陈立彤, 顾正平 [Chen Litong and Gu Zhengping], 工商局首次处罚不配合反垄断调查公司的警示 [First Time SAIC Punishes Company for Non-Cooperation with Anti-monopoly Investigation], 财新网 [*Caixin*], 21 January 2016, available at http://opinion.caixin.com/2016-01-21/100902263.html

Chen, Su, 'The Establishment and Development of the Chinese Economic Legal System in the Past Sixty Years' (2009) 23 *Columbia Journal of Asian Law* 109–36

程刚，崔丽 [Cheng Gang and Cui Li], 反垄断法草案有望通过，严禁国企和公用事业借垄断自肥 [Anti-monopoly Law Draft: State-owned Enterprises and Public Enterprises Strictly Prohibited from Relying on Monopoly to Fatten Themselves], 中国青年报 [*China Youth Daily*], 25 August 2007, available at www.sznews.com/news/content/2007-08/25/content_1457259.htm

Chin, Yee Wah, 'Mergers & Acquisitions under China's Anti-monopoly Law: Update' (Legal Research Paper No. 23/2012, Victoria University of Wellington, 21 February 2012)

'China Busy Preparing for WTO Entry', Xinhua, 9 March 2001

China Central Television, 发展改革委对合生元等乳粉企业反垄断调查 [NDRC's Anti-monopoly Investigation of Biostime and Other Infant Formula Businesses]

新闻直播间 [News Broadcast] 1 July 2013, available at http://tv.cntv.cn/vod play/015c07df1972448e915602c6c74c20b2/860010-1102010100

China Central Television, 新闻30分 [News 30'], 9 November 2011 (李青 [Li Qing]) available at http://news.cntv.cn/program/C20692/20111109/107411.shtml

我国明确七大行业将由国有经济保持绝对控制力 [China Clarifies Seven Industries Where the State-owned Economy Will Have Absolute Control], 新华社 [Xinhua News Agency], 18 December 2006, available at http://finance.people.com.cn/GB/1037/5184638.html

'China Inaugurates its 3rd, 4th Circuit Courts', *China Daily*, 28 December 2016, available at www.chinadaily.com.cn/china/2016-12/28/content_27805067.htm

'China Investigating Foreign Companies over Security', Xinhua, 21 August 2013, http://english.peopledaily.com.cn/90778/8371655.html

'China Makes New Anti-Inflation Move', *China Daily*, 14 January 2008, available at www.chinadaily.com.cn/bizchina/2008-01/14/content_6393131.htm

'China Overview', The World Bank, 6 April 2016, available at www.worldbank.org/en/country/china/overview

China Telecom Corporation Limited, 'Announcement' (Hong Kong Stock Exchange Announcement, 2 December 2011)

China Unicom, 'The Red Chip Companies of China Unicom and China Netcom Are Successfully Merged and China Unicom Telecommunications Corporation Limited Is Established in Beijing' (News Release, 15 October 2008)

中国联通与中国网通重组 国资委监管企业调整为141户 [China Unicom and China Netcom Reorganises, SASAC Supervised Businesses Adjusts to 141 Units] (7 January 2009) State-Owned Assets Supervision and Administration Commission, available at www.sasac.gov.cn/n2588035/n2641579/n2641660/c3753973/content.html

China Unicom (Hong Kong) Limited, 'Announcement' (Hong Kong Stock Exchange Announcement, 2 December 2011)

'China Vows Tough Regulation after Apple's Disputed Repair Policies', Xinhua, 28 March 2013, available at www.china.org.cn/china/Off_the_Wire/2013-03/28/content_28390858.htm

'China's 12th Five-Year Plan: How It Actually Works and What's in Store for the Next Five Years' (APCO Worldwide, 10 December 2010)

'China's Anti-monopoly Law: The Story So Far – And What's Next?' (Freshfields Bruckhaus Deringer, September 2015) available at http://knowledge.freshfields.com/m/Global/r/882/china_s_anti-monopoly_law_-_the_story_so_far___and_what_s

'China's NDRC and SAIC Intensify Non-Merger Antitrust Enforcement', Freshfields Bruckhaus Deringer, 24 October 2013, available at www.freshfields.com/en/knowledge/China%E2%80%99s_NDRC_and_SAIC_Intensify_Non-merger_Antitrust_Enforcement

'China's Reform Leading Group Holds First Meeting', *China Daily*, 22 January 2014, available at www.chinadaily.com.cn/china/2014-01/22/content_172 52345.htm

Cho, Young Nam, 'From "Rubber Stamps" to "Iron Stamps": The Emergence of Chinese Local People's Congresses as Supervisory Powerhouses' (2002) 171 *The China Quarterly* 724–40

Clarke, Donald C., 'Corporate Governance in China: An Overview' (2003) 14 *China Economic Review* 494–507

Clarke, Donald C., 'Legislating for a Market Economy in China' (2007) 191 *The China Quarterly* 567–89

CNOOC Limited, 'CNOOC Limited to Withdraw Unocal Bid' (Press Release, 2 August 2005)

'CNOOC Withdraws Unocal Bid', Xinhua, 3 August 2005, available at www.china.org.cn/english/2005/Aug/137165.htm

Cohen, Jerome A., 'Reforming China's Civil Procedure: Judging the Courts' (1997) 45 *The American Journal of Comparative Law* 793–804

'Competition Law in East Asia: A Month in Review' (Norton Rose Fulbright, January 2017)

*Conducting Government Affairs in China: Best Practices* (US–China Business Council, 2008)

反垄断法暂无望二审 [Currently No Hope for Second Review of the Antimonopoly Law], 经济观察网 [Economic Observer Online], 13 October 2006, available at www.eeo.com.cn/2006/1013/41491.shtml

Dabbah, Maher M., 'Competition Law and Policy in Developing Countries: A Critical Assessment of the Challenges to Establishing an Effective Competition Law Regime' (2010) 33 *World Competition* 457–75

Dabbah, Maher M., 'The Development of Sound Competition Law and Policy and China: An (Im)Possible Dream?' (2007) 30 *World Competition* 341–63

Dabbah, Maher M., *The Internationalisation of Antitrust Policy* (Cambridge: Cambridge University Press, 2003)

Dai, Lian, 'Food Safety Regulators Reshuffled', Caixin, 18 November 2011, available at www.caixinglobal.com/2011-11-18/101016303.html

Dai, Yan, 'Foreign Takeover Controversial', *China Daily*, 11 April 2006, available at www.chinadaily.com.cn/china/2006-04/11/content_565382.htm

Dai, Yan, 'Making of Anti-Trust Law Is Speeded Up', *China Daily*, 28 October 2004, available at www.chinadaily.com.cn/english/doc/2004-10/28/content_386300.htm

单素敏 [Dan Sumin], 许昆林: 亲历重大反垄断案 [Xu Kunlin: Personally Experienced a Major Anti-monopoly Case], 瞭望东方周刊 [*Oriental Outlook*], 25 June 2015, available at www.lwdf.cn/article_1473_1.html

腾讯诉360案宣判: 奇虎停止发行360隐私保护器 赔偿腾讯40万 [Decision in Tencent vs 360 Case: Qihoo to Stop Issuing Its 360 Privacy Protection Tool,

Pay Tencent 400,000 Compensation], 财经网 [Caijing], 26 April 2011, available at www.caijing.com.cn/2011-04-26/110702615.html

Delmestro, Manuél E., 'The Communist Party and the Law: An Outline of Formal and Less Formal Linkages between the Ruling Party and Other Legal Institutions in the People's Republic of China' (2010) 43 *Suffolk University Law Review* 681–700

Deng, Fei, H. Stephen Harris, Jr and Yizhe Zhang, 'Interview with Ning Wanglu, Director General of the Anti-monopoly and Anti-Unfair Competition Enforcement Bureau under the State Administration for Industry and Commerce of People's Republic of China' [2011] (February) *The Antitrust Source* 1–5, available at www.americanbar.org/content/dam/aba/migrated/2011_build/antitrust_law/feb11_ningintrvw2_23f.authcheckdam.pdf

Deng, Fei, H. Stephen Harris, Jr and Yizhe Zhang, 'Interview with Shang Ming, Director General of the Anti-monopoly Bureau under the Ministry of Commerce of the People's Republic of China' [2011] (February) *The Antitrust Source* 1–5, available at www.americanbar.org/content/dam/aba/migrated/2011_build/antitrust_law/feb11_shangintrvw2_23f.pdf

Deng, Fei, H. Stephen Harris, Jr and Yizhe Zhang, 'Interview with Xu Kunlin, Director General of the Department of Price Supervision under the National Development and Reform Commission of People's Republic of China' [2011] (February) *The Antitrust Source* 1–6, available at www.americanbar.org/content/dam/aba/migrated/2011_build/antitrust_law/feb11_xuintrvw2_23f.authcheckdam.pdf

Deng, Fei and Cunzhen Huang, 'A Five Year Review of Merger Enforcement in China' [2013] (October) *The Antitrust Source* 1–18, available at www.americanbar.org/content/dam/aba/directories/antitrust/oct13_deng_10_29f.authcheckdam.pdf

Deng, Fei and Gregory K. Leonard, 'The Role of China's Unique Economic Characteristics in Antitrust Enforcement' in Adrian Emch and David Stallibrass (eds.), *China's Anti-monopoly Law: The First Five Years* (Alphen aan den Rijn, The Netherlands: Kluwer Law International, 2013) 59–74

Deng, Fei and Yizhe Zhang, 'Interview with Shang Ming, Director General of the Anti-monopoly Bureau under the Ministry of Commerce of the People's Republic of China' [2014] (April) *The Antitrust Source* 1–6, available at www.americanbar.org/content/dam/aba/publishing/antitrust_source/apr14_shang_intrvw_4_8f.pdf

Deng, Fei and Yizhe Zhang, 'Interview with Xu Kunlin, Director General of the Bureau of Price Supervision and Anti-monopoly under the National Development and Reform Commission of the People's Republic of China' [2014] (August) *The Antitrust Source* 1–9, available at www.americanbar.org/content/dam/aba/publishing/antitrust_source/aug14_xu_intrvw_7_23f.pdf

Deng, Feng, 'Indigenous Evolution of SOE Regulation' in Benjamin L. Liebman and Curtis J. Milhaupt (eds.), *Regulating the Visible Hand? The Institutional*

*Implications of Chinese State Capitalism* (New York: Oxford University Press, 2016) 3–28

Deng, Guosheng and Scott Kennedy, 'Big Business and Industry Association Lobbying in China: The Paradox of Contrasting Styles' (2010) 63 *The China Journal* 101–25

Deng, Yongheng and Bernard Yeung, 'China's Stimulus May Be a Curse in Disguise', *Forbes*, 25 August 2010, available at www.forbes.com/2010/08/25/china-soe-real-estate-property-markets-economy-stimulus.html

Dickson, Bruce J., *Wealth into Power: The Communist Party's Embrace of China's Private Sector* (New York: Cambridge University Press, 2008)

反垄断法短期内难见效 [Difficult for Anti-monopoly Law to be Effective within the Short Term], 华夏时报 [*China Times*], 27 June 2006, available at www.china.com.cn/chinese/news/1256769.htm

'Domestic Aviation Companies' Price Alliance Collapses', *People's Daily* Online, 21 September 2009, available at http://english.people.com.cn/90001/90778/90857/90860/6763625.html

'Draft New Foreign Investment Law', Freshfields Bruckhaus Deringer, 26 January 2015, available at http://knowledge.freshfields.com/en/global/r/1159/draft_new_foreign_investment_law

'Drafting Work Begins on Drafting Auto Industry Antitrust Guidelines, Preliminary Draft in One Year', *Economic Information Daily*, 18 June 2015, available at http://news.xinhuanet.com/finance/2015-06/18/c_127928081.htm

"十二五"期间反价格垄断取得重大进展 [During the Twelfth Five-Year Plan, Anti-Price Monopoly Made Significant Progress] (3 April 2016) 中华人民共和国国家发展和改革委员会 [National Development and Reform Commission] available at www.sdpc.gov.cn/xwzx/xwfb/201603/t20160304_791938.html

全国人大常委会法制工作委员会经济法室 [Economic Law Division of the Legal Affairs Commission of the Standing Committee of the National People's Congress (ed.)], 中华人民共和国反垄断: 法条文说明、立法理由及相关规定 [The Anti-monopoly Law of the People's Republic of China: Explanation of the Articles, Legislative Reasons, and Related Regulations] (北京大学出版社 [Peking University Press], 2007)

Economic Situation Analytical Taskforce of the Macroeconomic Research Institute of the National Development and Reform Commission, 当前经济形势及2005年的政策取向 [Current Economic Situation and Policy Direction for 2005] (7 January 2005) 中国中小企业信息网 [www.sme.gov.cn] available at www.sme.gov.cn/cms/news/100000/0000000223/2005/1/7/ycqywyuytmhwghxskfw1104366671998.shtml

Economic Situation Analytical Taskforce of the Macroeconomic Research Institute of the National Development and Reform Commission, 发改委专家: 明年增长降到8% 调控力度难办 [NDRC Expert: Next Year's Growth to Drop to 8 Per cent, Difficult to Control], 瞭望新闻周刊 [*Outlook Weekly*] 1 November 2004, available at http://news.sina.com.cn/c/2004-11-01/19144107872s.shtml

'Editorial: Anti-monopoly Investigations Should Be Conducted Openly and Independently', *News China Magazine* (January 2012)

Elhauge, Einer and Damien Geradin, *Global Competition Law and Economics*, 2nd edn (Oxford: Oxford University Press, 2011)

Emch, Adrian, 'Chinese Antitrust Institutions – Many Cooks in the Kitchen' (2014) 10 *Competition Policy International* 217–46

Emch, Adrian, 'Taking It with a Grain of Salt – China's Commitment to Breaking Up Monopolies', Kluwer Competition Law Blog, 30 May 2016, available at http://kluwercompetitionlawblog.com/2016/05/30/taking-grain-salt-chinas-commitment-breaking-monopolies

Emch, Adrian, 'The Antimonopoly Law and Its Structural Shortcomings' [2008] (1) *CPI Antitrust Chronicle* 1–14

'Entrepreneurs' Presence Grows at CPC Congress', Xinhua, 12 November 2012, available at www.chinadaily.com.cn/china/2012cpc/2012-11/12/content_15919473.htm

EU–China Competition Cooperation, 'EU–China Competition Policy: Competition Weeks', available at www.euchinacomp.org/index.php/competition-weeks

European Union Chamber of Commerce in China, 'European Chamber Releases Statement on China AML-Related Investigations' (Press Release, 13 August 2014)

Evans, David S., Vanessa Yanhua Zhang and Howard H. Chang, 'Analyzing Competition among Internet Players: Qihoo 360 v. Tencent' [2013] (1) *CPI Antitrust Chronicle* 1–25

'Fact Sheet: 25th US–China Joint Commission on Commerce and Trade', United States Department of Commerce, 19 December 2014, available at www.commerce.gov/news/fact-sheets/2014/12/19/fact-sheet-25th-us-china-joint-commission-commerce-and-trade

国家工商总局公平交易局和反垄断处 [Fair Trade Bureau and Anti-monopoly Division of the State Administration for Industry and Commerce], 在华跨国公司限制竞争行为表现及对策 [Competition Restricting Conduct of Multinational Companies in China and Countermeasures] (2004) 5 工商行政管理 [Biweekly of Industry and Commerce Administration] 42–3

Fang, David, 'Bureaucrats Stall Anti-monopoly Law', *South China Morning Post*, 12 January 2005, available at www.scmp.com/article/485151/bureaucrats-stall-anti-monopoly-law

方乐迪 [Fang Ledi], 央企行政级别有门道 国资委hold不住央企 [There's a Knack to Central SOE Administrative Ranks, SASAC Cannot Hold onto

Central SOEs], 大公报 [Ta Kung Pao], 1 July 2013, available at http://news.takungpao.com/mainland/focus/2013-07/1727688.html

Farmer, Susan Beth, 'The Evolution of Chinese Merger Notification Guidelines: A Work in Progress Integrating Global Consensus and Domestic Imperatives' (2009) 18 *Tulane Journal of International and Comparative Law* 1–92

Farmer, Susan Beth, 'The Impact of China's Antitrust Law and Other Competition Polices on US Companies' (2010) 23 *Loyola Consumer Law Review* 34–53

Feng, Qihua, 'Anti-monopoly Legislation Urged', *China Daily*, 16 March 2002, available at www.chinadaily.com.cn/en/doc/2002-03/16/content_111189.htm

反垄断法实施5年: 公平竞争市场环境的有力维护者 [Five Years of Implementing Anti-monopoly Law: Strong Protectors of a Fair Market Competition Environment] 工商总局 [State Administration for Industry and Commerce] 29 July 2013, available at www.gov.cn/gzdt/2013-07/31/content_2458835.htm

反垄断法热点问题聚焦—全国人大常委会法工委有关负责人谈反垄断法热点问题 [Focus on Anti-monopoly Law Hot Spot Issues – Legal Affairs Commission of the Standing Committee of the National People's Congress Responsible Person Talks about Anti-monopoly Law Hot Spot Issues], 新华网 [Xinhuanet], 9 September 2007, available at www.npc.gov.cn/npc/xinwen/lfgz/lfdt/2007-09/30/content_372832.htm

Fox, Eleanor M., 'An Anti-monopoly Law for China – Scaling the Walls of Government Restraints' (2008) 75 *Antitrust Law Journal* 173–94

'Frequently Asked Questions About Merger Consent Order Provisions' (Answer to Question 40), US Federal Trade Commission, available at www.ftc.gov/tips-advice/competition-guidance/guide-antitrust-laws/mergers/merger-faq#Hold%20Separate%20Orders

Fu, Hualing, 'Autonomy, Courts, and the Politico-Legal Order in Contemporary China' in Liqun Cao, Ivan Y. Sun and Bill Hebenton (eds.), *The Routledge Handbook of Chinese Criminology* (London: Routledge, 2013) 76–88

Fu, Jing, 'Foreign Firms' Monopolies Cause Concern', *China Daily*, 8 December 2005, available at www.chinadaily.com.cn/english/doc/2005-12/08/content_501524.htm

Fu, Jing, 'Stiff Penalties for Price Rigging', *China Daily*, 29 August 2007, available at www.chinadaily.com.cn/cndy/2007-08/29/content_6063449.htm

符迎曦, 史怀特 [Yingxi Fu-Tomlinson and Steven R Wright], 商务部附条件批准沃尔玛收购案—它对沃尔玛、1号店以及VIE结构的未来意味着什么? [MOFCOM's Conditional Approval of Wal-Mart's Acquisition – What Does It Mean for Wal-Mart and Yihaodian and for the Future of the VIE Structure?] (2012) 64 中国法律透视 [China Legal Review] available at http://hk.lexiscnweb.com/clr/view_article.php?clr_id=70&clr_article_id=888#eng

# BIBLIOGRAPHY

'FY 2016 Budget Request at a Glance' (Antitrust Division, US Department of Justice, 30 January 2015), available at www.justice.gov/sites/default/files/jmd/pages/attachments/2015/01/30/19_bs_section_ii_chapter_-_atr.pdf

Gal, Michal S., *Competition Policy for Small Market Economies* (Cambridge, MA: Harvard University Press, 2003)

Gal, Michal, 'The Ecology of Antitrust: Preconditions for Competition Law Enforcement in Developing Countries' in Ana María Alvarez et al. (eds.), *Competition, Competitiveness and Development: Lessons from Developing Countries* (Geneva: United Nations Conference on Trade and Development, 2004) 21–52

Gao, Yongqiang and Zhilong Tian, 'How Firms Influence the Government Policy Decision-Making in China' (2006) 28 *Singapore Management Review* 73–85

耿振淞 [Geng Zhensong], 国家工商局换牌称总局 晋级为正部 [SAIC Changes its Nameplate to General Administration, Upgraded to Ministry], 北京青年报 [Beijing Youth Daily], 11 April 2001, available at www.people.com.cn/GB/jinji/32/180/20010411/439009.html

Gerber, David J., 'Constructing Competition Law in China: The Potential Value of European and U.S. Experience' (2004) 3 *Washington University Global Studies Law Review* 315–31

Gerber, David J., 'Economics, Law & Institutions: The Shaping of Chinese Competition Law' (2008) 26 *Journal of Law & Policy* 271–99

Gerber, David J., *Global Competition: Law, Markets, and Globalization* (Oxford: Oxford University Press, 2010)

Gerber, David J., *Law and Competition in Twentieth Century Europe: Protecting Prometheus* (New York: Oxford University Press, 1998)

Gillespie, John, 'Developing a Decentred Analysis of Legal Transfers' in Penelope (Pip) Nicholson and Sarah Biddulph (eds.), *Examining Practice, Interrogating Theory: Comparative Legal Studies in Asia* (Leiden: Martinus Nijhoff Publishers, 2008) 25–70

'Global 500 – 2015', *Fortune*, available at http://fortune.com/global500/2015

Godwin, Andrew, 'The Professional "Tug of War": The Regulation of Foreign Lawyers in China, Business Scope Issues and Some Suggestions for Reform' (2009) 33 *Melbourne University Law Review* 132–62

Goldman, Merle and Roderick MacFarquhar, 'Dynamic Economy, Declining Party-State' in Merle Goldman and Roderick MacFarquhar (eds.), *The Paradox of China's Post-Mao Reforms* (Cambridge, MA: Harvard University Press, 1999) 3–29

Gough, Neil, 'In China, Concern About a Chill on Foreign Investments', *New York Times*, 2 June 2013, available at http://dealbook.nytimes.com/2013/06/02/in-china-concern-of-a-chill-on-foreign-investments

Gu, Weixia, 'The Judiciary in Economic and Political Transformation: *Quo Vadis* Chinese Courts?' (2013) 1 *The Chinese Journal of Comparative Law* 303–34

横向垄断协议案件宽大制度适用指南 (征求意见稿) [Guideline on the Application of Leniency in Cases Involving Horizontal Monopoly Agreements (Consultation Draft)] (People's Republic of China) National Development and Reform Commission, 2 February 2016, available at http://jjs.ndrc.gov.cn/fjgld/201602/t20160203_774287.html

Guo, Yong and Angang Hu, 'The Administrative Monopoly in China's Economic Transition' (2004) 37 *Communist and Post-Communist Studies* 265–80

Hammond, Scott D. and Belinda A. Barnett, 'Frequently Asked Questions Regarding the Antitrust Division's Leniency Program and Model Leniency Letters' (US Department of Justice, 19 November 2008) available at www.justice.gov/atr/public/criminal/239583.htm

Hamrin, Carol Lee, 'The Party Leadership System' in Kenneth G. Lieberthal and David M. Lampton (eds.), *Bureaucracy, Politics, and Decision Making in Post-Mao China* (Berkeley: University of California Press, 1992) 95–124

Han, Michael and David Boyle, 'Antitrust Enforcement: China Ups the Ante' [2014] *Competition Policy International: Asia Antitrust Column* 1–10, available at www.competitionpolicyinternational.com/antitrust-enforcement-china-ups-the-ante

Han, Michael and Richard Hughes, 'Merger Control in China: Developments in 2012' [2013] (2) *CPI Antitrust Chronicle* 1–10

Han, Michael and Jessica Su, 'China's Antimonopoly Law: Status Quo and Outlook' [2008] (1) *CPI Antitrust Chronicle* 1–14

Han, Michael and Janet (Jingyuan) Wang, 'Due Process in Chinese Competition Law Regime' [2014] (1) *CPI Antitrust Chronicle* 1–10

Han, Michael and Zhaofeng Zhou, 'MOFCOM's Approach to Merger Remedies: Distinctions from Other Competition Authorities' [2012] *Competition Policy International: Asia Antitrust Column* 1–6, available at www.competitionpolicyinternational.com/assets/Free/cpiasiaantitrusthan.pdf

Han, Wei, 'Merger Remedies in China: Past, Present, and Future' [2013] (2) *CPI Antitrust Chronicle* 1–11

Hao, Qian, 'The Multiple Hands: Institutional Dynamics of China's Competition Regime', in Adrian Emch and David Stallibrass (eds.), *China's Antimonopoly Law: The First Five Years* (Alphen aan den Rijn, The Netherlands: Kluwer Law International, 2013) 15–34

Hao, Qian, 'Trade Associations and Private Antitrust Litigation in China' [2013] (1) *CPI Antitrust Chronicle* 1–9

Harris, H. Stephen, Jr, 'An Overview of the Draft China Antimonopoly Law' (2005) 34 *Georgia Journal of International and Comparative Law* 131–42

Harris, H. Stephen, Jr, 'The Making of an Antitrust Law: The Pending Antimonopoly Law of the People's Republic of China' (2006) 7 *Chicago Journal of International Law* 169–229

Harris, H. Stephen, Jr, et al., *Anti-monopoly Law and Practice in China* (New York: Oxford University Press, 2011)

Harris, H. Stephen, Jr and Rodney H. Ganske, 'The Monopolization and IP Abuse Provisions of China's Anti-monopoly Law: Concerns and a Proposal' (2008) 75 *Antitrust Law Journal* 213

Harris, H. Stephen, Jr and Keith D. Shugarman, 'Interview with Shang Ming, Director General of the Anti-monopoly Bureau under the Ministry of Commerce of the People's Republic of China' [2009] (February) *The Antitrust Source* 1–7, available at www.americanbar.org/content/dam/aba/pub lishing/antitrust_source/Feb09_ShangIntrvw2_26f.authcheckdam.pdf

Harris, H. Stephen, Jr and Kathy Lijun Yang, 'China: Latest Developments in Anti-monopoly Law Legislation' (2005) 19(2) *Antitrust* 89–94

商务部反垄断局负责人关于《关于经营者集中附加限制性条件的规定（试行）》的解读 [Head of the Ministry of Commerce Anti-monopoly Bureau's Interpretation of the 'Regulation on the Imposition of Restrictive Conditions on Concentrations of Business Operators (Trial)'] (People's Republic of China) Ministry of Commerce Anti-monopoly Bureau, 17 December 2014, available at http://fldj.mofcom.gov.cn/article/j/201412/20141200835988.shtml

Healey, Deborah, 'An Anti-monopoly Law for China: Weapon or Mirage?' (2008) 16 *Competition & Consumer Law Journal* 220–45

Healey, Deborah, 'Anti-monopoly Law and Mergers in China: An Early Report Card on Procedural and Substantive Issues' (2010) 3 *Tsinghua China Law Review* 17–58

Healey, Deborah, 'Mergers with Conditions in China: Caution, Control, or Industrial Policy?' in Lisa Toohey, Colin B. Picker and Jonathan Greenacre (eds.), *China in the International Economic Order: New Directions and Changing Paradigms* (Cambridge: Cambridge University Press, 2015) 245–67

央企"一把手"行政级别有多高 [How High are the Administrative Ranks of Central SOE Leaders?], finance.ifeng.com, available at http://finance.ifeng.com/news/special/gqybs

Howell, Thomas R., et al., 'China's New Anti-monopoly Law: A Perspective from the United States' (2009) 18 *Pacific Rim Law & Policy Journal* 53–95

'HR Key Figures Card – Staff Members' (European Commission, 2016), available at http://ec.europa.eu/civil_service/docs/hr_key_figures_en.pdf

胡鞍钢 [Hu Angang], 国有企业是中国经济崛起的"领头羊"—基于历史和国际两个视角的分析 [State-owned Enterprises are the 'Leaders' in the Rise of China's Economy – Analysis from Historical and International Perspectives] [2012] (19) 红旗文稿 [Red Flag Manuscript], available at www.qstheory.cn/hqwg/2012/201219/201210/t20121011_185632.htm

胡鞍钢详解"十二五"规划制定过程: 大体11个步骤 [Hu Angang Details the Process of Formulating the 12th Five-Year Plan: Roughly 11 Steps], 新华网 [Xinhuanet], 29 October 2010, available at www.china.com.cn/economic/txt/2010-10/29/content_21228169.htm

胡锦涛 [Hu Jintao], 讲话 [Speech] (Speech delivered at the 纪念党的十一届三中全会召开30周年大会 [Thirtieth Anniversary Ceremony Commemorating the Third Plenum of the Eleventh Chinese Communist Party Central Committee], Beijing, 18 December 2008, available at http://cpc.people.com.cn/GB/64093/64094/8544901.html

Huang, Cary, 'How Leading Small Groups Help Xi Jinping and Other Party Leaders Exert Power', *South China Morning Post*, 20 January 2014, available at www.scmp.com/news/china/article/1409118/how-leading-small-groups-help-xi-jinping-and-other-party-leaders-exert

Huang, Yong, 'Coordination of International Competition Policies: An Anatomy Based on Chinese Reality' in Andrew T. Guzman (ed.), *Cooperation, Comity, and Competition Policy* (New York: Oxford University Press, 2011) 229–64

Huang, Yong, 'Pursuing the Second Best: The History, Momentum, and Remaining Issues of China's Anti-monopoly Law' (2008) 75 *Antitrust Law Journal* 117–31

Huang, Yong and Richean Zhiyan Li, 'An Overview of Chinese Competition Policy: Between Fragmentation and Consolidation' in Adrian Emch and David Stallibrass (eds.), *China's Anti-monopoly Law: The First Five Years* (Alphen aan den Rijn, The Netherlands: Kluwer Law International, 2013) 3–11

Huo, Yongzhe, 'Nation Poised to Hammer Out Anti-monopoly Law', Business Weekly, *China Daily*, 28 January 2003, available at www.chinadaily.com.cn/en/doc/2003-01/28/content_154221.htm

Huo, Zhengxin, 'A Tiger without Teeth: The Antitrust Law of the People's Republic of China' (2008) 10 *Asian-Pacific Law & Policy Journal* 32–61

对滥用市场支配地位行为的认定—分组审议反垄断法草案发言摘登 （二）[Identifying Abuse of Dominant Market Position Conduct – Speech Excerpts of the Group Deliberations of the Draft Anti-monopoly Law (2)], 29th Session of the Standing Committee of the Tenth National People's Congress, 24 August 2007

'Infant Formula Found Contaminated', *China Daily*, 22 July 2012, available at http://usa.chinadaily.com.cn/china/2012-07/22/content_15606682.htm

'Inside the Bureau of Competition', Federal Trade Commission, available at www.ftc.gov/about-ftc/bureaus-offices/bureau-competition/inside-bureau-competition

坚持稳中求进，锐意改革创新，促进经济持续健康发展和社会和谐稳定—全国发展和改革工作会议在京召开 [Insist on Progress Whilst Maintaining Stability, Commit to Reform and Innovation, Promote Sustained and Healthy Economic Development and a Harmonious and Stable Society – National Development and Reform Commission Work Conference Held in Beijing], 15 December 2013, available at www.sdpc.gov.cn/xwzx/xwfb/201312/t20131215_570441.html

方便面涨价被调查始末：三次会议助推涨价 [Instant Noodle Price Increases Investigated: Three Meetings Helped Increase Prices], 新京报 [*The Beijing News*], 17 August 2007, available at www.chinanews.com/cj/xfsh/news/2007/08-17/1004121.shtml

机构设置 [Institutional Arrangements], National Development and Reform Commission Bureau of Price Supervision and Anti-monopoly, available at http://jjs.ndrc.gov.cn/jgsz/

内设机构 [Internal Structure], Anti-monopoly Bureau of the Ministry of Commerce, 13 March 2010, available at http://fldj.mofcom.gov.cn/article/gywm/200811/20081105868495.shtml

International Competition Network Merger Working Group, 'ICN Recommended Practices for Merger Analysis' (2009, rev 2010)

International Competition Network Merger Working Group: Analytical Framework Subgroup, 'Merger Remedies Review Project' (Report for the Fourth ICN Annual Conference, Bonn, June 2005)

解读《关于禁止滥用知识产权排除、限制竞争行为的规定》 [Interpretation of 'Regulation on the Prohibition of Abuse of Intellectual Property Rights to Eliminate or Restrict Competition'] (3 August 2015) State Administration for Industry and Commerce, available at www.saic.gov.cn/fldyfbzdjz/zcfg/xzgz/201508/t20150803_233534.html

Jeffs, James H., 'A Short Comparison of Certain Provisions of the New NDRC and SAIC Regulations' [2011] (2) *CPI Antitrust Chronicle* 1–7

Jenny, Nicolas, 'The Politics of China's Anti-monopoly Investigations', *International Policy Digest*, 17 September 2014, available at www.internationalpolicydigest.org/2014/09/17/politics-china-s-anti-monopoly-investigations

蒋安杰 [Jiang Anjie], 中外专家为反垄断法实施建言献策—第三届中国竞争政策论坛综述 [Chinese and Foreign Experts Offer Advice and Suggestions on Anti-monopoly Law Implementation – The Third Forum on China Competition Policy], 法制日报 [*Legal Daily*], 28 May 2014, available at http://epaper.legaldaily.com.cn/fzrb/content/20140528/Articel09002GN.htm

姜伯静 [Jiang Bojing], 商务部警示联通网通合并涉嫌违法凸显中国法制进步 [MOFCOM Warns China Unicom/China Netcom Merger Might Be Illegal, Highlights Progress in China's Legal System], 人民网 [*People's Daily Online*], 4 May 2009, available at http://it.people.com.cn/GB/42891/42895/9229575.html

江国成 [Jiang Guocheng], 发改委价格监督检查与反垄断局局长谈反价格垄断 [Director-General of the NDRC Price Supervision and Anti-monopoly Bureau Talks about anti-price Monopoly], 新华网 [Xinhuanet], 4 August 2013, available at http://finance.qq.com/a/20130804/003640.htm

江涌 [Jiang Yong], 警惕部门利益膨胀 [Be Wary of the Expansion of Industry and Sector Interests] [2006] (41) 瞭望新闻周刊 [Outlook] 33–5

Jiang Zemin, 江泽民在中国共产党第十四次全国代表大会上的报告 [Report of Jiang Zemin at the Meeting of the Fourteenth National Congress of the Communist Party of China], 12 October 1992, available at http://cpc.people.com.cn/GB/64162/64168/64567/65446/4526308.html

Joekes, Susan and Phil Evans, 'Competition and Development: The Power of Competitive Markets' (International Development Research Centre, 2008)

Jourdan, Adam, 'Starbucks under Media Fire in China for High Prices', Reuters, 21 October 2013, available at www.reuters.com/article/2013/10/21/starbucks-china-pricing-idUSL3N0IB4BG20131021

Jung, Youngjin and Qian Hao, 'The New Economic Constitution in China: A Third Way for Competition Regime?' (2003) 24 *Northwestern Journal of International Law & Business* 107–71

Kahn-Freund, Otto, 'On Uses and Misuses of Comparative Law' (1974) 37 *The Modern Law Review* 1–27

Kallay, Dina, 'Reflections on China's New Anti-monopoly Law' (Remarks presented at the IBA/SVK 'Europe and the Globalisation of Antitrust' Conference, Berlin, 30 June 2008)

Kao, Ernest, 'Luxury Brands Still Reaping Big Rewards in China', *South China Morning Post*, 18 February 2013, available at www.scmp.com/news/china/article/1153131/luxury-brands-still-reaping-big-margins-china-market

Keith, Ronald C. and Zhiqiu Lin, 'Judicial Interpretation of China's Supreme People's Court as "Secondary Law" with Special Reference to Criminal Law' (2009) 23(2) *China Information* 223–55

Kendall, Brett, 'US Court Throws Out Price-Fixing Judgment against Chinese Vitamin C Makers', *The Wall Street Journal*, 20 September 2016, available at www.wsj.com/articles/u-s-court-throws-out-price-fixing-judgment-against-chinese-vitamin-c-manufacturers-1474391092

Kennedy, Scott and Christopher K. Johnson, 'Perfecting China, Inc.: The 13th Five-Year Plan' (Center for Strategic and International Studies, 2016)

2016年价格监管与反垄断工作要点 [Key Points of NDRC Bureau of Price Supervision and Anti-monopoly's Work in 2016] [2016] (2) 中国价格检查与反垄断 [Price Supervision and Anti-monopoly in China] 5–6

Kovacic, William E., 'Designing and Implementing Competition and Consumer Protection Reforms in Transitional Economies: Perspectives from Mongolia, Nepal, Ukraine, and Zimbabwe' (1995) 44 *DePaul Law Review* 1197–224

Kovacic, William E., 'Getting Started: Creating New Competition Policy Institutions in Transition Economies' (1997) 23 *Brooklyn Journal of International Law* 403–53

Kuang, Lei, 'Celebrating with a Damp Squib: China's Public Competition Enforcement' (2016) 4 *Journal of Antitrust Enforcement* 411–38

Lan, Xinzhen, 'State Seeks Control of Critical Industries', *Beijing Review*, 9 January 2007, available at www.bjreview.com.cn/print/txt/2007-01/09/content_52480.htm

郎朗 [Lang Lang], 电信联通反垄断调查或搁浅 [China Telecom/China Unicom Anti-monopoly Investigated or Stranded], *21st Century Business Herald*, 21 November 2011, available at http://tech.sina.com.cn/t/2011-11-21/23596361616.shtml

Lardy, Nicholas R., *Markets over Mao: The Rise of Private Business in China* (Washington, DC: Peterson Institute for International Economics, 2014)

Lawrence, Susan V. and Michael F. Martin, 'Understanding China's Political System' (Congressional Research Service, 31 January 2013)

'Laws Necessary to Counter Monopoly', *People's Daily*, 15 November 2004, available at www.chinadaily.com.cn/english/doc/2004-11/15/content_391618.htm

'Lawyer Appeals to Gov't Over Instant Noodle Price Hike', *China Daily*, 31 July 2007, available at www.chinadaily.com.cn/china/2007-07/31/content_5446492.htm

律师上书国家工商局申请对腾讯展开反垄断调查 [Lawyers Petition SAIC to Launch an Anti-monopoly Investigation into Tencent], 每日经济新闻 [*Daily Economic News*], 5 November 2010, available at www.ce.cn/cysc/tech/07hlw/guonei/201011/05/t20101105_20538202.shtml

Legrand, Pierre, 'The Impossibility of "Legal Transplants"' (1997) 4 *Maastricht Journal of European and Comparative Law* 111–24

Leutert, Wendy, 'Challenges Ahead in China's Reform of State-owned Enterprises' (2016) 21 *Asia Policy* 83–99

李斌 [Li Bin], 多部门出面"叫暂停" "3Q 之战" 中场休息 [Many Departments Call for a "Time Out", Intermission in the "3Q War"], 京华时报 [*Beijing Times*], 5 November 2010, available at http://media.people.com.cn/GB/13134342.html

Li, Cheng, 'China's Midterm Jockeying: Gearing Up for 2012 (Part 1: Provincial Chiefs)' [2010] (31) *China Leadership Monitor* 1–24

Li, Cheng, 'China's Midterm Jockeying: Gearing Up for 2012 (Part 2: Cabinet Ministers)' [2010] (32) *China Leadership Monitor* 1–24

Li, Cheng, 'China's Midterm Jockeying: Gearing Up for 2012 (Part 4: Top Leaders of Major State-owned Enterprises)' [2011] (34) *China Leadership Monitor* 1–31

Li, Cheng, *Chinese Politics in the Xi Jinping Era: Reassessing Collective Leadership* (Washington: Brookings Institution Press, 2016)

Li, Fangchao, 'Food Group Slammed for Price Collusion', *China Daily*, 17 August 2007, available at www.chinadaily.com.cn/cndy/2007-08/17/content_6030552.htm

Li Fangfang and Li Fusheng, 'Automakers Lower Prices Following Monopoly Concerns', *China Daily*, 29 July 2014, available at http://usa.chinadaily.com.cn/epaper/2014-07/29/content_18206559.htm

李镭 [Li Lei], 总结经验，继往开来，开创制止价格垄断工作新局面 [Lessons Learned, Continue Opening Up, Create a New Situation to Stop Price Monopoly] (22 July 2008) National Development and Reform Commission, available at www.sdpc.gov.cn/fzgggz/jggl/zhdt/200808/t20080829_248411.html

李丽 [Li Li], 惠氏、雅培奶粉提价10% 众多品牌不跟风 [Wyeth and Abbott Increase Prices by 10 Per cent, Many Brands Do Not Follow], 经济观察网 [Economic Observer Online], 5 July 2011, available at www.eeo.com.cn/2011/0705/205356.shtml

李莫言 [Li Moyan], 让反垄断法少些遗憾 [Let Anti-monopoly Law Have Fewer Defects] [2006] (7) 大经贸 [Foreign Business] 24

Li, Qing, 'New Developments in the Enforcement of Anti-monopoly Law by NDRC' (Speech delivered at Asian Competition Association Conference, Beijing, 21 October 2012)

Li, Qing, 'The Relationship between the Anti-monopoly Law and the Price Law', in Adrian Emch and David Stallibrass (eds.), *China's Anti-monopoly Law: The First Five Years* (Alphen aan den Rijn, The Netherlands: Kluwer Law International, 2013) 77–82

Li, Richean Zhiyan, 'Unraveling the Jurisdictional Riddle of China's Antitrust Regime' [2011] (2) *CPI Antitrust Chronicle* 1–7

李荣融: 以朱镕基为榜样 以普京为偶像 [Li Rongrong: Zhu Rongji as a Role Model, Putin as an Idol], 人民日报海外版 [People's Daily Overseas Edition], 8 September 2010, available at http://cpc.people.com.cn/GB/64093/64102/12672016.html

Li, Yuwen, 'Judicial Independence: Applying International Minimum Standards to Chinese Law and Practice' (2001) 15(1) *China Information* 67–103

Li, Zhuowei and Ying Zhou, 'MOFCOM's Wal-Mart Decision and Its Wider Implications' [2013] (2) *CPI Antitrust Chronicle* 1–8

Liang, Fei, 'More Drug Firms Receive Govt "Visits"', *Global Times*, 2 August 2013, available at http://en.people.cn/90778/8350806.html

Liao, Jiehua, 'Controversial Air Ticket Pricing System Collapses', Economic Observer, 22 September 2009, available at www.eeo.com.cn/ens/Politics/2009/09/22/152023.shtml

Lieberthal, Kenneth, *Governing China: From Revolution through Reform*, 2nd edn (New York: W. W. Norton, 2004)

Lieberthal, Kenneth G., 'The "Fragmented Authoritarianism" Model and Its Limitations' in Kenneth G. Lieberthal and David M. Lampton (eds.), *Bureaucracy, Politics, and Decision Making in Post-Mao China* (Berkeley: University of California Press, 1992) 1–30

Lieberthal, Kenneth and Michel Oksenberg, *Policy Making in China: Leaders, Structure, and Processes* (Princeton: Princeton University Press, 1988)

Liebman, Benjamin L., 'Assessing China's Legal Reforms' (2009) 23 *Columbia Journal of Asian Law* 17–34

Liebman, Benjamin L., 'China's Courts: Restricted Reform' (2007) 21 *Columbia Journal of Asian Law* 1–44

林红梅 [Lin Hongmei], 中国民航局澄清: 中国民航运价政策没有发生变化 [Civil Aviation Administration of China Clarifies: China's Civil Aviation Pricing Policy Has Not Changed], 新华社 [Xinhua News Agency], 21 April 2009, available at www.gov.cn/fwxx/ly/2009-04/21/content_1291265.htm

Lin, Li-Wen and Curtis J. Milhaupt, 'We Are the (National) Champions: Understanding the Mechanisms of State Capitalism in China' (2013) 65 *Stanford Law Review* 697–759

Lin, Ping and Jingjing Zhao, 'Merger Control Policy under China's Anti-monopoly Law' (2012) 41 *Review of Industrial Organization* 109–32

林远 [Lin Yun], 反垄断执法新目标: 知识产权滥用 [New Target of Anti-monopoly Enforcement: Abuse of Intellectual Property Rights], 经济参考报 [*Economic Information Daily*], 24 March 2015, available at http://jjckb.xinhuanet.com/2015-03/24/content_541963.htm

灵戈 [Ling Ge], 联通网通合并案涉嫌违法? 追究责任要全面彻底 [China Unicom/China Netcom Merger Suspected Illegal? Quest for Accountability Must Be Complete and Thorough], 人民网 [*People's Daily* Online], 4 May 2009, available at http://it.people.com.cn/GB/42891/42895/9232735.html

Liu, Jie, 'Rising Costs Prompt Calls for Action on Prices', *China Daily*, 14 August 2007, available at www.chinadaily.com.cn/cndy/2007-08/14/content_6025017.htm

刘菊花 [Liu Juhua], 李毅中: 工信部正抓紧处理360与QQ纠纷事件 [Liu Yizhong: MIIT Currently Handling 360/QQ Dispute], 新华网 [Xinhuanet], 10 November 2010, available at www.yicai.com/news/595608.html

刘娜 [Liu Na], 反垄断法如期初审, 行政性垄断内容再写入草案 [Initial Review of the Anti-monopoly Law as Planned, Administrative Monopoly Content Restored in Draft], 经济观察报 [Economic Observer Online], 24 June 2006, available at http://finance.sina.com.cn/g/20060624/22332678790.shtml

Liu, Sida, 'Client Influence and the Contingency of Professionalism: The Work of Elite Corporate Lawyers in China' (2006) 40 *Law and Society Review* 751–81

Livdahl, David, et al., 'NDRC's Recent Enforcement of the PRC Anti-monopoly Law: A More Aggressive and Transparent Direction', China Matters: Paul Hastings' Newsletter for Investing and Operating in the People's Republic of China, 25 April 2013, available at www.paulhastings.com/publications-items/details?id=9311de69-2334-6428-811c-ff00004cbded

Lohr, Steve, 'Unocal Bid Opens Up New Issues of Security', *New York Times*, 13 July 2005, available at www.nytimes.com/2005/07/13/business/worldbusiness/13unocal.html

卢延纯: 反垄断法要促进行业经济发展 [Lu Yanchun: Anti-monopoly Law Needs to Promote Industry Economic Development], auto.sina.com.cn,

29 November 2012, available at http://auto.sina.com.cn/news/2012-11-29/12241071631.shtml

Lubman, Stanley, 'Bird in a Cage: Chinese Law Reform after Twenty Years' (2000) 20 *Northwestern Journal of International Law & Business* 383–423

Lubman, Stanley, 'Introduction: The Future of Chinese Law' (1995) 141 *The China Quarterly* 1–21

Lubman, Stanley, 'Looking for Law in China' (2006) 20 *Columbia Journal of Asian Law* 1–92

Lui, Chunfai, 'A Landmark Court Ruling in China: Resale Price Maintenance as Examined in the Johnson & Johnson Case' [2013] (2) *CPI Antitrust Chronicle* 1–10

马红丽 [Ma Lihong], 许昆林: 反垄断维护市场竞争秩序保护公众利益 [Xu Kunlin: Anti-monopoly Maintains Market Competition Order and Protects the Public Interest], 经济日报 [Economy], 27 September 2013

Manion, Melanie, 'When Communist Party Candidates Can Lose, Who Wins? Assessing the Role of Local People's Congresses in the Selection of Leaders in China' (2008) 195 *The China Quarterly* 607–30

Mao, Xiaofei, 'An Overview of the Anti-monopoly Practice in the People's Republic of China' in Hassan Qaqaya and George Lipimile (eds.), *The Effects of Anti-Competitive Business Practices on Developing Countries and Their Development Prospects* (New York: United Nations Conference on Trade and Development, 2008) 497–542

'Market Says Goodbye to Foul Play', *China Daily*, 9 January 2002, available at www.chinadaily.com.cn/en/doc/2002-01/09/content_101213.htm

Martina, Michael, 'Exclusive: Tough-talking China Pricing Regulator Sought Confessions from Foreign Firms', Reuters, 21 August 2013, available at www.reuters.com/article/2013/08/21/us-china-antitrust-idUSBRE97K05020130821

Martina, Michael, 'Insight: Flexing Antitrust Muscle, China is a New Merger Hurdle', Reuters, 2 May 2013, available at www.reuters.com/article/2013/05/02/us-mergers-regulation-china-insight-idUSBRE94116920130502

Martina, Michael and Matthew Miller, '"Mr Confession" and His Boss Drive China's Antitrust Crusade', Reuters, 15 September 2014, available at www.reuters.com/article/us-china-antitrust-ndrc-insight-idUSKBN0HA27X20140915

Masseli, Markus, 'The Application of Chinese Competition Law to Foreign Mergers: Lessons from the Draft New Guidelines' (2012) 3 *Journal of European Competition Law & Practice* 102–9

Mehra, Salil K. and Yanbei Meng, 'Against Antitrust Functionalism: Reconsidering China's Antimonopoly Law' (2008) 49 *Virginia Journal of International Law* 379–430

Mehta, Pradeep S., Manish Agarwal and V. V. Singh, 'Politics Trumps Economics – Lessons and Experiences on Competition and Regulatory Regimes from Developing Countries' (CUTS International, CUTS Institute for Regulation & Competition and CUTS Centre for Competition, Investment & Economic Regulation, 2007)

Mehta, Pradeep S. and S. Chakravarthy, 'Dimensions of Competition Policy and Law in Emerging Economies' (Discussion Paper, CUTS Centre for Competition, Investment & Economic Regulation, Jaipur, 2010)

孟斌 [Meng Bin], 王文超在全市要求加强党建工作做大做强国企 [Wang Wenchao Called for the Strengthening of Party Building Work and for SOEs to Become Bigger and Stronger], 郑州日报 [Zhengzhou Daily], 22 June 2007, available at www.zynews.com/2007-06/22/content_454693.htm

Meng, Yanbei, 'The Uneasy Relationship between Antitrust Enforcement and Industry-Specific Regulation in China' in Adrian Emch and David Stallibrass (eds.), *China's Anti-monopoly Law: The First Five Years* (Alphen aan den Rijn, The Netherlands: Kluwer Law International, 2013) 259–70

'Mergers Reduce China's Central SOEs to 123', Xinhua, 5 August 2010, available at www.chinadaily.com.cn/bizchina/2010-08/06/content_11107199.htm

Milhaupt, Curtis J., 'Beyond Legal Origin: Rethinking Law's Relationship to the Economy – Implications for Policy' (2009) 57 *American Journal of Comparative Law* 831–46

Milhaupt, Curtis J. and Katharina Pistor, *Law and Capitalism: What Corporate Crises Reveal about Legal Systems and Economic Development around the World* (Chicago: The University of Chicago Press, 2008)

Miller, Alice, 'The CPC Central Committee's Leading Small Groups' [2008] (26) *China Leadership Monitor* 1–21

Miller, Alice, 'More Already on the Central Committee's Leading Small Groups' [2014] (44) *China Leadership Monitor* 1–8

百万豪车国外只卖30多万 价格差巨大谁在获取暴利 [Million Dollar Luxury Cars Only Sell for 300,000 Overseas, Who Is Profiteering from the Huge Price Differences], 新华网 [Xinhuanet], 29 July 2013, available at http://finance.people.com.cn/n/2013/0729/c70846-22364060.html

Ministry of Commerce, 'Mission', 7 December 2010, available at http://english.mofcom.gov.cn/column/mission2010.shtml

Ministry of Commerce, 商务部条法司有关负责人介绍反垄断立法情况 [MOFCOM Department of Treaty and Law Responsible Person Introduces the Anti-monopoly Law Situation] (Press Release, 11 January 2005)

Ministry of Commerce, 2013年商务工作年终述评之三: 努力做好经营者集中反垄断审查 维护公平竞争秩序 [MOFCOM's Review of 2013 Work (Part 3): Improve Review of Concentrations of Business Operators, Protect the Fair Competition Order] (Press Release, 4 December 2013)

Ministry of Commerce Information Office, 2016年商务工作年终综述之十二: 全面推进反垄断工作 营造法治化营商环境 [Summary of the MOFCOM's 2016 Work (Part 12): Comprehensively Promote Anti-monopoly Work, Create a Legalised Business Environment], 11 January 2017, available at www.mofcom.gov.cn/article/ae/ai/201701/20170102499312.shtml

会议纪要指定经营者,工商机关首次行使建议权 《反垄断法》剑指地方政府排除限制竞争—广东省工商局调查滥用行政权力排除、限制竞争案纪实 [Minutes of Meeting Designate Operators, SAIC Authorities Target Their Recommendation Powers under Anti-monopoly Law at Local Governments That Eliminate or Restrict Competition for the First Time – Case Report of Guangdong AIC's Investigation of Abuse of Administrative Power to Eliminate or Restrict Competition], 中国工商报 [China Business News], 27 July 2011, available at www.saic.gov.cn/zt/jg/fldybzdjz/201209/t20120918_219847.html

Mitchell, Tom, 'China Dream Sours for Foreign Companies', *The Financial Times*, 10 August 2013

商务部反垄断局将承担反垄断委员会的具体工作 [MOFCOM Anti-monopoly Bureau Assumes the Specific Work of the Anti-monopoly Commission], 中国新闻网 [China News], 1 August 2008, available at www.chinanews.com/cj/gncj/news/2008/08-01/1333119.shtml

商务部反垄断局局长尚明谈 推进反垄断执法工作 维护市场公平竞争 [MOFCOM Anti-monopoly Bureau Director-General Shang Ming Talks, Advance Anti-monopoly Enforcement Work and Maintain Fair Market Competition] (5 December 2008) 访谈—中国政府网 [Interview – Chinese Government Website], available at www.gov.cn/zxft/ft155/wz.htm

商务部"反垄断工作"专题新闻发布会 [MOFCOM 'Anti-monopoly Work' Special Press Conference] (Ministry of Commerce, 27 February 2014), available at www.mofcom.gov.cn/article/ae/slfw/201402/20140200502174.shtml

商务部就可口可乐收购汇源反垄断审查决定答问 [MOFCOM Q&A on Anti-monopoly Review Decision of Coca-Cola's Acquisition of Huiyuan] (24 March 2009) available at www.gov.cn/gzdt/2009-03/24/content_1267595.htm

商务部报告: 中国尚无行业真正被外资垄断 [MOFCOM Report: No Real Foreign Monopolies in Chinese Industries Yet], 中国新闻网 [China News Online], 9 September 2007, available at http://finance.people.com.cn/GB/6236466.html

'MOFCOM Seeks to Streamline and Clarify the Chinese Merger Control Process – Draft Regulations Published' (Briefing Note, Clifford Chance, April 2013), available at www.cliffordchance.com/briefings/2013/04/mofcom_seeks_to_streamlineandclarifyth.html

'MOFCOM Solicits Comments on Draft Rules Regarding "Simple" Transactions', Cleary Gottlieb, 16 April 2013, available at www.clearygottlieb.com/news-and-insights/publication-listing/mofcom-solicits-comments-on-draft-rules-regarding-simple-transactions2

Montinola, Gabriella, Yingyi Qian and Barry R. Weingast, 'Federalism, Chinese Style: The Political Bias for Economic Success in China' (1995) 48 *World Politics* 50–81

'More SPC Circuit Courts Start Business', *Shanghai Daily*, 31 December 2016, available at www.shanghaidaily.com/nation/More-SPC-circuit-courts-start-business/shdaily.shtml

'National Competition Policy', National Competition Council, available at http://ncp.ncc.gov.au/pages/overview

National Development and Reform Commission, 'Main Functions of Departments of the NDRC: Department of Price', available at http://en.ndrc.gov.cn/mfod/200812/t20081218_252212.html

National Development and Reform Commission, 'Main Functions of the NDRC', available at http://en.ndrc.gov.cn/mfndrc

National Development and Reform Commission, 顺利实现价格预期调控目标, 价格改革和监管工作取得积极成效 [Price Control Targets Successfully Reached, Price Reform and Supervision Work Achieved Positive Results] (News Release, 24 January 2014) available at www.sdpc.gov.cn/xwzx/xwfb/201401/t20140124_576928.html

全国价格监督检查与反垄断工作会议日前召开 [National Price Supervision and Anti-monopoly Work Conference Recently Held] (9 January 2013) National Development and Reform Commission, available at www.sdpc.gov.cn/fzgggz/jgjdyfld/jjszhdt/201301/t20130109_522664.html

'Nature and Position', The National Committee of the Chinese People's Political Consultative Conference, available at www.cppcc.gov.cn/zxww/2012/07/03/ARTI1341301557187103.shtml

Naughton, Barry, '"Deepening Reform": The Organization and the Emerging Strategy' [2014] (44) *China Leadership Monitor* 1–14

Naughton, Barry, 'Inflation, Welfare, and the Political Business Cycle' [2011] (35) *China Leadership Monitor* 1–12

Naughton, Barry, 'Reform Agenda in Turmoil: Can Policy-Makers Regain the Initiative?' [2015] (48) *China Leadership Monitor* 1–8

Naughton, Barry, 'Since the National People's Congress: Personnel and Programs of Economic Reform Begin to Emerge' [2013] (41) *China Leadership Monitor* 1–11

Naughton, Barry, 'The State Asset Commission: A Powerful New Government Body' [2003] (8) *China Leadership Monitor* 1–10

Naughton, Barry, 'Strengthening the Center, and Premier Wen Jiabao' [2007] (21) *China Leadership Monitor* 1–10

Naughton, Barry, 'Two Trains Running: Supply-Side Reform, SOE Reform and the Authoritative Personage' [2015] (50) *China Leadership Monitor* 1–10

发改委"出手"康师傅联合利华暂缓涨价 [NDRC Acts, Master Kong and Unilever Suspend Price Increases], 财经网 [Caijing], 1 April 2011, available at www.caijing.com.cn/2011-04-01/110680850.html

发改委反垄断局: 继续督促电信联通反垄断整改 限期3–5年 [NDRC Antimonopoly Bureau: Continues to Urge China Telecom and China Unicom to Undertake Anti-monopoly Rectification, Time Limit of 3-5 Years], 证券时报 [Securities Times], 25 September 2013, available at www.cs.com.cn/xwzx/hg/201309/t20130925_4153920.html

国家发展改革委价监局 [NDRC Bureau of Price Supervision and Anti-monopoly], 2016 年价格监管与反垄断工作要点 [Key Points of NDRC Bureau of Price Supervision and Anti-monopoly's Work in 2016] [2016] (2) 中国价格检查与反垄断 [Price Supervision and Anti-monopoly in China] 5

NDRC Bureau of Price Supervision and Anti-monopoly, 江苏省两家混凝土企业不服反垄断处罚败诉 [Two Concrete Enterprises in Jiangsu Province Not Satisfied with Anti-monopoly Punishment, Lose Lawsuit] (News Release, 8 December 2014)

发改委否认宽带垄断案和解, 称已获得核心证据 [NDRC Denies Settling Broadband Monopoly Case, Says It Has Already Gathered Core Evidence], 新京报 [*The Beijing News*], 22 November 2011, available at http://finance.sina.com.cn/g/20111122/075410857808.shtml

国家发展改革委发出紧急通知 要求切实加强婴幼儿奶粉价格监管 [NDRC Issues Emergency Notice, Requests Strengthening of Infant Formula Price Supervision] (News Release, 19 September 2008) available at http://www.ndrc.gov.cn/xwtt/200809/t20080919_236575.html

国家发改委就价格监管与反垄断工作情况举行新闻发布会 [NDRC Holds News Conference on Price Supervision and Anti-monopoly Work] (19 February 2014) available at www.china.com.cn/zhibo/2014-02/19/content_31502397.htm

发改委就发展生产性服务业促进产业结构升级召开新闻发布会 [NDRC Holds Press Conference on Developing and Promoting the Structural Upgrade of Producer Service Industries] (6 August 2014) available at www.china.com.cn/zhibo/2014-08/06/content_33139708.htm

发改委约谈六家"洋奶粉"企业表示属例行工作 [NDRC Talks with Six Foreign Infant Formula Businesses, States That It Is Routine], 广州日报 [*Guangzhou Daily*], 9 May 2011, available at www.chinanews.com/cj/2011/05-09/3024728.shtml

发改委彻查进口豪车"低价设限" 车价全球最高被疑垄断 [NDRC Thoroughly Investigates Imported Luxury Cars 'Minimum Price Restrictions', Car Prices Are Highest Globally, Suspected Monopoly], 人民网 [people.cn], 19 August 2013, available at http://news.ifeng.com/gundong/detail_2013_08/19/28768765_0.shtml

发改委拿方便面开刀? 政府价格监管风暴正升级 [NDRC to Use Instant Noodles as a Weapon? The Government Price Regulation Storm Upgraded], 华夏时报 [*China Times*], 18 August 2007, available at http://news.enorth.com.cn/system/2007/08/19/001830080.shtml

Nestlé SA, 'Nestlé to Enter Partnership with Chinese Confectionery Company Hsu Fu Chi' (Press Release, 11 July 2011) available at www.nestle.com/media/pressre leases/allpressreleases/nestle-to-enter-partnership-with-chinese-confectionery-company-hsu-fu-chi

Nestlé SA, 'Nestlé to Enter Partnership with Chinese Food Company Yinlu' (Press Release, 18 April 2011) available at www.nestle.com.au/media/pressreleases/ nestletoenterpartnershipwithchinesefoodcompanyyinlu

Ng, Wendy, 'The Independence of Chinese Competition Agencies and the Impact on Competition Enforcement in China' (2016) 4 *Journal of Antitrust Enforcement* 188–209

Ning, Susan, et al., 'NDRC's Enforcement in 2016' [2017] (3) *CPI Antitrust Chronicle* 1–12

Ning, Susan, et al., 'Review of Merger Control and Merger Remedies Regime in China: From 2008–2013', China Law Insight: Antitrust & Competition, 23 August 2013, available at www.chinalawinsight.com/2013/08/articles/ corporate/antitrust-competition/review-of-merger-control-and-merger-rem edies-regime-in-china-from-2008-2013

'NPC to Continue Making Laws to Comply to WTO Rules: Li Peng', *China Daily*, 9 March 2002, available at www.chinadaily.com.cn/en/doc/2002-03/09/con tent_110119.htm

O'Connell, Jim, 'The Year of the Metal Rabbit: Antitrust Enforcement in China in 2011' (2012) 26(2) *Antitrust* 65–77

OECD, *Governance in China* (Paris: OECD Publishing, 2005)

OECD, *Review of Innovation Policy: China* (Organisation for Economic Co-operation and Development and the Chinese Ministry of Science and Technology, 2007)

OECD, *Reviews of Regulatory Reform: China: Defining the Boundary between the Market and the State* (Organisation for Economic Co-Operation and Development, 2009)

Office of the Leading Group of the State Council for the First National Economic Census, 'Communiqué on Major Data of the First National Economic Census of China (No. 1)', National Bureau of Statistics of China, 6 December 2005, available at www.stats.gov.cn/english/NewsEvents/200603/t20060301_ 25734.html

Office of the Leading Group of the State Council for the Second National Economic Census, 'Communiqué on Major Data of the Second National Economic Census (No. 1)', National Bureau of Statistics of China, 25 December 2009, available at www.stats.gov.cn/english/NewsEvents/200912/ t20091225_26264.html

Office of the Leading Group of the State Council for the Third National Economic Census, 'Communiqué on Major Data of the Third National Economic Census (No. 1)', National Bureau of Statistics of China,

16 December 2014, available at www.stats.gov.cn/english/PressRelease/201412/t20141216_653982.html

Ohlhausen, Maureen K., 'Antitrust Enforcement in China – What Next?' (Remarks delivered at the Second Annual GCR Live Conference, New York, 16 September 2014)

Ohlhausen, Maureen K., 'Taking Notes: Observations on the First Five Years of the Chinese Anti-monopoly Law' (Remarks delivered at the Competition Committee Meeting of the United States Council for International Business, Washington, DC, 9 May 2013)

Oliver, Chris, 'Can China's Stimulus Plans Really Help?' MarketWatch, 23 August 2012, available at http://cbonds.com/news/item/591863

中央企业2010年度总体以及分行业运行情况 [Operations of Central SOEs in 2010, Overall and by Sector], State-owned Assets Supervision and Administration Commission, 14 October 2011, available at www.gov.cn/gzdt/2011-10/14/content_1970139.htm

Owen, Bruce M., 'Competition Policy in Emerging Economies' (SIEPR Discussion Paper No. 04-10, Stanford Institute for Economic Policy Research, 2005)

Owen, Bruce M., Su Sun and Wentong Zheng, 'Antitrust in China: The Problem of Incentive Compatibility' (2005) 1 *Journal of Competition Law and Economics* 123–48

Owen, Bruce M., Su Sun and Wentong Zheng, 'China's Competition Policy Reforms: The Anti-monopoly Law and Beyond' (2008) 75 *Antitrust Law Journal* 231–66

Paler, Laura, 'China's Legislation Law and the Making of a More Orderly and Representative Legislative System' (2005) 182 *The China Quarterly* 301–18

Pate, R. Hewitt, 'What I Heard in the Great Hall of the People – Realistic Expectations of Chinese Antitrust' (2008) 75 *Antitrust Law Journal* 195–212

Pearson, Margaret, 'The Business of Governing Business in China: Institutions and Norms of the Emerging Regulatory State' (2005) 57 *World Politics* 296–322

Peerenboom, Randall, *China's Long March toward Rule of Law* (Cambridge: Cambridge University Press, 2002)

Peerenboom, Randall, 'Judicial Independence in China: Common Myths and Unfounded Assumptions' in Randall Peerenboom (ed.), *Judicial Independence in China: Lessons for Global Rule of Law Promotion* (Cambridge: Cambridge University Press, 2009) 69–94

Pei, Minxin, 'The Dark Side of China's Rise', Foreign Policy, 17 February 2006, available at www.foreignpolicy.com/articles/2006/02/17/the_dark_side_of_chinas_rise

'President Xi to Lead Overall Reform', *China Daily*, 30 December 2013

价格监督检查与反垄断工作取得新成绩 [Price Supervision and Inspection and Anti-monopoly Work Achieves New Results] (13 February 2013) National

Development and Reform Commission, available at www.ndrc.gov.cn/xwzx/xwfb/201502/t20150213_664544.html

《关于汽车业的反垄断指南》(征求意见稿) 公开征求意见 [Public Consultation for 'Anti-monopoly Guideline for the Auto Industry (Consultation Draft)'] (23 March 2016) National Development and Reform Commission, available at www.sdpc.gov.cn/fzgggz/jgjdyfld/fjgld/201603/t20160323_795741.html

Qi, Fang, Marshall Yan and Yan Luo, 'Consideration of Economic Evidence by Chinese Courts in Antitrust Litigation' [2014] (1) *CPI Antitrust Chronicle* 1–15

Qian, Yingyi, 'How Reform Worked in China' (William Davidson Working Paper No. 473, The William Davidson Institution at the University of Michigan Business School, June 2002)

Qian, Yingyi, 'The Process of China's Market Transition (1978–1998): The Evolutionary, Historical, and Comparative Perspectives' (2000) 156 *Journal of Institutional and Theoretical Economics* 151–71

Qian, Yingyi and Barry R. Weingast, 'China's Transition to Markets: Market Preserving Federalism, Chinese Style' (1996) 1 *Journal of Policy Reform* 149–85

Qian, Yingyi and Jinglian Wu, 'China's Transition to a Market Economy: How Far across the River?' in Nicholas C. Hope, Dennis Tao Yang and Mu Yang Li (eds.), *How Far across the River? Chinese Policy Reform at the Millennium* (Stanford: Stanford University Press, 2003) 31–63

Qin, Xiaoying, 'Law to Protect Public Interests from Monopoly', *China Daily*, 13 July 2006, available at www.chinadaily.com.cn/chinagate/doc/2006-07/13/content_640069.htm

Qualcomm, 'Qualcomm and China's National Development and Reform Commission Reach Resolution' (Press Release, 10 February 2015) available at www.qualcomm.com/news/releases/2015/02/09/qualcomm-and-chinas-national-development-and-reform-commission-reach

Quinn, James, 'Diageo's Paul Walsh Cracks China', The Telegraph, 24 March 2013, available at www.telegraph.co.uk/finance/newsbysector/retailandconsumer/9950082/Diageos-Paul-Walsh-cracks-China.html

Ren, John Yong and Jet Zhisong Deng, 'Developments in Anti-monopoly Agreement Enforcement and Suggestions Regarding Compliance Programs in China' [2013] (2) *CPI Antitrust Chronicle* 1–9

Ren, John Yong and Ning Yang, 'The Imminent Release of China's Anti-monopoly Law – What to Expect' [2005] (7) *China Law & Practice* 26

Renard, François and Michael Edwards, 'China Merger Control Practice: A Comparative Analysis' in Adrian Emch and David Stallibrass (eds.), *China's Anti-monopoly Law: The First Five Years* (Alphen aan den Rijn, The Netherlands: Kluwer Law International, 2013) 167–93

全国人大法律委员会关于《中华人民共和国反垄断法 (草案二次审议稿)》审议结果的报告 [Report of the Law Committee of the National People's Congress on the Outcome of Anti-monopoly Law of the People's Republic of China (Second Deliberation Draft) Deliberations], 29th Session of the Standing Committee of the Tenth National People's Congress, 24 August 2007

全国人大法律委员会关于《中华人民共和国反垄断法 (草案)》修改情况的汇报 [Report of the Law Committee of the National People's Congress on the Revision of the Anti-monopoly Law of the People's Republic of China (Draft)], 28th Session of the Standing Committee of the Tenth National People's Congress, 24 June 2007

全国人大法律委员会关于《中华人民共和国反垄断法 (草案三次审议稿)》修改意见的报告 [Report of the Law Committee of the National People's Congress on Views Regarding the Revision of the Anti-monopoly Law of the People's Republic of China (Third Deliberation Draft)], 29th Session of the Standing Committee of the Tenth National People's Congress, 29 August 2007

限制竞争还是技术局限—泉州广电捆绑销售机顶盒、智能卡案件追踪 [Restriction of Competition or Technical Limitations – Following the Quanzhou Radio and Television Set-Top Box and Smart Card Tying Case], 中国工商报 [China Industry & Commerce News], 21 May 2014, available at www.saic.gov.cn/zt/jg/fldybzdjz/201405/t20140521_219942.html

Rodriguez Galindo, Bianca, 'Presentation' (Speech delivered at the International Seminar Review of Anti-monopoly Law, Hangzhou, China, 19–21 May 2006)

Ross, Lester and Kenneth Zhou, 'Administrative and Civil Litigation under the Anti-monopoly Law' in Adrian Emch and David Stallibrass (eds.), *China's Anti-monopoly Law: The First Five Years* (Alphen aan den Rijn, The Netherlands: Kluwer Law International, 2013) 317–34

SAIC Anti-monopoly and Anti-Unfair Competition Enforcement Bureau, 司局介绍 [Introduction to the Bureau], available at www.saic.gov.cn/fldyfbzdjz/sjjs

工商部门迄今查办垄断案60件 [SAIC Investigates 60 Anti-monopoly Cases to Date], 法制日报 [*Legal Daily*], 27 April 2016, available at http://epaper.legaldaily.com.cn/fzrb/content/20160427/Articel04006GN.htm

国家工商总局专案组对微软公司进行反垄断调查询问 [SAIC Special Investigation Team Makes Enquiries of Microsoft on its Anti-monopoly Investigation] State Administration for Industry and Commerce, 5 January 2016, available at www.saic.gov.cn/fldyfbzdjz/gzdt/201601/t20160105_205359.html

Saich, Tony, *Governance and Politics of China*, 3rd edn (Houndmills: Palgrave Macmillan, 2011)

盐业改革方案获发改委通过 2016年将废止盐业专营 [Salt Industry Reform Plan Approved by NDRC, Salt Industry Franchise Abolished in 2016], 证券日报 [Securities Daily], 30 October 2014, available at http://finance.people.com.cn/n/2014/1030/c1004-25934904.html

Schroeder, Paul E., 'Territorial Actors as Competitors for Power: The Case of Hubei and Wuhan' in Kenneth G. Lieberthal and David M. Lampton (eds.), *Bureaucracy, Politics, and Decision Making in Post-Mao China* (Berkeley: University of California Press, 1992) 283–307

Sections of Antitrust Law and International Law and Practice, American Bar Association, 'Joint Submission to the Ministry of Commerce of the People's Republic of China', 15 July 2003

Sections of Antitrust Law, Intellectual Property Law and International Law, American Bar Association, 'Joint Submission to the Ministry of Commerce of the People's Republic of China', 19 May 2005

Serger, Sylvia Schwaag and Magnus Breidne, 'China's Fifteen-Year Plan for Science and Technology: An Assessment' (2007) 4 *Asia Policy* 135–64

服务群众服务发展 [Serve the Public, Serve Development] (21 April 2015) National Development and Reform Commission, available at www.ndrc.gov.cn/xwzx/xwfb/201504/t20150421_688874.html

山东省济南市历下区人民法院一审维持山东省局行政处罚决定 [Shandong Jinan Lixia District People's Court First Instance Hearing Maintains Shandong AIC's Administrative Penalty Decision], 6 September 2016, available at www.saic.gov.cn/fldyfbzdjz/gzdt/201609/t20160906_205297.html

Shang, Ming, 'Antitrust in China – A Constantly Evolving Subject' (2009) 3 *Competition Law International* 4–11

商思林 [Shang Silin], 反垄断法: 化解知识产权国际压力的中国利器？ [Antimonopoly Law: China's Weapon to Resolve International Pressure on Intellectual Property Rights?], 南方周末 [Southern Weekend], 6 July 2006, available at http://finance.sina.com.cn/roll/20060706/1449784438.shtml

沈丹阳 [Shen Danyang], 商务部召开例行新闻发布会 (2011年9月20日) [Regular Press Conference of the Ministry of Commerce (20 September 2011)] Ministry of Commerce, 20 September 2011, available at www.mofcom.gov.cn/article/ae/ah/diaocd/201109/20110907748307.shtml

沈丹阳 [Shen Danyang], 商务部召开例行新闻发布会 (2013年3月19日) [Regular Press Conference of the Ministry of Commerce (19 March 2013)] Ministry of Commerce, 19 March 2013, available at www.mofcom.gov.cn/article/ae/ah/diaocd/201303/20130300059439.shtml

Shen, Jia, 'The Invisible Obstacle', *News China Magazine* (January 2011)

Shen, Samuel and Pete Sweeney, 'Japanese Car Makers Cut Parts Prices in China after Anti-monopoly Probe', Reuters, 9 August 2014, available at www.reuters.com/article/us-china-autos-antitrust-idUSKBN0G90H520140809

Shi, Chenxia, 'Recent Ownership Reform and Control of Central State-owned Enterprises in China: Taking One Step at a Time' (2007) 30 *UNSW Law Journal* 855–66

Shi, Chenxia, 'Self-Regulation of Business Associations and Companies' (2010) 2 *Peking University Journal of Legal Studies* 182–207

Shi, Chenxia and Dong Kaijun, 'The Proposed Antitrust Law and the Problem of Administrative Monopolies in China' (2004) 12 *Trade Practices Law Journal* 106–13

时建中 [Shi Jianzhong], 反垄断法修改审查组专家: 反行政垄断不能删除 [Antimonopoly Law Review and Deliberation Group Expert: Prohibition on Administrative Monopoly Cannot Be Deleted], 新京报 [*The Beijing News*], 9 July 2006, available at www.southcn.com/news/china/zgkx/200607100074.htm

Shih, Willy C., 'Prepared Statement' (Prepared Statement for the US–China Economic and Security Review Commission Hearing on 'China's Twelfth Five-Year Plan, Indigenous Innovation and Technology Transfers, and Outsourcing', Washington, DC, 15 June 2011)

Shirk, Susan L., *The Political Logic of Economic Reform in China* (Berkeley: University of California Press, 1993)

Sichuan Provincial People's Government, 2007年做大做强煤炭产业 [Coal Industry Becoming Bigger and Stronger in 2007] Sichuan Yearbook 2008, 14 May 2009, available at www.sc.gov.cn/scgk1/jj/gy/mtgy/200905/t20090514_735500.shtml

Skeel, David A., Jr, 'Book Review: Governance in Ruins' (2008) 122 *Harvard Law Review* 696–743

Sobel, Yuni Yan, 'Domestic-to-Domestic Transactions (2014–2015) – A Narrowing Gap in China's Merger Control Regime' [2016] (February) *The Antitrust Source* 1–6, available at www.americanbar.org/content/dam/aba/publishing/antitrust_source/feb16_sobel_2_12f.authcheckdam.pdf

Sobel, Yuni Yan, 'Domestic-to-Domestic Transactions – A Gap in China's Merger Control Regime?' [2014] (February) *The Antitrust Source* 1–12, available at www.americanbar.org/content/dam/aba/publishing/antitrust_source/feb14_sobel_2_20f.pdf

'SOE Reform Essential to a Stable Economy', Xinhua, 9 November 2013, available at www.chinadaily.com.cn/china/2013cpctps/2013-11/09/content_17093214.htm

Sokol, D. Daniel, 'Merger Control under China's Anti-monopoly Law' (2013) 10 *New York University Journal of Law & Business* 1–36

Song, Bing, 'Competition Policy in a Transitional Economy: The Case of China' (1995) 31 *Stanford Journal of International Law* 387–422

发言摘登: 反垄断法草案 [Speech Excerpts: Draft of the Anti-monopoly Law], 22nd Session of the Standing Committee of the Tenth National People's Congress, 27 June 2006

Stallibrass, David and Jenny Xiaojin Huang, 'Brands, Consumer Protection, and Antitrust – Why China is Special' [2012] (2) *CPI Antitrust Chronicle* 1–10

State Administration for Industry and Commerce, 'Mission', available at www.saic.gov.cn/english/aboutus/Mission/index.html

State Administration for Industry and Commerce, 机构 [Organisation], available at www.saic.gov.cn/jggk

国务院反垄断委员会关于垄断协议豁免一般性条件和程序的指南(征求意见稿) [State Council Anti-monopoly Commission Guideline on General Conditions and Procedures for the Exemption of Monopoly Agreements (Consultation Draft)] (People's Republic of China) National Development and Reform Commission, 12 May 2016, available at http://jjs.ndrc.gov.cn/fjgld/201605/t20160512_801559.html

国新办就反垄断执法工作情况举行吹风会 [State Council Information Office Briefing on Anti-monopoly Law Enforcement Activities] (11 September 2014), State Council Information Office, available at www.china.com.cn/zhibo/2014-09/11/content_33487367.htm

'State Council Organization Chart', english.gov.cn (The Chinese Government's Official Web Portal), available at http://english.gov.cn/state_council/2014/09/03/content_281474985533579.htm

'State Council Policy Briefing' (State Council Information Office, 27 March 2015), available at http://english.gov.cn/news/policy_briefings/2015/03/27/content_281475078591808.htm

'State Owned Enterprises in China: Reviewing the Evidence' (Occasional Paper, OECD Working Group on Privatisation and Corporate Governance of State Owned Assets, 26 January 2009)

'Statistical Communiqué of the People's Republic of China on the 2013 National Economic and Social Development', National Bureau of Statistics of China, 24 February 2014, available at www.stats.gov.cn/english/PressRelease/201402/t20140224_515103.html

Su, Jessica and Xiaoye Wang, 'China: The Competition Law System and the Country's Norms' in Eleanor M. Fox and Michael J. Trebilcock (eds.), *The Design of Competition Law Institutions: Global Norms, Local Choices* (Oxford: Oxford University Press, 2013) 194–231

Supreme People's Court of the People's Republic of China, 'Judicial Reform of Chinese Courts', 3 March 2016, available at http://english.court.gov.cn/2016-03/03/content_23724636.htm

Sweeney, Pete and Paul Carsten, 'China Seen Probing IBM, Oracle, EMC After Snowden Leaks', Reuters, 16 August 2013, available at www.reuters.com/article/2013/08/16/us-china-ioe-idUSBRE97F02720130816

Swider, Sarah, 'Building China: Precarious Employment among Migrant Construction Workers' (2015) 29 *Work, Employment and Society* 41–59

Szamosszegi, Andrew and Cole Kyle, 'An Analysis of State-owned Enterprises and State Capitalism in China' (Research Report, US–China Economic and Security Review Commission, 2011)

Tan, Wei, 'SOEs and Competition', *CPI Asia Column*, 10 December 2012, available at www.competitionpolicyinternational.com/assets/Columns/cpi-asia-antitrust-column-tanFINAL.pdf

Tanner, Murray Scot, 'The Erosion of Communist Party Control Over Lawmaking in China' (1994) 138 *The China Quarterly* 381–403

Tanner, Murray Scot, 'How a Bill Becomes a Law in China: Stages and Processes in Lawmaking' (1995) 141 *The China Quarterly* 39–64

Tanner, Murray Scot, 'The National People's Congress' in Merle Goldman and Roderick MacFarquhar (eds.), *The Paradox of China's Post-Mao Reforms* (Cambridge, MA: Harvard University Press, 1999) 100–28

腾讯宣布装有360软件电脑将停止运行QQ [Tencent Announces That Computers Installed with 360 Software Will Stop Running QQ], 财经网 [Caijing], 3 November 2010, available at www.caijing.com.cn/2010-11-03/110558875.html

腾讯诉360不正当竞争 北京朝阳法院正式受理该案 [Tencent Sues 360 for Unfair Competition, Beijing Chaoyang District Court Formally Accepts the Case], 中国经济网 [*China Economic News*], 3 November 2010, available at www.ce.cn/cysc/tech/07hlw/guonei/201011/03/t20101103_20536304.shtml

Teubner, Gunther, 'Legal Irritants: Good Faith in British Law or How Unifying Law Ends Up in New Divergences' (1998) 61 *The Modern Law Review* 11–32

The National People's Congress of the People's Republic of China, 'Special Committees', available at www.npc.gov.cn/englishnpc/Organization/node_2849.htm

The National People's Congress of the People's Republic of China, 'Working and Administrative Bodies of the Standing Committee', available at www.npc.gov.cn/englishnpc/Organization/node_2850.htm

'The Objectives of Competition Law and Policy and the Optimal Design of a Competition Agency – China' (Note Submitted by China at the OECD Global Forum on Competition, 9 January 2003)

'The Way of the Dragon', *The Economist*, 23 June 2005, available at www.economist.com/node/4102015

田兴春 [Tian Xingchun], 最高法通报近年来人民法院审理商标和不正当竞争案件有关情况2012年法院审理商标民事案19815件 年增长率超50% [Supreme People's Court Reports on Trademark and Unfair Competition Cases Heard by the People's Courts, Court Hears 19815 Trademark Civil Cases in 2012, Annual Growth Rate of over 50 Per cent], 人民网 [people.cn] 28 March 2013, available at http://legal.people.com.cn/n/2013/0328/c42510-20950833.html

中国中央企业国有资本超过2万亿元 [Total Assets of the SASAC Companies Exceed 2 Trillion Yuan], 新华网 [Xinhuanet], 12 August 2010, available at http://finance.eastmoney.com/news/1350,2010081289688835.html

'Trust-Busting in China: Unequal before the Law?', *The Economist*, 23 August 2014, available at www.economist.com/news/business/21613348-chinas-antitrust-crackdown-turns-ugly-foreign-carmakers-forefront-unequal

US Chamber of Commerce, *Competing Interests in China's Competition Law Enforcement: China's Anti-monopoly Law Application and the Role of Industrial Policy* (2014)

US Department of Commerce, Office of Public Affairs, 'Fact Sheet: 25th US–China Joint Commission on Commerce and Trade' (Press Release, 19 December 2014)

'US Lawmakers Meddle in CNOOC's Unocal Bid', *China Daily*, 6 July 2005, available at www.chinadaily.com.cn/english/doc/2005-07/06/content_457677.htm

US–China Business Council, 'Competition Policy and Enforcement in China' (September 2014) 14–15, available at www.uschina.org/reports/competition-policy-and-enforcement-china

US–China Economic and Security Review Commission, *2015 Report to Congress of the US–China Economic and Security Review Commission* (114th Congress, First Session, November 2015)

USCBC 2014 China Business Environment Survey Results: Growth Continues Amidst Rising Competition, Policy Uncertainty (US–China Business Council, 2014)

van Rooij, Benjamin, 'China's System of Public Administration' in Jianfu Chen, Yuwen Li and Jan Michael Otto (eds.), *Implementation of Law in the People's Republic of China* (The Hague: Kluwer Law International, 2002) 323–42

Vandermeulen, Jackie and Philippe Perron-Savard, 'Law and Capitalism: A Book Review' (2009) 67 *University of Toronto Faculty of Law Review* 327–57

Waha, Marc, 'MOFCOM Simple Cases: The First Six Months' [2015] (1) *CPI Antitrust Chronicle* 1–7, available at www.competitionpolicyinternational.com/mofcom-simple-cases-the-first-six-months

王毕强 [Wang Biqiang], 联通网通合并涉嫌违法 [China Unicom/China Netcom Merger Suspected Illegal], 经济观察网 [Economic Observer Online], 30 April 2009, available at www.eeo.com.cn/industry/it_telecomm/2009/05/01/136645.shtml

王毕强 [Wang Biqiang], 三大修改尘埃落定《反垄断法》有望八月通过 [Dust Settles after the Third Major Amendments to the Anti-monopoly Law, Expected to Be Passed in August], 经济观察网 [Economic Observer Online] 24 August 2007, available at www.eeo.com.cn/2007/0824/81095.shtml

王毕强 [Wang Biqiang], 国资委人士称央企重组不需商务部反垄断审查 [SASAC Official Says MOFCOM Anti-monopoly Review Not Required in Central SOE Restructuring], 经济观察网 [Economic Observer Online], 2 August 2008, available at http://finance.sina.com.cn/roll/20080802/09455160451.shtml

王毕强 [Wang Biqiang],《反垄断法》草案二审: 反垄断前路漫漫 [Second Review of the Anti-monopoly Law: A Long Road Ahead for Anti-monopoly Law], 经济观察网 [Economic Observer Online], 2 July 2007, available at www.eeo.com.cn/2007/0702/74098.shtml

王毕强, 刘伟勋 [Wang Biqiang and Liu Weixun], 涉操纵机票涨价 发改委调查中航信 [Suspected Manipulation of Airfare Price Increases, NDRC Investigates TravelSky], 经济观测网 [Economic Observer Online], 17 May 2009, available at www.eeo.com.cn/finance/other/2009/05/16/137823.shtml

王毕强，郑猛 [Wang Biqiang and Zheng Meng], 今年人大预算报告反对票数创记录 审议频遭冷场 [Opposing Votes for the Budget Report at this Year's NPC Set a Record: Review Frequently Meets with Awkward Silence] [2012] (9) Caijing, available at http://news.hexun.com/2012-03-26/139730819.html

Wang, Elizabeth Xiao-Ru and Sharon Pang, 'A Discussion of MOFCOM's Competitive Analysis in 2012 from an Economic Perspective' [2013] (2) *CPI Antitrust Chronicle* 1–12

Wang, Peter J., 'Chinese Merger Control' [2006] *The Asia-Pacific Antitrust & Trade Review* 29

Wang, Xiangwei, 'Beijing Must Back NDRC in Probe of Telecoms Giants', *South China Morning Post*, 14 November 2011, available at www.scmp.com/article/984757/beijing-must-back-ndrc-probe-telecoms-giants

王晓玲 [Wang Xiaoling], 《反垄断法》: 把立法难题留到执法中解决—访中国社科院规制与竞争研究中心主任张昕竹 [Anti-monopoly Law: Defers Resolution of Difficult Legislative Issues to Enforcement – Interview with Director of Chinese Academy of Social Sciences Centre for Regulation and Competition Zhang Xinzhu] [2005] (17) 商务周刊 [Business Watch Magazine] 47–9

黄小伟 [Wang Xiaowei], 反垄断法二审: 良法仍有希望 [Second Review of the Anti-monopoly Law: There Is Still Hope for a Good Law], 南方周末 [Southern Weekend], 4 July 2007, available at www.infzm.com/content/7581

王晓晔 [Wang Xiaoye], 入世与中国反垄断法的制定 [Accession to the WTO and the Drafting of the Anti-monopoly Law] [2003] (2) 法学研究 [CASS Journal of Law] 122

王晓晔 [Wang Xiaoye], 中华人民共和国反垄断法详解 [Detailed Explanation of the Anti-monopoly Law of the People's Republic of China], (知识产权出版社 [Intellectual Property Publishing House], 2008)

王晓晔 [Wang Xiaoye], 我国反垄断立法宗旨 [The Legislative Purpose of China's Anti-monopoly Law] [2008] (2) 华东政法大学校报 [Journal of East China University of Political Science and Law] 37–41

Wang, Xiaoye, 'The China Telecom and China Unicom Case and the Future of Chinese Antitrust' in Adrian Emch and David Stallibrass (eds.), *China's Anti-monopoly Law: The First Five Years* (Alphen aan den Rijn, The Netherlands: Kluwer Law International, 2013) 467

Wang, Xiaoye, *The Evolution of China's Anti-monopoly Law* (Cheltenham: Edward Elgar, 2014)

Wang, Xiaoye, 'Highlights of China's New Anti-monopoly Law' (2008) 75 *Antitrust Law Journal* 133–50

Wang, Xiaoye, 'Issues Surrounding the Drafting of China's Anti-Monopoly Law' (2004) 3 *Washington University Global Studies Law Review* 285–96

Wang, Xiaoye and Adrian Emch, 'Five Years of Implementation of China's Anti-monopoly Law – Achievements and Challenges' (2013) 1 *Journal of Antitrust Enforcement* 247–71

Wang, Xiaoye and Jessica Su, 'China's Anti-monopoly Law: Agent of Competition Enhancement or Engine of Industrial Policy?' in Daniel Zimmer (ed.), *The Goals of Competition Law* (Cheltenham: Edward Elgar, 2012) 379

Wang, Xing and Chen Limin, 'Minister: Internet Companies' Spat Immoral, Irresponsible', *China Daily*, 10 November 2010, available at www.chinadaily.com.cn/business/2010-11/10/content_11526774.htm

Wang, Xue Zheng, 'Challenges/Obstacles Faced by Competition Authorities in Achieving Greater Economic Development through the Promotion of Competition – Contribution from China – Session II' (Note Submitted by China at the OECD Global Forum on Competition, 9 January 2004)

王晔君 [Wang Yejun], 航空汽车电信医药纳入发改委反垄断视野 [Aviation, Auto, Telecommunications, and Pharmaceuticals Included Within NDRC's Anti-monopoly Field of Vision], 北京商报 [Beijing Business Today], 25 November 2013, available at http://finance.eastmoney.com/news/1355, 20131125340227256.html

Wang, Yuhua, *Tying the Autocrat's Hands: The Rise of the Rule of Law in China* (New York: Cambridge University Press, 2015)

王子约, 马晓华 [Wang Ziyue and Ma Xiaohua], 中国掀反垄断风暴 央企无豁免权 [China Whips Up an Anti-monopoly Storm, Central SOEs Are Not Exempt], 第一财经日报 [First Financial Daily], 16 August 2013, available at www.yicai.com/news/2013/08/2942628.html

Watson, Alan, 'Legal Change: Sources of Law and Legal Culture' (1983) 131 *University of Pennsylvania Law Review* 1121–57

Watson, Alan, *Legal Transplants: An Approach to Comparative Law*, 2nd edn (Athens: University of Georgia Press, 1993)

Watson, Alan, *Society and Legal Change*, 2nd edn (Philadelphia: Temple University Press, 2001)

Wei, Min, 'State Monopoly Too Hard a Nut to Crack', *China Daily*, 17 April 2001, avaliable at www.chinadaily.com.cn/en/doc/2001-04/17/content_51654.htm

Wei, Shen, 'Will the Door Open Wider in the Aftermath of Alibaba? – Placing (or Misplacing) Foreign Investment in a Chinese Public Law Frame' (2012) 42 *Hong Kong Law Journal* 561–93

Wen, Philip, 'China's Xi Jinping Compared to Deng Xiaoping as His Power Base Grows', The Age, 18 November 2013, available at www.theage.com.au/world/chinas-xi-jinping-compared-to-deng-xiaoping-as-his-power-base-grows-20131117-2xp3y.html

"国有重要骨干"有企哪些? [Which Are the "Important Backbone SOEs"?], 新华网 [Xinhuanet], 30 January 2015, available at http://news.xinhuanet.com/video/sjxw/2015-01/30/c_127440169.htm

Williams, Mark, 'China' in Mark Williams (ed.), *The Political Economy of Competition Law in Asia* (Cheltenham: Edward Elgar Publishing, 2013) 88–118

Williams, Mark, *Competition Policy and Law in China, Hong Kong and Taiwan* (Cambridge: Cambridge University Press, 2005)

Williams, Mark, 'Foreign Investment in China: Will the Anti-monopoly Law Be a Barrier or a Facilitator?' (2009) 45 *Texas International Law Journal* 127–56

Wong, Edward, 'Contaminated Milk Is Destroyed in China', *New York Times*, 26 December 2011, available at www.nytimes.com/2011/12/27/world/asia/contaminated-milk-is-destroyed-in-china.html

Wong, Stanley, 'Effectiveness of Technical Assistance in Capacity Building on Competition Law and Policy: The Case of China' in Adrian Emch and David Stallibrass (eds.), *China's Anti-monopoly Law: The First Five Years* (Alphen aan den Rijn, The Netherlands: Kluwer Law International, 2013) 357–74

The World Bank and the Development Research Center of the State Council, the People's Republic of China, *China 2030: Building a Modern, Harmonious, and Creative Society* (Washington, DC: The World Bank, 2013)

World Trade Organisation, 'WTO Successfully Concludes Negotiations on China's Entry' (Press Release, Press/243, 17 September 2001) 1, available at www.wto.org/english/news_e/pres01_e/pr243_e.htm

Wu, Changqi and Zhicheng Liu, 'A Tiger without Teeth? Regulation of Administrative Monopoly under China's Anti-monopoly Law' (2012) 41 *Review of Industrial Organisation* 133–55

Wu, Qianlan, *Competition Laws, Globalization and Legal Pluralism: China's Experiences* (Oxford: Hart Publishing, 2013)

吴晓锋 [Wu Xiaofeng], 反垄断法是反'垄断的行为'而非'垄断的状态' [Anti-monopoly Law Opposes 'Monopoly Conduct' and Not 'Monopoly Status'] (26 November 2007) 中国人大新闻—人民网 [National People's Congress of China News – www.people.com.cn], available at http://npc.people.com.cn/GB/6574653.html

Wu, Zhenguo, 'Perspectives on the Chinese Anti-monopoly Law' (2008) 75 *Antitrust Law Journal* 73–116

惠氏奶粉最高降价二成 洋奶粉反垄断调查效应初现 [Wyeth's Maximum Price Decrease of 20 Per cent, Foreign Infant Formula Anti-monopoly Investigation Sees Initial Effects], 南方日报 [*Southern Daily News*], 4 July 2013, available at http://finance.chinanews.com/cj/2013/07-04/5001321.shtml

习近平 [Xi Jinping], 关于《中共中央关于全面深化改革若干重大问题的决定》的说明 [An Explanation of 'Decision of the Central Committee of the Communist Party of China on Some Major Issues Concerning Comprehensively Deepening Reform'], Third Plenary Session of the 18th Central Committee of the Communist Party of China, 15 November 2013

习近平 [Xi Jinping], 为建设世界科技强国而奋斗 [Striving to Build a World Power in Science and Technology] (Speech delivered at National Science and Technology Innovation Conference, Biennial Conference of the Chinese

Academy of Sciences and Chinese Academy of Engineering, and Ninth National Congress of the China Association for Science and Technology, Beijing, 30 May 2016) available at http://news.xinhuanet.com/politics/2016-05/31/c_1118965169.htm

习近平：全面贯彻党的十八届六中全会精神 [Xi Jinping: Comprehensively Implement the Spirit of the Sixth Plenum of the 18th CPC Central Committee], 11 November 2016, available at www.court.gov.cn/zixun-xiangqing-29261.html

谢晓冬 [Xie Xiaodong], 《反垄断法》草案减负"反行政垄断"被整体删除 [Draft Anti-monopoly Law Reduces Its Burden, 'Administrative Monopoly Prohibition' is Entirely Deleted], 新京报 [Beijing News], 11 January 2006, available at http://finance1.people.com.cn/GB/1037/4017283.html

新华社调查电信联通涉嫌垄断案，称系"神仙战" [Xinhua Investigates China Telecom/China Unicom Suspected Monopoly Case, Calls it the 'Battle of the Gods'], 新华网 [Xinhuanet], 11 November 2011, available at www.dezhoudaily.com/news/folder1004/2011/11/2011-11-17305760.html

Xu, Kunlin, 'Gradually Establishing the Fundamental Status of Competition Policy' (2015) 2 *International Antitrust Bulletin* 12–15

许昆林 [Xu Kunlin], 宽大政策适用于纵向垄断协议 [Leniency Policy Applies to Vertical Monopoly Agreements], 中国经济导报 [China Economic Herald], 31 October 2013, available at www.ceh.com.cn/xwpd/2013/10/255896.shtml

Yang, Jijian, 'Market Power in China: Manifestations, Effects and Legislation' (2002) 21 *Review of Industrial Organization* 167–83

Yang, Lillian, 'Anti-monopoly Bill for Review', *South China Morning Post*, 7 November 2006, available at www.scmp.com/node/570629

杨维汉、陈菲 [Yang Weihan and Chen Fei], 最高人民法院公布中国首部反垄断审判司法解释 [Supreme People's Court Announces China's First Judicial Interpretation on Anti-monopoly Trials], 新华网 [Xinhuanet], 8 May 2012, available at www.china.com.cn/policy/txt/2012-05/09/content_25337524.htm

Yang, Zi, 'Why China Decided to Abolish Its State Salt Monopoly', *The Diplomat*, 12 November 2014, available at http://thediplomat.com/2014/11/why-china-decided-to-abolish-its-state-salt-monopoly

Yao, Yang and Linda Yueh, 'Law, Finance, and Economic Growth in China: An Introduction' (2009) 37 *World Development* 753–62

叶碧华 [Ye Bihua], 发改委释疑惠氏免遭重罚：首先降价率队认错 [NDRC Explains Why Wyeth Was Exempt from Penalty: First to Reduce Price and Make Admissions], 21世纪经济报道 [*21st Century Business Herald*], 8 August 2013, available at http://finance.sina.com.cn/chanjing/gsnews/20130808/022816379184.shtml

Ye, Clare Gaofen, 'Combating Monopoly Agreements Under China's Anti-Monopoly Law: Recent Developments and Challenges' [2014] (1) *CPI Antitrust Chronicle* 1–10

叶逗逗 [Ye Doudou], 工信部主管媒体痛批央视 称其电信反垄断报道混淆视听 [MIIT Controlled Media Criticises CCTV, Says that the Telecommunications Anti-monopoly Report Misled the Public], 财新 [Caixin], 11 November 2011, available at http://china.caixin.com/2011-11-11/100324903.html

Ye, Juliet, 'QQ-360 Battle Escalates into War', *The Wall Street Journal*, 5 November 2010, available at http://blogs.wsj.com/chinarealtime/2010/11/05/qq-360-battle-escalates-into-war

Yin, Pumin, 'Medicine Price Reforms', *Beijing Review*, 23 June 2015, available at www.bjreview.com.cn/nation/txt/2015-06/23/content_693280.htm

于华鹏，沈建缘，张向东 [Yu Huapeng, Chen Jianyuan, and Zhang Xiangdong], 电信业风起反垄断 [Anti-monopoly Trend Blows through the Telecommunications Industry], 经济观察网 [Economic Observer Online], 12 November 2011, available at www.eeo.com.cn/2011/1112/215612.shtml

俞岚，周锐 [Yu Lan and Zhou Rui], 中国反价格垄断获突破性进展 已调查案件49起 [Breakthrough Developments in Anti-Price Monopoly in China, Already Investigated 49 Cases], 中国新闻网 [China News Online], 4 January 2013, available at http://finance.chinanews.com/cj/2013/01-04/4454595.shtml

原金 [Yuan Jin], 发改委谈反垄断困境: 有协会上来就拍桌子 [NDRC Talks About Anti-monopoly Dilemmas: An Industry Association Approached and Pounded the Table], 每经网 [nbd.com.cn], 27 August 2013, available at www.nbd.com.cn/articles/2013-08-27/768536.html

Yuen, Samson, 'Taming the "Foreign Tigers": China's Anti-Trust Crusade against Multinational Companies' [2014] (4) *China Perspectives* 53–9

Yum! Brands Inc., 'China's Ministry of Commerce Approves Yum! Brands Proposal to Acquire China's Little Sheep Restaurants' (Press Release, 7 November 2011), available at www.yum.com/press-releases/chinas-ministry-of-commerce-approves-yum-brands-proposal-to-acquire-chinas-little-sheep-restaurants

Yum! Brands Inc., 'Proposed Privatization of Little Sheep at HK$6.50 Per Scheme Share' (Press Release, 13 May 2011) available at www.yum.com/press-releases/proposed-privatization-of-little-sheep-at-hk6-50-per-scheme-share

曾建徽: 适应入世要求，及时修改制定有关法律 [Zeng Jianhui: To Comply with WTO Requirements, Promptly Revise and Formulate Relevant Laws], 人民网 [*People's Daily* Online], 4 March 2002, available at www.people.com.cn/GB/shizheng/7501/7507/20020304/678785.html

Zeng Xianwu, and Bai Lihui, 'Variable Interest Entity Structure in China', King & Wood Mallesons, 9 February 2012, available at www.chinalawinsight.com/2012/02/articles/corporate/foreign-investment/variable-interest-entity-structure-in-china

Zhan, Hao and Song Ying, 'At the Cutting Edge of PRC AML Private Litigation' [2016] (1) *CPI Antitrust Chronicle* 1–10

Zhang, Angela Huyue, 'Antitrust Regulation of Chinese State-owned Enterprises', in Benjamin L. Liebman and Curtis J. Milhaupt (eds.), *Regulating the Visible Hand?: The Institutional Implications of Chinese State Capitalism* (New York: Oxford University Press, 2016) 85–108

Zhang, Angela Huyue, 'Bureaucratic Politics and China's Anti-Monopoly Law' (2014) 47 *Cornell International Law Journal* 671–707

Zhang, Angela Huyue, 'Problems in Following EU Competition Law: A Case Study of *Coca-Cola/Huiyuan*' (2012) 3 *Peking University Journal of Legal Studies* 96–118

Zhang, Angela Huyue, 'Taming the Chinese Leviathan: Is Antitrust Regulation a False Hope?' (2015) 51 *Stanford Journal of International Law* 195–228

Zhang, Angela Huyue, 'The Enforcement of the Anti-Monopoly Law in China: An Institutional Design Perspective' (2011) 56 *The Antitrust Bulletin* 631–63

Zhang, Hao, 'Price Noodling Turns Spotlight on Food Cartels', Caijing, 31 July 2007, available at http://english.caijing.com.cn/2007-07-31/100025733.html

张黎明 [Zhang Liming], 中央三部委争立《反垄断法》 今年出台无望 [Three Central Ministries Fight for the Anti-monopoly Law, No Hope for Enactment This Year], 北京晨报 [Beijing Morning News], 11 January 2005, available at www.southcn.com/news/china/zgkx/200501110126.htm

张穹 [Zhang Qiong], 国务院法制办公室张穹副主任在反垄断立法国际研讨会闭幕式上的讲话 [Closing Remarks of Deputy Director of the Legislative Affairs Office of the State Council Zhang Qiong at the International Symposium on the Anti-monopoly Legislation] (Closing Remarks, Beijing, 9 October 2005), available at http://tfs.mofcom.gov.cn/article/bc/200510/20051000525406.shtml

Zhang, Vanessa Yanhua, 'CPI Talks ... Interview with Mr Handong Zhang, Director General of the National Development and Reform Commission (NDRC) of PR China' [2017] (3) *CPI Antitrust Chronicle* 1–3

Zhang, Xian-Chu, 'An Anti-monopoly Legal Regime in the Making in China as a Socialist Market Economy' (2009) 43 *The International Lawyer* 1469–94

张向东 [Zhang Xiangdong], 发改委有请 [NDRC Has a Request], 经济观察网 [Economic Observer Online], 30 April 2011, available at www.eeo.com.cn/eobserve/Politics/beijing_news/2011/04/30/200332.shtml

张晓松 [Zhang Xiaosong], 案件数量逐年递增，民生领域成为重点—工商总局副局长孙鸿志谈反垄断法实施五年案件查办等情况 [Cases Are Increasing Each Year, Emphasis to be on Sectors Related to the People's Livelihood – SAIC Deputy Director Sun Hongzhi Talks about the Investigation of Cases in the Five Years of Implementing the Anti-monopoly Law], 新华社 [Xinhua News Agency], 29 July 2013, available at www.gov.cn/jrzg/2013-07/29/content_2457600.htm

张晓松 [Zhang Xiaosong], 工商总局副局长谈反垄断法实施5年案件查办等情况 [SAIC Deputy Director Discusses Anti-monopoly Law Investigations and

Other Matters in the 5 Years of Implementation], 新华社 [Xinhua News Agency], 29 July 2013, available at www.gov.cn/jrzg/2013-07/29/content_2457600.htm

张晓松 [Zhang Xiaosong], 工商总局确定2014年市场监管重点, 力促公平竞争 [SAIC Determines the Focus of Market Regulation in 2014, Promotes Fair Competition], *Xinhua*, 26 December 2013, available at www.gov.cn/zhuanti/2013-12/26/content_2594573.htm

张晓松 [Zhang Xiaosong], 工商总局公布12起垄断案件 [SAIC Publishes 12 AML Cases], Xinhua, 29 July 2013, available at http://politics.people.com.cn/n/2013/0729/c70731-22369568.html

Zhang, Xinzhu and Vanessa Yanhua Zhang, 'The Antimonopoly Law in China: Where Do We Stand?' (2007) 3(2) *Competition Policy International* 185–201

Zhang, Xinzhu and Vanessa Yanhua Zhang, 'Chinese Merger Control: Patterns and Implications' (2010) 6 *Journal of Competition Law and Economics* 477–96

Zhang, Xinzhu and Vanessa Yanhua Zhang, 'New Wine into Old Wineskins: Recent Developments in China's Competition Policy against Monopolistic/Collusive Agreements' (2012) 41 *Review of Industrial Organization* 53–75

赵杰 [Zhao Jie], 反垄断法草案删除关于行政性垄断章节 [Anti-monopoly Law Draft Deletes Administrative Monopoly Chapter], 第一财经日报 [First Financial Daily], 8 June 2006, available at http://finance.people.com.cn/GB/1037/4448654.html

赵谨, 李蕾 [Zhao Jin and Li Lei], 工信部下属两家媒体驳电信联通涉嫌垄断报道 [Two Media Outlets under the MIIT Refute Reports of Alleged Monopolisation by China Telecom/China Unicom], 新京报 [*The Beijing News*], 12 November 2011, available at www.chinanews.com/it/2011/11-12/3455659.shtml

Zhao, Yinan, 'Antitrust Office Beefs Up Price Fixing Squad', *China Daily*, 12 December 2013, available at http://usa.chinadaily.com.cn/business/2013-12/12/content_17170067.htm

Zhao, Yong, 'Will Protectionists Hijack China's Competition Law?' (2004) 23 *International Financial Law Review* 21

Zhe, Wan, 'End of Salt Monopoly Opportunity for Private Firms', *Global Times*, 5 January 2017, available at www.globaltimes.cn/content/1027370.shtml

Zheng, Wentong, 'Transplanting Antitrust in China: Economic Transition, Market Structure, and State Control' (2010) 32 *University of Pennsylvania Journal of International Law* 643–721

Zheng, Yongnian, 'Central–Local Relations: The Power to Dominate', in Joseph Fewsmith (ed.), *China Today, China Tomorrow: Domestic Politics, Economy, and Society* (Lanham: Rowman & Littlefield Publishers, 2010) 193–222

Zhong, Oliver Q. C., 'Dawn of a New Constitutional Era or Opportunity Wasted? An Intellectual Reappraisal of China's Anti-monopoly Law' (2010) 24 *Columbia Journal of Asian Law* 87–128

Zhou, Fay, John Eichlin and Xi Liao, 'International Standards of Procedural Fairness and Transparency in Chinese Investigations' [2015] (1) *CPI Antitrust Chronicle* 1–10

Zhou, Lisha, 'Beijing IP Court Has Handled Six Antitrust Lawsuits Since Inception' (The Fifth China Competition Policy Forum: PaRR Special Report, October 2016)

周萍 [Zhou Ping], 破除市场垄断、倡导公平竞争—全国工商机关反垄断执法综述 [Break Monopolies, Promote Fair Competition – A Review of Antimonopoly Enforcement by the SAIC] (17 September 2008) 中国工商报 [China Industry & Commerce News], available at www.saic.gov.cn/zt/jg/fldybzdjz/200809/t20080917_219814.html

周锐 [Zhou Rui], 工商总局披露利乐案调查内情: 恢复一些被删邮件 [SAIC Discloses Inside Details of Its Tetra Pak Investigation: Restored Some Deleted Emails], 中国新闻网 [China News Online], 31 July 2013, available at www.chinanews.com/gn/2013/07-31/5108197.shtml

周望 [Zhou Wang], 中国'小组'政治模式解析 [China's 'Small Group' Political Model Analysed] [2010] (3) 云南社会科学 [Social Sciences in Yunnan] 14–8

Zhou, Xiaoyuan, 'Why are Chinese Goods More Expensive at Home Than Abroad?', *People's Daily* Overseas Edition, 9 April 2012, available at http://english.people.com.cn/90780/7781053.html

朱剑红 [Zhu Jianhong], 发改委: 多家奶粉企业涉嫌价格垄断被调查 [NDRC: A Number of Infant Formula Producers Suspected of Price Monopoly are Being Investigated], 新华网 [Xinhuanet], 2 July 2013, available at http://news.hexun.com/2013-07-02/155693324.html

Zhu Rongji, 'Report on the Outline of the Tenth Five-Year Plan for National Economic and Social Development' (Address delivered at the Fourth Session of the Ninth National People's Congress, Beijing, 5 March 2001) available at http://en.people.cn/features/lianghui/zhureport.html

# INDEX

abuse of dominance, 79–91. *See also* economic analysis
  competitive effects, 90–1
  consequences, 62
  dominant position, 81–5
  legitimate reasons, 88–90
  market definition, 80–1
  types of conduct, 85–8
    excessive pricing, 87–8
    imposing unreasonable conditions, 87
    tying and bundling, 86–7
abuse of market power. *See* abuse of dominance
administrative enforcement. *See* abuse of dominance; administrative enforcement structure; administrative monopoly; enforcement decisions; merger control; Ministry of Commerce; monopoly agreements; National Development and Reform Commission; State Administration for Industry and Commerce
administrative enforcement structure, 138–47
  AML drafting process, 214–19
  criticisms of, 12–14, 308–10
  enforcement power, struggles for, 247–59, 298–300
  institutional design issues
    bureaucratic rank, 185–7
    capacity constraints, 175–7, 303–4
    cooperation and coordination, 179–82

    knowledge constraints, 177–8, 303–4
    multiple roles and responsibilities, 182–5
  public enforcement, 244–7
administrative monopoly, 91–6
  AML drafting process, 224–9
  economic reform, 158–9
  fair competition review system, relationship to, 293–4
  industry monopoly, 110–11
  regional monopoly, 158–9
administrative power, abuse of. *See* administrative monopoly
administrative rank. *See* bureaucratic rank
*Alpha V/Savio*, 40–1, 45–6
AMC. *See* Anti-monopoly Commission
AML drafting process, 202–13
  administrative monopoly, 224–9
  competition law experts in, 209–13
  coordination in, 241–2
  dynamics of, 241–2
  enforcement power, struggles for, 214–24, 241
    administrative enforcement structure, 214–19
    regulated industries, 219–24
  foreign investment, 238–40
  industrial policy, 232–5
  industry associations, 235–8
  international norms, 211–13
  legislative history, 202–5
  national security, 238–40
  policy influences on, 207–9
  political commitment, 205–7

regulated industries, 219–24
  enforcement power, 221–3
  exemption, 220–1
  sector-specific laws, relationship with AML, 223–4
  role of the state, 229–32
    state-owned enterprises, 230–2
  timeline of, 332–4
anti-competitive agreements. *See* monopoly agreements
Anti-monopoly Commission (AMC), 147–9
  AML drafting process, 218–19
  composition, 147–8
  as coordination mechanism, 301
  expert advisory group, 148
  functions, 148–9
Anti-Monopoly Law (AML)
  abuse of dominance, 79–91
  administrative enforcement structure, 138–47
    criticisms of, 12–14, 308–10
  administrative monopoly, 91–6
  AML drafting process, 202–13
  AUCL, overlap with, 122–3
  criticisms, 4–16, 305–11
    administrative enforcement structure, 12–14, 308–10
    due process, lack of, 14–16, 310–11
    foreign companies, discrimination against, 9–12, 307–8
    non-competition factors, 6–7, 305–6
    state-owned enterprises, protection of, 8–9, 306
  existing analytical approach, 20–2
  international norms, 4–5, 211–13
  knowledge of, 107–8, 115–16, 303–4
  legal and economic analysis under, 28–59, 64–96
  legal transplant, 16–18
  merger control, 28–59
  monopoly agreements, 64–79
  political economy analytical framework, 22–4

Price Law, overlap with, 122–3, 288–9
  private enforcement, 161
  societal context, 20–2
Anti-Unfair Competition Law (AUCL), 121–2, 144, 146, 182
  AML, overlap with, 122–3, 184–5, 257–9
AUCL. *See* Anti-Unfair Competition Law
auto industry, public enforcement in, 292, 302–3

*Baxter/Gambro*, 40–1, 45–6, 52–3
behavioural conditions, 47–56. *See also* merger conditions; structural conditions
  exclusive dealing, 54–5
  exercise of rights, 55–6
  existing agreement, 52–3
  long-term hold separate, 50–2
  market expansion, 53–4
  regulatory nature, 286–8
  supply or access commitment, 48–50
  tying and bundling conduct, 54–5
bureaucratic rank, 105–6, 156, 185–7, 279–80, 286, 304

capacity constraints, competition authorities, 175–7, 303–4
central government
  economic reform, 157–8
  local government
    enforcement responsibility, division of, 181–2, 247
    relationship with, 196
  state-owned enterprises, 103–5. *See also* central SOEs
central SOEs, 103–5. *See also* state-owned enterprises
  public enforcement, 278–80, 282–3, 306
*Chifeng TobaccoTying*, 86–7
*China Telecom/China Unicom Abuse of Dominance*, 83, 254–6, 278–81, 300, 302, 306

Chinese People's Political Consultative Conference (CPPCC), 114
Coca-Cola/Huiyuan, 10–11, 59, 266
Communist Party of China (CPC), 187–91
  bureaucratic rank, 185–7
  five-year plans, 192–4
  leading small groups, 132–3, 190–1
  *nomenklatura* system, 106–7, 188–9
  policy, 191–2, 261–2
  relationships with
    government, 166–7, 188–91
      private companies, 114–16
      state-owned enterprises, 106–7, 132–3
  supervision within government, 189–90
competition analysis, under AML. *See* abuse of dominance; administrative monopoly; economic analysis; merger control; monopoly agreements
competition authorities, 138–47. *See also* administrative enforcement structure; Ministry of Commerce; National Development and Reform Commission; State Administration for Industry and Commerce
  capacity constraints, 175–7, 303–4
  competition law knowledge, 177–8, 303–4
  cooperation and coordination, 179–82
  enforcement power, struggles for, 247–59, 298–300
  multiple roles and responsibilities, 182–5
competition law. *See also* Anti-Monopoly Law
  context, 16–20
  legal transplant, 16–18
competition law experts, 167–74

AMC expert advisory group, 148
AML drafting process, 209–13
  Chinese academics, 167–9, 209–11
  economists, 172–4, 211
  foreign experts, 169–72, 211–13
competition law knowledge, 303–4
  AMC expert advisory group, 148
  competition authorities, 143–4, 146–7, 177–8
  competition law experts, 167–74
  foreign companies, 116
  judges, 178–9
  private companies, 115–16
  state-owned enterprises, 107–8
concentration of business operators. *See* merger control
constraints. *See* capacity constraints; knowledge constraints
context, of competition law, 16–22
coordination, of competition policy and other policies, 259–77, 300–1
  fair competition review system, 293–4
  foreign investment policy, 273–5
  industrial policy, 232–5, 260–8
  innovation and innovation-driven development, 260–8
  people's well-being and livelihood, 275–7
  regulatory policy, 268–73
courts, 161–7
  Communist Party of China, relationship with, 166–7
  competition law knowledge, 178–9
  decisions, 163–4
  hierarchy, 161–2
  independence, 164–5
CPC. *See* Communist Party of China
CPPCC. *See* Chinese People's Political Consultative Conference

# INDEX

demand-side stakeholders and dynamics
  foreign companies, 113–17
    foreign investment, 124–8
    governance gap, 120–3
      pre-existing competition laws, 121–2
    industry associations, 118–20
    industry regulators, 109–13
      industry monopoly, 110–11
      sector-specific laws, 112–13
      state-owned enterprises, relationship with, 111–12
    key stakeholders, 102–20
    policy environment, 124–34
      foreign investment, 124–8
      industrial policy, 133–4
      role of the state, 128–9, 133
      state-owned enterprises, 128–34
    private companies, 113–16
    state-owned enterprises, 102–9
      bureaucratic rank, 105–6
      central SOEs, 103–5
      Communist Party of China, relationship with, 106–7
      competition law knowledge, 107–8
      governance, 104
      industry regulators, relationship with, 111–12
      local SOEs, 104–5
      policy environment, 128–34
      role of, 130–1
      State-owned Assets Supervision and Administration Commission, 104–7
discrimination, against foreign companies, 9–12, 307–8
dominant market position. *See* abuse of dominance; economic analysis
dual accountability system. *See tiao kuai* system
due process, under AML, 14–16, 251–3, 310–11

economic analysis
  competitive effects, 34–42, 71–2, 90–1, 94
  market concentration, 35–6
  market control, 83–4
  market entry, 36–7, 84–5
  market share, 35, 82–3
  dominant market position, 81–5
  market definition, 32–4, 80–1
  theories of harm, 37–42, 50
    coordinated effects, 39–41
    foreclosure effects, 41–2
    unilateral effects, 37–9
economic reform, 120–1, 157–8
economic theories of harm, 37–42, 50
  coordinated effects, 39–41
  foreclosure effects, 41–2
  unilateral effects, 37–9
enforcement authorities, for AML. *See* administrative enforcement structure; Anti-monopoly Commission; competition authorities; Ministry of Commerce; National Development and Reform Commission; State Administration for Industry and Commerce
enforcement decisions
  *Alpha V/Savio*, 40–1, 45–6
  auto industry, 292, 302–3
  *Baxter/Gambro*, 40–1, 45–6, 52–3
  *Chifeng TobaccoTying*, 86–7
  *China Telecom/China Unicom Abuse of Dominance*, 83, 254–6, 278–81, 300, 302, 306
  *Coca-Cola/Huiyuan*, 10–11, 59, 266
  *Fushun TobaccoTying*, 86–7
  *Google/Motorola Mobility*, 56–7, 263–4
  *Infant Formula RPM*, 78, 291–2
  *InterDigital Abuse of Dominance*, 264–5
  *Liaoning Cement Clinker Cartel*, 73–4
  *Merck/AZ Electronics*, 42
  *Microsoft/Nokia*, 38–9, 55–6, 263–4

enforcement decisions (cont.)
  by Ministry of Commerce, 315–19
    compared to other competition authorities, 63–4
    overview, 31–2
  by National Development and Reform Commission, 319–27
    compared to Ministry of Commerce, 63–4
    overview, 63–4
  Nokia/Alcatel-Lucent, 55–6, 263–4
  Novartis/Alcon, 40, 52–3
  P3 Shipping Alliance, 59
  Panasonic/Sanyo, 45–6
  pharmaceutical industry, 271–3
  Qualcomm Abuse of Dominance, 82–4, 86–8, 91, 264–5
  salt industry, 271
  Seagate/Samsung, 39–40, 44–57
  Shanghai Gold and Platinum Jewellery Cartel, 281–2
  by State Administration for Industry and Commerce, 328–32
    compared to Ministry of Commerce, 63–4
    overview, 63–4
  TravelSky Cartel, 256–7, 279–80, 300, 306
  Wal-Mart/Newheight, 269–70, 274–5, 300
  Western Digital/Hitachi, 39–40, 44–57

fair, reasonable, and non-discriminatory (FRAND), 49, 264
fair competition review system, 293–4
  administrative monopoly, relationship to, 294
  review criteria, 293
FCS. See fiscal contracting system
Financial and Economic Affairs (FEA) Committee, 151–2
fiscal contracting system (FCS), 157–8

five-year plans, 130, 192–4
foreign companies, 113–17. See also foreign investment policy
  AML drafting process, 239–40
  competition law knowledge, 116
  discrimination against, 9–12, 307–8
  foreign investment, 124–8
  national security, 238–40
  public enforcement, 273–5
foreign competition law experts, 169–72, 211–13
foreign investment policy, 124–8, 273–4
  AML drafting process, 238–40
  public enforcement, consideration in, 273–5
FRAND. See fair, reasonable, and non-discriminatory
Fushun Tobacco Tying, 86–7

Google/Motorola Mobility, 56–7, 263–4
government, 156–60. See also central government; local government
  central-local relations, 156–60, 196

Huang Yong, 167–9, 204, 210

indigenous innovation, 262
industrial policy
  AML drafting process, 232–5
  innovation-driven development, 260–8
industry associations, 118–20
  AML drafting process, 235–8
  quasi-governmental nature, 118–19
industry regulators, 109–13
  AML drafting process, 219–24
  industry monopoly, 110–11
  Ministry for Industry and Information Technology, 110
  public enforcement, involvement in, 247–59
  sector-specific laws, 112–13, 223–4
  state-owned enterprises, relationship with, 111–12

*Infant Formula RPM*, 78, 291–2
innovation-driven development, 260–8
  brands, 266–8
  indigenous innovation, 262
  intellectual property rights, 262–6
intellectual property rights (IPRs), 262–6
*InterDigital Abuse of Dominance*, 264–5
international competition law norms, 211–13
IPRs. *See* intellectual property rights

judges. *See* courts
jurisdiction
  AML drafting process, 214–24
    administrative enforcement structure, 214–19
    regulated industries, 219–24
  defined, 214
  public enforcement, 244–59
    competition authorities, division of responsibility, 244–7
    other government authorities, involvement in, 247–59

knowledge constraints, 177–9, 303–4

LAO. *See* Legislative Affairs Office
lawyers. *See* legal practitioners
legal practitioners, 174–5
legal transplant, 16–18
Legislative Affairs Office (LAO), 155
  AML drafting process, 202–5
*Liaoning Cement Clinker Cartel*, 73–4
local government, 156–60
  central government
    AML enforcement responsibility, division of, 181–2, 247
    relationship with, 196
  economic reform, 157–8
  public enforcement, 247
  regional monopoly, 158–9

  state-owned enterprises, 104–5.
    *See also* local SOEs
  local SOEs, 104–5. *See also* state-owned enterprises
  public enforcement, 280–2
lower-level government. *See* local government

macroeconomic regulation and control, 191–4
  AML drafting process, 229–30
  public enforcement, 286–92
    merger conditions, regulatory nature of, 286–8
    price supervision and regulation, 288–92
market definition. *See* economic analysis
*Merck/AZ Electronics*, 42
merger conditions, 42–58
  behavioural conditions, 47–56
  consultation and consensus, impact of, 250
  regulatory nature, 286–8
  review, 56–8
  revocation, 56–8
  structural conditions, 44–7
  variation, 56–8
merger control, 28–59. *See also* economic analysis
  analysis under AML, 28–59
    competitive effects, 34–42
    market definition, 32–4
    theories of harm, 37–42, 50
  conditional approval. *See* merger conditions
  other government policies, 263–4, 266–70, 273–5
  prohibition, 58–9
  review process, 247–53
    consultation and consensus, 248–50
    delays, 251–3
    due process, 14–15
    simple cases, 29–30, 252–3
merger remedies. *See* merger conditions
*Microsoft/Nokia*, 38–9, 55–6, 263–4

MIIT. *See* Ministry for Industry and Information Technology
Ministry for Industry and Information Technology (MIIT), 110
  *China Telecom/China Unicom Abuse of Dominance*, 255–6
  merger review, consultation during, 248–9
  *Tencent/Qihoo 360*, 146, 257–9
  *Wal-Mart/Newheight*, 269–70, 275
Ministry of Commerce (MOFCOM), 141–4
  AML administrative enforcement structure, 142–3
  AML drafting process, 203–5, 207–8, 214–21
  capacity constraints, 175–7, 303–4
  competition law knowledge, 143–4
  enforcement activity, 28–59. *See also* behavioural conditions; merger conditions; merger control; structural conditions
    consultation with government authorities, 247–53
    merger conditions, regulatory nature, 286–8
    other government policies, 263–4, 266–70, 273–5
    state-owned enterprises, 282–6
  enforcement decisions, 315–19
    compared to other competition authorities, 63–4
    overview, 31–2
  knowledge constraints, 177–8, 303–4
  multiple roles and responsibilities, 181–2
  State Economic and Trade Commission, 203–5
monopoly agreements, 64–79. *See also* economic analysis
  consequences, 62
  determination of, 65–70
  exemption, 72–5

leniency policy, 76–9
prohibition, 70–2
types of conduct, 68–70
  market sharing, 69
  price fixing, 68–9
  resale price maintenance, 70

National Development and Reform Commission (NDRC), 139–41
  AML administrative enforcement structure, 142–3
  AML drafting process, 216–19
  capacity constraints, 175–6
  cooperation and coordination between central and local authorities, 181–2, 247
    with State Administration for Industry and Commerce, 179–81, 243–6, 298–9
  enforcement activity. *See also* abuse of dominance; administrative monopoly; monopoly agreements
    merger control, consultation in, 247–9
    non-merger conduct, 59–96
    other government authorities, involvement in, 253–7
    other government policies, 263–4, 269–73, 275–7, 294
    price supervision and regulation, 288–92
    state-owned enterprises, 277–81
  enforcement decisions, 319–27
    compared to Ministry of Commerce, 63–4
    overview, 60–1
  knowledge constraints, 177–8
  multiple roles and responsibilities, 182–3
  price supervision and regulation, 182–3, 288–92
National People's Congress (NPC), 149–54. *See also* Standing Committee of the National People's Congress

INDEX

Financial and Economic Affairs (FEA) Committee, 151–2
Law Committee, 151–3
Legislative Affairs Commission, 152–4
national security, 238–40
NDRC. *See* National Development and Reform Commission
*Nokia/Alcatel-Lucent*, 55–6, 263–4
*nomenklatura* system, 106–7, 188–9
non-competition factors, consideration in AML, 6–7, 305–6
non-merger conduct, 59–96. *See also* abuse of dominance; administrative monopoly; monopoly agreements
  analysis under AML, 59–96
  consequences, 62
  enforcement responsibility, 60, 244–7
  investigation process, 253–9
    due process, 15
    other government authorities, involvement in, 253–9, 263–4, 269–73
  state-owned enterprises, 277–81
*Novartis/Alcon*, 40, 52–3
NPC. *See* National People's Congress

*P3 Shipping Alliance*, 59
*Panasonic/Sanyo*, 45–6
people's well-being and livelihood, 275–7
pharmaceutical industry, public enforcement of, 79–80, 271–3
political economy analytical framework, for AML, 22–4, 297–8. *See also* demand-side stakeholders and dynamics; supply-side stakeholders and dynamics
pre-existing competition law regime, 120–3. *See also* Anti-Unfair Competition Law; Price Law
  AML, overlap with, 122–3, 182–5, 257–9
Price Law, 121–2, 140, 183
  AML, overlap with, 122–3, 182–4, 288–9
price supervision and regulation, 288–92
private companies, Chinese, 113–17
  Communist Party of China, relationship with, 114–16
  competition law knowledge, 115–16
  public enforcement, 60–1, 81
provincial government, 156–60. *See also* local government
  central government
    AML enforcement responsibility, division of, 181–2, 247
    relationship with, 196
  economic reform, 157–8
  public enforcement, 247
  regional monopoly, 158–9

*Qualcomm Abuse of Dominance*, 82–4, 86–8, 91, 264–5

regional monopoly, 158–9. *See also* administrative monopoly
  AML drafting process, 224–9
regulated industries. *See also* industry regulators
  AML drafting process, 219–24
  public enforcement, 268–73
restrictive conditions. *See* behavioural conditions; merger conditions

SAIC. *See* State Administration for Industry and Commerce
salt industry, public enforcement in, 271
SASAC. *See* State-owned Assets Supervision and Administration Commission
SCNPC. *See* Standing Committee of the National People's Congress
*Seagate/Samsung*, 39–40, 44–57
SETC. *See* State Economic and Trade Commission

*Shanghai Gold and Platinum Jewellery Cartel*, 281–2
Sheng Jiemin, 125, 167–8, 204, 210, 217
Shi Jianzhong, 167–9, 204, 210
simple case mergers, 29–30, 252–3
socialist market economy
  Communist Party of China, 187–91
  five-year plans in, 130, 192–4
  industrial policy, 133–4, 208–9, 232–5, 249, 260–8
  macroeconomic regulation and control, 191–4, 286–92
  public ownership, 128–9
  relationship between state and market, 191–2, 277–94, 301–3
  role of the market, 191–2
  role of the state, 128–9, 133, 191–4, 229–32, 286–92
SOEs. *See* state-owned enterprises
Standing Committee of the National People's Congress (SCNPC), 149–54. *See also* National People's Congress
  AML drafting process, 203–5, 208–9, 221–3, 227–40
  composition of, 150–1
State Administration for Industry and Commerce (SAIC), 144–7
  AML administrative enforcement structure, 144–5
  AML drafting process, 203–5, 207–8, 214–21
  AUCL, 121–2, 144, 146, 182
    AML, overlap with, 122–3, 184–5, 257–9
  capacity constraints, 175–6
  cooperation and coordination
    between central and local authorities, 179–82, 244–7, 298–9
    with NDRC, 179–81, 243–6, 298–9
  enforcement activity, 59–96. *See also* abuse of dominance; administrative monopoly; monopoly agreements
    non-merger conduct, 59–96

  other government authorities, involvement in, 253–4, 257–9
  other government policies, 266, 271–3, 275–7
  state-owned enterprises, 280–1
  enforcement decisions, 328–32
  compared to Ministry of Commerce, 63–4
  overview, 60–1, 63–4
  knowledge constraints, 177–8
  multiple roles and responsibilities, 182–3
State Council, 154–5
  AML drafting process, 202–5, 208, 217–24, 226–9, 233
  Legislative Affairs Office, 155
State Economic and Trade Commission (SETC), 203–5
State-owned Assets Supervision and Administration Commission (SASAC), 104–7, 133–4
state-owned enterprises (SOEs), 102–9. *See also* central SOEs; local SOEs; State-owned Assets Supervision and Administration Commission
  bureaucratic rank, 105–6
  central SOEs, 103–5, 278–80, 282–3, 306
  Communist Party of China, relationship with, 106–7
  competition law knowledge, 107–8
  governance, 104
  industry regulators, relationship with, 111–12
  local SOEs, 104–5, 280–2
  policy environment, 128–34
  protection of, 8–9, 306
  public enforcement, 278–86
  reform of, 131–3
  role of, 130–1
  State-owned Assets Supervision and Administration Commission, 104–7

structural conditions, 44–7. *See also* behavioural conditions; merger conditions
  crown jewel provisions, 47
  divestiture, 45–6
  fix-it first provisions, 45–6
supply-side stakeholders and dynamics
  Anti-monopoly Commission, 147–9
  Chinese competition authorities, 138–47
    Ministry of Commerce, 141–4
    National Development and Reform Commission, 139–41
    State Administration for Industry and Commerce, 144–7
  Communist Party of China, 187–91
  competition law experts, 167–74
    AMC expert advisory group, 148
    Chinese academics, 167–9
    economists, 172–4
    foreign experts, 169–72
  courts, 161–7
    Communist Party of China, relationship with, 166–7
    hierarchy, 161–2
    independence, 164–5
  industry regulators, 113
  institutional design issues, 175–87
    bureaucratic rank, 185–7
    capacity constraints, 175–7
    cooperation and coordination, 179–82
    knowledge constraints, 177–9
    multiple roles and responsibilities, 182–5
  key stakeholders, 137–75
  legal practitioners, 174–5

  local government, 156–60, 196
  policy environment, 187–96
    central-local relations, 196
    macroeconomic regulation, 191–4
  provincial government, 156–60, 196
  Standing Committee of the National People's Congress, 149–54
  State Council, 154–5
Supreme People's Court. *See* courts

technical assistance, 171–2
*Tencent/Qihoo 360*, 173–4, 257–9, 300
*tiao kuai* system, 194–5
transparency, lack of, 14–16, 95–7, 281, 310–11
*TravelSky Cartel*, 256–7, 279–80, 300, 306

value-added telecommunications services (VATS), 53, 269–70, 274–5
variable interest entities (VIEs), 273–4
VATS. *See* value-added telecommunications services
VIEs. *See* variable interest entities

*Wal-Mart/Newheight*, 269–70, 274–5, 300
Wang Xianlin, 167–9, 204, 210
Wang Xiaoye, 167–9, 204, 210
*Western Digital/Hitachi*, 39–40, 44–57
World Trade Organization (WTO), influence on AML drafting, 206–7
Wu Hanhong, 172–3, 204

Zhang Weiying, 172–3
Zhang Xinzhu, 172–3, 204